Kyle Christmas 2014
Love
Mary

© Sigrid Estrada

MAC GRISWOLD is a cultural landscape historian and the author of *Washington's Gardens at Mount Vernon* and *The Golden Age of American Gardens*. She has won a Guggenheim Fellowship and has written for *The New York Times, The Wall Street Journal,* and *Travel + Leisure*. She lives in Sag Harbor, New York.

Additional Praise for *The Manor*

"Meticulous . . . An impressive chronicle." —*Chicago Tribune*

"After reading Griswold's haunting new study, *The Manor: Three Centuries at a Slave Plantation on Long Island,* it is difficult not to see the ghosts of seventeenth-century colonists, native Manhansetts, and enslaved Africans mingling with the summer crowds. . . . Long Islanders curious about the history of the land we now occupy will be moved by her layered account." —*Newsday*

"Astonishing . . . The layers of history uncovered at Sylvester Manor show that slavery in the North was not just a passing phenomenon. . . . A step toward restoring these once-forgotten souls to a place in our shared history." —*The Daily Beast*

"Absorbing . . . The parallel stories of the homeowners and their bondservants interweave to form a moving tale of life in the New World, and the author enriches her narrative with meticulous examinations of items unearthed at the manor, from porridge bowls to old cobblestone pathways. Griswold brings American history home in this fascinating volume." —*Publishers Weekly* (starred review)

"One of the most detailed examinations of the culture of slavery and slave-owning and its deep influence on the development of the American colonies . . . A deeply researched, painstakingly detailed story of a forgotten chapter of our nation's history. Highly recommended." —*Kirkus Reviews* (starred review)

"So much history is trampled ground, but this is both fresh and urgent material." —*Library Journal*

"A work of enormous importance and energy, erudition, and humanity."
—David Margolick, contributing editor to *Vanity Fair* and author of *Strange Fruit: Biography of a Song*

"Griswold's flawlessly researched book presents a startling and comprehensive account of colonial interracial relationships and the way that people of widely distinct cultures held ties to the same land. *The Manor* is a superbly written and important book for readers of American history."

—Maryalice Huggins, author of *Aesop's Mirror*

"*The Manor* is an extraordinary account of a house in all its domestic splendor and squalor. Its physical presence is beautiful to behold, but the people in it—victim and victor alike—are evidence of all that has gone wrong since that fateful day in 1492. And in focusing our attention on this part of the Northeast, Mac Griswold reminds us how our understanding of the United States of America must be deeply and widely intertwined with the presence of the African. This is an important book, for it is not just about a house. It is about the world and the destruction we have caused in it, all for the sake of making that place called home—or, in other words: the Manor."

—Jamaica Kincaid, author of *See Now Then*

The MANOR

The MANOR

Three Centuries at a Slave Plantation on Long Island

Mac Griswold

Picador Farrar, Straus and Giroux New York

With thanks to Furthermore grants in publishing, a program of the J. M. Kaplan Fund.

Furthermore:
a program of the J.M. Kaplan Fund

Printed in the United States of America. For information, address
Picador, 175 Fifth Avenue, New York, N.Y. 10010.

www.picadorusa.com
www.twitter.com/picadorusa • www.facebook.com/picadorusa
picadorbookroom.tumblr.com

Picador® is a U.S. registered trademark and is used by Farrar, Straus and Giroux
under license from Pan Books Limited.

For book club information, please visit www.facebook.com/picadorbookclub
or e-mail marketing@picadorusa.com.

Owing to limitations of space, illustration credits can be found on pages 459–61.
Frontispiece: Julia Dyd Havens Johnson, housekeeper at Sylvester Manor.
Maps on pages ix, 14, 71, 148, and 149 copyright © 2013 by Jeffrey L. Ward.

Designed by Jonathan D. Lippincott

The Library of Congress has cataloged the Farrar, Straus and Giroux edition as follows:

Griswold, Mac K.
The manor : three centuries at a slave plantation on Long Island /
Mac Griswold. — First edition.
pages cm
Includes bibliographical references and index.
ISBN 978-0-374-26629-5 (hardcover)
ISBN 978-1-4668-3701-0 (e-book)
1. Sylvester Manor Plantation Site (N.Y.) 2. Slavery—New York (State)—Long Island—History. 3. Plantations—New York (State)—Long Island—History. 4. Plantation life—New York (State)—Long Island—History. 5. Excavations (Archaeology)—New York (State)—Long Island. 6. Shelter Island (N.Y.)—History. 7. Long Island (N.Y.)—History. 8. Plantation owners—New York (State)—Long Island—Biography. 9. Long Island (N.Y.)—Biography. I. Title.

E445.N56 G75 2013
974.7'21—dc23

2013005463

Picador ISBN 978-1-250-05020-5

Picador books may be purchased for educational, business, or promotional use.
For information on bulk purchases, please contact Macmillan Corporate and Premium Sales
Department at 1-800-221-7945, extension 5442, or write
specialmarkets@macmillan.com.

First published in the United States by Farrar, Straus and Giroux

First Picador Edition: April 2014

10 9 8 7 6 5 4 3 2 1

To Emma Tara Johnston Lee

Contents

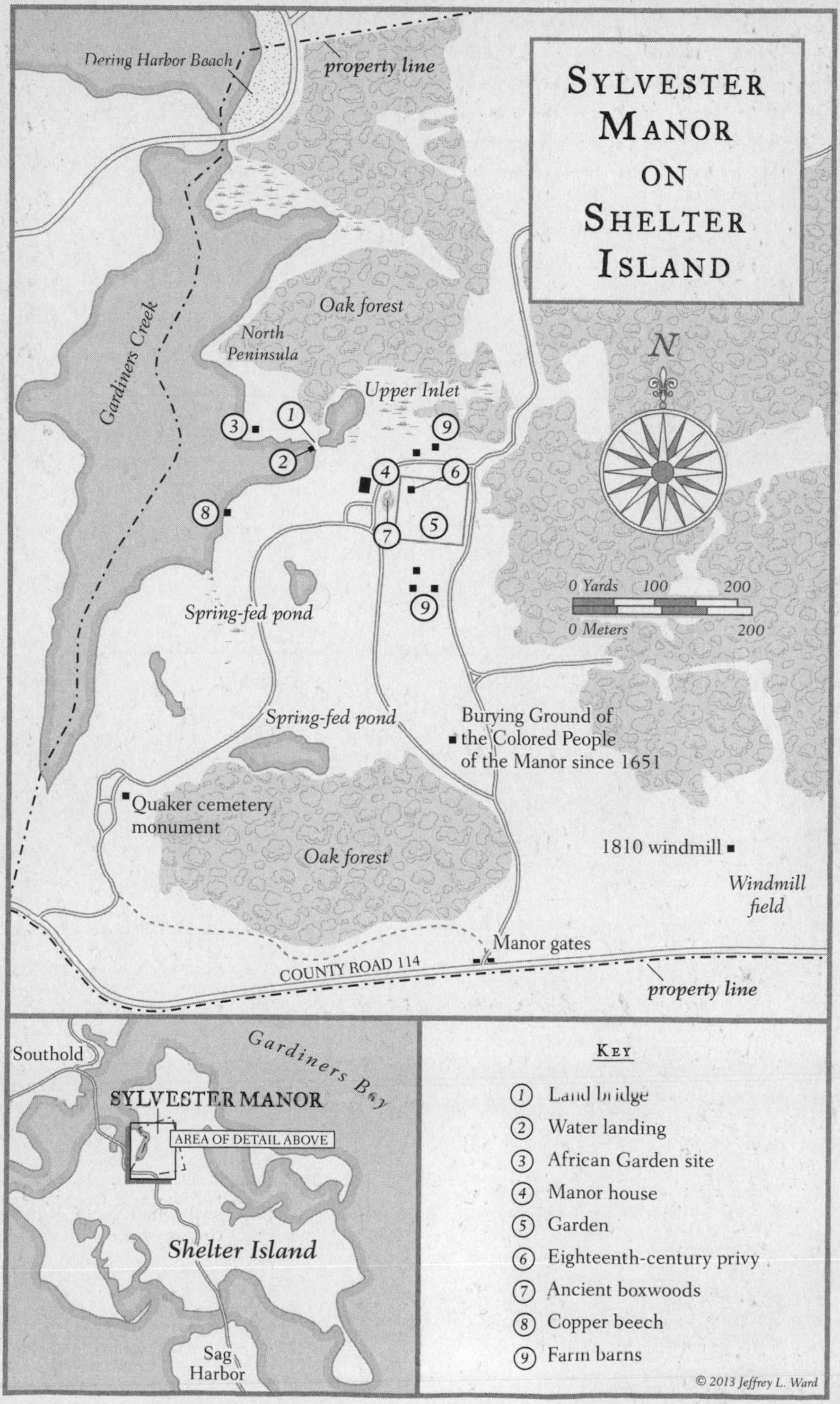

Sylvester Manor on Shelter Island
Dering Harbor Beach
property line
Oak forest
North Peninsula
Gardiners Creek
Upper Inlet
N
0 Yards 100 200
0 Meters 200
Spring-fed pond
Spring-fed pond
Burying Ground of the Colored People of the Manor since 1651
Quaker cemetery monument
Oak forest
1810 windmill
Windmill field
Manor gates
COUNTY ROAD 114
property line
Southold
Gardiners Bay
SYLVESTER MANOR
AREA OF DETAIL ABOVE
Shelter Island
Sag Harbor
Key
1 Land bridge
2 Water landing
3 African Garden site
4 Manor house
5 Garden
6 Eighteenth-century privy
7 Ancient boxwoods
8 Copper beech
9 Farm barns
© 2013 Jeffrey L. Ward

Descendants of Nathaniel Sylvester at Sylvester Manor

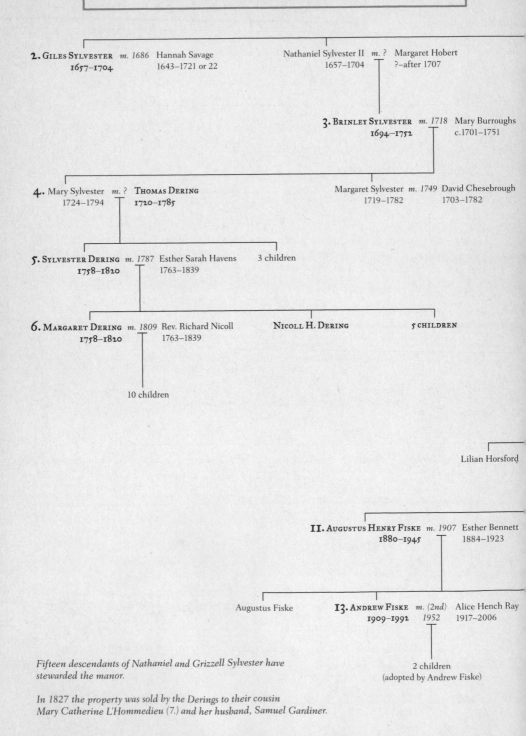

2. Giles Sylvester *m. 1686* Hannah Savage
1657–1704 1643–1721 or 22

Nathaniel Sylvester II *m. ?* Margaret Hobert
1657–1704 ?–after 1707

3. Brinley Sylvester *m. 1718* Mary Burroughs
1694–1752 c.1701–1751

4. Mary Sylvester *m. ?* **Thomas Dering**
1724–1794 **1720–1785**

Margaret Sylvester *m. 1749* David Chesebrough
1719–1782 1703–1782

5. Sylvester Dering *m. 1787* Esther Sarah Havens
1758–1820 1763–1839

3 children

6. Margaret Dering *m. 1809* Rev. Richard Nicoll
1758–1820 1763–1839

Nicoll H. Dering

5 children

10 children

Lilian Horsford

11. Augustus Henry Fiske *m. 1907* Esther Bennett
1880–1945 1884–1923

Augustus Fiske

13. Andrew Fiske *m. (2nd) 1952* Alice Hench Ray
1909–1992 1917–2006

2 children
(adopted by Andrew Fiske)

Fifteen descendants of Nathaniel and Grizzell Sylvester have stewarded the manor.

In 1827 the property was sold by the Derings to their cousin Mary Catherine L'Hommedieu (7.) and her husband, Samuel Gardiner.

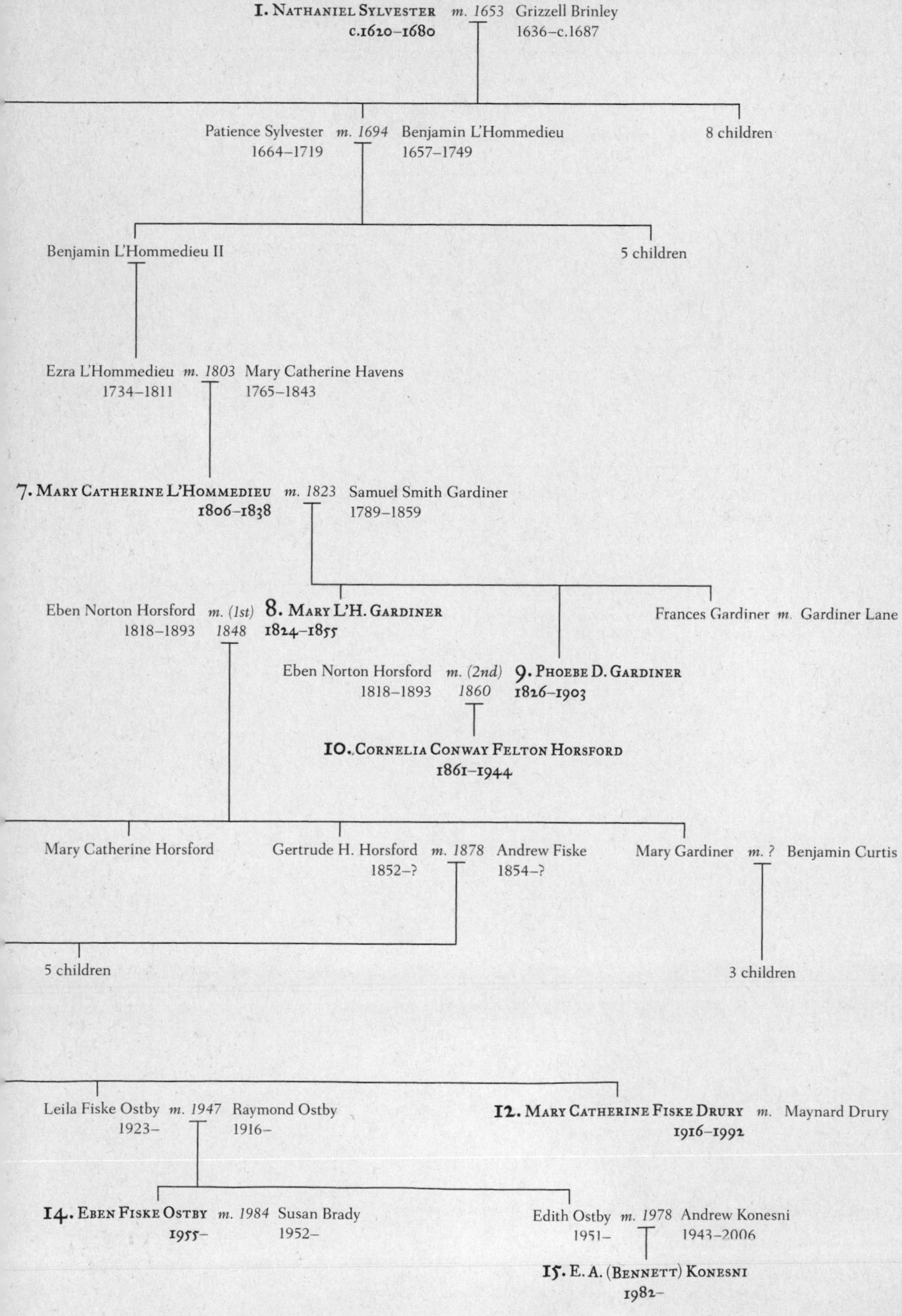
1. Nathaniel Sylvester m. 1653 Grizzell Brinley
c.1620–1680
1636–c.1687
Patience Sylvester m. 1694 Benjamin L'Hommedieu
1664–1719
1657–1749
8 children
Benjamin L'Hommedieu II
5 children
Ezra L'Hommedieu m. 1803 Mary Catherine Havens
1734–1811
1765–1843
7. Mary Catherine L'Hommedieu m. 1823 Samuel Smith Gardiner
1806–1838
1789–1859
Eben Norton Horsford m. (1st) 1848 8. Mary L'H. Gardiner
1818–1893
1824–1855
Frances Gardiner m. Gardiner Lane
Eben Norton Horsford m. (2nd) 1860 9. Phoebe D. Gardiner
1818–1893
1826–1903
10. Cornelia Conway Felton Horsford
1861–1944
Mary Catherine Horsford
Gertrude H. Horsford m. 1878 Andrew Fiske
1852–?
1854–?
Mary Gardiner m. ? Benjamin Curtis
5 children
3 children
Leila Fiske Ostby m. 1947 Raymond Ostby
1923–
1916–
12. Mary Catherine Fiske Drury m. Maynard Drury
1916–1992
14. Eben Fiske Ostby m. 1984 Susan Brady
1955–
1952–
Edith Ostby m. 1978 Andrew Konesni
1951–
1943–2006
15. E. A. (Bennett) Konesni
1982–

Preface

When I began my research for this book in 1997, I became the tourist that the cultural geographer J. B. Jackson described as "the solitary, uninformed traveler, setting out, hardly knowing why, in search of a new kind of pleasure and a new kind of knowledge." I found both at Sylvester Manor on isolated Shelter Island, set between the North and South Forks of Long Island. It is the only former slaveholder's plantation north of the Mason-Dixon line that still exists with papers, architecture, and landscape all in one place to tell its story. The property remains in the hands of the eleventh generation of the European colonists who settled there in 1651. The graves of Africans and Manhansett Indians lie quietly under the pines.

Though I have walked through dozens of historic landscapes, some abandoned and others restored, I never felt the immediacy of history so intensely as at Sylvester Manor. What sounds did these Shelter Islanders hear? What did they eat, how did they talk, what did they smell (and smell like)? Which cultural traditions, social ambitions, and political forces had shaped their experiences? I needed to get a clear picture of how oppression, war, religious beliefs, and a morality that accepted chattel slavery had operated at Sylvester Manor. At first I saw only that a line ran from the canals of Amsterdam to this handsome, smallish house and to scientists and poets in nineteenth-century Cambridge, Massachusetts. Soon the manor landscape swelled outward to include the Atlantic World as far as the West Indies and the slave-trade castles of the African Gold Coast. What I saw at the manor was connected to the flow of people, ideas, plants, and animals from a dozen other landscapes on four continents.

The written history of the manor has lasted for more than three and a half centuries, but half of this book is devoted to its first eighty years, because, as Richard Rabinowitz, who in 2005 mounted the first exhibition about the pervasive presence of slavery in New York, said, "The founding of Sylvester Manor is as exciting as the moment when people stepped across the Bering Strait. Here African, European, and Native American people came together to build an economic enterprise that was rooted in an ecology, a technology, and a set of racial hierarchies that continue to mark our lives today."

I made many discoveries. To find out where slaves such as Reuben and Chloe slept, I tiptoed through an ancient probate inventory, reconstructing the path of the appraisers through each nook and cranny of the house. A man at the Plimoth Plantation museum, near where the Pilgrims landed in 1620, sang a psalm tune for me that Nathaniel Sylvester had sung as a child in 1620s Amsterdam. A snowfall picked out in white a lost eighteenth-century entrance drive. I learned that the most lethal malarial mosquito in colonial Jamestown (where Nathaniel spent almost a year in 1644) had striped legs. On a June morning, I opened the door to the secret vault where priceless family documents were kept and smelled rotting paper (the antique plumbing above had burst). We saved them.

One midnight I asked myself, Why do we say "slave plantation"? It is, as one friend said, "as if they were growing slaves" like cotton or sugar or tobacco. It's a dehumanizing phrase we've come to live with, to romanticize. When I started to write, I was aware that my family tree, like that of many white Americans, includes generations of slaveholders who migrated across the South from Virginia to Texas. As my understanding of manor life deepened, I was seduced by the beauties and terrors of the place. By the time I finished writing about this Northern plantation, my bones had been rattled by the everydayness of slavery and its long legacy in our country.

I have written this study of a single piece of land and its inhabitants expecting that it will light up a long stretch of our American history. I hope my sensory impressions, combined with the historical facts—the moral paradoxes, combined with my guesses as a writer—remain as fresh and startling for the reader as they were when I gathered them.

The MANOR

1

The Discovery

Boxwood

It has taken us about twenty minutes to get into Gardiners Creek from a mooring in the town harbor of Shelter Island, set snugly between two peninsulas, the North and South Forks of Long Island, New York, whose tips stretch out to touch the western edge of the Atlantic Ocean, where the Gulf Stream runs close to the continent as it flows north and east toward Europe.

The tide is full as we ease the dinghy through a big pipe that supports a bridge, a bridge so low to the water that we have to flatten ourselves on the thwarts to get through without banging our heads. The pipe acts as an echo chamber, even for a whisper. It is too narrow for us to use the oars, so we brace our hands on the curve of the low ceiling and push. A friend has brought me here to see "something," but he won't say what. It is a summer day in 1984.

Finally out in the light, we see nothing but woods looming down to the water. Then, about a half mile off, at what seems to be the end of the inlet we have found our way into, phragmites and cattails fringe the shore. On our right are a few roofs, half hidden in the trees. On our left, toward the east, lies only a salt marsh where white egrets stalk in the long grasses. No houses. Not even a dock, a boat, or a mooring. Gulls wheel above a low hill covered with large trees: oak, hickory, walnut. Turning east means seeing land set back in time, so far back it looks as if it had never been inhabited. We blink, feeling tension rise between the modern world we've left behind so abruptly and the past we are rowing into.

A mudbank lies ahead, lurking under shallow water, and we get stuck, briefly. It is only when we steer into the tide channel, stirring up silty brown clouds in the water as we pole ourselves with the oars, that we first see the big yellow house. From its hip roof and big brick chimneys to its well-proportioned bulk, the house quietly acknowledges its eighteenth-century origins. I'm in a time warp.

As we cautiously approach, rowing as quietly as we can, hulking blackish-green boxwoods suddenly loom above the corner of a porch. *Buxus sempervirens*, or common box, these shrubs look to be an astounding twelve feet tall. Is this an illusion created by looking up from such a small boat? No, it isn't. They're gigantic. We're used to seeing boxwoods as frilly edging around flower beds, or modest green bosses set to either side of a front door. Slow-growing boxwoods do well in this moderate climate, tempered by the surrounding waters of the Atlantic, but they seldom exceed eight feet north of the Mason-Dixon Line. As a landscape historian and a gardener, I feel that these linebacker giants must be very, very old. Boxwoods, one of the few shrubs that in optimum conditions can live for hundreds of years, are like the guardians of history. The dense evergreen foliage of specimens like these seem to hold memory in each small, shining leaf.

Boxwoods, seen here in a family photograph taken before 1908, have guarded the central garden path at Sylvester Manor for at least two hundred years.

The reflection of the house in the glassy water doesn't tremble. No wind. I hold my breath too, as if the building itself would disappear if the water moved.

My friend idles his oars. As we pull closer to shore, we see what looks like a place to land. Apparently a crude boulder wall, it has a few stone steps rising from the water. Nobody is around. Can't resist. I climb the steps; my friend waits, amused but concerned that I'm going to get caught trespassing. However, he's used to my marauding tactics in deserted gardens.

Once up the steps, I see that the wall is actually a land bridge carpeted with grass. Wonderfully strange. On the far side of the bridge, another part of the inlet we've ventured into continues. A track runs down from the woods we just rowed past, heading for the house. I follow it. I knock softly at the front door, then louder. I call. Still no answer, nobody home. Great. So I check out the gangling, rusty windmill and water tank on stilts near a big barn, and an old cannon facing the water, sitting on a crude wooden carriage. Where the heavy lower branches of a gigantic copper beech have reached the ground, they have taken root and sprung up into a copse surrounding the mother tree. The tree bulks almost as large as the long, elegant house that was clearly built over many generations, lying composedly in the sun on a summer afternoon.

On the east side of the house, away from the water, white pickets protect a rambling flower garden. The big boxwoods I glimpsed from the boat flank the garden gate. Now that I am close to them, I see they are indeed twelve feet tall, and fifteen feet broad. Inside, the garden is cut by a central path running straight and narrow through two lines of more boxwoods. The far end of the path telescopes to a distant gate, a view that seems to stretch back at least two hundred years. Grand gardens were built like this then, fenced rectangles on axis with the main house.

I climb back into the rowboat, stunned. This place isn't self-consciously "historic"; it's not restored in any sense. It has simply *been here*, waiting for time to pass. Waiting for me.

Suddenly we hear water moving. The Atlantic tide begins to empty itself in a thin silver coil from the inlet above the stone bridge. Twice a day, every day, for how many years? This place stands still, outside any ordinary dimension of time or space, but tide and time move through it. We row out of Gardiners Creek, moving with the tide.

•

Curious to find out exactly where I'd been in the dinghy, I checked a map of the island to get my bearings, and asked the owner of the local sandwich joint if he knew who owned the place: an Andrew Fiske, and his wife, Alice. I wrote asking to meet them. I had trouble with my letter, trying out various versions of "Who are you and what is this place?" At last I settled on something economical and true, but pitifully inadequate to express the curiosity I felt. "Dear Mr. and Mrs. Fiske," I wrote, "I rowed into the creek below your house and could not resist walking around your lawns and garden," and I finished by saying I was a garden historian and would like to meet them and learn about the history of their house. Several months and three letters later, I received a reply, and an invitation to visit.

I pulled through the white-painted cement gates opposite Shelter Island's lone supermarket and rattled down the long wooded driveway, two worn sandy tracks separated by a grass ridge. Not much traffic here, that was clear. I wondered whether the couple I would meet could possibly match the magic of my waterside introduction.

To the Staircase

Two small figures stand under the front portico, one in a wrinkled linen jacket and open-necked checked shirt, the other in skirt and blouse, with a chintz mobcap topping the ensemble. Sensible shoes on both, and an air of the fifties about them. Pleasant greetings, a swift assessment from Andrew's pale blue eyes, a big lipsticked smile from Alice. As they invite me into the darkened front hall, light hits the polished brass doorknob. A large key gleams in the heavy, square lock. I step across the threshold and into a history project spanning eleven generations, three and a half centuries, and four continents. Here, where the Hamptons, jittery playground of the rich and famous, are only eight miles away, I am astonished to learn I'm meeting a member of a family that has lived on this tranquil-seeming property in an unbroken line since 1652.

Alice, clearly a character and perhaps the boss, departs for the garden. Andy asks whether I'd like to see the house. As we continue to stand in the front hall, he regales me with his romantic version of a family story passed on to him and shaped mostly during America's Colonial Revival, between 1876 and the twenties, by his great-grandfather Eben Norton

Horsford and his youngest daughter, Cornelia Horsford. I would review and reassemble this history many times.

Eventually I combined the results of a decade of research into Andy's documents with information from oral and traditional histories; intellectual, economic, agricultural, and architectural history; and archaeology, dowsing, and dendrochronological analysis of the timbers of the house. This book offers an interpretation of the Sylvester Manor site that is more startling, more full of gaps, and more complex and paradoxical than Andy's tale—and it still leaves the place and its history open to further study. The colorful Andy version rings with a certainty that my version doesn't possess, but I would discover many disconcerting errors and gaps in his tale.

His account runs like this: In 1652, the dashing Nathaniel Sylvester, son of an English merchant family, sailed north from Barbados, where his family owned sugar plantations that depended on the labor of hundreds of Africans. With him came his teenaged bride, Grizzell Brinley, daughter of Charles I's court auditor, Thomas Brinley. After a dramatic shipwreck, the newlyweds landed on Shelter Island, where a large and comfortable house (built previously by Nathaniel and his servants) stood ready to receive the young couple. Nathaniel and his brother Constant and two other Barbadian planters, Thomas Middleton and Thomas Rous, had bought the island from Stephen Goodyear, the deputy governor of New Haven Colony, who had bought it as a speculative venture in 1651 from the estate of the Earl of Stirling, its first English owner, for 1,600 pounds of the unrefined brown sugar known as muscovado. Andy carefully explained that even though Nathaniel and Grizzell were not Quakers themselves, a sense of noblesse oblige moved them to offer their isolated island as a sanctuary for the earliest Friends fleeing the savage persecution of Boston Puritans. The young couple invited George Fox, the Quaker founder, to visit in 1673 and preach the Inner Light. Because Grizzell's father, a high civil servant who served in the Royal Exchequer, had the ear and the gratitude of the king, Charles II, the persecution stopped. The Sylvesters enjoyed good relations with the Indians and respectfully purchased the island again from the local Manhansett chief, Youghco. They hobnobbed with, and married into, New England's ruling elite. Last but not least, Grizzell bore twelve children, eleven of whom lived to maturity, thereby begetting the long line that led to Andy Fiske.

Andy fast-forwards two generations to Nathaniel's grandson, the fashionable Brinley Sylvester, born in Newport, who inherited in 1733. To Brinley, the ramshackle eighty-year-old family mansion seemed very out of date; he tore it down and built this house. We are standing in the east parlor as Andy tells me this, a room of extraordinary beauty and strangeness. Beautiful because the proportions and the fully paneled walls are exquisite, and all the more so for being so very early Georgian high style in this now remote corner of the world, once part of a thriving maritime economy. Strange, because there are only two coats of paint on these walls, through which the silvery old wood shows in patches. The bottom coat is that acid blue-green so fashionable in the mid-eighteenth century. The top coat is a modest biscuit color, emblematic of good taste, applied sometime in the 1840s, just before wall colors turned dark and Victorian. How peculiar and lucky it is that no one put on a third coat, I think to myself.

On one wall hangs a dingy portrait of a solemn man with a very large nose, Andy's notable ancestor Ezra L'Hommedieu, Nathaniel Sylvester's great-grandson, an American statesman who died in 1811. As we turn away from the painting, I am startled to see the same nose confronting me in the flesh—on Andy's face. The doubling of past and present doesn't stop with the portrait. Andy gently coaxes me to notice that the same blue and white pearlware basket depicted in the portrait of a little girl in red over the mantel now sits safely on a shelf behind the parlor door. Despite the past, how strangely lived-in this room feels, with its big bunch of plastic daffodils, box of mah-jongg tiles, and folding card table, vintage 1950.

It hits me that Andy and Alice are living in a place that is hidden away from the outside world—but in plain sight. Everything is simultaneously ghostly and absolutely present. I've lost my bearings and have no idea how to deal with the vast world laid out before me. But because I'm a landscape historian, and landscape historians always look out the window to see what's there, I peer through the east window. Yes, the axial garden path that marches through the giant boxwoods *does* align exactly with the view from this window, meaning there is a good chance that the builder of the house knowingly connected the two. I feel I could follow this slim lead on the ground and backward into history. We head into the library, dimmed by half-drawn blinds, where the rare histories of rail that are Andy's passion stand shelved beneath a sepia photograph of a fur-hatted "Papa" Horsford, as Professor Eben Norton Horsford, Andy's great-grandfather, is called by the family. The personal fortune of this self-made man gave the manor a sorely needed boost in the 1850s. I'm told that a framed crewelwork strip hanging beside the photo came from a set of eighteenth-century bed hangings. Andy says that the bed once furnished a room on nearby Gardiners Island, a sister manor first settled in 1635 by Lion Gardiner, a Dutch-trained English fortifications engineer. A Gardiner descendant married the girl in the red dress, a Sylvester descendant. I nod. Of course.

The next stop is a blank wall in the front hall, or so it seems. Andy waits a beat, which allows me to see the outline of a secret jib door cut into the garlanded silk wallpaper. He then creaks open the thick panel to reveal a walk-in safe, a vault that Andy has been told could withstand the hottest flames for six hours. I can barely keep from saying that fire would probably consume this wooden house in minutes, the timbers are so old and dry. The vault ceiling is about seven feet high, and the walls—lined with high dark chests and file cabinets—press in on us from every side. Old trunks crowd the red-tiled floor. By the single sixty-watt bulb, I can pick out one with a curved top painted the same acid blue-green as the parlor undercoat; another is covered in hide. Thousands of documents are housed here in these trunks and many others, in drawers, and in albums in which Andy has flattened some several hundred of his most precious ones, decoding them over countless Sunday mornings. (Andy, quietly determined not to be a churchgoer like his wife, has found a convincing escape.) Other papers have not been read since the original recipients broke the wax seals, or slit the envelopes, and then bundled them up with ribbon or string for reference someday. Someday in 1690, or 1790, or 1890, or today.

Andy opens what he calls "the object case." Each dark metal shelf is loaded—a framed letter from Thomas Jefferson to Ezra L'Hommedieu about "the Hessian fly," a crop pest, an antique meerschaum pipe; an Indian treaty of 1654, written on both sides of the parchment paper and signed with the "marks" of many Indian sachems. And there are things that are counted as treasures only by those who have stashed them here: a woman's long, fat braid of light brown hair, a tarnished metal spirit level barely an inch long with the bubble still intact. Silver candelabra lord it over prosaic metal file cabinets. In glass-front cupboards, display dishes are heaped with brooches, strands of beads, and earrings, a stone block incised with the date 1777, a small yellow brick, sets of porcelain cups, pincushions bristling with pins. As Andy puts each precious artifact into my hands, he tells me its story, making the past as vivid for himself as for me.

We take the heaviest album into the dining room, where there is more light. I watch while Andy quietly smooths out on the mahogany table the original parchment charter for what had once been an 8,000-acre water-bounded domain—the entire island. Blobs of red wax, the personal stamps of the various parties, dot the wide sheet, from which dangles a large, handsome governmental seal. Signed in 1666 by Richard Nicolls, the first governor of the English colony of New York, the document defines the place, "by the Indyans formerly called by the name of Manhansucke Ahaquatzuwamocke and now commonly known as by the name of Shelter Island." The island, and 435-acre neighboring Robins Island, had previously been conveyed "into the hands of Constant Silvester of the Island of Barbadoes Esqr, and Nathaniell Silvester now Inhabiting and residing in Shelter Island aforesaid Merchant," and their two other partners in 1651. But Nicolls's signature now affirms more than mere ownership: "NOW KNOW YEE That . . . I do hereby . . . Give Grannt and Confirme . . . that the said Island & premises, now is, and forever hereafter, shall be . . . deemed, reputed, taken and held as an absolute Intire, Infranchized Township mannor and place of it selfe in this Government." (Governor Nicolls and his home government mistakenly imagined that the feudal system of hereditary rights bestowed with the land itself would take root across America.) For the powerful privileges of manorial squires, which included the appointment of a magistrate and exemption from taxes and military levies, the two Silvester (later Sylvester) brothers paid Nicolls a hefty sum, £150 sterling in beef and pork, probably raised on the island. I briefly wonder what happened to the other two partners, then discard the thought—there are too many other questions crowding my mind.

Such as: Why isn't this incredible document about the very earliest colonial history of this country in a museum or a library? Like the several hundred acres of open land that Andy still owns, reduced from the original 8,000-acre domain, the creased old charter has survived intact for more than three centuries through a combination of design and accident and pure luck. I was brought here by water to be shown an eighteenth-century house and a landscape seemingly unchanged by time; I am now about to discover a great deal more. Before my eyes, the written history of this refined eighteenth-century house has now been pushed back about a hundred years to a highly experimental period of European settlement. Andy Fiske carefully slides the charter back into its heavy red leather housing.

In the west parlor, we gaze at a gorgeous nineteenth-century French panoramic wallpaper: snowy peaks, garden terrace balustrades topped with overflowing urns of flowers, and peacocks. I sign the guestbook and turn to admire the mantel. To the left of it is a closed door with two oval holes cut in the transom panel above. Walking toward the door, Andy says, "This leads to the slave staircase," as if it were the most natural thing in the world to have a slave staircase in your early Georgian house on Long Island. A breeze suddenly blows through the window that overlooks the creek, lifting the organdy curtains like a breath. The openings in the transom become eyeholes in a mask, studying us.

The staircase behind this door spirals up to the attic, Andy remarks, pointing out how narrow and high the steps are. But nobody walks up this pinched back staircase any longer: the steps are blocked by a collection of small vases and dishes, mostly crystal and metal, which glitter in the light from a glassed side entry. Later I can't help but notice the luxurious treads of the front stairs, whose four-inch risers are so shallow I seem to float effortlessly upward.

It begins to sink in: the "servants" who Andy said built the house were slaves. So were those who lived in the house built by Nathaniel and his wife in the 1650s. In common seventeenth- and eighteenth-century American parlance, slaves were often called servants, as were indentured servants, whose terms did not last for life and whose children would be free. As I listen to Andy's glancing mention of the staircase, I realize I am face-to-face with slavery in the North.

In 1984, Andy was among the comparatively few who were aware of Northern slavery. His family had lived with that knowledge as his ancestors had lived with their captives. The door to memory had never closed.

Human bones were discovered in 1991 in New York City about a mile and a half north of Wall Street as builders began to clear the ground for another skyscraper. The struggle to stop construction occupied many column inches in every newspaper. Archaeologists who excavated only a portion of the area estimate that as many as ten thousand people may have been interred there. During a long century (the burial ground was opened in the late 1600s and closed in 1794), burials may have stretched for miles beyond the original five- to six-acre plot. By 2003, 419 human remains exhumed from what was identified as the old "Negro Burial Ground" had been carefully analyzed by Howard University. Nearly half of them were those of children under twelve. Placed in wooden coffins hand-carved in Ghana, once the grisly center of the West African slave trade, all 419 were reburied at the site and mourned publicly by some ten thousand visitors. The discovery of the African Burial Ground brought with it the dawning recognition that wealthy colonial society in the North—epitomized perfectly by the Sylvesters' lucrative Long Island plantation—was initially shaped by generations of captive people, until 1827, when slavery was finally abolished in New York State.

Did slaves live in the attic of this house? Andy assures me they did. I pose my questions politely and ask whether I might see it. To avoid the knickknacks on the lowest flight of the slave staircase, we take a different route to reach the second floor. In the top hall hangs a photograph of James Russell Lowell, a committed abolitionist, his snowy beard spread comfortably over his waistcoat. He looks at me. What does Mr. Lowell think about slaves at the manor, I wonder. And why is he here?

On we go, Andy and I, through a bedroom door that leads to the top flight of the slave staircase. Climbing the steep steps makes my calves ache. Or maybe it is just that I can't yet believe who climbed them. The attic is full of racks of clothes, colored lithographs in chipped but handsome frames, a tiger-skin rug complete with snarling head, a beautiful train set, hatboxes, and dozens of flowered china chamber pots. Andy says the slaves may have slept on the boards that rest on joists above our heads. Two crude ladders lie on the floor. Are they proof that somebody climbed up there? The spaces around the two massive chimneystacks are the warmest places in the house, Andy adds.

Andy is not unsympathetic to my interest in the slaves, nor is he apologetic about them. They are part of his history, his life, what roots him to this land. He is proud to have preserved all this and to know all he does about it. Standing in the dusty summer heat, he tells me about the earliest slaves, twenty-four people who are listed as property of Nathaniel Sylvester or of his partners, in Nathaniel's 1680 will. But Andy is more interested in pointing out the detailed images of ships, probably scratched with a penknife, in the whitewashed sheathing inside the attic dormers. A sailor himself, Andy admires the knowledge of hulls and rigging displayed by the unknown carver. One dormer looks out over Gardiners Creek. Who wanted to sail away from here?

Burying Grounds

Now Andy wants to lead me outdoors on a walk to what his family calls the Quaker Graveyard. We leave the house by the front door. As we turn to follow a deeply cut turf track that runs south through some woods, Andy pauses, looks back, and points to a tall stone standing in the lawn near the giant boxwoods. "The First House stood there," he says with certainty. Well, of course, I say to myself, Nathaniel Sylvester, the hardy seafarer and merchant who came to the island in 1651 and died here in 1680, couldn't have lived in this fine Georgian structure. It will turn out that Nathaniel's dwelling was more than the standard, modest, one-over-one First Period house that still can be seen occasionally in New England. Much later, I will discover it was described as "the late mansion house of Captain Nathaniell Sylvester" and stood surrounded by a throng of outbuildings. But Andy is moving on into the woods. So I leave my phantom Jacobean house, its mullioned windows glittering in the sun, to follow him. We emerge at the top of the creek, where a low metal railing encloses a small cemetery. From here we can look back toward the bridge that my friend and I had rowed under.

From what I have seen this morning, I get an uneasy sense of a history that has been prettified and mummified in family stories like the ones I just heard from Andy. This graveyard memorializes Nathaniel Sylvester and his clan as protectors of oppressed Quakers. Only later will I discover that, contrary to what Andy had told me, they were in fact Quakers themselves—and slaveholders, the ultimate contradiction. The top of an imposing table monument erected in 1884 bears a family coat of arms and a list of the manor's proprietors—which, to my surprise, acknowledges the island's original inhabitants, the Manhansetts. Scattered around the monument are a few gravestones. Some are carved with the winged skull that reminded seventeenth-century believers of where they came from and where they were headed, dust to dust. But Nathaniel and Grizzell's remains are not among them. More questions . . .

We leave the graveyard via a bridle trail cut through a grove of tall white pines. The path is carpeted with soft reddish-brown needles; we make no sound as we walk. We skirt a freshwater swamp edged with pepperidge trees and fragrant summersweet. The fine south front of the manor house appears from time to time through the trees and across a wide meadow.

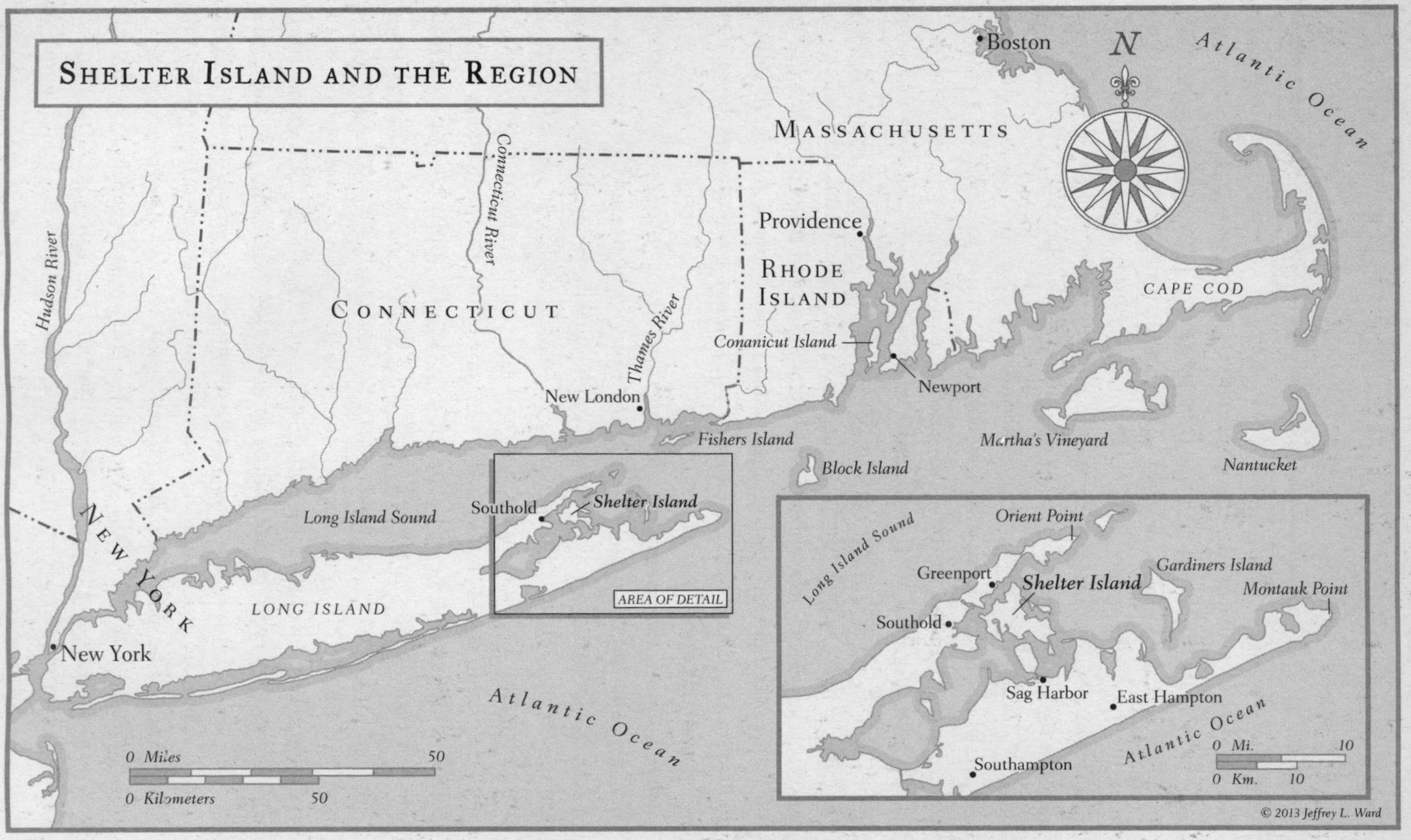

SHELTER ISLAND AND THE REGION
N
Atlantic Ocean
Boston
MASSACHUSETTS
Providence
RHODE ISLAND
Conanicut Island
Newport
CAPE COD
Martha's Vineyard
Nantucket
Block Island
Fishers Island
CONNECTICUT
Connecticut River
Thames River
New London
Hudson River
NEW YORK
New York
Long Island Sound
LONG ISLAND
Southold
Shelter Island
AREA OF DETAIL
Atlantic Ocean
0 Miles 50
0 Kilometers 50
Long Island Sound
Orient Point
Greenport
Shelter Island
Gardiners Island
Montauk Point
Southold
Sag Harbor
East Hampton
Southampton
Atlantic Ocean
0 Mi. 10
0 Km. 10
© 2013 Jeffrey L. Ward

The penumbra of beauty and power that vibrates around this house bears little relation to its compact size. The south front measures only forty-two feet across. From this angle, so different from my first water view of it, the serene shingled mass and ample hip roof are perfectly framed by the two mighty chimneys just behind the ridge. Why does this place create such a profound impression? Partly because it has all apparently survived—house, garden, landscape, papers, stories, and people still around to tell those stories. In this day of You Are Here restorations and re-creations, it's a potent mix. And partly it's a matter of perfect proportions. Early Georgian architectural harmony and symmetry triumphed with the first flowering of the British Empire. The sense of domination over the physical world, the aura of special grace, and the confidence of the Enlightenment are twined with that empire, and with this structure. More than anything else, however, my sense of this place comes from my visit to the attic with Andy, the stories he has told me, and my queasy sense of more to come. And all this is made increasingly extraordinary because we are in a Long Island enclave where ostentatious beachfront houses on tiny parcels of land that cost millions of dollars are built, torn down, rebuilt, and flipped every year.

The unknown people who lived here and helped create this place step forward when Andy and I reach what he says some call the slave graveyard, others the Indian burying ground. As I drove in, I had noticed an old gray fence line, but missed a big boulder lying closer to the main drive. Now I see an inscription carved on the flat side: "Burying Ground of the Colored People of the Manor since 1651." There are no gravestones in this graveyard under the pines. Andy tells me that more than two hundred people may be buried here. I don't ask where are the records, why are there no markers? I can guess the answer. These are the ones who slipped soundlessly through history.

In later conversations, Andy will expand on what he knows about the manor slaves, acknowledging that the forced labor and hardships of many people helped to make possible the building of this fine yellow house and the fortunes of this family, still in residence after nine generations. For now, all I see is that he keeps the interior of the fenced rectangle comparatively free of underbrush. The fence is in good repair. Andy opens the fine little gate on the northeast side. The metal gate latch clicks crisply behind us. We are back outside.

Reading a Plantation Landscape

Although the lure of the manor was undeniable, it was not until I was writing a book about George Washington that I grasped what I had seen on Shelter Island. Results of documentary and archaeological research at Mount Vernon drove home the obvious: that often when Washington said "I," he was talking about the slaves who did the work of shaping his immense plantation landscape.

Before the discovery of New York's African Burial Ground, slavery in the North had generally been considered a passing phenomenon pushed by a pressing need to clear the land, not as a powerful social structure that lasted for more than two hundred years. Northern slavery was largely obliterated from memory because it didn't serve the North's version of the Civil War. Although the fight for African American freedom began in New England, the story of race relations in this region was put aside. Slavery became the skeleton in the attic.

New York City slavery comprised only one aspect of the system. By the time Andy's house was built in the 1730s, Long Islanders owned more human chattel than any other group of colonists in the North. In outlying areas such as Shelter Island, up to half the workforce was enslaved. After the Revolution, in 1799, the new state enacted agonizingly complex graduated manumission laws. New York State's last slaves were set free on the Fourth of July, 1827, only thirty-four years before the outbreak of the Civil War. Buying and selling continued through the years of graduated manumission: Sylvester Dering, Andy's forebear and lord of the manor between 1785 and 1820, purchased a "Negro man Joseph" in 1810. In 1821, Dering's widow would emancipate London, the last of the slaves at the manor. Because there was never a single cash crop nor a united slaveholding oligarchy to point a finger at, the ubiquitous presence of slavery, which shaped New York physically, financially, and socially in profound ways, was obliterated. After the Civil War, the legend of a victorious Abolitionist North expanded. As the struggle for an appropriate monument to the cemetery continued in New York City, and even before my Washington book was published in 1999, I found myself longing to be back in the Sylvester Manor vault.

Andy died of cardiac complications in 1992, at the age of eighty. Alice, in her late seventies by the time I returned in 1996 to do some research for an article about the manor garden, was still wearing a version of the remarkable mobcap she had worn when we first met in 1984. It turned out to be her daily attire, one of dozens in chintz or plain fabric made up for her by her dressmaker. She also wore fifties-style plastic poppit beads carefully matched to her blouse and skirt, along with diamonds and gold bracelets. And wrist-length white gloves. People on the island said, "Alice dresses up to go to the post office." Indeed she did. On summer afternoons, crisply clad in white, she also whacked croquet balls across the part of the garden lawn dedicated to the game. She brushed her hair a hundred strokes every day, as instructed by her mother long ago, and often demonstrated to me how she could put her hands flat on the floor from a standing position. No doubt she owed her flexibility to the many years in the garden that occupied so much of her time and affection, those two acres where she dug and sweated, hollered and gave orders. An autocrat, she was also smart, funny, manipulative, outspoken, observant, and, on occasion, tactful and empathetic. She was very much the lady of the manor, loving both the place and the status it gave her.

When Alice and Andy met, both of them were just emerging from their first marriages. He was land poor, owning little except the island property and a great book collection. To economize, he lived in the back bedrooms of his house, shutting off much of it in winter to save money. Alice, the only heir to a compressed-gas fortune, saved him and his place from penny-pinching, land sales, and slow decay. Still, theirs was a love match and more; the marriage had lasted for fifty-four years.

By the time I returned to the manor, Alice was searching for a way to memorialize him. Andy, who had loved his family papers so dearly, had also loved archaeology. Fortuitously, I had just hired Gresham O'Malley, a graduate student at the New York Botanical Garden, to make measured drawings as illustrations for my article, a narrow look at the manor's Colonial Revival garden history. While Gresham and I tugged on strings and tape measures and yelled at each other across the hedges, he told me about his digger brother-in-law, Professor Stephen Mrozowski of the University of Massachusetts, Boston, who had excavated at Jamestown and other seventeenth-century sites in Virginia and New England.

As Gresham talked over our sandwiches about his brother-in-law's excavations, Alice realized this might be the way to keep Andy vividly close to her. The methodology of an archaeological dig struck us both as a way of continuing Andy's dig among his papers—and with the same intention to discover things and make connections. Later, I asked Gresham if he thought Steve would like to visit, maybe even consider Sylvester Manor as a project.

On a drizzly winter day, Steve drove up with his wife and kids, absolutely prepared, he later told me, to say no, but as we walked toward the house, he bent down and, from among the pebbles on the back drive, picked up a piece of creamware pottery and then a piece of eighteenth-century blue and white porcelain. Then he met Alice, who with her characteristic mix of down-home style and ceremony offered Pringles in a silver bowl as just the right pre-luncheon hors d'oeuvre. That clinched the deal.

Field archaeology requires squads of people, wads of money, and a lab to process the "finds." Alice soon funded a research center at UMass in memory of Andy. Ruddy, balding, and bearded, invariably dressed in shorts, T-shirt, and sandals, and often visibly excited by what he found, Steve came to the manor with a preliminary team in the summer of 1998. Fieldwork would continue for eight more years.

Steve is a historical archaeologist, which means he studies the recent past, not prehistory. Although historical archaeology is sometimes also described as the study of cultures that have a written record, ironically, in the Americas, it has proved most effective at revealing the lives of those who had little chance to enter that record because they were illiterate: native and enslaved people and the poor—laborers, factory workers, common soldiers, migrant workers. Steve, like others in his field, was digging to expose what James Deetz, who was considered the world's foremost historical archaeologist until his death in 2000, called "the spread of European cultures throughout the world since the fifteenth century, and their impact on and interaction with the cultures of indigenous peoples." On Shelter Island, Steve's team focused on the Indians of the East End, both before Europeans arrived (the "pre-contact era") and after, as well as on traces of the voiceless Africans.

Although Alice encouraged and cheered Steve's endeavors, she was hunting primarily for ancestors and real estate. She wanted to find Nathaniel's lost grave and authenticate the location of the vanished "First House." Buildings—even long-gone ones like this one—have a special place in American history: appearing so solid and reassuringly tangible, they are also roosts for folklore and speculation as well as repositories of the facts and dates from which we imagine we have built "the past."

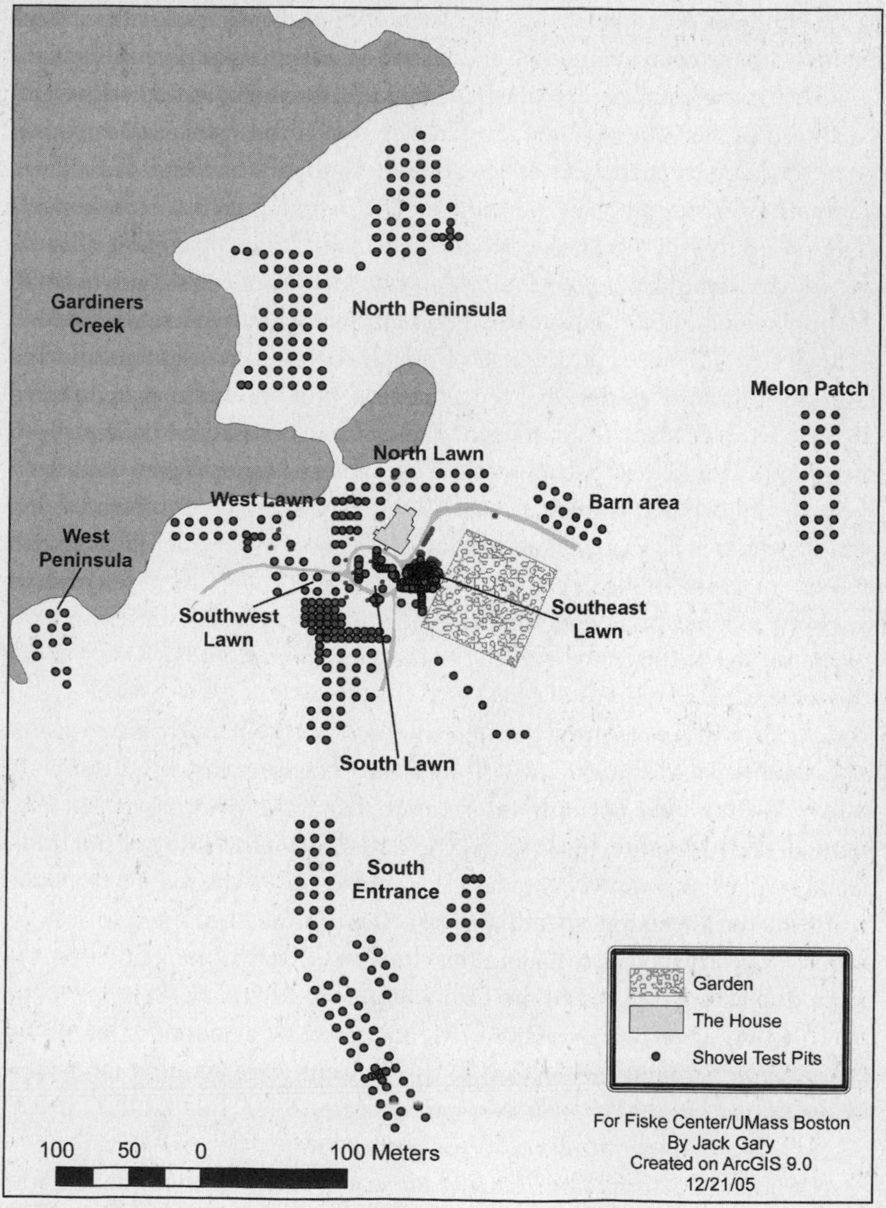

Shovel test pits (archaeology's first marks in the soil at any excavation) mark the eight years (1999–2006) of archaeological summer field schools at the manor by the University of Massachusetts Boston.

Steve's eight summer field schools undoubtedly will prove to be only the first phase of excavation on the incredibly rich site. He and his team came with the intention of unearthing what they called a multicultural Northern provisioning plantation that dates to the earliest days of European settlement on the Eastern Seaboard. Calling a farm in the North a "plantation" startled me, as did the concept that such places were specifically set up to provision West Indian sugar plantations powered by slaves. Steve's digs would unearth the often voiceless "conversations" that had taken place on Shelter Island between Europeans, Indians, and Africans, struggles over power and the use of space revealed by artifacts and the faint, multilayered evidence of fences, roads, and buildings.

Once the UMass team started, the Sylvesters' ease as travelers and merchants would also become visible as artifacts were teased out of the ground: English and European ceramics of every description, coins of five nations, Dutch clay pipes and bricks, a German silver stickpin, pounds and pounds of Caribbean coral, stockpiled as a vital ingredient for making mortar. Evidence of an enormously wide and adventurous world of people on the move rose up from beneath the manor's green front lawn, so smooth and settled.

Within the first year of the dig, my own path became clear. I asked Alice if she would agree to my writing a three-century history of the place that would include not only information from the documents but also some of the excavation results, and the day-to-day processing of the finds. For several years, however, "reading the landscape" of the manor as a landscape historian meant spending most of my time studying old letters, deeds, and other papers, hoping for clues to what had happened on the ground. The paper trail led me to many places where the Sylvesters had lived, worked, or merely visited. Meantime, out of doors, sticking up everywhere through the surface of the present were genuine landscape history question marks such as a garden gate to nowhere and a curious six-inch level change running across a meadow.

Steve and I had much to learn from each other. He, too, delved into the written history of the place, and he found, tucked away in the vault, a precious 1828 map of the existing house and its outbuildings that I had missed. And I discovered the thrill of thinking about this place as a dig site that sometimes supported the written evidence, sometimes proved it wrong. This island, Manhansucke Ahaquatzuwamocke—translated from the Algonquian as "island sheltered by islands"—was thickly inhabited by the Manhansetts before the Sylvesters settled it as part of a larger business project that foreshadowed modern global capitalism. It was a system born in what a new cadre of scholars term "the Atlantic World," a restless, constantly evolving web of ship-born connections, not the isolated New World of settlement that Andy—and many historians before him—had considered to be the core of early American history. Money—how the Sylvesters made it, married it, lost it, kept it over three centuries—is also part of the tale. From their Atlantic World mercantile beginnings, Nathaniel's descendants would become colonial—and then American—lawyers, magistrates, revolutionaries, soldiers, government officials, speculators, and scientists. They also continued to farm, although it was never their sole occupation.

From a contract Nathaniel and his partners had drawn up in 1652, it was clear that the four had initially envisioned the island not only as a place to raise livestock for the Caribbean market but also as a trading post for the exchange of goods with the Indians and with Europeans: the Dutch in New Amsterdam, for instance, or the Swedes, who had colonized Delaware, or with anyone else who was staking a claim in what was still essentially very contested territory in the 1650s. Nathaniel, younger than the three others, and with his fortune still to make, became the resident partner. Archaeology would show that his settlement evolved restlessly over almost thirty years, with buildings being moved, demolished, and rebuilt as needed. His polyglot establishment circled the same spot by Gardiners Creek, like a dog circling its bed before finally lying down.

So a big question now arose for me: Who exactly were those first Sylvesters? Andy and Alice knew that Nathaniel and his brothers and sisters, children of English expatriates, were born and raised in Amsterdam, but that was it—why they lived there and for how long, why and how they left, seemed relatively unimportant to them. The Dutch information coming out of the soil didn't connect with the eighteenth-century American colonial landscape I walked through every day. How could I write a book about these implacably disconnected fragments of an older Atlantic World?

I found funding for a Dutch graduate student to hunt down references to the family in the Netherlands. She located thirty-three precious Sylvester documents in the Amsterdam notarial archives. Transcribed and translated from the seventeenth-century Dutch, they charted the birth and growth of a far-flung trade network in which men like Nathaniel and his five brothers spent more time afloat than ashore. Their canny merchant father, Giles, remained in Amsterdam, the center of their operations. Demonstrably fluent in Dutch as well as English and powered by a fierce mercantile drive, these Atlantic adventurers operated with ample credit, relying on kinship and contacts to manipulate the levers of power—and injustice.

Shelter Island was hardly unique as a provisioning plantation. There were scores of such ventures along the coast of New England long before the monster establishments of the South were created. Nathaniel employed a heterogeneous force of indentured servants, enslaved Africans, and nominally free but virtually enslaved Indians. They shaped white oak timbers into staves, which he shipped south to the Caribbean to make barrels, the indispensable containers of the day. They bred and broke horses that were sent to carry sugar from mill to port. The grain they grew would feed man and beast. They butchered, salted, and casked cattle, sheep, and hogs, which were also shipped south to feed the hundreds of slaves who powered the sugar operations of the Sylvesters and their partners—and any other West Indian planters to whom they could sell their goods. Sugar, rum, and molasses came back to the manor or went to New England or Amsterdam or other European ports. There, sugar in its various forms was converted into cash to buy manufactured goods of all kinds to send back to New England and the Caribbean.

Sylvester Manor is the earliest of the Northern provisioning plantations to survive in such complete form. I learned that it has an integrity few others possess, retaining its original water access, land, architecture, and documents. But the larger interest collects around the American—the human—polarities that the place displays: the slave burial ground and the Quaker cemetery, the impulse to exploit versus the exceptionalist city-on-a-hill resolve that we could start over in the New World and this time do it right. The house and its landscape are where these opposites meet. Wrestling with the Sylvesters' problems of good and evil means wrestling with ours: What drives us to the crucial moment when one force overcomes the other? Interpreting the sketchy personal data available, taking historical events into account and making character judgments, I found that this question loomed over the full range of centuries and cultures at the manor. My answer would be very different from Andy Fiske's.

Telling the Tale

Andy had told me his version of the story as he had received it from his nineteenth-century forebears, the first people to look back at their history as history. For them, the house, its landscape, and the carefully preserved contents of the vault were what mattered. What I found mesmerizing in the vault were the fleeting references to what Andy's family historians didn't value: the stories of generations of slaves. As I wrote, the outlines of slavery in New England, of which Shelter Island was considered a part for the first century of settlement, began to take shape for me. Despite much recent scholarship, it's still a history that is harder to grasp than that of the plantation slavery system in the American South. This is partly because slavery did indeed take a different and less overtly vicious form here. Because the numbers of slaves were fewer and the labor arrangements and tasks more varied, the Northern system seemed at first to offer a greater range of freedom and choice. But whether it was crueler or kinder, Americans ceased to know anything about it.

By contrast with the rubbed-out actuality of Northern slavery, I found that many of the places people had left to come to Shelter Island exist weirdly unchanged. In Banda, near the Volta River in Ghana, where slave coffles once crossed on their way south to the slave castles of the Gold Coast, a rural life continues: field after field of cassava, outdoor cooking fires flickering, children dancing and shrieking in the last minutes of daytime play, yam stew and peace under a neem tree as the light fades and the earth cools. The steep thatched roof of the replica of an Asante fetish shrine museum in Besease still guards a mediating spirit, an *obosom*, who resides in a tree in the courtyard. On Barbados, Constant Plantation continues to be planted in sugar. (The local telephone directory lists hundreds of people named Sylvester.) In sleepy little Charlton Adam, in Somerset, the tithe barns and meadows that Nathaniel's father left when he emigrated to the Netherlands still stand. Nathaniel would have no trouble recognizing the houses I saw along Amsterdam's Singel Canal, where he lived. In London, and in Datchet, near Windsor, I walked among the landmarks of Grizzell Brinley's childhood.

As I arrived back on Shelter Island from travels in Europe, Africa, and Barbados, the unusual name of one of the manor's first Africans, Semonie, jumped out at me again and again from the pages of later local church records on Long Island. Someone carried this precious name down the generations. At the manor, archaeologists unearthed huge animal bones and the unbroken top half of a Manhansett pot from a slaughter pit beneath the lawn. A garden set aside for the slaves to cultivate as their own was discovered only inches under the brambles. The heron, the red-winged blackbirds, and the deer of Shelter Island appeared—and still appear—at the secret time of day when flowers of the imagination open, pale as X-rays.

2

Living with the Indians

Blood and Magic

It was still an Indian world when Nathaniel and Grizzell set foot on the island in the early 1650s. And yet among the several hundred documents that I've looked at so far, perhaps only a dozen—mostly land treaties and account books—deal directly with the Indians who lived here, with how they lived before the Sylvesters came, with how they lived both with the Sylvesters and with the Africans. The Manhansetts, the Algonquians of Shelter Island, and their neighbors, the Montauketts, Shinnecocks, Corchaugs, and other peoples of the East End of Long Island, thought of themselves as members of the Ninnimissinuok, or, loosely translated, "the people who lived in Southern New England," which for them and for the Sylvesters included most of Connecticut, Rhode Island, Massachusetts, Long Island, and the islands in the Sound. On Shelter Island they reveal themselves as sharp silhouettes, flickering by the fiery light of the complaints and grievances that make up most of their sorry colonial history. Every once in a while the light is bright, as when the Grand Sachem of Long Island, Wyandanch, the English colonists' ally, comes to Shelter Island from his Montauk home to witness a land deal. His signature is two stick figures: two men clasping hands in friendship, a white man and an Indian. It is the mark of a man who believed that the compacts he signed would hold.

The politics, the dance of alliances and betrayals, the astonishing bloodshed, the unspoken threats of violence on both sides, are all integral to a complete view of unfolding events in New England in the early 1650s. But it's hard to determine who was more violent, more "savage," the English or the Indians. "The confrontation between the American Indians and the

English colonists is almost always presented as a meeting between admirable but extremely primitive people and the representatives of a vastly superior culture," writes historian Karen Ordahl Kupperman. To right the comparison, just think of the criminals' heads lawfully displayed on London Bridge until they rotted that were an accustomed sight in Grizzell Brinley's England, or of the wartime massacre of every single man, woman, and child in the Dutch town of Naarden by the Spanish duke of Alba's son in 1572, a bloodbath still remembered fifty years later when Nathaniel was a little boy.

What brings the general acceptance of violence closest to peaceful Shelter Island for me are the severed Indian "fingers and thumes," thirty of them, that were offered to William Coddington, Grizzell's brother-in-law, then governor of Rhode Island. These bloody digits were the gift of the Narragansett sachem Canonicus, who wished to ally his people with the Newport colony by proving his warriors' ability to disarm or dispatch native enemies of the English. Almost as eye-opening as the tribute itself is Coddington's calm, matter-of-fact tone in a letter to Massachusetts governor John Winthrop: "Pesecus [another sachem] nore Canonecus have not sent unto me sence I rejected a present of 30 fingers and thumes . . ." This terse postscript doesn't say whether Coddington's refusal sprang from disgust or, more likely, political expediency. It illustrates the casual acceptance of violence as part of daily life that we know existed as a threat during Nathaniel and Grizzell Sylvester's decades on the island. Even though an uneasy peace held throughout their lifetimes, they lived with a background of fear, calculating that blood would be spilled again as the balance of power between natives and Europeans wavered.

Wyandanch, sachem of the Montauketts of eastern Long Island, came to Shelter Island to witness a sale document in 1658 for what we now call Lloyd Neck in Huntington, Long Island. He signed with his mark, the figures of two men clasping hands in agreement.

Kupperman says colonists feared not only Indian military attacks "but also that the Indians might use magic against them. They and the Indians believed in a world peopled with supernatural forces which could affect their lives." Algonquian accusations of witchcraft were taken seriously enough to be heard in English courts. The Salem witch trials, late in the seventeenth century, demonstrate forcefully that the colonists believed as much in the supernatural as any Indian who believed that the Pennacook sachem, Passaconway, a *powwaw*, or priest, could "make water burn, the rocks move, the trees dance, metamorphose himself into a flaming man."

To the North Peninsula

I'm at my desk in a ground-floor back bedroom at the manor, studying the family papers. Outside, winter's bareness exposes the mound north of the house, across the Upper Inlet; the part of Gardiners Creek spanned by the land bridge. Leafless trees frame the curve of the mound, a low hill that blunts the north wind shaking the old house. I watch the track crossing the stone bridge and disappearing into the woods. The mound, which the archaeologists call "the North Peninsula," seems remote, mysterious. I turn back to the papers, hoping to find more about the Indians who lived here.

In my hands is an untidy late-nineteenth-century manuscript written by Eben Norton Horsford, a layer cake of information about Shelter Island and the Sylvesters that has been stored in an old broken-backed cardboard box. Horsford, the Victorian patriarch on Andy's library wall, tells his version of the Sylvester Manor story in colorful prose—colorful at least by the standards of modern archaeological and anthropological reports. I'm not sure how much to believe him. When he gets to the Indians who lived on the mound in the seventeenth century, he writes:

> In the account of one of his visits to Sylvester Manor, George Fox mentions that he preached in front of the Manor House, to an audience of an hundred Indians. It must have been comparatively easy to send an invitation to a large body of the native inhabitants of the Island. The visit of Mr. Cushing, of the Ethnological Bureau at Washington, whose researches during his long residence at Zuni have given him an unprecedented skill in tracing indications of Indian occupation, has resulted in a solution of how this may have

been. Mr. Cushing finds the long mound East of the entrance to Dering water [the harbor beyond Gardiners Creek], was the site of an Indian village surrounded by a stockade . . . He also pointed out the path leading from end to end through the enclosure, along which were the sites of wigwams marked by abundance of shells and the dark earth covering the kitchen middens. A spade brought from one of them numerous fragments of pottery, bits of charcoal and bones, grains of corn, etc. The outline of the stockade which enclosed the cluster of wigwams was traceable. At one end of the mound a previous excavation by Dr. N. B. Derby had revealed the presence of Indian skeletons, and marked the site of the Indian graveyard . . . In times gone by great numbers of flint arrow heads, belts, knives, fragments of pottery, hammers, pestles and an Indian stone pipe have been gathered on the top of this mound . . . the long ridge looking across the mouth of Dering water toward Greenport, was the site of the stockade village of Youghco, the Chief of the Manhansetts, at the time of Capt. Sylvester's purchase, and the neighboring landlocked cove the sheltered yard of his fleet of war canoes and fishing craft. The depth to which the trail leading to the spring was worn, points to the occupation of the village site for centuries, and it is not improbable that the grave yard at the Southern extreme of the ridge has served for chiefs and clansmen, sachems and warriors, and their families from a date indefinitely early.

It all sounds so implausibly complete as a history. The nineteenth century stands in my way at Sylvester Manor, with its confident and conclusive explanations of events and motives. And what about the casual mention of George Fox, the Quaker founder, on Shelter Island? Anything else in the passage is momentarily overwhelmed by the presence of his name. Fox carried his incendiary Quaker doctrine throughout the Caribbean and up through the coastal colonies—that I knew. He was often better treated by the Indians than by his fellow Englishmen. On Shelter Island clearly he drew crowds. In his autobiography and other contemporary accounts, Fox seems like an English version of Passaconway, a man with the power to make the trees dance or to "metamorphose himself into a flaming man."

Suzan Smyth is with me in the manor workroom as I set aside my excitement over Fox and puzzle over what Horsford has to say about the

Indian village. The descendant of generations of a local Long Island family and the keeper of the history room at the nearby Sag Harbor library, she is also an archaeologist. "Why don't we go have a look?" Suzan says, nodding toward the North Peninsula.

As we walk across the land bridge, a blue heron flies over Gardiners Creek. The sky is dark gray; the trees are dripping, the ground is beginning to thaw; rampant bittersweet vines, greenbrier tangles, and blackberry canes fill every open area, making it hard to stray from the track. At the top of the wooded hill we begin to see large windfalls—trees, Suzan says, that were probably downed in the 1938 hurricane. The undersides of the tipped-up root-balls are masses of brownish clay and black topsoil. Suzan says that such dark soil can indeed be a sign of long habitation, where food trash or any organic material has been transformed past compost, back into soil. She scratches one root-ball and a shower of shining things tumbles out. They look eerily white on this dark day. Besides fragments of shell, Suzan identifies a stone projectile point and some chips of stone, known to archaeologists as "flakes," the debris left over from making the tip of a tool or weapon.

Suzan and I lift our eyes. Any sense of the manor's quiet isolation in time and space disappears. Through the bare trees we can see Greenport, across from Dering Harbor. Later we will find that on a clear day we can make out a fuzzy line lying above the horizon—the faint landmass of the Connecticut shore beyond Long Island sound. No wonder the Manhansetts prized this mound, like the Sylvesters after them. Algonquians such as the Manhansetts had ancient connections—both of family and trade—that linked them with a broad geography. By canoe and on foot, these networks led them down the Atlantic coast and deep into the interior of the continent. From as far away as the Southwest came some of their great gods, like Cautantowwit, "aloof, impersonal, benevolent," as John Strong, the most prominent of Long Island's present-day Indian historians, describes him. Cautantowwitt created the first human being from a piece of wood; his venerated messenger, Conconchus, the crow, gave them corn and beans.

Pushed by their hopes that at least some of Horsford's nineteenth-century description of a native settlement may be true, the UMass team excavates the North Peninsula during one of their first field schools in 2001. Their results are both chastening and encouraging. The bad news is that a "wigwam" footprint turns out to be that of a nineteenth-century gazebo. The Fiskes have a photograph of the gazebo, I later discover, taken in the 1870s when the entire North Peninsula was a pasture, with clearer views of Greenport and Connecticut. The good news: on the north shore of the mound, plenty of potsherds give proof of habitation dating back seven hundred years. But if Horsford's "chiefs, sachems, warriors, and their families" do lie buried here, we haven't found them. For now, the archaeologists intend to leave them undisturbed.

Jim's Drink

The spot where the Sylvesters settled had been a magnet for centuries. Since prehistoric times, Indians had gathered here. The north side of the mound gave them safety—they could see who was coming. From the beaches they could head out to gather clams, oysters, and scallops, and fish the deep waters for sturgeon. The south side offered land ideal for cultivation and abundant springs. The mound village was probably only a seasonal encampment; in winter they moved into the middle of the island, where trees broke the force of wind and foul weather, and game was plentiful.

The landscape the Manhansetts knew had received its shape from the last of the glaciers, the Wisconsin, which started moving implacably southward over New England some twenty-two thousand years ago. When paleogeologists use the term "ice-shoved," they are referring to places like Shelter Island, where the power of the glacier dropped long lines of stone, gravel, and sand: moraines. Except for impressive cliffs that face northwest, the topography has an unfinished, gently lumpy look, as if the shear lines of the pushed-together blobs of earth and rocks have not been completely smoothed over. When the glacier ground its way back up north beginning ten or twelve million years later, it paused several times, leaving stony recessional moraines. The one that marks the glacier's southern limit forms the Ronkonkoma Moraine, the hilly east-west spine of Long Island's South Fork that finally runs offshore into the ocean.

When glacial melting finally slowed down some three to four thousand years ago, the rise in Shelter Island's seawater level slowed to a fraction of an inch per year. Beaches widened as sand piled up instead of being washed away. Coastal sandbars drifted in to reconnect the tops of morainal deposits, like Ram Island, back to the main island. Marshes thickened and were cut by channels; bogs formed; estuaries were shaped, creating rich intertidal zones that supported the fish and crustaceans that were mainstays of the Manhansett diet.

The island's freshwater supply comes from a single source, an upper glacial aquifer that is recharged only by rain. It seems prodigal that the tidal shoreline of Sylvester Manor is pricked in many places with spring holes where the water from that aquifer seeps upward into the salty bay. In his manuscript, Horsford gives hard-to-follow directions to several springs. One near the land bridge, he says, can be seen only at low tide, among loosely piled stones. When I try to find it at ebb tide, I find no sign of anything bubbling up.

Every day I'm at the manor, I walk my dogs. In fine weather, Jim and Ruby lie patiently leashed under some spruces, waiting for the big event. Sometimes we go along the low shore bank so they can get excited about the Canada geese, who rarely respond. Most of the time, neither dog will go down into the water—Irish terriers are convinced they will melt if they get wet. But sometimes in the spring, Jim will pad through the mud, hunting frogs. Today it's a full-moon low tide, with barely a skim of wetness over the foreshore. Jim lowers his head. He's drinking from the creek. Jim is too smart to drink salt water. Is he drinking from Horsford's spring? I scoop up a small handful of water; it is muddy but fresh. The almost invisible flow—the merest shimmer of movement—makes its way among the small, dark stones, sheeting the surface. The Manhansetts, who knew every inch of Shelter Island's coastline, would have been familiar with Jim's spring. At least on this one, Horsford got it right.

Youghco Resists, Wyandanch Assists

Youghco (d. 1653), sachem of the Manhansetts, Wyandanch's kinsman and a leader recognized by European colonists and Indians alike as powerful throughout Long Island, lived on Shelter Island. In June 1651, apparently without consulting Youghco or any other Shelter Islander, Nathaniel and his partners purchased the property from Stephen Goodyear of New Haven. Thirteen months later, perhaps as Nathaniel was beginning to clear and build, Youghco sent a representative to the New Haven Colony court in Hartford. (Shelter Island was nominally under New Haven's jurisdiction.) He complained that he and his people were "threatened to be forced off the said island, and to seek an habitation where they can get it," that they had never envisioned being "deprived of their habitation there," and that they had never sold their land. An accomplished translator, Checkanoe, who was also a Manhansett, may have been responsible for the sophisticated prose of this document, which predicts what would be the eventual result of countless treaties between Europeans and Indians. The Manhansett petition arrived in court on September 2, 1652, only eighteen days before the partners signed the twelve articles of agreement setting out the plan for their new venture.

The backstory of the Manhansetts' complaint dates to 1637, when Charles I issued the first English patent for Long Island and all the adjacent islands to William Alexander, Earl of Stirling. Stirling's land agent, James Farrett, took as his commission Shelter Island and nearby Robins Island (where the Manhansetts also lived) and sold both to Goodyear before returning to England. By the time Goodyear made his deal with the partners, English colonists feared that New Amsterdam was secretly arming Long Island's Indians for war against them. Anxious to keep Youghco as an ally, New Haven's authorities required the partners to purchase the island a second time.

Six months later, in March 1653, Youghco met with Nathaniel to officially ratify the transfer of the island with an Indian deed and an English ceremony. Nathaniel, perhaps in a good dark coat and breeches for the momentous occasion, would have advanced to meet the elderly man, who would die only a few months later. From contemporary accounts I can gather more about Youghco's appearance than Nathaniel's on that day. As chief sachem of Long Island, Youghco carried himself royally among his followers, as did one earlier Virginian leader: "For though hee hath no Kingly Robes . . . nor dayly Guardes to secure his person . . . yet doe they yeeld all submissive subjection to him . . . going at his command, and comming at his becke." If he wore face paint for this important moment, his characteristic sharp cheekbones and prominent nose would have set the angles for the stripes of pigment. Most of his hair had probably been plucked from his head, face, and body, and what remained on his head was probably gathered into a *wuchechepunnock*, "a great bunch of hayre bound up behind," or possibly a *muppacuck*, a long lock hanging down. By the 1650s, some Indian men had begun to favor European cloth mantles and coats instead of furs and deerskins, or cloaks "made of the fairest feathers of their Neyhommauog, or Turkies, which commonly their old men make; and is with them as Velvet is with us." A breechcloth, leggings, and moccasins still completed a standard Algonquian outfit, with neck pendants and a belt of wampum added to honor ceremonial events or to denote rank.

What one commentator said about the Jamestown Indians also offers a vivid impression of coastal Algonquians in those years: "They are a very understanding generation, quicke of apprehension, suddaine in their dispatches, subtile in their dealings, exquisite in their inventions." Roger Williams of Rhode Island, discussing the local Indians' taste in English cloth, added an observation on their temperament. He wrote that rather than admire "Cloth, inclining to white," they preferred "a sad [dull or sober] coulour without any whitish haires, suiting with their own naturall Temper, which inclines to sadnesse [meaning what we think it means regarding temperament]."

Dispossession was a step-by-step process. When Youghco gave Nathaniel a "turfe and twige," the clump of island soil and a branch that "according to the usual custom of England" signified the consummation of a land sale, the sachem "with all his Indians that were formerly belonging to said island . . . did freely and willing depart." Nathaniel was becoming a landowner for the first time; it's not at all clear what the ritual meant to Youghco. Certainly the ceremony illustrates an important metamorphosis: common land was becoming private property. British law and custom superseded Indian tribute ceremonies, in which gifts of wampum had sealed treaties and deeds over rights and use. In any case, after this formal ritual had taken place, many Indians either remained on the island or soon returned. But as their hunting and fishing grounds were lost to colonial occupation, they became ever more dependent on trade goods such as cooking kettles, hatchets, shoes, cloth, and above all liquor. Shelter Island was not only home, but also a place where they found employment as a permanent underclass of servants, slaves, and freemen. They worked as messengers, butchers, whalers, field hands, whalers, domestics, and livestock herders and handlers. For some, the island seemed preferable to a mainland taken over by growing numbers of white households and controlled by stringent and unfamiliar English regulations. At least on Shelter Island, there was only one family and one law—the Sylvesters'—to contend with.

Even before he officially relinquished the island, Youghco had understood that his world would be very different with Europeans in it. Unlike

Wyandanch, he resisted. Lion Gardiner, the Sylvesters' near neighbor, Wyandanch's friend, and his close collaborator in many land deals, later wrote that when Wyandanch asked the elder sachem to hunt down Indians who came to Shelter Island who were accused of killing colonists or of plotting against the English, Youghco either refused, enabled the fugitives to elude capture, or helped prisoners to escape. (English courts routinely sentenced Indian offenders to death without regard for tribal codes of justice.)

Visiting

At the Manhansett settlement, wigwams were dwarfed by forest giants, forebears of the oaks and hickories still here today. The rounded roofs followed the curves of their frames: arched saplings, usually black locust or red cedar, strong yet supple, whose fire-hardened tips were stuck firmly in the ground. Red maple saplings tied to them on the inside braced the structure. Woven mats or laboriously flattened bark were lashed onto the frame with bark or root ties. Pine resin sealed the tie holes. The early New England chronicler William Wood said wigwams "deny entrance to any drop of rain, though it come fierce and long, neigther can the piercing North winde finde a cranny." Elliptical or circular in plan, household wigwams were small—the largest only fifteen by twenty feet in diameter. Calabashes, carved wooden implements, nets, baskets, woven bags, bows strung with animal sinew, and arrows of elder wood hung on walls and tent rafters, alongside a wealth of dressed skins, some painted in bright vegetable colors.

The hearth was in the middle of the floor, vented through a hole in the roof for smoke—very like the arrangement in many English houses before "the Great Rebuilding" of the sixteenth century, which introduced fireplaces set against an outside wall. Daniel Gookin, who served Massachusetts Colony as Indian commissioner for more than three decades (1652–86), writes that he had often stayed overnight in wigwams and had always found them to be as warm as any English house. (This comparison was easy to make in favor of the Indians, given the rudimentary heating in seventeenth-century houses all over Northern Europe, where firewood was beginning to run short, especially for the ordinary man.)

Indian domestic fires burned day and night, just as they did in any colonial household. By night, on wide raised platforms circling the central fire in the wigwams, the Indians slept on sweet-smelling woven reed mats heaped with furs and skins—otter, beaver, bear, lynx, deer, raccoon, fox. The soft mesh of darkness was often interrupted: some woke to sing, or sit upright out of their sleep and murmur, startled, from a dream. Sometimes there was a lament—*mâuo*—sorrow for the dead. Not that nighttime in Amsterdam, the African Gold Coast, or London was any less noisy. But the comforting, expected blanket of night sounded different to the newcomers. Huge bonfires also lit up the night sky from time to time, signaling festivals and feasts, meetings and attacks. The meanings of the fires were clear to the Manhansetts and the other coastal Indians, but again, not to foreigners.

The setup of a native village was equally foreign to the Sylvesters. An Indian visitor who reached the North Peninsula in the summer of 1653, when Grizzell first set foot on the island after her marriage, would have seen an orderly, productive encampment, whose inhabitants frequently shifted their wigwams around within the village, changing locations to find a cleaner site and to leave lice and fleas behind. On occasion, large parties set up campsites for seasonal hunting or fishing trips; wampum and pottery workshops moved closer to sources for shells or clay. By winter, all would have disappeared from the summer village, having migrated inland to the "warme and thicke woodie bottomes." But the supreme architectural advantage engineered by the Algonquians—mobility—made the English uneasy, since to them such impermanence was the earmark of a savage society, not a civil one. The English found language to express their unease with this Indian vanishing act. Even an observer as well disposed toward the Indians as John Josselyn could write, "I have seen half a hundred of their wigwams together in a piece of ground and they shew prettily, within a day or two, a week they have all been dispersed." Despite his admiration, Josselyn is asking a question: Could the impermanence of the village reflect some flaw, some lack of solidity, in the society as well?

All the same, Kupperman writes that Algonquians in fact met the standards by which seventeenth-century Englishmen judged a civil society. They had a complex language, government by hereditary rulers, and organized towns. They tilled the soil and providentially stored up food for winter and hard times. English visitors wrote admiring accounts of preservation methods, from smoking lobsters on scaffolds over a slow fire to bagging huge quantities of shelled dried corn and threshed beans in "Indian barnes." Serving the same purpose as the eighteenth-century root cellar excavated at Sylvester Manor, these "barnes" were underground pits as deep as six feet, lined with clay, grasses, and mats. Once the pit was filled with stores, sand or earth was piled on top to seal it.

"Friendly Joyning"

An Indian garden or field was a movable carpet, changing shape or location as soil became depleted. The fields were cleared by girdling and burning the trees, then chopping the burnt remains and leaving stumps to rot. This was a big job: "All the neighbors, men and women, forty, fifty, a hundred, joyne, and come in to help freely. With friendly joyning they break up their fields." Unlike an English field or garden, whose whole area would have been cultivated, Indians broke their plantings into small patches about three feet across, almost like raised beds, a custom the English soon followed in their first fields. Nonetheless, English observers who found this practice disorganized and wasteful cited it as more evidence that the Indians didn't deserve their land.

In summer, women bent over the young corn, piling earth up around the base of the stalks to steady them; bean vines climbed the stalks. (Together, corn and beans supply complete proteins—all nine essential amino acids.) The end of April and the month of May were called "when the corn is set," or "the planting month." Shelter Island Indians also planted by the stars: when the Pleiades finished their winter journey across the sky, and disappeared in the first week of May, corn was sown. But there were other planting signs as well: when dogwood leaves were the size of a squirrel's ear, when the alewives—small Atlantic fish that spawn in the fresh water where they were born, like salmon—choked the streams. June was "the weeding month," when women got out their clamshell hoes, "not suffering a choaking weede to advance his audacious head above their infant corn, or an undermining worm to spoil [it]." The Pleiades' reappearance in October signaled the harvest.

Manitoo! God Appears as Men, Women, Birds, Beasts, Fish

The indigenous Americans on Shelter Island were fishermen long before they took up agriculture. Shell middens—deep heaps of discarded shells—lie everywhere along the shore. The waters beyond the creek were more than fishing grounds, however. Out in the deep, the underworld opened to the home of Hobbemok, the god both of death and of everyday life. While Cautantowwit, creator of mankind, remained remote from human affairs but steadily benevolent, Hobbemok was unpredictably present. Even as believers blamed him for misfortune, they called on him for help. In his ambiguity and restlessness, he seems a peculiarly modern god. Cautantowwitt and Hobbemok, cast simply as God and Satan by the English, were both animated by *manitou*, a highly unpredictable shape-shifting force. "There is a generall Custome amongst them, at the apprehension of an Excellency in Men, Women Birds, Beasts, Fish &c. to cry out Manittoo A God," wrote Roger Williams.

The Manhansetts believed that they inhabited a three-layered circular cosmos—sky, earth, and underworld—supported and connected by a giant cedar tree. Possessed by *manitou* and aided by fasting, tests of physical endurance, incantation, music, and dance, human beings could penetrate mystical depths and heights. At the outer edges of the earthly world—whether inhaling the thick smoke of a ceremony or fishing on the long ocean swells past Montauk—a person could step across the threshold into mythic time and place.

How much the Manhansetts revealed of their beliefs to the Sylvesters—or how much the Sylvesters wanted to hear about "heathen" practices—is debatable. John Updike wrote that "description solidifies the past and creates a gravitational body that wasn't there before. A background of dark matter—all that is not said—remains, buzzing." The first Sylvesters lived their lives against that buzzing sound.

Mâuo: *A Lament*

The story of that early life when power hung in the balance between Native Americans and Europeans is as hard to put together as a pot in a thousand pieces. First of all, the disastrous loss of population meant that Indian New England was changing so fast that it is almost impossible to describe it except as a dissolving point on a trajectory: of the roughly ninety thousand Indians in the Northeast alive in 1600, nine-tenths had died by 1650 of epidemic diseases such as smallpox and measles, diseases that were entirely new to them. While the regional native population shrank to 9,000, the total of English inhabitants had already swelled to 18,500 by 1640. Even though Indians regrouped their decimated societies and reshaped their territorial boundaries and alliances after 1650, the psychological dislocation and disempowerment caused by the devastating losses increased the sense (among colonists as well as natives) that God had deserted the Indians.

Eastern Long Island's Indians never had their own early European chroniclers as did New England's: no William Bradford, no John Winthrop Jr., nor any of the host of lesser-known observers who recorded so many details of Algonquian life. Above all, they had no Roger Williams (1603–1683), the reporter I trust the most. The son of an English shopkeeper, Williams was a protégé of the brilliant jurist Sir Edward Coke and a highly respected scholar in England—what we might call a public intellectual. Only four years after Williams came to Massachusetts in 1631, the Bay Colony's Puritans kicked him out. While Williams is best known popularly for stating that civil authorities had no right to persecute their citizens over their differing religious beliefs (a basic tenet of the argument against the union of church and state), the reasons for his banishment were as much political as theological. Massachusetts feared the unwanted attention from the crown and authorities in England that Williams's strident insistence that the colony separate publicly from the Church of England would bring. Politically canny, the Bay oligarchy preferred to keep their heads down on this subject. Williams also loudly held that Charles I had no right to confiscate Indian land—thus denying the validity of the colony's precious patent. Massachusetts wasted no time in banishing him; Williams headed for the friendly Narragansetts, in Rhode Island.

In his *A Key into the Language of America*, published in 1643, a sort of Christian guide and Algonquian phrasebook (he spoke the language), Williams draws sympathetic and acutely observed portraits of the Narragansetts "from their Birth to their Buriells." Williams called his *Key* an "Implicite dialogue." Some entries read like cheerful Berlitz exchanges: coming into an Indian village by night, Williams asks *Yo nickowemen?* or "Shall I sleep here?" and receives the answer *Wunnegin, cowish*: "Welcome, sleepe here." Sometimes a single word can describe the wrenching cultural shift under way even as he wrote; in the section titled "Of Buying and Selling," Williams observes "*Cuppaimish* I will pay you . . . is a word newly made from the English word pay." When the team excavated a Spanish "cob," a roughly milled bit of silver, from the jumble of European roof tiles and ceramics in the midden, they found one side incised with an angular drawing, a potent Native American religious emblem: a thunderbird. The European power of money—silver—had been rephrased in another language.

The spoken language throughout southern New England was Algonquian. Most speakers, from whatever nation, could understand one another. Discovering this was a relief; I felt easier about pulling details from Williams and other Rhode Island and Massachusetts sources. Connections ran across Long Island Sound, so that Algonquians in Connecticut, Rhode Island, and the Cape were the neighbors, not those surrounding and north of New York City. (The shortest distance across the Sound is about ten miles, while New York City is eighty miles from Shelter Island by car.)

Long Island Indians had been shielded from direct dealings with Europeans by the dominant Connecticut Pequots, who extracted tribute from them in exchange for protection until 1637, when Pequot power was extinguished following an escalating series of New England colonial demands to avenge the deaths of two English traders. The struggle culminated in genocide. English-led forces and some Indian allies attacked a stockaded Pequot village in Mystic, Connecticut, and set it afire; a massacre and an ensuing bloody pursuit killed off most of the tribe's warriors. Those men who survived, including the boys, were sold to the West Indies as slaves. The women and girls were sold by lot to the victorious and eager New Englanders, setting a precedent on Long Island as well for Indian slavery that would last until the nineteenth century, notwithstanding ineffectively enforced legislation against it as early as 1679. "Pequot" was outlawed as a tribal name, and those Pequots who survived were absorbed into other Indian communities. Such total extermination was new to the Indians. The effects of the Pequot War also reverberated through the marriage of Indian women who found partners among enslaved Africans, increasing the mix of races already begun.

The Manhansetts, who had stayed out of the Pequot struggle as much as possible, weighed the outcome and sent tribute to the English a few weeks after their final victory. Previous to this conflict, the decades of Pequot protection, uneasy and difficult as they had been for the vassal nations, may have led Long Island Indians to assume that the English would also abide by the treaties they negotiated, which they did not. Early land sale agreements required European goods and sometimes currency—such as Old Peter Minuit's "twenty-six dollars and a bottle of booze" for the island of Manhattan—in exchange for wampum to seal the terms of the deal. Contrary to what Rodgers and Hart wrote, however, wampum and hatchets and desirable "trade cloth" were treated by the Indians as ceremonial offerings that didn't represent actual property values, but were considered to pave the way for alliances. Like the seals on English government documents for the English, exchanging gifts acted as acknowledgments of agreement over rights. To the English, on the other hand, such gifts confirmed the transfer of ownership, or, more precisely, complete control of the land.

Wampum beads—small polished purple and white hand-drilled cylinders made from two species of shellfish that thrived almost exclusively in Long Island Sound—were the original big attraction for the English besides land. Wampum had originally been so sacred it was handled only by sachems, but it gradually became a currency that spurred the growth of the European fur trade, the first exchange commodity. Wampum has been found as far north as Maine and westward to the Ohio River. Coastal Algonquians such as the Montauketts and Manhansetts were in a sense enslaved by the need to produce more and more wampum and to pay more and more tribute, first to their Pequot overlords and then to the English. After Europeans began to manufacture wampum with steel drills, inflation eventually took its toll. By 1661, wampum was no longer legal tender in Massachusetts, for example, where it had been institutionalized in 1637 as currency at a rate of six beads for a penny.

Long Island's wampum supply, fertile soils, and many harbors drew English settlement by the 1640s. Miantonomi, a Narragansett sachem from Rhode Island, prophesied in 1641:

> ye English . . . Say broth^{r} to one anoth^{r}, So must we be one as they are, oth^{r}wise we shall be all gone shortly, for you know our fathers had plentie of deare, & Skins, our plaines weare full of dear as also our woods and of Turkeies, and our Coves full of fish and foule, but these English having gotten our land, they with Sithes cut downe ye grass, and with axes fell the trees their Cowes & horses eat ye grass, and th^{r} hoggs spoyle our Clambanks, and we Shall all be starved . . .

The supply of desirable land was soon exhausted, as Long Island measures only 113 miles long and 23 wide at its widest point. There were no distant forests and fields for Indians to retreat to. Miantonomi's prediction, and his plea for unified resistance, came true. Algonquians of Connecticut, Rhode Island, and Massachusetts did band together in 1675 to wage what is called King Philip's War, undertaken to force the colonists out of America. By then, the East End tribes were too divided and weak to join in. They had already lost. *Mâuo*, indeed.

Cattails and Phragmites

A dirt track runs along an earthen causeway built to carry farm equipment across the Upper Inlet to the big flat north fields of Sylvester Manor, closing off the large freshwater spring that fed it. Most of the inlet has become a brackish marsh, overgrown with phragmites, the invasive, non-native common reed. But since the causeway isn't quite watertight, a thread of fresh water supports a thin trail of cattails weaving through the taller phragmites. Common cattails, which grow only in fresh water, can't compete with phragmites, whose rhizomes, often fifty feet or more in length, flourish in both fresh and salt water and choke out other species. Those cattail stragglers are losing the ecological battle here in the Upper Inlet.

I find myself studying these reeds because I've left the manor house to clear my head after reading early Italian explorer Giovanni da Verrazzano's description of his encounter with Rhode Island Indians in 1524. Gliding along through his overwhelming description of that meeting, I feel the beauty and power of the Indians as Europeans first saw them. These were not the violent and drunken people Nathaniel Sylvester complained about in 1672 after he had paid their wages for years in hard cider and West Indian rum, or the romanticized "red men" that Eben Horsford imagined two hundred years later. Verrazzano's Algonquians were utopian figures. They were pagan demigods, stepping out of ancient myth to embody a Golden Age:

> Before entering [a harbor], we saw about twenty small boats full of people, who came about our ship, uttering many cries of astonishment . . . Among them were two kings more beautiful in form and

> stature than can possibly be described; one was about forty years old, the other about twenty-four, and they were dressed in the following manner: The oldest had a deer's skin around his body, artificially wrought in damask figures, his head was without covering, his hair was tied back in various knots; around his neck he wore a large chain ornamented with many stones of different colors. The young man was similar in his general appearance. This is the finest looking tribe, the handsomest in their costumes, that we have found in our voyage . . . They exceed us in size . . . their faces are sharp, and their hair long and black, upon the adorning of which they bestow great pains; their eyes are black and sharp, their expression mild and pleasant, greatly resembling the antique.

"Two kings": to me they represent Youghco and Wyandanch. On my way back to the house, instead of gazing across the phragmites/cattail battle in the marshy inlet, I look down into the big spring on the other side of the causeway, a shallow hole about forty feet in diameter thickly surrounded by wineberries and blackberries and weeds. Standing in the middle are about a hundred more cattails, silent and brown and completely unexpected. I stop breathing for some long seconds. I am looking at a remnant population of the increasingly rare cattail. Maybe I hadn't noticed them before, or maybe the extremely wet spring has given them the extra inch of fresh water they needed to germinate and flourish? They must have been there for months. Walking to the fields so often, I must have passed them many times.

I imagine the Indians often existed just like this for the first Sylvesters: always present, but only sometimes visible. Sometimes they were powerful, then powerless; sometimes dangerous, then accommodating and friendly: sometimes needed, and sometimes desperately wished—or legislated—away. The Indians, for their part, must sometimes have come into full view only when they wanted to be seen. I snap out of my vision and see just a bunch of cattails, bulwarked for the time being, by fresh water and the causeway, from invasive rhizomes and extinction.

3

Amsterdam

Earth, Water, Fire

By 2000, the UMass team has excavated hundreds of yellow bricks, whole and in fragments, from almost every section of the dig that has now pockmarked the lawns on all sides of the manor house. The archaeologist Paul Huey, the "brick man from Albany," once visited and said that there was more yellow brick at Sylvester Manor than at all the Dutch sites he had dealt with in New York State put together. "Yellow" is a relative term here: these small bricks, about 1.5 × 2 × 6 inches, range in color from dun to ocher to a soft honey to a dispirited salmon. Their color indicates where they were made: in Gouda, of clay dug from the bed of the IJssel River ("Eye-sel"). High-fired bricks have a hard surface that withstands wear when they're laid as pavers and a density that prevents rising damp from seeping into their core. Many of these bricks, however, are creased, dented, torqued out of shape because the IJssel clay was worked while still soft or the firing temperature was too high or low. Shelter Island's acid soil has eaten away at the glaze until the surfaces look like sliced meat loaf on a cafeteria steam table.

Yellow bricks went wherever the Dutch did. In seventeenth-century Dutch genre paintings, they floor tranquil city gardens and backyards. In present-day Amsterdam, rain-polished yellow bricks shine on the residential quays. New York–bound trading vessels often carried Dutch bricks as ballast. In New York City, once New Amsterdam, they still turn up among the cobblestones of SoHo. Nathaniel and his partners used this sturdy material in the first buildings erected on Shelter Island, probably in foundations and chimneys.

Yellow bricks dovetail neatly with our image of the sturdy, benevolent, enterprising Dutch Golden Age—the decades between 1600 and 1672 when the Netherlands ruled the seas, enjoyed a higher standard of living than any other in Europe, and saw an explosion of artists and thinkers. Another set of these same bricks, however, yanks us into the murky back room behind the starched housewives and laughing cavaliers. At the Dutch trade castle Elmina, in Ghana, the steps leading up to the governor's quarters are built of yellow Dutch brick. During that same Golden Age, the Dutch also efficiently took control of the Atlantic slave trade. Footsteps on Elmina's brick steps echo the sound of merciless bureaucracy.

On a visit to Amsterdam's National Maritime Museum, I look at extravagantly beautiful Dutch maps and sea charts, along with books like Dierick Ruyter's *Torch of Navigation* (1623), which provided key information to sailors on trade routes to Africa. (I am startled to find that by 1614, Adriaen Block, a Dutch trader and navigator, had already mapped Long Island, the islands offshore, and the Connecticut coast.) A 1646 chart depicts Europe, Africa, and the east coasts of North and South America—Nathaniel's world on paper. The labels in Dutch and English point out various inscriptions; one reads *om slaven te halen*: "(in order) to buy slaves." The lettering runs across the South Atlantic, marking the slave carrier's route to Brazil. And there is "Mina St. George," Elmina, on the coast of Guinea. Across the North Atlantic, the mapmaker has labeled Adriaen Block's Island (Block Island). And between the forks of Long Island, precisely drawn but unnamed, lies Shelter Island.

The yellow bricks at Sylvester Manor speak not only of the extent of Dutch power, but also of the scope of Nathaniel Sylvester's ambitions. By the time Nathaniel walked out of his new house on Shelter Island in the early spring of 1653 to receive the ceremonial "turfe and twige" from Youghco, the Manhansett sachem, he had sailed around the Atlantic World for a decade as a "merchant factor," a man in charge of buying and selling goods, his own and others'. Now, for the first time in his life, he was a propertied man. The moment must have resonated with power.

Nathaniel's Amsterdam

Nathaniel was born in Amsterdam around 1620, when the city reigned as Europe's center of wealth, culture, and trade. By 1634 one goggle-eyed English traveler reported that five hundred ships left Amsterdam every week. Treasure crammed the warehouses and storerooms: gold, silk, pearls and emeralds, precious spices and dyes. But nothing was more precious in Amsterdam than land. Beginning in the twelfth century, the city had literally been raised out of the marshes and rivers. Pilings shoved into the peat or the stable layer of sand thirteen feet below the surface of the mucky water formed the foundations of many buildings. Worn-out ships were filled with stones, sunk, covered with soil, and paved over. Tiny building lots exploited every square foot of made land; each inch above sea level offered incrementally more safety from the continual threat of flooding. Nathaniel lived with everyday reminders of the dangers of water: the creak and roar of windmills on the defense walls told him that water was constantly being pumped out of Amsterdam. He heard locks opening and closing to flush the canals of garbage and sewage. The city's fluid environment was at best brackish; drinking water came at a premium. Barges delivered it to your door, or, if you were rich enough, a tiled cistern in your basement collected rainwater from the roof, the only free water in town. When Nathaniel first scouted Shelter Island, nothing could have pleased him more than the many fresh springs and ponds he found. Nothing would have seemed more familiar than the tide flushing the Upper Inlet.

Nathaniel's parents, Giles and Mary Arnold Sylvester, lived at various addresses during their thirty-eight years in Amsterdam. Giles had emigrated to the Netherlands sometime in the first years of the new century. Mary, nineteen when she married him in 1613, was the daughter of Nathaniel Arnold, a well-to-do English merchant who had moved to Amsterdam from his native Lowestoft, England, about seven years earlier. As immigrants, Giles and Mary were not alone: during the first half of the seventeenth century, 39 percent of all newlyweds in Amsterdam came from abroad. The English, who made up one of the smaller groups of foreigners and were scattered throughout the country, numbered in the tens of thousands.

Tracking the number of English merchants in Amsterdam is no easy task: church lists, marriage records, citizenship registrations, and even the notarial archives in which the Sylvesters are so well recorded don't always give a profession; the numbers fluctuated between 1613, the date of Giles and Mary's Amsterdam marriage, and 1651, the last mention of Giles in the notarial archives. Identifying them by English-sounding names doesn't work: Arnold becomes "Aernouts," Johnson often simply "Jansz." Between thirty and forty seems a safe estimate, however. Like a number of others, the Sylvesters were termed "interlopers," belonging to no guild or merchant association, English or Dutch, paying duty only to the Dutch state. When the Merchant Adventurers, the monopolistic English cloth guild, agitated for the expulsion of interlopers from Amsterdam, the Dutch authorities ignored them, eager to retain the extra trade.

A House on the Singel Canal

In 1634, Giles and Mary and their five sons and two daughters were living on the Singel, or "belt," Canal, an unusually wide and busy commercial thoroughfare that opened directly onto the harbor. This was not a fancy neighborhood. But it was respectable enough, and on the "good" west side of town. The next canal over, the entirely residential Herengracht, "Gentlemen's Canal," was Amsterdam's Park Avenue. Famous architects designed grand establishments on the Herengracht and enriched their brick façades with orgies of white stone columns, carved masks, and obelisk-crowned gables. Teenaged Nathaniel had only to walk around the corner from his family's home for a preview in brick and stone of where ambition and drive could take him. Residents of the Herengracht had rear gardens and private coach houses nearby. By contrast, dwellings and warehouses facing the Singel backed onto a mix of *achterhuizen*, humble trade and domestic buildings, passageways, and blind alleys, or *gangen*. On the canal itself, the sound of haggling over mussels, fish, fruit, coopers' and carpenters' wares, and chandlers' stores for ships mingled with the clang of small manufactories.

Amsterdam's houses often stood as tall as five stories. The Sylvesters, like their neighbors, packed family life and business into one building. Goods came to the quay by water on barges or other small craft, as well as by land on sledges or wheelbarrows. When the basement was full, a projecting crane in the front gable hoisted bulky merchandise up to the attic storeroom. When Nathaniel moved to Shelter Island, his tight clustering of the plantation housing and outbuildings within ten acres of home ground may owe as much to his memory of this Dutch economy of space as to the need for security and safety against attack by Indians or other colonists, particularly the Dutch. Despite the allure of other sites on the island's 8,000 acres, neither he nor his descendants ever budged from this spot.

Five Barrels of Tobacco

On a bright May morning in Amsterdam, I head into the street with a translation of one of the documents concerning the Sylvesters' early lives there. I hope to track down the location of Nathaniel's house by following one Evert Pietersson, a "common carter," who in mid-January 1634 lugged five barrels of tobacco on a wooden sledge from the city's central Stock Exchange to the Sylvesters' house. Each barrel stood about four feet tall and weighed 400 to 800 pounds. A notary's record of his route survives because Pietersson filed a deposition with Amsterdam's master of tobacco duties. According to the young carter, Giles Sylvester had broken the law by failing to pay duty on the tobacco, which had been loaded off a barge from Delft. The streets and many of the houses along the way still exist. I locate the bend in the Singel where the Sylvesters lived by finding the Jan Roodenpoortstoren, a tower mentioned in Pietersson's deposition.

To retrace the journey of the alleged contraband, I leave the sunny cobbles outside the Exchange and cut west around the Nieuwe Kerk, a Gothic church, to the tiny Vogelsdwarsstraat, where Pietersson and his heavy sledge—accompanied by the Delft captain's servant and one of Sylvester's employees—first ran into trouble. A *producent*, a municipal functionary from the customs office, flagged them down. Shouting ensued. The *producent* said that the captain of the barge from Delft had not paid the requisite duty. Pietersson got nervous—would anyone pay his wages if the duty went unpaid? His escorts insisted that Sylvester would hand over his *stuivers* on delivery. They instructed Pietersson to go on, and he did. Furious but outgunned, the *producent* went off to find help. He came back with Jacob Marssen, a bailiff. Marssen caught up with the fugitives at the Molsbrugge crossing on the way to the Singel. He commanded them to halt so that he could impound the five barrels. Apparently, this failed to impress Pietersson, Sylvester's henchman, or the captain's servant. The angry little procession of five men and the sledge pressed on—as do I. I arrive at the Singel and spot the Jan Roodenpoortstoren—or rather, its ghost. The brick tower was demolished in the nineteenth century and only white cobbles block out its footprint on the Torensluis, the wide bridge it once straddled. A summery café scene crowds the canal quay: tables and chairs, bright umbrellas, students and tourists in shorts, bicycles, the occasional dog. Music, the murmur of coffee or beer drinkers having a good time. But I am back in the January chill, hearing the rumble of sledge runners against stone and Pietersson's labored breathing as he drags all five barrels to the top of the arched bridge, around the gate tower, and across to the far quay. The yells of the enraged bailiff and the *producent* ring in my ears.

Then Pietersson, nearing Sylvester's house, anxiously asks again who is going to pay him. The collector sees his chance to stake a claim on the barrels. "*I* will pay you," he says, handing the sweaty Pietersson eight *stuivers*—two more than the stipulated payment. The tobacco is now in the possession of the law, momentarily. The *producent* and the bailiff—and probably a relieved Pietersson—tip the unwieldy barrels off the sledge. At this moment Sylvester pops out of his door, sees the barrels, and faces off with the *producent*. The court recorder compressed Pietersson's oral account of this encounter into one stately sentence: "A dispute arose between [the *producent*] and the said Gillis Silvester, who finally, with the help of the captain's servant and the worker and his own servant, managed to roll the five barrels of tobacco back unto the sledge and brought them to his cellar, even though they had been impounded . . ."

Did young Nathaniel witness this fracas? What did he think? Here was his father, fifty years old, a merchant with an account at the Amsterdam Exchange Bank and a ranking position in his church organization, shouting and engaging in what amounted to physical combat with the law.

Ships unloaded their cargoes, such as tobacco, at Amsterdam's Dam (see dot at left). The Jan Roodenpoortstoren (dot at right) marks the spot where Nathaniel's father had a fight with a bailiff over five barrels of Virginia tobacco.

It's not known what happened to Giles, if anything, as a consequence of Pietersson's testimony, and the notarial records give only a few other clues to what might have been Giles's characteristic behavior. On other occasions he was cited in court for nonpayment of debts, as were his sons. A family ship evaded the import duties of the Dutch West India Company (WIC); another got a new mast and sheathing and was seized, briefly, for nonpayment to the shipwright. But this was par for the course in a world in which it took at least six weeks to consummate a transoceanic deal involving multiple ports; bills of exchange and IOUs were sometimes held for years. On the other hand, Giles acted as a trusted interpreter for other English merchants, stood surety for fellow traders, and maintained powerful business contacts among his compatriots in the Netherlands, London, and Barbados. He's called "the honorable Giles Sylvester" or "Mr." and appears as a creditable witness "known to me" by the notary.

Giles's business dealings recorded in the notarial archives date to 1614. Although he may have brought capital from England, it's likelier that his in-laws financed him initially. Giles did well in Amsterdam, laying a basis of wealth and connections that would help his sons to become part of what the historian Robert Brenner has called the New Merchants, the founding fathers of American colonial commerce. Often younger sons of English country gentry or prosperous yeomen, they wanted to take their chances without the protection of the state or the privileges, market monopolies,

Global traffic crowds the harbor in Pieter van der Keere's 1618 *Profile of Amsterdam Seen from the IJ.*

and fees of the established guilds and the London merchants' chartered trading companies.

Such freedom went hand in hand with religious freedom, a characteristically Dutch tightrope act involving both church and state authorities, according to the historian Simon Schama. Where the church condemned, the state overlooked, and vice versa, whether the issue was the status of immigrants, regulation of trade, or acceptance of prostitution as a fact of life in a port city. Whatever acceptance the Sylvesters won in Amsterdam thanks to the flexible quality of Dutch culture, they were nevertheless outsiders (and determined to remain so), set apart by their extreme puritanism and their desire to safeguard their English national status. Nathaniel would also resist being an insider: during his lifetime, Shelter Island remained largely in a fluid boundary-crosser's realm while the Dutch, English, and Indians maneuvered against one another, mounting conflicting claims. At the same time, as a merchant he resorted to the law in his trade dealings with other merchants when absolutely necessary or when expedient. And after his conversion in 1657 to the nascent Society of Friends he supported the tight, persecuted community of his fellow Quakers.

The Sylvesters' Atlantic transactions began small, with a single load of Virginian tobacco that Giles Sylvester offered to buy from a Dutch trader in Amsterdam in 1626. The entire cosmopolitan family was fluent in Dutch, which would serve them well within the Netherlands' seaborne empire. Over the next sixty years, as Nathaniel and his elder brother, Constant, planted themselves on Shelter Island and Barbados, the ocean itself also remained home. The speed and frequency of their travels run counter to our conception of the American colonist braving the dangers of waves and wilderness, settling in the New World, and never leaving the farm. After Giles's death in 1651, his wife, Mary, went to live in London. She then may have spent time on Barbados with Constant, by then already a successful sugar planter, before returning to London, where she died before June 1664 at the ripe old age of sixty-nine. Daughter Mercie had emigrated to Bedfordshire by 1657. By the 1650s, two of the younger sons, Peter and Giles II, had also returned permanently to England from Amsterdam but joined their older brothers in the family business, continually crisscrossing the Atlantic. Nathaniel and Grizzell would also make a trip to England in 1661. Not rootless, but peripatetic and relentlessly entrepreneurial, Nathaniel and his five brothers were elbows-out businessmen, carrying every commodity from horses to salt to wine from port to port, taking advantage of each opportunity to broaden their trade circuits, always jockeying for the best prices.

God's Word

We have no idea how and why Giles left the tiny village of Charlton Adam, Somerset, where he was born around 1584. Assessing his chances as a young man without apparent capital or connections who wanted to become a merchant, he may have wanted to escape the stranglehold of the English mercantile companies. Or, like Plymouth's Pilgrims, he may have fled religious persecution at home. Or both. Certainly he and his wife's family, the Arnolds, defined themselves spiritually as members of a dissident Protestant sect that had fled England to escape persecution in 1596. One of the sects that were lumped together as "Brownists" or "Anabaptists" by their Anglican adversaries, also called Separatists because they had split with the Church of England, these exiles settled in a part of Amsterdam known as the Binnen Amstel, an area that had then only recently been enclosed within the city walls. Not a particularly desirable neighborhood, it attracted immigrants of all nationalities with cheap housing. Most Separatists were miserably poor, having left behind their English livelihoods; few spoke Dutch on arrival. Within his own congregation, Nathaniel saw the marginal existence that dissenters were willing to endure for their faith.

Giles and Mary's stretch of the Singel was a "better" neighborhood than the Binnen Amstel. Besides giving Giles ready access to wheeled traffic on a major "bridge street," this property lay close to the Rouen Quay, a key location for dealings in the French trade. It was a forty-minute walk to church in the Vlooienburg. One of an archipelago of made islands that included industrial districts, the Vlooienburg probably had a gritty, lonely feel, but it was a safe haven for religious nonconformists. The Separatists, who called themselves the Ancient Church, worshipped in members' houses before building the Englelse Kerk in 1607 on the Lange Houtstraat. Jews, Mennonites, Huguenots, and the occasional Muslim also lived and worshipped nearby, tolerated by the authorities though hardly embraced. Just a bit farther to the northeast stood the city leprosarium.

At thirty-two feet, Amsterdam's first English church was about the width of a mansion on the Herengracht. In 1610 the Pilgrim leader William Bradford (then living in Leyden) numbered the booming Separatist congregation at three to four hundred—a tight fit for so compact a building. Within a mere thirteen years, however, schism after schism would splinter the church: a 1623 report stated, "Of this sect there is not above 80."

The European religious world between 1560 and 1660 boiled with nonconformist sects, some with political agendas: in England alone there were Familists, Arminians, Baptists and Anabaptists, Behmenists and Barrowists and Brownists, Ranters, Muggletonians, Grindletonians, Adamites, Quakers, and a half dozen others. These often coalesced around a single charismatic preacher. Many sects were short-lived. In England, most aimed to "purify" post-Reformation Protestantism, hence the name under which they have all been lumped: Puritans. They sought to sweep aside ceremonies, rituals, ordained priests, vestments, central authority, governmental ties, and above all the Book of Common Prayer. They intended to rely on a covenant organized within each congregation that used only the Bible as its guide. Some groups denied private property rights, the existence of original sin (and therefore the need for baptism), the imposition of tithes, the power of the law, and the sanctity of oaths. (Quakers would hold that swearing a judicial oath imposed a double standard of truth, one for the courtroom and one outside it.) Others espoused communal living and were frequently accused of wife swapping and free love.

In England from the 1580s through the 1630s, orthodox Anglicans panted like dogs for schismatical red meat—and they got it. Three founders of the Sylvesters' church had been accused of high treason and two were executed in England before their congregation fled for their own lives. The third, Francis Johnson, who would become the church's first pastor in Amsterdam, languished in prison for four years without accusation or trial. He was freed only on condition that he go into exile.

Separatist life in Amsterdam, inside and outside church, was seldom placid. Keith Sprunger, the most insightful of the Separatists' historians, describes them as "some of the hardiest and most single-minded souls of the times . . . Separatists were ideological people who had staked everything on religion, and for them compromise was a thing of the past." Sprunger notes that the Separatists' major failings were "schism and bad manners." Within Giles's lifetime, believers had willingly suffered martyrdom for the sake of the Ancient Church. With God and justice on your side, what was a bout with a bailiff over some barrels of tobacco?

Nothing illuminates young Nathaniel's world or is more important to understanding his development than the religious pamphlets of Amsterdam, the tabloids of their day. The cheapness, speed, and availability of print—combined with Dutch authorities' general laxity toward English religious publications—produced a fantastic spout of ink. Some pamphlets frothed over the minutiae of outer display: Does the wife of an imprisoned minister flout religion if she wears a velvet hat? Others pondered true doctrinal considerations: whether marriage is a religious or a civil ceremony, or whether an entire congregation is stained by the sins of one member. An anti-Separatist pamphleteer outed one Elder of the Ancient Church for upholding the practice of severely beating those who worked for him by citing Exodus 21:120, "that if a man smite his servant, or his maid, with a rod, and they die not under his hand, but continue a day or two dayes, he should not be punished because they are his money." Though this was intended as a smear, invoking biblical authority for the rights of ownership would soon justify the extreme treatment of enslaved human property.

As early as the time of Giles and Mary's marriage in 1613, the Ancient Church had begun its decline. Over the next decades, most of the substantial English merchants defected to the respectable "English Orthodoxicall" Reformed Church, where the formidable John Paget, a onetime army chaplain, shot telling pamphlet arrows against the Separatists while maintaining his own congregation's useful relationship with the Dutch Reformed Church. Giles and Mary remained pillars of the quarrelsome covenant in the Vlooienburgh, bound to it not only by faith but also by family ties. This "left the Separatist assembly increasingly a circle of 'buttonmakers and weavers'—people 'seemingly but Ordinary.'" In 1636, Mary's oldest brother and Giles arranged for a loan of three thousand guilders for the benefit of the Ancient Church, using its building as collateral. (Judged by the standards of rich Dutch merchants, this sum is small, but the ability to raise it demonstrates that among their covenant, the Sylvesters and Arnolds had good financial contacts and reputations.) Two other brethren were also Giles's brothers-in-law. Surrounded by uncles and aunts and many cousins in the flock, Nathaniel was a third-generation member of the church. This religious community lit a spark in Nathaniel that lasted his lifetime.

Household prayers were said morning and evening, and Sunday services stretched from eight to noon and then from two to five or six o'clock (as they would in New England meetinghouses). According to an approving William Bradford, during these long hours "one ancient widow . . . sat in a convenient place in the congregation, with a little birchen rod in her hand, and kept little children in great awe from disturbing the congregation." Besides the brilliant hellfire preaching, fervent praying, and noisy general discussion, young churchgoers did get to enjoy one sensual pleasure—the music of their own voices—thanks to pastor Henry Ainsworth. An accomplished Hebrew scholar, he gave his congregation a new metrical translation of the Book of Psalms, set to well-known tunes of his choosing.

Masters and Pupils

As up-and-coming young merchants, the Sylvester boys learned to write swiftly and legibly in the classic script known as "secretary hand," but each son made the style his own. (I'm drawn again and again to the marks of ink on the page, simultaneously trying—and denying to myself that I'm trying on such slim evidence—to distinguish individual personalities.) In Nathaniel's nine surviving letters to John Winthrop Jr., the signature begins with an extra-long, fluid upstroke that sweeps across a quarter of the sheet. More flourishes embellish his pages than those of his brothers,

Nathaniel Sylvester's signature from a letter to Governor John Winthrop Jr., August 8, 1653. (Courtesy of the Massachusetts Historical Society)

as if he put more stock in formality and self-presentation. As if he were watching himself write. The Sylvesters' writing masters were English ministers and elders of the Separatist church, many of whom were Cambridge-educated. They taught their pupils from a copybook, with woodcuts or copperplate engravings of various penmanship styles. Nathaniel most likely learned how to cut a quill, mix ink, and set pen to paper under the watchful eye of elder and sometime preacher Jean de l'Écluse, a printer as well as a teacher.

When Nathaniel was about twelve, another teacher arrived: John Canne, the church's first new pastor since Ainsworth's death. What Nathaniel absorbed from Canne, however, were probably life lessons rather than formal schooling. Both a writer and a printer, Canne published a stream of incendiary books excoriating the Church of England (eight during a six-month period of 1637–38 alone, for example) before returning to England in the late 1640s. Canne had emigrated to Amsterdam in 1632 along with other radical Protestants; they increasingly feared persecution at the hands of their new king, Charles I, who wished to strengthen the Church of England and return his Puritan countrymen to the Anglican fold. After his appointment as Archbishop of Canterbury in 1633, the ultraorthodox William Laud sent agents to the Netherlands in search of religious refugees such as Canne, whom they constantly harassed, seizing books from his house in 1638. Though Canne proved wily—"[He] makes him selfe out of the way and is not to be found"—he was jailed, briefly, for illegal printing. From Canne, Nathaniel learned firsthand the dangers as well as the importance of speaking out for one's beliefs or taking actions to defend them "for conscience' sake."

The Sylvesters in Amsterdam were part of a literate community of restless men and women who listened directly to the voice of God and whose radical ideas reached each other all over the Atlantic World—in print. Practically swaddled in religious paper (broadsheets, pamphlets, and books), Nathaniel Sylvester had reading as a birthright. The 1680 Shelter Island probate inventory made after his death lists the number of books he owned—sixty—although, sadly, not the titles. The size of this library places Nathaniel among the upper half of colonial book owners in 1680. His brother-in-law Francis Brinley of Rhode Island assembled an impressive 217 volumes between the 1670s and 1713. Many colonists owned books, but usually fewer than five, most often a Bible and religious tracts. Nathaniel's sixty probably all dealt with religious topics. But since religious discourse in the period touched on a wide range of subjects, secular as well as spiritual, he had access to a great variety of ideas about the self and the world, as well as the language needed to frame an argument and make a convincing case.

Separatists had to be strenuous debaters, because Anglicans gave as good as they got. The orthodox frequently damned radical Puritans as "Anabaptisticall." This term arose from the heretical belief that human beings are born free of original sin and therefore do not require the spiritual cleansing of infant baptism, but can choose to be baptized as adults. Anti-Anabaptist hysteria fed upon memories of the infamous Münster Rebellion of 1534, when a radical group of millennial peasants and clerics took over the Westphalian city for eighteen months of legalized polygamy, communal property ownership—and adult rather than infant baptism. Amsterdam had its own Anabaptist outbreak the following year. Forty men and women seized the town hall, ran naked through the streets to proclaim their prelapsarian innocence, and were promptly executed.

The Ancient Church was not "Anabaptisticall"; it did baptize infants and did not rebaptize adult converts. But because for a decade after Henry Ainsworth's death, the Ancient Church was unable to find a cleric who satisfied all their members or who was willing to preside over their fractious flock, no baptismal entries exist for many of the Sylvester children, leading historians to believe they were Anabaptists. And since no records survived the disbanding of the Ancient Church in 1701, what we know of the birth order or ages of Nathaniel and his brothers and sisters can only be determined from evidence in wills and marriage records.

To the New World

"An infinite number of ships not to be numbered lie here," an amazed Sir William Brereton wrote on a visit to Amsterdam in 1634. Seventeenth-century panoramas of the city (and every bird's-eye view and city map of the period) invariably include a view of the harbor on the IJ, the great estuary that stretches far inland. Pieter van der Keere's *Profile of Amsterdam Seen from the IJ* (1618) shows a harborside forest of masts pricking the sky.

By the time Brereton wrote, the seagoing Dutch controlled the global trade monopoly previously held by Spain and Portugal. (When Antwerp fell into Spanish hands in 1585, the Jewish community there who had found refuge from the Inquisition in Spain left for Amsterdam along with many other southern Dutch merchants, carrying the knowledge of Portuguese and Spanish maritime routes.) At almost exactly the same time, a new type of vessel, the *fluyt,* or flute—longer and less beamy than the chubby merchant vessels called *cogges*, and therefore easier to sail close to the wind—had given the Dutch an immediate advantage. The invention of the wind-driven sawmill, which produced planks to sheath hulls much more quickly and cheaply than hand labor, revolutionized shipbuilding.

Seagoing ships did not sail out of Amsterdam directly but made their preparations for departure or unloaded cargo at Texel, largest of the string of islands between the Zuiderzee and the North Sea. The city's inner harbor was silting up: to get to the metropolitan piers or naval facilities for refitting, large ships arriving before or after high tide had to be lifted by "ships' camels," floating docks that raised their keels and guided vessels across the sandbank—a painstaking, time-consuming process. Hence the importance of the deeper waters and loading facilities at Texel. Moreover, the winds that safely blew the Dutch ships out of the shoaly English Channel and onward to the west crossed this island before reaching Amsterdam. For outbound voyages, hundreds of vessels took on everything from hardtack to cannons. Merchant captains or factors, like Nathaniel and his elder brother, Constant, sometimes waited for weeks, hoping for winds to take them around the rim of the Atlantic, or to the Baltic, or the Mediterranean, or simply across the Channel to England. Waiting in the Texel "roads," as offshore anchoring grounds are called, they were stuck aboard, unable to risk returning to the city in case a breeze sprang up.

"Texel" is pronounced "Tessel." The soft, almost slushy sound of the name feels like a reminder of the softness, the ambiguity, of the Dutch environment: Is it water? Is it land? Is it somewhere in between, still emerging from marsh, or dissolving, on the verge of a flood? I visit Texel in May, to see how the Sylvesters prepared themselves for a merchant voyage to the New World. The island is insanely green and covered with sheep. It's just past lambing time by about a month, and lambs are running, playing, nursing, wagging their tails, sleeping in the sun. I remember that on Shelter Island, Nathaniel kept five hundred sheep, both for wool and for mutton to salt and ship to Barbados.

The topographical map I bought in the city marks the island's all-important "sweet wells," where boats used to stock up on barrels and barrels of water for the weeks of travel ahead. The past is coming closer.

In the little maritime museum in Oudeschild, the old fishing harbor, the Texel Roads panorama displays model boat making at its height. The display also obsessively records the power of the VOC, the Dutch East India Company, over several centuries. Not recorded here is the parallel course of the WIC, the Dutch West India Company, founded in 1621, which enjoyed its only splashy success shortly after its founding. In 1628, the renowned privateer Admiral Piet Heyn captured half the Spanish silver fleet on its way home from the Americas. Heyn's booty of 11.5 million guilders was enough to give the WIC shareholders a whopping 50 percent return on their money and to finance the Dutch army for eight months. Heyn's success apart, the tale of the WIC appears dowdy, not glamorous, its carrying trade of hats and shoes, grain and pelts eclipsed by the splendor of the VOC's traffic in Eastern spices, silks, and jewels. Eventually, however, what the Americas produced for the Dutch exceeded the spices of the East, especially after the WIC reformed itself in 1674 to focus on the highly profitable African slave trade and the remaining Dutch possessions in the Antilles.

Texel's museum display is laid out on a big table like a model railroad. The room is dark. The theatrically lit scene shows sea and shore crowded with maritime activities of 1660–70 (a bit late for the Sylvesters' endeavors in the forties, but not too late to get the idea). The sound track gives us seagulls' cries and wind and waves. We spectators are making ourselves small enough to fit through the eye of history's needle. There's no wharf or dock in this harbor. Lighters carry every cask and bale and all the passengers and crew from the beach to boats several hundred yards offshore. A winch lowers barrels of water from the top of the seawall to the shore below. In just this way, food, water, and cargo to ship to the West Indies—barrels of salt meat, sacks of grain, animals on the hoof (mostly horses), and bundles of staves—were rowed out from the shallow Shelter Island plantation landing to seagoing vessels anchored in deeper water.

On the mini-Texel's plaster waves, in a gaff-rigged *galjoot*, a navy supply vessel, sits the artist Willem van de Velde the Elder. From him and other marine painters we know what many of the boats looked like. Here are models of the *fluyt*, the Dutch maritime workhorse, to study close-up. About 80 to 150 feet long, and typically manned by a crew of six to twelve, these vessels crossed the Atlantic without difficulty. The Sylvesters'

Seerobbe, the Seal, was another class of vessel—a ship, meaning it had a flat stern, or transom—but many of their other carriers were probably *fluyts*, the favored Dutch commercial transport.

In the Texel display, small pinks with narrow, snipelike sterns and bulging sides dart about, carrying local traffic. In New England much larger pinks, some forty-five to fifty feet long, transported goods as far as the West Indies or even Europe. The three-ton craft Nathaniel would commission in 1653 from a boatwright in "ye Bay" was probably a pink. As soon as it was finished, he wrote to Governor John Winthrop Jr., he would carry his bride, Grizzell, across Long Island Sound for a visit.

The day turns bright and breezy; I board a waiting tourist sailboat, the *Texelstroom*, for a three-hour trip along the shore. The wind freshens as we move out of the harbor. Now we head for the deep water where Nathaniel and Constant would have anchored to wait for the wind. Although captains chose this place because they could have fathoms of anchor chain to play with in heavy storms, when their ships lay too close to each other they often crashed and sank. As we sail only fathoms above the carcasses of such vessels, the dangerous past comes alive.

Back aboard the ferry that will take me to the mainland, a rusty-black crow perches on the foredeck windscreen. Sitting there quietly for the entire ride, he is a reminder of the *Swarte Raven*, the Black Raven, one of three Dutch vessels mentioned in the Amsterdam record that were trading on the James River in Tidewater Virginia in 1644. Nathaniel, then about twenty-four years old, was on the James too, buying tobacco to load aboard his family's ship, the *Seerobbe*.

The great coastal rivers of Virginia swarmed with Dutch traders during the first half of the seventeenth century. International traffic moved up and down the colonies as well: one Dutch vessel, the *Oranjeboom*, shuttled regularly from Nansemond, Virginia, to New Amsterdam. Dutch supplies—from muskets to Madeira wine to copper pots—were crucial to English colonies, especially during the English Civil War years when trade with the mother country dwindled. Nathaniel, fluent in Dutch as well as English, probably seemed more Dutch in Virginia than he did in Amsterdam, where he was unmistakably an Englishman.

In 1644 the Netherlands and England considered each other firm Protestant allies, linked by memories of decades-long combat against

Papist Spain. Relations between their New World colonies were sometimes strained by territorial disputes, but they steered clear of outright war. When, for example, the Dutch explorer David Pieterzen de Vries ventured south from New Amsterdam to Virginia in 1633, he enjoyed "a Venice glass of sack" with the English governor, Sir John Harvey. The two politely sparred over boundaries, with Harvey allowing that there was land enough for both. If the Dutch "did not come too near us," he said, then the two nations should "be good neighbors with each other."

During the month of February 1644 the *Seerobbe*'s Dutch captain, Sijmon Dircxsz, steered up and down the Chesapeake's treacherous tidal rivers, stopping at plantation wharves to load heavy hogsheads of cured leaf. Nathaniel would have seen a few black faces at wealthier plantations, but the Virginia that he viewed from the James was still largely a place where a freed servant could farm a small tract with a few white bondsmen. (Slaves were in short supply, as slave traders were more interested in supplying South America and the Caribbean.) Those small operations would largely vanish in the following two decades, to be replaced by large plantations worked by Africans as England entered the transatlantic slave trade with enthusiasm.

Although miles of "sweet-scented tobacco" lined the riverbanks, the tobacco market fluctuated violently in the early seventeenth century. De Vries noted, "He who wishes to trade here must keep a house here and continue all the year, that he may be prepared when the tobacco comes from the field to seize it," but at other times an oversupply caused a depression. Nathaniel and a consortium of other buyers got shorted on this trip: they had contracted to take on a hundred and fifty barrels, but were able to load only forty-three.

As required by law, Nathaniel had stopped first at the colony's capital, "Jemston," as the Dutch record spells it. There he had offloaded "Commodytyes" so desired by planters, such as hats, both "Browd & brimd," and "thred stockens . . . new fashioned shoes . . . pinnes . . . tufften Holland" (a fine Dutch linen), and "wines and spirits." Prosperous "James Cittie," then in its fourth decade, had survived starvation, drought, epidemics, bankruptcy, hostile government takeovers, and Indian attacks. After this halting start, Jamestown was on its way as the urban center of the Tidewater region. Long before 1644, the first miserable Virginia Company settlement of 1607 had burst out of the original palisaded fort and spread into a "New Towne" with a church, warehouses, shops, taverns, stocks, gallows, and a single brick house considered "the fairest that eer was knowen in this countrye," which would surely not have impressed Amsterdam-bred Nathaniel. As of 1643, it also boasted the first bicameral representative government in the colonies.

Nathaniel probably kept his mouth shut on his religious and political views in Virginia, an Anglican colony loyal to the crown. In April, two weeks before the *Seerobbe* sailed for home, David de Vries witnessed two London ships manned by Parliamentarians engage a fly-boat (a fast frigate) from Bristol filled with royalist sympathizers in a sharp firefight. The short battle ended in a draw, but afterward the Londoners feared to land "because all the people of the country were in favour of the king" and left Virginia without a shred of tobacco. Given Nathaniel's Separatist upbringing, what wonder is it that in 1651 he and his partners, all Parliamentary sympathizers, set up their plantation in the Puritan homeground of New England (of which Long Island was then considered a part)?

His Virginian stay lasted some months, perhaps even as long as a year—certainly long enough to get a taste of the climate. Much later, writing to John Winthrop Jr., the governor of Connecticut, from Shelter Island, he remarked that Tidewater winters were more moderate than those up north, but that Virginia "is more Unhelthie than N. England." Nathaniel may have contracted what we now know is mosquito-borne malaria, then thought to be caused by noxious swamp vapors. In a much later letter to Governor Winthrop, a noted apothecary and healer, Nathaniel complained of chronic bouts of ague, nausea, and stomach pain—all symptoms of malaria. Winthrop carefully labeled this missive as "Capt Sylvestters note about his Sicknesse."

Two weeks before the *Seerobbe* sailed from Kecoughtan, leaving Nathaniel to face the "Unhelthie" summer, coastal Virginia had exploded in war, the third attempt by the region's united Indians to push the English out. Some of the major attacks occurred on the lower side of the James River, where Nathaniel was trading at Blunt Point, some thirty-five miles downstream from Jamestown. Four to five hundred colonists were killed. The English retaliated with a summer campaign, destroying villages and burning fields. The Indian leader Opechancanough, Powhatan's brother or cousin, was captured, imprisoned, and shot in the back by a soldier.

"He Would Rather Lose His Right Hand"

Nathaniel made his way from Virginia to the West Indies by the spring of 1645, where the *Seerobbe* picked him up on another transatlantic round, either on Barbados or St. Kitts, the last port on a typical Caribbean trading circuit. Trading partnerships like the Sylvesters' kinship network made for voyages that stopped in many ports as they carried shorthaul freight from island to island as well as long Atlantic trips. It was in St. Kitts that Arent Gerritss, a longtime West Indies Company employee, hopped aboard for the fifteen-week trip home to Holland. The company designated him as its supercargo, or official representative, on this trip, meaning that the *Seerobbe* sailed under WIC orders.

Two years later, Gerritss and Reijer Evertsen, the steersman of the *Seerobbe*, testified to the company's board of directors that there were 2,911 rolls of tobacco in the ship's hold. Each roll bore a merchant's mark or initials or had been set aside as a crewman's share. (One hundred rolls were marked NS, for Nathaniel Sylvester.) There were also forty-five prime beaver pelts, twenty-four bales of cotton, thirty-four casks of candied fruit (Evertsen ate some, he confessed), eight and a half hogsheads of sugar, a hundred and forty pounds of indigo (property of the captain), and half a hogshead of cochineal, an expensive crimson dye. Everything listed could have been produced or grown in the Caribbean or South America except the beaver skins, which had to have been taken in North America. My bet is they came aboard in Virginia, thanks to Nathaniel. Evertsen watched as Captain Dircxsz signed the bills of lading to deliver the goods from St. Kitts to Amsterdam, "which would be the right place to unload." Similar documents were diligently signed at every port and duly noted by Evertson or Gerritss.

The Sylvester documents in the Amsterdam notarial archives record contracts, executed or broken, as well as infringements of the law, disputes (Giles and his barrels), and complaints. It's rare that the accused looks good in them. Their abundant detail often makes them seem tantalizingly clear, but I have to remember they have been wrenched from their seventeenth-century context and were written for purposes that often don't exist on the page. Gerritss's and Evertsen's testimony, which stretches over two long documents and a period of years, is a good example. It's pretty clear that the company was "shadowing" the Sylvesters. Indeed, the family already had a record for illegally evading payment of

WIC duties in 1646, when Gerritss first alerted his superiors. Curiously, there is no record of any punishment or fine levied against the Sylvesters, even though the file remained open: in 1649, a duplicate report was sent to the WIC director, who had heard Evertsen's testimony. Beyond that, nothing.

Dutch maritime regulations stipulated that the merchant who owned a ship had the right to set its course. (If the merchant wasn't aboard, the captain had to follow a plan laid out in the original contract.) In November, when the *Seerobbe* neared the European coast, Nathaniel took charge.

"On the way back here," Gerritss testified, "having arrived at the Channel of England, at forty-nine degrees and some minutes North altitude, the said captain and merchant changed course to La Rochelle in France or the island of St. Martin opposite to it, even though the wind was more expedient for sailing into the Channel than for sailing to France, and they would have arrived soon[er] than at St. Martin." Nathaniel and his ship were just south of Land's End, approaching the mouth of the English Channel, closer, given the wind conditions, to Texel than to France. "Also they did not need light, sails, ropes, water, food or anything else," Gerritss added, "[They went] of their own will alone, under pretext of looking for a convoy [for protection against privateers]." The French port of La Rochelle and the smaller harbor of St. Martin on the Île de Ré, less than half a mile off the coast at La Rochelle, lay outside WIC jurisdiction. Nathaniel could escape WIC taxes on any goods he unloaded.

Then the clincher: "the merchant having said before that he would rather lose his right hand than not come to France on that trip." Here is the unmistakable voice of Nathaniel, whom I will hear again throughout his life. Even with Gerritss aboard, Nathaniel apparently was willing to gamble on the chance that the WIC authorities in the Netherlands would not catch up with him—or he didn't care if they did. At twenty-six or so, this Calvinist merchant had the stuff of a stubborn renegade.

4

The Other Island: Barbados

Merchant's Mark

Two field school students stand over a wheelbarrow at the manor, shaking a wood-framed screen that sieves soil particles into a wheelbarrow below, leaving on the mesh whatever is too big to pass through. A small, dark blob glows among the pebbles. Vaguely oval, it's about three-eighths of an inch long. Steve Mrozowski picks it up and pronounces it a bale seal, made of lead. Soft lead folds easily: what was cast as a rough blank about the size of a nickel was then stamped and crimped securely over baling string. The markings on this one are illegible. The trail of such ID tags runs from Russia to South America, from the thirteenth century to the nineteenth. They marked commercial goods in transit and kept track of mixed shipments such as those the *Seerobbe* carried. Combinations of initials, numbers, and armorials, as well as symbols like a fleur-de-lys or cross, distinguished each "merchant's mark."

No recognizable Sylvester insignia are stamped on the bale seals found at the manor, but Nathaniel's elder brother, Constant, drew his mark in the margin of a 1659 letter from Barbados to John Winthrop Jr., whom he had just visited in Connecticut, thanking Winthrop for "ye many civilities." Constant sent him a "Case of Such Sugars as my plantation doth yeeld." Constant used the device as a personal emblem, almost a coat of arms, just as the Sylvesters of Burford, the center of England's wool trade, used similar marks as heraldic devices on their tombs in the sixteenth century.

So far, no connection has emerged between the branches of the family, but the marks and the name clearly link them. These kinfolk also knew about the New World. In 1569 the husband of Agnes Sylvester, Edmund Harman, had a startling family memorial carved in the Burford church. Around the central cartouche, four sexy naked men and women in feather crowns, perhaps representing Tupinambas from coastal Brazil, dangle bunches of what look like gourds and bananas. Lithe and ferocious, these figures once exhaled the exotic fragrance of "the Indies," an alluring mix of riches, wonders, danger, and the barbarous, beauteous "Other" that had penetrated deep into European consciousness a century before the Sylvesters sailed into Bridgetown, Barbados.

On the Island of Barbados

By July 1646, when Nathaniel and the *Seerobbe* returned from La Rochelle to Barbados, his family had been doing business there for seven years. His father, Giles, was directly involved in Barbadian trade as a purchaser on his own account and as a broker as early as 1639. By 1646, the island had seen the beginnings of the changeover from cotton, indigo, and tobacco as staple crops, grown and harvested mostly by white indentured servants or small farmers, to sugar, produced by a labor force of enslaved Africans. By 1646, Nathaniel's elder brother, Constant, had already purchased plantations and a plot for a warehouse on the Bridgetown harbor waterfront. The family network was smoothly transitioning to sugar.

As Nathaniel sailed back across the Caribbean, the island, a soft mound of dense tropical green only 166 square miles in extent, would have appeared before him, floating on the sea. I followed him there. The island was green—uniform cane fields surrounding a ragged mountainous spine—not

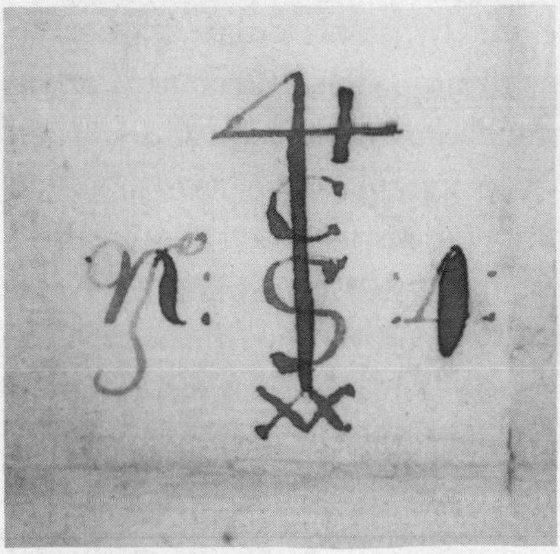

To the left of Constant Sylvester's merchant's mark, "C.S.," are the much smaller initals "N.S.," which probably stand for "Nathaniel Sylvester."

the patchwork of remaining forest and fields of cotton, tobacco, indigo, and cane that Nathaniel first knew in the 1640s. Constant Plantation, one of the three that belonged to Constant Sylvester, still produces sugar today, and just as at Sylvester Manor, an eighteenth-century house still stands.

I hunted through the Barbadian archives to track down the growth of the Sylvesters' wealth and to research the politics that catapulted the four partners into purchasing Shelter Island in 1651, a purchase made possible by sugar and paid for in sugar. In 1651, as Barbados became embroiled in the English Civil War, Parliamentarians such as Constant Sylvester and Thomas Middleton were exiled. They bought Shelter Island as a bolt-hole in case the monarchy won and they lost their plantations. But only months later, in January 1652, Oliver Cromwell's fleet conquered Barbados in a nearly bloodless siege. Constant and Middleton rushed back to Barbados, became members of the Barbados Council and Assembly, and positioned Nathaniel on Shelter Island to develop it. The Barbadian plantations provided start-up capital for Shelter Island and the primary market for what Nathaniel produced. Just as he was the junior partner, so his island (as he came to think of it) was of secondary importance.

In the Barbadian National Archive, in the hot, high-ceilinged, white-painted main room where scores of people quietly turned pages of the ancient deeds registers, I learned that it was from Constant and other planters that Nathaniel came face-to-face with the practice of slavery. From the first he was apparently prepared to stock the Northern plantation with Africans. West Indian planters' profit-driven brutality and savage disregard for human life are not news; an immense literature exists on the subject. But what I found out about slavery at seventeenth-century West Indian plantations became the information that must stand in for all I *don't* know about the control—through coercion, cruelty, and fear—of enslaved labor on Shelter Island during the first thirty years of European settlement. Without comprehending the conditions that Nathaniel must have seen and grasped on Barbados, my speculations about the Sylvesters' early Shelter Island life are worth little. Long Island's different imperatives included controlling a volatile mixed workforce of enslaved Africans and Indians, and a few indentured white servants, living together under crowded conditions in a cold climate—and growing crops less valuable than the sugar that made Barbadian slaves expendable and easily replaced. The concept of human chattel as the predominant source of labor was the same on both islands. Edgar McManus, author of *Black Bondage in the North*, notes that "the principal formative influence on slavery came from the West Indies," although, he continues, "the North did not adopt the harsh codes of the islands completely, for some changes had to be made for local needs and conditions."

Richard Ligon's *A True and Exact History of the Island of Barbados* provides the most comprehensive record of the island as it became a sugar colony between 1647 and 1650. About his arrival from England, as his ship "past along the shoar" toward the island capital of Bridgetown in 1647, Ligon wrote, "The nearer we came, the more beautiful it appeared . . . There we saw the high large and lofty trees, with their spreading branches and flourishing tops . . . return their cool shade to secure and shelter them from the Suns heat, which without it would scorch and dry away." Mangroves flourished in coastal wetlands. Beaches were fringed with sea grapes dangling

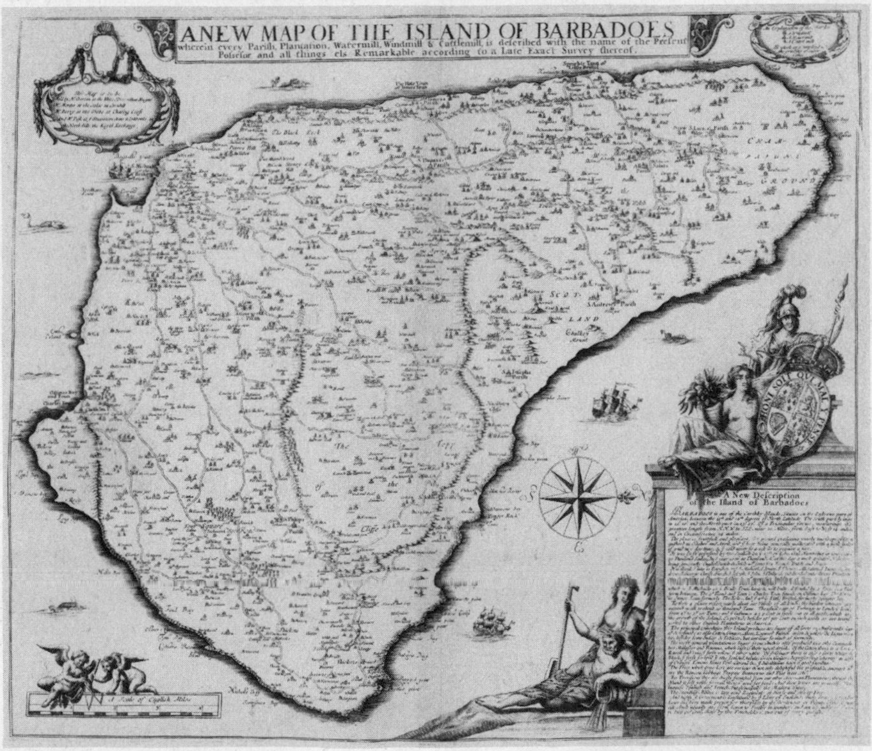

The several hundred plantations whose sugar mills are shown on Richard Ford's 1674 *A New Map of the Island of Barbadoes* had made the island the most successful of all British colonies by that date. Bridgetown, the principal port where Constant Sylvester's shipping warehouse stood, is at left, above Needham's Point. (Map courtesy of the John Carter Brown Library at Brown University)

their long bunches of fruit, and by salt-tolerant trees such as whitewood, flushed with pale pink trumpet flowers, and manchineel, whose sap was used to make poison for Carib and Arawak arrows. Smooth-skinned manatees, the Rubenesque mermaids of seafarers' sex-deprived imaginations, grazed placidly on seaweed. Hummingbirds "not much bigger than an humble Bee" hovered at the flowers, "never sitting, but purring" with their wings. Poisonous scorpions, their jointed limbs as translucent as moonstones, dreamed under the bark of trees, or scuttled, barbed tails raised like banners, from beneath the leaf litter of the forest floor. For white colonists like the Sylvesters or Richard Ligon (who became a plantation manager), the immense, florid wilderness contained as much danger as beauty and promise.

The appearance of tropical abundance was deceptive: the ecology of a seasonal rain forest is fragile and its soils are easily depleted once tree cover disappears. By 1646, deforestation was well under way. In the decades following their initial settlement in 1627, colonists planted market crops for export—tobacco, cotton, ginger, indigo—as well as food for themselves and their white indentured servants, and African slaves. Disease and Spanish slavers had eradicated the Amerindian population by 1536, so the settlers had no natives to contend with. Commercial sugar production was still a trial-and-error affair in the late 1640s, although by 1644 James Drax, Barbados's richest planter, had grown, processed, and sold enough sugar to pay for thirty-four Africans. By 1654, not long after Nathaniel had made another trip to Barbados from New England, Drax would have two hundred Africans slaving on his lands. Ligon singles out Drax and another major planter, Humphrey Walrond (whose daughter Grace would marry Constant in 1660 or 1661), as models of prosperity and success.

When the protective tree canopy disappeared, the repeated pounding of heavy tropical rains compacted much of the remaining soil. What remained after severe erosion became impoverished with the constant replanting of sugar. But the crop was too lucrative to abandon, despite the environmental and human costs. Planters compensated with innovative techniques of fertilization, soil conservation, and planting, all of which required that slaves work harder and longer. Sugar producers did not suffer: they simply sold more sugar, satisfying the increasing global demand for the commodity. And the supply of forced labor could be expanded at little cost to them, since the price of slaves dropped over time.

The first Africans to arrive on Barbados—a handful of people captured from a Spanish ship—had come with the first Europeans in 1627.

A 1645 census tallied 23,980 inhabitants: 18,300 white men and 5,680 Africans. By 1650 the number of slaves had more than doubled to nearly a third of the island's total population. Between 1645 and 1672 a total of 56,800 Africans were imported, an average of 2,030 people per year. Because they were so poorly fed and housed, and the planters considered their lives expendable, slaves on Barbados died faster than they could reproduce. Year after year, slave traders supplied their replacements.

Between 1640 and 1646 the value of agricultural acreage rose tenfold; during the next four years, the purchase price of a fully equipped sugar plantation increased more than twenty times. Shelter Island's 8,000 unimproved acres were worth only 1,600 pounds of the cheapest brown sugar in 1651. Little more than a year later, Constant paid 40,000 pounds of sugar for a 67-acre Barbadian working plantation. Measured in sugar, an acre on Shelter Island was worth less than a quarter of a teaspoonful; each of Constant's new Barbados acres—even taking into account the expensive housing and sugar works—surpassed 200 cups.

Making a Fortune

The Sylvesters' Dutch base gave them a jump on most transoceanic settlers. Dutch capital was more easily available to them, and repayment terms more flexible; Dutch ships were better designed; and Holland's import duties were lower than England's. Historians continually debate which nation introduced African slavery to Barbados, but they virtually agree that Dutch shippers cornered a major share of the early markets for European goods and American produce.

By 1665, Barbados was exporting more than 15,000 tons of sugar a year. In the oft-quoted words of Caribbean historian Eric Williams, "Little Barbados . . . was worth more to British capitalism than New England, New York, and Pennsylvania combined." Meanwhile the Sylvesters' trading network expanded throughout the Atlantic Basin. How their father's death affected the Sylvesters can't be assessed, except to say that the loss of a family base in Amsterdam, the passage of the English Navigation Acts of 1651–52 and 1660, the huge success of Constant's sugar plantations, and the purchase of Shelter Island saw the focus of operations shift to the New World, while the European foothold became London.

Besides what provisions Nathaniel sent south from Long Island, Con-

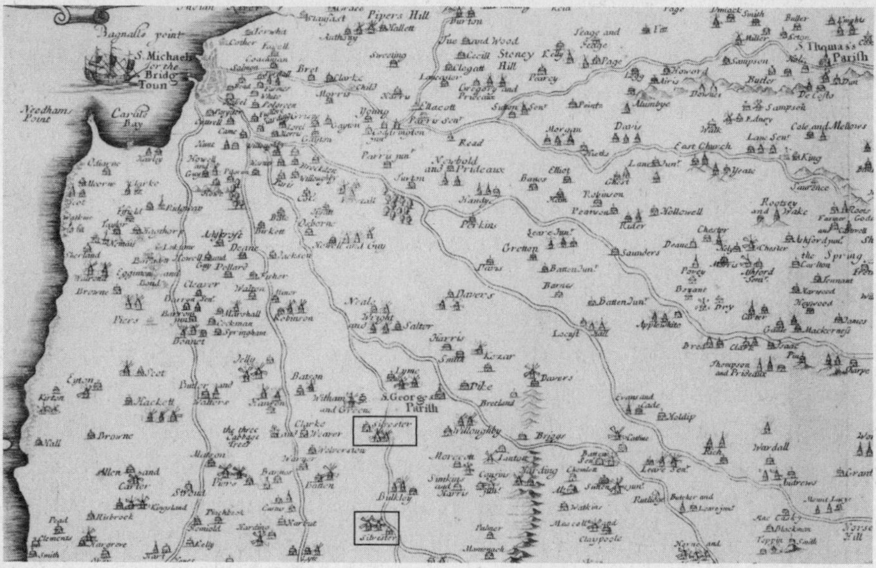

A detail from Richard Ford's 1674 map shows the two Sylvester plantations, each with two windmills, on the island's richest sugar soils, in St. George's Valley. By 1679, the Sylvesters were among the wealthiest families on the island, with a total of 695 acres, 260 African slaves, and 11 indentured white servants. Sugar and slaves were the engine of Shelter Island's first European economy.

stant shipped sugar, molasses, rum, and ginger to Amsterdam, New England, and England. Salt for preserving meat from Nevis went to New England; wine from the Azores traveled to Europe, New England, and the West Indies; and manufactured goods from Europe came to all colonial ports where they could be sold profitably. They had good credit and access to the right people in Amsterdam, London, and Rhode Island, which rapidly became a major West Indian shipping depot. With a trusted family member as factor aboard ship or in almost every major port, they profited from every trip across the Atlantic.

"They Choose Them as They Do Horses in a Market"

Before African captives went on sale at the Bridgetown docks, sellers groomed their merchandise to be as presentable as possible. Oil made skin shine, rust and gunpowder concealed sores, anuses were corked to hide the leakage caused by the deadly "bloody flux." At a well-documented

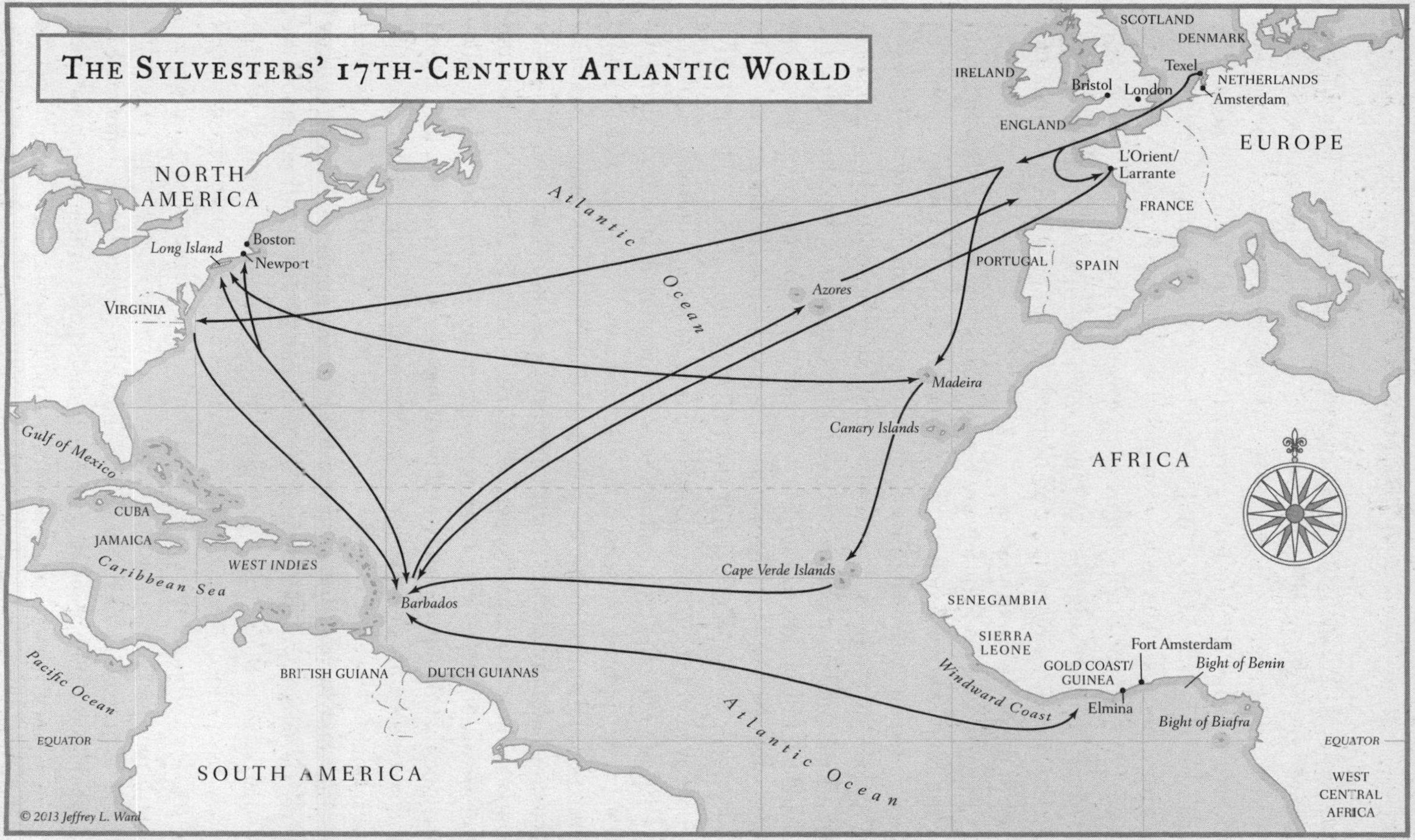

Global maritime traffic united four continents in the seventeenth-century Atlantic World.

vendue of 251 Africans in 1644, the largest purchaser was James Drax, followed by William Hilliard, a partner of a Bristol merchant, Samuel Farmer, who became Constant's friend and one of his executors. When Hilliard returned to England, Farmer took on the management of Hilliard's Barbadian plantation and agreed to supply it with "90 slaves within fourteen months." The most economical way for Farmer to do so was by slaving himself, or buying shares in an African venture. Nathaniel may also have been seeking to stock family plantations or make a profit by selling slaves to other planters when he made a trip from Barbados to Africa aboard the *Seerobbe* in 1646.

Ligon writes, "When they are brought to us, the Planters buy them out of the Ship, where they find them stark naked, and therefore cannot be deceived in any outward infirmity; they choose them as they do Horses in a Market; the strongest, youthfullest, and most beautiful, yield the greatest prices . . . [The men] are very well timber'd, that is, broad between the shoulders, full breasted, well filletted [muscled], and clean leg'd and may hold good with Albert Durers rules" (the artist Albrecht Dürer). He faults the women for figures that fall short of the German's standards: "I have seen very few of them, whose hips have been broader than their shoulders."

Twenty-five of every hundred men and women usually died during the first twelve months of "seasoning," the arduous three-year process of acclimation. Recent arrivals fell prey to malnutrition and disease, and to a "fixed melancholy." Felix Christian Spoeri, a Swiss doctor who visited the island in the early 1660s, observed: "When slaves come first to Barbados and are forced to work they often die of hunger [by refusing to eat]. They imagine that if they die they will go to another land where riches, honor, and splendor will not be lacking and where there will be an abundance of everything."

But those who survived seasoning kept memories of African culture alive by shaping a creole community that gained strength from each wave of newcomers. Black resistance also thrived. Absent a single slave testimony from those years, Barbadian legislation offers the clearest insight into plans for black rebellions—and the fears of white masters. Laws enacted from 1646 onward forbade slave-run markets, as well as large-scale black festivals and funerals. Complete enforcement proved impossible. Even though drums, horns, and conch shells (all familiar in Africa) were outlawed as instruments of revolution, the law was often broken: people made music, danced—and plotted—late on Saturday nights, aware that a mounted militia could be watching. They defiantly mourned their dead. Slave women continued to sell their produce in Bridgetown and at plantation corners, enjoying a few hours of independent public existence. Runaways "marooned" themselves in caves and woods until the island's deforestation eliminated safe long-term hiding places, meaning that if slaves took up arms, the bare choice was victory or death. People continued to slip away for days at a time, however, to visit friends and relations on other plantations, a practice that continued (and was punished) on Barbados, and in all slave societies, as long as slavery lasted. Stealing from whites occurred regularly, often by night when "their bodies black, they [could] scape undiscern'd." Africans on Long Island would offer similar calculated resistance.

Several well-conceived black plots on Barbados—betrayed or found out only days before their scheduled execution—exposed a revolutionary life hidden under the eyes of unsuspecting whites. To set a harsh example, authorities tortured or executed slaves for a suspicious word, even a whisper. One old black man was burned alive for frightening his mistress, following the discovery of a 1675 conspiracy. The biggest scare, in 1692, led to the arrests of several hundred slaves "many [of whom] were hang'd, and great many burn'd." The Barbados Council authorized an Alice Mills to castrate forty-two black men and paid her ten guineas for the job. In New York Colony, where rebel slaves would also be mutilated, tortured, and then executed as "examples," the laws enacted to control the slave labor force were modeled on legislation in the West Indies.

By 1660 the sugar island's population was almost equally divided between white and black, and by the 1690s, when Constant's widow owned the Sylvester properties, the numbers stood at about 18,000 whites to 49,000 enslaved Africans and creoles. Fearful whites had walled themselves in against the chances of revolt long before: a siege mentality was expressed in architecture as well as legislation. Ligon describes planters' houses "built in the manner of Fortifications [with] Lines, Bulwarks, and Bastions to defend themselves, in case there should be any uproar or commotion in the Island, either by the Christian servants, or *Negro slaves*."

Even plants had useful defensive capabilities: the "Lime Tree . . . is like a thick Hollybush in England and as full of prickles: if you make a hedge of them, about your house, 'tis sufficient proof against the Negroes; whose naked bodies cannot possibly enter it." Ligon, who wanted to promote colonization, nonetheless manages casually to introduce the subject of slave uprisings in a discussion of hydraulics: "Water they save likewise from their houses, by gutters at the eves, which carry it down to cisterns. And the water which is kept there, being within the limits of their houses . . . serves them for drink whilst they are besieged as also, to throw down upon the naked bodies of the Negroes, scalding hot."

Slaves and servants found ways to retaliate that could appear to be accidents. Worst of all preventable disasters—from the planters' point of view—were cane fires, where "whole lands of Canes and Houses too, are burnt down and consumed, to the utter ruine and undoing of their Masters." Everyone smoked a pipe—men, women, slaves, servants, and masters—and a careless or malicious smoker might start a blaze, with "every knot of every Cane, giving as great a report as a Pistol." Ligon wrote that "Mr. Constantine Silvester . . . had not only his Canes, but his house burnt down to the ground. This, and much more mischief has been done, by the negligence and wilfulness of servants." Only a few lines before, Ligon had extravagantly praised another planter's kindness to his slaves and servants, adding that such "care and charity" paid off, not only in the "love of his servants," but also in "foreseeing and preventing mischiefs." Ligon was a deft and politic writer on a small island in an inferior position (not a planter, but a manager): perhaps he was in no position to criticize a powerful man directly. I read his description of "Mr. Constantine Silvester's" fiery disaster (from which he soon recovered, building another house and still greater wealth) as a statement that Constant mistreated his workers—and paid for it.

Satanic Mills

The basic layout for a successful Barbadian sugar plantation was well developed by the 1650s. Near the typical planter's house stood the sugar works, as close by as Nathaniel's warehouse and other outbuildings stood to his Shelter Island dwelling. The two-hundred-and-fifty-acre spread where Ligon lived and worked from 1647 to 1650 had an "Ingenio," or mill (powered by oxen or horses), to press the canes, along with "boyling house, filling room, Cisterns and Still house, carding house, stables, Smith's forge, and rooms to lay provisions of Corn, and Bonavist" (a kind of bean). He counted a workforce of "96 Negroes and three Indian [perhaps Guyanese] women with their children" in addition to "28 Christians." Two hundred acres of cane fields yielded a crop that a single sugar mill could effectively process.

Every part of the sugar-making "machine" wore out, especially the living parts. The biggest maintenance cost was the annual replacement of human and animal cogs, totaling as much as 37 percent of all outlays. Once cut, cane must be processed within forty-eight hours or the juice dries, so the mills operated twenty-four hours a day, six days a week. During the hellish nights, straw was burned for light. Exhausted workers sometimes fell into cauldrons of boiling sugar, which scalded them to death. Every mill had axes for chopping off hands or arms that got caught in the rollers.

Oxen and horses that were hitched to booms to power the mills died in their harness traces. Without replacements, work stopped. Because island breeding programs had little success, most draft animals were shipped in at great expense from New England, Britain, and the Netherlands. Nathaniel's 1680 inventory lists forty horses, many more than could have been used on Shelter Island, where oxen were generally used for plowing and pulling heavier loads and horses only for lighter draft and travel. Shipping livestock to the West Indies probably generated much of Nathaniel's income.

"Negro Yards," the Barbadian plantation villages where slaves lived, belonged to the same complex as the "mansion house" and sugar works. At both Sylvester plantations in St. George, where more than a hundred people lived, some twenty-five to fifty slave huts clustered around the sugar works. Each village probably stood on about five acres. The housing arrangements on Shelter Island would differ because of the difference in numbers of people, climate, and work requirements: slaves slept in the attic or the barn lofts for warmth, meaning, among other things, that they had no home hearth for themselves. But the nucleated pattern of life and work—and surveillance—that Steve Mrozowski and his team unearthed on Shelter Island revealed the same tight spacing of house, outbuildings, and work areas (which persisted through the centuries). Black Barbadian villagers created their own commonwealth of family, friends, lovers, and enemies. They raised chickens, guinea fowl, and sometimes a pig. As on Shelter Island, they laboriously ground their ration of corn—a pint per person per day—by hand between two stones.

Some areas were set aside to grow food for slaves. Besides the plots that surrounded their houses, they were allocated a few acres, often on the worst land and at the outskirts of the plantation. This "Negro ground" or "Negro garden" was usually divided into separate family allotments. Here, as in their tiny house gardens, blacks exercised one of their few freedoms: choosing what to plant. Given dawn-to-dusk work hours, that meant Saturday afternoon and Sunday. On Shelter Island, Nathaniel apparently followed this pattern and laid out a "Negro garden" that continued to be cultivated as such at least until 1856, twenty-nine years after slavery ended in New York. Planters also laid out a third area, the "provision ground," where blacks grew basic foodstuffs under white direction, so that—ideally—they would "maintain themselves without burdening their master." In fact, because the provision ground usually comprised only about 15 percent of a plantation's land, it often did not provide enough food to sustain the slave population.

"They Are Happy People, Whom So Little Contents"

Observant, curious, and a humanist, Ligon paints more portraits of individual enslaved Africans than of planters. Occasionally, however, his observations reduce them to mere aesthetic objects, as when he writes, "But 'tis a lovely sight to see a hundred handsome Negroes, men and women, with every one a grasse-green bunch of these fruits [plantains] on their heads, every bunch twice as big as their heads, all coming in a train one after another, the black and green so well becoming one another. Having brought this fruit home to their own houses, and pilling off the skin of so much as they will use, they boyl it in water, making it into balls, and so they eat it. One bunch a week is a Negroe's allowance. To this, no bread nor drink, but water . . . They are happy people, whom so little contents. Very good servants, if they be not spoyled."

Those "happy people" were in fact gravely malnourished—sometimes actually starving—in every season except "crop time," when vegetables were more plentiful and blacks were allowed to chew cane and drink the sugar skimmings. To keep costs down, planters fed slaves barely enough to enable them to work efficiently. The two hundred and sixty enslaved people at Constant's two plantations would have survived almost entirely on carbohydrates, such as plantains, though their rations doubtless included a small amount of (often rancid) salt fish shipped from New

England. (White servants and overseers ate most of the salt meat Nathaniel shipped.) Ligon noted that "if any cattle dyed by mischance, or by any disease: the servants eat the bodies, and the *Negroes* the skins, head, and entrails which was divided amongst them by the Overseers; or if any horse [died], [then] the whole bodies of them were distributed amongst the *Negroes*." Wars, embargoes, shipwrecks, crop failure, plagues of worms, long droughts, and "Horicanes" frequently decimated imported and homegrown supplies.

Because slaves were chronically hungry, food theft was common. James Drax's son, Henry, in a 1679 directive to his overseer, instructed that "if att any time there are any taken Stealling Sugr Molasses or Rum which is our Money and the finall productt of all our Endewors and Care the[y] must be Sewerely handled theire being No punishment tooe terrible on Such an octation as doeth Not deprive the party of Either life or Limbs." Father Antoine Biet, a French Catholic priest visiting Barbados in 1654, wrote, "As these poor unfortunates are very badly fed, a few occasionally escape during the night and go to steal a pig . . . from a neighboring plantation . . . If they are discovered there is no forgiving them . . . One of these poor Negroes . . . his hands in irons, the overseer had him whipped by the other Negroes until he was all covered with blood. The overseer, after . . . seven or eight days, cut off one of his ears, had it roasted, and forced him to eat it." Whether or not Nathaniel practiced such outrageous cruelty on Shelter Island is unknown; he would certainly have been aware of the treatment routinely inflicted on slaves in Barbados. In New York Colony, colonial law sanctioned any punishment meted out by a slave's master or mistress excepting dismemberment or death. All enslaved people knew this.

Homecoming

The Barbadian and Shelter Island plantations were in full swing in the late 1660s when Constant left Barbados for England, where he had bought property in the Midlands. Like many another Barbadian planter, he may have been "desirous to suck in some of the sweet air of England." Despite his Dutch birth and many years in Barbados, Constant considered England his true home. West Indian colonials yearned for cool weather, soft fields of wheat instead of sharp-edged cane, and English country sports and rambles. Having created a living hell for uprooted Africans, such men longed to escape Barbados themselves. In England, they intended to become landed gentlemen, marry off their children well, and transform sugar wealth into the foundations of a family dynasty. Constant would die in Brampton, a small village in Huntingdonshire. His New World venture would end with a carved burial stone inside an obscure English church. He would exchange his family's merchant mark for a modest escutcheon but never gain knighthood. His most enduring legacies in Barbados would be the system of West Indian slavery he had helped to forge—and the hundreds of Sylvesters listed in the Barbados phone book today who may or may not be his descendants.

5

Nathaniel's Middle Passage

To the Coast of Guinea

After their short stay in Barbados during the summer of 1646, Nathaniel and the *Seerobbe* set sail for a different cargo: slaves. From the time he had already spent at his brother's plantation he was well aware what life would offer to the Africans he purchased. "From there [Barbados] this ship went with English orders and crew, and some French crew, to the coast of Guinea," is how Reijer Evertsen, the steersman, finished his deposition before the West Indies Company about the Sylvesters' evasion of duties. ("Guinea" loosely described the West African littoral from Ivory Coast eastward to Benin.) The Transatlantic Slave Trade Database, the magisterial CD-ROM compilation of all such known voyages, does not list the *Seerobbe* or this trip to "Guinea," but the adroit Nathaniel may have succeeded in staying under the radar.

Most slavers traveled south from Europe to Africa, then west to Brazil and the Caribbean, selling their human cargo there and loading up with sugar and other local products before returning to Europe with the help of the Gulf Stream and the trade winds. The stock phrase for this sequence, "the triangular trade," has the virtue of simplicity, but in fact the ocean was crisscrossed by ships in every direction, making multiple stops and, in the early days before the construction of specialized slave ships, handling gold, ivory, dyewood, hides, beeswax, and spices as well as slaves.

The *Seerobbe* had reached Barbados just as a lesser-known ocean current began its annual change of direction. Captain Dircxsz, like all Atlantic World sailors, would have known about the Gulf Stream, which curves up the American coast and then eastward toward Europe as part of the circular North Atlantic Current. The South Equatorial Current, which carried slavers westward from Angola to northern Brazil, defines the northern boundary of the South Atlantic circle. The North Equatorial Countercurrent (NECC), a seasonal phenomenon, slips between the two larger currents and begins to flow eastward across the South Atlantic toward Africa; its flow is strongest from July to September. By steering south from Barbados toward the South American coast, the *Seerobbe* would have caught the NECC in early August at an opportune moment.

The Sylvesters' ship would have arrived off the African coast in time to travel on the 1646 late summer or early fall surge of the eastbound Guinea Current. Slavers coasted past the rocky points and sandy beaches of the Gold Coast, now Ghana, hunting for cargo. The Gold Coast, named for the precious mineral from upcountry mines, was thickly studded with European fortresses, or "castles," built on land leased from local Africans. With gun ports pointing out to sea, they were originally built as early as the 1450s by the Portuguese to guard against threats to the gold trade from other Europeans. However, whether hunting for gold or slaves, European traders were dependent on their African hosts and landlords who controlled the flow of commodities from the interior. European slavers were reluctant to go inland because they instantly succumbed to African killer diseases such as yellow fever.

Competition for these European footholds in Africa sharpened as the slave trade grew. Prime locations changed hands often, and African slave vendors willingly entered into contracts with rivalrous European buyers. A ship like the *Seerobbe* would make many stops to fill her holds, buying a few slaves at each place. Although the Dutch then controlled the bulk of the Atlantic trade, Nathaniel found Englishmen trading directly in view of Dutch forts such as Elmina, "the Mine," the major gold entrepôt, which the Dutch had captured from the Portuguese in 1637. Elmina's governors reported tersely to the Netherlands that between February 1645 and January 1647 nineteen English ships, most of them belonging to interlopers like the Sylvesters, were anchored offshore and engaged in slaving. Most of these ships could carry about a hundred captives each. The *Seerobbe* and her captain were Dutch; the crew was English. Aboard as a merchant factor, Nathaniel could take advantage of both his English and Dutch ties. As interlopers, the Sylvesters ran risks, but they also operated outside any effective control by the WIC or English trade organizations.

Palaver and Preparations

Aboard the *Seerobbe*, Captain Sijmon Dircxsz and Nathaniel Sylvester would have waited for lithe African open boats to come alongside and take them ashore to pay their respects and conduct business with local Africans. As it still does today, the reef would have bared its stone teeth when the combers reared up to crash ashore. White slavers, who understood the hazards of piloting their own boats, relied on "the Negro [to] count the seas and know when to paddle safely on or off." It was the rainy season—probably September or October—so humidity would have reached 95 to 100 percent, but with a daytime temperature of only about 85 degrees Fahrenheit, cooler than in Barbados. First the tricky beach landing, then up into the fort, then step by step up the wide yellow brick treads of the governor's staircase. After a palaver with the African dignitaries and merchants about current prices, taxes, and duties, Captain Dircxsz would have seen that goods were rowed ashore—textiles, rum, tobacco, and anything else from the Sylvesters' Barbados warehouse that Africans would accept in exchange for slaves.

If the seasonal rain cleared off and the sea breeze picked up, the upper terraces of the slave castle would have been pleasant enough for Europeans clad in dark, tight-fitting serge or velvet. Orchards and kitchen plots carpeted the surrounding slopes. The fort gardens held delicious salad crops, cabbages and cauliflowers grown from imported seed, and fruit trees from tropical Asia and America. Fields bulged with starchy crops such as yams, cassava, and maize or guinea corn (*Sorghum bicolor*). The *Seerobbe* would have taken on tons of such staples in amounts narrowly calculated to keep slaves alive on the ocean crossing.

Dinner would have been served between three and four o'clock, the hottest time of day. The hosts most likely entertained Captain Dircxsz and Nathaniel as they did other slavers, with a certain amount of ceremony. Picking up human cargo at Elmina in 1693, Captain Thomas Phillips wrote in his journal of the welcome he received:

> Dinner being over . . . we were invited . . . to take a walk, where the Negroes use to dance, about a quarter of a mile from the fort under two or three very large cotton-trees, of which their canoes are made . . . thro' which they made a hideous bellowing, another

> in the mean time beating a hollow piece of brass with a stick; then came Mrs. Rawlisson the [Dutch] factor's wife, a pretty young Mulatto, with a rich silk cloth about her middle and a silk cap upon her head, flower'd with gold and silver, under which her hair was comb'd out at length, for the mulattos covet to wear it so in imitation of the whites, never curling it up or letting it frizzle as the blacks do; she was accompany'd . . . with the second's and doctor's wives, who were young blacks, about 13 years of age . . . After the English had saluted them they went to dance by turns, in a ridiculous manner, making antick gestures with their arms, shoulders and heads, their feet having the least share in the action; they began the dance moderately, but as the[y] continu'd it, they by degrees quickened their motion so, that at the latter end they appeared perfectly furious and distracted.

Phillips is disdainful as he describes the Afro-Dutch society. But he in fact spent a great deal of time talking to himself in his journal about how he could morally participate in the slave trade. A telling phrase in this description is "furious and distracted," which in seventeenth-century vernacular meant *overtaken by an animal frenzy.* So, at the conclusion of his moral deliberations, by relying on the innate human ability to dehumanize those he saw as different, Phillips ended by having few qualms about buying or selling anyone he saw as a pagan savage incapable of rational, civilized behavior.

Like other seventeenth-century Europeans, Phillips would also have looked to the Bible. According to the Old Testament, Ham was cursed by his father, Noah, for gossiping about the sight of Noah naked and drunk in his tent. For this (and for other unspecified trespasses, perhaps sexual ones), the descendants of his son Canaan were to be slaves forever. One version has it that Ham's name meant "dark" or "black," an explanation that traders like Phillips may have used to justify their purchase of Africans.

While Dircxsz and Nathaniel were dining or haggling, the *Seerobbe*'s carpenter would have refitted the hold, building bulkheads to divide the space into two main compartments. One compartment, forward of the mainmast, was for men and boys; the other, aft, for women and children. Pregnant women, and maybe the sick, were confined separately. Only a few grated hatches and portholes lit and ventilated the dark hold. Dirczsz's windowed, comparatively spacious cabin sat above the slave deck;

Nathaniel may have shared it with him. The crew slept in bunks built into odd corners if they were lucky, or in hammocks slung behind the slave quarters or even on the open deck in longboats, or in gangways, if the vessel was crowded.

The *Seerobbe* was not a small vessel for her day: Dutch records describe her as about eighty to ninety feet long with a beam, or width, of perhaps twenty to twenty-five feet—roughly the same size as present-day fishing boats off Shelter Island. The hold measured about ten to twelve feet deep at its lowest point. Casks of food and drinking water filled the bottom level of the hold as well as parts of the main 'tween deck fore and aft of the space for slaves. Any expansion of that space meant losing room for essential supplies.

In the 1640s many slavers carried mixed shipments of goods as well as people, and they did not modify their ships to carry a full load of captives. But a vessel like the *Seerobbe*, if the interior was rebuilt especially to carry human cargo, could have loaded between one hundred and two hundred slaves, in addition to the officers and crew (the general rule of thumb being ten to fifteen slaves per crewman). Twenty or so cannon—to ward off pirates—were carried aboard.

A slave hold was only five feet high, maximum. The central space served as an alley, with only enough headroom to crouch, or at best to walk with knees deeply bent. Horizontal "shelves" that doubled the size of slave accommodation ran along both sides of the hull for the full length of the compartment. These ledges had about as much headroom as bunks. With a width of about eighteen inches allotted to each prone body, people crawled or were shoved into these spaces at night, the men constantly chained. In foul weather, all would lie below or creep hunched over, day and night.

A Pocket History

When Nathaniel dropped anchor at Elmina, he was participating in an ancient international trade. African and Arab merchants and rulers had been buying and selling slaves north across the Sahara and east up the Indian Ocean for more than six centuries. The Atlantic slave trade began slowly, shortly after the discovery of the Americas at the end of the fifteenth century. But until the second half of the sixteenth century, indigenous Americans seemed the more logical slave workforce for

Central and South America. Only after newly introduced diseases killed off millions of American Indians did European colonizers turn to Africa for replacements.

Like other New England Indians, the Manhansetts, even if they were not contractually enslaved, were impressed by the Sylvesters into labor arrangements roughly similar to Spanish and Portuguese *encomienda* or agricultural vassalage practices in the Southwest. Indian slavery in New England grew out of the original European (and Indian) thinking of war prisoners as slaves, the fruits of a "just war." New York passed legislation in 1679 against Indian slavery, but many Indians continued to be listed as chattel in wills and probates as late as 1796. Over time, as Indian power and status declined on Shelter Island, the Manhansetts who had possessed the power to insist that Nathaniel must purchase the island from them in 1653 had become "his Indians" by 1675. Marriages (not recognized by whites) between enslaved Africans and nominally free Manhansetts or other local Indians further complicated the standing of many who were raised as Indians. In 1684, a boy variously described as "Indian" and "negro," meaning he was the son of an African or creole and a native, was seized as chattel from Nathaniel and Grizzell's eldest son, Giles, in payment for taxes levied by Suffolk County authorities. With tribal systems of law and justice subordinate to English colonial law and generally ignored, virtually no one defended Indians against chattel slavery until the early nineteenth century.

Within Africa, in various countries and in many different periods, prisoners of war and criminals were sold into slavery, as were people designated as sacrificial offerings to gods or oracles. Debtors turned over members of their families to satisfy liens. Tax payments could take the form of human property. Unprotected agricultural villages were often raided in wars, or on the pretext of war, and in times of famine, the young, old, and weak were sometimes sold by their own starving kin.

African slavery clearly differed from New World plantation slavery, however. Black Africans bought and sold each other, but African slavery was not a matter of color, as it became in America. In many parts of Africa, the children of free fathers and enslaved mothers often won acceptance as legal members of their fathers' families. In North America, this happened only during the earliest days of slavery, and rarely. Slave labor in Africa—domestic tasks or craft production in shops rather than work in the fields—involved many more women and children than men.

Slaves in Africa never comprised as large a proportion of the population as in the American South. I have to wonder what chances the first African Shelter Islanders—people like Tammero or Semonie or Oyou, who are mentioned by name in Nathaniel's 1680 will—might have hoped for in their own lives as slaves in America, and in those of their children, given the cultural expectations they brought with them from their native lands.

All of the mechanisms that existed in Africa were adaptable to the toxic transformation of the Atlantic trade. When the *Seerobbe* arrived in 1646, the Gold Coast market was tipping toward slaves as the principal export because the demand for sugar and sugar profits in Europe had stimulated interest in cheap African labor. Before the abolition of slavery in Europe and America during the nineteenth century, an estimated 12.5 million African people had been transported across the Atlantic.

The People

What sort of captives came aboard the *Seerobbe*? European traders and planters touted the superior strength and endurance of "Coromantees," or Cormantines, from the Gold Coast area around Fort Amsterdam, a British fort active between 1631 and 1665. African sellers and European buyers agreed that captives from the Gold Coast and the Bight of Benin also withstood the Middle Passage better than other Africans. Later in the century, it became regular practice for ship captains to purchase "Gold Coast guardians" to police their other captives aboard ship, which it appears they reliably did. But no matter what nationality or ratio of male to female slaves West Indian planters might request, their preferences had little to do with what they got. Customers were dependent on African sellers and African conditions. African traders preferred to keep women to sell on the domestic market, so most Atlantic exports were men. Strong young people, no matter where they came from, sold at a premium.

Whether he landed at Elmina or elsewhere, a European ship's captain, physician, or merchant factor, such as Nathaniel, personally scrutinized the merchandise on offer. "Eyes met eyes as buyers studied corneas for signs of fever and jaundice. Teeth, gums and tongue were checked, muscles probed, skin inspected. The classic marks of good health were 'a glossy sleekness of unblemished skin, clear eyes, red tongue, open chest [and] small belly.'"

The same African canoes that brought Nathaniel and Captain Dircxsz ashore would have loaded up with roped or fettered captives to carry them through the surf to open water. Willem Bosman, a Dutchman who spent fourteen years (1688–1702) on the Gold Coast and rose to be chief factor at Elmina, described how, as slaves were prepared for transport, African sellers would "strip them of all that they have on their backs, so that they come aboard stark naked, as well women as men."

Captives would have been transferred from the canoes into the *Seerobbe*'s longboat, which held more people and was manned by English crew, and from there up into the ship, some ten feet above water level. Any inexperienced sailor who has climbed from a dinghy or a launch into a larger vessel knows this tense moment, when the two boats plunge and yaw, sometimes touching each other and sometimes feet apart. At just the right second, the boarding party must willingly abandon the safety of the dinghy to grab for the slippery boarding ladder.

The people being transferred would not have been willing. As the *Seerobbe*'s English crew briefly unroped or unchained them, the Africans would have seen a last chance to escape. In his journal, Captain Phillips wrote, "The negroes are so wilful and loth to leave their own country, that they have often leap'd out of canoes, boat and ship, into the sea, and kept [themselves] underwater till they were drowned."

Once on board, the men, though not the women and children, were shackled together with leg irons, two by two, and forced into the hold. The Capuchin priest Father Denis de Carli, aboard a Portuguese slaver making a trip from the Congo in 1666, wrote: "It was a pitiful sight to behold how all those people were [stowed]. The men were standing in the hold, flattened one to another with stakes, for fear they should rise and kill the Whites. The women were between the decks, and those that were with child in the great cabbin, the children in the steeradge and pres'd together liked herrings in a barrel, which caus'd an intolerable heat and stench."

Depending on which fort was the first or last stop on the coast for the *Seerobbe*, or somewhere in between, the slaves that Nathaniel purchased could have languished in the hold for as long as seven months with Africa only a few yards away. Security remained tight until the *Seerobbe* was eight days out of port on her westward journey, when eyes that still searched the eastern horizon could no longer see the coast. Out at sea, weather permitting, slaves came on the main deck in the morning, eating on the ship's open deck and taking part in forced exercise, which often meant dancing the dances they knew from home. Dutch slavers bought African drums to accompany these macabre performances.

Water and Food, Life and Death

Statistics vary as to how much water an average person needs per day—that is, when he or she is not battling dysentery (the primary killer on a slave ship) or fever, both of which cause extreme dehydration. Dehydration was aggravated by vomiting, brought on by seasickness and the stench of urine and ordure. In the close confinement of a slave ship's hold, people sweated continually in temperatures that at times reached 100 degrees Fahrenheit. Based on figures calculated by the slave trade historian Herbert Klein (and if the *Seerobbe* carried as many as 150 slaves), about ten tons of water were loaded aboard. Small wonder that, along with the ship's carpenter, the most important man on board after the captain would have been the cooper. He checked the water casks, making sure they were tight and clean enough to keep the water sweet throughout the voyage.

The captain, healthy crew members, and Nathaniel ate European foods such as biscuit, salt beef, hard cheese, and smoked meat, often served with three pints of wine per day. The captain and Nathaniel got the best and freshest fare. Slave rations of beans, corn, or yams were stirred into a gruel made with water or fish stock and thickened with cornmeal or flour. Occasionally, fresh or salt fish and meat were added. The crew doled out this porridgelike soup twice a day, and water, three times daily. A plantain or an ear of corn sometimes varied the diet, and some enlightened captains administered a daily mouthwash of lime juice or vinegar to ward off scurvy.

By Northern European standards, except for the lack of fresh vegetables, this was a fairly healthful diet, not so different from peasants' standard winter fare. The majority of deaths resulted from common illnesses aggravated by chronic malnutrition in Africa, the arduous journey to the coast, and the rigors of being penned ashore. Diseases of every kind, though mostly gastrointestinal, exploded with epidemic force aboard the slave ships. Even modern medications would be hard-pressed to impose control under similar conditions. If it was windy enough, crews tried to ventilate the hold with a sort of windsock sail that funneled air to the

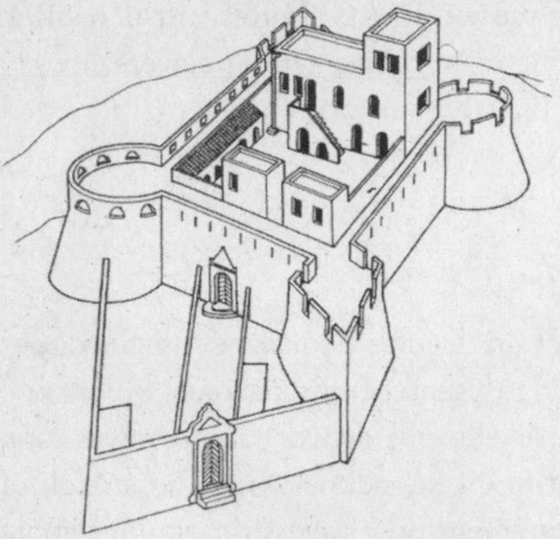

Fort Amsterdam was in English hands in 1646 when Nathaniel made his trip to the Gold Coast, now Ghana. Captives from the coastal areas and from the interior were kept in the windowless "trunk," or dungeon, while they awaited the terrible voyage to the Americas, now known as the Middle Passage.

slave deck below. Slave quarters were scraped out and cleansed periodically; Captain Phillips wrote that he had the job done daily, but such attention was rare on other slave ships. Corpses were thrown overboard.

Fort Amsterdam

Today, Elmina and other Ghanaian slave forts such as Cape Coast Castle or the lesser-known Fort Amsterdam bask in the blinding African sunlight. (Fort Amsterdam, where the *Seerobbe* would have stopped, as it had recently become the British headquarters on the coast, was originally known as Fort Cormantine, after the area, but was renamed by the victorious Dutch in 1665.) The landscape is nondescript: not tropically green but oddly gray, with stunted growth, low hills and swamps, straggling villages, and the occasional roadside stand. From the road near the village of Abanze, a square tower is visible between the tops of the palm trees. This view from African soil is not what Nathaniel would have seen from the *Seerobbe*. But the stumbling, hungry, frightened men, women, and children roped or chained together saw this tower from afar. Many served as beasts of burden on their last African journey. On their heads and backs they carried heavy payloads: beeswax, pepper, dyewood, elephant tusks, gold.

Today, Fort Amsterdam exists as a partially restored ruin, as impressive as a crusader castle in the Mediterranean, with solid-looking walls and redoubts. The empty window frames of its tallest tower look out over the harbor and fishing beach. This was the first Gold Coast fort with an interior prison. The English constructed it in 1645, the year before the *Seerobbe* sailed to Africa, so they could house growing numbers of slaves.

Fort Amsterdam "had two round and two square bastions . . . The fourth bastion . . . which has now disappeared, was hollow and had a grated ventilation hole in the roof (or platform)." Captives were imprisoned inside this tall stone drum, or "trunk," as the English called such dungeons. In the early years after 1645, British needs were satisfied by local Fanti slave traders, who initially dealt mostly in prisoners of war and convicts from within a fifty-mile range of the coast, although as the trade expanded, it's not possible to say from how far inland captives journeyed.

Where the hollow bastion crumbled into the Gulf of Guinea there is a sheer drop of some one hundred feet to the beach below. From the battlements the huge white bulk of Cape Coast Castle, about twelve miles away, is visible as a pearl-gray blob on the horizon. Half a dozen forts used to stand between here and there—a reminder of how fiercely contested this slice of coast once was. A fleet of beautiful wooden boats shaped like oversized canoes lies on the beach. As the last of the morning fishermen expertly cut their path through the breakers, the keels of their craft sink onto the sand with a grinding crunch. Nets are laid out to dry, men stretch themselves after their hard work, women walk around with basins of big silver fish on their heads. Life is a pulsing mix of community, tradition, family, skills, music, market, barter, and poverty. These are the men, women, and children whose ancestors were *not* forced into Atlantic slavery.

Seventeenth-century coastal traders and fort officials described in detail the sections of the Gold Coast they knew. In 1602 the Flemish trader Pieter de Marees, writing at a time when commerce was still confined mainly to gold, ivory, salt, and spices, described the gorgeous, familial Africa he visited in the "Gold Kingdom of Guinea." Half a century later, the German Wilhelm Müller, based at the Danish fort, Frederiksborg, in the Fetu kingdom just east of Cape Coast Castle in the 1660s, borrowed from de Marees but added his own observations. More broad-minded than most visiting Europeans, the two found much to admire. The "fine, upright men" with "bodies as strong as trees . . . learn easily, understand quickly and when they see something demonstrated, will copy it as quickly as one could wish." Handsome women, dignified managers of purse and household, draped themselves in yards of fine textiles, printed

Indian calico, and striped African cloth and dressed their hair high and shining with palm oil. The sabers worn by rich men gleamed with gold and seashells, but even a poor man wore yards of coarse linen, a necklace of cowries, a cap of straw, and armbands of copper or iron. De Marees observed that the children were "stout and fat" and could "walk and speak within their first Year, nay . . . speak and walk much earlier than our children." Muller wrote that fathers "took their sons with them from boyhood onwards, whenever a public assembly or court-day is held" in order to see how justice was done. Trains of slaves snaked through the coastal towns with loads of goods on their heads from upcountry dealers—but then returned to the locales they had come from. Though many of the mud and wattle houses were humble, their earthen floors were polished to a high shine and the walls painted with red, black, and white patterns. Everyone washed thoroughly—daily (a practice that puzzled Europeans). By night and day, the air reverberated with the sound of bells, royal drums, and roaring elephant horns. The day began with a friendly embrace: "Going out in the morning and meeting one of their friends or acquaintances," wrote de Marees, "they will take each other in their arms and give each other the first two fingers of the right hand, putting them together and making them click twice or thrice against each other and saying 'Auzy, Auzy,' which in their language means 'Good day.'"

Tammero and Semonie and Oyou, and so many others on Shelter Island who had lost their African names, had left Africa. But how could their Africas ever leave them? They lived a double life, one in memory and the other in their Northern isolation. The remembered world of that "Good day" embodies what they and so many others like them had lost.

Pagans

Nathaniel and his partners would have felt few misgivings about enslaving Africans. Their first line of argument was that all human beings could be enslaved as prisoners taken in "just wars." (The English word "slave" has its roots in the Byzantine Greek *sklavos*, and its identification with servitude dates to eastern European wars of the ninth century, when many Slavs were captured and enslaved.) Captain John Smith was captured in a skirmish with the Tartars and sold as a slave to a Turk in Istanbul in 1602; Nathaniel's good friend Colonel Lewis Morris had been

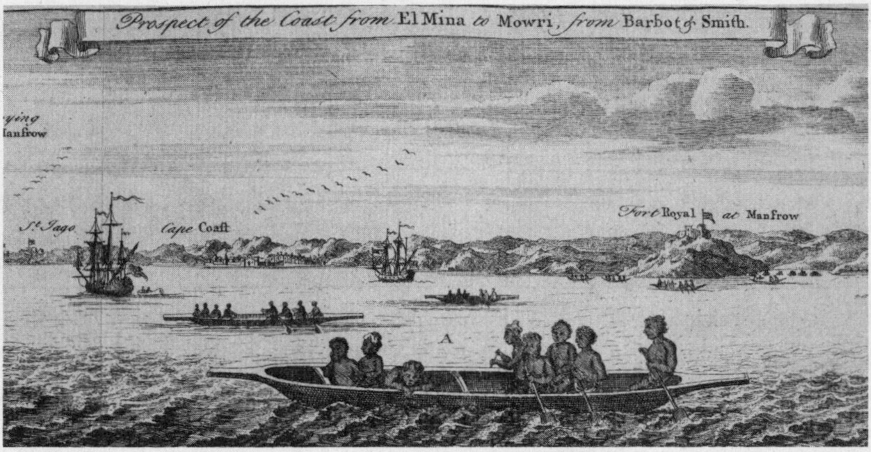

One of the captive Africans being rowed to a waiting slave ship puts hand to cheek in sorrow, while another leans over the gunwale. Many preferred drowning to leaving their families and native lands. (Detail, *Prospect of the Coast from El Mina to Mowri*, engraving by Jean Barbot, in *Description of the Coasts of North and South Guinea* [London, 1732])

captured by Barbary corsairs, was imprisoned in Algiers for six months, and may have served time as a galley slave. Pequots conquered in 1637 were sent as slaves to the West Indies; Irish men and women were sent to America and Barbados as slaves during Cromwell's Irish wars. Planters and colonists like Nathaniel found it easy to say that Africans who arrived in the Americas were presumably first taken prisoner in Africa's internal wars. That Providence made them available to Nathaniel was a mark of God's favor.

The second rationale arose from the nature of early modern Christianity. According to seventeenth-century European and American churchmen, all non-Christians got what they deserved, be it slavery now or eternal hellfire later. The neat trick for a Christian slaveholder, who could not enslave a fellow believer, was to prevent the conversion of the pagans he owned. This no longer mattered once colonials, chiefly in North America, tied slavery more pragmatically to skin color. By the 1670s, when some of the enslaved people whom Nathaniel and Grizzell lived alongside had become Christians, they nonetheless remained slaves, as did their children and their children's children.

The historian Patrick Manning, in his bitter and enlightening *Slavery and African Life*, refuses to reduce the fraught subject to a simple morality play peopled by a cast of characters divided into innocent Africans pursued by evil Europeans, demonstrating how every African understood that slavery was deeply embedded in family structure, religion, government, war, taxation, and systems of justice. The same rapidly became true on Shelter Island, as it did in every coastal American colony from Maine to Florida and throughout the Caribbean. The larger tragedy was not just the suffering of captives sent overseas, or African nations' loss of generations of young men and women, but the complicit transatlantic creation of an African world where "people were forced to think of how much they could get for selling a neighbor, or how much they would pay to ransom a loved one," and where, on both sides of the Atlantic, both sellers and buyers, as Manning puts it, "lubricated and disguised the flow of slaves with a hundred euphemisms, proverbs, equivocations and outright lies."

For a hard-driving merchant like Nathaniel, physical intimacy with someone he had purchased would have become nearly inevitable at some point—in the barracoons (slave pens), on the beach, or aboard ship. At that moment, another human being stared back at him. From all we know about Nathaniel (a man soon to become a Quaker but one who owned slaves), from Captain Phillips and so many other slave traders' accounts, we can conclude that whatever moral qualms Nathaniel might have felt were soon dispelled. In 1758, more than a century after the first Africans arrived on Shelter Island, the members of a Philadelphia Quaker meeting, many of whose families owned slaves or had been engaged in the trade, finally reached a consensus about abolition that was based on self-interest: "that no Quaker could keep a slave without risking damnation, since no master could be expected to resist the temptation to exploit the slave."

6

Before the Whirlwind

Hunting for Grizzell Brinley

At the manor, one of the UMass field school archaeology students carefully brushes off a dusty metal button dug from the front lawn. Four stout tulips and their leaves wreathe the surface in a bold symmetrical design. Much of the gilt has worn off, leaving the brass underneath to turn to verdigris during its centuries underground. In Nathaniel and Grizzell's day it probably shone on a man's coat. Back then, buttons did more than fasten a garment. They were also sewn on as ornaments, dispersed in rows or clustered in patterns that signified the bearer's social rank. As badges, they became insignia of the all-encompassing hierarchy of service. The Duke of Buckingham, King Charles I's most trusted courtier, wore white and sky-blue satin velvet "sett all over both suite and cloak with Diamonds," on his trip to Paris to bring home the monarch's bride, Princess Henrietta Maria of France. Grizzell Sylvester's father, Thomas Brinley, also the king's servant, was one of the seven auditors of the royal revenue.

Hunting for Grizzell's childhood, I visit her London parish of St. James Clerkenwell, where Thomas and his wife, Anne Wase, produced most of their brood of twelve children. Today, a chaste eighteenth-century church replaces the hulking medieval structure Grizzell knew, which had originally belonged to an Augustinian nunnery before Henry VIII dissolved the Roman Catholic monasteries in England in 1536. The Brinleys brought their infants to St. James to be baptized, perhaps by walking up the hill through Jerusalem Passage from their house on St. John's Lane.

I walk away from the church and slip down into the dense shade of a fortresslike gate built in 1504 for the priory of the Knights Hospitaller of

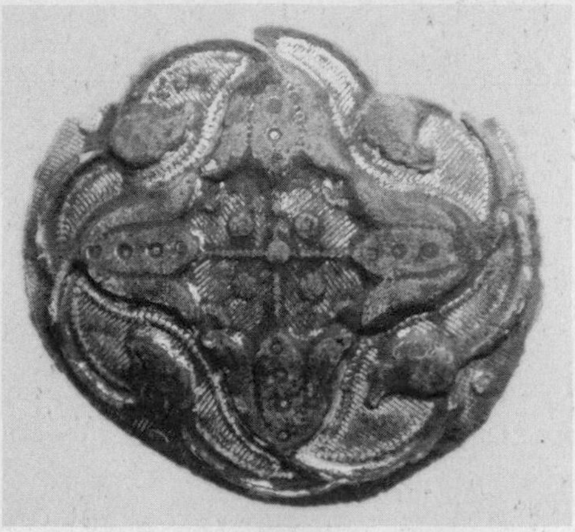

Though its surface has been tarnished and eroded by the manor's acid soil, this chased and gilded button still gleams as it once did on a high-style seventeenth-century garment.

St. John of Jerusalem, a crusader military order. Beyond the arch, narrow St. John's Lane, once the main entrance to the priory, feels like a private road. In the early nineteenth century, Albion Place was cut through the center of what had been the Brinleys' property, and the house where Grizzell was born in 1636. But nearby streets still preserve the shape of the ancient neighborhood and record the names of a few residents from Grizzell's day. When St. John's became crown property after the Dissolution, courtiers and well-heeled city folk colonized the Hospitallers' palatial buildings and grounds. The area resembled an aristocratic club when the Brinleys moved there in 1629: the inner precinct north of St. John's Gate boasted ten titled households.

William Cavendish, Earl of Newcastle, cultivated, extravagant, and eccentric, exemplified those grander neighbors. A romantic landscape gardener ahead of his time, he planted amid the crumbling arches of a Gothic cloister. The author of court masques (and Ben Jonson's greatest supporter after the king), he was also a master of fencing and horsemanship, a patron of the sciences, and above all a passionate musician (he owned four harpsichords, an organ, and twenty-two stringed instruments). In 1641, five-year-old Grizzell might have seen—and heard—the glittering pageantry of his daughter's wedding at St. James Clerkenwell as the bridal party made their way to and from Newcastle House. But Grizzell also would have glimpsed a rougher London close-up: the stain of "the Fleet," the notorious debtors' prison, spread up to the bottom of St. John's Lane below her house. Tumbledown tenements there provided a dangerous rookery for criminals and prostitutes. Taverns lined the streets, while a little farther south the open space of Smithfield hosted a huge livestock market and public executions.

"A Dwelling House . . . Several Coach-Houses and Stables, & the Residue as a Garden"

The noble Berkeley family lived next door to Grizzell. An engraving by Wenceslaus Hollar, who recorded much of London in the 1660s before the Great Fire, shows Berkeley House as a three-story brick edifice with Jacobean gables and ornate chimneys. Documentary evidence for Grizzell's adjacent house and garden is sketchy, but there is enough to suggest the establishment was sizable, although it was not designed to be impressive. On a map of 1676 the Berkeleys' front courtyard is shown flanked by imposing brick wings, while Grizzell's house, less than half the size, stood modestly end-on to the lane. Outbuildings and stable yards that her family shared with the Berkeleys were clustered between the two houses. When the property was sold as a teardown in 1685, the 115-by-279-foot plot

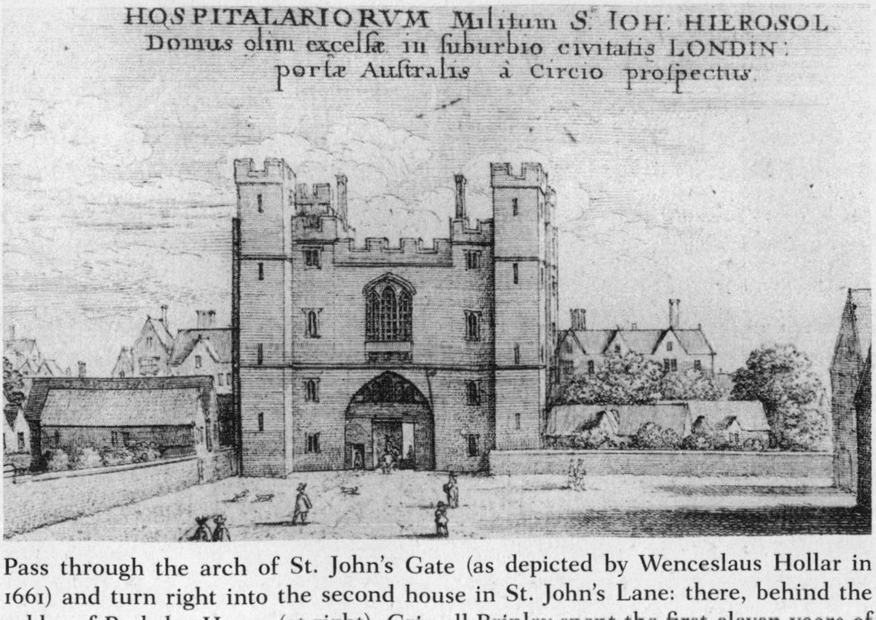

Pass through the arch of St. John's Gate (as depicted by Wenceslaus Hollar in 1661) and turn right into the second house in St. John's Lane: there, behind the gables of Berkeley House (at right), Grizzell Brinley spent the first eleven years of her life.

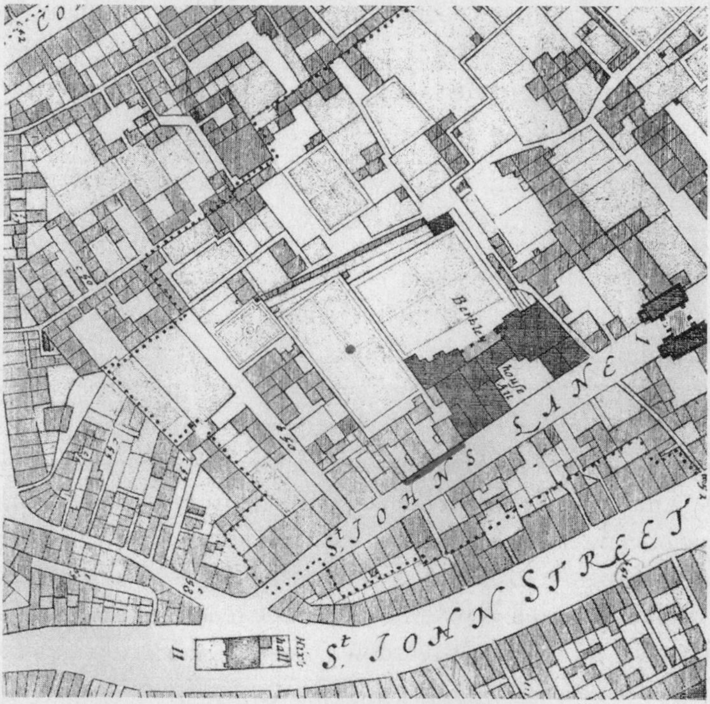

A dot marks the center of the Brinleys' large garden behind the house complex fronting on St. John's Lane. Ogilby and Morgan's 1676 London map was the first accurate and detailed map of the city, with all the buildings represented in the plan.

accommodated "a Dwelling house . . . with several coach-houses and stables, & the residue as a garden to the said late house." The house was probably brick, two or three stories tall, and, like its grander neighbor, had gabled roofs and towering brick chimneystacks.

Results of excavations of both the Berkeley and Brinley sites published in 2004 by the Museum of London Archaeology Services revealed underground cesspits reached by chutes from indoor privies, which allowed the diggers to learn much about what people ate, tossed, or mislaid. The Berkeleys and the Brinleys ate very well: archaeologists have unearthed the bones of fallow deer (game reserved for royalty and peers) and swans, along with the remnants of common cattle, sheep, pigs, cod, whiting, herring, and plaice.

The back of the Brinley house faced west, catching the last rays of the setting sun, a boon when candles were a luxury and Little Ice Age winters were frigid. Elizabethan domestic architecture had glorified glass as a stylish and expensive building material, opening windows into tall banks of light. (Cavendish's grandmother, the redoubtable Elizabeth Hardwick, had built the Glass House of her day: "Hardwick Hall, more glass than wall.") It's likely the Brinleys had at least one large window at the rear of the second floor, the typical location for a "long room," or gallery, from which the entire garden panorama could be admired at a glance.

"The Best and Surest Herbe"

The size of the Brinley garden behind the house may have come as a surprise to visitors: the same 1676 map reveals that the space was as large as that of the Berkeleys' garden, maybe even a bit larger. Other nearby houses are depicted on the map with orchards and knot gardens laid out in patterns, probably of cut turf and gravel, but these two areas are shown as simple rectangles. Paradoxically, what begins to make Grizzell's London life come alive for me as a landscape historian are the two straight lines that quarter the plot, dividing the long space into four equal parterres, an ancient and handsome design appropriate for a court official such as Thomas Brinley. Tubbed topiary trees (cypress, bay, or juniper) would have punctuated the corners of the plats. Glistening boxwood—that evergreen shrub so revered in later centuries at Sylvester Manor—would have been set as hedging or edging.

Britons had known boxwood for centuries before Grizzell's time. Man-sized ancient *Buxus sempervirens* specimens still grow wild in Surrey, skinny druids on the chalky slopes of Box Hill above the North Downs. Geoffrey Chaucer, appointed a royal forester in the 1390s, mentions box as a common woodland tree. Clipped specimens flanked a London doorway in 1490, and low hedges rimmed garden beds as early as 1500.

Tall-growing boxwood, *Buxus sempervirens*, is known as "standard" or "tree" box and was for long the only species the English knew. The giants at Sylvester Manor are standard box. The slower-growing "dwarf" or edging strains of box, *Buxus sempervirens* L. var. *suffruticosa*, are denser, shorter, and have smaller leaves. They were either hybridized or discovered as "sports," or natural mutations, by French and Dutch horticulturists shortly before English gardeners began to import the plant in the first quarter of the seventeenth century for royal and upper-class gardens. In

1629, John Parkinson, botanist to King Charles I, wrote about "French or Dutch Boxe" he had seen in the gardens of plant collectors. He condemned its "unpleasing sent which many mislike," an aroma some say reeks of cat piss and others savor as the bitter fragrance of history. (Scientists have at last identified the source of the smell, a volatile organic compound containing sulfur, also present in Sauvignon Blanc!) Parkinson nonetheless wholeheartedly recommended it for edging beds as "the best and surest herbe to abide faire and green in all the bitter storms of the sharpest Winter and all the great heates and droughts of Summer." Thomas Brinley would have seen an abundance of it in the royal palaces where he served, and Grizzell could not have stepped out of her garden door in Clerkenwell without brushing against boxwood of some kind, a furry little green creature, a household companion. Not that this necessarily means she carried a rooted cutting with her from England, as Cornelia Horsford, the early twentieth-century chatelaine of the manor and its gigantic boxwoods, would have it. Boxwood, alone among the plants that early colonists brought with them to America, has no discernible medicinal or culinary value. So why would Grizzell have carried it with her? Familiarity, or homesickness—and status value—are reasons that spring to a speculative historian's mind.

Grizzell was a woman who saved what she could from the past and looked to the future. Years later, on Shelter Island, she bequeathed a precious teething toy she surely had brought from England, "the Child's Corall w. ch. hath silver bells on it," to "the first son of any of my Sons, who bears his grandfathers name," meaning her husband, Nathaniel, whose name she wanted remembered by future generations. But in truth, if the ancestors of the boxwoods now growing at the manor's garden gate reached the island at that early date, they might as easily have traveled from the Netherlands with Nathaniel, an arriviste eager to advertise his gentility and, as a merchant with ships, well placed to order direct.

In the Brinley garden, seeds of garden favorites such as primroses, opium poppies, and violets were found in one archaeological deposit, along with those of the ghostly gray wild fumitory, which creeps along the ground like smoke. Well-rotted manure enriched every inch of planting space. All paths would have been graveled for drainage in London's wet weather, and to ensure dry footing for the pleasure of "walking up and downe, and about the garden." Brisk walks were also thought to expel unwholesome humors from lungs and head. In troubled times to come during the Civil War, Thomas could stroll in his garden "for the delight and comfort of his wearied mind." Just closing the door on the noisome street outside to be welcomed by the fragrance and order within would have cheered anyone in seventeenth-century London.

Divinely Ordered

From late spring into early summer, the greatest floral flourish in gardens such as the Brinleys' was a cumulus cloud of fruit blossom, promising sweetness. Sugar was precious and fresh fruit seasonal. Lawson advised that the roots of fruit trees be "powdered with strawberries, Red, White and Green," and beds planted with berry bushes "hanging and dropping with . . . Raspberries, Barberries, Currans." Familiar fruits—apples, cherries, pears, peaches, and plums—as well as mulberries, figs, medlars, and sloes, which are exotic eating today—were trained in pots or to grow as regular patterns of branches that were pruned for maximum fruiting and espaliered against rosy brick walls. This orchard spoke to the satisfying human control over nature ordained by God since the Garden of Eden. Rank and class pervaded the seventeenth-century natural world in a hierarchy that descended from the regal rose to lowly weeds. John Parkinson advised gardeners to lay out their plots "as may be fit and answerable to the degree they hold [in society]," like sumptuary laws for the garden.

When Grizzell was born, five of her brothers and sisters were under ten years old; Anne no doubt assigned her children tasks like pulling carrots, picking fresh "sallet" greens, or finding and squishing cabbage worms. In the Brinleys' square brick-lined cesspit, archaeologists have found the remains of *Leprisinus varius*, a beetle that lives in ash trees. The Hollar view of St. John's Gate shows a row of small trees standing on the far side of the wall that abuts the gate tower; beyond rise the rounded crowns of larger trees—perhaps ash?—obscuring all but the gables of Berkeley House. Bees did the work of pollination, traveling in and out of their "warm and dry Bee-house, comely made of Fir-boards." "Bird pots," home to martins, swifts, and starlings, hung from trees or were attached to house walls. They supplied the kitchen with eggs and nestlings: "Four-and-twenty blackbirds baked in a pie" is not just a nursery rhyme.

William Lawson, author of *A New Orchard and Garden* and its companion, *The Countrie House-Wife's Garden* (issued ten times between

1617 and 1683), wrote, "The skill and Paines of Weeding the garden with weeding knives or fingers, I refer to herselfe, and her maides, willing them to take the opportunity after a showre of raine; with all I advise the Mistresse, either to be present herselfe or to teach her maides to know hearbes from weedes." The mistress of the Brinley house and garden, of course, was Anne Wase Brinley. Anne may not have done much gardening herself, but she was expected to know the work well enough to direct it. Gentry like the Brinleys hired "weeder women" (Lawson's "maides") in addition to professional gardeners. Women of every class were familiar with the garden as both larder and medicine chest. Even ornamental flowers had useful properties to recommend them; Lawson praised clove pinks for "comforting the spirits, by the sense of smelling."

Archaeologists also identified a compost pit by the seeds it contained. Macrofossils of garden plants are hard to identify, as the seeds of wild plants are almost indistinguishable from those of closely related cultivars, but when verifiable seeds of stinking chamomile, black bindweed, and other common weeds turn up together in a single deposit, it means someone was weeding.

Service, Servitude, and Slavery

The Brinleys' status as "metropolitan gentry" meant that they employed a number of servants. Live-in domestics, they were usually young, ranging from children of ten or twelve to adults. Indeed, most young people in seventeenth-century England were servants or apprentices of one kind or another, learning skills and saving wages while receiving room and board. Even the gentry and aristocracy sent their sons to "serve" in other families of similar or higher rank. "The institution of servants and apprentices helped solve the problem of what to do with children between puberty and marriage," as the historical anthropologist Alan Macfarlane has written. Like the words "service" and "servant" (Thomas Brinley was "the king's servant"), "family" was defined more broadly in the seventeenth century than it is today. The English term comes from the Latin *famuli*, meaning "slaves living under one roof who make up the *familia*," or a man's "whole property, both real and personal, houses, lands, money, cattle, slaves, etc." Both the tradition of service as an honorable but temporary condition of life shared by thousands, and the ancient concept of family as *familia*, or whole property, including slaves, would travel to America.

Grizzell Brinley's comfortable childhood seems as remote from the Africa of the Middle Passage as it does from Shelter Island. However, black domestics were not unknown in London in the 1640s. An alderman employed "three blackamore maids"; a brewer gave his black servant, Frauncis, a decent burial in the Aldgate parish graveyard. At the court of Elizabeth I, aristocrats had employed black personal attendants outfitted in fantastic garb, like the queen's "lytle Blackamore" dressed in "white Taffeta, cut and lined with tincel, striped down with gold and silver."

The number of "Indeans, Moores, Moreans, Neygers" and mulattos living in England from as early as the Tudor period testified to the expansion of travel, trade, and imperial exploration. Slavery was made officially but ineffectively illegal within England in 1569: the law was generally construed only to limit the savagery with which slaves could be treated, not the question of ownership, so people of color inhabited an uneasy up-and-down world in which they could still be bought or sold. Queen Elizabeth had twice ordered "blackamoors" out of England, claiming they took English jobs, while others were treated as figures of fun, as if they were jesters and dwarves, and a few, like Captain Pedro Negro, "a Spaniard," received honors for secrets they passed along from foreign enemies; still others were simply rated as domestic property.

For an image of a black person treated matter-of-factly as chattel, Grizzell needed look no farther than her own parish church. St. James Clerkenwell housed "a costly stone altar-tomb, with Corinthian pillars, to the memory of Lady Elizabeth Berkeley, one of Queen Elizabeth's Ladies of the Bedchamber, whose effigy lay in state with the head of a negro at her feet." A variation on the carved dogs that had faithfully attended generations of tomb figures as footrests, this grotesque head was already apparently part of the everyday order of things. So from childhood onward, Grizzell may have been no stranger to black faces and the concept of African servitude.

The Ascent of the Auditor

Between 1626 and 1641, Grizzell's father occupied a solid pew in the Anglican establishment and a lofty desk at the Royal Exchequer. A descendant of minor Staffordshire gentry, he had benefited from his marriage into a family with strong civil service connections. He clerked for his wife's great-uncle, Richard Budd, one of the seven auditors who supervised all crown accounts, before becoming one himself. Land and property made up much of the crown's great wealth, but Tudor and Stuart monarchs were constantly short of cash. The auditors' primary job had been to visit the king's estates to assess and collect rents, but increasingly they were also required to value the crown lands, make contact with buyers, and negotiate sales to boost the royal coffers. They became real estate agents, collecting commissions and, as opportunities arose, buying properties and making deals for themselves.

Thomas reached the peak of his career in 1636, when in the course of his duties he and Charles Harbord, the royal surveyor general, and other partners received a royal grant as part of the king's negotiations with Sir Cornelius Vermuyden, a Dutch embankment engineer, to drain some eighteen square miles of fenland in Yorkshire, Nottinghamshire, and Lincolnshire. The profits of a total of 12,459 acres of crown lands, including all existing "houses, buildings, stables, dovecots, [and] gardens," were to be divided among six lucky men "and their heirs and assigns." Had the war not intervened, even a fractional share of that acreage would have given Thomas, as a prominent landowner, the opportunity to gain a knighthood, and perhaps more, through skillful political maneuvering and illustrious alliances for his children.

The Air Grizzell Breathed: Spectacle, Science, and Magic

In his role as a royal servant, Thomas Brinley observed the king's splendors—or, as his auditor, at least could estimate what they cost. As a child, Grizzell would have heard from him about glamorous masques at Whitehall, Charles I's favorite palace, in which even the king and queen danced and sang, conjuring up a mythic microcosm where a beneficent monarch ruled over amicable subjects. The ideal world onstage melted into the real. In Aurelian Townshend's *Albion's Triumph*, the stage set morphed from a scene of the ancient Roman republic into a shimmering "prospect of the King's palace of Whitehall and part of the city of London."

Meanwhile, a different sort of drama began to take place in gardens. The Renaissance discovery of classical antiquity and fresh ideas of perspective and symmetry arriving from the Continent transformed English landscapes into theaters. The lead roles went to exotic flora that proclaimed England's prowess in global exploration, trade, and colonization. Gardeners, scientists, scholars, and collectors drawn to natural rarities and oddities were esteemed as "the curious."

As part of the new and passionate intellectual interest in science and natural history, the British began to shape what became known as "natural philosophy," a new way for "the curious" to connect with their surroundings. Natural philosophy's atmosphere of free inquiry and intellectual independence was first advanced by Sir Francis Bacon at the beginning of the seventeenth century and was fostered by empirical scientists such as Robert Boyle, one of the first proponents of a mechanical universe.

Boyle and his fellows—the Connecticut alchemist Governor John Winthrop Jr. among them—held that only rigorous and repeated experimentation, accompanied by skepticism, could deliver the truths of nature. Alchemy, now popularly marginalized as an occult search to transmute base metals into gold, in fact sought to refine material to its elemental forms using basic laboratory techniques, a perfectly scientific aspiration. At the same time, as the colonial historian Walter Woodward writes, "a world of wonders is almost by definition a world of magical possibilities." Leading thinkers, confident that "all parts of nature—minerals, plants, stars, animals, humans—were alive and correspondent with each other," easily reconciled a magical cosmic view with the scientific concept of a mechanical universe.

The New World was a lesson for Europe about the extent of the possibilities of creation. Believers accepted the infinity of real American "monster" animals such as the armadillo or the manatee that were described or brought back by explorers, confirming that such creatures still walked the earth and swam the seas. Imagination ran wild: the gentlest monster, the "Scythian lamb" or "borametz," which reportedly grew on a stalk like a vegetable, was presented as fact on the frontispiece of John Parkinson's compendium, *Paradisus in Sole, Paradisus Terrestris* (1629).

Curiosity and Delight

Unlike most women who came to America in the first generations of settlement, Grizzell was no English provincial growing up in what the historian

Carol Berkin has called "the comforting sameness of a parish or village life." She belonged to a worldly and well-educated metropolitan gentry family with court connections, and as such, unlike many of her cohort, she was, until the age of fifteen when she emigrated, inevitably immersed in the richness and flamboyance of England's late Renaissance.

The usual assumption about New England's earliest women settlers is that they were heroically bent on reproducing the households they had left behind. Of course they were. They believed that the tasks of shaping a home and bearing children were their godly mission. Their bodies were their destiny. But because they quickly became aware of how much their new environment could shape them, they were forced to come to grips with a nature foreign to them—peoples and their cultures, animals, plants, and the very different seasons—and to adapt. And because English colonists "recognized the power of the inspirited natural world to both harm and heal them," writes the historian Susan Scott Parrish, women (and men) also acknowledged immanent supernatural forces, whether manifested in other humans as witches and changelings, or in the unknown forests, or in the mighty power of the Lord to assist in famine or sickness.

Few colonial women's diaries or letters from before 1750 have been found. The first women's "travel" writings were memoirs of captivity, such as Mary Rowlandson's bestselling account of her travails as a prisoner of the Narragansett Indians in 1676. Memorable female characters speak up from time to time in early colonial court and town records, often retailing trenchant gossip about Goody This and Goodman That. But their voices say little about the natural world except as an endurance trial.

Despite the lack of evidence, and our predisposition to frame these women in very pragmatic terms, is it possible that some of them felt a flash of excitement or admiration, however brief, for the spectacle that unrolled around them? I want to ask if there was room or time enough for Grizzell to be amazed and delighted in the New World, given the intellectual climate of her English youth and her background as a young gentlewoman.

Whether the ultimate spiritual quest that led Grizzell to the Society of Friends began with her hearing family discussions about religion, philosophy, or the new science is a highly speculative question. Certainly two of her brothers, Thomas and Francis, were intellectuals. The younger, Thomas, became a Cambridge don and part of a circle that explored the far reaches of mysticism and inward spiritual experience. When Thomas died in 1672 he left his books, which included some of the most extreme writings of the period on religion, politics, and social protest, to his older brother. Francis, four years older than Grizzell, left England at the same time she did, moved to Rhode Island, and created one of the largest libraries in America at the time. His 217 books, according to a list he compiled when he was eighty-one years old, included works on the law, literature, travel, science, and medicine. Francis Brinley kept his brother's incendiary books even though, as a staunch conservative, his own opinions, expressed in action, print, and personal correspondence, ran absolutely counter to their contents. He clearly wanted to know all sides of every question. His lifelong reading habits reveal a humanist searching everywhere for "the capacities of human reason to grasp the patterns of nature and the requirements for a flourishing life for both the body and the soul."

Grizzell, like Nathaniel in Amsterdam, thus grew up in a family where readers and knowledge were valued. As a grown woman, she possessed her own Bible, so we know she was literate. Although the exercise of female intellect was generally regarded askance as Eve's "fatal curiosity," a woman could freely indulge in reading popular garden manuals, a relatively new literary genre only steps away from the natural histories and travel accounts and topographies that were just beginning to emerge in print. Books such as William Lawson's *The Countrie House-Wife's Garden* dealt with more than the practical science of growing plants and the art of laying out beds and paths in Clerkenwell—or anywhere. "Far from being tedious prescriptions, the early English gardening books were full of dreams of nature—and men's dreams for themselves," writes the historian Rebecca Bushnell.

The sensuality in the fiercely sexy poetry of Donne and Marvell also permeated ordinary garden manuals, though the language was more decorous. Inevitably, Nature, with a capital *N*, was cast as a woman. The herbalist John Gerard rhapsodized over the pleasures of a queenly virgin earth "apparelled with plants, as with a robe of embroidered worke, set with orient pearles, and garnished with great diversitie of rare and costly jewels [in a] varietie and perfection of colours," even as he ardently also stressed that the intellectual pleasures of gardening led to a deeper knowledge of the Creator. Grizzell, as a girl entering womanhood, would have grasped that such power and beauty were also to be hers, however humbly she was meant to accept them as God's gift.

Tradescant's Ark

Grizzell's childhood London contained the loveliest, most accessible, and liveliest proof of the mix of old magic with the new scientific observation: "Tradescant's Ark," in South Lambeth, London, so nicknamed because it aimed to gather all creation under one roof. It opened as England's first public natural history museum, Tradescant's Rarities, in 1631 and quickly became a regular city sight for visitors and London citizens alike, along with the royal armory, the wild beasts of the Tower of London menagerie, criminal executions and hangings, and the tombs of Westminster Abbey. (Westminster Abbey's cloisters housed the offices of the Exchequer where Thomas Brinley worked.) One prominent pedagogue praised London as the best place "for the full improvement of children in their education, because of the variety of objects which daily present themselves to them, or may easily be seen once a year, by walking to Mr. John Tradescant's, or the like houses or gardens, where rarities are kept." By the early 1640s, Grizzell, then six, was old enough to visit the Ark on an outing, like any other young Londoner with enlightened, well-off parents. Getting there was not difficult: there were abundant light craft to hire on the Thames, operating out of the many water stairs between Whitehall and London Bridge, where Grizzell might have hopped aboard.

Tradescant's rarities combined a *Wunderkammer* (a cabinet, or chamber, of natural and artificial wonders) with a botanical institute and trial garden. A sixpence admission charge let visitors gaze at hundreds of exhibits indoors and out. While every *Wunderkammer* was meant to show off the power of knowledge and the miracles of God's creation, the John Tradescants, father and son, were also intent on studying the cultural world in microcosm through each object they gathered, just as empirical scientists investigated the natural world with their new instruments—microscopes and telescopes.

I imagine Grizzell walked through the pair of bleached whale ribs, towering white and high over the moated entrance, then into the courtyard where she passed "a very ingenious little boat of bark"—perhaps an American Indian canoe. Indoors, walls were hung to the ceiling with "rarities" of all sorts, spears, bows, arrows, shields, little boats and paddles, tacked up next to the domed shells of giant sea turtles, snake skins, and grinning desiccated alligators. Other walls were papered with paintings. Every flat surface was crammed with ostrich eggs, medals, coins, antiqui-

The Scythian lamb, *Cibotium borametz,* grew on a stalk and grazed only in the fabulous pages of travel and natural history books. (From Henry Lee's *The Vegetable Lamb of Tartary* [London, 1887], after Claude Duret [1605])

ties, natural malformations, fossils, statues, crystals, beautiful scientific instruments, and intricate chiming mechanical toys. The Ark's 1656 catalogue matter-of-factly listed a piece of the skin of a borametz, *Agnus scythicus*, the stalk-bound vegetable lamb!

"Pohatan, King of Virginia"

After gawking at a dragon's egg, a mermaid's hand, and a fragment of the True Cross, Grizzell would have found her way to a large brown cloak: "the robe of the king of Virginia." (Today, as the single most famous object to survive from the Tradescants' collections, the "robe" is exhibited with other remnants of their hoard in the Ashmolean Museum in Oxford.)

By the 1640s Virginia was a known quantity to Londoners. They eagerly consumed travelers' information about Native Americans and their exotic ways. When Captain John Smith met Powhatan, Smith was impressed by his noble bearing, "proudly lying uppon a Bedstead [with] such a grave and Majesticall countenance, as drave me into admiration to see such state in a naked Salvage." As the historian Karen Kupperman writes, Smith admired him, and the *werowances*, or kinsmen and leaders who owed Powhatan allegiance, "in part because he could not trust them. He saw their alternating friendliness and hostility as evidence of policy and as part of their toughness." (The Sylvesters' neighbor, Lion Gardiner, expressed similar wary admiration for the Indians of New England.)

Whether the cloak belonged to Powhatan is debatable, as it is unclear who brought it to the Ark. Some even think of it as a wall hanging rather than a garment. But whoever its owner was, and whatever its purpose, this southern Algonquian treasure is what Smith saw in Virginia and described as "large mantels of Deare skin . . . Some imbrodered with white beads," made from local shells and worn by "the better sort." About seven and a half feet long and five feet wide, the mantle is the right size for a six-footer (Smith described Powhatan as "a tall well proportioned man, with a sower looke, his head somewhat gray . . . His age near 60; of a very able and hardy body to endure any labour").

The Tradescant robe consists of four tanned deerskins stitched together with sinew, which is also used to attach the beads. Some of the beads have fallen off, but the design is clearly visible. The figure of a man flanked by a deer and a wolf stands dead center, facing the viewer. Scholars have identified the Indian as a major chief, probably Powhatan, and other parts of the design as a map of Tidewater Indian communities. The clue to a probable Powhatan connection lies in the thirty-four small beaded roundels surrounding the central figure. Each circle may represent a district under the chief's command. Sure enough, in his *Historie of Travell into Virginia Britania* (1612), William Strachey, secretary of the Virginia Company in 1609, wrote that Powhatan's "petty Weroances in all, may be in nomber, about three or fower and thirty."

Even if Grizzell viewed the deerskin cloak only as barbaric raiment, she would nevertheless have grasped that its mysterious figures and circlets had something to do with kingly power, just as those who admired the Duke of Buckingham's diamond buttons could read their social meaning. She was surrounded by British royal iconography. The deliberate "branding" of Queen Elizabeth I, for instance, had generated hundreds of images of the monarch in print, paint, and embroidery, and on coins and fabric. It's an easy jump to the worlds of power and beauty embroidered on the Virginia chieftain's cloak—or to the regalia that Wyandanch, the Montauket leader, and his followers wore when they came to Shelter Island in 1658 for a ceremonial meeting with Nathaniel.

Other coats, of feathers and bear and raccoon skins, hung in the museum, along with "Black Indian girdles made of Wampum peek, the best sort," six sorts of "tamahacks . . . Virginian purses imbroidered with Roanoke," and a stuffed "black bird with red shoulders and pinions," the natty red-winged blackbird that arrives every spring on Shelter Island and sings its sweet, piercing song as it swings on a cattail in the marsh.

The garden around the museum teemed with living discoveries. The two John Tradescants, father and son, were first and foremost plantsmen; by the time Grizzell would have visited in the 1640s, they had amassed an astounding collection. As gardener at the royal palace of Oatlands, John the Elder had hunted specimens obsessively for himself and his powerful patron. From the New World, North American plants poured into his three-acre trial plots. John the younger, who followed in his father's footsteps at Oatlands, brought back additional hundreds of American species from his three trips to Virginia.

When Grizzell wandered the paths of the Ark's garden, she would have observed American flowers she later came to know more intimately. Alabaster-pale *Sanguinaria canadensis*, the ghost flower of March or April, named bloodroot for the gory juice that drips from every broken stem, probably existed in South Lambeth as only a clump or two; in the New World it spreads in thousands of blossoms, whitening the black woodland leaf mold. By the late 1640s the Tradescants' single tulip poplar (*Liriodendron tulipifera*) had probably reached twenty feet and borne a few flowers, a contrast to the mottled trunks of tulip poplars on their native soil, which soar 150 feet, their branches lit from top to bottom in May with small, deep cups of greenish yellow. The red trumpets of American honeysuckle (*Lonicera sempervirens*), which decorously climbed a wall or trellis next to the Tradescants' English roses, would have greeted Grizzell's first American July by raging through sunny woodland edges like a summer firestorm.

Given the seventeenth-century conviction that certain plants were always ready to jump the barrier from vegetal to animal species, Grizzell had good reason to scrutinize some of the odder American plants in the Tradescants' garden. Autumn visitors to the Ark beheld the gaunt, scraggly form of a fast-growing staghorn sumac (*Rhus typhina*) holding up thick, flushed drupes packed into pyramidal "candles." Coming across sumac in its native habitat, it is impossible to resist running a hand over its clublike branches, shaped like a young buck's antlers and clad just like them in a dense, alluring reddish-brown velvet. When the temperature drops suddenly in the evening, a branch clothed in that soft fur still feels warm to the touch, like a human hand or arm. At the edges of forest clearings, in natural meadows and especially in sandy soil, staghorn sumac colonizes quickly, its flat-topped tribes growing to twenty-five feet and spreading even wider.

The rarities of South Lambeth would become the stuff of everyday life during Grizzell's more than thirty years on Shelter Island. No doubt her take on the Manhansetts who lived and worked within the Sylvesters' domestic compound would alter drastically over the decades, as familiarity eroded her wonder and curiosity and as the English ceased to respect the local Indians or to depend on them as needed allies.

In reviewing what Grizzell was exposed to in her early life, we can ask if she shared the inquisitive spirit of her times. The age was afire with willingness to explore the unknown, whether an entire continent or the unlimited interior reaches of the human head and heart. Brought up to expect a settled English life, Grizzell would be forced by the events of the Civil War to become an economic refugee in America and to set out on a dangerous and often lonely adventure, an adventure in which all she had learned, absorbed, or breathed in her young life that had helped her to read the world and trust her powers would come in handy to read a new language of signs.

7

The World Turns Upside Down

I'm back at the manor. My footsteps echo off the clay tiles as I approach the vault's only source of light, a rickety floor lamp. Large leather-bound albums hold the most important documents, unfolded and pressed flat by Andy Fiske in the course of his many years of effort. The heavy covers of one album are lined with lead. Page one. The will of Grizzell Sylvester, the only document in which she tells us directly about herself, so we must read backward from it to find out about her. A sheet of finely ribbed paper folded in quarters to make four pages, it was written on May 7, 1685, when Grizzell was forty-nine years old. Two of her brothers, Francis and William, were among the executors; her witnesses included two of her five sons. Scanning the regular lines of the clerk's handwriting, I find standard phrases that to Grizzell were more than the formulas they typically are today. She defined herself first and foremost, as did all seventeenth-century Europeans, by her religious beliefs. Pay dirt for me is on the last page, where she signed her name in the small, well-formed script she had learned in England as a child: Grizzell Sylvester.

In calling her Grizzell, her parents honored a distant cousin, reusing the name after their first Grizzell died soon after birth in 1631. (Baptizing another baby with a treasured family name was a frequent practice when infant mortality was high.) The name originated in a popular fairy tale: Patient Griselda, a Cinderella in reverse, was the poor, virtuous, and beautiful heroine whose cruel princely husband tested her fortitude by kidnapping their children, telling her they were dead, exiling her to her peasant cottage, and threatening to marry her sister, or, in another version, their own daughter. Grizzell's name must have taught her, as well as generations

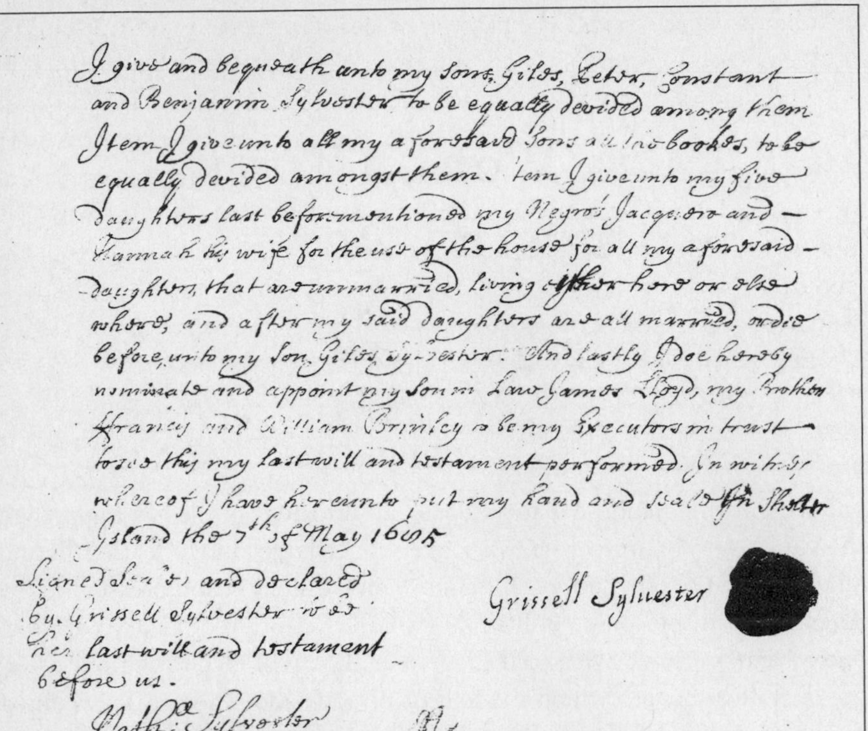
I give and bequeath unto my sons Giles, Peter, Constant
and Benjamin Sylvester to be equally devided among them
Item I give unto all my aforesaid Sons all the books, to be
equally devided amongst them. Item I give unto my five
daughters last beforementioned my Negros Jacquero and
Hannah his wife for the use of the house for all my aforesaid
daughters that are unmarried, living either here or else
where; and after my said daughters are all married, or die
before, unto my Son Giles Sylvester. And lastly I doe hereby
nominate and appoint my Son in Law James Lloyd, my Brother
Francis and William Brinley to be my Executors in trust
to see this my last will and testament performed. In witness
whereof I have hereunto put my hand and seale in Shelter
Island the 7th of May 1685

Signed Sealed and declared
by Grissell Sylvester to be
her last will and testament
before us.

Nath: Sylvester
Simon Grover
Jacques Guillot
Peter Sylvester

Grissell Sylvester

Newport in Road Island the 2d June 1685.
Grizzell Sylvester then appeared before me and
declared the abovewritten will to be her voluntary
act and deed, and that she did signe and seale
the same.

Henry Bull Gov.

Grizzell's signature on her will is as legible and well-formed as the handwriting of the official copyist who took down her last wishes. Two of her sons, Nathaniel II and Peter, acted as witnesses.

of other little girls, about the passive virtues of composure, self-discipline, and resilience—as well as godly acceptance of the unexpected.

The modest firmness of Grizzell's signature contrasts with her tumultuous last years in England. Nathaniel's roots in striving entrepreneurial Amsterdam and his crucible relationship with plantation slavery shaped Sylvester Manor. Grizzell's early adolescence was spent in the bloody uproar of the English Civil War. She saw the end of her father's career and endured the loss of family stability. So far as we can tell, the threats of war, loss, and uncertainty appear to have made her resourceful and steady. Within the demands and restraints set out for a seventeenth-century woman, she would fashion a life for herself and her household on Shelter Island very different from that of most of her female New England colonists, who lived next door to each other in close, supportive communities.

The Royal Route to Civil War

King Charles I and his people struggled with each other for twenty-four years. Between 1625, when he was crowned, and 1649, "the people," as represented by Parliament, denied the king many powers—governmental, fiduciary, and military—that he considered royal prerogatives. He fought back.

An increasing number of his subjects were alienated from the Church of England after the king appointed William Laud as Archbishop of Canterbury in 1633. With the king's encouragement, Laud strengthened episcopal powers and used the secret proceedings of the Star Chamber to harry Puritans, who fled abroad (hence the pamphlet war waged by clerics such as Amsterdam's John Canne, Nathaniel's pastor). Laud also reintroduced as High Anglican practices the lace-cassock-and-incense rituals that had been banned with Catholicism at the Reformation. Public fears that the nation was headed back to the Roman Church had already been aroused by the king's marriage in 1625 to the French royal princess, Henrietta Maria, a devout Catholic.

By 1636, the year of Grizzell's birth, England was seven years into the so-called Eleven-Year Tyranny, also known as King Charles's Personal Rule, during which the monarch governed by executive privilege, refusing to summon Parliament after a catastrophic session in 1629 when most of his requests for subsidies were questioned, denied, cut back, or grudgingly granted. The cash-strapped king partially solved the ensuing credit crisis by pawning the crown jewels, by squeezing the country with demands for money unauthorized by Parliament (promptly condemned as taxation without representation), and by the sale of royal lands. He waged underfunded, unsuccessful, and therefore unpopular wars led by his favorite, the first Duke of Buckingham, against Spain and France, and against the Scots in 1640.

Grizzell was four when the historic Long Parliament, so called because it remained in power for so long, was finally summoned in 1640. It enacted legislation intended to control the monarch. He retaliated with more royal edicts. The Irish, seeing a chance to escape English domination, raised a rebellion, whereupon Parliament saw *its* chance, taking over official responsibility for national defense from the king. In August 1642, the two sides—Parliamentarian Roundheads and Royalist Cavaliers—took to the battlefield. And for nine years, bouts of war alternated with fitful outbreaks of peace.

Upside Down

Grizzell was eight when the royal household fled London in 1642 at the start of hostilities, and Charles settled on Oxford as a safe place to establish an ad hoc court. He reassembled the cumbersome apparatus of royal governance around him, but only two auditors obeyed his summons. The others, including Thomas, either retired discreetly to their country estates or stayed in London, as Thomas did at first. Life in Clerkenwell continued at the same tranquil pace, but the sense of uneasiness increased beneath the daily round. Unluckily for Thomas, his northern properties lay within a major theater of war. In 1644, parliamentary forces gained control of Yorkshire. In an age when armies lived off the land and commanders turned a blind eye to pillage, Thomas must have feared for his distant holdings.

How Thomas Brinley's certainties crumbled has little to do with any romantic drama of Cavaliers and Roundheads. Each side in the combat drew supporters from all social strata and almost every Christian denomination, as well as adherents who switched allegiances. And for every unwavering loyalist in either camp, a dozen others lay low or hedged their bets. Of the twenty-nine auditors and clerks in the Exchequer, only twelve, including Thomas, were avowed Royalists. Ten were more or less neutral, and seven were out-and-out Parliamentarians.

Early in the summer of 1646, Oxford surrendered to Oliver Cromwell's forces and the king turned himself in as a prisoner. In November 1647 he escaped and fled to the Isle of Wight, where the governor whose sympathies he had counted on instead held him politely captive. Secret plans Charles laid from prison resulted in the final round of war, but meantime Parliament, firmly in the hands of his enemies, began to pursue prominent Royalists in government service. Many, including Thomas, now bowed to the inevitable, accommodating themselves as best they could without entirely compromising either their principles or their safety.

In restive London, an uneasy heartbeat of revolution—Puritan against Anglican, commoner against courtier, poor against rich—throbbed at the lower end of St. John's Lane. In 1647, unrest surged uphill into exclusive Clerkenwell. "Lady Bullock's house, on Clerkenwell Green, was attacked by soldiers who stole fifty pieces of gold and tore five rich rings from her ladyship's fingers. Dr. Sibbald, the incumbent of Clerkenwell, who resided near, remonstrated with the Parliamentary soldiers from his window but the only reply was three musketballs at his head, which they narrowly missed."

The family fled to the safety of Datchet, Buckinghamshire, where his wife Anne's family lived. Sixteen forty-seven was also the year that Grizzell's youngest brother, little William, was born and baptized in Datchet, not in Clerkenwell. Thomas lay low somewhere, either in Datchet or in Eton, across the Thames, a town familiar to him as a young man when he had first begun to work for his wife's uncle, Richard Budd.

After a three-day prayer session in November 1648, grim Puritan leaders hit a flash point, defending their decision as just retribution for the agonies of the Civil War (in which more English lives were lost, proportionately to the population, than in World War I), Calling on Charles as "Charles Stuart, that man of blood, to account for the blood he had shed," they executed him as a monarch who had made war on his own people—the one thing that a king must not do.

The Final Struggle

By this time, 2004, I had tracked the progress of the war and visited Datchet, still a village, up the Thames from London, where Thomas had long perched with some of his fellow auditors when he was not working for the king at the Exchequer in London or on his rounds to collect rents. Grizzell had cousins and aunts and uncles there, a comfortable nest of relatives.

I return to the manor to check on some documents in the vault that might help make sense of Grizzell's last three years in England. A minuscule handle projects just above the hallway wainscot. I turn the key halfway in the keyhole. Pulling open the close-fitting heavy panel is a struggle; then the door lunges toward me, crying out with a gothic screech.

A short, slight, bearded man steps forward: Charles I, king of England, Scotland, and Ireland. He walks through the tall second-story window of his banqueting hall at Whitehall Palace and onto the executioner's scaffold specially constructed for this day, January 30, 1649. He wears two shirts so he won't shiver and look as if he's afraid. Of all his decorations and honors, he wears only one, the glittering silver star of the Order of the Garter—the star of St. George the Martyr. He lays his head calmly on the block and the hooded executioner raises, then swiftly lowers his ax. The body of the anointed sovereign slumps. The crowd groans, then falls silent. There is no rejoicing.

On that cold morning, almost nobody wanted the king to die—in fact, few in the nation had thought he would. But Cromwell's austerely Puritan son-in-law, Henry Ireton, had gained control of the army, and in December 1648 he had purged the House of Commons of MPs who might vote against the execution. In the following month, more than a hundred additional members absented themselves from Westminster to avoid being involved in the show trial of the king, thus creating what was later derisively known as the "Rump" Parliament of about eighty members, the remains of the Long Parliament, which stayed in power until 1653. An obscure provincial judge presided over the trial, the only one who agreed to do the job. A threadbare parliamentary quorum signed the execution order.

The darkness of the manor vault thickens with a swirl of snow, and I hear the lapping of river water. In an early February storm, oarsmen bend their backs to row a barge, laden with the royal corpse, up the Thames for a hasty and secret burial by night under the floor of St. George's Chapel at Windsor. (The king's head has been sewn back on.) No prayers, because parliamentary officers stop the royal chaplain from accompanying the tiny cortege into the church.

Immediately across the Thames and far below the towering mass of Windsor Castle lies sleeping Datchet. Asleep, but hardly tranquil: as many as four thousand troops are quartered in the area with as many as twenty to forty soldiers in some houses. The castle, ancient stronghold of kings, is now Cromwell's headquarters; his New Model Army is drilling in Windsor Great Park. The dead king's auditor, probably concealed nearby, could not have missed the telling reversal.

On this night, the surrounding landscape is picked out in snow. An owl in flight looks down on the clustered village of Datchet and its gabled manor house, the farms with their gates, hedges, and enclosed gardens, the rough common shared by all, the open fields striped light and dark in fallow, stubble, and plow. (Every year the authorities stake the bounds of each strip.) He swoops over the hairy blackness of the Great Park where the king and his court hunted fallow deer and villagers are permitted to gather fallen forest branches for firewood. He soars above the Thames, bordered by rich water meadows that are harvested according to specified haying rights.

Everything that makes Datchet home for thirteen-year-old Grizzell is bounded and parceled out according to laws, rights, duties, privileges, customs, and feudal endowments. (The same will be true on Shelter Island, but the Manhansetts' practices will be unfamiliar to the colonists, and often misunderstood and abused.) On this February night, she lies in her Datchet bed, unconscious of the final act of the drama taking place, although by now she undoubtedly is aware of King Charles's beheading. Pillowed in family and the familiar, Grizzell has no idea that she will soon leave home.

"The Said Anne"

"Mr. Auditor" Thomas Brinley had last been recorded doing royal business in April 1641, when he certified the receipt of some £67 or so in fines levied on the queen's properties in Yorkshire. Fifty years old, this diligent royal servant found his world beginning to crack. He continued going about his business amid news of money shortages, discontented troops, and the movement of horses and wagons already preparing for a fight. But by 1644, after Thomas's job had vanished and his close connection to the crown made him suspect, it was clear he could lose everything he had worked for. His income as auditor has been estimated as £600 annually, or £55,000 (about $100,000) in current money.

By then, having "just cause to be very apprehensive of the danger of the tymes," he and his wife, Anne, turned to a successful merchant with trade interests in Europe and Virginia, John Bland. It was "the said Anne," not Thomas, who "did repaire to the Complainant [Bland] & acquaint him with some parte of her feares." "Shee or her servant" asked him to entrust "some money [an initial £400] for the benefit of her said children in the hand of some friend beyond the seas" so that "whatever might happen to these defendants . . . the said children might have somewhat wherewith to subsist."

The money was invested for them in Spain, Bland stated, and over the next several years, the Brinleys made further investments that realized returns. But in 1649, according to the court case, the connection turned sour when the Brinleys sought to draw out £200 "to be given as the marriage portion of their daughter," probably Anne, who married Governor William Coddington of Rhode Island in January 1650, a year after the death of the king. (Marriage portions were probably uppermost in the Brinleys' minds: their boys would be able to take care of themselves, but the girls had to have respectable funds to marry well.)

Bland countered that the Brinleys had illegally sent their funds abroad to evade seizure and charged Anne's brother, William Wase, with laundering the couple's money. Most dangerous of Bland's allegations, given the political climate, was that Anne had accused Laurence Brinley, Thomas's brother, of becoming "a very unkinde brother [who] would destroy" Thomas and Anne and "any of theire estate yt he could seize on." Laurence, a London merchant, was by this time active in the Commonwealth cause.

In court, Anne stoutly denied "that she did desire ill in respect of any unkindnesse of Laurence." She dealt with her brother William's involvement by saying that he was not called in to cover her tracks (a doubtful statement), but as trustee for his nieces and nephews. Wase himself testified that he had brought the case on the Brinleys' behalf to force Bland to produce the marriage portion. Anne was not the only wife to take charge during the war; many capable women did the same, managing estates and family while their husbands fought. But in an era when married women generally could not own property or speak publicly, that women like Anne stood up in place of men is proof of desperate times. Whatever the outcome of the case, enough money appears to have been salvaged from the wreck to provide funds for Anne and Grizzell in the New World.

Cromwell's total victory was not long in coming. In early September 1651, Charles II, who had been hastily crowned in Scotland five days after his father's execution, commanded his troops at Worcester, where the Royalists went down in final defeat. Charles made a daring escape, hiding overnight in an oak tree near the hunting lodge of Boscobel, in Shropshire, then fleeing across England. After a month of desperate concealment, on October 15 he sailed to France on a coal boat, and into nine years of European exile. Could Thomas have been part of the circle that accompanied Charles abroad to form an unhappy, peripatetic shadow court? An American genealogical researcher who thoroughly examined the records in the early twentieth century for Cornelia Horsford found no trace of Thomas on the Continent.

It is true that after Charles II came to the throne in May 1660 he promptly reappointed Thomas to his old position at the Exchequer, but Thomas did not regain most of the lands that had been confiscated under the Commonwealth. Perhaps the new regime didn't value his services enough to aid him; more likely Thomas's grant holdings in the north had been seized by the Commonwealth and sold to pay off its enormous war debt. The king, ruling a barely reunited nation, would have been reluctant to press new owners to return properties they had purchased only to give them to a former Royalist supporter. Or maybe Thomas, dead within eighteen months of Charles's coronation, had too little time to press for reparation.

The Civil War's larger-than-life antagonists fill history's screen: battling, bleeding, dying or escaping death, enduring mutilation and imprisonment for their religious beliefs and political convictions, crying out in letters, diaries, pamphlets, and prayers. Thomas and Anne flicker in and out of view. I feel an odd sympathy for this frightened, displaced pair, hiding in their own country, trying to preserve some measure of protection for their children. How nightmarish it must have been, after a lifetime of security, to make their way in a world of conflict where allegiances shifted overnight, inviting treachery, denunciation, imprisonment, or worse: where a troop of horses could blow over the hill or onto the end of the street, borne on the winds of religious fanaticism and greed for plunder. The monarchy—an institution that had endured for nearly seven centuries—had crashed, and with it the Brinley family. Thomas and Anne had played by the old rules, but now they faced a new harsh order.

My Loving Brother

Fortunately for his brother Thomas, Laurence was a moderate Presbyterian, a powerful layman in his influential London church and a steady supporter of the efforts to remove (but not execute) the king. As events turned out, this was exactly the right kind of Protestant to be during the unsteady twenty years from 1641 to 1660. As such, he was at the forefront of the political struggle to control Parliament in the winter of 1641–42. It is probably thanks to Laurence that Thomas later met with more lenient treatment than others equally close to the crown, and even retained some of his assets.

By the end of 1650, Cromwell commanded England and was on his way to crushing resistance in Scotland and Ireland. Thomas Brinley's connections were useless as a means to advance his children. It was time to make new alliances. Laurence stepped in. He probably helped Anne and Grizzell get a start in life after the loss of Thomas's post and estate by reaching out to the Atlantic community of Puritan merchants and colonizers such as Matthew Craddock and Samuel Vassall, to which the Sylvesters also belonged. The early 1650s marked the zenith of New England's Puritan confidence and power as godly colonists. They were breathing easy. They flexed their muscles, hardened by years of iron determination, since Laud's persecutions began, to see every event as deserved punishment or reward doled out by an inscrutable but just Lord God. Looking around them in the new clear light of vindicated righteousness, they viewed the Commonwealth as God's reward and welcomed it as their own.

William Coddington had arrived in New England in 1630 as one of the first colonists of the Massachusetts Bay Company, founded in England as a trading company in 1629. (He was thus known to Craddock and Samuel Vassall, both founding partners of the Company.) The Bay Colony's fourth-richest citizen, and the colony's treasurer until a break with Massachusetts's religious policy forced him out in 1638, he left Massachusetts for Rhode Island, where he prospered. In 1649, Coddington sailed back to London in search of a new charter for Rhode Island that would put him in control of the colony, and a new (third) wife. He stayed for three years, reveling in the new freedoms for Puritans like himself, and running into old friends such as Stephen Winthrop, brother of Governor John Winthrop Jr. of Connecticut. Laurence Brinley must have seen the bluff Rhode Islander as an excellent catch for his niece, Anne, in the new dispensation. She was then about twenty-four years old, and he twice that, not unusual in the day of serial wives, due mostly to their death in childbirth. They were married in January 1650 in Datchet.

Grizzell, at most fifteen and a half years old and now almost a woman of marriageable age, set sail for America with the Coddingtons and their infant son sometime before June 1651. Our final view of Thomas comes from a phrase in Grizzell's will. She describes "my loving Brother in Law Mr. William Coddington of Road Island to whose care and custody I was committed by my father Mr. Thomas Brinley at my departure from him." As the father entrusted his two girls to this robust Puritan so different from himself and said goodbye, he and his daughters must have understood that they might never see one another again. Thomas was seventy when he died in Datchet in November 1661. (Grizzell went back to England that year, accompanied by Nathaniel—her first visit home in ten years—but it is not certain that she arrived before the death of her father.) The phrases of his will tell us he died faithful to the Church of England.

Four Brinley children out of the brood of twelve—Francis and William, Anne and Grizzell—crossed the Atlantic to find new lives. Anne and Grizzell's migration and their marriages to men whose politics and beliefs were so unlike Thomas's bear striking testimony to the English political shakeup. Anne Wase Brinley, so intrepid and outspoken in protecting her children and their interests in 1650, suffered little but sickness and loss as the years passed. She wrote from London four years after Thomas's death to her "sonne Francis" in Rhode Island about the death of his sister Rose in England. Reflecting on her children, she lamented that "I have but them two now left in old England to bee a comfort to mee." She was old, she was ill— "I have kept my chamber all this winter and doe at this present writing . . . think [I am] in a consumtion [tuberculosis] for all my flesh is gone from mee & I think I shall never write to you more." Not quite true—she would last another five years. But she would never see the constellation of children who, in another time, might have clustered around her in her old age, in her own house.

8

"Time of Longing"

To Newport

Andy Fiske, who led me through the manor house in 1984, always kept marine charts handy, like every Shelter Island sailor. In unrolling them, he had also unrolled memories of summers on Peconic Bay, the Sound, out to Block Island, and beyond. "Once you leave the tip of Montauk behind, you are already in Rhode Island waters," he used to say. (Andy died in 1992.) As the crow flies, it's only about forty-eight miles from the manor harbor to Newport. By the time Grizzell arrived at her first home in the New World, Nathaniel Sylvester would already have known the place as a convenient port for West Indies traffic.

Driving across the pair of high bridges that connect Rhode Island's mainland with Aquidneck Island, I glance down at Conanicut Island, where Francis Brinley and William Coddington had farms and pasturelands. The wrinkled waters of Narragansett Bay stretch out below me in all directions: a map will tell you that the real estate of Rhode Island is half water, fringed by the safe, desirable harbors and coves that extend from Point Judith all the way up to Providence on the west side of the bay and back down to Newport and Sakonnet on the east. Everyone—English or Indian—hopped into a boat as the easiest and fastest way to travel. The coastal lands of Rhode Island cradling the bay comprise some of New England's finest soils. The climate is the mildest in the region. Thanks mostly to Roger Williams's respectful cultivation of local Indian leaders, relations with the dominant Narragansett tribe on the west side of the bay and the Wampanoags to the east were fairly harmonious for decades. Both Massachusetts and Plymouth fought for possession of this territory in the 1650s. But Rhode Island survived the conflict intact and independent, fat with livestock and trade, proud of its traditions of "soul liberty" and the separation of church and state—and not yet stained by its ascendance as the colony with the biggest slave trade in North America.

As I swoop down from Newport Bridge, what I can see of Aquidneck Island, spotty with development, doesn't look like "the garden of New England" that a Mr. Harris described in the 1670s. "Old Newport," huddled at the tip of Aquidneck, is a collection of fine Georgian and Federal architecture. Somewhere here, close to the edge of the harbor that made Newport a magnet for settlement, I will find the site of William and Anne Coddington's house (built in 1641), where Grizzell spent her first two years in America.

We last saw Nathaniel in 1646, aboard the *Seerobbe*, sailing from the African coast with a cargo of slaves. By 1653, Nathaniel and his partners had purchased Shelter Island and drawn up their contract as to how they would operate their island provisioning plantation. Who would set the place up, who would run it? For Nathaniel, the junior partner of the four and the only one who hadn't rooted himself in a piece of land, this was his big chance.

He and his brother Giles left Barbados, perhaps with a shipment of sugar, rum, salt, and other Caribbean products, for Newport late in the winter of 1653. They sailed in the *Swallow*, a ship capable of carrying twenty-two guns and as many as seventy-six people. The same Stephen Goodyear who had sold Shelter Island to the partners had bought the *Swallow* in 1647 after the old vessel was decommissioned by the Dutch, and this venture from Barbados was probably the return trip of a routine trading voyage. As was almost always the case, the risk was shared with others, including the master of the vessel, Greenfield Larrabie of Saybrook, Connecticut. No passenger list or cargo manifest survives, only court depositions about the fate of a cabinet belonging to Nathaniel.

A merchant's cabinet held his account book, copies of contracts, correspondence, and valuables such as jewelry and coins. Small enough to be portable, solidly impervious to theft, and often decoratively inlaid with rare woods, such cabinets often had drawers of various sizes and a secret compartment. For a traveler like Nathaniel, his cabinet was both his desk and proof of his fortune. They were at sea when, according to the testimony of Stephen Daniel (probably a crew member), Nathaniel, "perceiving his cabbinet to recive Some harme by Some wette it had taken caused the Said Cabbinet to be caried up into the Round hous where it did remaine till the day that the Ship was cast away."

It was a late afternoon sometime in February or early March; the *Swallow* had sailed to within only a few hours of Newport. Suddenly, something—a gust of wind, the current, or a storm—rammed the ship sideways into the middle of the main harbor channel, where the current runs strongest, and then westward in a matter of seconds into the shoal waters of Conanicut Island. At that point, as Bernard Collins, an indentured servant of Nathaniel's, and one of the two court witnesses, reported, "the Swallow was Driven near the Rock at Connanicott Iland . . . & in great danger to be cast away." As soon as the *Swallow* hit the rocks, "Captain Nathiell Silvister with severall others & the Deponant" were "goieinge ashore of the afore said iland of Cannaniucott." A dinghy was hastily put over the side, and Nathaniel courageously took off in the dark to fetch help, attempting to reach Newport, a two-mile stretch across the water.

Nathaniel returned in the morning with a "shallop with Horsers" to relieve Larrabie and his men "in gitting of [off] your ship ffrom the rocks." (Horsers were flat bargelike boats used to transport livestock.) But help came too late—the *Swallow* had broken up in the darkness and freezing cold, timbers shrieking against the rocky coast. Larrabie, having presumably made what efforts he could to save her, floundered ashore with the rest of the crew and passengers, including Giles Sylvester and "the rest of Capt: Nathaniell Silvisters servants." Larrabie's next move broke the proverbial first law of salvage: to "return to the stream of commerce the goods of any owner, for the benefit of the owner, not the salvor." Instead, Collins said, "Greenfeild Larrabie tould ye Deponant & the rest of Capt: Nathaniell Silvister's servants yt now the ship was cast away, yt thay were all free men, & no longer servants under ther Master A [and?] Declaring yt what came out of the Reck ashore of Captaine Nathaniell Silvisters goods, was as much thars as thar Masters and as ffree for them to take as it was to the Master." A looting free-for-all ensued.

Larrabie reportedly confessed later to Nathaniel that he had "Consented unto the opening of your cabinett." The servant Collins recalled an outraged Nathaniel stating that his cabinet had been "broke open, and yt all his rings and other things of vallew yt was in it, whare stollen out." And, Collins added, "ye severall writings which was in the cabinet, aftar being broken open ware thrown too & againe [to and fro against] the rocks where being torn in peeces & blown away by the violnt wind & further nott." This after Nathaniel had asked Larrabie to take particular care of his cabinet in exchange for his risking his own life by rowing at night to Newport in treacherous currents and storm waves.

Worse yet, Collins testified, in Nathaniel's absence Larrabie had turned to young Giles and said, "Now Mr. Giles Silvister now is the time for you to make your selfe of what Goods Comes ashore of your Brothers Capt. Nathaniell Silvister for now you are in a place wher I beleeve your Brother Capt Nathaniell Silvister will not assist you or look after you Any More." After Nathaniel's return, Larrabie began to regret his rash action and assured Nathaniel that what was stolen would be "restored againe." Nathaniel filed suit against Larrabie, who was quickly found guilty in May by a New Haven Colony court and made liable for £125, a huge sum, and court costs. These proceedings burnished the wronged merchant's stature as a man to be reckoned with—just in time to score points with Governor William Coddington, the guardian of the woman he might already have hoped would be his bride.

William Coddington was a power to reckon with: intelligent, outspoken, ruthless, persevering, and well schooled in the law. Deeply religious throughout his long life, he remembered the heat and light of the Puritans' original desire for a mystical union with God. Yet in political matters he was out for all he could get. Born in 1601, Coddington was Nathaniel Sylvester's superior both in age and social standing. He had a profound knowledge of what setting up a thriving plantation entailed. Although no correspondence between the two men who were to become brothers-in-law has been found, it is likely that Nathaniel would have depended on Coddington for advice in such matters. Everyone else did. By 1653, after the purchase of Shelter Island, Coddington would have taken stock of Nathaniel Sylvester as an up-and-coming young Puritan, a merchant with land, able partners, good political connections in England, and a brother, Constant, with sugar plantations on Barbados. Through Constant's continued ties to Amsterdam, Nathaniel may also have had access to international credit markets. As for Nathaniel himself, in 1653, when he contracted to marry Grizzell, the auditor's daughter, it surely mattered more to him that Coddington was to be his brother-in-law than that Thomas Brinley had been a royal servant to the late Charles I.

Grizzell's Newport

The center of the nine-year-old community of Newport had already taken shape by 1650. A navigable river ran through the middle of town into the harbor, where wharves extended into "Nanhygonsett [Narragansett] Bay which is the largest and safest port in New England, nearest the sea and fittest for trade." The houses of the "big men," including Governor Coddington, faced one another, clustering around the town spring and mill. Widely and irregularly spaced, with barns, stables, enclosed fields, and gardens set between them, the frame houses had rambling extensions and steeply pitched roofs that gave them a brooding, medieval cast.

A muddy little sketch drawn shortly before the Coddington house was torn down in 1835 shows a three-story dwelling with a deep second-story overhang similar to those of the ancient London houses downhill from St. John's Lane in Grizzell's day. The huge exterior masonry chimney, embellished with Elizabethan-style fluting and pilasters, that makes up most of the gable wall contained flues for three or four fireplaces. The rooms they warmed—probably two up and two down, with an attic above—made this a mansion in a town of mostly one-room houses. The front door would have led directly into the hall or Great Room. Small casement windows with leaded panes and wooden shutters, often closed against the cold or Indian raids, let in a little daylight. Clear-burning beeswax tapers were saved for best; smoky tallow candles or guttering rushlights sufficed for everyday use. The furnishings of the low-ceilinged hall—tables, chairs, benches, and a large curtained bed—accommodated every family activity: cooking, eating, writing, praying, sleeping. It was also the room for making love, nursing infants, and dying, as well as public matters that a Rhode Island man of consequence like Coddington dealt with continually.

After her arrival in 1651, Grizzell lived for two years in a household where colonial leaders parleyed with Narragansett sachems and where English voices mingled with those of Algonquians—and of the Coddingtons' multilingual slaves. Throughout the Atlantic World, the "charter generation" of slaves, as the historian Ira Berlin calls them, did not form a culturally cohesive group. Arriving in New England after crossing the Atlantic to the West Indies or Brazil, they thought of themselves not as Africans, but as Coromantee, Fanti, Oyo, Mandinga, or one of many other nationalities. Besides their native tongues, some also spoke enough of the language of their enslavers—Spanish or Portuguese, Dutch or

French—to communicate with them. They also spoke variants of a common creole language—called *fala de Guiné* or *fala de negro*—that had evolved swiftly and dramatically since the earliest Iberian voyages to Africa, Brazil, and Central America. Some of the slaves in the Coddingtons' house in the late summer of 1651 probably had enough life experience on both sides of the Atlantic to understand how crucial it was to study the structure of the society they had been forced to join in order to find ways to influence it to their benefit. So they probably watched this pale fifteen-year-old English girl with interest as she rocked her sister Anne's baby boy to sleep or went about other chores. As for Grizzell, she found herself living with those she would only have glimpsed as outlandish strangers on the streets of London, or in stony effigy as a carved head on a tomb in her former parish church in Clerkenwell.

Matchmaking

I stroll to Ocean Coffee Roasters, around the corner from the Coddingtons' old address. Inside, six men talk sailing while they eat their three-egg omelets. With a mix of fatalism and amusement, one of them pinpoints exactly where he ran aground in the harbor a few weeks ago—on Conanicut's rocks. When I step outside, a skim of fog glides lightly across the blue-gray waters at the end of the street. Whitethroat sparrows on their way north are singing in the trees. It feels like spring, like the spring soon after the wreck when Grizzell and Nathaniel considered each other as partners for life.

Although we don't know exactly how or when the marriage was agreed to, those green months of Grizzell and Nathaniel's betrothal as the season ripened into summer were the appointed "time of longing," a time for "the affections to settle in," as Thomas Weld, the minister of Roxbury, Massachusetts, wrote in his commonplace book. Even an arranged match could include falling in love, and a Puritan match definitely presumed love as a primary duty of married life, although the common understanding was that love would follow marriage, not precede it. The man made the choice; the woman merely got the chance to agree or disagree. If a woman felt she could never love the man selected for her and spoke out decisively and promptly enough (not an easy move for females trained to silent obedience), she could refuse him. The Reverend Hugh Peter, Cromwell's chaplain and the Puritans' Puritan in England and New England, coldly warned his only daughter against choosing her own spouse, saying she should marry "in and for the Lord. The sensual part of that condition can never answer the encumbrances that attend it. Let Christ be your Husband, and He will provide you one to His own Liking." However, from the vast amount of cautionary advice available, it's clear that young women in New England did not always subordinate love (or lust) to the service of God in picking mates. In Grizzell's case, I can only guess that the choice was made by Coddington, with approval from her parents.

What are the chances that Grizzell and Nathaniel slept together before their marriage? Now that we read "Puritan" to mean "puritanical," there's reason to consider the question. Carol Berkin, author of *First Generations: Women in Colonial America*, observes that "the official 'prudishness' that later generations would see as the core of 'Puritanism' was confounded by a steady record of sexual and moral offenses that suggests that the bawdiness of seventeenth-century English culture had survived the Atlantic voyage," and that "traditions such as pre-bridal pregnancy and marital infidelity proceeded unabated," if only because "the immediacy of sexuality and procreation in cramped spaces gave these behaviors a logic that the Puritan code of morality could not erase." The historian Edmund Morgan writes, "Food, drink, sleep, sex, safety—as long as the ultimate end was the service of God, all lusts were necessary, but if [men or women] forgot God, they became lusts of the flesh."

The general unspoken expectation was that couples like Grizzell and Nathaniel would probably desire each other "improperly," although there are as many different accounts of how premarital sex was viewed in early New England as there are historians. Society cut engaged couples some slack: Edmund Morgan writes that if a betrothed pair "could not restrain their sexual impulses, they were forgiven more readily than couples who were not espoused (and the number of cases in which couples confessed to fornication during the period of their espousals suggests that Puritans possessed no more restraint than other human beings)."

Grizzell, although reared to be modest, may well have overheard gossip her father brought home from the libertine royal court. Would such talk have served as a cautionary tale for her regarding safeguarding her virginity? We don't know. Young women were not always able to defend themselves sexually in a society that taught women to believe that they were innately more sinful than men, who were their superiors and must be obeyed.

Nathaniel was almost certainly sexually experienced before he met Grizzell, however. In Amsterdam, on his way home from the docks, he would have had trouble avoiding "the most impudent whores . . . who would if they saw a stranger . . . pull him by the coat and invite him into their house." On Barbados, planters made sex with female slaves readily available.

Once they had made the decision to marry, Grizzell could have done no better than to consult the Reverend Thomas Hooker (1586–1647) of Hartford, Connecticut, as to what she might hope for from Nathaniel as a husband in godly New England. An electric, optimistic preacher, Hooker was the author of the immensely popular *The Poor Doubting Christian Drawn unto Christ* (1629). A self-help book *avant la lettre*, it went through seventeen editions by 1700. "The man whose heart is endeared to the woman he loves," Hooker wrote, "he dreams of her in the night, hath her in his eye and apprehension when he awakes, museth on her as he sets at table, walks with her when he travels and parlies with her in each place where he comes." Such a husband cradled his wife's head on his bosom, and "his heart trusts in her . . . the stream of his affection, like a mighty current, runs with ful Tide and strength."

"The Shell of the Soul"

That spring, Grizzell was a desirable young English heiress whose handsome fortune (and the higher ratio of men to women in New England) made it unlikely that Nathaniel would have been her only suitor. Seventeen when she married, she was four or five years younger than most brides of her generation in New England. Nathaniel's age that spring is conjectural. Because the Amsterdam Separatists' baptismal records disappeared, his birth can only be pegged to his parents' marriage in 1613. The genealogist Henry B. Hoff tentatively offers a date of 1620 for Nathaniel's birth as the third child, which would mean he was thirty-three when the teenaged Grizzell first laid eyes on him, past his youth but not yet middle-aged.

Only a handful of portrait artists were working in seventeenth-century New England. No pictures or verbal descriptions remain of Nathaniel or Grizzell, if they ever existed. But a good idea of how they carried themselves, how they dressed, and how they behaved toward each other—or thought they should—can be pieced together from contemporary sources. In their world, costume and comportment not only spoke of social status; they also articulated a person's inner spiritual state. As the royalist poet Francis Quarles wrote, "The Body is the Shell of the soul, Apparel is the Husk of that Shell, the Husk often tells you what the Kernel is."

Nathaniel's florid penmanship suggests a striving for gentility; the belabored salutations and closing phrases of letters to his longtime correspondent and social superior John Winthrop Jr., which are deferential even for that period, make him come across to my ear as somewhat stiff, maladroit, and ill at ease. In his element at sea, or in rough foreign ports—and tough and fit enough to make the stormy crossing to Newport in a dinghy—it's doubtful he was cut out to play the mannered lover. He probably wore a sword, like almost every other gentleman. (When he became a Quaker, he and Coddington may have continued to do so for a few years, along with a number of other very early Friends, until the Peace Testimony of 1660.) But if he dressed the way he wrote, he's unlikely to have exuded the nonchalance—"weareing your cloathes in a careless, yet a comelie forme"—advised by contemporary books of manners.

In England and on the Continent during the first half of the seventeenth century, men's clothing devolved from the tautness and exposure of earlier styles to an elegantly draped amplitude. "Skin-close" breeches passed from fashion, as the Puritan divine Samuel Purchas noted approvingly. Gone from view were the polished thigh, the tight knee, the smoothly modeled derrière of an earlier century. Nathaniel probably appeared in Newport looking presentable enough but baggy in an outfit of handsome dark plush. Black cloth was fashionable throughout the first half of the century for Puritans and Cavaliers alike, in part because expensive black dye showed off the wearer's worth. It is difficult to imagine Nathaniel or Coddington in the yards of braid or lace, the rows of gold or silver buttons, or the bunches of ribbon that some fellow Parliamentarians sported in England at the time, but respectability called for a modicum of show even in New England. Take the Pilgrim leader William Bradford: after his death in 1657, his estate listed an "old Violett Coullered cloak," a red waistcoat, and a "stuffe [worsted] suite with silver buttons & a coate." For a New England woman, it was neither immodest nor ungodly to quietly call attention to a fine figure with a close-fitting velvet "wastcoate."

The young woman who stepped into the Coddingtons' Newport hall to greet Nathaniel would have hoped to mirror the seventeenth-century ideal of beauty that New England's Reverend Seaborn Cotton described in his commonplace book under the heading "For to Make a Hand som Woman." Cotton's ideal had "light brown hair, a high, straight brow, narrow black eyebrows, round hazel eyes, pure vermilion cheeks, a small mouth and coral lips, the underlip a little fuller than the upper, a pretty long white neck, a small waist, middle-sized hips, small legs and feet, and long hands, and 'to be rather taller than shorter.'"

Between the reigns of Elizabeth I and Charles I, women's fashions changed dramatically. The wasp figure of the old queen, with its stinger of a bodice pointing downward to a rigid farthingale, faded from sight. Women's bodies appeared to swell into muffins. The bunch of heavy pleats massed and dropping from a slightly raised (but still corseted) waistline enhanced the belly and pushed it forward, making a ledge where a woman could fold her hands. Sometimes a gown or a coat was hiked up in back for easier walking, or pinned into a soft bustle, emphasizing the buttocks. Bare necks and forearms and escaping curls held a new erotic charge.

For Englishwomen of the Brinleys' rank, fashions changed more slowly than in aristocratic circles. So, in general, the costume historian Aileen Ribeiro's observation about English dress in the 1640s applies to the early 1650s as well: "Women of the gentry and the middle class continued to wear the tightly laced open gown (black for Sundays and special occasions)." A 1645 portrait of Hester Tradescant, John the younger's second wife, depicts her pulling aside the edge of her black silk skirt to show off a white petticoat embroidered with flowers in russet thread. Both Hester Tradescant and Grizzell Brinley would have worn thin, lace-edged linen neckerchiefs or "whisks," pinned around the neck with the points dropping halfway to the waist. However, an etching titled *Autumn*, one of a set of the four seasons by Wenceslaus Hollar, shows how a sudden movement, or the wind, could displace a woman's kerchief to expose the curve of her pushed-up breasts above the low neckline beneath.

Hester wears a black beaver hat atop a lace-trimmed linen cap. Beneath such a cap, Grizzell probably dressed her hair in "spaniel's ears," with the sides loosely falling almost to the shoulders and the rest gathered up into a lustrous knot. This hairstyle, combined with the kerchief that makes shoulders look as if they were sloping, creates, as Ribeiro writes, "a kind of submissive modesty." Grizzell, as she shyly advanced toward Nathaniel in the Coddingtons' hall in Newport, may have looked like

Hollar's drawings of a young Englishwoman in side and back views, with her drooping curls, downcast eyes, eyebrows slightly lifted, and a string of beads or pearls around her neck. If there is anything sexy about Hollar's tender drawing, it's the exposed nape of the young woman's neck.

Beneath her bodice and stays, under his doublet and shirt, Grizzell and Nathaniel wore white linen shifts, their sole undergarments, which were cut to a shapeless unisex pattern. When made from the finest bleached linen called lawn, a shift's whiteness evoked innocence and virginity, but its near-transparency revealed the flesh beneath. A shift was the only article of clothing either Grizzell or Nathaniel would have changed and had laundered regularly. Outer clothing stiffly kept its owner's shape and smell for decades. Between 1347, when the bubonic plague first struck Europe, and about 1750, physicians opined that the best defense against pestilence was an impermeable skin with pores safely sealed by an encrustation of dirt and sweat. Bathing left the body defenseless.

The flax from which linen is spun was believed to absorb excess dirt and perspiration, and the middle and upper classes spared no expense for keeping linen white. Early seventeenth-century views of London show laundry laid out to dry and bleach in the fields beyond Clerkenwell. In Newport, Grizzell would have become familiar with the Coddingtons' washing routine, which relied on fresh water from the nearby town well. Nathaniel would have been careful to wear a clean collar band and shirt when he came courting.

Nathaniel and Grizzell wouldn't have considered themselves unkempt or unclean; their grooming simply didn't involve much water. People washed their hands, especially before eating, their faces, and sometimes their feet. They dug particles of food out of their teeth with toothpicks or knives; the fastidious cleaned their teeth by rubbing them with a cloth. The slightest move of a well-dressed body must have produced an acrid, revolting stench. Both men and women wore pomades and perfumes to mitigate the effect.

The cultural connotations of what is "clean" or "dirty" have always operated on various frequencies. When Robert Herrick's Julia (whoever she was in real life) unlaces her stays, the poet writes, the air fills with the fragrance of musk and amber exhaled by her body. Her sweat smells like lilies and spikenard. Her lips are sweet and "cleane." Either the poet believes his muse smells that sweet or he is trying to convince himself that she does. There's room to believe that everything Herrick lovingly catalogues about Julia is precious to him, arouses him, because it is hers. If Nathaniel and Grizzell found each other "suitable," they would have smelled delicious to each other for the same reason.

Startlingly enough, the moment they first heard each other's voices would have been a homecoming. Their accents and speech patterns were doubtless very similar, despite their different origins and the wildly varying regional dialects of England. Nathaniel grew up in Amsterdam with a mother from Lowestoft and a father from Somerset, but he was taught how to speak correctly by schoolmasters, scholars, and preachers worried about preserving the Englishness of their expatriate charges. Grizzell's London and Datchet childhood, and her father's occupation, meant she conversed in the "best" spoken English. This, as early as 1589, was defined by a contemporary to be "the usuall speech of the Court, and that of London and the shires . . . about London within sixty miles." From clues in variant spellings as well as metrical and rhyme evidence, modern linguistic experts at Plimoth Plantation in Massachusetts have painstakingly (yet still tentatively, they insist) reconstructed various English dialects spoken by the Pilgrims for their costumed interpreters. They agree that "this 'courtly' speech . . . was taught in the schools, used by poets, men of letters and printers, and mimicked by the socially ambitious."

John Kemp, the director of interpretation at Plimoth Plantation, assures me that present-day Americans would have understood Grizzell and Nathaniel, and that they would have understood us. Martyn Wakelin, an English sociolinguist who has helped steer Plimoth's research, disagrees. He says that certainly if the site's interpreters were to speak in the deepest seventeenth-century dialects, visitors would find it extremely hard to grasp their meaning. In a recording, Wakelin reads—with relish—a passage from William Bradford's *Relation* (of the Pilgrims' Atlantic journey and their hard landing on Cape Cod) in pure Somerset. Only because I'm familiar with the story can I follow along. Wakelin makes hooting, bonging, and bagpipe-drone noises; he pauses for strange interrogatory moments, and scampers up and down the tonal scale in a single sentence.

But I *can* understand a recording of two Plimoth interpreters, a man and a woman, speaking early modern Londonese. As I crudely transcribe it, the man says, "Is dis he which teaches you to speak French?" and then remarks that the teacher doesn't look French. She says: "It is becaws he is so plainly clawth-ed. It is not de weave dat maaketh de mohn. Ahl dey dat ahr clawth-ed with silk and are braav [finely dressed] are not awlways de most sufficyent. Awftentames mahr larning is fawnd in one meanly apparelled dan in dem dat have auwtward braahvery . . . Mye mother . . . hath chawsen rether a man of understanding withawt silk then a silken man withawt understanding." She ends by warning him to pay no attention to "megnefical sweggering." Unsurprisingly, he says he can't stay for a moralizing dinner.

Cawing Cockney Londoners, twanging Appalachian hillbillies, soft-voiced black Americans—I hear traces of them all in the interpreters' voices, and I am touched by the possibilities of my ancient, ever-changing language. Kemp calls the vigorous medley of Pilgrim English "a musical instrument." I assume that the particular music of early seventeenth-century London is what Grizzell and Nathaniel played together.

The Newport house of Governor William Coddington and his wife, Anne, Grizzell's older sister, seen here in a much later sketch, was Grizzell Brinley's home for the first two years of her American life, 1651–53.

The wedding probably took place inside the Coddingtons' house. William Coddington may have married them himself, since Puritan marriages were secular contracts, covenants between bride and groom, not religious alliances. Grizzell's sister Anne and twenty-year-old brother Francis were there, and no doubt there was a feast. Afterward, Nathaniel and Grizzell probably spent their wedding night in the scant privacy of a curtained bedstead in the Coddingtons' ground-floor parlor room. "Sexual experience had not yet acquired the ceremonial sanctity of a separate setting," writes Laurel Thatcher Ulrich. "Even if the notion had suggested itself, there was little possibility of segregating sex in the larger sense from the daily round of life. Procreation was everywhere, in the barnyard as well as in the house."

"To Be at . . . My Said Wifes Dispossal for Ever"

Wills are a form of autobiography. Since in Grizzell's case it is the only document in which we hear her own voice, it is worth a very careful read. Only by looking at the end of her life can we see its domestic beginnings, as well as the rights and possessions that would circumscribe her existence. Five years after the death of her husband, thirty-two years after her wedding, she walks through the rooms of her house planning the distribution of its contents to her sons and daughters. As a single woman over the age of eighteen and later as a widow, Grizzell counted under English law as a *feme sole*, a woman entitled to possess property in her own right and to enter into contracts. But the minute she married she became a *feme covert*, whose entire identity was "covered," or merged with her husband's.

In both England and New England, the land, cash, houses, goods, and chattels a bride brought to her marriage could legally be designated either as dowry or jointure. Anything classed as dowry automatically became her husband's property. A jointure, however, preserved some of a married woman's rights. Almost invariably negotiated with the bridegroom before the wedding by a male relative (in Grizzell's case, probably Coddington), a jointure promised the bride the use of funds she brought into the marriage. Grizzell received a life interest in her joint estate with Nathaniel: the use of one hundred pounds sterling a year—a fortune for her "better comfortable livelyhood." Her bed and board would be Nathaniel's responsibilities. (If their marriage had ended in divorce—and divorce did occur in Puritan New England—Grizzell would have had her jointure to fall back on.)

Like a venture capital agreement, a jointure also rested on hope. Nathaniel and Coddington were making a bet that profits would flow from the success of the island plantation and its company trade; Grizzell's estate would be her investment in that venture. A wife's ability to hang on to jointure rights depended partly on her family's power to enforce them, and partly on the mutual trust that she and her husband brought to the arrangement. No signs of wariness, no self-protective clauses, appear in either of the Sylvesters' wills; their long marriage appears to have been peaceful, generous, and affectionate.

Under Nathaniel's will, Grizzell would inherit the entire island and everything on it for the remainder of her life, including the "Negroes . . . and their increase." Her ownership did not include the eventual disposition of assets after her death, however; it was Nathaniel, in his will, who planned in painstaking detail the partition of slaves, land, and livestock that would take place then. Following general custom, he did not specify gifts of domestic furnishings: "all my household goods to be to and for the use of my said Deare Wife."

Also excluded from Nathaniel's bequests was a family of three: Jacquero, Hannah, and their daughter, Hope. "Being my Wifes owne," they were "to be at her my said Wifes dispossal for Ever." They were almost certainly the first people of African descent to set foot on Shelter Island, arriving in 1653 with Grizzell after her marriage.

Property law is the clue. If Jacquero and his family belonged to Grizzell under her jointure—"the Deed left in the hands of my Brother William Coddington," which unfortunately has not survived—then they were hers outright. But if she purchased them as a married woman out of her annual allowance, or "pin money," her unequivocal ownership would have been in doubt, because the reading of a woman's separate property rights narrowed over time. For example, a 1674 English case for assigning such assets to the husband reads: "So long as the husband and wife do cohabit . . . if the wife out of her good housewifery do save anything out of it [her "allowance"]; this will be the husband's estate and he shall reap the benefits of his wife's frugality." Furthermore, in most cases, larger expenditures such as real estate, housing, or chattel (as slaves were classed) were judged as more than a woman needed for "her better comfortable livelyhood" and thereby became her husband's property or inheritance.

The names of the three, in the case of Jacquero, at least, tell us something about events in their lives before they arrived on Shelter Island. Jacquero, an Iberian-sounding version of the French name Jacques and the English John, is an Atlantic creole's name; he surely acquired it in Afro-Portuguese Africa, or Brazil, or the French West Indies before arriving in New England. Hannah and Hope, Jacquero's wife and daughter, may have been given these biblical names by English colonists.

Nathaniel singled out Jacquero and Hannah's second daughter as his property, not Grizzell's, which means she was "increase," born on the island after the earlier purchase of her parents and sister. He bequeathed "my Negro Girl Isabell being the Daughter of Jaquero and Hannah his Wife" to his sixth child, daughter Elizabeth, "when shee shall bee twentie one years of age or at her Marriage if it be before."

The rights that were so carefully safeguarded for Grizzell (and the land and possessions bequeathed to her children) did not exist for Jacquero, Hannah, Hope, and Isabell. The Sylvesters' temperaments and experiences eventually led them to the Society of Friends, but if we think that meant that slave families could count on not being broken up, or that individual family members would not be sold separately, we are mistaken. Everything depended on the Sylvesters' needs and wishes, which would trump Quakerism. As parents, Jacquero and Hannah would be powerless to protect their daughters or arrange their futures for them. Hope and Isabell would be forced to understand that this was so whatever strategies their parents might devise to try to keep them safe from harm.

Nevertheless, as Ira Berlin writes, "the slaves' history—like all human history—was made not only by what was done to them but also by what they did for themselves. All of which is to say that slavery, though imposed and maintained by violence, was a negotiated relationship."

At the kitchen hearth on Shelter Island, in the birthing room, in the garden rows, on the threshing floor, and most of all within the echo chambers of their hearts and minds, Jacquero and Hannah negotiated with Grizzell for thirty-two years. But she did not free them by the terms of her will, as some masters did. She wrote, "Item I give unto my five daughters [the eldest, Grizzell, had married] . . . my Negro's Jacquero and Hannah his wife for the use of the house for all my aforesaid Daughters that are unmarried . . . and after my said daughters are married or die . . . unto my son Giles Sylvester," that is, for the rest of their lives. Then she adds, "And my mind is, the warming pan should remain for the use of the family in general." By 1685, Grizzell would have become accustomed to the idea that slaves, like the warming pan, were "for the use of the family"—her own family.

9

Where They Lived

"A Comfort unto Each Other"

"Sir . . . it hath pleased god to change my Condition by mariage," Nathaniel wrote to John Winthrop Jr. "In which, praysed be his name, I finde myselfe very happie, and hope in god we may be a Comfort unto Each Other." By early August 1653, about a month after the wedding, Nathaniel and Grizzell had sailed over from Newport to Shelter Island—and into their new life. He sent his letter from the island, where the time of the Manhansetts' green corn festival had just ended. As I read through the faded nineteenth-century transcription in the vault, Nathaniel's happiness overflows the page; he spreads his wings with wishes; he is transformed into a whole man. He wishes Winthrop would come visit—"Worthey sir, I should be very Glad if it might be my happines onc to see you here on our small spot of ground"—and he proposes a return visit to the Winthrops in New London as soon as his new "bote of 3 ton" is finished.

Grizzell lived in a time when women gained most of their daily support and comfort from the company of other women neighbors—female relatives and friends. On Shelter Island she would not enjoy that sociable community life, which included everything from lending a helping hand or a kettle to overcoming melancholy (depression) and anger. Once she became a Quaker (probably as early as 1657), she would be further separated from the women of East Hampton, Southold, and Southampton, the nearest towns, by her radical beliefs as well as by a boat ride. Her children were apparently not baptized: early Friends believed that all infants are baptized with the Holy Spirit, simply by being born. On the island, few of the female Africans or Indians, if any, spoke more than a smattering of English or shared her Christian beliefs. Nothing in her life so far (except practice in Christian fortitude) would have prepared her for this particular solitude.

In her other roles as consort, mother, and mistress of a household, and even sometimes as what the historian Laurel Thatcher Ulrich calls a "deputy husband" when Nathaniel traveled, Grizzell must have found recompense. She also effectively became the young matriarch of her family, since no top-dog mother-in-law lived with her, or nearby. Like other first-generation colonial women, she successfully adapted to new foods, new ways of cooking, and other major changes in hallowed routines. Besides the everyday work she and her domestics did together, such as baking, pickling, and preserving, churning butter, spinning, weaving, and sewing, there were other tasks: preparing medicines, tending the sick, solemnly closing the eyes of the dead and washing their bodies for burial. But other New England women, unlike Grizzell, as the historian Carol Berkin notes, "moved freely among their neighbors' homes. They borrowed and they lent; they kept each other company while going about their chores; they assisted at the birth of one another's children; and they disciplined their neighbors' sons and daughters as if they were their own."

An entire community of women could gather to assist at a childbirth, an exclusively female ritual. "A New England woman often gave birth sitting in another woman's lap, or supported by the steady arms of friends as she squatted on the midwife's low, open-seated birthing stool." Given the short intervals between the births of Grizzell's babies (often less than two years), as well as the upper-class reliance on wet nurses, it's probable that another woman on the island—perhaps a Manhansett or an African—breast-fed at least some of her children. The first baby, also named Grizzell, arrived on August 12, 1654, thirteen months into the Sylvesters' marriage. The size of their family—eleven surviving children out of twelve born between 1654 and 1675—was not unusual in seventeenth-century English culture on either side of the Atlantic, but the rate of survival was much higher in New England than elsewhere, thanks to a bracing climate, clean water, and an absence of most epidemic diseases.

The challenges of isolated island living for young parents became alarmingly clear a year after little Grizzell's birth, when a frantic Nathaniel dashed off a note to Winthrop. His "Yongest Child," Nathaniel wrote, had been "taken with an Extream stoppinge in y^{e} Nose in so much as that it is Not able to fetch its breth through y^{e} nostrils wch dooth disinable y^{e} poor infant to suck and is Not able to Eat without great payne wch causes

The Children of my Brother Nathaniell Sylvester when
they were Borne which is as Followeth
Grizzell Sylvester was Borne the 12th of August 1654
Giles Sylvester was Borne the 19th of August 1657
Nathaniell Sylvester was Borne the 31th of December 1661
Peter Sylvester was Borne the 26th of July 1663
Patience Sylvester was Borne the 31th of August 1664
Elizabeth Sylvester was Borne the 11th of September 1666
Mary Sylvester was Borne the 31th of July 1668
Ann Sylvester was Borne the 27th of February 1669/70
Constant Sylvester was Borne the 1st of December 1671

"The Children of my Brother Nathaniell Sylvester when they were Borne" may have been penned on Shelter Island by Nathaniel's brother, Joshua Sylvester. Three children are missing from the list: Mercie (born c.1673), Benjamin (born c.1675), and an unnamed infant who probably died in 1655, the only one not to survive to maturity.

the child to falle away exceedingly; and beinge ignorent in givinge of it anything wch may cause comfort unto ye child I have made bould humbly to crave your advise, with such means as y^{u} in your discretion may think most fitting." The baby, Grizzell and Nathaniel's second, was two months old. Nathaniel begged his friend, the region's leading physician, to rush advice and medicine across the Sound: "Our Greif is Great to see the Child lay in ye sadd Condition . . . and heer wee are quite out of ye Ways of help." At the earliest, Winthrop's advice and medicine could only have arrived some three days after Nathaniel sent his plea. The baby must have died, apparently the only one of the Sylvester brood not to survive infancy. The historian Martha Saxton writes that the women of early New England were "strong, self-contained, emotionally subdued, literate and sometimes well-educated women who . . . considered themselves equal to men in the eyes of God and in their chance for salvation." Grizzell would have gathered some grim strength from the constant self-examination and strenuous battles for belief and humility expected of every good Christian—and solace from her confidence that such infant deaths were the Lord's will.

It appears that in 1655, Grizzell put little trust in her female domestics, including Hannah and Hope, "to doe any busenes about ye house." In the same urgent plea for medical help, Nathaniel inquired about an "Irish wooman" living in his friend's household. (Cromwell's subjugation of Ireland in 1641, and the brutal "Irish clearances" that followed, during which "troublemakers" were evicted and English tenants were settled on Irish land, meant that thousands of Irish men and women were sold as slaves and shipped to the colonies in the following decades.) Assuming she was competent, and Winthrop willing to part with her services, would he, Nathaniel asked, "lett me have her resonable?" If so, he added, "I would have her before winter." On Shelter Island, the October cold was creeping indoors, a baby was crying, and little comfort was at hand.

Where They Lived

Nathaniel had been living aboard ship or elsewhere in the rough Atlantic World for a decade by 1653, but nothing, not even Grizzell's brief years in Newport, could have prepared her for the accommodations that had probably been readied for her on Shelter Island. Where they lived in the first years is a matter for guesswork, even after nine summers of UMass excavations. The articles of agreement signed by the Shelter Island partners in September 1652 state only "That until such time as the place can and will board the charge nothing shall be done about building but what needs might be done for conveniency's sake, to wit, a house with six or seven convenient rooms." What a gigantic house for the period, when a one-room dwelling was the norm! There's a conditional twist to the sentence, however: "nothing *shall be done* about building but what needs might be done *for conveniency's sake*." So who knows whether the proposed mansion actually could have been built less than a year after the signing? More likely, Grizzell and Nathaniel, and Francis Brinley, who came to visit for a year, along with whatever other (male) visitors or family such as Nathaniel's brother Giles may have dropped in—and Jacquero, Hannah, and Hope, and indentured servants such as Stephen Daniel and Bernard Collins, all lived together in at most a two-room-over-two house with some crude outbuildings. Even for those used to a standard of privacy startlingly lower than today's (many people, sometimes including unrelated men and women, slept together in one bed, for example), this "starter house" was a crowded domicile.

Only from Nathaniel's will, written in 1680, do we learn about the full array of plantation buildings built and modified over time in addition to a dwelling: a warehouse, barn, tide mill, salt house (for storing enough of the precious substance to preserve meat and to sell), and even piles of bricks set aside for the chimneys of his sons' future homes. What emerged from the archaeological evidence of the earliest days was not a house, but what Steve Mrozowski called "a dynamic, multi-cultural landscape," by which he means a plantation employing people of different cultures and skills who lived, ate, and worked virtually on top of each other. We did not learn precisely where the Sylvesters and these dozens of other people lived, but we did get an unparalleled look at *how* they lived together from the beginning.

Before archaeologists put a shovel in the ground, they are prone to have what the UMass field school dig supervisor, Katherine Howlett Hayes, a graduate student who became the "memory" of the project over the years, once called "feature fantasies." (Features are what remain of man-made structures and contain artifacts that give context or indicate use.) In 1998, to establish the datum, or base, for the project grid—a map of the landscape from which all findings would be plotted throughout the full nine summers of excavation—Steve picked a corner of a four-foot-long stone half buried in the lawn by the plantation landing. We fantasized that it had been a threshold for the door of one of the dozen buildings mentioned in Nathaniel's will. They set up a handsome yellow-legged surveyor's tripod with an electronic distance measuring instrument (EDM) that captured locations of any points on the site in three-dimensional coordinate space relative to the location of the instrument via infrared beams. From their "datum stone," across which I imagined Nathaniel may have stepped, the small advance team of archaeologists and students thus shot their digital coordinates to create the first computerized map that would eventually orient the grid excavation structure for the entire dig.

Steve then sank a first shovel test pit right in front of the house. Such a pit, the standard investigative unit for the first phase of archaeology, usually measures about sixteen inches square and deep, and when it is freshly cut, the vertical interior faces of the hole are layered like a cake. Archaeologists descend through time in the soil via the stratigraphic differences, which they call "horizons," from each level into the next below.

When a larger area is opened up, excavators follow across a single horizon, noting the soil's color and consistency as well as its contents, before exposing the next layer. "Don't assume any information is trivial when you write up field notes," Steve cautioned his students. "Record everything, even the weather." In order to avoid subjective color identification such as "chocolate" or "cream," diggers keep a set of colored tags handy. Called a Munsell Soil Color Chart, they are "paint chips for dirt," explained the UMass archaeologist David Landon, who joined the field team in 2000. Each plastic chip has a little hole above the color sample: a fingertip mounded with earth and poked carefully through the hole will tell the truth about the color match.

None of us could have dreamed up the abundance Steve instantly found in that first shovel test pit. Under the rich black loam—which Nathaniel and Grizzell's grandson Brinley Sylvester had spread to make smooth green lawns around the house he built after tearing down his grandparents' dwelling around 1737—Steve had hit the center of a midden, or trash heap. Used by the first two generations of Sylvesters, it was also the repository for piles of building materials that Brinley salvaged from the outmoded original house but never reused. Like privy deposits, middens are archaeological bonanzas, revealing much about cultural as well as physical life.

Steve's upbeat mantra about middens—and about archaeology in general—is that nothing is ever lost. As the midden excavation broadened, the seventeenth and eighteenth centuries tumbled out of the ground from a roughly 120-square-foot rectangle on the lawn facing the front door: 158 clay tobacco pipes, many of them Dutch; coins of five nations; upholstery tacks; brass harness ornaments; ceramics from as far off as Turkey; fragments of a redware candlestick; and a Spanish "cob," a roughly milled bit of silver, typically South American, with a Manhansett thunderbird image scratched on it. One afternoon, Alice Fiske returned home from her errands in her white Cadillac at the very moment when a giant key (some six inches long) emerged from the soil, which Alice, today's householder and lady of the manor, took as a salute directly from Grizzell, that "first lady," who would have held all the keys to her supplies and stores as well as to the house itself.

Further digging revealed that the midden thinned out as it stretched out over traces of some of the manor's earliest European buildings and fences, an area later used mostly for work and storage. Shattered ceramic fragments that had been smeared as much as six yards apart from each other by subsequent landscaping efforts were patiently "mended" by Steve and his crew. Scraps of narrow wrought-iron window muntins and bits of the panes they held prove that the Sylvesters had glazed casements, like all those of the middle class and above who could afford more than shutters. Some ground-level floors were laid with terra-cotta pavers. Fragments of red roofing pantiles have turned up by the thousands. Shaped differently from English or Dutch tiles, they may have been made nearby or shipped from Barbados. Everything dug up inside the nineteenth-century driveway that circles the lawn in front of the extant manor house confirmed a fury of building and rebuilding during the first eighty years of settlement.

That constant activity, and the many microlayers of soil, trash, and architectural debris deposited onsite made it hard to find what Alice wanted so badly to unearth: the "first house." Not unreasonably, given traditional accounts of colonial settlement, she saw her husband's ancestors as "first settlers" who built a fine homestead right away, set up housekeeping, and necessarily enlarged their dwelling over time: "So many children!" she exclaimed. She sometimes referred to the house where she lived as "the new house."

Alice had read the available histories and heard the many tales of the manor. She had visited the Winterthur Museum in Delaware, and "colonial villages" such as Old Sturbridge and Williamsburg, where every effort has been made to represent and explain the material culture of the past truthfully and to display its actual remnants. Andy Fiske had collected everything he could find about the manor in manuscript and print. From such sources, she could select elements and build Nathaniel and Grizzell's house in her imagination in a minute. For her, and for me, too, until we bumped our noses against the hard facts, the "first house" had a tiled roof, massive brick chimneys, and window frames and doors imported from England. Inside—ah, inside—Alice and I both imagined the warm light of fires and candles flickering on plastered walls, on children's faces, and against the crooked panes while snow and wind raged outside. In summer, in the tidy garden we dreamed up, sanded paths wound between the giant boxwoods, and the fragrance of herbs and flowers rose in the air. What we really wanted to know about wasn't *House and Garden* but the inner life of the house. From various unreliable later descriptions—all of which had some truth to them—we made that life come alive for ourselves.

Everyone who visits this marvel of a place is momentarily seduced by the urge to leap over the gaps, simplify, conjecture, or even make it all up.

The first printed Long Island history appeared in 1824; by then "the manor of Shelter Island" was more than a century and a half old, and the existing house had stood for at least eighty years. "The twilight zone that lies between living memory and written history is one of the favorite breeding places of mythology," writes the historian C. Vann Woodward. Such mythology has its uses. Family stories, so concentrated, potent, and clear, cluster around ancient places and make us want to preserve them. For that reason alone, we can take a group pass for our urge to mythologize, and not be too hard on ourselves about our willingness to reconstruct a past "as it ought to have been."

Testing the Myths

By the end of the 1999 season, the midden had yielded some eye-popping treasures. To the southwest, but still within the drive circle, the archaeologists found trenches, possibly for posts for a fence or a small building, but no significant foundations for a "manor house." Excavation slowed while procedures were evaluated. In 2000, they decided on smaller wire mesh to sieve the midden to make sure no pins, bones, or beads slipped through. Because the temporal aspects of different periods revealed by the dig as it continued downward through the soil seemed so jumbled and cryptic, Steve took to digging in hard-to-see spoil layers of five-centimeter increments, or about 2.5 inches, peeling back the strata patiently with a sharp trowel and a brush. We were joined in the field by David Landon, a zooarchaeologist (for faunal remains), and Heather Trigg, a paleobotanist (for plant remains), who also analyzed the findings at the Center for Archaeological Research that Alice had established at UMass in memory of Andy.

A bare five weeks in the field each summer (followed by another five in the UMass lab in Boston) were proving too short to do what Steve wanted: broaden the search beyond the core area around the house. (On the North Peninsula, excavation also proceeded every year on prehistoric and pre-contact native sites.) Extra funding opened up a tempting possibility: that summer, Ken Kvamme, a geophysical testing expert from the University of Arkansas, arrived with what looked like large carpet sweepers and lawn trimmers to create noninvasive guides to future excavation. With the technologies of magnetometry, ground-penetrating radar, and electrical soil resistance, he would search delicately for signs of vanished structures at different depths underground. The spaces had to be smooth and uninterrupted by trees or shrubs. The locations were designed to tie into the UMass GPS survey. Kvamme tested not only the several acres of lawns surrounding the Fiskes' house but also parts of the garden left uncovered by Alice's extensive plantings, and an area that had been clear-cut and manicured on another peninsula jutting out into Gardiners Creek south of the manor house, where one traditional account had sited Nathaniel's grave. He detected no human remains. Those who expect definitive results from archaeology come, over time, to learn how very difficult it is for an archaeologist to dig without expectations and to come to a single conclusion.

For me, as a landscape historian, the most interesting and understandable results were produced by electrical resistance testing, which "reads" what's underground via probes set at one-meter intervals that inject a current into the soil. This detects subsurface soil compaction and porosity, as well as the presence of brick or stone. Kvamme came up with a startling alternative to Alice Fiske's vision of a substantial "first house": *two* possible "first houses"! His experienced eyes organized the blots and dots of electric resistance images of the area immediately around the manor house into two sets of parallel lines and right angles. "Nature doesn't generally make square corners," Kvamme said. He read them as the remains of two sets of rectangular structures that crossed under the existing house, and he tentatively suggested that a major change in plantation layout had occurred in the early years. It's an idea that remains to be "shovel-tested," as archaeologists call it, meaning excavated for confirmation.

It quickly became apparent that the scale of the site and the mingled evidence of three cultures made it impossible to excavate fully in brief summer sessions. At the manor, untrained undergraduates worked for four to five weeks under the direction of a PI—a principal investigator, Steve Mrozowski; a field superintendent, Kat Hayes; and trained graduate students. (Almost all field schools are made up of undergraduates: some just want a fun summer, others are already hooked on archaeology as a discipline.) Each summer, the results were taken back to the lab in Boston, and for up to five additional weeks, with support from the National Science Foundation, the field school participants would get a taste of analysis and cataloguing procedures.

Kvamme's electric resistance readings of the north and west slopes

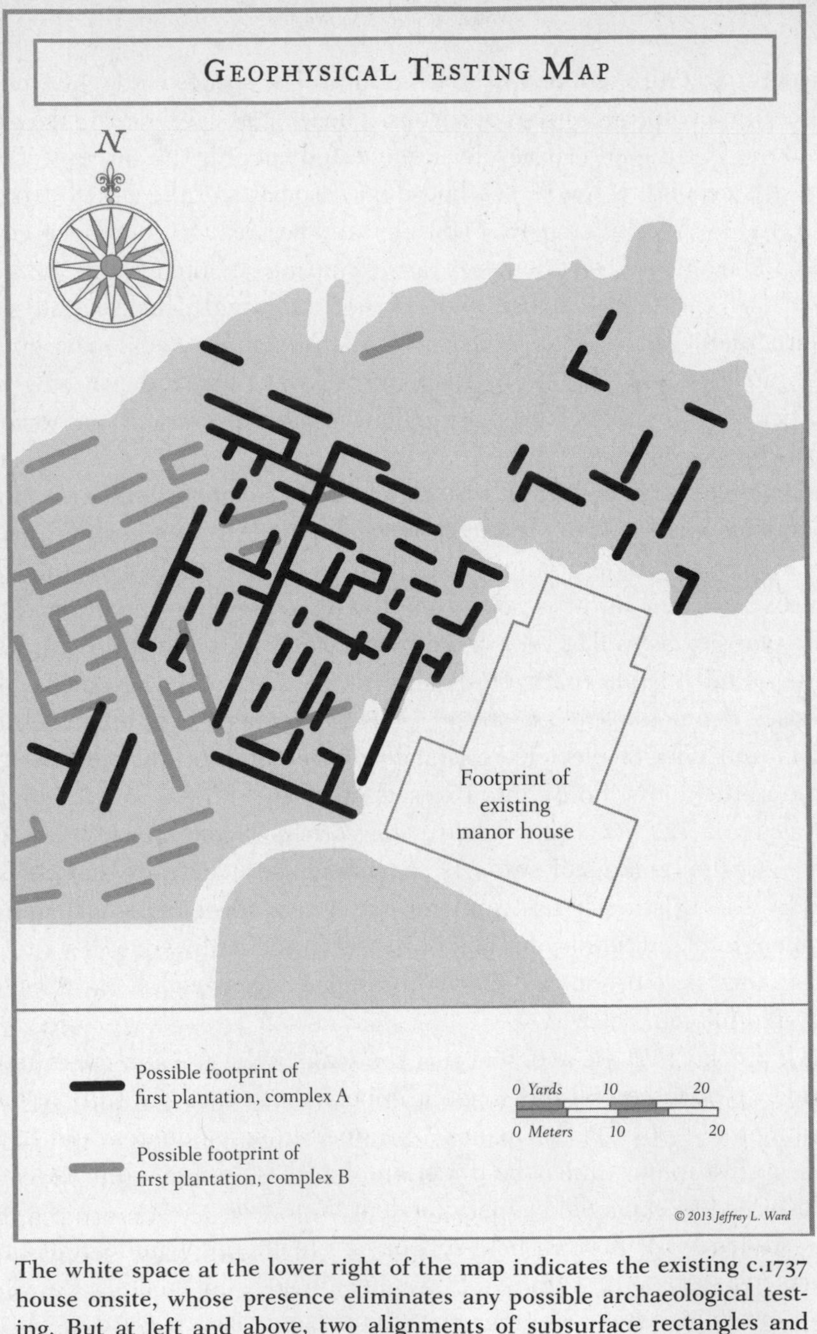

The white space at the lower right of the map indicates the existing c.1737 house onsite, whose presence eliminates any possible archaeological testing. But at left and above, two alignments of subsurface rectangles and straight lines point in different directions. The dark set (A) points right (northeast), the lighter set (B) to the left (northwest). Since both apparently date to the manor's first period of settlement (1651–80), they may indicate two different plans for a first house complex, built successively by Nathaniel Sylvester.

running down to the creek, also as yet unexcavated, revealed a landscape totally different from today's green and blue stillness. He found "a plethora," as his otherwise unemphatic report puts it, of straight lines and right angles beneath the slightly lumpy lawn that stretches to the water. They produced strong signals, evidence that suggested stone—walls, footings, or foundations, or the compacted soil surfaces of floors, lanes, and paths—the possible remains of as many as eighty buildings. Thinking about even half that number of structures (all doubtless did not exist at the same time) made the work of "provisioning" visible, as it had been to me in the historical display on Texel Island. On Shelter Island, gangs of skilled workers—slaves, indentured servants, local natives, the Sylvesters themselves—loaded skittery little boats to ferry cargoes to a ship waiting in the deepwater harbor outside quiet Gardiners Creek, returning with sugar, salt, and rum, or with European goods. Nathaniel or his brothers stored everything for safekeeping in the buildings whose shadowy footprints were partially sensed by Kvamme's electric probes.

Steve's reports and analyses confirm the existence of an all-purpose outpost that served as both family living quarters and a trading post for transactions with the Indians and with Europeans from other colonies who heard news of the Sylvesters' abundant imported goods. It included an ad hoc "first house" and several other structures, all located inside the present driveway circle or under the existing manor house. The first buildings had no footings, but were "earth fast" structures, meaning rough timber poles were rammed into the ground and the framing rested on hewn wooden sills laid on the ground between the posts. Indoors, a hearth and perhaps a threshold, such as the long shaped stone by the water landing, would have constituted the only masonry. After a building was demolished, the valuable hewn timbers were often lifted out of the ground and reused, leaving their faint traces in the soil. Stones and bricks were also salvaged, leaving compacted areas that archaeologists call "robbed" foundations, which also have geophysical testing signatures. Of the possible eighty structural remains Kvamme estimated were under the west and north lawns, many may have been robbed for reuse.

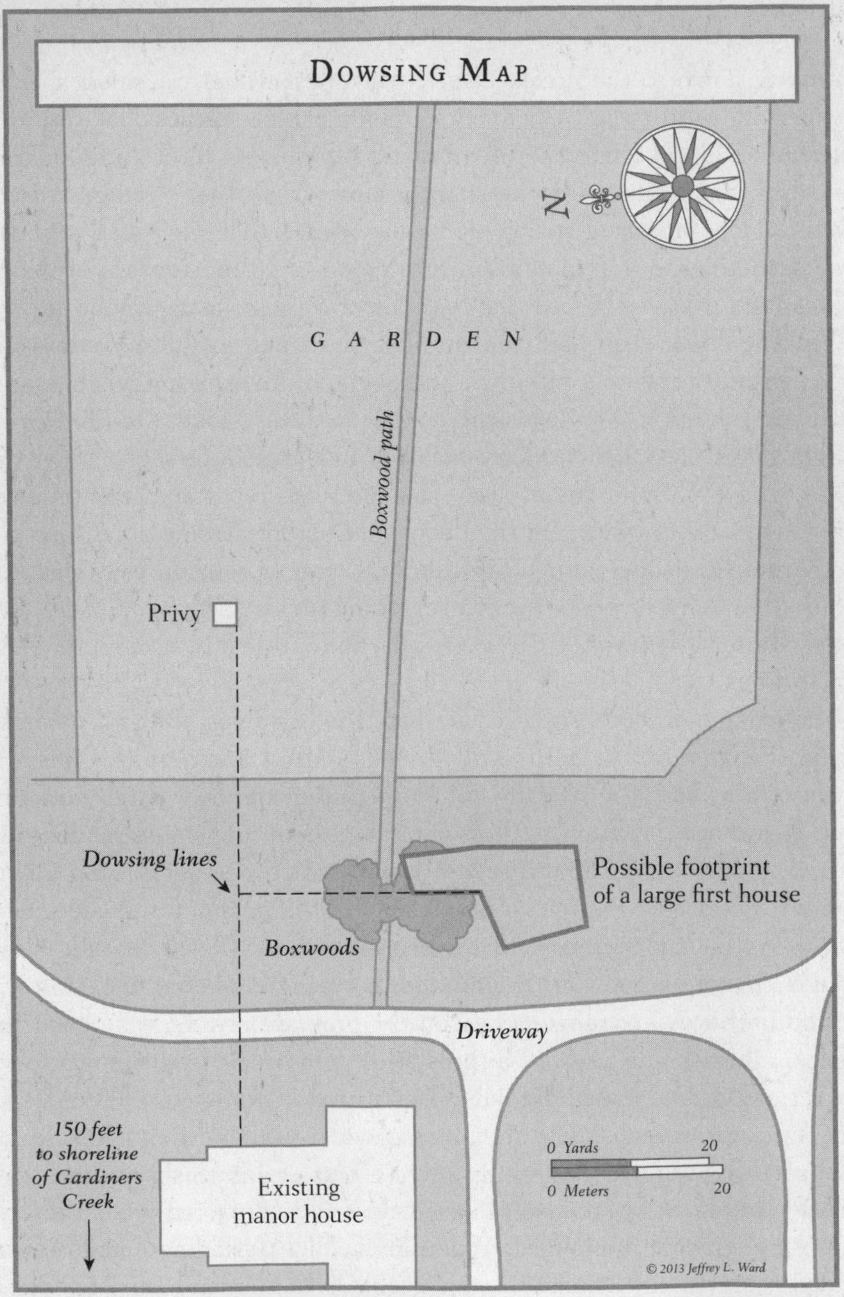

A dowser's divining rod supposedly senses underground water or minerals. Some say a rod held by a dowser can also detect differences in soil texture and compaction, such as those left by wall foundations. On the flat lawn near the garden where Dr. David Jacques conducted his dowsing procedure, a crude outline was revealed where traditional accounts placed a "first house."

"But I Am a Dowser"

Family and local lore contradict archaeology, clinging tightly to the idea that the first house stood on the lawn south of the great boxwoods, near Alice's modern garden on the southeast lawn, not inside the drive circle. In his unfinished manuscript, Professor Horsford wrote that the edge of a foundation could be seen skimming the green grass beneath a pear tree. A standing stone marked the spot, he added. A tall stone still stands on the southeast lawn, and eureka: a photograph from the vault showed the vanished pear tree—but nothing else. Reading Horsford's account, I found myself in sympathy with the storytellers and wanted the foundation to be there. I understood that this was a "feature fantasy" we shared. The very least we wanted was a single grounded certainty about this vanished house and life.

Before UMass excavated on the southeast lawn, I had the chance to try another, very alternative testing method, hoping to locate a building that matched Alice's expectations for Nathaniel Sylvester's "mansion house." Alice and I invited my colleague, the eminent British landscape historian David Jacques, an expert in seventeenth- and eighteenth-century landscape design, to visit Sylvester Manor. He arrived one snowy February day in 2003. I asked if his knowledge of small English manor complexes could offer clues to the possible layout and functions of a colonial counterpart: house, garden, courtyard, workspaces, and outbuildings. He politely replied that the commercial aspect of the site—the warehouse, the salt house, the considerable provisioning operation, and the landing—made such comparisons dicey. A brief silence followed.

Then, to my surprise, Jacques said, "But I am a dowser." The best case for dowsing, an ancient but often disparaged practice of divination, is that a successful response can depend on the human diviner's personal sensitivity to a magnetic field as it is transmitted to the divining rod (just an ordinary stick) through his or her hands. The procedure, according to Jacques, who admits it is hardly foolproof, is a kind of natural "geophysical testing." He believes that the stick supposedly reacts to different densities in the soil, so it can detect the presence of compaction, water, or stone. (Like most dowsers, Jacques had simply tried it one day as a kid, was successful, and got hooked.)

Before I could begin to tell him what we were looking for, Jacques quickly said, "Don't tell me anything about what you want to find—or where." We ripped a flexible forked branch from the nearest tree, and off he walked, this don in a gray cardigan with elbow patches and drooping pockets, holding one of the two branching ends of his divining rod loosely in each hand and pointing the "nose" directly ahead. Back and forth he went, across a stretch of the southeast lawn that I told him I had randomly selected. Slowly, as I poked pink plastic gas-line marker flags through the snow and into the ground wherever Jacques's stick dipped decisively, a bulky outline emerged.

The line that Jacques roughly plotted out had a bend or bulge in it about midway along its length. In her will, Grizzell mentioned a "closet or porchamber," indicating that by 1685 her house had evolved into one of the few domestic buildings in the colonies built on what the *Field Guide to American Houses* calls a Jacobean cross-plan with a shallow two-story bay, or "porch tower," projecting from the entrance façade. Whether the ground floor "porch" was an open space with corner columns or a fully enclosed room, it would have served as a vestibule. The room overhead—the "closet," then a term for a small private room for reading, correspondence, and prayer—was clearly Nathaniel's domain because Grizzell in her will noted that it contained a cabinet, maybe the same one salvaged from the wreck on Conanicutt's shore. Could the bulge Jacques divined be where a south-facing front porch once stuck out, I asked myself? Cross-plan houses often had a rear projection corresponding to the porch. As Jacques moved north, his pointer nosed downward repeat-

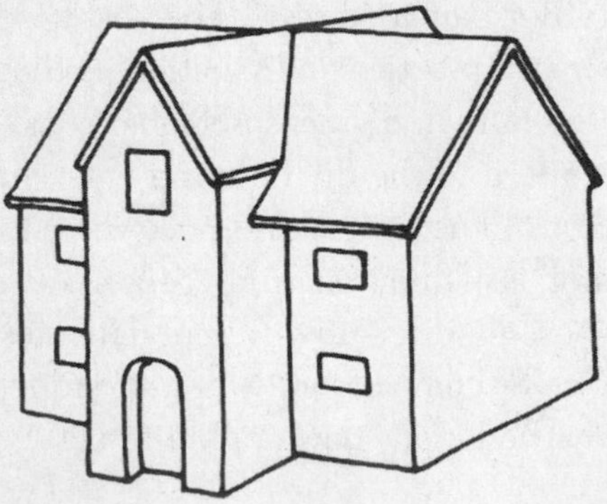

Only a few houses were built in the American colonies on this elaborate Jacobean cross plan. (From Virginia and Lee McAlester, *A Field Guide to American Houses* [New York, 1984])

edly, sketching out what appeared to be precisely that: a narrow perpendicular ell.

That June, although strongly disinclined to regard the results of Jacques's foray as scientific findings, the UMass team obligingly recorded the dowser points on their official grid and opened a few units. In 2005 they excavated the area more fully and indeed found two huge postholes and a quantity of shell-plaster debris, indicating a sizable building with some finished interior walls. They also unearthed a pair of large boulders—possibly cornerstones, they said. A line of smaller postholes crossed the site. But absent the footprint of a hearth or much domestic debris in the surrounding area, the archaeologists were inclined to interpret the large structure as a barn or other farm building.

Later in that summer of 2005, however, before the field school ended, Steve walked me through the freshly exposed area and floated a new hypothesis. As is standard archaeological practice once a feature has been fully excavated, the exposed surface is swept as clean as a kitchen floor in preparation for the official field photographs. The smooth, sandy area had been bleached pale by the sun. The big postholes cast ochre shadows into their deep interiors. The two boulders sat exactly where they had been found.

Steve's new proposal comfortably fits into the swirl of continual building and rebuilding that characterizes the seventeenth-century site. The first area of European occupation appeared to have been in front of the existing house and probably extended under Alice's dwelling, Steve said, but another structure, where Jacques's stick had outlined a building, was built sometime later. Steve referred to it as a "manor house," and he interpreted the line of smaller holes that crossed the space as evidence of later fence lines erected after that "manor house" was taken down. I wondered if that had happened when Brinley Sylvester tore down his grandfather's house and built his own.

Archaeologists are more comfortable with open questions than laymen are, and the question "Where was the first house?" will probably remain unanswered even if and when digging resumes. (The last field school took place in 2006.) The solid reality of the present manor house sits squarely atop the intersection of Kvamme's two visionary electrical resistance grids. In 1908, Cornelia Horsford, the tenth family proprietor, further complicated matters by having the notable American architect Henry Bacon totally revamp the existing manor house cellar and solidly reinforce every surface with concrete. No one was willing to suggest to Alice that the concrete that coats—and probably by now partially supports—her cellar walls be torn off to check for the possibility of earlier material evidence of the "first house." She might have agreed!

10

How They Lived

A Stone Carpet

The archaeologists and I agreed that the original house was splendid by the time Nathaniel died. But the handsome porch and luxurious interiors that his inventory lists—ten beds complete with "furnishings," or hangings; a couch and a dozen chairs upholstered in English "turkey work," floral embroidery in the manner of Turkish or other oriental carpets—were not all that signaled wealth and status. An amazing fragment of pavement was excavated in 1999 on the south lawn. Alternating squares of large and small rounded cobblestones made from local quartz are bordered neatly with narrower stones. Invasive tree roots and Victorian driveway builders had destroyed the short ends of the pavement, so we don't know the original length, but an impressive thirty-one-foot section remains. Judging from the intact edges on the long sides, which are finished with rows of slightly larger cobbles, the pavement was originally eleven and a half feet wide. The craftsman who laid the stones followed the standard European method of setting tapered cobbles point-down, burying most of the stone for stability and leaving only a single face visible.

From the Middle Ages on, cobbled paving existed throughout Britain and Europe on roads, in city squares, and in courtyards both urban and rural. Cobbles supported heavy wheeled traffic, channeled drainage, and kept feet off muddy ground. Pavings were sometimes set in squares outlined with edging stones for additional strength. But at Sylvester Manor, where the squares are set in a pattern of large and small cobbles, the decorative effect is startling, and clearly intentional. Whatever useful purpose it served—a dooryard? a courtyard? a road to somewhere?—this baroque stone carpet also reflects the ambitions of a man who knew it would proclaim the skill, sophistication, and costly labor required to make it. The variation in cobble size from square to square produces a tonal contrast, as if mimicking the black-and-white paving depicted in Dutch genre scenes and church interior views. Certainly on Long Island, the pavement must have been a wonder in its day. No comparable example from that period is known to survive in New England.

Whether seen from the major excavation area on the front lawn or from the footprint of Jacques's dowsed outline, the pavement's strong diagonal movement comes across as a diamond or "diaper" pattern. The effect of that insistent geometry virtually reorients the site from north/south to northeast/southwest, making me wonder how it was originally intended to be viewed. I can't help thinking of one of Kvamme's two grids, which has the same orientation.

Steve carefully lifted a few cobbles at one corner to confirm what we all hoped: this paving was laid very early in the manor's development, since beneath it he found only pre-contact Indian ceramics. Steve recognized the pale brown low-fired clay sherds by the characteristic glint of "temper," either crushed local shell or mineral, added to make raw clay stiffer when a pot is shaped and stronger after firing. For more than two centuries, the gleaming cobble pattern had been hidden under a scatter of trash from the nearby midden and a layer of landscape loam that was smoothed over the entire site when the new house went up.

Once archaeologists have finished drawing and photographing a feature, they commonly rebury it. But the pavement was left exposed—like a trophy—because it was so beautiful and so rare. Weeds sprouted between the stones; frost and sun quickly began to do their damage. Everyone, including me, couldn't resist stepping onto it, just to see what it felt like to time-travel to the seventeenth century. In 2008 this witness to past grandeur was again covered with a few inches of soil, to be revealed again only if some protective method of display can be found.

It is an archaeologist's article of faith that momentous events, such as dynastic succession, trigger major alterations in architecture and landscape. The creation of this extraordinary pavement probably marked some milestone—perhaps the birth of Nathaniel and Grizzell's first son in 1657, or the Sylvesters' attainment of the freedoms of a royal manor in 1666 (no military levy, no taxes, the right to appoint a magistrate), which essentially gave them the status of a little fiefdom. Just what Nathaniel wanted.

The laborers who laid these beach cobbles gauged the size of each stone, had a geometric design in mind, and followed it to make this patterned pavement, which was concealed for centuries under a few inches of soil on the manor's lawn.

Steve is equally speculative about the motives for laying the pavement. Once, thinking of all the colonists who returned to England or moved on, Steve said, "Maybe it's when Nathaniel decided to stay."

Most of the rest of this chapter is not about the Sylvesters; instead, it reveals the little we can learn about the character and lives of those who produced the Sylvesters' wealth. North of the pavement, and below the parlor windows, Kat Hayes found shell fragments left over from wampum production, rolled copper beads, European straight pins, and fish scales and bones mixed together in one archaeological stratum. So Kat was looking at events taking place in the same space and time. Kat deduced that this was one of the sites where Manhansetts worked for the Sylvesters, carving from shells what was common currency in the 1650s and '60s. In other words, the Sylvesters had their own mint in their backyard, until inflation caught up with them. The amount of zinc and lead in the copper beads—half-inch to two-inch-long curled metal scraps, not solid beads as we think of them today—indicates that they were probably cut from European copper kettles (copper kettles figured in countless land deals between Indians and English settlers). Hundreds of pins have come to light. Both men and women used them to fasten clothing, even after buttons began to be used more frequently in the Renaissance. Pins also secured documents and shrouds, and they possessed a voodoolike power, it was said, to cast and ward off spells.

The fish scales and bones in Kat's excavation hole tell us what some people ate while others carved wampum, or perhaps cast a spell, or simply shed a pin from a doublet as they hurried about their daily rounds. Craig Cipolla, a graduate student with a profile like a Medici prince under a backward-facing baseball cap, once looked up from his work and mentioned that he was analyzing a vertebra as big as a silver dollar from a fish the size of a large tuna. That fish (which it may be impossible to identify) hurtled me back into the never-never New England of John Josselyn's seventeenth-century oysters: "long shell'd . . . nine inches long from the joint to the toe . . . Oyster[s] . . . that were to be cut into three pieces before they could get them into their mouths, very fat and sweet." Such riches from the sea must at first have been proof of a mythic world of plenty for the Sylvesters, as they were for Josselyn, before they became ordinary fare, as they were for the Manhansetts.

Samp: the Heart of a Creole Household

A web of sounds that soon became familiar to a half dozen different cultures, European, African, and American, netted this creole space. *Weskhunck, tackhunck*, the Algonquian words for a stone or wooden mortar to crush corn, sound like the thud of a pestle pounding all day long. For anthropologists, "creolization" denotes the process of creating hybrid cultures. Applied to people, the English word "creole," in the seventeenth century, didn't mean "of mixed race," a common misconception today. The term was coined in the sixteenth century to describe children of Spanish colonists born in the Americas, and it came to apply loosely to all whose parents had emigrated from Africa and Europe. Although the word sometimes took on racial overtones, throughout the Caribbean it described—and still describes—a culture derived from many sources as well as the region's people, their language, and their cuisine. In that early sense, the Sylvester children were Atlantic creoles—American-born offspring of foreign parents—just like the black children born on the island. Language kept changing, however, and soon the Sylvester children would become "colonials"; children of African-Indian parentage, "mustees"; and those with both white and African blood, "mulattos." The ethnic slur "half-breed" was the most common label for the children of white and Indian unions.

Before the roar of a mill was heard grinding grain on the island or at Nathaniel's mill in Southold, the thud of pestles produced the food that united everyone in the Sylvesters' settlement. At its busiest, the plantation fed as many as forty to fifty people. Besides Nathaniel and Grizzell and their children, the numbers included Nathaniel's brothers Joshua, who lived permanently with the family, and Giles Jr., who stayed there often enough between transatlantic trips to sometimes style himself "of Shelter Island"; Grizzell's brother Francis; and whatever Quakers were traveling through the colonies to and from New England and Barbados—as well as white indentured servants such as Bernard Collins and up to twenty-four slaves.

Although they probably never all sat down at once at the same table, we can gather something about community *and* prejudice from a 1704 journal of a trip from Boston to New York. Madam Knight observed that farmers in coastal Connecticut were "too indulgent (especially the farmers) to their slaves: sufering too great familairity from them, permitting them to sit at Table and eat with them (as they say to save time) and into the dish goes the black hoof as freely as the white hand."

All drank cider and beer, although as investors in the Azores wine trade, the Sylvesters may also have poured fortified wines such as port and madeira. Fragments of Rhenish pottery jugs and "case bottles" for spirits, with flat sides for easy packing and minimal breakage, have emerged from the dig. Barbadian rum was measured out as pay for Indians and an incentive for slaves. The masters doubtless ate prime cuts of roast meat off pewter plates; the slaves got stew in pottery bowls. Fine Indian cornmeal—*nokake*—was mixed with water to make the corn porridge called *nausamp*. Everybody ate the steaming hot "samp," a comforting bridge between three cultures. Samp was reheated for days, and the lacy brown crust at the edge of the iron kettle was a delicacy. The flavor of the dish varied with the additions of slivered meat or fish.

A single startling phrase associated with samp—"niggering corn"—conjures up the uglier side of that creole world. The term would have meant nothing to anyone except inhabitants of the western rim of the North Atlantic for a few decades in the colonial period. Before Long Island colonists built gristmills, they used another method for producing cornmeal that was reportedly used by the Indians. A white-oak stump was hollowed out to form a giant mortar, and a heavy block was mounted above it like a pestle, at the end of a hinged pole. The block was raised and dropped again and again, crushing the corn placed inside the stump. It could take a day to pound half a bushel of dry kernels into coarse meal. On Long Island plantations, this arduous, monotonous process became work for slaves.

The reasons for the existence of slavery, the rationales that whites offered for enslaving blacks, and the treatment slaves endured were constantly redefined in every period of the system's history as the needs for labor changed in the many different locations where it took hold. Ira Berlin has made famous the distinction between "slave societies," like that of Barbados, and "societies with slaves," like New England's, where slaves were marginal to the central productive processes. Shelter Island plantation between 1651 and 1680 was shaped as a "society with slaves" in two ways: the number of Africans was small by comparison with a West Indian operation, and a single crop, such as sugar, did not form the basis of the economy. But both Africans and Manhansetts were crucial to production.

In 1652, when the four partners set up their Shelter Island provisioning plantation, three of them—Thomas Rous, Thomas Middleton, and Nathaniel's brother Constant—were seasoned planters who had been among the first to set up the slave society of Barbados. From the time he had spent there, Nathaniel was somewhat familiar with such large-scale endeavors. But neither he nor any of his partners had any New England experience. Nathaniel, as resident plantation manager, could rely on advice (and English grass seed and breeding stock) for those who, like his brother-in-law William Coddington, had been experimenting for a dozen years in the North, producing crops for export using what labor, slave or free, they could find. According to Nathaniel's will, however, the three others seem not to have provided enough labor for their start-up operation: "where as the planting field behinde the Orchard Containeing about fourtie akers and the planting feeld called Mannanduck Containing about twentie five akers doth wholly belong unto mee having subdued the same with my owne Estate for want of Negros or other servants to performe it." Easily as important to Nathaniel as housing were the imperatives of getting the farm and a trade with the West Indies under way. The cost of labor in the colonies was higher than in England. Labor of any kind for hire was scarce, since the abundance of cheap land everywhere meant people wanted to work for themselves, not for others, making white indenture and Indian and black slavery valuable systems. For Nathaniel and his partners, making a go of their provisioning plantation meant helping themselves to labor wherever they found it, and as economically as possible: Africans direct from Africa or from the West Indies; Manhansetts and other local Indians; perhaps Irish slaves from Cromwell's Irish Wars and the Clearances, as well as a few indentured Europeans. At least one early colonist probably got his Shelter Island start as an indentured servant at the manor: Jacques Guillot, the Frenchman who eventually owned his own farm.

The Slaughter of the Animals

Close to the site of Jacques's ghost outline on the southeast lawn, and some five feet beneath it, the UMass team excavated a deep thirteen-foot-square midden whose contents tell us a great deal about the pressing requirements for labor on the island, and about what it may have meant to some of those who did the work. Once the pit had been filled with trash, it was capped with clay and sand to seal it, perhaps as late as the 1670s. Opened in 2005, the site revealed a scene dating to the earliest period of Sylvester occupation. In one of three dense strata of butchery trash, thousands of fragmentary jaws, teeth, tibias, and skulls attested to a single livestock slaughter. Lab analysis at UMass accounted for some thirteen hogs, plus lesser numbers of cattle, sheep, and goats. Though a small number by contrast with what is slaughtered daily in a commercial abattoir today, it would have required many plantation hands for the job. Specific butchering cuts mean that most of the 1,300 pounds of dressed meat was destined to be salted and barreled for shipment to the West Indies: food for sugar plantation slaves.

At the center of the upper stratum of the welter of bones, the archaeologists unearthed a large, smooth-bodied clay pot whose neck is heavily collared with distinctive decorative frills, a stylistic innovation that reveals historical information about the period. These embellishments mark it as Fort Shantock ware, named after the first similar pots found at the eponymous Mohegan Indian fort in Connecticut. The style spread across Southern New England in the mid- to late seventeenth century (what anthropologists and archaeologists call the "late post-contact period.") Reading ceramics as cultural history, archaeologists think that the spread of the decorative style may be an affirmation of pan-Indian identity, a blurring of tribal lines as catastrophic losses from epidemic diseases and the Pequot War caused the fragmented native communities to fuse together, and as relations with the English about land and settlement became more hostile.

Almost half of the vessel remained intact, as if it had been set carefully upright rather than thrown onto the pile as trash. As the pot was carefully removed from the soil and bones surrounding it, a telltale lump halfway down its curved side became visible. It marks the beginnings of a handle, but one structurally so weak it would have been more ornamental than utilitarian. Because pre-contact native pots had no handles, unlike both African and European pots, Steve explained, this vessel dates to the Sylvester plantation era (1651–80) and is testimony to the fusion of the manor's cultures and experimental identities.

While Steve suspected that it was most likely heaved into the trash because it was broken, in the same breath he also speculated that the container may have been placed among all these bones for a purpose. His remark made me speculate further than he would have: What did the Manhansetts think of this "provisioning"? The placement of that pot seemed like an acknowledgment of the animals killed here, and a reminder of their own traditions.

Traditional European slaughters took place in November or December, when livestock was at its fattest. Autumn slaughter fed people through the winter and economized on seasonally scarce fodder. The promise of winter plenty was welcome. But having axed and plucked a few turkeys myself, I know something about what those few cold, early winter days of bloody mayhem felt like. The entire job happened quickly. The beasts were as strong as their butchers: hogs screamed, sheep bleated, heifers mooed wildly. Then the speed and flash of the knife or ax, and the ebb of the struggle, clouds of steam and breath, the stench and stickiness and spatter of blood and guts everywhere. Split-open animals were hung by their hind feet, the way beef quarters are hung in commercial cold lockers today, or as hunters still hang deer. A tall wooden scaffold stands in the back fields of Sylvester Manor, and a buck or a doe, fresh-killed and gutted, hangs there almost every week of deer season. It's a startling sight, an altar to a distant past.

Africans and Europeans were accustomed to breeding domestic animals, feeding and caring for them, and then killing them. Cattle, sheep, and hogs all came to North America with the colonists. North American natives kept dogs and sometimes ate them when food was scarce, but had no other domesticated animals. For meat and hides, they relied mostly on deer, and given the opportunity, they would kill as many as they could—fawn, buck, or doe, including the pregnant does. So the Manhansetts were very familiar with killing for food, and with mass killing. In laboring for the Sylvesters, however, they also learned to husband and watch over the plantation's flocks and herds. Although they were more exquisitely knowledgeable than any Englishman about every detail of the game they hunted, from deer to the smallest rodent, this kind of domestic care was new. They were unsentimental about taking life in order to eat, being strangers neither to death nor to hunger. But they took their game while respecting the rule of Mesingw, "Master of Animals."

The historian John Strong, a trusted advocate for the East End Indians today and an expert in their history and lore, describes Mesingw, the "mask being," whose memory the Lenni Lenape of western Long Island took with them on their forced migrations westward. Strong says that the

East End tribes revered this strange and powerful deity who rode through the woods in human guise on the back of a stag. His face had the shape of a large mask, painted black on the left side, red on the right. Black hair covered his body. He watched the hunters, who prayed to him for continued plenty and a successful chase. Mesingw also watched over their quarry, to ensure that they were killed with humility and valor, honor, and gratitude. The rites of supplication enacted before a big deer hunt found everyday counterparts in the continual asking and receiving, the unstinting generosity in Indian culture that almost every European observer remarked on. Anyone who asked for food, shelter, or clothing received it. The same expectations applied to what their gods would provide when ritually asked and thanked.

The early winter darkness falls, and butchering ends for the season. I see Nathaniel turning indoors to his own hearth. Then, while the island's Manhansetts and Africans dump the last of the bones into the pit, Mesingw gallops soundlessly through the leafless woods, pausing, watching through his narrow masked eyes.

More than Their Names

"The history of silence" is a term Steve finds handy to use when artifacts and customs are concealed by those of another, dominant culture. Twenty-four Africans, or the children of Africans, lived as slaves on Shelter Island in 1680, four or five times as many people as were enslaved by any other colonists in the area. (Somewhat unusually, Nathaniel's will includes the names of both parents, not just the mothers.) But none of the obvious indicators of such a large African presence that the UMass team at first thought they would find, such as cowrie shells, or certain kinds of beads or amulets, or small in-ground storage pits for stashing precious belongings, have been located.

Kat Hayes has taken this "bundle of silences," as she calls the gaps in the archaeological record, and made it speak by looking closely at technologies used in Sylvester Manor's early plantation period to make stone tools, mortar, and ceramics. In ceramics alone, for example, evidence of the heretofore "invisible" first-generation Africans is striking: she concludes that they brought with them expertise that markedly changed the quality of pottery made on the island. Among the 2,400 "native" sherds found at the manor spanning some four thousand years, Kat was able to identify a range of plantation-period examples that show specific differences in temper (the incorporation of ground shells), and firing (higher temperatures and more skilled control). At least one or more of the slaves were probably familiar with common African smelting and ironworking practices; any one of them who had been forced to work as a boiler tender in Barbados was all too familiar with controlling high-temperature fires, the kind needed to fire the thinner, stronger ceramics Kat examined.

The post-contact wares she analyzed, Kat argues, are only one example of the exchanges between Manhansetts and Africans that have been overlooked as historians (and archaeologists) stressed the singularity of different minority populations. She makes a persuasive argument for "a flow of knowledge" that took place at the seventeenth-century manor in a common social space where "small acts of sharing led to an intertwined history" that existed for more than a hundred years. In the nineteenth century, new political and ethnological takes on colonial history deemed "blood" (as in the "full-blooded Indian") as the ultimate marker of "race," producing isolated histories of white, black, and Indian.

Kat agrees that placing the broken castellated pot so prominently among the bones in the slaughter pit may indeed have been a deliberate act. For the Manhansetts, she says, it may have signified mourning or anger: the slaughter stratum where the pot was found is close to the top of the pit. The clay pipes used by archaeologists as reliable chronological markers that were found in the same layer date to the 1660s or 1670s, so it's possible to give a date somewhere around the time of "King Philip's War," the last large-scale Indian conflict in New England (1675–76). In 1675 a government official observed that Shelter Island's Indians were "very sullen." For the slaves, the placement of the Shantock pot with its African handle may well have been an announcement of solidarity with the Manhansetts. The pot shaped by two cultures and set purposely on top of the midden could thus be read as a wordless statement by both minorities. Their captors, the uneasy Sylvesters, would have been alert to any sign of collusion, even one as enigmatic as this.

But where was the other direct and incontrovertible evidence we expected about the Africans? Sylvester Manor was the first Northern provisioning plantation to be systematically excavated. Working at first on the supposition that from its beginnings, the Sylvester compound would have included separate slave quarters, Steve and his team dug shovel test pits in the old melon field to the east, in the briars under the pines near the slave cemetery, on the point of the North Peninsula, on a smooth patch of grass close to the barns. "Hindsight being 20/20," Kat wrote a year after these disappointing attempts, "it now seems clear to us that we fell into the most obvious trap: we were guessing at the location of slave quarters based on what we know from Southern plantation sites, without knowing anything from the written history about how different Northern sites might look."

The team had to revise their ideas, and they came to believe that Nathaniel and Grizzell lived with the people they kept in slavery in their own house and its outbuildings. Stunning news. We all slowly comprehended what this meant: a different understanding of personal and social space, the questionable preservation of African languages and family structure (even the neat nuclear families in Nathaniel's will began to look different), queries about cross-cultural exchanges and compromises in the close confines of the house, about the meanings of race and class structure. So how was this situation "racial" if Africans were not segregated from Europeans? (Until it became very clear from the mass of evidence that the Manhansetts also played an intimate role, we consistently left them out of the domestic equation.) It would take years—nine to be exact, until Kat finished her thesis—to parse the subtle evidence of what "living together" might have meant at the manor. Even then, as many intriguing questions as solid answers remain.

Common housing also turned out to have been the case for the very earliest planters of Virginia and Maryland, whose history of shared space has generally been obscured by later practices. At Rich Neck Plantation, an intact seventeenth-century site, archaeologists uncovered movements through space told in the marks of fence lines erected by three different owners between the early 1640s and the 1680s. Rich Neck's initial configuration (seventeen slaves living with their owners and white servants in two structures, main house and kitchen, on a single fenced acre) was similar to Sylvester Manor's in Nathaniel and Grizzell's day. Archaeologists used the evidence of lines of Virginia postholes to chart the advance of fences across the land, tracing how slaves moved out of the "big house" into the separated spaces that became a signature of the Southern plantation as early as the 1670s, as the perceived need for the owners' privacy, increasing racialization, and the numbers of slaves increased. But Northern landowners cultivated fewer acres than in the South, experienced shorter crop seasons, and planted multiple crops that, unlike tobacco, didn't require year-round attention. Therefore they owned fewer slaves. At Sylvester Manor, masters and slaves appear to have lived together at least until the mid-eighteenth century.

In shared accommodations such as those at Rich Neck and Sylvester Manor, which anthropologists call "contested spaces," people from different cultures played out day-to-day dramas with "the other." Depending on who you were, the act of simply stepping into a room or walking through a garden could hold immensely different significance. The design of buildings is always freighted with meaning, and Africans, no less than anyone else, saw living spaces as symbolic. The manor house the Sylvesters erected—perhaps after converting the temporary settlement of the 1650s into an auxiliary work site or tearing it down—advertised their status as gentry and masters and their intention to create something that would last. For first-generation slaves especially, that alien assemblage of space and materials must have felt uncomfortable and intimidating. Sleeping on a straw mattress in the attic, on a stair landing, in dark corners and dank storerooms, or huddling in barn lofts where oxen, horses, and sheep breathed welcome animal heat up between the floorboards, Africans encountered daily reminders of how far they had traveled from home.

For the Sylvesters, the identity of Shelter Island's first black community must necessarily have been based partly on assessments of slaves' abilities and skills, and maybe even on their character—unknown valuations that mattered most when the plantation was running full steam. (After Nathaniel's death, those human lives were appraised purely at market price: a total valuation of £258, the third-highest amount on the list after the land and livestock.)

But how to find out what the slaves thought of themselves and their labor? Within the black community, and certainly more important to them than what their employers thought, the first black Shelter Islanders would have first based their identities on kinship, and on whatever status each person might have possessed within his or her own society. Crafts such as ironworking and animal husbandry passed down from generation to generation within families much as they did in European guilds. Africans probably came to Shelter Island with diverse skills and acquired more as the decades passed, and those skills were part of what defined identity—for themselves as well as for the Sylvesters.

Since social identity is shaped and constantly reshaped in the practices of daily life, we must briefly look at the dry phrases of Nathaniel's will to see what they might reveal about the identity of Shelter Island's black community. Kvamme's data has indicated the presence of various structures crowding the west slope down to the inlet: the cider press and cider mill, salt house, barn, and warehouse all noted in Nathaniel's will would have stood on or near the waterfront for loading the plantation's products and unloading the incoming sugar, salt, and manufactured goods, Nathaniel's trade staples. The smallest details give insight into the qualities and skills required for daily life and work. For example, brick-making, burning charcoal, and slaking lime for mortar require knowledge of specific technologies. Loading vessels required more than muscles. Although a puncheon of molasses could weigh 1,300 pounds, a sack of flour some 280 pounds, and a barrel of salt beef half a ton, each had to be carefully placed in a small boat, then heaved or winched up and over the gunwales of the large ship out in the deep harbor. Breaking a restive young horse took intelligence, dexterity, courage, and patience. Shuttling live-stock on and off the island by boat was a dangerous test of reflexes and timing. Horses had to be shod, farm equipment constructed and repaired, and iron hoops made for wooden casks.

Whatever staves for barrels or water buckets or other vital containers a black cooper or carpenter could turn out were probably for use on the island. In the early years, producing staves in the near-industrial quantities needed for West Indies sugar, molasses, and rum would have taken away from the essential work of setting up the plantation, so Nathaniel looked off-island, apparently without much initial success. He wrote several times to John Winthrop Jr., hoping to have "a prsell [of staves] from yor towne [New London]," and to pay for them with "Salt and English Goods" that he expected to receive shortly at Shelter Island. But by the 1660s he was shipping thousands of staves from Southold.

Tammero (or Tomeo), the husband of Oyou and father of four children, may have been one of the three indispensable men on the Shelter Island plantation. His name, like other African names in the documents, offers little clue as to his African identity. Tomeo may be the standard form for Bartolomeo, indicating that he, like Jacquero, is an Atlantic creole who came to the Americas through the Iberian slave trade. But whatever his ethnicity, perhaps Tammero proudly acknowledged it, just as Oyou might have said "I am Oyo" when she described herself, meaning she

Division of Slave Families According to the Will of Nathaniel Sylvester, 1680
Sylvester Manor Archives and Shelter Island Historical Society Copy of Will

ENSLAVED	SYLVESTER FAMILY MEMBERS TO WHOM THEY WERE ASSIGNED IN 1680, WHEN FAMILIES WERE BROKEN UP
Jacquero and Hannah	*Grizzell Sylvester (wife of Nathaniel)*
Hope	*Grizzell Sylvester (wife)*
Isabell	*Elizabeth Sylvester (daughter)*
Tony and Nannie	*Giles Sylvester (son)*
Hester	*Patience Sylvester (daughter)*
Abbey	*Mary Sylvester (daughter)*
Grace	*Ann Sylvester (daughter)*
Semnie	*Mercie Sylvester (daughter)*
Japhet and Semnie	*Nathaniel Sylvester II (son)*
Tammero and Oyou	*Peter Sylvester (son)*
Child 1	*Constant Sylvester (son)*
Child 2	*Constant Sylvester (son)*
Child 3	*Benjamin Sylvester (son)*
Child 4*	*Benjamin Sylvester (son)*
Black John and Maria	*Grizzell Sylvester (wife)*
Prescilla	*Grizzell Sylvester (wife)*
J.O. and Marie	*Grizzell Sylvester (wife)*
Negro Jenkin	*Grizzell Sylvester (wife)*

In March 1680, when the Quaker convert Nathaniel Sylvester wrote his will, the family and community bonds of most of those listed here were given little consideration.

*One of these children is Obium (d. 1757); another probably Tom as per Isaac Arnold and James Lloyd to Nathaniel Sylvester II, Sept. 20, 1687, SMA, NYU, I/A/140/20.

came from the powerful Oyo Empire, an inland state the size of England in what is now Nigeria. If we can suppose for a minute that these two guesses are true, we are looking at what happened often in America and surely on Shelter Island also: two people from different cultures, each of whom spoke a native language as well as a creole lingua franca, were creating a new domestic order and a new collective identity for themselves and their children.

The binding conditions of ownership in Nathaniel's will demonstrate his high regard for Tammero. "Whereas Tammero the Negro was . . . formerly my owne," Nathaniel wrote, "[I] yeelded [him] to goe into partnership [with brother Constant and Thomas Middleton]," but only on the condition that "he should upon dividing of the Negros in partnership be returned to mee againe as my owne negro." If Tammero had been on Shelter Island since the partnership began in 1652, as Nathaniel's will implies, it means he might have lived there for thirty-six years. The place must have become his home. The premature death in 1697 of a Sylvester son, Peter, to whom Tammero had been bequeathed, caused yet another loss. Tammero, his wife, and one of their sons, Obium—the one black islander of his generation known to read and write—were sold to James Lloyd, the husband of Nathaniel and Grizzell's daughter Grizzell, who lived in Boston. As Michael Gomez notes in *Exchanging Our Country Marks*, each African who was enslaved came out of a "socially stratified, ethnically based identity directly tied to a specific land." But on Shelter Island, Africans were forced to learn that skin color alone would henceforth define them in the eyes of their captors.

Symoney, Semnie, Siminje, Simene

In early April 1674, Captain Richard Smith of Narragansett, Rhode Island, owner of a thriving Indian trading post and a friend of the Sylvesters and the Coddingtons, wrote to Fitz John Winthrop, the Connecticut governor's son. Describing a trading trip around Long Island Sound, Smith said, "We had some good fraight on board namely, Mistress Sylvester and her daughter Mistress Grisell, and negro Symoney to attend them, whom we saufly landed at Rhode Island."

"Negro Symoney" sounds like a known figure; she was not merely "a negro," or a nameless servant. She was included in the "good fraight." On this trip, Symoney accompanied the Sylvester women as a lady's maid, meaning she was familiar with the exalted routines of dressing the two Grizzells and herself for a visit to the Coddingtons in Newport. "Mistress Sylvester" was by this time thirty-eight years old, a settled matron; she may then have been pregnant with her last baby, Benjamin. "Mistress Grisell," eighteen and highly marriageable, was a year older than her mother had been when she left Newport for Shelter Island as a bride, so Symoney may have doubled as a watchful duenna. Smith's jocular tone suggests that this was a pleasure jaunt for the three women breaking out of Shelter Island's winter isolation, when the strait of the Peconic Bay between Shelter Island and Southold often froze solid. The closed circle of Symoney's two worlds—her own family on the island and the Sylvesters, with whom she lived in claustrophobic intimacy—opened out, in Newport, to include other companions, black and white.

The presence of Symoney's uncommon name, alternatively written as Semnie or Semenie, in Nathaniel's will may offer a glimpse of a slave exercising a rare privilege—naming a child, as the will also records a second Semnie among the other slaves. One, a married woman listed without children, is probably the person who traveled to Newport. The other is a girl whose three sisters had conventional English names. What are the odds of two people having this unusual name, just by chance, on tiny Shelter Island in 1680? One scholar has proposed that the senior Semnie is the grandmother, but even if the two are not related by blood, it seems pretty clear that little Semnie's parents must have named her after the elder woman. Eighteen years later, when the first census was taken on the East End, there they are, the two Semnies together in Southold. Their Shelter Island society had vanished with the deaths of Nathaniel and Grizzell. But the power of their name lived on in the baptismal and death records of the East End. The name repeats like a tolling bell once in every generation down to 1805, then fades to silence. Semnie, Symoney, Semonie, Semone, Simene, Simmany.

"Semnie" appears in no dictionary of proper names—English, French, Portuguese, Spanish, or Dutch—and if it is African, corruption has taken it far from a recognizable original. The only name I've found that even comes close is Siminje (pronounced "See-MIN-yeh"), that of a Guyanese Indian woman enslaved in Barbados in the 1640s. One clue as to why this odd name may have had such a long life comes from Richard and Sally Price, anthropologists steeped in the history of the Guyanas and the world of the Saramaka Maroons (still-extant forest communities in Suriname founded in the seventeenth century by Africans who successfully escaped slavery). The Prices offered a word used by the Saramakans in the African secret language, Komanti: *sêminí* or *osêminí*, which refers to a class of warrior spirits. Perhaps the name traveled from Africa to the forests of South America to Shelter Island; whatever route it took, the name casts a spell of spiritual power. On the Shinnecock Indian Nation's reservation in Southampton, Long Island, old "Poppy" Terry, who claimed to be the grandson of a Barbadian slave, called his wife, a Long Island native whose real name was Thelma, Semmie until the day she died in 2005.

11

In the Ground

Under the Pines

In the vault, sorting through stacks of early-twentieth-century letters, I open a small envelope without a name or address. It contains four half-sized sheets covered in Cornelia Horsford's loopy, acrobatic scrawl. Cornelia inherited the manor upon her mother's death in 1903. Her letter is dated Sylvester Manor, August 26, 1915, but has no salutation. I keep reading, hoping for clues regarding Cornelia's correspondent, although I don't expect to find more than family gossip. Indeed, the letter describes a visit to the manor by a cousin, General Sylvester Dering II. But on page three Cornelia writes, "I took him to see the old slave burying ground which grows more interesting day by day as new graves are brought to light from under the heavy brush, some mounds, some fallen in, all with their headstones and footstones." Headstones and footstones? Unbelievable. No headstones or footstones have ever been remarked on by anyone as far as I know. The fenced "African burial ground," as the archaeologists call it, is now kept weed-whacked to a shaggy twelve inches or so; all that honors the two hundred or so people reportedly interred there are the fence and the boulder monument with its carved inscription, BURYING GROUND OF THE COLORED PEOPLE OF THE MANOR SINCE 1651.

I read Cornelia's breathtaking sentence to a student archaeologist, Elizabeth Newman, who is helping me with the document inventory. The two of us drop everything and head outside to investigate through a sleety rain. We pound up the soggy, puddled drive to the graveyard under the pines and fumble our way through the gate, half expecting to find regular mounds and hollows, headstones and footstones, where we've never seen them before. Neither; nothing. Just brambles, withered field grasses, and poison ivy on the uneven ground. As we walk around, wondering what lies beneath our feet in this sacred space, we stare down at every step, feeling gullible, disconsolate. Elizabeth kicks a small stone like a kid. Then she says, "God, there are so many rocks in here, I guess because this area hasn't been tilled, and the glacial rocks haven't been cleared . . ." Her voice trails off, and a light goes on. The two of us—she, an archaeologist, and I, a landscape historian—are used to scrutinizing the earth for different patterns. We missed this one until Cornelia gave us the clue: we are stumbling over an army of small glacial boulders and fieldstone pebbles, many more, at a cursory glance, than anyplace else we have examined on the property. The largest have rolled or been rolled against the fence; the little ones are scattered underfoot, many half buried in the ice-glazed soil. Are these Cornelia's "headstones and footstones"? Early Dutch settlers on Long Island used fieldstones as grave markers, sometimes carving them with names or initials and dates. As part of their doctrine of "plainness," or simplicity, early Quakers sometimes also placed

The inscription "Burying Ground of the Colored People of the Manor Since 1651" was probably carved on a glacial erratic boulder in 1884, when the current generation of Sylvester descendants publicly celebrated their Brinley and Sylvester ancestors and the manor itself. The boulder lies next to the fenced burying ground and is visible from the drive.

such uncarved stones on graves, although the very earliest Friends, such as Grizzell and Nathaniel, apparently chose burial without markers of any kind. The body was a vessel for the soul, and when the soul was gone, the body had no meaning.

The people laid to rest in the "Burying Ground of the Colored People" underwent what the historian Orlando Patterson has famously called "social death," meaning that the society in which they lived rejected them as full human beings. But as they lie here, unmarked, they are also vividly present. As Jerome Handler and Ira Berlin have written about funeral practices in the Caribbean and the North American colonies, the slaves' exclusion from segregated white cemeteries meant that their own graveyards became free spaces, repositories of African religious and cultural traditions. Resourceful, thoughtful people, slaves used funeral rites to remember the arts of dying and the chain of ancestors that connected them to their homelands.

For the first Africans and their American-born children on Shelter Island, this ground would have meant something quite different from what it meant for the Sylvesters. It seems entirely unlikely that Nathaniel and Grizzell, despite their Quaker sensibilities, would have been sensitive to African cultural traditions. Although they had the upper hand—after all, they could physically punish or sell troublesome slaves, or ship them back to the West Indies, the ultimate threat—the Sylvesters were nonetheless far outnumbered. Practically speaking, in order to extract labor and ensure their own safety from those they held in bondage, they had no choice but to reach some kind of accommodation: perhaps more lenient treatment, better food, an increased rum ration, extra liberties, a gift of new clothing—or the chance to name a child. In considering the role of the African "guardians" whom slaver captains employed to control their captives aboard ship (and Shelter Island was like a ship, separated by water and with its sole authority, Nathaniel, as captain), Stephanie Smallwood writes, "Presumably, a preventive strategy was not only the best defense against slave insurrection, but also arguably the only reliable defense." The Sylvesters, by following a custom that had originated in Barbados—authorizing a place for slaves to bury their own dead—legitimized one outlet for powerful emotions.

There's no record of major uprisings, murders, or massacres occurring on Shelter Island during the entire history of slavery on the island, as first happened in New York City in 1712, when some twenty-five to fifty black men and women met at midnight to carry out the first stages of a well-organized plot to kill all the whites and destroy the city. Nine whites were killed; after the rebellion ended, thirty-one rebels were dead. Six had committed suicide; twenty-four were hanged, burned, or broken on the wheel; and the last, a pregnant woman, was allowed to give birth before she, too, was executed. The events of 1741, in which more than a hundred black New Yorkers were imprisoned, more than two dozen executed, and seventy sold as slaves in the Caribbean, has been shown by the historian Jill Lepore to be less a conspiracy than a hysterical overreaction to a (mostly imagined) plot. Despite subsequent restrictive legislation, urban slaves continued to gather in numbers, in defiance of the law.

Enslaved people nonetheless would have had many ways to retaliate short of outright rebellion: they could break or steal tools, pretend to be sick, or, in innumerable ways, do a work slow-down, interfering with the economic health of the plantation, despite whatever punishment might have been offered, including the cat-o'-nine-tails. Shelter Island's social dynamic probably involved delegating some authority to a trusted slave, already a leader in the black community, someone with a facility for language—African (particularly Akan), Creole, or newly acquired Algonquian, and of course English or Dutch—who could be counted on to inform Nathaniel of any threats to him and his family. No arms are listed in Nathaniel's inventory—were they locked up? As a Quaker who eschewed violence, did he have none? We don't know, but the absence is surprising. Through whatever means, a delicate balance seemingly held between the couple and their large black labor force.

Since the discovery of New York's African Burial Ground in 1991, other Northern slave burial sites, both private and public, have been identified and tidied up. In Orient, New York—a fifteen-minute ferry ride across Peconic Bay from Shelter Island—the Hog Pond Cemetery, which dates to the 1830s, recently acquired a new historical sign and had the toppled boulders of its old wall reset. Within it, the two imposing carved monuments of Dr. Seth Tuthill and his wife, Maria, face those of their "former servants," with whom the white couple wished to be buried, according to oral history and family research. The disparity between the masters' smooth tablets and their ex-slaves' blank, rough fieldstones in neat rows embodies a "family" hierarchy that the Tuthills, despite their apparent ecumenicism, would clearly have felt uncomfortable about erasing on earth, if not in heaven.

In this cemetery under the pines, investigation has at last begun: in March 2013 UMass initiated geophysical testing, the most respectful and least invasive initial approach. The site may have been an Indian burial sanctuary long before the Sylvesters and Africans arrived—Manhansetts and Montauketts reportedly lie there too. Although the manor team has been very careful to keep good relations with local tribal councils, they are understandably uneasy about allowing anyone to disturb the peace of the dead here: they have fresh memories of other Indian graveyards on the East End that were discovered in the course of construction and hastily covered up without ceremony. If testing indicates that human remains are present at the manor, archaeological excavation will proceed with tribal assent. Body positions and funeral ornaments may clarify the ethnicity of any remains; signs of age and gender may emerge; the effects of labor and nutrition may turn up in teeth and bones—although in the island's acid soil, "remains" might only be stains in the sand. Some corpses may have been buried only in shrouds, others in coffins. As at New York City's African Burial Ground, buttons and other fasteners may indicate what the dead wore to their graves; beads with sacred African meanings may be found looped around wrists and waists. The pattern of pins underground may show how a vanished shroud was carefully folded. In the African Burial Ground, the body of an infant cradled in the crook of its dead mother's arm had a tiny shroud secured with many more pins than necessary, as if the multitude of fasteners marked an outpouring of protectiveness.

"Byron Griffing [Shelter Island's town supervisor, 1892–1905] has the names, which I mean to have carved on a rough boulder on the crest of the slope at the head of Julia's grave," Cornelia's letter continued. No stone confirms the presence of the remains of Julia Dyd Havens Johnson, the manor's longtime housekeeper and the daughter of a former slave, who died in 1907. And the only known monument, at the bottom of the slope near the driveway, fails to record a single name. This incident is a perfect illustration of why archaeologists point out how misleading documentary evidence can be. Plans that get written down don't always get carried out. A search for Cornelia's list of names and for Griffing's records produced discouraging news: the farmhouse where his papers were stored was burned to the ground. The list, if it existed, was lost.

I'm angry at Cornelia's careless exaggeration about proper headstones and footstones, and her inability to carry through with honoring Julia, someone Cornelia had known all her life. Given that people so often don't do what they say, rage seems unreasonable. Yet both Cornelia's professed good intention and her inaction put her gesture where it belongs: in the category of condescending and sentimental racism typical of her class and day.

"The Negro Garden"

If death, its rituals, and the dense shade of the pines have consecrated the "Burying Ground of the Colored People of the Manor," everyday life, the seasonal rites of agriculture, and bright sunlight hallow the spot of earth that two nineteenth-century manor proprietors called the Negro Garden. For their makers, both grave and garden carried the sweetness of order, an order that the slaves themselves created out of the disorder and powerlessness of their lives. In death, Africans believed, the spirits of those they buried would be free to return to Africa; every spring, the seeds they chose to plant on Shelter Island would sprout from the ground. Digging the first spadeful of earth—the same act performed in both places, life and death answering each other—restored harmony and gravitas to the world.

In a daybook entry for May 7, 1856, three years before his death in 1859, Samuel Smith Gardiner, the husband of Nathaniel and Grizzell's great-great-great-granddaughter, Mary L'Hommedieu, noted matter-of-factly that he "Planted Six rows of corn in the Negro garden." By then, twenty-nine years after the end of slavery in New York State, the term "Negro garden" had lost its original sense as the only ground that plantation slaves were permitted to cultivate for themselves. But when the first Sylvesters began to import Africans, probably through the West Indies, both masters and slaves would have known of such plots in Barbados. While traces and records of many "Negro gardens" can be found on plantations in the South, few besides this one have even been mentioned in the North, where plantations run with slave labor were fewer to start with, and where, once free African Americans decamped for the cities, the ground was used for other purposes.

Those gardens provided more than physical sustenance. The Barbadian planter Henry Drax instructed his overseer, "For the enabling Negroes to go through their work with cheerfulness there must be great care taken that they have plantation provisions enough, besides the constant provision-ground of their own. The quantity and most convenient place for the Negroes Garden you must allot, which should be in the outskirts of the plantation." Drax added that better food—particularly food they'd grown themselves—made his slaves better workers.

But what crops familiar to Africans from a tropical climate could survive on Shelter Island? First on the list would have been Indian corn, or maize. This Native American grain, introduced into West Africa by the Portuguese as early as the second half of the sixteenth century, was loaded into the holds of slave ships as a durable staple food for the long westward passage. Slaves would also have been familiar with beans, yams, sorghum, and squash in Africa, some of which had originally been brought from the Americas by Europeans. They could have grown these plants for themselves on Shelter Island, particularly with Manhansett collaboration and encouragement in adapting to the climate.

Creating "social death" for Africans in America required shearing off the African past. The naked, possessionless people who stumbled off slave ships were regarded by the white colonials who greeted them as blanks, except for crude general observations as to which Africans were strongest or most suited to certain kinds of labor, or which were more likely to rebel. Similarly, American colonists conveniently classed the land they were claiming as an uncultivated wilderness, even though Indian land management was both sophisticated and intensive. Both false concepts were useful for Europeans intent on framing themselves as the legitimate masters of the new territory and its inhabitants.

African American scholars had long written in specialized journals about the role of Africa and Africans in the making of the Atlantic World (to borrow John Thornton's title). But it was only in the 1970s, after the civil rights movement and the publication of Philip Curtin's seminal *The Atlantic Slave Trade: A Census* (1969), that a wave of contemporary historians began to look backward for what anthropologists call *habitus*, the system of socialization beginning in childhood that weaves person and place into a single sociocultural structure. In the context of Africans arriving on Shelter Island in the 1650s and 1660s, habitus could mean things as diverse as carrying a body memory of how they held themselves in pride, sorrow, or joy, or of how to behave toward children and elders, or how to recognize familiar plants such as maize or any leafy plants that resembled callaloo, favored greens in the West Indies. Not all familiar crops would have thrived. Even if an African captive somehow managed

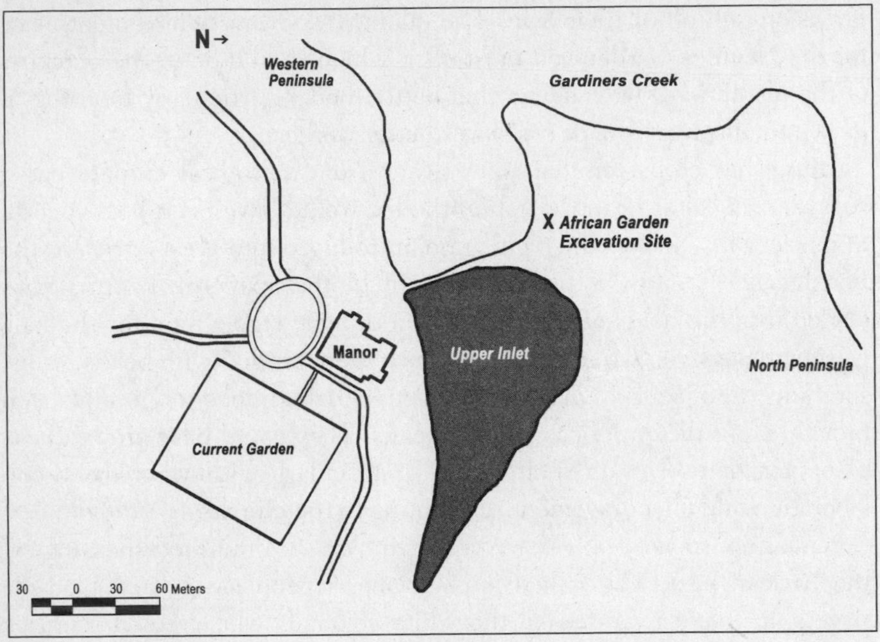

The African Garden site excavated by the University of Massachusetts team may be that of "the Negro Garden," as Samuel Gardiner called it in 1856. The area faces south on a gentle slope, with a low-tide spring nearby.

to smuggle a root of cassava, the bread of the tropics, to Shelter Island, frost would have killed it.

The first arrivals in colonial America, European and African alike, sought replication, not adaptation—until they learned that adaptation meant survival. "One is not born with a disposition to recollect," writes the neurologist Oliver Sacks. "This comes only with changes and separations in life—separations from people, from places, from events and situations, especially if they have been of great significance, have been deeply hated or loved . . . Discontinuity and nostalgia are most profound if, in growing up, we leave or lose the place where we were born and spent our childhood, if we become expatriates or exiles, if the place or the life we were brought up in is changed beyond recognition or destroyed."

So where on Shelter Island was this locus of love, labor, and memory, the "Negro garden"? Samuel Gardiner's bare notation gave no clue. We had to depend on his less reassuringly literal son-in-law, Eben Norton Horsford. Writing thirty years after Gardiner's daybook entry, he described the paths, tidal spring, shoreline indentations, and Indian village and graveyard of the North Peninsula, finishing with a flourish: "Between the spring and the end of the graveyard, runs the old hawthorn hedge, the office of which has been evident as it forms the limit of the Negro Garden, immemorially so called, and indicated the distance to which the servants might extend their spading the ground." (Horsford applied the word "servant," as did both Nathaniel Sylvester and Andy Fiske, to enslaved as well as free laborers.) There are now a number of paths, springs, and silted-up marshy areas but no visible signs of Manhansett burials or a hedge, as the entire peninsula has become a weedy succession forest.

The first tantalizing clue on the ground appeared when Steve and two graduate students, Anne Hancock and Lee Priddy, who would help lead the first summer of exploratory fieldwork, drove down from Boston on a cold March day in 1998. We walked together across the land bridge to the North Peninsula, which Steve, on the basis of the Gardiner and Horsford descriptions, had picked as a dig site for the season. Over the winter the ground had frozen, then thawed, heaving up stones and artifacts. We crossed the deep-cut old wagon road that runs from the stone bridge to the far side of the North Peninsula. Anne stooped down for the first find, a piece of a white-and-red-glazed pot. Then, quite a few steps farther on, she picked up a sherd that fitted it exactly. Lee spotted something brownishly different from the brown leaves and soil. She turned it over in her hand, and then, in a star turn only an archaeologist can pull off, said, "It's a piece of a clay colander, glazed inside, unglazed outside. The irregular holes tell me it dates to the seventeenth century." On track to become an archaeologist from childhood, Lee had been washing potsherds at Colonial Williamsburg since she was fifteen. I held the fragment in my hand: it became the fine indented foot and fat belly of a colander basin. The interior glaze gleamed. It looked rather like the colanders at Williams-Sonoma.

For Steve, Anne, and Lee, as historical archaeologists, this was only a piece of a European utensil without a material frame of reference to tie it to a specific ethnic use or period of manor settlement. It could have been brought to the North Peninsula at any time since it was made. It could have been dumped here as a broken piece. For me, this colander was a gathering basket. Garden produce is picked, washed, and sorted in a colander. Were we in the Africans' garden? I felt the tension between the archaeologists' thoughts and mine.

"Ground-truthing" is the term archaeologists automatically reach for when information they receive from outside a dig—from documents, for example—must be verified against what they find with shovel and trowel, followed by microscopic or chemical analysis. It's not just that archaeologists are a skeptical lot, suspicious of anything outside their own discipline (which they are), or that they chafe under what they perceive to be the unfair primacy of history as a discipline (which they do). It's also that they have a valid point. A written description in a letter like Cornelia's, or even in a court order dangling with seals, won't yield the same truth as the earth. As for geophysical testing—it produces "evidence," all right. For example, "resistance" (a change in soil compaction) on the West Lawn near the water *did* mean that Kvamme's testing gadget had registered a different material composition—but what material, exactly? What might first promise to be the footprint of the long-sought seventeenth-century warehouse may easily turn out to be nineteenth-century cast-iron pipes, as did in fact happen at the manor. Often only digging will tell.

For archaeologists, an area of flat ground may indicate past habitation and use. Absent other indicators, when first scanning a prospective site, their eyes rest on level areas. I began to read every flat place on the North Peninsula as an Indian village, or a plot that the Africans of the first generation gardened. Rereading Horsford's description of the North Peninsula, though, I found it confusing and vague; I wasn't sure he was actually describing this peninsula as the site of the Negro Garden. Could it have been closer to the seventeenth-century house? Every linear hump or ridge in the lawns around the existing house could mark a vanished fencerow; each line of more than four trees, no matter what the species, began to look like the ghost of a hedge. The landscape seemed unwilling to give up its secrets, or even to admit it had any secrets. It was time for me to give up on looking for the Negro Garden for a while and return to the documents.

It's May 2000, and I'm staring out the window of the ground floor back bedroom, my workroom. I've been sorting, transcribing, and inventorying Sylvester family papers since 1997, the year that Steve first visited the manor, even though I'm not sure that the story I'm interpreting from these fragments is a story, or makes sense, or is true. I tell myself, "I must not exaggerate; I must not underestimate." Is it too big a picture for me to comprehend? From the canals of Northern Europe and the slave castles of the African Gold Coast the line runs to this handsome, smallish house whose serene forehead also hides secrets, and to scientists and poets in nineteenth-century Cambridge, Massachusetts.

To the north, across the Upper Inlet, something has changed today. The pale green hillside is splashed with foamy white. I step outdoors to have a look. In searching for the hedge that "forms the limit of the Negro Garden," I hadn't previously paid much attention to some of the understory trees growing in the scrubby woodland on the other side of the land bridge—trees I could easily have identified, given my horticultural knowledge. Too tall for a hedge—about twenty-five feet in height—they are struggling and unhealthy: their papery-smooth bark is scarred, scabbed, pocked with borer holes, and many of the multistemmed trunks are decaying or rotten. They look like they need more sun. My eye moves upward. Today the canopies are blazing white with flowers, hawthorn flowers. Competition from taller succession-forest trees—black locusts and wild cherries—has forced this "hedge," if that is what I'm really looking at, to lift itself up into the air to find light. The line of trunks has been scattered and broadened by seedlings that sprouted from the pips of blackberries the birds ate and deposited in their droppings. I now remember tall treelike hawthorns in Wiltshire, in England. No longer useful as hedges, they mark the ghost edges of ancient pastures thrown together long ago to make bigger ones. They carry the same blaze of flowers in May, and have the same bittersweet, foxy perfume.

I break off a branch of frilly, shiny, two-and-a-half-inch-long deeply lobed leaves and serious two-inch thorns to take home for conclusive identification. Michael Dirr's *Manual of Woody Landscape Plants* confirms my guess: *Crataegus monogyna*, singleseed hawthorn, one of the two most common English hedging plants, originally used to keep livestock out of cultivated fields and imported into America in the seventeenth century. Peter Banks, a professional plowman and trainer of "heavy horses" (draft breeds such as Shires and Percherons), has told me that hawthorn hedge is still used today in England for livestock fencing and is sometimes interplanted with alder, holly, and blackthorn for additional strength. Could these really be Horsford's hawthorns? Could they indicate for us, at last, the site of the Negro Garden?

I must check out other parts of the property while the trees are still in flower, to see if this is the only place on the 243 acres where singleseed hawthorns grow in quantities large enough to sustain the memory of a hedge. Feeling the slow crawl of ticks, less sluggish in the warmer weather,

I head through the manor woods and along field edges adjacent to the home grounds. I find only one large hawthorn, by the cattail spring at the top of the Upper Inlet. But on the North Peninsula, 142 specimens stand in a broad, ragged line stretching from the south-facing slope of the Upper Inlet north toward the mouth of Gardiners Creek. I mark each tree with a pink plastic bellyband. Some trunks are less than three inches in diameter, some more than eighteen.

Using a laser beam shot from a transit atop a surveyor's tripod to a reflector set at the base of each hawthorn tree, the UMass graduate students input the location of every trunk as part of a GIS (Geographic Information System) program. The program is one of the many that digitally record all the excavated units that were first drawn painstakingly to scale by hand, then backfilled, and then input, throughout all the years of the dig. The GIS program also holds information about each unit in what are called geodatabases, which provide such information as the area of each individual rock or root. Such maps can be seen on a computer screen in sequence (in time) or in layers (in spatial depths).

This particular map includes rough outlines of all the blocks the archaeologists have excavated so far, the existing features of the man-made landscape—house, drives, outbuildings, garden, and the enormous boxwoods that were my first key to the age of the manor—and, within the outline of the North Peninsula, shown in bright green, one hundred and forty-three little light brown specks—the hawthorn trunks—in a wide, curving constellation.

A photograph taken around 1900, after Cornelia Horsford had rebuilt the land bridge, shows her proudly atop it. Behind her is the North Peninsula, a startlingly bald hump cleared of all vegetation but closely cropped grass; apparently it was being used as a pasture. Maddeningly, the photographer has framed out of the picture the rest of what we want to see: the westward portion of the peninsula that presumably—wishfully—contained the Negro Garden, and the area Horsford described as the site of the Indian burial ground. But in the left corner of the picture a few small trees stand in a straight line exactly where the thickest clump of present-day hawthorns is flowering.

In the fall of 2000, the New York Botanical Garden sent two experts from the Bronx to "core" the hawthorns—to determine their age by measuring annual growth rings—and to "observe the landforms," which is more or less what the Sylvester brothers and their partners did when they

At the far left of this detail of a c.1900 photograph stands a line of small trees, possibly a remnant of the hawthorn hedge mentioned by E. N. Horsford that "formed the limit of the Negro Garden." It is just east of the UMass African Garden excavation. The land bridge in the center of the picture was built or reconstructed at this time by Horsford's daughter Cornelia, perhaps the unidentified figure standing on the bridge.

first scouted Shelter Island as a provisioning plantation. Long, lean men of a recognizable arborist type, dressed in NYBG dark green, arrived at the manor on a bright sunny day. From a small case they pulled out a Matson increment borer, a simple corkscrewlike device that, without harming the trees, produces five-millimeter-thick, multicolored corings that document the growth of each trunk, from the pinkish heartwood out to the dark bark. The corings of several ancient-looking hawthorns were carefully transferred to soda straws and taken back to the lab to be dried, dissected, and analyzed. These trees in fact proved too young to be Eben Horsford's hedge, but the scientists concluded they are very probably descendants of the original hawthorns that have grown up on or close to the site of that planting. Nearby terrain provides confirming evidence about the possible sites of the Indian cemetery and garden.

Any farmer knows that a gentle south-facing slope, favored by early spring warming and abundant exposure to sun, is a good place for agriculture. Erosion patterns suggest that the area south and east of the hawthorns was kept cleared and cultivated for a long time, but the linear imprints of cultivation have been softly etched away.

In order to place the hawthorns in context, more corings were taken from trees on the northwest side of the wagon road: two large native hardwoods, a black walnut and a red oak. Both are too young for Horsford to have seen them in the 1880s when he wrote his description. Walnut and oak are forest trees; the trees on the southeast side of the track, where the arborists cored the hawthorns, are smaller in stature and mostly varieties that colonize previously disturbed soil. So the vegetation distinctly differs from one side of the track to the other. The NYBG researchers were confident in saying that the soil surrounding the oak and walnut "has not been used for some time for agriculture."

We walked farther north and west, toward the top of the hill and the mouth of Gardiners Creek. The trees, almost all natives—oaks, maples, and walnuts—grow taller here. They are the guardians of this site. Maybe the scientists are right: no one dug or plowed this higher ground. Was it perhaps because tradition said "Do not dig here," even if the reasons behind the warning had been long forgotten?

The UMass team opened units down along the south shore of the creek to seek evidence of the Negro Garden. In the steamy summer days, shrieking with mosquitoes, Craig Cipolla led a team that cautiously cleared the thick brambles, bittersweet, saplings, and poison ivy and then even more cautiously lifted dense matted roots and topsoil. Faint traces of cultivation can be as powdery as moths' wings—the marks of wooden plows or hoes are far less stable than those left by stone foundations. When Craig found long, shallow, crumbly scratches in the earth—"plow scars"—he called me away from the workroom to come see. They resembled the lines of a child's secret letter written in lemon juice, whose invisible script appears only when the paper is held over heat—except here it was Craig telling me what I was looking at that made me see it. The team went on to uncover possible planting pits or fence postholes and a larger pit containing ceramics dating to the late seventeenth and early eighteenth century, but not a trace of food waste—a good sign, since they were looking for a garden rather than a dwelling where people cooked and ate what they grew. A second season of excavation produced more inconclusive yet tantalizing evidence: a few more lines in the soil that were tentatively identified as plow scars, as well as finds ranging from pre-contact lithics (chipped stone artifacts) to antebellum ceramics from the era when Samuel Gardiner planted his "six rows of corn in the Negro garden."

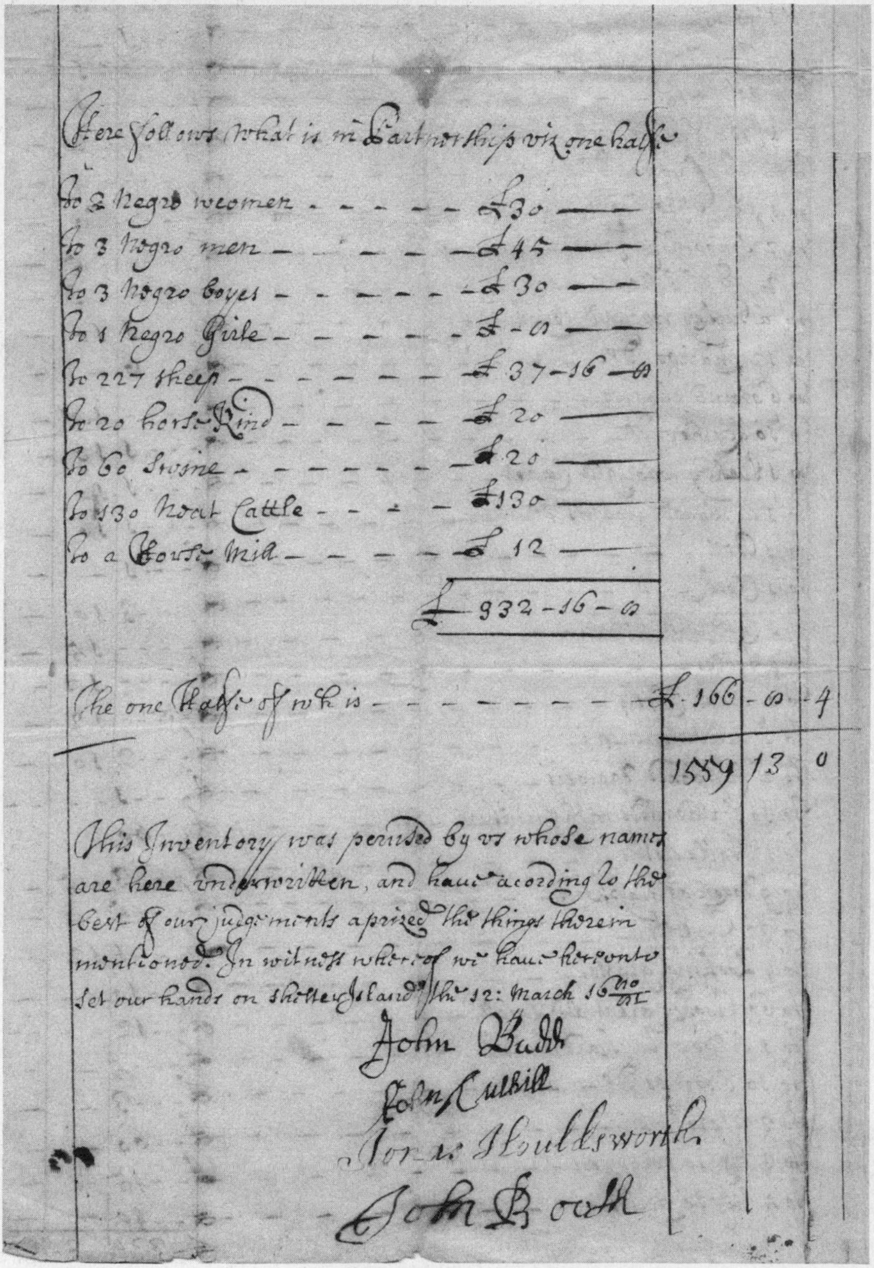

Here follows what is in Partnership viz one halfe

To 2 Negro weomen	£30
To 3 Negro men	£45
To 3 Negro boyes	£30
To 1 Negro Girle	£01
To 227 sheep	£37-16-0
To 20 horse kind	£20
To 60 Swine	£20
To 130 Neat Cattle	£130
To a Horse Mill	£12
	£332-16-0

The one halfe of wh is — £166-0-4

1559 13 0

This Inventory was perused by us whose names are here underwritten, and have according to the best of our judgements aprized the things therein mentioned. In witness whereof we have hereunto set our hands on Shelter Island the 12: March 16 80/81

John Budd
John Cutbill
Jonas Houldsworth
John Booth

On September 22, 1680, after Nathaniel's death, appraisers came to assess the value of his estate, including the women and men, the boys and girls, who had contributed to his wealth with their labor. The nine listed here were held "in partnership," meaning they were nominally owned by the heirs of Nathaniel's brother Constant and Thomas Middleton. (The other fifteen people are noted elsewhere in the probate as Nathaniel's or Grizzell's property.) The partners were dead, but their claim of ownership of people as chattel lived on.

Work and Wealth

By 1664, when Great Britain conquered New Netherland, enslaved and free blacks already accounted for about 5 percent of the colony's overall population; in New York City, they comprised 10 percent of the total. The Dutch West India Company had begun to import slaves to New Netherland as early as the 1630s, laying the basis of what would become the largest African population of any Northern colony. Only in the mid-eighteenth century would the proportion of blacks (then almost all enslaved) in Charleston surpass the percentage of blacks in New York City's population.

A fair number of free blacks and mulattoes lived in seventeenth-century New York under Dutch rule. And, despite the passage in 1665 of English legislation dubbed the Duke's Laws, which imposed harsher versions of Dutch precedents, a handful of people of African descent continued to marry whites, own land, and enjoy some of the privileges New Netherland had granted them. Over the decades that followed, a few slaves were freed, almost always by the terms of their owners' wills after a lifetime of service, or they managed to buy their way out of bondage. A scant number even became landholders and employed white labor.

By 1698, Suffolk County's census listed 558 blacks in a total population of 2,679, or about 20 percent. (Among them were Shelter Islanders Tony and Maria; the two Semnies; Hope, Jacquero and Hannah's daughter; and two other women named in Nathaniel's will as girls, Prescilla and Grace, all now listed as in Southold.) By the end of the seventeenth century, Long Islanders owned half the slaves in New York Colony, and slave ownership was widely dispersed throughout all levels of society. It remained rare to find establishments on Long Island like that of the first-generation Sylvesters (the region's largest seventeenth-century slave holding) because the average smaller farm required fewer slaves. When more slave children were born than were needed, it was profitable to sell them, or hire them out, with the master pocketing the profits as a matter of course.

Nathaniel's estate, valued in probate in 1680 at almost £1,560, was colossal by East End standards. He carefully specified in his will (as the appraisers would also do in the probate) what didn't belong solely to him on the island, the biggest divisions being the land (4,000 acres at £700), half the value of the slaves (£113, or nine people), and half the livestock (£207).

Shelter Island had been held in common since 1651, when the four merchants initially signed their contract. One of the original partners, Thomas Rous, sold out quickly to a John Booth (whose descendants still live in Southold today); Booth then ran into debt and sold his share to Nathaniel and Constant, meaning that by 1660 the brothers owned three-quarters of the island between them, with Middleton retaining his quarter share. In 1680, when Nathaniel wrote his will, the claims of the heirs of Constant and Thomas Middleton had to be respected—at least on paper—which was what happened. Even as Nathaniel described the partners' legal claims ("the said Moyetie or halfe part of Shelter Island . . . and of the Stock Negroes horses, Mares Cattle, Sheep, etc."), in the next breath he disputed them. He complained that he had made "great disbursments" to improve the partners' half as well as his own; that Constant owed him "great sums of Money"; and that he had been forced to pay to the Dutch a £500 penalty on his partners' shares, thereby extinguishing his partners' claims. The only resident partner who had worked for thirty years to create the island's wealth and stability as a provisioning plantation, Nathaniel was, in fact, claiming the entire place, which, it appears, he loved. None of the rightful heirs turned up to dispute his ownership until 1733, when Grace Sylvester renounced her claim on behalf of young Henry Lloyd, her first cousin once removed, who conveyed it to Brinley Sylvester.

Using a price index adjusted for inflation, the inventoried items would now be worth $311,817, but the buying power of Nathaniel's estate in 1680 would have been several times greater than this indicates. Consider, for example, the true worth of the Sylvesters' clock (an expensive, almost certainly imported rarity in a seventeenth-century colonial household), listed at £3. That amount equaled 2 percent of the appraised value of all manor housing, a ridiculously disproportionate amount by modern standards.

If we include Nathaniel's partners' shares in the value of his estate, bringing it to £2,426.4.4, a comparison with the estates of roughly contemporaneous merchants and planters will illustrate his financial standing among his peers. William Brenton of Rhode Island, a merchant and farmer in the same livestock and provisioning business as Nathaniel, inventoried his estate at £10,768.13.4 a year before his death in 1673. In 1691, Nathaniel's friend and fellow Quaker Colonel Lewis Morris, of Barbados, New Jersey, and New York, left an estate valued at £4,915, excluding his considerable landholdings. Barbadian sugar merchants like Constant and Thomas Middleton had accumulated still larger estates and enjoyed more lavish incomes. I don't think Nathaniel made such comparisons; he had started off as the junior partner on a remote island, and he died feeling sure—if no one came along to challenge him, at any rate—that he had become master of all he surveyed, as he expected his children would be after him.

Nathaniel's annual income, estimated at approximately £200 sterling (some £365,000, or $589,000 if valued today), which was derived from shipping ventures, the resale of sugar products, and the sale of farm goods, livestock, manufactured imports, and perhaps even slaves, was eight to ten times that of a skilled English craftsman in the building trades. Grizzell's considerable jointure of one hundred pounds per annum also boosted the income stream indirectly. In 1658, Nathaniel sold a firkin (56 pounds) of butter, two gallons of cider, and a bushel of pears for twelve shillings, sixpence. Had he needed to purchase groceries to supply his own household, instead of producing food on Shelter Island, he would have run through his income fairly quickly. And even though he incurred initial capital costs—for importing cattle, say, or pear tree grafts—most of the labor was unpaid.

Like every colonist, from the smallest smallholder to the largest landowners of New England or the South, Nathaniel kept much of what he owned in woodland (for timber and fuel) and in pasture (for animals he could sell on the hoof or as salt meat). Many acres lay in valuable salt marsh for hay; others in swamp, bog, and freshwater ponds. The economy of the plantation was a delicate balance between supply and demand for the staples the island produced and the sugar products and manufactured goods Nathaniel imported and resold. He could have purchased more slaves from the West Indies, had he thought he needed to in order to produce more for the market. He didn't, so it seems the balance worked for him. He also planned that parts of the island were to be improved by his sons as their homesteads.

Most property owners, when they had cash to spare, bought more land as investments. By 1665, Nathaniel was financially secure enough to option Hog Neck (now Lloyd Neck) in Oyster Bay, Long Island, for £400. By 1667 he owned the mill at Tom's Creek (Hashamomack) in nearby Southold and had planted an orchard there. He possessed other lots on the North Fork and on Block Island, and he was one of the group (almost all of them religious dissenters of one sort or another) who bought miles of land in New Jersey in 1665. As of 1671 he was listed as a merchant of Newport as well as Shelter Island.

Planting, harvesting, and threshing the sixty-five acres of "planting feelds," and planting meadows and grazing land with English grasses, produced precious, sometimes irreplaceable crops. In the first week of April 1678, Nathaniel found his "meadows and mowing land" trampled and despoiled by "divers strange horses" that had "come over to his island" by swimming the narrow strait from North Haven. A peninsula barely attached to the mainland, and therefore desirable as common pasture once the "neck" was fenced and predators killed, North Haven belonged to the nearest town to the west, Southampton. Nathaniel politely notified the citizens of Southampton that "hee, being very desirous to still continue the good corespondence with this said town . . . and very loth to offer violence to any neighbors' horses or horse kind that may at any time (unknown to them) make escape to his island, thought good to . . . procure the same to bee published." Nathaniel wanted those horses off the island, but "in regard to the present busie time of sowing and planting hee yet gives liberty to the neighbors of Southampton . . . until the last day of the third month (called May) . . . to fetch off their horses from his said Island." Otherwise, he said, he would have to destroy the animals, "the which he doth declare he is exceedingly loth to doe." Nathaniel honored his neighbors "busie time," but he also cared for his meadows and fields, probably sown with English grasses for summer grazing and winter hay to feed all his stock. A whole year's worth of labor in the island fields may have been at stake.

What meaning could their own labor have had for those who got no share of the profits? Tilling an acre of ground with a horse-drawn single-share moldboard plow means walking twenty-one miles, says Peter Banks. A seventeenth-century English field strip measured about five to six acres. (What's called the "windmill field" at the manor today is four acres.) Because of the inexorable green logic of growth, Banks points out, "you wouldn't want to take longer than a week to plow any field—you want to harvest it all at the same time." A suitable "heavy" horse, such as Banks's big, handsome Major, a registered Shire, who stands six feet four inches at the withers (the high point between a horse's shoulders), has shod feet that weigh at least ten pounds apiece. When Banks drives this well-broken creature to the plow, he lengthens his own stride to keep up, holds the reins chest high, and is carried springily along the furrow by the powerful advance of his two-ton partner. "Steady, steady," Banks practically whispers when they reach the end of a furrow. "A well-trained horse can turn around almost in his own tracks," Banks explains, and Major does just that, his giant, shining haunches shifting steadily, almost in place, from side to side as he turns.

Inevitably, when a solitary Tammero, or Tony, or Negro Jenkin, or Black John, or J.O. plowed a manor field, back and forth, back and forth, he knew he was retracing his own steps, with no escape and no reward. But sometimes even within the poverty and powerlessness of his life, when he walked behind an animal like Major (or a team of oxen), he could instead have felt—for a brief, beautiful moment—in step with himself and his work, and in control.

12

"Oppression upon the Mind"

"God in Every Man"

In the Quaker cemetery at the top of Gardiners Creek, spangled shadows cast by high oaks flick across the lichen-crusted nineteenth-century stone table monument to Nathaniel Sylvester. The inscription commemorates him as one who sheltered Friends "Persecuted for Conscience' Sake" in New England. Not as the slaveholding Quaker he was. Only a half mile separates this spot from the "Burying Ground of the Colored People," a short distance that underlines the disorienting, dislocating contradiction for anyone today between the words "Quaker" and "slaveholder."

How can it be that Quakers, the first Americans to abolish slavery in the eighteenth century, were themselves originally slave owners and—in some cases—even slave traders? Questions about the morality of slavery had been raised early on by George Fox. Soon after his convincement (as Quakers call conversion) in England in 1647, he preached, "There is that of God in every man." A decade later he published an epistle, "To Friends Beyond Sea, that have Blacks and Indian Slaves," reminding his coreligionists that God "hath made all Nations of one Blood."

In Barbados, in a teaching later published as "Gospel Family-Order" that Fox preached when he was staying at the sugar plantation of Shelter Island partner Thomas Rous, Fox expounded on 1 Corinthians 7:22: "He that is called in the Lord, being a Servant, is the Lord's free Man." Fox urged planters to bring their slaves to meeting, as Quakers call their form of church service; those Friends who did so, including Thomas Rous, were heavily fined by the authorities. Fox's explosive words could make a slave believe that conversion to Christianity entitled a "free Man" to freedom from more than "Sin and spiritual Bondage." Fox also spoke for slaves' rights to humane treatment and the sacrament of marriage. Aware that planters were listening to what they considered very subversive teachings, Fox cautiously proposed that they *eventually* liberate their Africans—after nearly a lifetime of service. His most direct appeal to slaveholders simply adapted the Golden Rule: "Consider with your selves, if you were in the same Condition as the Blacks are . . . you would think it . . . very great Bondage and Cruelty . . . And therefore consider seriously of this, and do you for them and to them, as you would willingly have them or any other to do unto you."

Completely altering the social system was not Fox's goal. He sought to shape a religious organization and win converts who, struck by the Inner Light, would radically change their own lives and act more humanely. When Barbadian planters and clergy pounced on the perils of advocating manumission, Fox equivocated. Far from teaching "the Negars to Rebel . . . a thing we do utterly abhor and detest in and from our Hearts," he wrote, a true Quaker should admonish slaves "To be Sober, and to Fear God, and to love their Masters and Mistresses, and to be Faithful and Diligent in their Masters Service and Business."

As slavery in American and West Indian colonies expanded at an explosive rate over the first decades of the Society's growth, a few doubts, a very few doubts, about the institution were expressed during the seventeenth century—by Quakers or anyone else. Quaker William Edmundson, pompous and unlikable (Roger Williams said he had "a flash of wit, a Face of Brass, and a tongue set on fire from the Hell of Lyes and Fury") but a hero nonetheless, launched the first American attack on the immorality of slavery in 1676. He addressed a meeting of slave-owning Newport Friends who regularly gathered at the Coddingtons' and who almost certainly didn't want to hear what he had to say. As an Irishman, Edmundson drew a direct connection between African slavery and his compatriots' brutal subjugation to English rule. He spoke out after the end of King Philip's War in the region in 1676, when Indian captives were shipped to the Caribbean—just as Irish slaves had been shipped to America throughout the 1650s—under the old rationale that prisoners of war deserved this fate. Debate briefly flared up over the legitimacy of lifelong servitude for Indians who were *not* prisoners of war. "And many of you count it unlawful to make slaves of the Indians, and if so, then why the negroes?" thundered Edmundson, asking his slave-owning listeners to "consider their condition of perpetual slavery, and make their condition your own

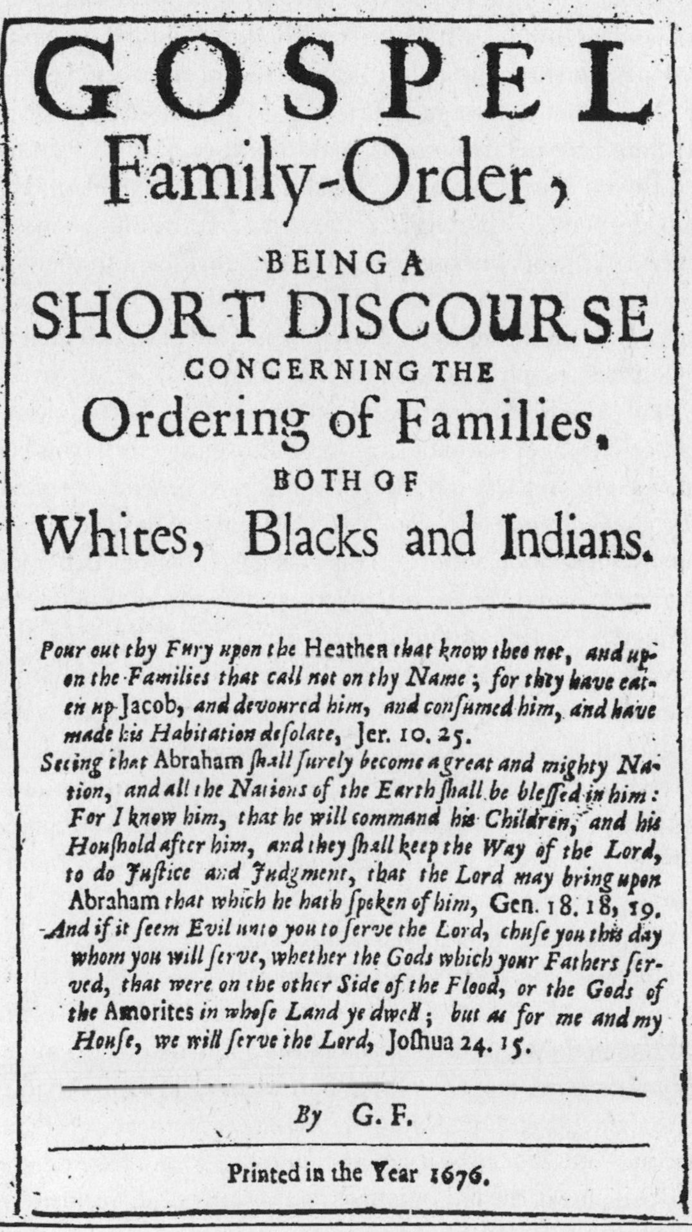

GOSPEL
Family-Order,
BEING A
SHORT DISCOURSE
CONCERNING THE
Ordering of Families,
BOTH OF
Whites, Blacks and Indians.

Pour out thy Fury upon the Heathen *that know thee not, and upon the Families that call not on thy Name; for they have eaten up* Jacob, *and devoured him, and conſumed him, and have made his Habitation deſolate,* Jer. 10. 25.

Seeing that Abraham *ſhall ſurely become a great and mighty Nation, and all the Nations of the Earth ſhall be bleſſed in him: For I know him, that he will command his Children, and his Houſhold after him, and they ſhall keep the Way of the Lord, to do Juſtice and Judgment, that the Lord may bring upon* Abraham *that which he hath ſpoken of him,* Gen. 18. 18, 19.

And if it ſeem Evil unto you to ſerve the Lord, chuſe you this day whom you will ſerve, whether the Gods which your Fathers ſerved, that were on the other Side of the Flood, or the Gods of the Amorites *in whoſe Land ye dwell; but as for me and my Houſe, we will ſerve the Lord,* Joſhua 24. 15.

By G. F.

Printed in the Year 1676.

Preaching on Barbados in 1671, George Fox envisioned a "Government of Families" that included "those bought with money," meaning both indentured servants and slaves.

[i.e. free them] . . . for perpetual slavery is an agrivasion [*sic*], and an oppression upon the mind." After leaving Rhode Island, the itinerant Irish missionary passed through Shelter Island, holding a meeting there as the guest of "Nathaniel Sylvester, a Friend"—who was also the possessor of twenty-four slaves. The outspoken Edmundson must have raised the subject with his hosts. As observant Friends, Nathaniel and Grizzell would have respected "openings" of the spirit like Edmundson's as communications from God without feeling obliged to adhere to them as absolute commandments. Even if the Sylvesters acknowledged, in the silence of meeting and within themselves, where their belief in spiritual equality could lead, it was simply a possibility to ponder.

Why didn't the Sylvesters free their slaves? The short answer is that like other early Quaker slaveholders—and like "early Christians" or members of an opposition party that becomes the government—they had been something else before. They were slaveholders who derived their wealth and status from the people they held as chattel. And after "convincement," Nathaniel and Grizzell continued to live as they previously had.

Their quarter century of Quaker activism does not seem to have made them sensitive to the plight of their slaves. Although Nathaniel listed black families with their children in his will, neither he nor his wife held those relationships sacrosanct: all the offspring of Shelter Island slaves suffered the same fate as Hope and Isabell, Jacquero and Hannah's girls. Separated from their parents and from each other, they were property, to be tossed back and forth after Nathaniel's death as various family debts got paid off.

They seem hypocritical to us, accustomed as we are to regard the Friends as people who observe a higher spiritual standard. They enjoyed the economic benefits of owning human property while professing their belief in the sacredness of the individual, the ability of every person to find an inner path to God, and the perfectibility of each life. Even the details that set Quakers apart outwardly—the democratic *thees* and *thous*, their refusal to take off their hats to show deference to another person—run counter to the idea of enslavement based on skin color. Only after a century of debate, and arising from the slow conversations among Friends about the nature of property and human nature, did any American Quaker meeting outlaw members who owned slaves. The Philadelphia Friends did so in 1776, the year that also saw the declaration (written primarily by the slaveholder Thomas Jefferson) that says "We hold these truths to be self-evident, that all men are created equal, that they are endowed by their Creator with certain unalienable rights, that among these are life, liberty, and the pursuit of happiness."

"Offensive Carriage Concerning the Saboth"

Nathaniel personified what the Quaker historian Rufus Jones called "prepared ground": the right man in the right place at the right time to give what would become the Society of Friends a foothold in America. Brought up as a religious nonconformist, Nathaniel would have been open to the radical message brought to the New World by Friends traveling first to Barbados in 1655. He chose the right place to settle: Long Island's East End, where the towns only nominally adhered to the strict religious covenant of the New Haven Colony. The watery, uncertain miles between New Haven and Long Island gave dissidents room to feel estranged from the colony's particularly godly and restrictive form of Puritan governance. They fretted over New Haven's cumbersome and centralized judiciary and what they saw as misuse of tax revenues. Most of all they wanted the opportunity to vote in general and local elections, denied them because they were merely landholders, not full church members, or "saints," as the Puritan church called their elect. ("Freemen," as voting members were called, formed only a small percentage of Southold's inhabitants.) Southolders in particular were guilty of "high miscariages." In March 1653, for example, Nathaniel and his new young Shelter Island partner, Ensign John Booth, swore that the local pastor's son had threatened to recruit sixty Indians and "make a garrison at Southhold to defend him against the power of Newhaven."

Similar threats of revolt against the colonial government shake many pages of New Haven and Southold's court records, a mix of what today would be police blotter reports and criminal trial proceedings. More often than not, the accused admitted guilt, repented publicly, confessed to having "feared that in his passion and distemper he might speake such things as are charged," and appealed for a light sentence. This was Nathaniel's strategy in his first litigious encounter with New Haven in 1654, when his defiance erupted, a sign that his resentment of church-and-state regimes predated his Quaker convincement by at least three years. New Haven's general court accused him of calling the colonial government "tyrannical," and declared his "carriage concerning the Saboth & ordinance" in Southold "offensive." (It sounds as though he spoke out against a requirement that all attend church or pay to support the minister.)

Even before he faced Governor Theophilus Eaton and the gathered deputies and magistrates of the colony, including Deputy Governor Stephen Goodyear (the same Stephen Goodyear who had sold the island to the partners), Nathaniel had already "shewed much passion and hight of spirit [before a lesser bar], to the courts great dissatisfaction." Worse yet, furious over rumors that Southold was about to ban him from the town, he had threatened that "if any mett him in the streets and medled with him he would pistoll [shoot] them." A sidebar conference with Governor Eaton persuaded Nathaniel to back down. Admitting that he was guilty as charged, he expressed regret for "too much bitterness of speech, wch he now sees the evil of and hopes to walk inoffensively for time to come." The bench informed "Capt. Silvster that [it was] willing to take satisfaction, hopeing he sees his evill." This moment in court was Nathaniel's one stab at getting along with the New Haven regime. From then on he used the law to further his commercial enterprises and to conduct political and military maneuvers, but he refused to be held accountable to the state for his beliefs.

The Darkness Within

In 1656, two years after Nathaniel's trial, eight English Quakers took passage to Boston aboard the *Speedwell*. Upon arrival, they were imprisoned for eleven weeks for sedition and heresy and shipped back home at the captain's expense. It seems almost too good to be true for this story that another passenger on the *Speedwell*'s westward voyage was twenty-three-year-old Francis Brinley, Grizzell's brother, returning to the colonies from England, given his expressed distaste for Quakers in general. If Nathaniel and Grizzell hadn't previously heard of the Friends from Thomas Rous and his son, John, among the first Barbadian Quaker converts, Francis certainly would have brought news of his shipmates to Shelter Island. The Quakers' daily shipboard prayer meetings surely repelled this conservative young gentleman. They shouted and moaned, recounted their "night-journeys," spoke in tongues, urgently embraced one another, and fell to the deck. Being struck by the Inner Light—the presence of God within every human soul—was a physical assault; men and women found this encounter as unsettling and painful as it was joyful. The "children of the light," as they styled themselves, swam to America on a sea of dreams. God's hand hovered overhead and every journey gave proof of miraculous escapes, proving that the Lord guided the traveler to safety "as a man leads a horse by the head."

To most present-day Americans, Quaker history embodies a magnificent struggle within the colonies for the rights to free speech, religious toleration, and the separation of church and state. Our Quakers are Gary Cooper as a pacifist refusing to fight in the Civil War in *Friendly Persuasion*, or the painter Edward Hicks's chummy lions and lambs in multiple versions of *The Peaceable Kingdom*. The historian Barry Levy offers George Fox (1624–1691) as a classic frontier hero, even before he left the Old World for the New. "In his story," Levy writes, drawing on the journal that Fox published late in life, "a young shepherd from Leicestershire with a divine call rides on horseback through the edges of England, restoring insane women to inner peace, frightening cosmopolitan ministers from their pulpits, piercing judges into anguish with his eyes, enduring repeated riots and stonings without recanting or even changing his facial expression. He invades the center of cosmopolitan life, London, where he earns the respect of the country's leader, Oliver Cromwell . . . The journal is spiced with amazing tales, home remedies, egalitarian values, atrocious spelling, and a larger than life manly, gentle folk hero dressed in leather britches."

Fox's accounts of his mystical experiences and the certainty of his faith fired many converts, who, like him, came "up in spirit through the flaming sword into the paradise of God" and found that "all things were new, and all the creation gave another smell unto me than before." Fellow Quaker Robert Barclay wrote that in meetings, "there will be such a painful travel [travail] found in the soul, that it will even work upon the outward man, so that . . . the body will be greatly shaken, and many groans sighs and tears. Sometimes the Power of God will break forth into a whole meeting." Anyone, man or woman, could obtain mercy from God and become "an heir to His kingdom, a member of His body, a minister of His Spirit, and an inheritor of His Eternal rest blessed forever." Fox's crusade, "the Lamb's War," was first a war against the darkness within. When a Massachusetts inquisitor asked one *Speedwell* Friend where this "dark place" was, the prisoner placed his hand over his heart and answered, "It is under my hand."

Like Francis Brinley, the Puritans viewed Quakers as anything but heroes. Puritans saw them as dangerous subversives intent on infecting every aspect of existence with their seditious beliefs. Saying they always spoke the truth and had no need to swear to it, Friends would not take an oath, which eliminated them from government service and made them suspect in business dealings to anyone but fellow Quakers. According to the authorities, a particular communal failing—since Indians were considered a constant threat—was their refusal to take up arms to defend themselves or their communities.

Alarmed magistrates and ministers saw the Quakers as an incoming wave of wild sectarians, like those who had proliferated during the runup to the English Civil War in the tumultuous 1640s. This fear inspired repressive legislation: only nine years after Fox first preached in England, Massachusetts enacted its first anti-Quaker law in October 1656, imposing an enormous fine of £100 (about $16,000 today) on any ship captain who brought foreign Friends into the colony. The law also required that he transport these undesirables out of the Bay Colony at his own cost. Resident Quakers faced fines as well as incarceration, whipping, forced labor, and restricted public speech. Legislation in 1657 mandated branding, boring the tongue with a red-hot poker, and the cropping of ears. In 1658, nonresident Quakers were sentenced to banishment on pain of death. Other New England colonies followed suit, although none hounded Quakers as vengefully as did Massachusetts.

The earliest Puritan apologia for such persecution (published in 1659) painted Quakers as heretical lunatics and dangerous anarchists. Friends fired back with *New England Judged* (1661), portraying the Puritans as sadists and hypocrites. Historians have rounded up the considerable reasons why the Puritan establishment found Quakers so toxic—and why much of what Friends preached sounds alluring today. Quakers denied original sin and proclaimed their own salvation to be unconditional. They insisted that any convinced man or woman could find divine truth and preach it as well as a university-trained minister. They welcomed women as preachers and itinerant "witnesses to truth" who willingly left home and family. They believed that spiritual rebirth lifted the curse Genesis had laid on women, making them equal partners in marriage "as they were before the Fall"—an earth-shattering heresy for Puritans and most other Christians. Quakers also rejected orthodox assertions that God had inflicted the pain of childbirth as punishment for Eve's disobedience; instead, they argued, this was but another part of incomprehensible suffering throughout the world. Puritans warned that such challenges to conventional rules of family order doomed women to the flames of lust and adultery.

As alarming for Puritans as the number and kind of converts the Friends attracted was the freewheeling community they enjoyed. Quakers served and supported each other as "children of the light" who would carry out the holy work of conversion. Quakers wrote to each other with an ecstatic ardor that can sound steamily erotic. A feverish, almost physical heat emanates from their religious transports. Their correspondence does not distinguish between the sexes, impose any hierarchy on family relationships, or differentiate degrees of friendship—all are lovers. Although they embrace each other first and foremost as lovers of Christ, they also prize one another's courage, fortitude, spiritual insights, and suffering. The tender rapture Quakers shared in the trenches helped them to overcome distance, isolation, and fear.

For the Massachusetts Bay colonists, determined to forge a commonwealth with a strong work ethic and an ironclad chain of command, these free-floating, fire-breathing enthusiasts were "masterless men." Vagrancy, homelessness, and idleness represented gross social and religious disorder in their Puritan world. Poverty signified God's displeasure. It didn't help that many early Quakers came from the lesser ranks of society and had little education: they were tenant farmers, servants, weavers, shepherds, cobblers, plowmen, and yeomen before leaving those lives behind. Last but never least, Quakers were often suspected of witchcraft: "If the heretics were witches, their success at converting English men and women to their blasphemous views was much easier to explain," writes the historian Carla Gardina Pestana.

Colonial Puritans read about the civil disobedience that Quakers in the mother country used to expose "false worship"—meaning any religion but their own Quaker faith. English Friends with ash-smeared bodies and faces burst into churches and tore their clothes to shreds. Quaker women walked through the streets "going naked for a sign" (probably meaning that they stripped to their short transparent shifts) to signify their Edenic spiritual purity. In Boston, Friends smashed bottles to smithereens on a Puritan meetinghouse floor in 1658 to show how the Lord would smash all who ignored their teachings. Refusing to pay tithes to "hireling" ministers, Quaker missionaries accused Puritan clergymen wholesale of lying to uphold the institutional power that blocked believers from God's truth. John Rous, Humphrey Norton, and other Friends who sought to break open the colonies for the Lord headed to New England, where resistance was strongest. Henry Fell, an early visitor to Shelter Island, wrote, "The word of ye lord came to mee that I should goe to New England there to be a witness for him . . . For his word was as a fire & a hamer in me." Savage persecution only intensified Friends' zeal. For Quakers, as for early Christians, the idea of valiant suffering was deeply ingrained. William Penn, the founder of Pennsylvania, titled his first book, written in the Tower of London after his convincement, *No Cross, No Crown*.

Puritans denounced Quaker meetings as savage and as uncivilized as Indian powwows. Roger Williams, who detested what he saw as Quaker intolerance and pride, wrote that Fox displayed a "loose and wild spirit" in a debate with university-educated New England ministers. The Friend leaped and skipped from topic to topic "like a wild satyre or Indian, catching and snapping at here and there a sentence." In fact, Friends and Indians got along remarkably well. The missionary John Taylor, a Yorkshireman convinced by Fox, "came late into an Indian Town" one evening on his way to Shelter Island in 1659. He was invited to spend the night in a "Wigwam or House." One tribal elder lay ill next door, and "by and by came a great many lusty proper Men, Indians all, and sat down, and every one had a short Truncheon Stick in their hands pretty thick, about two foot long. So they began to *Pow-wow* as they called it . . . They all spake very Loud, as with one Voice and knock'd on the Ground with their Truncheons; so that it made the very Woods ring and the Ground shake." Taylor interrupted the ceremony to say that the healing deities ("dark Infernal Spirits") they sought would not come while an Englishman was present. But, he added, once he got to Shelter Island he would "send one that should Cure him, which I did." The sick man recovered, giving Taylor, on his next journey through the Indian town, the chance to deliver his Quaker message to receptive ears—"and they heard me soberly and did Confess to the Truth I spake by an Interpreter that was my Guide."

Of Shelter Island, Taylor wrote, "We were received very kindly by one Nathaniel Silvester . . . this island was his own: And he had a great many Indians lived on it, and they were Friendly and Sober and made Serviceable to Friends for Guides." (Although he was respectful toward the Indians he encountered, like all the Quaker missionaries, Taylor had evidently met some who were neither friendly nor sober.)

The Puritans also feared the Quakers because they preached in beautiful, gripping, and accessible language. What Governor John Winthrop of Massachusetts had warned about the seductive speech of earlier dissenters from the Boston Covenant was equally true of the Quakers: "They would . . . pray with such soule-ravishing expressions and affections, that a stranger that loved goodnesse, could not but love and admire them, and so be the more easily drawne after them; looking upon them as men and women as likely to know the secrets of Christ, and bosome-counsels of his Spirit, as any others." Although Quakers shared the Calvinist tradition of self-examination as a precondition for enlightenment, they rejected the continual punishment of self-doubt and abasement. Once they had seen the light, they were saved. During Fox's spiritual struggle to shape himself as a Quaker, he saw within his being "an ocean of darkness and death" and "the natures of dogs, swine, vipers, of Sodom and Egypt" before beholding "an infinite ocean of light and love, which flowed over the ocean of darkness."

In early February 1658, Humphrey Norton, one of North America's first "Public Friends," or preachers, made his way to Southold to spread the Quaker message. New Haven Colony, unlike Massachusetts, hadn't codified punishments for Quakers. But something had to be done about Norton, who marched into the "steeple-house" one Sunday, broke up the service, reviled the colony's magistracy and government, and denounced the pastor. The miscreant was hauled off to New Haven, where he refused to answer the official charges, demanding that charges of his own be read instead (they were not). He was locked up in an outdoor jail (in February in New England) for three weeks. On March 10, during what Quakers later termed his "frivolous trial," a large iron key was bound over Norton's mouth, symbolically locking it shut. He was then whipped, branded, fined, and banished from the colony. New Haven hastily passed anti-Quaker laws modeled on those of Massachusetts.

During the same month as Norton's fracas in Southold, Nathaniel became embroiled in a dispute there with a Captain George Deakins. Their quarrel ostensibly concerned the insurance terms for some Shelter Island livestock to be loaded aboard Deakins's *Goulden Parrett*, but the real issue was Nathaniel's insistence that his island was sovereign territory. Ever since his chastisement by the New Haven court, he had apparently maintained that because New Haven Colony had refused to purchase the property before Stephen Goodyear sold it to the partners, it was exempt from any jurisdiction except his own. When Deakins proposed to Nathaniel that the local magistrates settle their differences, his adversary replied that "hee scorned to goe to Southold." Tempers rose. Nathaniel said he didn't care whether the cattle and sheep were loaded or not. Deakins countered, "I see you say, you are out of the reach of all power, both of Old and New England and namely the Lord Protectors [Oliver Cromwell] power?" Nathaniel answered, "And soe I am." Only three weeks later, Giles Sylvester apologized to the Southold magistrates for publicly stating that "all the ministers in New England were witches." Feisty Giles did not offer a full apology, however. His precise target, he explained, had been ordained ministers who were "formall and not spirituall"; in other words, those who preached from Scripture and not from direct divine inspiration, as Quakers did. Giles's language and Nathaniel's actions tell us that certainly by 1658 both men had been "convinced."

"A Place Called Shelter Island Yt Belongs to a Friend"

Along with Thomas Rous and Lewis Morris and the Coddingtons, Nathaniel and Grizzell ranked among the mere handful of prosperous first-generation Atlantic Quakers whose assets, social standing, and decisive actions gave incalculable aid to less fortunate brethren. Only as the Society of Friends solidified after 1665, and its members toned down their radicalism, would sizable numbers of middle-class converts join the fold. Rous and Morris offered the benefits of their government connections and respectability as major planters. Coddington's Rhode Island, that "Sinke into which all the Rest of the Colonyes empty their Hereticks," proved its official commitment to religious tolerance by refusing to persecute or extradite Quakers.

Nathaniel's unique and daring contribution was to create a lawful sanctuary in the very region where Quakers suffered the most severe persecution. His argument turned on a legal distinction regarding the purchase history of Shelter Island. When James Farrett took Shelter and Robins Islands as his agent's commission from the Earl of Sterling in 1639, he thereby removed them from colonial government control; when Stephen Goodyear later sold them to Nathaniel and his partners in 1651 (after New Haven Colony turned down Goodyear's offer), he did so as a private citizen, not as a New Haven Colony representative, thereby preserving their independent status. Nathaniel's narrow distinction held again in 1666 when Governor Richard Nicolls of New York bestowed the manor patent, confirming a certain independence from regional government.

What impelled an ambitious man with a wife and young children, heavy obligations to his business partners, and an uneasy equilibrium with his workforce to risk antagonizing his neighbors and regional governments as a religious extremist? Nathaniel knew the exaltations and comforts of belonging to a tiny, close-knit group of dissidents. His participation in the Separatists' sophisticated, far-flung print network would also have primed him to find similar sustenance in Quaker publications. And he had the support and encouragement of family, friends, and business associates. His brothers Giles and Joshua, who lived with him in the 1650s and '60s, apparently became Quakers. And there was his beloved island, his shield against persecution, which lived up to its name. Each meeting of Friends on Shelter Island pulsated with a reckless, communal energy. They were going to harvest the world for Jesus.

Nathaniel suddenly appears different from his younger self: he's more open, loving, and generous, a man who extends aid and succor to fellow believers. Take Joan Brocksopp, an English matron who, after hearing the call in her sixties, left her Quaker husband, Thomas, at home, traveled to America, and spent time on Shelter Island. In a letter to fellow Friend John Bowne of Flushing, Long Island, Thomas Brocksopp wrote, "As the Lord gives the opportunity, my dear love to Nathaniel Sylvester of Shelter Island, whose tender love and fatherly care of my wife when she was with him, the Lord God of my life render into his bosom an hundred fold." John Taylor likewise took leave "in much Love and Tenderness of *Nathaniel Silvester*, his Wife and Family, and all Friends there, leaving them to the Grace of God and ingrafted Word that is able to save their Souls." Lawrence and Cassandra Southwick—elderly, ill, and obdurate Quaker exiles from Salem, Massachusetts—fled to Shelter Island and lived in the Sylvester household until their deaths a year and a half later.

Grizzell, perhaps even more than Nathaniel, knew about life's uncertainties from her family experience. Brought up as an Anglican, she had traveled further than Nathaniel in joining the Quaker covenant. Like other Quaker converts, she would undergo an expansion of interior spiritual space that was as painful as it was rapturous. Both men and women took part in discussions of Scripture and theological works, working through their readings and beliefs with intellectual rigor. Grizzell wasn't a preacher, a Public Friend, like one of Nathaniel's sisters, Mercie Cartwright, or Boston's Quaker martyr, Mary Dyer. But there is no reason to assume that she differed from other female Quakers in the seriousness of her search for a new spiritual connection, or in her intellectual independence.

By 1659 the Quakers were everywhere in the English Atlantic World, and almost everywhere in trouble. On Shelter Island with Grizzell and Nathaniel, they could encourage each other, marvel at the cruelty of the authorities, preach God's vengeance on their abusers (in what we think of today as very un-Quakerish language), rejoice in the coming millennium, and recover from mutilations and imprisonment. They slept on feather beds and ate the plantation's ample fare (in prison they were often starved). They read the latest pamphlets and letters, meditated and prayed, held tumultuous meetings—and planned their next forays to find converts, or to "witness" the trials of fellow Quakers, and risk further incarceration. How these colloquies helped the little band shape themselves as Quakers can't be known at this distance, but the authors of the Quaker pamphlets called "sufferings" record many who sojourned at one time or another with Nathaniel and Grizzell Sylvester on Shelter Island.

A port of entry for ships carrying Friends from England and on to Rhode Island, Virginia, and Barbados, Shelter Island was now on the Quaker map as a place where captains could safely land such Quaker passengers with their combustible message. Risking everything, Nathaniel and Grizzell had gained new souls and shared the exhilarating company of kindred spirits. They were surely having the time of their lives.

Sylvester Manor on Shelter Island: the handsome early Georgian house stands at the edge of Gardiners Creek, the vital Atlantic connection that brought wealth to the family that has owned the place since 1651. Slaves slept in the attic, under the swooping roof.

From the water tower: on a snowy day, the boxwood maze and huge box specimens near the house stand out clearly in a pre-1908 bird's-eye-view photograph. Crop rows visible at left indicate that this garden was productive as well as ornamental; the clustered outbuildings recall the manor's history as a Northern plantation that shipped food to the West Indies to feed sugar planters and slaves.

Through the remains of the boxwood maze, a mowed path heads for a twentieth-century garden shelter, visible between a towering pair of overgrown yews. Sylvesters, slaves, and servants have gardened here since the seventeenth century.

Early-twentieth-century wooden rose trellises and arches stand witness to Cornelia Horsford's love for the Colonial Revival style, America's first evocation of a national past. Beyond, steps from what was once the chicken yard lead up to another garden level.

The roof of the beautiful garden privy, a three-holer, has tilted eaves that echo the eaves of the manor house. The interior is paneled and whitewashed.

An 1884 table monument stands among seventeenth-century grave markers. The carving on top commemorates Sylvester forebears; the slab below lists the manor's owners, including the Manhansett Indians who once owned the entire island; around the steps run the names of Quakers, including that of the martyred Mary Dyer, who sheltered here from the persecutions of the Boston Puritans in the 1650s.

Mary Sylvester: painted as a shepherdess by the English artist Joseph Blackburn in 1754, this great-granddaughter of Nathaniel Sylvester represents the epitome of eighteenth-century colonial gentility. As Mrs. Thomas Dering, she and her family would flee the ravages of the British invasion of Shelter Island during the Revolutionary War. (Courtesy of the Metropolitan Museum of Art. Gift of Sylvester Dering, 1916 [16.68.2])

On the mantel in the paneled parlor, beneath the portrait of heiress Mary Catherine L'Hommedieu (also a Sylvester descendant), sits a china fruit basket. The same basket appears in the portrait itself, which was probably painted in 1810 by an anonymous artist when Mary Catherine was about four years old. The fragile vessel has remained here for more than two hundred years.

The Horsford Girls: only Cornelia, still a child, stares straight at the camera, at ease in her black mourning clothes. Born in 1861, she inherited the manor in 1904 and firmly stamped the house and garden as her own. Her older sisters stare off into the middle distance so beloved by Victorian photographers.

Bennett Konesni, born in 1982 and the fifteenth Sylvester steward of the manor, walks the old farm road that crosses the far end of the garden and leads to the fields. The property, 243 acres today, once encompassed the nearly 8,000-acre island.

Traces of the original mid-eighteenth-century blue paint are visible on the walls of paneled rooms upstairs and down. The glass on a framed piece of embroidery over the bedroom mantel has caught many reflections, such as this one, of those who passed by.

Sunlight glows through a side door that leads to darkness, the slave staircase that winds up three flights to the attic. The air-circulation holes cut into the wooden transom study us like eyes in a mask. An opulent French scenic wallpaper first blocked in 1849 wraps around the walls.

Slavery in the North: generations of enslaved African, African American, and Indian laborers climbed the steep flight of steps to sleep.

Isaac Pharoah, a Montauket Indian indentured at the age of five in 1828, called the little attic room between these white oak walls his home. The rough wooden door that gave him privacy now stands at left, off its hinges.

The west porch, added by the architect Henry Bacon in 1908, enjoys a view of the light fading quietly over Gardiners Creek. Along the shore, nineteenth-century chroniclers noted shell mounds, or middens, the remains of Manhansett Indian feasts. Today's archaeologists have found traces of busy seventeenth- and eighteenth-century mercantile life beneath the lawn. Immigrants from Europe and Africa probably first stepped ashore at the landing beyond the posts and gate that are silhouetted against the water.

13

Quaker Martyrs, Quaker Peace

The Antinomian Controversy

Massachusetts's Puritan elect trembled and burned at the emergence of the Quakers for very good reasons. Etched in their memory was the religious feud that had torn their infant Boston community apart in 1636, only twenty years before. Now, with the Quakers in their midst, they again foresaw looming political anarchy, social chaos, and satanic temptations (carnal as well as theological). The 1636 dispute—known as the Antinomian Controversy, so called from the Greek *anti*, against, and *nomos*, law—concerned the merits of grace versus works, a subject for theological debate since the beginnings of Christianity. In 1637, a colonial court condemned Anne Hutchinson (1591–1643), a member of Boston's elect and a respected healer, for heresy and banished her and many of her followers and adherents, including William Coddington, from Massachusetts. Hutchinson's accusers (who were also her judges) hated her for her certainty of her eternal salvation through grace alone, that gift of God that could free men and women from the obligation to do good on earth, and for her refusal to serve their ministers and observe church law with the exactitude they required from her. They also hated Hutchinson for her intellectual agility. Governor John Winthrop called her "a woman of a haughty and fierce carriage, of a nimble wit and active spirit, and a very voluble tongue, more bold than a man."

After the civil court found Hutchinson guilty, she was tried by Boston's church elders. The Reverend John Cotton, whom Hutchinson had followed across the Atlantic from England, turned against her to save his reputation, claiming that the religious views of this middle-aged matron and mother of thirteen would lead her into adultery. When she had been formally excommunicated and rose to leave the meetinghouse alone, her friend and follower Mary Dyer rose and walked out too, holding Hutchinson's hand.

A year before the church trial, Dyer had given birth to a stillborn infant. Hutchinson, who had assisted the midwife, Jane Hawkins, buried the body secretly with Cotton's help. Hawkins later revealed what she knew. Governor John Winthrop, well aware of Dyer's support for Hutchinson, had the corpse disinterred. He described the decayed remains as those of a "woman child, a fish, a beast, and a fowle" with claws and horns. Modern medical historians have concluded that the child suffered both from spina bifida and anencephaly (in which a baby is born without a cranium, and with small or missing brain hemispheres). Winthrop circulated the news by letter, and although he did not publicly label Dyer's misfortune a "special providence," or a warning from God about how Hutchinson's wickedness brought God's wrath on her followers, he hardly needed to, in an age that put equal faith in divine intervention and witchcraft.

The banished Hutchinson and her family moved to Rhode Island. Soon after (in 1638), she herself spontaneously aborted an anencephalic fetus. Winthrop, alerted to the mishap, hunted down the Rhode Island doctor who witnessed the birth and arranged for a report to be circulated that "30. [*sic*] monstrous births [occurred] at once; none . . . of humane shape." Here was "God's casting voice . . . testifying his displeasure . . . as cleareły as if he had pointed with his finger."

Following her husband's death in 1642, and after Massachusetts threatened to annex Rhode Island, the unstoppable and heroic Hutchinson moved her family west to Yonkers, in New Netherland, and to safety, or so she thought. The Dutch were at war with the Siwanoy Indians, who warned Hutchinson not to settle among them, but she had faith that God would protect her. Barely a year later, she and six of her children were slaughtered by a Siwanoy war party in 1643 as they retaliated against the Dutch.

"Quaker Martyrs"

Mary Dyer was as spiritually driven and intellectually active as Hutchinson. Her contemporaries repeatedly described her as "comely," an adjective that then connoted feminine beauty and modesty matched by moral grace. Winthrop, for example, recalled her as "a very proper and comely young woman," as if to underscore his astonishment that this paragon could commit the transgressions for which she had been banished. Gerard Croese, a Dutch minister, later praised Dyer as a "person of no mean extract and parentage, of an estate pretty plentiful, of a comely stature and countenance, of a piercing knowledge in many things, of a wonderful sweet and pleasant discourse, so fit for great affairs, that she wanted nothing that was manly, except only the name and the sex."

With the rest of the Boston outcasts, Dyer moved to Rhode Island and lived there for a decade. In the early 1650s, shortly after the birth of a sixth child, she left her husband, Edward Dyer, and their children for England. When she returned to Boston in February 1657 as a Quaker preacher, the authorities arrested her. Edward secured her release on payment of a £100 bond and the promise that she would not return to Massachusetts, on pain of death. But Dyer soon reappeared in Boston to hurl herself against the colony's 1658 capital law. Quickly imprisoned, she was sentenced to be hanged with two younger Friends, Marmaduke Stevenson and William Robinson. Quakers from all over New England converged on Boston; one woman brought winding sheets for the martyrs' corpses. On October 27, sixty-four armed soldiers surrounded the three as they walked a mile to the scaffold. They went "hand in hand, all three of them, as to a Wedding Day," Dyer in the middle. Onlookers said that their faces shone with joy. By official command, military drums rolled incessantly, so that only those closest to the gallows could hear the heretics' last words. Robinson and Stevenson rejoiced that they would be at rest with the Lord; Dyer spoke of the "sweet incomings and refreshings of the Spirit." Robinson stepped up to the platform; the hangman adjusted the noose, and after he pulled the ladder away, Robinson's body jerked, writhed, and was still. Then came Stevenson's turn. Having watched her companions perish, Dyer ascended. Her face was covered with a handkerchief, her arms and feet bound. Theatrically, improbably, a long pause followed. The hangman took off Dyer's blindfold. Unmoving, and seemingly unmoved, she continued to stand with the halter around her neck. She had to be forcibly escorted from the platform, even after hearing that the magistrates had reprieved her.

Unbeknownst to Dyer, they had granted this pardon some days before but kept the news secret in order to pull off the grisly charade. Perhaps the magistrates feared that hanging a woman would increase sympathy for the Quakers; perhaps they wished to look magnanimous. Dyer was banished again, set on a horse, and escorted to the Rhode Island border. Another return to Massachusetts, she was informed, would result in her execution. She made her way home, but she didn't stay there for long. Shortly before the Quaker missionary John Taylor left Shelter Island in late 1659, Mary Dyer arrived. Taylor found Dyer, then in her late forties, to be still "a very Comely Woman," as well as "a Grave Matron" who "ever shined in the Image of God," and the two led several meetings together. By the end of the following April she decided to return to Boston, to burn as a candle for the Lord, traveling north through Providence to avoid visiting her husband and children.

The six months or so that Dyer spent with the Sylvesters may have been the happiest, most dedicated, least fractured time of her life. Her actions embodied her faith; all the rest of life's concerns had burned away. Perhaps Nathaniel and Grizzell helped her into a boat, prayed with her and waved goodbye, then watched her disappear over the rim of the bay. They could have had no doubt that she was voluntarily, knowingly, headed for death. By late May she was back in Boston's jail. On June 1, 1660, Dyer mounted the scaffold under a big elm tree on Boston Common. As her body dangled from the noose, her skirt quivered in the breeze. What a bystander scoffingly said at that sight would eventually stand as Mary Dyer's truth: "She did hang as a Flag for them to take example by."

The King's Missive

Ten months after Dyer's death, in March 1661, William Leddra, a young Quaker from Barbados, was also hanged for his faith on the Boston Common, becoming the last of his sect executed in the colonies. English Friends had appealed to Charles II (recently restored to the throne, in May 1660), but their plea was answered too late to save Leddra from the gallows. Although the Horsfords stoutly held to the notion that Auditor Thomas Brinley's access to the crown was what led to the cessation of the persecutions, it seems much more likely that Nathaniel's brother, Giles, was responsible—if any Brinley or Sylvester could take credit, that is. Only a month before Leddra's death, Giles, along with several other Quakers then in London, had signed a petition to the king that listed the sufferings of American Friends in graphic detail. The petition ground its way through the royal bureaucracy, at last reaching the Council for Foreign Plantations—on which sat the council member and Shelter Island partner Thomas Middleton! He may have sped the document along to help his partner on Shelter Island.

It seems an improbable move for radical sectarians like the Friends: appealing to the son of a monarch beheaded by radical Protestants. Astonishingly, however, the petition got a royal hearing. The king responded promptly, perhaps because Massachusetts Colony had also sent a petition to him, to defend their actions regarding the Quakers, appended to which was a note written by a Massachusetts functionary who was aware of the Quakers' appeal. The note scornfully dismissed the Quakers' request: "You will go to England to complain this year, the next year they will send to see if it is true, and by the next year the government in England will be changed." If anything was calculated to fire Charles up, it was just such a snide reminder of what changing government had brought to his father.

In response to the Quakers' plea, the king quickly drew up what is called a mandamus, a special royal writ—later commemorated in 1880 by the Horsfords' friend, the Quaker poet James Greenleaf Whittier, in his dramatic poem "The King's Missive." The document specifically commanded Massachusetts governor John Endicott to send any Quakers condemned to death "or other corporal punishment" to England for judgment, thereby superseding the colonial law of 1658—a blow to the Puritans, who dreaded interfering monarchs even more than they did Quakers. This was a royal warning, clear and simple, that Massachusetts had overstepped its jurisdiction. The Quakers raised £300 for Captain Ralph Goldsmith, a Quaker of London (and later of Southold), to set sail in his ship, whether he had a load of goods to carry or not, and carry the writ to Boston without delay.

"With a prosperous gale," Goldsmith's vessel arrived in Boston toward the end of November. Boston's authorities, seeing a ship entering the bay flying English colors, soon boarded, and they found that the ship's passengers included Quakers who had been banished from Massachusetts. Did Captain Ralph Goldsmith have official letters? "Yes," he said, but told them he would deliver them the following day. The next morning, Goldsmith and one of the banished Quakers, Samuel Shattuck, went ashore. As George Fox wrote in his autobiography, the two men, closely guarded, "went through the town to Governor John Endicott's door, and knocked . . .

They sent him word that their business was from the King of England, and that they would deliver their message to no one but the governor himself."

Inside Endicott's house, a hastily summoned government meeting was weighing a politic response to the shipload of heretics. Shattuck and Goldsmith entered, hats firmly upon their heads. Endicott ordered the two to uncover, but they didn't stir. A servant threw the offending headgear onto the floor. Shattuck handed the governor the letter ordering him to stop the persecutions. Aghast at seeing the king's signature, Endicott took off his own hat and had Shattuck's and Goldsmith's returned to them. "We shall obey his majesty's commands," the governor said.

One popular version of the Boston martyrs' story concludes triumphantly that the royal order effectively protected the Quakers. Charles did, in fact, prevent further executions, although Massachusetts's chief colonial court simply shifted responsibility for other corporal punishment of Quakers to lower jurisdictions. Visiting Friends were again tied to the backs of carts and whipped from town to town to the colony's borders. But now an unsympathetic royal eye was trained on freedoms that the Puritan colony had enjoyed since the start of the English Civil War. Within another twenty years the colony's charter would be revoked and Anglicans, Baptists, and Quakers would lawfully establish congregations. By 1680, the year of Nathaniel's death, exclusively Puritan rule had ended.

While Giles was in London, helping to shepherd the Quaker petition through the government in 1661, Nathaniel was contending with local repercussions from the Boston hangings. Two days before Mary Dyer's death, the New Haven General Court had unsealed a "slanderous & blasphemous letter" from Nathaniel "written with his owne hand." Branding him a self-professed Quaker, the court also accused Nathaniel of "sundry calumnious and opprobrious speeches uttered at Southold against yt courts & magistrates of New England, as well as o'selves in pticular." (Nathaniel had apparently put himself on record as a Friend for the first time, as if the bloody events in Boston and his powerlessness to protect Friends once they left his island had impelled him to step forward.) Furthermore, he was a "frequent harbourer . . . to yt cursed sect, who fro his island have frequently taken opportunity to come amongst our people, soweing the seeds of their pernicious doctrines & sometimes by grosse affronts, publiquely to make disturbance at Southold." Under New Haven law, seditious speech and harboring Quakers were punishable offenses. The magistrates ordered that £100 of Nathaniel's estate be "attached & seised & not to be released untill this court . . . have received satisfaction from him for these & such like offences, if proved against him." He was also summoned to appear in court that October to answer those charges, and, ominously, to respond to "what else shalbe charged against him." Nathaniel failed to turn up in October, or in May 1661, the second court date set for him.

New Haven retaliated by sending "divers persons under the Government of New Haven and by virtue of an order from the said Government" to raid Shelter Island. Yet again the invaluable Giles filed a petition with the Council for Foreign Plantations noting that none other than council member Middleton "by himself and partners did at their very great charges settle a plantation upon the said Island." Furthermore, the document claimed that the raiders broke open "your Petitioners' houses laying violent Hands upon the said Inhabitants . . . seized and confiscated all the Estates they could find of your petitioners . . . and do still most wrongfully detain the [goods]." The petitioners concluded with a request that they "may be restored to their said Lands and goods . . . and in future be preserved from the like violences and outrages." Whether restitution was made, whether Nathaniel himself was arrested or another attack occurred, isn't known. Maybe the very act of submitting this petition fired a loud warning shot across New Haven's bows. The Sylvesters would not have to fear New Haven much longer: by 1665 the colony had been absorbed into Connecticut, which was ruled by Governor John Winthrop Jr., Nathaniel's patron, friend, and ally.

Nonetheless, Nathaniel's safety and sovereignty had been breached for the first time. Throughout the 1660s and '70s, he aided Friends more discreetly, buying shares in the 1665 Monmouth County Patent in New Jersey, where Quakers and Baptists from Rhode Island and Long Island settled to enjoy religious freedom. He also encouraged other Friends, such as Captain Ralph Goldsmith, to settle on the East End. Visiting Quakers continued to stream through Shelter Island, and regular meetings were established in Newport and Oyster Bay, Long Island. After Great Britain acquired New Netherland by treaty in 1664, Governor Richard Nicoll incorporated the islands in Long Island Sound into a royal province under James, Duke of York, with laws that provided for nominal religious freedom, built on the existing Dutch precedent of religious toleration. Quakers still endured occasional discrimination, but not fanatical persecution. While Shelter Island no longer sailed as far offshore in solitary splendor as Nathaniel had envisioned, the privileges of the 1666 manorial grant—the power to appoint his own magistrate and freedom from military levy and taxes—largely compensated for the loss.

George Fox on Shelter Island

It is six o'clock on an August evening, hurricane season. The tail of a big one is just beginning to lash the East End. Alice and I sit in the long living room, gazing out the bay window at Gardiners Creek. The South Ferry will shut down soon if the storm gets bad, so I must get going. But before I do, I fix each of us a good stiff drink. Alice's preferred poison is two fingers of Mount Gay Barbadian rum—only Mount Gay will do—in a stemmed glass filled up with water, no ice. Andy died of cardiac complications several years ago and Alice is now even more the lady of the manor. (She has left all of Andy's clothes and shoes in his closet, however, and when she gets lonely, she tells me, she opens the door and inhales.) She is now in her eighties: her hair is brilliantly white, cut in a thick, handsome helmet with visorlike bangs down to her eyebrows. The sky has turned livid, the color of the sky in El Greco's *Entrance to Toledo*. That electric-shock hue flashes right into the room and dyes the pale green walls and wall-to-wall carpet. Big trees bend and toss to the breaking point; rain, branches, and unidentifiable objects begin to fly past the window, which suddenly seems very fragile. The wind, sweeping across the island from the south, shakes the walls. But we are safe: this house has seen so many storms in its two and a half centuries that we trust it.

George Fox arrived on Shelter Island in August 1672 after beating his way across the Sound from Narragansett through a big late summer storm, maybe even the tail of a hurricane like this. He wrote in his journal: "After we had stayed two months in and about Rhode Island and thereabouts . . . we took sloop and passed by Point Juda, and by Block Island, and from thence to Fisher's Island . . . The next day we went into the sound, and our sloop was not able to live in the water." The Rhode Island Friends traveling with him wisely "turned in again, for we could not pass, and so came to anchor again at Fishers Island two nights, and there was exceeding much rain, whereby we were much wet being in an open boat; and we passed over the two Horse Races waters (so called) and by Garner's [Gardiners] Island and the Gull's Island, and so came to Shelter Island which was twenty-seven leagues from Rhode Island." While Fox constantly had his eye on the heavenly kingdom, he seldom missed a grounding physical detail, from the head count of crowds who came to hear him to the ferocity of the Fishers Island mosquitoes, which kept him from camping onshore. When he preached in Providence on a simmering June day "in a great barn full of people," he duly noted that the heat of his preaching made him "so hot with sweat as though I had been sodden."

The Sylvesters would have been aware of Fox's whereabouts long before he attempted to reach them. It had taken a year for him and his disciples to make their way from Barbados up the North American coast, a journey during which "the eminent arm and power of the Lord . . . carried and preserved us through and over the fury of wild beasts and men, woods, storms, wildernesses, bogs, rivers, famine and frosts." He debated opponents, welcomed converts, and performed medical miracles. When a companion fell from his horse and stopped breathing, "his head turned like a cloth it was so loose," Fox recalled. "[I] took his head in both my hands . . . and I put my hand under his chin, and behind his head, and raised his head . . . with all my strength, and brought it in, and I did perceive his neck began to be stiff, and then he began to rattle, and after to breathe."

In Newport, Fox led a ten-day general meeting at William and Anne Coddington's house. He preached to crowds each day, "and yet by the continued coming in of people in sloops from diverse other colonies and jurisdictions it continued longer." Narragansett Bay must have been bright with sails, bringing believers, the curious, the bored, and even scoffers from as far away as Plymouth and Cape Cod. Streaming across the water in long canoes, Narragansetts, Mohegans, and Pokanokets joined them.

A few days later, Fox arrived on Shelter Island. This was a time of triumph, peace, and rejoicing for Nathaniel and Grizzell after witnessing their fellow Friends endure so much sacrifice, pain, and bloodshed. When Fox climbed out of the sloop onto their soil and Nathaniel, more than fifty years old, came to greet him, it was a moment of reward and glory. Grizzell, thirty-six years old, held year-old Constant, his uncle's namesake. Eight other Sylvester children would have stood around, ranging in age from five to eighteen, the "tender Plants" who "would stand and wait in the Simplicity" of a moment their parents hoped they would always remember.

Indians came too. Fox wrote, "I had a meeting at Shelter Island among the Indians, and the king and his council, with about one hundred Indians with him." This was by far the largest of the many gatherings with Native Americans that Fox recorded: every soul was another to exult over. (The multitude of local tribesmen surely speaks to the Sylvesters' easy relations with them, at least momentarily: a few halcyon days when so many worlds came together.) "They sat about two hours and I spoke to them by an interpreter, that was an Indian that could speak English very well and they appeared very loving, and they said all was truth, and did make a confession after the meeting of it." Their apparent readiness encouraged him to "set up a meeting among them once a fortnight and a friend Joseph Silvester [actually Joshua, Nathaniel's brother—Fox got the name wrong] is to read the Scriptures to them." Although Fox does not mention Africans being present, what he had already written about the importance of bringing slaves to meeting on Barbados strongly suggests that they, too, were included in the crowd.

The next day, "many of the world and priests' people [Puritans] . . . that had never heard friends before" came from the congregations of Southold, East Hampton, and Southampton, and probably from much farther away. Fox, the religious rock star of his day, wrote that "they was very much satisfied, and could not go away until they had seen me and spoke to me after the meeting, and I went down to them, and they was taken with the truth, and great desires there is, and a great love and satisfaction there among the people."

The preacher departed as he had come, wreathed in the Inner Light and violent weather, headed first for Oyster Bay, and then for John Bowne's refuge in Flushing, closer to New York City. Setting his course first for Plum Island, Fox got stuck in the fearsome rip at Plum Gut, "where there was a very great fog, and the tide did run so strong for several hours, I have not seen the like, though we had a gale we could hardly get forwards . . . We were driven a great way back again, near Fisher's Island . . . and a great storm arose." After a big meeting, a farewell brigade of Quakers often accompanied Fox toward his next stop. Perhaps Nathaniel, Joshua, and Grizzell went part of the way in their sloop before turning back to the reality of their lives, and other storms.

Three years after Fox's visit, in King Philip's War, a confederacy of New England's Algonquians united under Metacom, the Wampanoag leader known to the colonists as King Philip, burned ninety English communities in Maine, Connecticut, Massachusetts, and Rhode Island to ashes. Fewer than a thousand colonists had perished, as against at least two thousand Indians killed in battle or executed, another two thousand exiled, and three thousand casualties from disease, hunger, and other wartime hardships. Again, as after the Pequot War four decades earlier, the English sent vanquished Indians as slaves to the Caribbean, a thousand of them, this time to Bermuda. It took years for colonists to rebuild the towns; some only began to grow again after a generation. For the Algonquians of New England, Miantonomi's plea in 1641 for unity—"Say broth^r^ to one anothe^r^. So must we be one as they are"—had resulted in final defeat, and a breakdown in culture and ownership of what lands still remained to them.

In March 1675, as the war threatened to spread to Long Island, Governor Winthrop begged the Sylvesters to build a "palisadoed fortificacon" to protect themselves and their children. They refused to do so, even though Shelter Island's Indians were "very sullen and crosse," according to Winthrop's emissary. Perhaps Nathaniel and Grizzell, she again "big with child"—perhaps Benjamin, her last—had faith in whatever tenuous balance they had worked out with their fellow islanders, both African and Indian, and were prepared to trust in God. In doing so, the Sylvesters would have followed the Quaker Peace Testimony, framed by Fox in 1660: "The Spirit of Christ will never move us to fight and war against any man with outward weapons, neither for the Kingdom of Christ, nor for the Kingdoms of the World." As it happened, King Philip's War never crossed the Sound, petering out in 1676 with Metacom's death in a Rhode Island swamp. (His wife and child were among those sold as slaves in Bermuda.) The nonviolent Nathaniel who took Fox's words to heart was a very different person from the bristling man who in 1654 had threatened to "pistoll" any Southolder who stood in his way. By his lights, he had perhaps fought the darkness within himself and won.

The wind is really starting to blow now; rigid scallops of white froth etch the surface of Gardiners Creek. But before I hurry off to the ferry, Alice and I turn yet again to the Quakers. Only a few weeks ago, Steve Mrozowski and the field school dug unsuccessfully for Nathaniel's grave near the Quaker cemetery where, Alice says, family tradition places his burial. She and I agree that Nathaniel and Grizzell deserve a special niche in the history of the Friends. For Alice, however, Nathaniel exists not as a Quaker but as a "Quaker Protector." For Alice, as for the Horsfords, who had those words carved on the monument, Nathaniel personifies the selfless fighter for justice. Insisting on his role as a protector is a help to Alice—to anyone, really—who wants to reconcile Nathaniel the upright man with Nathaniel the man who owned other human beings. I still can't reconcile the two.

14

"A Duchman in His Hartt"

"A Duchman in His Hartt"

A year and a half after Fox's golden days on Shelter Island, some much less welcome visitors arrived to stay with Nathaniel and Grizzell. Dutch troops landed and spent the night in February 1674 on their second foray to Long Island after retaking New Netherland in the autumn of the preceding year, during the Third Anglo-Dutch War. Then, their fleet had visited the East End towns, but not Shelter Island. But in 1674—how strange it must have felt for Nathaniel to lie at the mercy of invaders who spoke the language of his childhood city, and in a place that he had made such mighty efforts to make secure.

"The Captaine Landed with about Fiftie Souldiers," Nathaniel wrote as he recalled the invasion, "and to strike the greater Dread in my familie they beset my house." The Dutch wanted £500 that Nathaniel owed them, and they probably paid themselves in "provisions of the country." They ransacked warehouse, storehouses, fields, and pens, as well as the house. "Horses and Mares, Cattle, sheep, hogs," and whatever movables—sugar, rum, salt, bales of cloth, furs and skins, salt fish, fathoms of wampum, barrels of tobacco, rugs and duffel blankets to pay his Indian workforce, precious European goods (imported pipes, pots, cutlery, copper kettles, spirits and wines) he had intended to sell to other colonists or tribesmen, and apparently also slaves, which counted as chattel—everything they could load into the holds of Dutch men-of-war, they took. Calculated against average annual earnings of the day, that's about £925, a huge amounts, more than four times Nathaniel's estimated £200 annual income. Nathaniel and his servants and slaves had to stand by in the face of such an overwhelming force of soldiers in cuirasses and helmets, armed with guns and sword. The children, and Grizzell, who during the Civil War had lived side by side with enemy soldiers quartered in her village of Datchet, must have been terrified. Where the soldiers slept is an open question.

The global conflict between England and the Netherlands for imperial dominion of the seas, which the British would eventually win, was waged in many theaters over half a century, beginning in 1652. The first two of the three short maritime Anglo-Dutch Wars did not require Nathaniel to take sides, but in 1673 and 1674 the third conflict took place close to home. In August 1673, six months before the soldiers arrived to ransack Shelter Island, a formidable Dutch fleet had sailed into New York Harbor, where Governor Francis Lovelace presided over defenses in such bad repair he could do nothing but yield after an hour's battle, to the joy of the city's mostly Dutch citizenry. (Much as they do today, Long Islanders had chafed at having to support the faraway metropolis, so they had not funded vital improvements for Fort James.) The victorious Dutch sent commis-

Nathaniel and his family had reason to fear the rampant lions on this coat of arms: Willem III, sovereign prince of Orange and stadtholder of Holland, was in power in 1673–74 when Dutch warships visited Shelter Island.

sioners to all parts of the colony to demand submission and elect new governments. Faced with possible bloodshed, and lacking any promise of help from other English colonies, the East End towns of Southampton, East Hampton, and Southold reluctantly pledged allegiance to the new regime, turning in their flags and staves, the emblems of office.

Within days of these events, Nathaniel rushed to Manhattan and appeared before the Dutch commanders, volunteering to take their pledge but also requesting confirmation of the privileges he had enjoyed under English rule. (The Dutch willingly maintained the status quo with many English colonists, as the English, on retaking New York, would also maintain with Dutch inhabitants.) As proof of those entitlements, Nathaniel exhibited an extract of the manor grant. "Where is the original?" asked the commanders. He had left it at home, Nathaniel said. The Dutch soon discovered that half of Shelter Island belonged to the heirs of Constant and Thomas Middleton, English subjects. "But after divers arguments pro & con," regarding Nathaniel's improvements to the island and the recompense that he claimed his partners owed him, they reached an agreement. The Dutch sold Nathaniel his partners' forfeited shares in "houses, lands, movables, negroes, and effects" and reaffirmed his manorial privileges. In return, Nathaniel signed a bond for £500, probably dated August 29, 1673, to be paid in "provisions of the country." He had traded the uncertainty of collecting debts from the heirs of his deceased brother and Thomas Middleton for what he saw as a businesslike arrangement to acquire the entire island. This would cost him a fat sum when the bond came due (probably in six months, as most such bonds were payable on three- or six-month terms), but who knew when that might be? Six months, almost to the day—the following dismal February—would be the answer.

Furthermore, by swearing obedience to the Netherlands that August, Nathaniel had, in his view, compromised himself no more than any other local landowner. Fellow Quaker Colonel Lewis Morris, the owner of many acres in the Bronx (and Nathaniel's ally in negotiations with the Dutch), and Nathaniel's neighbor David Gardiner (Lion's son) also took the oath as a pragmatic realignment with the Dutch. Because of Nathaniel's Netherlands background, many of his neighbors didn't see Nathaniel's assent in the same way.

An outraged Richard Smith of Narragansett—the same Richard Smith who in more peaceable times would soon carry Semoney and the two Grizzells to Newport—wrote to Connecticut's Governor Winthrop in

September 1673, "I understand Captt Sylvester hath submited himseluf to Yorke, the Duch. I wonder att him, onley he is a Duchman in his hartt I judge, or elce would not have dared to have done it. Its not his pretending he did it to prevent daingar will exceuse him when time shall serve, besyds he nowe lyes open to be pilliged by the Einglish, as being nowe an enimey to our King & Cuntry."

As soon as the Dutch war fleet left the East End in September 1673, Southold, Southampton, and East Hampton felt it was safe to reassert their loyalty to England. Events moved fast over the next few months, and Nathaniel found himself in a tight spot as a bilingual go-between. Almost at once, another Dutch foray to Southold took place, at the request of a hopeful Nathaniel and Lewis Morris. They had assured the new Dutch governor that the townfolk would once again "submit as dutiful subjects &c." But the Southolders now had the backing of Governor John Winthrop Jr. of Connecticut. An uncharacteristically bellicose Winthrop warned the Dutch that if they persisted in harassing helpless English civilians—"the Poore in their Cottages," he called them—he would "deale with your head quarters [in Manhattan]."

So when Dutch troops sailed back into Southold at the end of October 1673 (after Nathaniel had signed his bond), they were probably not surprised to find the ship of Captain Fitz John Winthrop, the governor's son, lying off Shelter Island. Coached by his father, the young officer had already asked Nathaniel for help in delaying direct action, to give Governor Winthrop more time to muster a defense. Nathaniel loaned a small boat to the Dutch commander and another to Captain Winthrop so that each could row to Southold and peacefully settle the dispute.

Governor Winthrop knew his man: Nathaniel, reared in Amsterdam and on familiar terms with New York's current administrators, could surely deal with these Dutchmen if anyone could. Furthermore, as a practicing Quaker, Nathaniel would feel conscience-bound to avoid violence. And he and his large young family were virtual hostages, their plantation temptingly stocked and vulnerable to Dutch pillage. But Nathaniel's peace parley did not take place. Southold's citizens mounted a sufficient show of arms to induce the Dutch to sail back to New Amsterdam, postponing their campaign to "reduce or destroy the townes on the East end of Long Island."

In late February 1674, Dutch warships again loomed on the horizon—four huge, silent apparitions, by far the largest and tallest objects most

East Enders would see in their lifetimes. The Dutch display terrified even the seasoned Captain Winthrop. He huddled on Shelter Island with the leaders of Southold's small militia. Nathaniel's brother-in-law Francis Brinley and Richard Smith (both hurried across the Sound as conflict threatened) had arrived from Rhode Island to offer advice and moral support. Their side clearly lacked the troops and firepower to defend both Southold and Shelter Island.

With wind and tide in their favor, the Dutch troops landed on Shelter Island. A few days after the raid, Captain Winthrop wrote in an official report that Nathaniel had found "himself in no condition to resist them." With their troops so few (and perhaps feeling that "Dutch" Nathaniel should be left to fend for himself regarding his person, family, and goods), the other colonists, including his own brother-in-law, Brinley, had decided not to protect him or his property. For Nathaniel, barely six months after he had agreed to pay his new overlords £500 in "this country's provisions," the moment of reckoning had come. By his lights he was a victim, not a debtor, a useful stance to demonstrate to his neighbors that he had suffered more from the Dutch conquest than anyone else.

As the Dutch loaded their ships with Nathaniel's stores, the tide ebbed. By sundown, the bulging vessels lay low in the water with no room to maneuver. The *Zeehond*, a warship, and the rest of the convoy remained at the island overnight. In the morning, Nathaniel boarded the *Zeehond* for the short sail to Southold. His last hope was to "prevent the shedding of blood" by some desperate last-minute negotiation. If ever there was a Quaker moment, this was it: Nathaniel's own soil had been invaded, his family terrified, goods commandeered (as Nathaniel probably saw it), and yet he was willing to make his best effort to avoid war. He probably also gauged the strength of the Dutch opposition—and the weakness of his own allies.

Even as the Dutch commander "placed his squadron in an handsome order, and whilst he was preparing to land his men, and bringing all his great guns to bear upon us," Captain Winthrop reported, Nathaniel appealed to the Dutchman, "endeavoring to divert his hostility." Unswayed, the commander ordered that Nathaniel be rowed ashore to deliver an ultimatum to Captain Winthrop, who had taken up his post to defend Southold: meet the Dutch demands for capitulation or face destruction "with fire and sword." Winthrop sent Nathaniel back to the warship with his answer: he would defend to the death every Southolder's right to English sovereignty.

"Capt. Sylvester being returned to his island" after he had delivered the uncompromising message, Captain Winthrop continued, the Dutch "filled their sloops with men, and made all preparations to land; which we easily perceived, and were ready to entertain them with 50 men, [in] which I placed a forlorn hope . . . [The Dutch commander] fired one of his great guns upon us; but the shot grazing by the disadvantage of the ground did no hurt to our men . . . I gave order to return [fire] but the shot falling at his fore foot did him no hurt—whereupon he fired 2 more great guns, and his small shot, which fell thick about us did us no hurt . . . We then presently answered with [a volley of small shot] and another shot from our ordnance; Many of our small shot hitting the ship as we could perceive, but know not of any hurt done him—Whereupon he presently weighed [anchor] and set sail, and being little wind, we had opportunity to observe his motions so far as 'Plumme gutt'—Since when our scouts have not discovered any of them in the sound—but I suppose he will convey the provisions [to] their quarters [in New York], and then return to do us what mischief he can, as he told Capt. Sylvester."

Winthrop's account of shot falling harmlessly here and there reads like Gilbert and Sullivan. Even in an age when firearms were still notoriously difficult to aim accurately, something about this almost farcical and harmless episode rings false. Had Southold's doughty few somehow persuaded the Dutch that they would need to maintain a garrison in the town if they hoped to suppress further rebellion? Did the Netherlanders' command interpret Connecticut's defense of Long Island as a signal that other New England colonies would soon join the fray? Or were the warships laden with Nathaniel's provisions enough to satisfy New Amsterdam's honor as well as the outstanding £500 debt? My bet lies with the latter, and with Nathaniel's powers of persuasion. The mighty Dutch could not back down entirely and lose face, but they could be persuaded to make a show of force, then back off.

More intriguing than Nathaniel's feints and countermoves during these events is the ambiguous relationship he maintained throughout his life with Governor Winthrop. Nathaniel had had good reason to thank Winthrop for "Favoirs that have so liberally from time to time been bestowed" and for all "ye love and Care which you have had for the preservation of me and my Familie in these Perrilous times."

The delicate steps of their dignified promenade together—astute readings of a changing political landscape—took place over a quarter century. No matter how cordial and respectful the Sylvesters' relations with the governor, Nathaniel was touchy about island autonomy, especially before he achieved his manorial patent. And Winthrop took note of this sensitivity. In London in 1663, while struggling to obtain a patent for Connecticut that would co-opt New Haven Colony, he sent a secret letter to his deputy in Hartford warning him to steer clear of proposing sovereignty over any nearby areas where "uncomfortable opositions and litigious controversies" might flare up, including "Mr Sylvesters."

The threats from Connecticut, masterminded by Winthrop and eventually supported by Massachusetts, routed the Dutch from Long Island and sent them scuttling back to home base in New Amsterdam. Nathaniel was thereby spared the further acknowledgment of Dutch sovereignty that he had been prepared to make. But Winthrop knew of other possible dangers when he had his son counsel Nathaniel to "declare before some fitt testimony his manifesting his allegiance to the King, in such way as may be a good safety to him." Boston privateers, as Winthrop had heard (and as Richard Smith had threatened), ever ready to jump at any likely pretext, were ready to pounce on a man who looked as if he had colluded with the enemy. By the same token, Winthrop also had reason to thank Nathaniel: by putting himself in danger as an ambassador for peace, he had helped prevent the Dutch from leveling Southold. Not a drop of blood had been spilled.

By May 1674, the Long Islanders were hearing whispers of peace, and at the end of October the Dutch relinquished their claim. The Treaty of Westminster, formally approved by both sides by early March 1674, in which the Netherlands yielded New York Colony to Great Britain, marked the end of the Dutch empire in continental North America. It also ended the seventeenth-century global conflict between the two nations in Europe and in every colonial arena they shared. The Dutch gained control of the West African slave forts, as well as Tobago, Saba, St. Eustatius, and Tortola, which, along with the important slave depot of Curaçao, left them a satisfactory position in the West Indies as well as an increasing hold on trade and territory in the East Indies.

For Nathaniel, probably of more immediate import was the issue of free trade versus mercantilism. Although the series of British Navigation Acts (1651, 1660, 1663, 1673, 1696) were intended to restrict American trade only to English vessels manned by English crews, and the shipment of all American products only to English ports, for decades the Dutch (and the American colonists) easily circumvented the laws, which were laxly enforced by an inadequate number of customs inspectors. Shippers and merchants connived to change the names of vessels, fired Dutch and hired English crew, and satisfied the requirement that all goods be bonded for delivery in England by various shady means. None of this would have been new to an experienced interloper like Nathaniel, and he probably took it in stride.

Intellectually supple, intensely curious, and broadly tactical, not to say devious, John Winthrop moved in a wider arena than Nathaniel did. Fifteen years older than Nathaniel, he had been accustomed to governing almost from the moment he landed in America in 1631 at the age of twenty-five. His superior status—because of birth, wealth, rank, and education—was burnished by a lifetime of achievement. A master of political dissimulation and passive resistance, accustomed to dealing with fractious fellow colonists, he assiduously avoided saying a direct no, explaining instead why he couldn't quite see a way to say yes. Winthrop was also a shrewd judge of character. He had watched Nathaniel build his small kingdom, and had been sympathetic to, or at least tolerant of, the Sylvester brothers' Quaker beliefs and activities.

Winthrop would die in 1676; Nathaniel would survive him by four years. By then, Shelter Island was no longer a distant outpost. Nor was coastal New England a perilous frontier. Nathaniel had watched the western rim of the Atlantic expand from a narrow strand of discrete points linked by sea to Europe, England, Africa, and the West Indies into a wide mesh stretching inland as well. He was not a loner in this Atlantic World—he had his large extended family, his religious fellowship, and his partners and other business associates. But he remained averse to living in any community other than the one he had set up on his island domain. He had seen trade become, as Bernard Bailyn writes, "an auxiliary to landowning and agriculture." He had laid the foundation for his descendants to become country gentlemen.

By turns grasping, sharp, tender, fearful, brave, resolute, and daring—but always devout—Nathaniel remains a difficult man to understand. All human beings are stubbornly irreducible, but in Nathaniel's case neither a diary nor sufficient correspondence exists to help fill in a biography or flesh out the man. In a commercial world where trust was a rare commodity and a transatlantic deal could take years to consummate, or could fail with a single shipwreck, he drove hard bargains and left a strenuous court record (though no more so than many other merchants). Within his family, to the very end, he ruled as an iron autocrat. He intended to supervise his sons' lives from the grave by driving them into theirs, at least figuratively, should they dare to challenge his will: if any one of them sold island property, Nathaniel wrote, it would be "as if the said Child so doeing . . . were dead before he made any such sale." On the other hand, Nathaniel never thought to entail his children's religious fidelity.

By 1700, only twenty years after his death, not a single Sylvester child remained a Quaker. Continuing as Friends on the East End would have been a lonely business in any case. Once the seventeenth century's missionary fever had broken, the nearest Quaker communities lay at least half a day's journey away on Long Island. Nathaniel had envisioned a close family of Quakers, which he had initiated with the betrothal of his eldest daughter, Grizzell, to Latimer Sampson, the son of an English Quaker from Bristol. Sampson died (but not before making a will that left all his property to his fiancée) and Grizzell married an Anglican, James Lloyd of Boston. Another daughter, Patience, married a Huguenot and attended Southold's Congregational church. (After the revocation of the Edict of Nantes in 1685, when Protestantism was made illegal in France, many Huguenot refugees came to America.) Their eldest son, Giles, was wed in Boston by a French Protestant minister who converted to the Anglican church; Nathaniel Jr. converted to the Church of England.

The difficulties of finding a suitable and well-connected mate (of any religious persuasion) for a young woman living on a remote island outside the orbit of her extended family in Newport were considerable. Elizabeth and Mercie did not do badly in their choice of husbands: Elizabeth married a Jonathan Brown of Southold; Mercie, a Jonathan Viall of Rhode Island. But in 1693 Mary, the seventh child, married a Matthew Carey in Boston, only to discover he had a wife in England. Such discoveries were quite frequent as men (and women) left their legal spouses behind, but it's not clear that many chose to do what Mary did. Even though her brother Giles petitioned in Massachusetts court that the couple be prevented from living together until Carey's English wife was proved dead (as he falsely claimed), Mary stayed with him.

Without Nathaniel and Grizzell, Shelter Island would lose both its center of gravity and its sense of forward momentum for a half century.

With them vanished an ardent, severe, and admirable religious longing that Nathaniel and Grizzell satisfied by joining the Society of Friends, the ultimate Puritan stretch of the individual's reach for God. What survived after their deaths were the island itself, the aging house and its compound, a profound sense of isolation, and the evolving American systems of race and class.

15

"Children of the Founders"

Decay

Dennis Piechota, a conservator with more than thirty years' experience in preserving archaeological artifacts but almost none in field excavation, has come up with an unprecedented experimental plan. He wants to move an intact block of soil from the manor's seventeenth-century midden to the Boston lab. Although measuring only sixteen by twenty inches across the top and bottom and twenty-four inches deep, his "soil sample" weighs an impressive eight hundred pounds. Dennis's subject is decay. Shelter Island's acid, sandy loam consumes many traces of organic matter—plants, flesh, wood, leather, textiles—leaving nothing to analyze except inert metal, stone, glass, brick, and a startling array of West Indian coral, probably hauled north as ballast and burned to make mortar for plaster and brickwork. Only some ten inches below the surface of Alice's lawn, chunks and piles of the stuff pock the midden layer, skeletal, ribbed, and pale from long burial.

Dennis wants to see if, under lab conditions, gaseous "plumes" attest to the past existence of vanished organic matter. Using chemicals, dyes, and light rays, he will analyze microscopically the soil formation and soil interactions with any buried artifacts. Ultrafluorescence will let him visualize the degraded proteins that cling to soil particles. For instance, Dennis says, even though it's impossible to differentiate between the Sylvesters' brocade or worsted and their slaves' coarse osnaburg, he might detect the former presence of some kind of textile—a ghost of seventeenth-century daily life in the form of evanescent gases, microscopic particles, and blooms of invisible light. As a conservator, Dennis usually thinks in terms of cleaning and preserving historical evidence. But here, he says, "the ultimate goal is the complete though orderly destruction of the object [the soil block] being 'cleaned'!" To transport his chunk of earth intact to Boston, Dennis has arrived in the summer of 2003 with an elegant plywood box painted bright green; it looks like a small photographer's trunk. Lifting blocks of soil has been done before, though in much smaller sizes and to preserve fragile objects (a Salvadorean calabash, for example), not to study soil processes. Dennis's box comes apart into sections: four sides, a top and a bottom, all with aluminum tongue-and-groove edges and steel clasps.

At one edge of the front lawn excavation area, Dennis has cut away three vertical faces of his block. To keep them from crumbling, he has bound them with poly sheeting. Next, he plans to free the bottom by sliding a metal guide plate we quickly dub the "cookie sheet" between the block and the ground underneath. Then he will cut the block away from the earthen wall behind it, severing its last attachment to Shelter Island. The least elegant aspect of this operation will be the last: brute force, supplied by members of the field school, to heave the encased block from the pit and high enough into the air to set it very, very carefully in the van.

Conservator Dennis Piechota's eight-hundred-pound soil block being encased at the manor for transport to the University of Massachusetts laboratory in Boston.

Since the dig began in June, it has rained hard every few days, and the soaked soil is holding together well. With her trowel, Kat Hayes pats the three exposed surfaces of the block as if she were smoothing icing on a cake, a cake filled with a three- or four-inch-deep layer of seventeenth- and early eighteenth-century trash. From this point on, things don't go quite as planned. All afternoon a circle of patient observers watches as first Dennis and then a succession of students whang the metal cookie sheet under the resisting chunk of history with a mallet.

The midden doesn't want to give up its secrets. It just doesn't want to travel to Massachusetts. The afternoon isn't hot, but everyone is sweating. At dusk, the air gets chilly and a flock of Windbreakers and sweatshirts appears. The cookie sheet has barely budged forward into the earth. This exercise suddenly seems fruitless, which somehow makes everyone relax. The archaeologists go off to smoke in little cabals, drink some beers. Alice, wearing her mobcap and a bright yellow slicker, sits in her director's chair a few yards from the excavation, enjoying every minute.

At last the cookie sheet has been pounded far enough to reach the back of the block. Everyone is very quiet. Will the whole chunk disintegrate when the bottom section of the box slides in above the cookie sheet? Nope. It goes in easily. The final step of releasing the block from its surroundings begins. Something, however, keeps it attached—something invisible that's lodged right in the middle of the back side of the block, about six inches above the bottom. Dennis takes a deep breath and says he wants to tip the entire sample forward on its base. Kat winces: although this will release the block, the action may mangle whatever attaches it to the side of the pit. Steve and a student agree to push back against the weight of the eight-hundred-plus pounds of soil to keep it from crashing forward. Strong arms push the block to a precarious forty-five-degree angle. Everyone grunts anxiously, sympathetically. Dennis, peering down into the darkness at the bottom of the pit, announces that the only thing keeping the chunk stuck in the ground is a yellow Dutch brick, a commonplace at this site. Out it comes.

Gray and exhausted, Dennis drives the last plywood section into the slot behind the block and snaps the final clasp. It is supposed to rain, and it does, but the big chunk of dirt gets to Boston in one piece. No whiff of textile or leather emerges from Dennis's yearlong excavation of the sample. But from my nonarchaeological point of view, the project reveals the incredible power of earthworms, and how their activities at the manor display a pattern in time. When organic matter such as coral, bones, and shells were tossed across the midden surface (following the routine colonial practice of throwing trash out a door or window), the pH level of the naturally acid soil turned alkaline, ideal for worms, who had a feast and left an astonishing two-inch layer of lacy castings, or excrement, between two midden layers. The very existence of these fragile droppings, sensitive as they are to rain splash and trampling, signals an interval, perhaps of some years, between the rubbish deposits. Dennis hazards that the worm-casting layer might have been protected by an overhanging roof, although its survival could also simply indicate neglect of the place as the nearly vacant manor grew still. The household of Brinley Sylvester, Nathaniel's grandson, may have added the second trash layer after they moved into the old manor house in 1719. And it was Brinley who buried this deposit, once he had built his new mansion, by spreading a layer of loam over the entire landscape, sometime between 1735 and 1750.

"The Children of the Founders"

Grizzell died at the age of fifty-one after a more adventurous life than she could ever have imagined for herself in Clerkenwell. After her husband's death in 1680, she wound up his affairs on the island in November of the following year by signing off on his inventory as executor. As a Quaker, she did not swear to the truth of the probate, but attested instead, "being," as she wrote, "a person that cannot take an oath for conscience sake." She made at least one more trip to Newport in June 1685, to confirm that her will was her "voluntary act and deed," and survived for another two years, dying sometime before September 10, 1687, on Shelter Island, when instructions were issued to probate her will in New York Colony. Her inventory, taken on Shelter Island a month later, is small: it includes the few things she had not bequeathed to her children—the wool of 138 sheep, two-thirds of a barrel of whale oil, and the "silver coral with bells," the teething toy she had brought with her from England. We don't know where on Shelter Island she is buried.

Giles, her eldest son, was thirty or thirty-one when he inherited the manor house and the surrounding forty acres of gardens and orchards. His brothers Peter and Constant (Benjamin, the youngest Sylvester son, born circa 1675, died of unknown causes before he turned twenty) built farmsteads with "housing, barns, and outhouses thereon," but they held no outright title, mindful of the departed patriarch's stringent plan for sharing the island's 8,000 acres. For thirteen years following his father's death, Giles apparently kept only sporadic accounts of payments for farm work to several Indians and one African, Black John, in exchange for cloth, "country pay" (farm products), and cider or rum. Then, in December 1693, Giles, who was spending most of his time in Boston, where he gambled and amassed huge debts, rented out the western half of his house to Edward Downing, "husbandman," for a seven-year term as tenant farmer.

According to the lease, Downing paid Giles with half his yield—cider "in good, strong, tight, and Sweet casks," butter, cheese, grain, livestock, and meat, which he brought to "ye landing place of ye farme" for pickup and sale. Two Sylvester hands from the 1650s—Jacques Guillot, who lived near the manor house in 1693, and John Collins—witnessed the lease along with Nathaniel Jr. Three of the Sylvester girls, Elizabeth, Anne, and Mercie, probably occupied the other half of the house, "ye Hall with ye chamber & ye garret over ye same and ye leanto therounto enjoyning," and may have lived part-time with their married sister Patience in Southold. The little seaport's 1698 white population had grown to 132 families, up from the dozen or so who founded the town in 1640. "Slaves, old & young" numbered forty, and the town's Indians had dwindled from a reported four hundred Corchaugs (a local North Fork tribe) in 1640 to a mere forty. But the total population had expanded to 881 residents, reflecting its rise as a bustling entrepôt for scores of farmers and small traders. By contrast, once-busy Shelter Island slowed down, as Giles, the head of the clan, no longer moved within his father's mercantile orbits abroad.

For the next three or four decades, the family would derive most of its Shelter Island income from land sales, not trade or agriculture. The dynastic monolith on which Nathaniel had insisted with such crushing force in his will ("as if the said Child . . . were dead before he made any such sale") was never realized. The vehemence of Nathaniel's phrase is extreme, even for an age in which Puritan parents loved their children but considered them depraved at birth by original sin. Parents were enjoined to break the will of their offspring to make them biddable and exact the reverence and awe due their elders. (Quakers rejected the doctrine of original sin, but Nathaniel, whatever his beliefs on the subject, ruled the roost as fiercely as any Puritan patriarch.)

The historian David Hackett Fischer notes that in the few existing New England autobiographies of the period, childhood was looked back on not with nostalgia, but with pain and guilt. Nathaniel may not have been an easy parent.

Whatever their reasons (besides the desire to make money) for wishing to get off the island, before 1700, Giles and Nathaniel Jr. circumvented their father's will by making quitclaims (transfers of land that release ownership rights) to each other, after which they sold off several thousand acres to outsiders instead of settling it with tenants. Nathaniel Jr. moved to East Hampton and then to Newport. Giles began to style himself "sometime of Shelter Island now of Boston." The younger daughters left as they married or went to live with relatives. In the 1690s both Constant and Peter, the two sons who had made their peace with the prospect of an island life lived under the commandments of their father's entail, died within a year of each other as very young men, unmarried and without issue.

Except for the younger Grizzell, who married the Boston merchant James Lloyd, the second-generation Sylvesters were unsuccessful, in any worldly understanding of the word. In describing Boston's second generation, the historian Bernard Bailyn could well have been writing about Giles: "The children of the Founders, however well-intentioned they might have been, knew nothing of the fire that had steeled the hearts of their fathers. They seemed to their elders frivolous, given to excess in dress and manners." Giles lacked the acumen to compete in the changing world of high-level English contacts and newly powerful colonial councils. He had no Thomas Middleton at the Council for Foreign Plantations, no Uncle Giles to carry the mercantile business in London, nor the standing that Nathaniel evidently enjoyed with John Winthrop Jr. While more enterprising second-generation colonials built on their parents' successes in commerce, and as the second stage of the big American land grab along the coasts and around emerging cities took place, Giles remained in the second rank, a true native colonial.

Giles was by no means a cipher: he became a judge of the Court of Common Pleas for Suffolk County and a member of a royal commission to investigate claims of the Mohegans in Connecticut. He added a working knowledge of the law to his skills, acting as an attorney (in a day when no special schooling or accreditation was required) in a number of cases in Connecticut, Massachusetts, Rhode Island, and New York. As Suffolk

County government began to muscle in on the manor's independence, Giles fought back successfully. However, letters he wrote as a young man to Fitz John Winthrop and his younger brother, Wait, with their high-flown sentiments—"I am at leisure for noebody but you"—and his talk of "excellent romances" and family escutcheons and crests, to the almost complete exclusion of the politics, commerce, wars, and religion that had occupied Nathaniel and his brothers, expose Giles's efforts to become, as Bailyn writes, "English as only British colonials can be English."

In 1686, Giles had married a Boston widow fourteen years his senior, the redoubtable Hannah Savage Gillam, a granddaughter of Anne Hutchinson. Their marriage was childless and unhappy, and they lived apart most of the time. Asked about this virtual separation, Hannah hinted at Giles's loathing for the island and its provincial society. "As for Mr. Sylvester's living from me he dare not live here [in Boston, where his creditors could jail him]," she wrote, "& [he] was ashamed I should go there [Shelter Island] . . . I have often wrote and told him of late years I would come & abide with him . . . but his answer was I should not live amongst such brutes."

It's a good guess that Giles was simply trying to keep his wife at arm's length. And yet his unfavorable comparison of Shelter Island to Boston also voiced the beginnings of a search that began in the 1690s for gentility, which historian Richard Bushman calls "the ideal of a cultivated and refined inward life." Moderation, decorum, and self-restraint would become the proper attributes of a polished New England gentleman at the beginning of the eighteenth century. Godliness, and the steely dignity (and inner anxiety) and sternness that accompanied godliness, had marked the seventeenth-century Puritan man.

Giles's desire to acquire that new gentlemanly polish collided with his blustering sense of entitlement as the eldest son of the respected Captain Nathaniel Sylvester of Shelter Island. What he did inherit of his father's rough-and-ready temperament made Giles an embarrassment and a burden to his family. James Lloyd, married to young Grizzell, wrote a chatty letter to Francis Brinley in Newport in 1693 asking him to buy "half a yard of the Greenish Stufe [that Grizzell] had had a gowne & pettycoat off [of]." Lloyd closed with a postscript headlined "a barbrous act." He describes how "Brother G: S: [Giles] owed Camble [Campbell?] some money: Camble arrested him for itt [in Boston]." Lloyd paid the bail to get Giles out of jail, he says, but then "Camble went to Long Island Giles met him in Est Hampton Shook hands with him & with a truncheon felled him he now spits blood: after [which] I arrested him [Giles] which Mr Nichols countenanced, scared him out of £5 mony." Lloyd's own brother-in-law had ambushed someone and had beaten him in cold blood with a big stick on a public street, behaving embarrassingly outside any gentleman's code of honor. Lloyd's brief account of this attack, and the specter of the money troubles behind it, vibrates with the disgust of a well organized, socially adept man writing about the family black sheep.

William Nicoll, who apparently often acted as Giles's "keeper," also became his executor. Born the same year as Giles, in 1657, Nicoll had served as a soldier in Europe and trained as a lawyer, marrying the wealthy widow of the Dutch magnate and landowner Kiliaen van Rensselaer of New York. A controversial but successful politician, Nicoll followed his father, Mathias, as speaker of the New York Assembly. By the 1680s he already owned the 51,000-acre freehold of Islip and had his eye on Shelter Island. He would buy 2,200 acres—about a fifth of the island, later called Sachem's Neck—from Giles in 1695.

Relatives' attempts to safeguard the island acreage against Giles's depredations had begun in 1686, when James Lloyd and Ephraim Savage, Hannah's father and Giles's soon-to-be father-in-law, signed a prenuptial agreement with Giles. This contract made over "all that messuage [farmstead] & house or Tenement upon Shelter Island aforesaid wherein the said Giles Sylvester doth now inhabitt" as well as half the entire estate to Hannah and to "the issue of the bodyes of the said Gyles and Hannah lawfully begotten . . . and then for want of such issue to . . . the right heirs of the said Gyles Sylvester," presumably his blood relations. (It's not clear what "half the estate" means, since Nathaniel's will explicitly stated that the island was to be held in common, except for the forty acres around the house.)

When I first read this indenture, inscribed on a two-foot-wide sheet of crisp vellum adorned with Giles's large signature and seal, I could almost hear his cosignatories sighing with relief: the watertight-sounding clauses surely would ensure that Giles's "right heirs" would inherit his vast property intact. Instead, Nathaniel Jr. and Giles juggled land with each other to make sales to outsiders that circumvented their father's entail. After Giles died in 1707, Hannah retained only 400-acre Ram Island, a hilly section of Shelter Island good only for pasture, which Giles stipulated as her "widow's third" of the estate.

Giles left all his remaining property, about half the island, to his executor, William Nicoll. The will charged him with settling Giles's "debts & funerall charges," of course, but it also granted Nicoll and his heirs "the overplus after my said Debts are paid to be disposed of as the said William Nicholls [*sic*] shall think fitt." With a stroke of a pen, Giles had freed himself of his father's island.

Obium and "the Mansion House of Capt Nathaniel Sylvester, Deceased"

The year Giles died, another man who had known "the mansion house of Capt. Nathaniel Sylvester" since childhood was living in Boston. A slave, one of the four children of Oyou and Tammero, he was called Obium, an African name of unknown origin. He had left Shelter Island for Boston in 1688 as a young man, the property of Grizzell Sylvester Lloyd and her husband, James. Some time thereafter, Obium ran away from the Lloyds' house, evidently on one of their horses. It was not uncommon for slaves to try to make their way back to familiar places near their former homes where they might find shelter and friends and secretly see their kin. Maybe homesickness—missing his family and community, and even the place itself, its sights, sounds, and silences—spurred Obium to think of Shelter Island, if not as a lost paradise, at least as his home. We can surmise that he was vaguely familiar with the stretch of New England he had seen on his journey north to Boston, to the Lloyds. But whatever his plan, nothing was going to protect him from the consequences of flight if he was caught.

Even on abominable Massachusetts roads, a post rider could cover as much as twenty-five miles a day. But the rare sight of a young black man hurrying on horseback would have turned heads, and word would soon have spread that a slave had gone missing. The most reliable sources for information about fugitives are newspaper advertisements, but none was published in New England until 1704, and the first advertisement for a runaway slave did not appear until the following year. We know about Obium's escape only from the record of a reward paid to someone of twenty shillings—one pound sterling, a large sum—"to find the horse Obium ran away with," noted in 1691 by an elderly Francis Brinley, who had become James Lloyd's executor and the general caretaker of the family's accounts. Lloyd's 1693 probate inventory confirms that Obium himself was captured and returned, but we don't know the details of his punishment. The list of contents for the Hall Chamber includes a "negro man named Obium" along with "a pallet bedstead & rug . . . 1 old chest, 1 table and other lumber in the closet." This is probably where Obium slept. A lonely life: no other human property appears among the hundreds of inventory items.

Assessed at the high price of £25 when he was still on Shelter Island, Obium must have been too valuable for the Lloyds to sell as damaged goods even after proving himself defiant and untrustworthy. All we know of the sixteen years following his capture is that during the first eight of them, the Lloyds hired him out to three different employers in Boston, his wages rising steadily year by year, earning more—not for Obium, of course, but for the Lloyd estate—each time a contract for his services was renewed.

Obium's time in Boston ended abruptly in 1709, when the Lloyds' eldest son, Henry, summoned him first to Newport, then to Lloyd Manor in Oyster Bay, Long Island, which Henry's mother, Grizzell, had inherited as her legacy from Latimer Sampson. Henry's father-in-law, John Nelson, with whom Obium was living in Boston before the move, wrote, "He seems to be something unwilling to part with us, but as it is in a maner the same familie I tell him that upon his future good behavior he may be assured of as good treatment he promisses his best Endeavors for your Servise &c."

Here is where the misery of accommodation to slavery comes in, and the poverty of trying to understand—today—the mechanisms of trust and distrust that made such accommodation work. Nelson wrote patronizingly, "You know how to deal with [Obium]. By praiseing or speaking well of him you may doe with him as you please." He was to be petted and managed like a child. But as Obium hesitatingly shares his fears with Nelson regarding this unequal relationship, he negotiates, preparing to make his "best Endeavors" in exchange for the possibility of better treatment. He has learned to make use of what the sociologist Anthony Giddens calls "practical consciousness . . . all the things which actors know tacitly about how to 'go on' . . . in social life without being able to give them direct discursive expression." For their part, Nelson and Lloyd would have taken their complete power over Obium as a given but still regarded themselves as kindly and enlightened men, considering the trust and latitude they were about to extend to him. The irony of it is that, some two decades after his escape, Obium, who had come to consider the Boston he had run away from as his home, now had little recourse but to accept the fate of being uprooted yet again.

Nelson gave Obium more clothes for his new existence on Long Island than many slaves would have received in a lifetime: "A Great Coate, Double brested Jackett, & a Coate, new and all lined: 2 pr Cloth Britches; 5 Shirtes . . . which . . . may want mending, 2 pr Stockings." Nelson explained, half jokingly, that he was sending a list "of what Obium brings with him for feare of Other disposals," meaning that he might sell off some of his new wardrobe while traveling alone. Nelson's smile vanishes with a final caveat: "Yett not trust him too much."

In 1737, while Obium was living with the Henry Lloyds in Oyster Bay, he surely heard that the house where he grew up was being torn down. Captain Nathaniel's grandson, Brinley Sylvester, Henry Lloyd's first cousin, who had moved back to Shelter Island (at most a day's sail from Lloyd Manor), was building a new house. Local traffic on Long Island's best highway—the Sound—ran freely. Blacks, slave and free, had their own private network of informants. News came through despite the punishments and fines against gathering together or even communicating with one another. From runaways and "night walkers" daring to visit their families or friends or lovers on other farms or plantations or towns, from black deckhands in the ports, from messengers on business for their owners, and from Indian informants, news sped round the region.

By this time, Obium knew how to read and perhaps also how to write. He owned an Anglican prayer book bound in leather and fastened with clasps. Small and worn, it was stained with dirt and sweat and tears, or raindrops, according to an antiquarian's article in the *Brooklyn Eagle* in 1888, when the book was last seen. My attempts at tracking this "curious old hymnbook" and the descendants of the Joel Gardiner to whom it belonged in 1888 have been fruitless. But according to the author of the *Eagle* article, Obium (or somebody else) had written at the foot of the opening page of the psalms: "Obium Rooe—his book—god give him grace—1710 or 11." (The old Roman Julian calendar year, which began on March 25, was slowly being replaced in public usage by the Gregorian calendar year, which starts on January 1, but many still hung on to the old system, simply marking the date for the first three months of the year as 1710/11, so the inscription reads as before March 25, 1711.)

A curved dormer board and a pair of original shutters found by the architectural historian Robert Hefner in the attic supplied clues to the chaste Newport-style appearance of the early Georgian south front, c.1737. The grand double front doors would have been framed by pilasters and a neoclassical pediment.

The book subsequently belonged to Jupiter Hammon, another Lloyd slave, a bookkeeper, a preacher, and the first published African American poet, born in October 1711, whose name was inscribed on the back flyleaf as Jupiter Lloyd. Jupiter's mother was probably Rose, some ten years younger than Obium. (She appears in the Lloyd family papers for the first time in 1687.) Obium came to Lloyd Manor when Henry Lloyd built his house there in 1711. Given the vagaries of eighteenth-century penmanship—where the upper loop of an *s* is sometimes so small that the letter looks like an *o*—it would be easy to misread Rose as Rooe. Recent research now holds that Obium and Rose were Jupiter's parents. Perhaps the pairing of their names commemorates the couple's union. If so, Obium made a gift of his own prayer book to his son. It was all he owned, all he could give. The concluding page of the psalms reads "If any be afflicted, let him pray: and if any be merry, let him sing psalms."

I am there with Obium at the razing of the old house and the building of the new. The manor house is still here today, but the past is being leveled to make way for the future. Obium had dwelled in that past. But his long life took him well beyond it. What I know about the seventeenth-century manor from a distance is what Obium knew close-up: the dark corners, the winding stairs, the white clouds of flowering orchards gleaming through the upstairs windows. As I imagine it, I hear him counting up the details he recalls of his deceased master's and mistress's comforts: what they had, what he didn't, what he and the twenty-three others had labored to create for the Sylvesters. The softness of fabric, flowers, and feather pillows; the smell of roasting pork; the warmth of a well-built fire. Looking up at the garret that is about to come down, does he remember exactly when he learned black was different from white? Does he still feel his thin bedding in that attic and hear the straw rustle, hoping that his body and those of his little sister and brothers curled next to him will make enough heat to keep off the chill until morning? He hears the voices of black and white children playing, and of his African parents speaking a soft creole patois together, and of Joshua Sylvester reading the Bible aloud to the assembled manor "family" as George Fox had asked him to do. He hears Mary Dyer and John Taylor praying together. Outdoors, the whump of corn being pounded in a mortar, the whickering of horses to each other; indoors, the scratch of Nathaniel's quill on paper in the quiet evening. I see Obium standing near Gardiners Creek some fifty years after he left the island, reflecting on liberty and how he tried to grab it.

We—Obium and I, in my imagination—watch while Brinley takes a last look at the old house. We wonder how he thinks about his improvident uncle Giles, and the years, expense, and effort it has taken Brinley to reclaim what he is about to destroy. The decades-long court case that reversed Giles's gift to Nicoll—and placed a thousand acres and the old house compound back in Brinley's hands—has ended. It's a big day, a great victory for him. Brinley is determined to build here, on this exact spot. He is going to reclaim his history but redefine his inheritance. He's going to topple the mossy chimneys; erase the gaping middens, muddy paths, tumbledown fences; pull the swaybacked outbuildings to the ground. It all happens in what Steve Mrozowski calls a "single event." The house and everything around it crashes with a scream of timbers, the roar and clash of bricks and roof tiles falling and shattering. The oak posts that held up the building are wrenched out of the ground, and what can't be razed or uprooted is burned. Brinley is a thrifty man; he salvages whatever stuff he can from the wreck. Usable bricks and other building materials are neatly stacked. He is erasing the outworn design for living along with its plaster, glass, nails, and lumber. We stare at the ghostly cloud of dust and smoke, vanished breath and movement hanging in the air.

Silence. Obium, one of the last surviving children, black and white, who grew up on Shelter Island in the first generation of European settlement, will outlive Brinley by five years. He was here at the beginning of slavery on the island, but he will not see its official end, seventy years after his death—and even then the business of black and white will not be finished. Next to where the new house will rise sit piles of white-oak logs and thick timbers, still green, and hauled out of the woods only a few months earlier. The tenets of slavery that shaped the old place will be hammered into the new, strengthened and ramified by the courts, by colonial legislation and town ordinances, buttressed by years and years of habit: slaves have their place; Brinley has his.

16

Illusion and Reality

Brinley's Enlightenment

In the house that Brinley built, on either side of the fireplace in the paneled parlor, capitals rise in tiers from twin Doric pilasters. The fluted shafts of these flat columns barely project from the wall. Their shallow relief looks like a sketch—the formulation of an idea. They look as if they were carved by a provincial carpenter-builder working from verbal descriptions of what Brinley envisioned rather than from a standard handbook of classical design. However crudely, their proportions embody an architectural understanding of the new Age of Reason, the sensibility of an era filtered through the sensibility of one man, Brinley Sylvester. The house is the man.

Brinley's pilasters shine with the glow of Newport's Enlightenment. In 1728, a decade or so before construction started, George Berkeley, the Irish philosopher and Anglican churchman, had come to Rhode Island to await parliamentary funding for his "Bermuda college," which never arrived. While waiting, he built Whitehall, a simple but fashionable Georgian house in the fields outside Newport, and lived there for four years before returning to London. Besides a fresh jolt of English culture and a coterie of intellectuals and artists, the genial and worldly Berkeley also brought to Newport his concept of Immaterialism. Everything in the physical world, he asserted—including Brinley's mantelpiece—exists only in the human mind. All phenomena consist of ideas, not matter, and only God's steady gaze maintains the physical existence we inhabit. It's very doubtful that Brinley or many of any of his coterie of Newport friends read Berkeley's *An Essay Towards a New Theory of Vision.* But Joseph Addison's triumphant hymn "The Spacious Firmament on High," published in the London periodical *The Spectator* in 1712, was a popular expression of that same belief in the underlying rationality of God's creation maintained unseen by God's all-seeing eye. Newport's cultivated citizens inhaled this invigorating early eighteenth-century Enlightenment atmosphere. They accepted the concept of the world as a splendid, shining machine operating by divine rules of reason and science within the spangled heavens. The youthful, gracious classicism of Brinley's pilasters and scores of similar ones in contemporary Newport bore witness to this rational although ethereal universe. As I stand in front of the parlor fireplace, the sturdy oak-framed house vibrates, and then—just for a second—levitates slightly.

Outside the east window, the boxwoods billow fatly along a path that runs straight for a quarter mile, cutting the long rectangular garden in half. Brinley incised this line on the earth not just as a way to get from one place to another, but as a mark of rational dominion: every eye and mind that follows the path tethers house to ground. He turned his mansion's front entrance away from the water so it faced south (the work buildings were moved a suitable distance to the north, apart from the house). Brinley laid another straight line along the axis that led from the front door to the main road that crosses the island. This was terrain on which to breathe the atmosphere of the Enlightenment, an oxygenated mix of mathematics, geometry, natural philosophy, and theological speculation.

"Mr. Silvester's Island"

Born in East Hampton in 1694, Brinley Sylvester moved to Newport with his father, Nathaniel II, and the rest of his family when he was ten years old. Nathaniel and Grizzell's only grandson to survive to maturity, Brinley was to be the manor's link to the next century. As an adolescent and then as a young man, he grew up with Newport itself and had entrée to its finest houses; the old house of his great-uncle William Coddington, once the town's grandest mansion, was a reminder of his family's long standing there. Over the next several decades, merchants thoroughly renovated or tore down many seventeenth-century buildings to make room for larger, sunnier, more symmetrical Georgian structures, both private and public. Houses glowed with precious Honduras mahogany and superb locally crafted silver, and their windows opened onto well-tamed "landskips."

Gardens brimmed with ornamental plants and apricots, plums, and other delicate table fruits. The local library loaned out Pliny's *Epistles* and Virgil's *Georgics* as well as Gerard's *Herbal* and books on "the Method of Improving Barren Lands."

Brinley kept his connections to Newport culture and style after moving back to Long Island sometime in 1718. On December 2 in Southold, he wed Mary Burroughs (c.1702–1751) of Jamaica, Long Island. A year later, they evidently moved into Nathaniel and Grizzell's old house with baby Margaret, the first of their two children, named after Brinley's sister and baptized by Mary's brother-in-law, the Rev. Woolsey. The couple were tenants of William Nicoll, to whom Giles had bequeathed the property in order to pay off his debts. But Brinley wanted to be more than a tenant; he wanted his grandfather's domain back as his own.

Luckily for him, Hannah and Giles's 1686 prenuptial agreement directing that the property go to "the right heirs of the said Gyles Sylvester" had recently been found in a chestful of Francis Brinley's old documents in Boston. (There's no way to know why Brinley's great-uncle Francis, so methodical about every detail regarding family and money, had not produced the document in 1707 when Giles willed his estate to Nicoll rather than to a member of his own family.) That ambiguous proviso, Brinley felt, might entitle him to ownership of the whole property. He believed he could win back at least some of the land if he sued Nicoll. Nicoll invited the couple to stay at the old place until the case was settled, and they promised to leave if Brinley lost. It sounds surprisingly reasonable, even gentlemanly. But Nicoll was confident of victory too. So confident that, one month after signing with Brinley, he made a new will leaving the manor house and its farm to one of his two illegitimate sons in the event of his death.

The Town of Shelter Island

The sell-off of Sylvester property that had begun with Giles and his brother Nathaniel's sale of a thousand acres to George Havens in 1698 continued through the first three decades of the new century as Brinley and William Nicoll battled. A few other small buyers purchased from George Havens's sons but continued to live on the North Fork, using their Shelter Island properties as remote pastures and woodlots.

Like other New York Colony landholdings that had been granted to one family—particularly those recognized as manors—Shelter Island developed slowly. It was first legislatively set off as a township in 1683, but no town government was set up and no officers elected. Finally, in 1729, New York's General Assembly commanded the handful of island freeholders to set up a government, but the place continued to be known colloquially as "Mr. Silvester's island."

The seventeenth-century fiefdom had irrevocably vanished, replaced by a settlement, a town. In the nearly three centuries that have passed between 1730 and the present, less has changed in terms of social hierarchy and local government than between 1651, when the Sylvesters and their partners made their purchase, and 1730. The outlines of many fields—some of them now covered with development—still exist. Except for a change in the north ferry landing, the major road, crossing the island in unending dogleg turns, is still recognizable. James Fenimore Cooper, who had stayed on Shelter Island and was a partner in whaling ventures with Charles Dering, a Sylvester descendant, was seduced by this same thick timelessness in 1849 when he wrote *The Sea Lions*.

At last, in 1735, the verdict came down from New York Colony's Supreme Court: Brinley had won back a thousand acres of land and his grandfather's old house. Nicoll, who already owned the largest land patent on Long Island, Islip Grange, 51,000 acres, went on to fry other fish as Speaker of New York's General Assembly, apparently remaining content with what lands he had on Shelter Island, including the 2,200 acres he had purchased from Giles in 1694, which he would leave to his son, William II, who moved to Shelter Island in 1726 upon his inheritance. Known as Sachem's Neck (and today the Nature Conservancy's Mashomack Preserve), the long point of land is the least arable and perhaps the most beautiful part of the island, where ridges of oak and beech rise from a skein of tidal ponds, and where the last nineteenth-century Indian who was born on Shelter Island lived.

Brinley, titular "lord of the manor" even during the years of struggle, fitted the mold of a New England country squire. His fellow Shelter Islanders (twenty-one families in 1730) respected him as such. They considered him "a very handsome man, distinguished for his courteous manners and general benevolence," as well as "a fine equestrian." An eminent livestock breeder, he paid a whopping £120 in 1745 for a "rhone [roan] stallion," to be transported with care from Sakonnet, Rhode Island. Brinley diligently noted every outlay for hay, freight, and stabling, and "oats to keep him while at Newport."

A model of law and order, comity and culture, in 1732 Brinley became town supervisor, an administrative position equivalent to mayor that had evolved from its designation as town treasurer sometime in the seventeenth century. He served in every government from then until his death, frequently holding multiple positions. He and William Nicoll II, the son of his old adversary, worked together, apparently quite amicably, in the town's government between 1734 and 1752, the year of Brinley's death.

Brinley was the local go-to man when the colony wanted someone of stature to "investigate the complaints of Indians at Montauk." (Even though the complaints—of deliberate encroachment on Indian lands and rights—were well founded, Brinley and his fellow commissioner predictably found them "baseless.")

He served as surrogate of Suffolk County and associate justice in the Court of General Sessions, which heard criminal cases, and he acted as the local banker. Because he was a port collector, real money flowed through his hands in all the varied currencies of the cash-starved colonies—"pieces of Gould," "pistoles," and "Spanish dollars," as well as standard English pounds, shillings, and pence.

Accommodating, cheerful, and well mannered, Brinley strove to help his neighbors frame a decorous, dignified society. For him, responsible government and organized religion were natural allies, even though they were no longer officially linked along the lines of the seventeenth-century Puritan theocracy. But on an island where five or six leading landowners held all the power, and nearly all of them, stoutly Presbyterian, attended the only house of worship (which they had paid to build), a de facto union of church and state persisted.

The "New Lights"

Meanwhile, the major religious revival movement of the century was pulsating wildly just across the water: the Great Awakening of 1739 to 1745. The "New Lights" (as devotees called themselves) considered a rapturous personal conversion the measure of salvation, abandoning the Puritan (and Quaker) insistence on rigorous self-examination and scrutiny by an elect. The Great Awakening also reacted against the Enlightenment:

many found its distant, rational God less enthralling than a radiant and immediate Presence. Revivalist preachers such as the English George Whitefield and the American James Davenport, the minister of Southold, filled the churches, barns, and fields where they spoke. The converts, the self-styled "wounded," were left in states not unlike those of the early Quakers' violent "convincements": convulsions, fainting fits, and profound trances, with the afflicted lying open-eyed, reading in "the Book of Life in Golden Capitals" the names of those who would end up in heaven. Mass rallies and new evangelical congregations broke down social and racial barriers.

Brinley's Anglican father, Nathaniel Jr., very likely reared his children in the Church of England. And as Brinley grew to manhood in Newport, God "withdrew slowly into the Newtonian stratosphere," so that Newport's famed acceptance of any and all faiths was further tempered by a neoplatonic largeness of vision, a sense that just as no one had God's will perfectly right, no one could corner the market in perfection. Although Brinley thus found himself prepared to join Long Island's Presbyterian mainstream, he was definitely not someone who could be "wounded" by the preaching of any "New Light" evangelist.

Neither was the Reverend William Adams, whom squire Brinley imported to his island as an antidote to radical contagion. Adams had no interest in public firebreathing, and, loath "to be encumbered with wife or parish," he freelanced for sixty years, about thirty of them in the safe, comfortable berth on Shelter Island where he officiated mostly as Brinley's private chaplain and had no official ministerial duties. An impression of "this amiable shepherd," short, stout, and equipped with an angler's rod, rambling the countryside in his white wig and cocked hat, conjures up Shelter Island's eighteenth-century pastoral calm.

"I Want to Make Sum Money"

Sylvester Manor's handsome steeds and table silver—like Newport's garden books and sandstone-and-brick houses—were bought with proceeds from the slave trade. Or so goes the story, which manages to be both true and false. The North American "Guinea trade" indeed centered on Newport, which sent some eighteen to twenty-two ships to the west coast of Africa for slaves and gold every year between 1732 and 1764. Most of Newport's top-tier investors bought shares in these voyages. The returns could justify the risks: "At a time when merchants considered 10 to 12 percent return on investments 'a noble thing' . . . the Champlins, a prominent Newport family, made 23 percent on a slaving voyage in 1773."

"How was it that this unpromising, barely fertile region, incapable of producing a staple crop for European markets, became an economic success by the eve of the Revolution?" asks Bernard Bailyn about New England. He answers his own question by describing the region's economy as "an annex, an offshoot, a service industry of the great powerhouse of the Atlantic economy in the pre-Revolutionary period: slave plantations and their workforce . . . Without the sugar and tobacco industries, based on slave labor, and without the growth of the slave trade, there would not have been markets anywhere nearly sufficient to create the returns that made possible the purchase of European goods, the extended credit, and the leisured life that New Englanders enjoyed. Only a few of New England's merchants actually engaged in the slave trade, but all of them profited by it, and lived off it."

The foundations of Newport's eighteenth-century fortunes rested on the coastal colonial and West Indian provisioning trades, which generated steady profits year after year, just as they had for Nathaniel. Because Rhode Island's tiny acreage could not furnish provisions and goods in the huge quantities needed for the West Indies trade, Newport's citizens established complex networks with other continental colonies from whom they purchased what they would then sell south at higher rates. Brinley did the same: he informed a nephew that he planned to ship beef and mutton to Boston, "for I want to make Sum money there Early in the Spring."

Brinley was no Newport Champlin, however. He operated regionally, running wheat, horses, and cattle to Boston, New York City, and points in between. What he shipped to Rhode Island, a collection point for the provisioning trade, undoubtedly found its way to the sugar islands, as did a shipload of goods for which he signed the clearances in December 1747 as "Deputy Collector, Surveyor & Searcher" of Southampton. The sloop *Hampton*, burden thirty tons, sailed for Jamaica out of the "East End of Long Island" with a cargo of over a hundred barrels of beef, pork, and tallow, as well as Indian corn, bunches of onions, staves, shingles, barrel hoops, and anchor stocks. Livestock aboard were twelve horses and seventy sheep. The venture was as typical of the West Indies trade on Long Island in the mid-eighteenth century as Nathaniel's much smaller shipments had been in the seventeenth.

Brinley also acted as a factor, or intermediary, for the wide Long Island community that he supplied with goods as small as "1 bottle of Beachman's Drops." The vessels of his cousin, Captain Benjamin L'Hommedieu of Southold, active in both the coastal and West Indian trades, brought Brinley necessities like salt, as well as luxuries such as "6 China Custerd Cups" and a mahogany tea table. Brinley also made a range of domestic goods to sell and occasionally branched out beyond the usual farm products. He asked his cousin L'Hommedieu to ship him "a Barrell of the Best of Tarr" from Mystic, Connecticut, to produce tar water (touted by Dean Berkeley as a medical panacea) for sale.

Brinley's direct connection with the West Indies is fleetingly revealed only once, in a note that Colonel George Bennett sent him from Jamaica in 1719 requesting an overdue payment of £68.17s for "rum, mollasses, and negros." But rum and molasses, the lifeblood of all slave-based international trade, flow through the account book Brinley kept between 1738 and 1746. In 1739, for example, he sold 170 gallons of rum, probably from Rhode Island, to a thirsty James Fanning. And as port collector for Southampton, New York—besides pocketing his official percentage from seizures of contraband rum, tobacco, and molasses—he earned an eight-shilling fee from the £4 duty imposed on every legally admitted slave.

Eighteenth-century slaveholders like Brinley and Mary regarded themselves as people of "sensibility," whose outward marks of refinement indicated an inner elevation. "The power of the genteel ideal lay in its transformation of personality; it lifted properly reared persons to a higher plane. At the same time gentility implicitly diminished the rest, creating differences which were difficult to forget," writes Richard Bushman. He is addressing tensions between polite and vulgar in mid-eighteenth-century colonial society at large, but his comments also apply to new lines being drawn between free and slave, white and black. The conditions in which slaves lived, the clothes they wore, while probably no worse than in the seventeenth century, fell further behind the ever more luxurious accouterments of their white masters. This new kind of distancing increasingly relegated blacks to a permanent underclass.

The last and largest entry in the 1752 inventory of Brinley's "movables" simply states "Negro slaves . . . £495," without any numbers, names, ages, or family relationships. During the second half of the eighteenth century, the average price for a slave on Long Island was £33.13s. (An adult male was valued at £38, a woman at a few shillings less, and a child at £24.) So a crude computation gives a figure of fifteen slaves at the manor in 1752. Long Island's total population more than quadrupled between 1698 and 1790 (the year of the first United States census), rising to thirty-seven thousand. The number of blacks rose more rapidly than the white majority. At the height of Brinley's prosperity, in 1749, the percentage of Africans and African Americans, enslaved and free, stood at 13.5 in Suffolk County, or approximately one black person for every six whites. On agricultural Shelter Island the percentage was probably higher.

The middle of the eighteenth century marks the nadir of Northern slavery, when the system was most tightly bound by custom, habit, and law. A freedman could no longer own property of any kind. Manumitting a slave required the master to post a £200 bond, ostensibly ensuring that the freed black would not become a public charge but in fact jamming the door to liberty. Slave owners' rights to inflict punishment expanded in New York Colony (which was known for the harshness of its criminal statutes) to the point where only maiming or murder was illegal. Slaveholders who exceeded the limits got off with light sentences. When one New York man beat his runaway slave to death, the jury judged this an accident caused by "the visitations of God."

The code, designed after slave legislation in the West Indies and Southern mainland colonies, where gang labor produced a single crop, didn't fit the North. Judging from the variety of products that Brinley shipped from Shelter Island, the black laborers at Sylvester Manor had to be quite highly accomplished, able to move from task to task with expertise and judgment, both in the busy farm seasons and during the slack winters. The ubiquitous practice of "hiring out" to give masters every farthing of possible profit offered slaves further opportunities to acquire diversified knowledge and skills. They became valuable or even indispensable, and therefore were able to negotiate their positions to some extent, as Obium clearly did in his relations with the Lloyd family after he ran away. Punishing a slave severely cost an owner labor as well as profit. Loopholes in the acts passed in the first half of the century allowed masters room in "correcting" their human property. Consequently, punishments such as branding slaves' bodies, forcing them to wear iron collars or shackles, and severe whipping—all legal—were often reduced to less than what New York law stipulated. For Brinley, as it had been for his grandfather, a working balance that included negotiation with his human property was essential. However, "negotiation" took place in an arena where the possibilities always existed that a master's implicit threats of force and cruelty could become reality, and where slaves' resistance could finally topple into sudden, violent action.

"Madam Sylvester"

When sixteen-year-old Mary married her handsome Brinley in 1718, she presented him with a magnificent covered silver porringer made for her father, the New York City pewterer Thomas Burroughs, in the 1690s. Its old-fashioned baroque heaviness contrasts with the later refinements of the offerings for his bride that Brinley purchased from the famed Newport silversmith Samuel Vernon three decades later. Vernon's two porringers and a tankard display linear dash and nervy delicacy that foreshadow the parlor paneling Brinley would later order. The provenance of these two wedding gifts, New York and Newport, are symbolic of the trajectory of Brinley's life: always in heart and style "of Newport" in New England, he now would become—at least as far as his commercial circles extended—a colonial New Yorker as well.

Porringers, small handled bowls for porridge, were often exchanged as wedding gifts. Later generations of Sylvester descendants had their names engraved on the bowl to celebrate their own marriages. (Covered Porringer, made in United States, New York City, 1680–1700, silver. Gift of Sylvester Dering, 1915. The Metropolitan Museum of Art, New York, NY)

The Nicoll lawsuit shadowed the young couple's lives. As they moved into Nathaniel and Grizzell's dilapidated house with their year-old daughter, Brinley had his dog shipped to him from Newport, along with a muff and gloves for Mary. Although the little family sounds cozily settled, their situation was tenuous because of the ongoing lawsuit with William Nicoll: neither the house nor a square inch of island soil belonged to Mary's husband. This would be the reality of her life for the next sixteen years.

"To be lawfully evictd out of the said estate" was the operative clause in Brinley's 1719 agreement with Nicoll. Mary had been reared to be lifelong mistress of a family domain, but instead she found herself the temporary manager of a house and haunted by the possibility of eviction. As Brinley's relations produced affidavits and quitclaims to support their kinsman in his fight, the long, costly, disruptive struggle to hang on to the place continued and must have taken its toll on Mary as well as her husband. The hefty payments Brinley made to successfully defend himself against ejectment (eviction) proceedings brought by Nicoll in 1727 and 1736 reflect the effort required. The latter was a large sum—£182 sterling.

After Brinley won his case and had evicted Nicoll's tenants, and while demolition of the old mansion and construction of Mary's future home took place, she evidently went to stay with her family on Long Island until the house was finished. But the day the new timber frame was raised—always a moment of celebration—"Mrs. Sylvester came from the west end to see the raising and a great feast was given on the occasion," wrote the later island chronicler Lodowick Havens.

For all its sunny gentility, the manor house conceals very dark spaces. The front, or south, four-room "box" exists much as originally built, despite a string of later northern extensions. Facing south, so as to get plenty of light and sun, were the family's handsome living hall, now the "paneled parlor," and what today is called the "landscape parlor," because of the nineteenth-century scenic wallpaper that replaced its original paneling. The kitchen and downstairs bedroom, which today have been rejiggered as parts of the dining room and the library respectively, broke the force of the north wind and faced the Upper Inlet. Running the north-south length of the house, just as it does today, a central entry hall enclosed the main staircase. Two six-foot-thick brick chimney stacks, opening into fireplaces north and south, heated all four major rooms, an arrangement that would have satisfied any eighteenth-century standard of comfort. The depth of the stacks creates extra rooms between the north and south

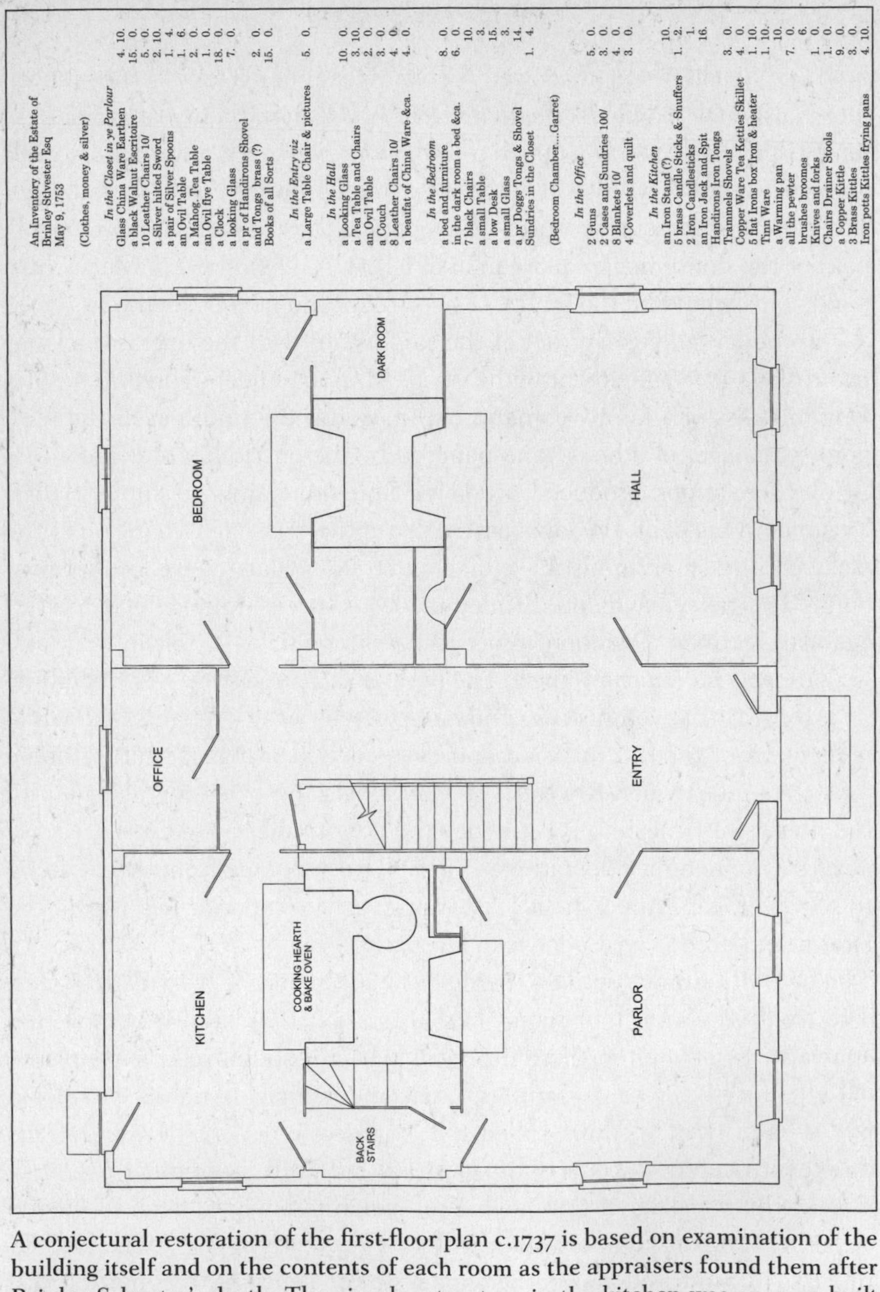
An Inventory of the Estate of
Brinley Stlvester Esq
May 9, 1753
(Clothes, money & silver)
In the Closet in ye Parlour
Glass China Ware Earthen 4. 10.
a black Walnut Escritoire 15. 0.
10 Leather Chairs 10/ 5. 0.
a Silver hilted Sword 2. 10.
a pair of Silver Spoons 1. 4.
an Ovil Table 1. 6.
a Mahog. Tea Table 2. 0.
an Ovil flye Table 1. 0.
a Clock 18. 0.
a looking Glass 7. 0.
a pr of Handirons Shovel
and Tongs brass (?) 2. 0.
Books of all Sorts 15. 0.
In the Entry viz
a Large Table Chair & pictures 5. 0.
In the Hall
a Looking Glass 10. 0.
a Tea Table and Chairs 3. 10.
an Ovil Table 2. 0.
a Couch 3. 0.
8 Leather Chairs 10/ 4. 0.
a beaufat of China Ware &ca. 4. 0.
In the Bedroom
a bed and furniture 8. 0.
in the dark room a bed &ca. 6. 0.
7 black Chairs 10.
a small Table 3.
a low Desk 15.
a small Glass 3.
a pr Doggs Tongs & Shovel 14.
Sundries in the Closet 1. 4.
(Bedroom Chamber....Garret)
In the Office
2 Guns 5. 0.
2 Cases and Sundries 100/ 3. 0.
8 Blankets 10/ 4. 0.
4 Coverlets and quilt 3. 0.
In the Kitchen
an Iron Stand (?) 10.
5 brass Candle Sticks & Snuffers 1. 2.
2 Iron Candlesticks 1.
an Iron Jack and Spit 16.
Handirons Iron Tongs
Trammels Shovels 3. 0.
Copper Ware Tea Kettles Skillet 4. 0.
5 flat Irons box Iron & heater 1. 10.
Tinn Ware 1. 10.
a Warming pan 10.
all the pewter 7. 0.
brushes broomes 6.
Knives and forks 1. 0.
Chairs Drainer Stools 1. 0.
a Copper Kittle 9. 0.
3 Brass Kittles 3. 0.
Iron potts Kittles frying pans 4. 10.
KITCHEN
OFFICE
BEDROOM
COOKING HEARTH
& BAKE OVEN
BACK
STAIRS
DARK ROOM
PARLOR
ENTRY
HALL

A conjectural restoration of the first-floor plan c.1737 is based on examination of the building itself and on the contents of each room as the appraisers found them after Brinley Sylvester's death. The circular structure in the kitchen was an oven built into the chimney. The "dark room," described below, is at right.

ranges of chambers, and the spaces to either side of each chimney accommodate the winding slave staircase and two closets.

In the 1752 inventory, one of these closets—a cubbyhole barely four and a half feet by six feet, opened off the ground-floor bedroom. Accurately labeled "dark room," this cramped, gloomy space was also unventilated. (A bookcase-lined alcove today, it has a door opening toward the garden.) The inventory itemizes "a bed . . . valued at £6" in the dark room. Ordinarily, a slave's straw mattress would have cost less, so this may have been a feather bed; whoever slept here had at some point received exceptional kindness. Even if the Sylvesters treated their human property with consideration—which the scant information available suggests that they did—the dark room and other coffinlike chambers deprived the people who slept in them of more than light and air. Every day, they rose earliest to silently and invisibly do their slumbering masters' bidding. On waking, whoever slept in the dark room glanced at the bedskirts and curtains housing the sleeping body of a captor. Even if Mary knew little about New York City's repressive Black Code, she would have remembered an incident that had jolted the entire colony. As a six-year-old in the town of Jamaica, she heard the story of how the Halletts and their five children in next-door Newton had been murdered by two household slaves as they slept.

Dear Daughter

Against such menacing shadows, some thirty humdrum letters—sent from the manor between 1718 and 1750—stand out for their wonderful domestic ordinariness. Mary tells her older daughter, Margaret (nicknamed Molly), who is staying with Boston cousins, that a harp is on its way to her. Mary prays that as Molly acquires a ladylike polish she will not forget to "be Dilgent in Making & Mending your Cloaths" and "Consider of the Things that belong to your Souls Peace." The enslaved people of the household figure casually in this correspondence: Reuben is "very Ill with a fevour & swelling," reports Mary to Molly, and Brinley writes, "we are all concerned for poor Chlo" and wonders "Wheather she is Living," since "Our Negros has got a notion she is ded, which I hope will not prove so." When the "dredful Surprise" of an earthquake shakes the house and rattles the "Cobard of Linnen," Mary mentions that "our Negrows . . . Say that both the kitchen doors flew open & put them in a great fright."

Death is ever present. As smallpox stalks Boston, Mary fears "what God is a bout to doe unto a World of Sinners." When Brinley's sister Grizzell Cotton expires after years of illness, he accepts "the Melancholy tidings" as almost everyone in his world greets death, with Christian resignation and a prayer that "God may be Sanctified to us all." Reports of smallpox, pirates, and blockades on the Sound periodically interrupt the years, while births and marriages thicken the ties of blood from Shelter Island to Oyster Bay, back to Newport, and north to Boston.

An account book records cheeses, tallow, lard, and candles produced for sale under Mary's supervision. Outgoing shipments of oats and live turkeys are balanced by incoming garden seeds (£4.10s. worth—a lot of seeds), two and a half yards of expensive lutestring silk for a dress, and coarse osnaburg linen for slave clothing. Mary longs to send Molly "a Jugg of Sweet Cream" from the farm. Drinking chocolate, "Butter Cups," and a breadbasket arrive, and a nephew searches for just the right new wig for the Rev. Adams. As a gift, Brinley orders "as good a white damask mantle lined with a white pealing as could be got in the City [New York]," but when the cloak is pronounced unfashionably short, he adds (ever the adoring father), "I am very sorry if it is not a good one, for I spared no cost to have it as Genteel & handsome as any could be had."

Tranquillity fills the place on a summer afternoon in 1740. A little dog barks and leaps—probably not Brinley's old dog from Newport, long dead, but another dog, one of many. (Alice's small black poodle is named Ezra L'Hommedieu, or ZuZu, after Andy's famous eighteenth-century forebear.) In the new house, Molly, sixteen, plays her harp and its notes carry on the little cool breeze that today still rises and crosses the creek on every hot evening as the temperature drops. The air blows through the west windows and the entire house and on toward the garden. A "linnen wheel" (Brinley has hired a weaver) whirs slowly to a stop somewhere in the background. Someone is sailing to the town harbor in the "Dorey," but the breeze has already carried the boat past the Negro Garden on the point, where a woman is weeding the rows; only the stern is visible now.

In Sickness and in Health

The tranquil appearance of Brinley and Mary's family life together as I first saw it differed from its reality. A shared tragedy begins to unfold for me from a single telling sentence in the Reverend William Throop's 1752 "Sermon on the death of Brinley Sylvester, Esq." Throop takes as his text "the merciful man" from the Book of Proverbs, eulogizing the departed in conventional terms as generous to the poor, "of an hospitable Temper . . . an indulgent father, a most compassionate Master, and an assured and faithful Friend." But then the boilerplate shatters: "He was a most tender Husband, and gave flagrant Evidence of the same, thro' a Scene of bitter Trial." Mary had died the previous year, but "flagrant Evidence" coupled with "bitter Trial" does not sound like a reference to some terminal disease. Throop's allusion to the "Trial" surely means that Mary's ordeal—a long struggle with mental illness—was general knowledge. The Rev. Adams, whom Brinley called his "Soul Friend," later remarked that the years he spent at the house of his "dear departed friend" had included "some of the most painful hours of my life."

As a conventional upper-class woman, Mary led a life of private domesticity. Her public appearances would have been at church in Southold, or at family events in Newport, Boston, and New York. Had a prominent man like Brinley undergone anything like Mary's travails, his condition would have drawn public comment, and an appointed guardian would have taken over his affairs. As it is, reports of Mary's psychotic breaks and treatment are confined to a few mentions in family correspondence, and two revealing letters from a doctor. The onset of her illness may have occurred in the summer of 1742. Mary had just turned forty. In a letter to Brinley freighted with news about a chaise and some chintz shipped to Shelter Island, and a promise of books and magazines to follow, his Boston cousin Thomas Hutchinson writes, "We are sorry Aunt Silvester does not enjoy her health better." He also politely inquires why no letter has come from Cousin Molly, who seems to have visited Boston a short time before. (My guess is that the news from Shelter Island may have been too painful for a young woman to tell even her relatives.) Only in hindsight does either of these circumspect remarks have any bearing on the struggle for sanity that would rule the rest of Mary's life.

In early April 1744, Brinley took his wife to see a Dr. John Smith of Rye, New York, a clergyman as well as a physician. Dr. Smith was, by his own account, "possessed of a Piece of Skill for the help of Distracted Persons," that is, the insane. It is unlikely that Mary would have had to travel far from home and enter a doctor's care unless her mental state had reached some crisis. But by the spring of 1744 Brinley and his daughters could no longer manage Mary's derangement at home, where most "madness" was still treated. Dr. Smith wrote that Mary agreed to treatment in his private asylum—"She is with us [as a patient] and chose after your departure to be so." What a parting from her husband that must have been.

At the end of May, Dr. Smith wrote, "My long Silence has been occasioned by the slow advances in Your Spouse's Case, not having much to write that was encouraging." He has had "uncommon difficulty in her Case; and tho She be now vastly beter than when She came here; yet such is the temper of her Mind, that when her case will be perfected is very uncertain." He goes on to acknowledge that "her Case I have never mett with," but notes that "her countenance is much altered for the better," and that "she grows very fleshy, looks well to what she did at her first coming hither." Although Mary has periods "of talking & acting very rationally . . . when she is more yeildable in her temper to my advices," she is, Dr. Smith concludes, "being very untractable." He advises that "of necessity [she] stay here longer . . . You may expect to hear . . . when I have anything . . . to write . . . Till then [I hope you will] wait with patience."

Dr. Smith, who was also the parson in Rye, was caring for the insane just at the end of the period when madness was considered an incurable "manifestation of a supernatural drama, with God, the devil, and the distracted person as the principal characters." Until the mid-eighteenth century, prayer and fasting were considered as efficacious as medical treatment or folk remedies. Before housing "the distracted" in asylums became accepted practice, living with them at large on the streets and at home appears to have been commonplace, although the violent and suicidal were sometimes chained in barns and outbuildings. Mental illness was just beginning to be associated with physical or psychological conditions that might respond to more specific and intensive medical treatments. If Mary wasn't so agitated as to require fetters, there's a chance that Smith's methods were relatively humane. As a specialist, Smith probably kept abreast of the latest procedures, which included bloodletting, purges, and forced vomiting to mitigate extreme "passions." Other therapies called for a "low diet"—virtual starvation. On doctor's orders, Mary may have had a piece of tape, or "seton," sewn through a fold of skin in her neck with a red-hot needle (to cauterize the wound), and left in place like a wick to drain away whatever poisoned her sanity. The father of

Mary Sewall of Maine had a "bunk made for M. to sleep in, with a lid to shut down."

Aware that darkness and isolation were standard remedies for "untractable" patients like Mary Sylvester, her family may have locked her in "the dark room." Was that £6 bed Mary's "bunk to sleep in"? Or would she have been housed in the equally dark "clossitt" adjoining an upstairs bedroom that also contained bedding? Either way, it seems hideously ironic that the proper place to confine a madwoman was an airless box otherwise deemed perfectly adequate for a slave.

Throughout Mary's progressive, chronic illness, Brinley appears to have tried hard to keep her in the life she had known. How long she remained with Smith, or whether she returned to him for further treatment, is unclear, but by 1749 she was back on Shelter Island. A brief respite occurred now and then, as when Brinley wrote to Molly, "Your poor mother has been with me . . . to wait upon her friends . . . & behaved very well." But more often it was, "Through the Goodness of God we are all well Except your poor mother, and she is much as She was when you left . . . She is often inquiring of me if I have hear'd anything of her Children, and now desires to be remembred to you."

The woman who had once penned such long, affectionate letters to her daughters was gone, had been long gone by the time Brinley wrote. I knew nothing of Mary's secret until my research was well under way; the worst I had imagined was that she had died of some common illness, at forty-nine, in 1751.

Brinley survived her by only two years. But he must have expected that he would have a long life in front of him: after Mary's death, he had written to a cousin in Boston to look out for a second wife for him. "I was in hopes and dreams to meet with an agreeable woman of about fourty of a good carector & family . . . for I find it very lonesome and uncomfortable to live as I do without a companion." Even though he was a methodical man (to judge from his detailed account books), he didn't make a will and expired intestate at the age of fifty-eight on Christmas Eve in 1752, only four months after he wrote that letter.

The manor house was left to tenants yet again, as it had been between 1693 and 1719. Ten years passed. Young Mary was not expected to remain alone without family on the island; she left for Newport, to visit her married sister, Molly, now Mrs. David Chesebrough.

Alice and I often talk of what went on in the beautiful house in those years, and of the furniture that remained there, and of how undusted and unpolished and uncared for things become in tenants' hands. If we are in the dining room, our eyes automatically go to the glittering gilded phoenix crowning the fine mahogany mirror that Brinley's son-in-law, Thomas Dering, brought to the house in 1762 when he moved to Shelter Island from Boston.

Thomas Dering, who married Mary Sylvester and moved to the manor in 1762, commissioned a sophisticated rococo bookplate for his library from Boston's finest engraver (Nathaniel Hurd. Bookplate of Thomas Dering. 1749. Engraving. Gift of William E. Baillie, 1920 [20.90.11(72)]. The Metropolitan Museum of Art, New York, NY)

17

The Doors

Thomas and Mary

From the mid-eighteenth century onward, in relating the history of the manor, I can turn to portraits, drawings, photographs, keepsakes—and this c.1737 house itself, the earliest Georgian house on Long Island. For the first time, faces survive to match the voices in Sylvester letters. English artists arrived to capture the colonial aristocracy in silk and lace. The English painter Joseph Blackburn, fresh off the boat, painted both of Brinley and Mary's daughters. Molly wears light blue with pink bows and a demure expression. Her younger sister, Mary, on the other hand, black-browed and black-haired, looks down knowingly from the tower of her long white neck. She is clearly as forward as they get, despite a dainty shepherdess's crook clasped lightly in one hand and a white lamb nestling in the folds of her blue satin skirt. Carrie Barratt, associate director for collections and administration at the Metropolitan Museum of Art, says: "The image itself is conflicted in a profound way: the lamb is virginal, but Mary is not, despite her white and blue. This dress never existed; there is a complete misunderstanding of female anatomy and of English costume as constructed and sewn. No corset, no fichu; dress apparently held together only with pearls; breast just about falling out of her bodice, hand cocked on her hip, elbow akimbo—altogether a very saucy, bold girl." (The frock is the kind of garment that the English aesthete Horace Walpole, writing about similar images by Lely and Kneller, called "fantastic nightgowns, fastened with a single pin.")

Alice Fiske, who has never thought about Mary in quite this way, loves both portraits; they are now in the Metropolitan Museum of Art, a Dering family gift in 1916. Handsome Mary's portrait in particular is a mainstay of Alice's costume drama of upper-class island life in the eighteenth century. That slender, finely wrought shepherdess's crook still leans against a door next to the slave staircase. Or does it? Like so much else at the manor, its history is more complex and must be disassembled, then pieced back together slowly.

In the case of the crook, this process begins only when Richard Barons, then the director of the Southampton Historical Society, pays a call. Alice and I gasp in horror when he grabs the shaft and twists off the finial—a metal screw top painted to look like wood! Not the carved wooden crook in the portrait, but a replica. When we check its appearance against a print of the painting, the finial design is clearly different. Among the hundreds of still-unsorted family snapshots in the vault, I now remember a two-inch-square early-twentieth-century black-and-white photo of a young girl standing in the manor driveway decked out in an eighteenth-century costume. She is one of Andy Fiske's many great-aunts or second cousins, dressed for a fantasy ball in her version of Walpole's nightie—Mary Sylvester, soon to be Mrs. Dering, come back to life during the Colonial Revival. A magnifying glass reveals that the crook she holds in her hand is the one with the metal finial.

In 1757, black-browed daughter Mary married merchant Thomas Dering (1720–1785). The Reverend Ezra Stiles, soon to be president of Yale, officiated at their Newport wedding. (Thirty-one years old when she married, Mary was old enough to have begun to worry whether she would ever find a husband.) At first the Derings lived fashionably in Boston, where Thomas and his brother Henry were merchant partners. A combination of bad luck, bad management, the failure of some creditors to pay them, and the loss of a family court case caused the Dering brothers' firm to fail; they dissolved their partnership in 1762. Thomas, Mary, and their three children moved to the bolthole of the thousand-acre family estate, taking up farming as their financial salvation.

Common Sense

If Alice and I could look into Thomas Dering's elegant looking glass and see his reflection as well as our own, we would be looking into the steady eyes of a mild-mannered, extremely devout, often sickly man who was the foremost American patriot of Shelter Island. Dering collaborated closely in the struggle for freedom with Ezra L'Hommedieu, who, like Dering's wife, Mary, was also a great-grandchild of Nathaniel and Grizzell. (L'Hommedieu is the man with Andy Fiske's nose in the portrait in the paneled parlor.) In the vault, a first-edition copy of Thomas Paine's *Common Sense* pamphlet, published in January 1776 and inscribed boldly on the cover by L'Hommedieu, tells us about the political beliefs of both Dering and L'Hommedieu. No longer "loyal subjects," they had become activists, revolutionary Americans who affirmed that the inherent natural rights of Englishmen belonged to them too. They called themselves Englishmen when they used the phrase "the rights of Englishmen," but their home country called them colonists. Without hesitation, both refused to take the British oath of allegiance to King George III. Working together, they played important roles in the war and took part in the formation of the new American government.

How did these two men come to challenge the power of the institutions and the laws they prominently supported and lived by? (It sometimes seems striking that there is less evidence of Americans being oppressed by the British than of Americans *feeling* oppressed—certainly the British thought the American colonists were doing very well—as indeed they were, by comparison with the Irish, for example.) In the 1750s and '60s, the colonies were reaching the breakpoint of what historian Jon Butler calls the "colonial dark ages," the seventy-five years before the Revolution, which have so often been skipped over in telling an American story that runs directly from the Pilgrims who challenged English religious discrimination to Sam Adams and the Boston Tea Party—the challenge to Great Britain.

Ezra L'Hommedieu, the son of Brinley's cousin, the well-to-do sea captain Benjamin L'Hommedieu, grew up in Southold, graduated from Yale in 1754, and established a successful law practice in Southold and New York City. As a lawyer, he was radicalized, like so many others, by what he perceived as repressive and illegal British tax legislation, and he was among the first on Long Island to jump into the fray. In 1765, at thirty-one, he had married Charity Floyd, sister of William Floyd, who held his first political office as a trustee of his home town, Mastic, Long Island, and went on to become a member of the second Continental Congress and a signer of the Declaration of Independence. Like Floyd, L'Hommedieu became a political figure and also served in the Continental Congress (1779–83). When the British occupied Long Island in 1776, L'Hommedieu exiled himself to Middletown, Connecticut, where he worked on the Committee of Safety to oversee the flight of Long Island's refugees across the Sound. From Middletown, he handled the loans Congress allocated to help the refugees. (George Washington had authorized repayment of expenses and living costs for the exiles.) But when funds failed to materialize, L'Hommedieu spent his own money. The man he worked most closely with from his perch in Connecticut was his friend, ally, and relative Thomas Dering.

Thomas Dering was prepared for the separation of the colonies from the mother country by his religious experiences. Across New England, conservative and radical ministers inspired by the Great Awakening struggled for control of their congregations. As the laity began to overturn established church governments and found scores of breakaway churches, they "developed novel arguments defending the rights of minorities, and they increasingly characterized the authority against which they were rebelling as illegitimate, even tyrannical." The colonial historian Patricia Bonomi writes, "The institutional disruptions and church separations of the Great Awakening thus provided a kind of 'practice model' which enabled the provincials to 'rehearse'—though unwittingly—a number . . . of the arguments . . . that would reappear with the political crisis of the 1760s and 1770s."

The Reverend William Adams, who had left Shelter Island after Brinley's death, returned with the Derings to his old position as family chaplain. Adams was not the only cleric to enjoy the comforts of the manor. Thomas Dering, struck by the revival movement, was a man who thirsted after God and enjoyed uplifting sermons—"I am almost starved for want of a preached Gospel," he complained to a young missionary friend in 1767. Preacher James Davenport's inspiration, the evangelical Englishman George Whitefield—the eloquent driving force behind the Great Awakening in 1740—visited Dering twice during his many tours of the colonies. Even if Thomas hadn't belonged to the political and intellectual Boston circles that rumbled against the British in the 1760s, Whitefield's convictions would have gone a long way toward strengthening those of his friend and disciple as New England's political temper rose. In 1764, as Whitefield was about to visit Shelter Island, he exclaimed in Boston, "O poor New England! There is a deep laid plot against both your civil and religious liberties"; a couple of years later he rejoiced in the repeal of the Stamp Act ("*Gloria Deo*," he wrote in 1766), and just before setting out on his seventh and last American tour in 1770, he inveighed from his London pulpit against "the great mischiefs the poor pious [Boston] people suffered lately through the town's being disturbed by the [British] soldiers," a reference to the Boston Massacre in March of that year.

Refugees

We can chart how fast the revolutionary fever reached Shelter Island from a letter a breathless young man wrote from New London, Connecticut, to his islander cousin, Nicoll Havens, only a week after the battles of Lexington and Concord. "Deliver with all Dispach," he scribbled on the envelope. The words of the letter still leap off the page. Twenty-one-year-old Thomas Fosdick wrote: "I Send you Inclosed the News Papers Containing the Most alarming News of the King's Soldiers Striking a Blow on the Americans. I've Recd. the News Last Night, & we are Fixing to go Immediately for Boston, So I have only Time to Let You know that I am one that is Going." Young Fosdick returned home to marry in the middle of the war, and he died on Shelter Island in 1811. It's a good bet he never forgot his own "famous day and year" when, already an American, he rushed to defend what was not yet a nation.

Only a few weeks after Fosdick wrote, almost all the island's freeholders, forty-three of them, "shocked by the bloody Scene, now acting in the Massachusetts Bay," signed their support for "whatever Measures may be recommended by the Continental Congress" and resolved "in the most solemn Manner . . . never to become slaves," using language that would eventually raise a national debate about the rights of all men. Thomas Dering's name heads the list.

After the Battle of Long Island was lost in August 1775, Shelter Island, like the rest of Long Island, was occupied by the British. Throughout the winter and into the next spring, more than five thousand Long Island refugees who had refused to take the British oath of allegiance fled across the Sound, crowding into the small towns of Connecticut. (Connecticut was held by the Americans, and the shoreline was fairly well fortified against British invasion.) With them they took what household effects they could carry aboard and what grain, hay, turnips, and potatoes they could get together, both to feed themselves and their animals and to keep supplies out of British hands. The Derings took with them twenty-one cartloads of goods, forty-nine "Large horne Cattle," and 204 sheep, along with twenty-six hogs and "powdering tubs" to salt the hams. It took

Captain James Jones four days to clean out his schooner, the *Elizabeth*. Two servants or slaves also made the trip; it's not known who they were. Like a large number of Shelter Islanders, the Derings ended up in Middletown, far enough up the navigable Connecticut River to be considered out of danger.

Like all refugees everywhere, the Long Islanders imagined their exile would be short. In fact, for the Derings, as for most, it lasted seven years—until 1783, the end of the war. As refugees, farmers lost the means of subsistence and their livelihood. Merchants and shopkeepers lost their shipping and markets. The West Indies trade was embargoed. Shelter Islanders left houses and farms to be watched over by a few tenants and by slaves, the slaves they themselves swore they would never become.

By February 1779, more than three thousand British troops were quartered in Southampton, Sag Harbor, and Southold. Reluctantly, American sympathizers who were unable or unwilling to leave swore fealty to the British crown. British adherents assisted the occupying troops while American intelligence and resistance efforts were organized behind the lines. Long Island militants returned across the Sound by night in their whaleboats to raid British encampments, taking arms and prisoners—and sometimes plundering the houses of their fellow refugees as well. Like the British, they fired without warning: Ebenezer Miller lost his only son, who was shot through the glass and curtains of an upstairs window by a Connecticut plunderer who saw a movement and thought it was a sniper. In the usual way of occupiers, the British looted and burned; abused and terrified helpless locals; ate whatever they could find; and commandeered transport. Fields were left untilled. Newport's proximity became a liability: the large British army quartered there regularly came to Long Island to fell timber and forage for supplies. As many as twenty-one British men-of-war anchored in Gardiners Bay.

Dering, by July 1776 already well in his fifties and always a frail man, did his utmost in the battle for liberty. He was a delegate from Suffolk County to the Fourth Provincial Convention of New York (1775–77), which unanimously adopted the Declaration of Independence. One of three men appointed as auditors for the refugee relief effort, Dering put his merchant training to good use, scrutinizing the mountains of accounting to present to the financially shaky American government for the refugees' stay in Connecticut. He spent laborious hours checking every invoice and receipt in hopes of ensuring fair repayment from the state to every request.

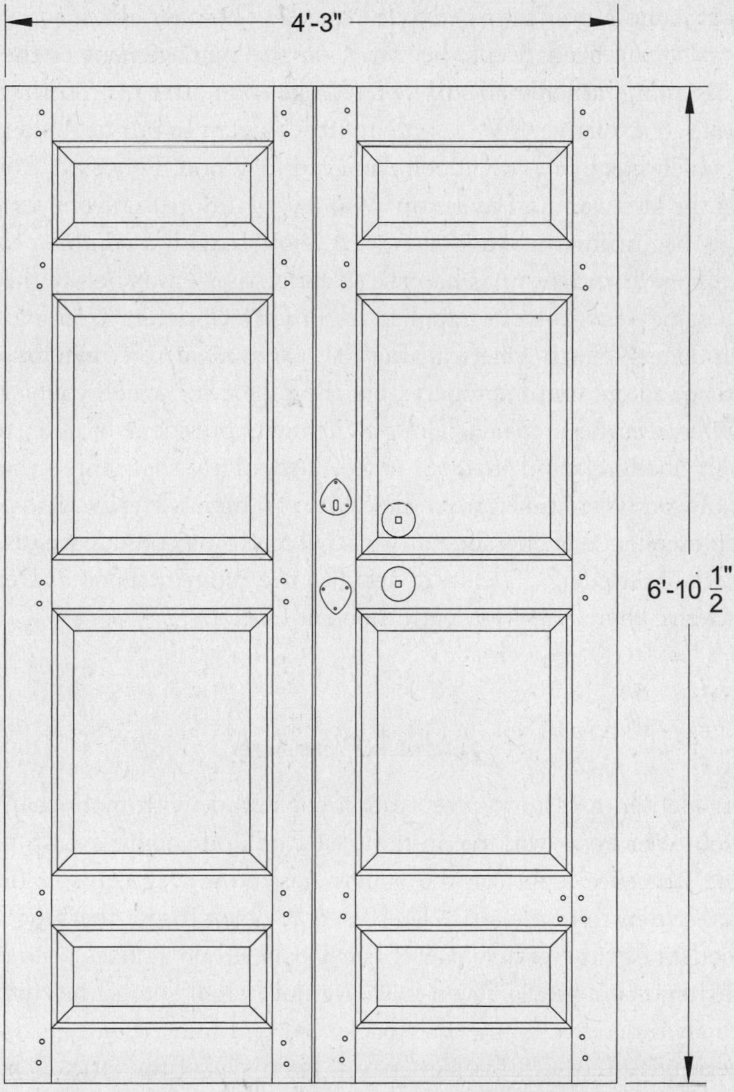

The double front doors that Brinley Sylvester had made for his c.1737 new dwelling tell us (and told his community) that he was setting himself up as the incoming "lord of the manor." Double doors usually appeared on a church, courthouse, or statehouse.

In 1783 the family returned to the manor. Thomas's eldest son, Sylvester (1758–1820), aged twenty-five, took on the management of the place from his ailing father, who suffered a stroke soon after his return. Sylvester wrote to a relative, "We . . . are returned again to our farm on this Island, which has been very much damaged in Wood, Fences & Buildings during the late war . . . I make this War a very unfortunate one for us, we are now beginning the world as it were anew & with a common blessing we shall put ourselves in as happy a situation as we was before the War." In the same year, Sylvester applied to Sir Guy Carleton, Commander of British Forces, North America, after the surrender at Yorktown for restitution for wood cut on the property, but the £1,400 for which young Dering petitioned was never paid. (Timothy Dwight, president of Yale, touring through Shelter Island in 1804, noted particularly that "three thousand cords of wood were taken from the estate of Thomas Dering, Esq., a man of such excellence of character as would, if anything could, have disarmed the spirit of plunder.") The list of debts on the estate of Thomas Dering in 1797, twelve years after his death, stood at £2,602.

Hidden in Plain Sight

Robert Hefner, a historic preservation consultant with more than thirty years of experience working on the East End and coauthor with me of a historic structure report on the manor, has found fragments of Brinley's original structure in the attic. These people never threw anything away if they could help it. A stately pair of heavy paneled doors have been hacked down from their nearly seven-foot original height. As a final indignity, somebody hinged them together backward and hung them upside down to act as a five-foot windbreak between two parts of the attic. Bob calculates the original height of the doors by assuming that the sawed-off bottom panels were mirrors of the unmutilated top ones (now upside down at the bottom of the windbreak), just as the center panels mirror each other. The combined width of the two door leaves is fifty inches, so there is plenty of room for them and a doorframe in the space between the nearest front windows of the two parlors. He concludes that the windbreak is indeed what remains of Brinley's double front doors.

In early-eighteenth-century New England, imposing double doors spoke the language of public buildings such as meetinghouses and town

When the house was renovated in 1839 by Samuel Smith Gardiner, who had married into the family, he removed the old front doors and reused them in the attic. On one leaf, someone scratched the date and an *X*, apparently meaning "remove but retain."

halls. They proclaimed Brinley's standing on Shelter Island as both the grandson of the founder of its English community and its prime public figure. (Indeed, at the time when the house was built, the only public building on the Island was Jonathan Havens's general store.) Up the Connecticut River Valley across the Sound, the grandees known as the River Gods also commanded double doors for their houses in the 1750s and '60s. But on the entire East End the manor's majestic portal was then apparently unique.

Even before a later manor owner removed these doors to remodel the entrance, they had seen hard use and neglect. The pine panels, stylishly grain-painted to look like mahogany, are heavily scuffed and scratched. As built, they were Brinley's statement of style as the lord of the manor. If we put the marks of wear on the same page with their later history, we can read the lifeless state of the house and the property when the Derings came home.

Bob keeps coming downstairs to the workroom with more discoveries. He has found the door of the delicate glass-fronted china cupboard that once fit into a corner of the paneled parlor. Cornelia's architect, Henry Bacon, opened a passage to the library in 1908. Juxtapose the contents of that china cupboard with the "Tea Table," and the "6 Teaspoons and Tongs" listed in Brinley's inventory: a party is taking place in this paneled room. The cupboard door's faint blue paint matches the parlor's fashionable hue.

Next, Bob arrives from the attic with a baluster from the original staircase—he found the full set in a cardboard box placed on top of the boards laid across the attic joists, where Andy Fiske said the slaves used to sleep. From the angled cut at the bottom of each baluster he can tell the height of the risers on the old stair.

Museums do this kind of reconnaissance work all the time, when objects or sets of room paneling come into their collections. House museums also conduct forensic inquiries, but this is a family house, which is different. This house is so lived-in. I feel that its many inhabitants have not only left their marks but are still here. It was their home, for better or worse, and it is now their abode.

Bob Hefner is now in the attic in a white overall suit and a mask: he has vacuumed out the insulation lining the cavity between the paneling in the bedroom below and the framing of the outer wall. Wielding a mirror exactly like an angled dentist's mirror, he peers down into the hole with a long flashlight. No nails. A good sign. The paneling in the bedroom below hasn't been removed and replaced, contrary to what the local historian Ralph G. Duvall wrote in 1932: "Much of the interior work such as the cornices, panels, wainscoting and the like was executed in England." No, it's American pine paneling on an American white-oak frame.

In the afternoon, master carpenter Nathan Tuttle examines the slave staircase. The contrasts between the airy front hall, where Brinley's stairway climbed grandly up (Samuel Smith Gardiner replaced it with the even grander flight that remains today), and the coiling darkness of this hidden one underline the increasing disparity between black and white, slave and free, as society grew more racialized and stratified.

Tuttle uses a midget handsaw to cut small sections of the finish boards off the corner posts to either side of the outer door so he can confirm the oak frame as original. It is. He moves to the dining room, where he performs the same operation on the cornice, looking at the staircase from the dining room side. He finds a wad of modern newspaper with a barcode lying in the cavity inside the wall next to the dining room chimney. Hmmmm. No apparent explanation for this one.

Alice has come home. It's late, she wants a restorative glass, wants to put her feet up, doesn't want to come admire the fine finish board Nathan has found that frames the top of the slave staircase door entry. Placed overhead and in darkness, it's invisible unless you climb up a few steps, turn around, and shine the flashlight on it. But Alice does come to peer at it, and is delighted. "Very smooth," she says, caressing it. Nobody would plane, chamfer, and sand a board like this for it to be seen only by the slaves and servants who used the staircase every day. It must be a piece of wood reused from Nathaniel and Grizzell's house, probably part of a casing for a ceiling beam in an important room.

As an aside, Alice tells us that the newspaper in the cavity near the dining room fireplace is there because quantities of newspaper have been rammed up both big chimneys, which are no longer used. There are no chimney caps, she says, "so the paper is scrunched up and rammed up from the fireplace with a rolled carpet. Keeps the birds out."

What is more significant is Bob's identification of four framing studs in the roof that are clearly reused exterior wall studs from the first manor house. They are pit-sawn in traditional English fashion, in the way that the first houses here were constructed in the seventeenth century, he says. Holes clearly indicate where the sheathing, whatever it was, was nailed onto them. "There are carpenter's marks on one which show these studs were pit-sawn," he says. (Pit-sawing is done in a deep hole, a sawpit: a big timber is laid across the hole so that two men, one standing in the pit and the other on top of the timber, can push and pull the saw vertically to produce a long cut.) "This means there was someone here, or perhaps a crew, who was familiar with traditional English house framing techniques," Bob adds. (Later housewrights dispensed with the niceties of sawing square studs and used saplings with the bark still on; bark still covers many of the other studs.)

So this is good news, that the reuse of timbers from Nathaniel and Grizzell's house is somewhat substantiated. Duvall had also written, "That which was serviceable of the prior homestead [was] worked into the new building." Sifting the documentary and material evidence, Bob has got to the bottom of a few of the stories that people have told themselves to remember, or resolve, or ignore the contradictions and gaps they faced every day.

Some weeks later, Bob finished the first stage of his technical examination of the structure. Now he has prepared a preliminary report, which he hands to me as we stand outside the front door in the sun. He has scrutinized the building inside and out. Besides lifting floorboards, prying out panels, and sawing through sections of corner-post casings, he has also calculated how many Atlantic white cedar shingles it would take to cover the outer walls—and then discovered an entry for exactly that many shingles in an account book in the vault. The first sentence of his report is a shocker: "An initial investigation of all exterior and interior building fabric of Sylvester Manor and the historic research accomplished to date have revealed that most of the exterior and interior building fabric dates from an 1835–1844 renovation [of the original circa 1737 structure] in the Greek Revival Style and a 1908 renovation in the Colonial Revival Style."

Bob is a man who fell in love with American history in the third grade. When he read about Daniel Morgan, the larger-than-life Revolutionary War hero, Bob's life course was set. Morgan, a rough-and-ready frontiersman, recruited a company of riflemen and marched them to Boston in August 1775, making sure his men's rifles were the latest models, lighter and more accurate than those of the enemy. Once on the battlefield, Morgan, a superb military tactician, ordered his men to pick off the Indians who guided the British troops through the rough terrain, and the British officers. The British, used to more polite warfare, complained. George Washington promoted Morgan to the rank of colonel, then brigadier general. Morgan topped his Revolutionary career with the battle of Cowpens, South Carolina, in 1781, considered the tactical masterpiece of the entire war.

Bob is Sylvester Manor's Daniel Morgan: he deploys his weapons to devastating effect. Sylvester Manor is a trophy, a precious hostage—"the earliest Georgian house on Long Island"—and as its ally he wants to cut to the ground the untruths and misapprehensions that have been marshaled around it. But in fact what we see—what Bob is talking about—is not all we have. He is correct in writing that "most of the exterior and interior fabric" is not original to 1737. Nonetheless, the most important structural elements are still here to tell the story of the 1737 house: the original oak frame, the old pine paneling upstairs and down, the slave staircase, and all the reused or saved fragments Bob has discovered that illuminate the house as Brinley built it.

The report also shocks Beverlea Walz, curator of the Shelter Island Historical Society, who is inputting papers on the workroom computer today. She has come outside to join us. Beverlea dresses up in a corset, fichu, and mobcap to take part in Revolutionary War reenactments up and down the East Coast. (A lover of textiles, she has let me finger an eighteenth-century embroidered cream silk waistcoat in the society's collections; the marks of the shoulder blades and back muscles of the man who first wore it, probably one of Thomas Dering's sons, are outlined in sweat and dirt on the back of the garment.)

For Bev, as for me—as for every visitor—Sylvester Manor is a treasure chest that still manages to encompass a fully intact history. "It's pre-Revolutionary," we say. "It's colonial," everyone says. "It's been standing since before our nation began." But the manor was also constructed from the inhabitants' ideas and dreams for the future. A widening gulf between Brinley and those who labored and suffered to realize his vision begins with the transformation of his hardheaded grandfather's mercantile outpost into a genteel country seat, ever more profitable and now newly elegant. The doors tell a version of the full story of Brinley's house from 1737 through the generation that inherited after the Revolution. By the time they landed in the attic in 1839, they had served the manor for a hundred years. But the previous century's promise of the Enlightenment had failed to materialize, either for the Sylvesters or for a republic sliding toward civil war. The portal to a rational, divinely ordained future no longer opened.

As we walk inside, I tell Bob and Bev about tragic, troubled Mary Burroughs Sylvester. "Are you going to tell us something terrible about Brinley too?" asks Bev, who has had enough revelations for one day. Like all who enter this house, Bev deeply wants the place to take her as straight as an arrow to its past, where comprehensible stories will unfold before her. I say no; Brinley's efforts to find treatment for his wife stand as a testimony to him. I step back into the paneled parlor they all knew. Behind the glass-paned doors of the mahogany secretary bookcase rests a jumble of choice antique pottery and porcelain—lusterware, salt-glaze, blue-and-white creamware—alongside valueless souvenirs made of papier-mâché and plastic. I open a cabinet door for a better look, puzzling over why some of these knickknacks have been granted such a place of honor. It's beyond me. They remind me of the figures of the century I have just traveled through—coarse or fine, cruel or kind, thoughtful or fatuous, sad, heroic, grotesque, beautiful, sometimes all at once. I close the door softly, without touching a thing.

18

Family and Slavery

"Commos Will Be a Plage to You"

It's summertime, already hot. I'm in the cool workroom when Steve Mrozowski walks in waving a thick bunch of papers, another document from the vault's innumerable and seemingly inexhaustible drawers, trunks, and crannies. Since I glimpse a court recorder's neat script and headings that list plaintiff and defendant, I can guess it's a transcript of a court proceeding. It's the story of a bitter loss: the pleasant, honorable, and much respected General Sylvester Dering (as he became), his wife, Esther Sarah, and their five children had not in fact "begun the world anew," as he had written on his return to the manor after the Revolutionary War. Even as they tried to repair the losses and move forward, the burden of inherited debt pressed on them. By 1827 the family had come on hard times.

After Thomas Dering's death, the 1,312-acre farm had been divided between his two sons, Sylvester and Henry. In 1827, seven years after Sylvester Dering's death, his share of that division, the manor house and its 578 acres, were sold at a public auction to Ezra L'Hommedieu's young daughter, the heiress Mary Catherine, and her lawyer husband, Samuel Smith Gardiner, a descendant of Lion Gardiner. The entire place, the property of Dering's children, went for $10,400 on the steps of an inn in Sag Harbor. Dering and her children considered Samuel Gardiner and his mother-in-law, the formidable Mrs. L'Hommedieu—a woman who watchfully managed her own (and her daughter's) investments and who was also Mrs. Dering's sister—to be responsible for this bitter family scandal. It is true that Sylvester Dering's children owed the L'Hommedieu estate nearly $6,000 (the rest of the auction profits may have gone to the government in taxes). Like other Shelter Islanders such as the Nicoll family, whose extensive property was auctioned by the heir Richard Nicoll and purchased by his brother Samuel, the Derings perhaps couldn't find other means to satisfy their debts among themselves.

After the sale, the Dering children scattered to points as close to the island as Sag Harbor and as distant as Rome, in upstate New York, making off with the portraits, furniture, silver, and many of the family papers. They left behind Thomas Dering's handsome glazed secretary-bookcase and a Queen Anne side chair in solid black walnut, which still stands on the landing at the top of the stairs. The Derings had lost their abiding treasures, the land and the house. And although the property remained "in the family"—Mary Catherine L'Hommedieu Gardiner being a descendant of Nathaniel and Grizzell through her great-grandmother, Patience Sylvester, a daughter of Nathaniel and Grizzell—the family rift never entirely healed. As I discovered in an innocent phone call to one descendant who told me he was still prepared to sue . . . and he wasn't joking.

For us, trying to understand life at the manor, the precious residue of the battle is the map included in the Gardiner family copy of the court proceeding to eject Sylvester Dering's widow from the "widow's third" of the land and house that she insisted she still owned according to her husband's will, despite the auction. She won, but she eventually moved to Sag Harbor anyway. Flipping through the document with Steve, I understand why he's transfixed by page four. I am too. It's a sketch plan of the house we stand in and its grounds in 1828. This single sheet of paper momentarily forces the limitations and difficulties of marrying documents and archaeology (where words say one thing and trowels another) to vanish. It all but says "Dig Here!"

Soon after this discovery, Steve and his team began excavating for the vanished structures indicated on Esther Dering's imperfectly scaled but tantalizing sketch plan. They tested the drawing by pocking the manor lawns with their usual sixteen-inch-square holes at the various locations that seemed to be indicated on the map. They found the vegetable cellar southwest of the house. And on the north lawn near the Upper Inlet, just where the sketch plan indicated that a dairy once stood, remnants of a dairy lay on top of one another, or mixed in together, from the nineteenth century back to a seventeenth-century stone floor. An undated early photograph taken looking toward the Upper Inlet from the front drive shows the top of the last dairy's roof. The rest of the building is hidden below a slight rise in the lawn. The layout of the farm buildings probably

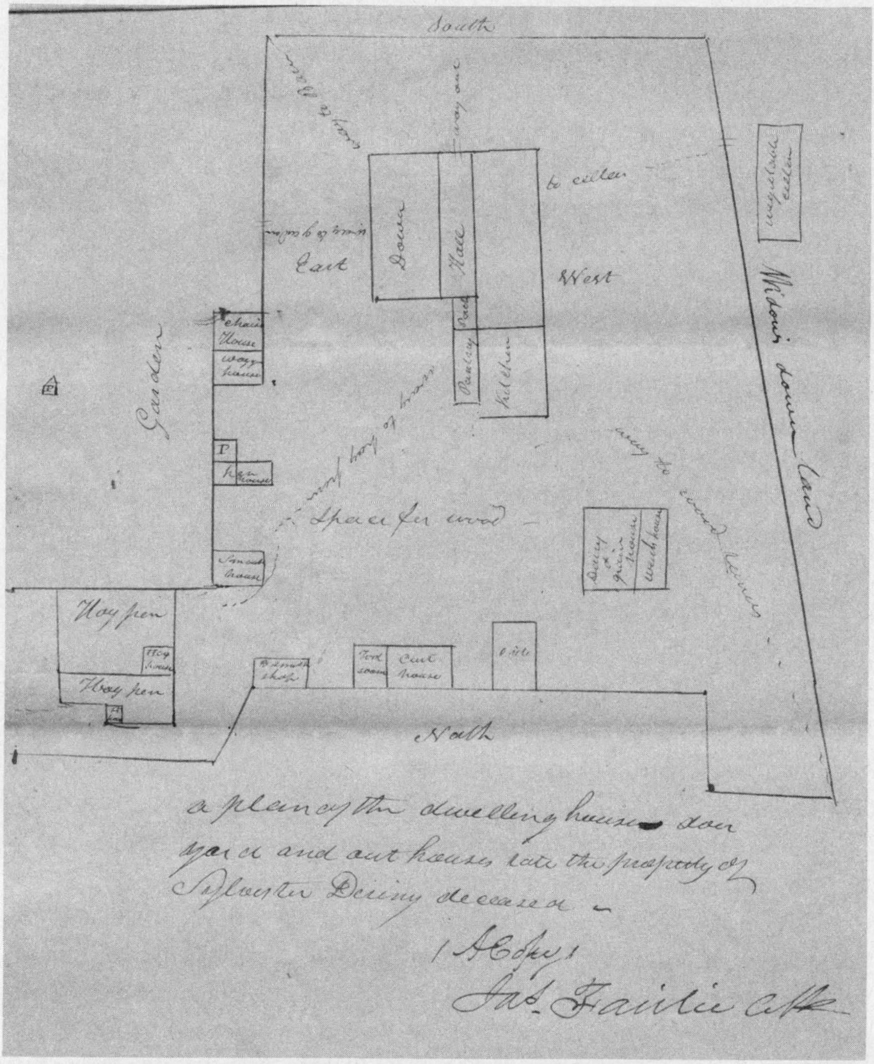

A Plan of the Dwelling House, Dooryard and Outhouses Late the Property of Sylvester Dering Deceased, detail. The scribbled legends on a hand-drawn plan, the most striking part of the drawing, show where Comus, Cato, Judith, London, Matilda, Hagar, and anonymous others worked their long hours. Comus was enslaved at Sylvester Manor from 1762 until his death in 1820, at which time slavery was still legal in New York.

resembled what Brinley had created in 1737, when he hid workaday areas from the front entry used by Sylvester guests. (Steve's eighteenth-century archaeological findings lie almost entirely behind the house along the Upper Inlet, where an 1867 map shows a line of small structures—an area still occupied by a tractor shed today.)

The "chaise house" described on the map, an elegant little shingled building for a single light carriage with racy lines—the Porsche of horse-drawn transport—still exists, although it has been moved away from the house. A single *P*, for "privy," presumably indicates the Georgian-style outhouse that still stands on the same spot in the garden. Long since torn down or reworked into other structures are the corncrib, the combination dairy-granary-washhouse, and the "smoak house," where pigs that rooted in the large pens and snored in the two "hog houses" were transformed into hams and bacon. The jog in a retaining wall where those hog houses impinged on the garden survives, as does the deep cavity of the hog pen, now filled with Alice's excellent compost. On the map, appendages to Brinley's beauteous box of a house stretch northward, not as large as Cornelia Horsford would later make them, but definitely there. The dates of these accretions aren't yet known, but Thomas Dering's 1786 probate inventory mentions a "Great Kitchen" and a "Little Kitchen." Dering's inventory listing of a dozen chairs in the Great Kitchen, six with leather bottoms, reveal it was more than just a place to cook.

Most gripping for me as a landscape historian are the scribbles showing where people walked every day doing their chores, following in the tracks of earlier generations. A man named Comus was purchased as a farm laborer by Thomas Dering in 1762 and died, still enslaved, seven years before slavery ended in New York in 1827. For fifty-eight years, or for as many of them as he was able, Comus would have carried slops and rotten apples on the "way to hog pen"; walked with his hoe and other tools along the "way to garden"; and used the "way to barn" for daily chores as well as the annual threshing that heaped the granary for winter, and for sale. The "way to woodlands"—the cart track that led past the site of the "negro garden and the Indian graveyard" located by Eben Horsford on the North Peninsula—and the vast "space for wood" bear witness to the imperative daily need for chopping and splitting fuel.

One of Thomas Dering's Massachusetts cousins, Hepzibah Edwards, may have advised him to purchase Comus in Massachusetts in 1762, in the months after the Derings' forced move from Boston to Shelter Island.

Once Comus had made the long trip, Hepzibah remarked in her characteristically pithy way, "as you say nothing of Comas [*sic*] I hope he behaves well." It wouldn't have taken Comus long to sense that his master's situation was at best shaky. A town-bred merchant short on funds for improvements to the property, Thomas was ill prepared for hands-on farming. His sister-in-law, Molly Chesebrough, had warned, "Dear Brother I must tel you that Except a farm is not manneged to advantage it is . . . a cirse [curse]: you must be Sence abel that it will take a Grat deel to Purchas Sarvants & Stock."

Things went badly between Thomas and Comus. Hepzibah Edwards wrote: "Dear Coz, I se by your Last that Commos [*sic*] will be a plage [plague] to you & suppose you intend to Sell him there or keep him as you dont say anything about him only of his rogry [roguery]." But despite her reference to his possible resale, Comus appears in a 1765 "Inventory of Personal effects now in possession of Thomas Dering at Shelter Island" along with Cato, Judith, a man and a boy both named London, and Matilda.

In the manor vault, a brief garden diary kept during some of Comus's years of servitude chronicles abundant harvests, a fruitfulness that demanded plenty of skilled laborers. The season began with currants and gooseberries flowering in early May and went on through entire fields of strawberries in June and July. (A drive today on the East End from Orient Point to Greenport on a blistering June afternoon passes strawberry fields dotted with Latino migrant labor stooped beneath that first cousin of slavery, debt peonage, under which a debtor must work for a creditor, usually his or her employer, until a continually mounting loan is paid off—or never paid off.) Later, the yield of dark "English cherries" was so great that off-island workers were hired, arriving by sloop with their ladders and baskets, making a party of the day of work. They were paid with half of what they gathered. It sounds like old-fashioned harvest festival fun, but beneath the bucolic pleasure lay the urgency of ripeness—cherries about to rot, or wheat and flax standing ready, demanding to be reaped before they fell. When Timothy Dwight traveled through Shelter Island in 1804, he remarked on a field of Sylvester Dering's that "yielded under a skillful husbandry between thirty-nine and forty bushels of wheat an acre." The "skillful husbandry" was directed by Dering, an Enlightenment farmer using the latest agricultural techniques, but the toil was almost entirely performed by chattel slaves.

The first Federal Census in 1790 listed ten slaves in the manor household of Sylvester Dering, Thomas Dering's eldest son. It would appear that he was farming big time, except that many of those slaves were far past their prime. The 1786 probate inventory for Thomas Dering's estate already listed "1 Negro man Blind (Comus)." Comus may have reached his seventies by 1812, when the island's Presbyterian church admitted him as a member, along with another manor slave, Matilda. He paid pew rent as a full subscriber ($2.50), but he sat in the four short rows reserved for his race at the back of the church.

On an island whose total population numbered only two hundred in 1790—less than that of many large Southern plantations of the same era—Comus was surely a familiar figure. But his local renown had been established as far back as the pre-Revolutionary period of Thomas Dering, judging from what a local historian, the Reverend Jacob Mallmann, relates:

> Among other possessions Mr. [Thomas] Dering owned a number of slaves, one of whom, by the name of Cato, was once caught in his wine cellar imbibing. Mr. Dering had him immediately brought before him for punishment, and in order to make his punishment as effective as possible, both on the guilty one and the rest of the slaves, had them all summoned, with all the whites whom he had in his employ, in the large servants' kitchen [the Great Kitchen]. Among the other slaves was one named Comus, who was remarkable for his keenness of intellect as well as for his immense stature, he being six feet and six inches tall. While the sin and punishment of Cato was being discussed, this giant of a slave rose up and asked permission to plead for Cato, and having received permission from his master, proceeded as follows: "Massa, you have pigs and you have corn, 'spose them pigs get in and eat some of that corn. The pigs are yours, and is not the corn yours just the same, if the pigs have eaten it? Now Cato is yours and the cider he drank was yours before, and is it not still yours after he drank it? I do not see why Cato should be punished." Mr. Dering rose and said: "Comus, thou reasoneth well. Cato, thou art discharged."

Mallmann wrote this in 1885, regaling readers with a tale that had been handed down for more than a century. It's a story told in many versions throughout the Atlantic slave world. The plot invariably turns on the issue of property. The subtext is resistance, couched as mockery of the legal fiction that people are things. Comus, as he rose in the Derings' kitchen, may have swelled to Paul Bunyan size in the island storytellers' imaginations, but before we dismiss Mallmann's portrait of the man as folklore, it's important to weigh Hepzibah Edwards's comments about Comus. Even though Edwards called Comus "a plage," Thomas Dering may well have had practical reasons to overlook a large, strong worker's bad behavior. What Hepzibah termed "rogry," her cousin may have come to value as intelligence and resourcefulness.

Mallmann's account of the kitchen tribunal makes both men shine. Thomas doubtless wished to be remembered as a just Christian master, and it appears he was. Comus had no say as to how he might be memorialized, but the thirty years before his death in 1820 at least granted him time to take satisfaction in his defense of Cato—a good story, one that evidently continued to sound as fresh to nineteenth-century islanders' ears, white and black, as if they'd never heard it before. These were two old fellows who had reached an accommodation with each other, wary, perhaps, but respectful on both sides, or so it appears. Forget for a moment Mallmann's jocular tone, and the high-flown biblical syntax he gives Thomas, and Comus's African American dialect. What did it take for Comus to stand up and contest Thomas's power? Mallmann presents Comus as a confident man who had fought to achieve a measure of self-respect and autonomy.

But not freedom. Comus was Thomas's property, and subsequently remained that of his son Sylvester. Becoming free was immensely difficult. Slaves had to negotiate and earn their freedom price, complete the contract or find someone to help them do so, register the bill of sale, and "secure approval from the courts or the Overseer of the Poor. New York slaves and independent blacks had no legal standing in the courts, and they often relied on third parties to undertake these tasks," as the historian of Long Island slavery Richard S. Moss writes.

The legislative progress of emancipation in New York State was agonizingly slow and circuitous, and so complex that even the simplest explanation of the various stages is almost unintelligible. Even New York's first antislavery law of 1788 outlawed slave importation and imposed heavy fines on offenders. In 1799, a Gradual Emancipation law ruled that children born to slave mothers after July 4 of that year would be considered free—with the proviso that boys serve their mothers' owners as indentured servants until age twenty-eight, and girls until twenty-five. The slaveholder could thus profit from a servant's most productive years without any loss of investment. Anyone born a slave before 1799 had to wait until 1817, when a second Gradual Emancipation law determined that all slaves born *before* July 4, 1799, would be freed on July 4, 1827. But children born into slavery between 1817 and July 4, 1827, were required to remain bound servants until they turned twenty-one. Incredible as it seems to us today, had that 1817 law not later been modified to grant freedom to all slaves, a person born on July 3, 1827, in New York would not have gained full freedom until 1848, only thirteen years before the Civil War.

"Few enslaved people got free by convincing their masters that slavery was wrong," writes the historian John Sweet; "many, however, did earn manumission as part of a more or less articulate *quid pro quo* . . . Still, any agreement forged by masters and slaves was effective only to the extent to which it could be enforced." Enforcement depended not just on the law or the prodigious efforts of slaves themselves, Sweet says, but on a shift in public opinion that began in the 1760s and owed as much to a new secular humanitarian altruism as to lofty religious reflections on the golden rule or Revolutionary-era concerns about the natural rights of all men. Humanitarian thinking grew directly out of the eighteenth century's culture of sensibility. As compassion and a reluctance to inflict pain became touchstones of civilization, white Northerners eventually questioned the morality of the whole system. The newly awakened emotional response to cruel treatment of fellow creatures often came first: "What is necesary, is to stir up the Sparks of Compassion in the human Breast." As Sweet tellingly observes, however, instead of confronting the central problem of race relations—equality—such an appeal to the heart instead "provided . . . a compelling correlative to the language of natural rights and Christian benevolence precisely because it evaded and obscured the question of equality." Pity seldom confers equality.

The House on the Creek

Julia Johnson worked sporadically as housekeeper at the manor for three generations of the Sylvester family. Born free between 1807 and 1811 in the last years of New York's slavery, she died in 1907. She was photographed as part of a suite of images—landscape views, documents, furniture, and small objects such as a portrait miniature and a snuffbox—for an 1887 magazine article about the manor by the historian Martha J. Lamb. Julia's expression is strained—no surprise, since taking a photograph required a long exposure. But eyes rolled heavenward, bowed shoulders, and hands clasped loosely in her apron—even the apron itself and her head kerchief, instead of Sunday clothes—cast Julia as a type, not an individual. She sits outside the manor's cellar door (a doorway that exists today). At the same time, elsewhere on the East End, many blacks and Indians headed to local photo studios in their best attire: in bustles, flowered and feathered hats and derbies, and dark three-piece suits. They themselves chose how they wanted to look for posterity. Julia was an illustration, costumed as a faithful domestic: the sentimentally inaccurate magazine caption reads "One of the last of the slaves."

The photograph of Julia sits in front of me as I transcribe documents at the manor dining room table. The crystal drops on the candelabra tinkle when I slide my box of papers across the mahogany. At the end of March, with snow blowing in soundless sheets across the creek, it is too cold to stay in the workroom. There is nobody else in the house today; Alice is away for Easter. The old furnace groans and mumbles and diligently blows gusts of hot air through the floor grate by the fireplace. The comforting sense of being inside and warm surrounds me.

One document more than a foot and a half wide is folded over to make four pages, with writing on all sides. It demonstrates how difficult it was for a free black man to hang on to land he had legally paid for. Dated September 30, 1828, this big sheet confirms a land sale transacted eight years earlier by Sylvester Dering and Comus Fanning, farmer. *Comus Fanning.* A second Comus, unrelated to the man who died in 1820. This man is distinguished by having a last name. He isn't a slave, he isn't called "Negro," or "Negro farmer"; just "farmer." Times are changing. Comus Fanning got both a surname and a start as a free man in 1796, when the will of his late owner, Captain Phineas Fanning, manumitted him. Fanning, who later lived on the North Fork in Laurel, a small village west of Southold, had been one of the two manor tenants in the 1750s, after Brinley's death and before the arrival of the Derings in 1762. It's not clear whether Comus Fanning was even alive at that time. But we know that

Comus (as I'll call him from here on) had moved to Shelter Island to work for Sylvester Dering at least as early as 1800, when the census lists one free person of color in the manor household.

For $35 per acre, Sylvester Dering sold Comus twenty-one and three-quarters acres of manor property, "beginning at a stake a little north of the outlet of Wilkinson Creek" with an existing "house . . . and garden . . . adjoining the meadow as the fence then stood." On September 15, 1820, Comus paid Dering in full—$750—a large sum for a former slave to have amassed. Only a week later, Sylvester, then sixty-two, took a fall from his horse, and he died from complications on October 8.

When Sylvester's heirs were forced to relinquish the manor because of estate debts in 1828, even though the bill of sale made note of the land sold to Comus, Sylvester's widow and executrix, Esther, signed another document confirming the 1820 transfer to him. "By inadvertance," however, she left out any mention of Fanning's payment. The illiterate farmer, who signed his own will with an X, would not have noticed the crucial omission, but the Derings did. It must have struck them all that Fanning's grip on his land could be slippery if the Gardiners came after him. Fanning was a black man holding a copy of a contract with a white man (by then dead for eight years) that acknowledged payment, but the executrix's later confirmation of the sale said nothing about it. Hence the four-page ratifying document signed in 1828 by the widow and her children that I found in the box.

Several months later, I discover a badly torn hand-colored map of the entire manor property rolled up in the vault. It had been completely hidden behind the largest and heaviest chest of drawers. (Restoring it to the point where it could be safely unrolled took more than a year.) On this map, an inlet a mile north of the manor house is simply marked "Creek"; a little rectangle is labeled "Tenant House." Can this be Comus Fanning's house? Confusion exists because the locals call this inlet "Dyd's Creek," not "Wilkinson." However, by now I know from a later description of Julia Dyd that she lived somewhere north of the manor. When I walk to the creek I find one of the most beautiful water views on the island. The property faces south, sloping gently to a calm expanse of water fed by fresh springs visible only at low tide. On the sandy, sunny bottom, small, almost transparent crabs dance sideways. Minnows and tadpoles flirt with their own dark shadows; the shadows of overhanging leaves flicker above them.

A blue heron stands in the shallows, watching. Swallows swoop through shining clouds of gnats, open-beaked, catching a meal. A fish lunges up at a fly. Louise Tuthill Green, who grew up on the island, remembers shrimping as a girl in this brackish tidal cove, which teems with life. A poem of a place: woods, water, pasture, sheltered harbor for small craft. In summer, no houses are visible: they are hidden in the deep green woods that spill down to the encircling bright stripe of salt marsh—sweet shrub, spartina, and salt grass.

I then discovered from Comus's will that Julia was the child of Comus's wife, Dido. The vanished tenant house shaded by the big oaks that still stand here was where Julia lived as a child. Next to the garden lay enough pasture for two cows. In Comus's years working for Sylvester while he saved his money, he may have spotted this ideal place or lived here: no sweeping views, no lofty heights—just soft, small perfection. His own good ground. To get to work at the manor he could have rowed about a mile, heading south from his own creek. Or, if he traveled on foot, he walked farther along the track that crossed the North Peninsula, climbing over the high pasture knob and skirting the Negro Garden and Indian Graveyard. Then the land bridge led him to the line of work buildings along the Upper Inlet. From there he traversed lawns and gardens, heading for the farm barns near the Burying Ground of the Colored People.

At Comus's death in 1831, his executor, Charles T. Dering, one of Sylvester and Esther's sons, oversaw the bequest of twenty-one acres to Dido, "my wife the woman I now live with," and after her death, "to a daughter of the said Dido named Julia who now resides with me . . . and to her heirs and assigns forever." The one-page testament Comus signed on June 2, 1831, marked a watershed moment simply because it exists—a rare example of the will of a freed black man on Shelter Island. And his legacy appears to have been the largest freehold owned by a black islander at that time. "Dido a colored woman being duly sworn in" to confirm the will as that of Comus, appeared in court to sign her affidavit with an X, "her cross."

Comus's probate outlines a neat and self-sufficient rural life that Jean-Jacques Rousseau or Henry David Thoreau would have admired. But seen another way, the Fanning family's meager effects are fewer than those accumulated by most first-generation New England yeomen. It had taken Comus thirty-six years as a free man—and however long Captain Fanning had let him work for hire—to become an extremely modest farmer. By the 1830s he had acquired a mattress, a bedstead, and a coverlet, three window curtains, a table (set with plates, cups and saucers, knives and forks, and six glasses), chairs, fire tools and a pair of andirons, a large iron kettle, and the chest in which he locked his will. The other possessions that made his life safe and profitable included a scow, a grain cradle, an ax, three tin milk pans, and two fine cows—at $25 each worth eight times more than his three-dollar gun, the second most valuable item. That "no money or notes belonging to the deceased have come to the knowledge of the executors" tells us that most of his family's economic well-being probably rested on barter.

Comus, Dido, and Julia belonged to a community of free black men and women. According to the 1790 census, the first to list free blacks on Shelter Island, they were almost as numerous as slaves, twenty-three as against twenty-four. That census marked the high point of the island's African American populace overall: forty-seven blacks out of a total of two hundred people. But only two black families—both headed by second-generation entrepreneurs—possessed their own houses. All other freedmen listed in the 1790 census lived in white households, probably those of their former owners. Like Comus, most adult slaves began their free lives with little or no education, meager or no savings, severely restricted voting rights, and lower wages than a white person would pocket for the same work.

Whites only reluctantly sold property to blacks, as the example of Matilda demonstrates. After thirty years of unpaid bondage at Sylvester Manor, Matilda began her life as a free woman in 1795 with no assets. Henry Packer Dering, Sylvester's brother, lent her $75—to be repaid with interest—so she could build a house. Dering stipulated that "as soon as the said Matilda pays . . . the said Note [she] shall be intitled to the said house or building [but to no land]." Even after paying off that debt, she still owed Dering annual rent of $10 for her land. He kept a ledger of her accounts, accurate to the penny. Earning too little to cover her rent and living expenses, until her death in 1818 Matilda was as much a prisoner of debt as any migrant worker today. Unlike Comus Fanning and Dido and Julia, although free, Matilda was not a freeholder. Barriers to land ownership had much to do with the decline of Shelter Island's black population. The railroad reached nearby Greenport in 1844, and every African American who could do so left for what then looked to be better opportunities in the cities. By 1870 only thirteen blacks are listed in a total island population of 632.

In his early-nineteenth-century memoir of Shelter Island, Lodowick Havens, born in 1774, reached back deep into his childhood to recall the slaves of his distant cousin, Nicoll Havens (young revolutionary Fosdick's correspondent), who died in 1783. Lodowick wrote, "In them days all kept slaves as could afford it." His list includes a Dido—after the name of the Numidian queen of Carthage, the heroine of Virgil's *Aeneid*—a name that was frequently given, ironically, to black female slaves by classically minded captors eager to flaunt their knowledge.

The Shelter Island Presbyterian church records list a Dido, aged sixty-two, who died in 1834. Because Julia, who had married a Morris Johnson at an unknown date, sometimes used Havens as her surname, it seems likely that this Dido was the same woman mentioned by Lodowick Havens and the mother of Julia. At other times Julia was known as Julia Dyd, using a matronymic, a common pattern used in slavery to recognize the mother but not the father of a black child. Like other slave states, New York refused to recognize marriages between people in bondage (and even those who had been freed) until 1809. The children of such unions were therefore officially bastards. Who was Julia's father? Dido never identified herself as Dido Havens, and no male parent for Julia is mentioned in Comus's will or any other document. Was Julia the child of a Havens slave, or of a white Havens owner? Dido took the answer to her grave in 1834. Julia left us only her trail of names to wonder about.

19

Summer Colony

Suitable Alliances

Against a wall inside the vault stands an old steel safe coated in cream enamel and filled with relics. Softness brushes my hand as I unfold a crumpled tissue packet: out falls a foot-long trail of blond ringlets and a glossy brown braid tied with twine. Might either have belonged to the same Mary L'Hommedieu Gardiner whose fortune kept the manor in the family in 1827? She died of a fever at age thirty-two in the landscape parlor. During the nineteenth century, a woman's hair was often shorn when she was ill or after a difficult birth, supposedly to conserve her strength for healing. When a body was prepared for burial, the bereaved clipped a lock or two to make a hair bracelet or brooch to keep memory warm. Mary's mother wrote down a sad little postmortem list of her clothes, which—unremarkably—includes shawls, a light silk dress, a loose calico gown, and some capes. But when I read about Mary's white silk stockings, her pairs of "draws," and the "baby things," she comes too close to me. I'm supposed to be inventorying the lifeless contents of this safe, but their owners refuse to lie still. I catch my breath when I open a box and see something quivering inside it. It's a still-pristine white shirt, one that belonged to Mary's husband. Who would think that starch could last for two hundred years—long enough for the slight inhalation caused by lifting the box lid to suggest a chest heaving under the double organza ruffles that Samuel Gardiner wore? Longer than today's dress shirts, this garment must have hung down to midthigh.

Gardiner's ruffled front invokes the man. Born soon after the end of the Revolution, he died in 1859, two years before the Civil War. He carried the fashions of his youth deep into the Victorian era, and he contin-

Young and in a hurry, an unidentified woman walks through the shaggy lawn edging the boxwood path in the manor's garden.

ued to send his shirts to be starched and pressed by a local laundress, who still knew how to perform such tasks. His young granddaughters were wonderstruck at his outfits; Lilian remarked lovingly on his attire in a memoir, so it's no wonder that one of his shirts was carefully saved for posterity.

Samuel Smith Gardiner was the last proprietor to live at the manor year-round until Andy Fiske took up residence almost a century later. Gardiner's eldest daughter, Mary, moved to Cambridge, Massachusetts, as a twenty-four-year-old bride in 1848, soon after her marriage to the Harvard chemistry professor Eben Norton Horsford, who at twenty-nine had just set forth on his academic career. Mary died only a few months after giving birth to the couple's fourth child, and in 1860 Eben married Mary's sister Phoebe, who was two years younger than Mary. The youngest Gardiner sister, Frances Eliza, had wed a Bostonian, George Martin Lane, three years before. Although Samuel Gardiner had granted his children equal shares in his estate, Eben became his de facto successor. The Horsfords, the Lanes, and their offspring all used Shelter Island as a summer place, but the Horsfords took center stage as lord and ladies of the manor. With the Horsfords' move to Cambridge, the family returned to thinking of themselves as New Englanders, as Nathaniel and Brinley had done, while Sylvester Dering and Samuel Gardiner had allied their interests more with New York.

Eben—appointed Rumford Professor of Chemistry at Harvard's newly established Lawrence Scientific School in 1847—brought the exhausting, admirable exuberance of the nineteenth century to Shelter Island. With a polymath's intensity, he interested himself in everything that crossed his path, but particularly science and history. What eighteenth-century books remain in the house are predominantly religious or political; the nineteenth-century mind disports itself in the dark upstairs hall, where a floor-to-ceiling bookcase houses works of ethnology, archaeology, metallurgy, geography, geology, anthropology, and genealogy, leavened by some poetry and fiction and a dash of art history. More than two dozen of Eben's thin notebooks bound in marbled paper detail in his minuscule handwriting and drawings a lifetime of experiments and scientific observations. There are volumes in Latin and Greek, in French and Italian, and many in German. Before taking up his position at Harvard, Eben had spent two years at the University of Giessen, studying with the distinguished chemist Justus von Liebig, who invented nitrogen fertilizer (and dismissed the role of humus in soil health).

Although he was an active member of the conservative Protestant Shepard Church of Cambridge (named after the Reverend Thomas Shepard, one of Anne Hutchinson's most vigorous persecutors), Eben's life search was not a religious one. He was an inventor. He wanted to improve the human condition, to make life faster, easier, more efficient, and more economical. His many patented discoveries and methods—acid phosphate (a nineteenth-century "energy drink" and cure-all), antichlorine, yeast powder, and a process for condensing milk among them—were intended for immediate use as well as the long-term profits they could generate for his family. In 1863, forty-five years old and the father of five daughters, he quit Harvard, turning with zest to launching business ventures. Rumford Baking Powder (named after the American scientist who founded the Harvard chair) was Eben's most successful and lucrative product. A stable calcium biphosphate compound that replaced baking soda and cream of tartar, it raised the family fortunes just as it raised biscuit dough. Sylvester Manor's remaining 243 acres have stayed in his descendants' hands in large part because the nineteenth- and twentieth-century generations never needed to sell off the rest of the land for financial survival.

The Horsfords swirled about in the invigorating intellectual and social currents of Cambridge. Eben attended dinner meetings of the Saturday Club, the leading literary society of Cambridge, of which Emerson, Hawthorne, Longfellow, Whittier, and Lowell were founding members. He served on exhibition juries in Vienna and Philadelphia and took his daughters along. The family visited Newport and other fashionable New England watering spots, and they crossed the United States in a private railroad car. Distant cousin Helen Hunt Jackson, the author of *Ramona* (1884), the influential novel about Mexican colonial life in California, was a frequent summer guest at the manor. She shared Eben's enthusiasm for Indian life and ways and invited some of the Horsford girls to rough it with her on camping trips in the West, where they met members of local tribes.

Rocking Chair Sagas

The family came to Shelter Island and bathed in the formidable quiet. They reshaped the story of the manor to suit themselves, savoring the place and its history as the Past while introducing indoor plumbing, electricity, window screens, and newfangled contraptions: the island's first telephone, the latest metal windmill, and a "touring motor." They toyed with new names for their beloved homestead. What had been simply "the Gardiner farm" became Woodstock at one point, inspired by Sir Walter Scott's Cavalier-and-Puritan romance of that title and by the female Horsfords' visions of their ancestor, Auditor Thomas Brinley. Sylvester Manor eventually stuck, grandly emblazoned on writing paper and on new entrance gates that stand at the main road today.

Over the years, the Cambridge intelligentsia descended in droves. Poet friends arrived—Longfellow, Whittier, Lowell. So did Annie Fields, editor, publisher, and host of Boston's most distinguished salon, accompanied by her more famous lover, Sarah Orne Jewett, who would chronicle literary New England's Golden Age in memoirs and biographical sketches. Jewett's work, at its most luminous in *The Country of the Pointed Firs* (1896), generated an interest in atmospheric locales and characters, part of a national post–Civil War nostalgia for the innocence of a rapidly vanishing rural past. The Shelter Island that Jewett first visited in 1883

In the summertime shade of the big trees near Gardiners Creek, Phoebe, Kate, and Lilian Horsford enjoy their rocking chairs, a solemn Dr. Morrill Wyman meditates, and Professor Horsford points out a detail of the manor house to an unidentified woman.

would have seemed just as gently untouched by modern times as the coastal New England she depicted, with its old salts and ancient turns of phrase.

During the long summers, the Horsfords and their guests from Boston and New York exchanged the latest gossip, discussed the great issues of the day, and dwelled lovingly on the manor's history. The men and women gathered there included pioneers of philanthropy, advocates of social justice, and champions of female higher education. Henry Fowle Durant, who, with his wife, Pauline, founded Wellesley College in 1875, was Eben Horsford's best friend; Horsford, the president of the Board of Visitors, established the scientific curriculum and provided salaries and sabbaticals. (Oddly, none of the Horsford girls attended college—but then higher education was widely considered unnecessary for upper-class women who didn't need to earn a living.)

No doubt partly as a relief from the brute realities of nineteenth-century capitalism, they eagerly worshipped the past together. The house itself became a member of the Horsford family, like a beloved old aunt.

They adorned her with rescued trophies. When the American elm on Cambridge Common under which Washington had taken command of his troops was felled, the Horsfords had an armchair crafted from some of the wood and affixed a commemorative brass plate to its back. When Justice Oliver Wendell Holmes's venerable family house in Cambridge was torn down, the Horsfords brought a mantelpiece to Shelter Island and installed it in the room where Longfellow slept, attaching yet another brass badge of provenance. Alice told me that Longfellow once complained that his coffee cup was too small; they *had* to find a bigger one. And so the corner cupboard of what she called the Longfellow Room now holds a supersized Royal Worcester cup. "Longfellow's," said Alice. Ordinary objects reverberated with talismanic national overtones that had not accompanied the keepsakes of previous generations.

Summer also meant pageants in which the Horsford girls dressed up and played their ancestors—a sentimental form of time travel linked to the nineteenth century's fascination with motion of every kind, from new forms of transport (trains, steamboats) to Eadweard Muybridge's photographic series on locomotion. The Cambridge contingent was delighted to watch Shelter Island glide before their eyes like a sequence of brightly lit lantern slides. The landscape parlor's French wallpaper, installed in the 1880s, a dazzling panorama of Andean peaks and florid jungle called "El Dorado," was meant to be viewed in a stately circuit of the room.

The lead actor in one such tableau vivant—someone the author of "Hiawatha" no doubt appreciated meeting—was Isaac Pharaoh, a Montauket indentured to Samuel Gardiner "of his own free and voluntary will" in 1829, when he was five years old. Although free to leave the manor at twenty-one, he spent his entire life there and is interred in the Burying Ground of the Colored People. Looked at one way, Pharaoh had a safe berth for life at a time when most Montaukets scrambled for a living. But even though Gardiner had contracted to "teach him to read or write or cause him to be taught," the cultural conditioning of being a second-class citizen that hooded Isaac Pharaoh probably limited his ability to strike out on his own. In winter he lived in the manor house attic or by the kitchen fireside, in summer on the North Peninsula. His circumscribed pattern of seasonal habitation (merely crossing the Upper Inlet to get to the peninsula and back again) echoed—in a melancholy minor key—his ancestors' spring and fall migrations across the entire island, their trips across the Sound, and their free-roaming treks from Montauk Point to

Southampton. It was Isaac who scratched the outlines of dozens of fully rigged ships into the attic dormer walls—the carvings Andy had so proudly shown me. Light reflected from the creek shone up through the crooked old panes; boats bobbed up and down at their moorings, ready to set sail—as Isaac did not.

Nineteenth-century Bostonians admired American Indians but preferred them as "figures in literary aspic." Longfellow, a dedicated student of Indian languages, described the Sauk warriors who in 1837 visited Cambridge as "savage fellows . . . with naked shoulders and red blankets wrapped about their bodies; the rest all grease and Spanish brown and

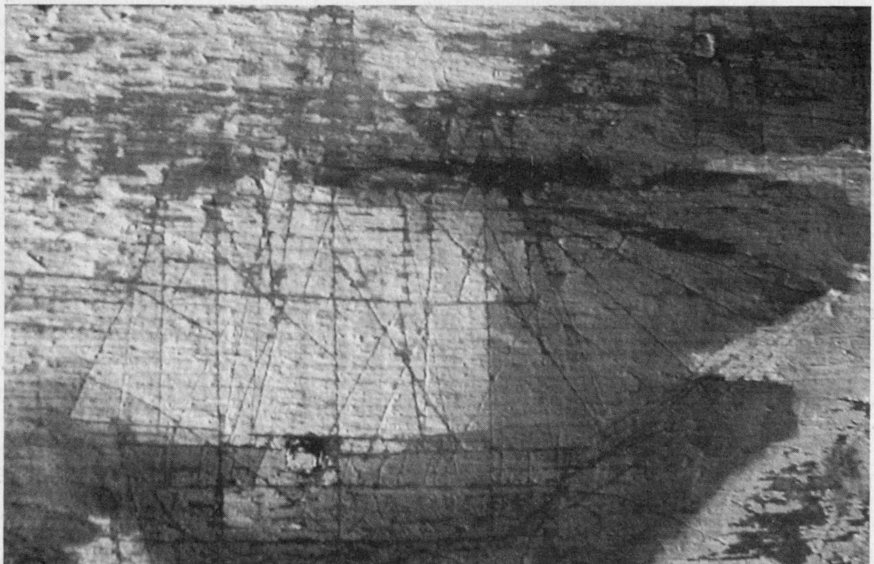

The sloop that the Montaukett Indian Isaac Pharoah scratched in outline on a dormer board in the attic sails through storm clouds of whitewash. Approximately 60 to 70 feet long at the waterline and between 50 and 100 tons burden, such vessels were typical of small New England craft in the African trade. (*Right*: From Richard C. Youngken, *African Americans in Newport*, 1998)

vermillion." But Isaac, whom Eben dubbed the "last of his royal race," was a sort of court jester to the Sylvester Manor family, the least threatening, the best loved of Indians.

Eben and Ethnology

Eben was also the benefactor of the anthropologist Frank Hamilton Cushing, arguably America's first great modern ethnologist. Employed by the Smithsonian, Cushing began his groundbreaking fieldwork with the Zunis of New Mexico in 1879. Tribesmen initiated him into their most secret rituals and he adopted the Zuni lifestyle, calling himself "1st War Chief of Zuni, U.S. Asst. Ethnologist" and suiting up in native outfits, silver jewelry, and weapons. Eben, however, recognized Cushing's genius despite his tendency to go earnestly overboard. An enthusiast himself, Eben enjoyed, understood, and endorsed the role of "participant observer" as a new and valuable anthropological methodology. On Shelter Island, Cushing whetted Horsford's interest in archaeology with interpretive walks, spade in hand, along the North Peninsula, where they dug for the remains of the Manhansetts.

Eben was beset by the antiquarian's desire to explore and then clearly define the past. This led him to confident overstatements about history—and to an error of a comic order. An honored guest at the manor in the 1870s was Ole Bull, an acclaimed Norwegian violinist and champion of his nation's fight for independence from Sweden. To Yankee eyes, Bull was another Leif Eriksson, the first European to reach American shores, and by the 1870s, Eben and Bull busily set about rediscovering that medieval New World, Vinland. Over three centuries, Eben claimed, as many as ten thousand Norsemen had settled throughout Massachusetts and in coastal New Hampshire and Maine, building settlements, dams, canals, and piers. Although Eben enlisted supporters and issued publications substantiating a Norse city of Norumbega-on-the-Charles (the statue of Leif he erected on Boston's Commonwealth Avenue still stands), his findings were quickly called into question. By the beginning of the twentieth century, his conclusions no longer had any credence. (Norumbega, a name that first showed up on maps of northern New England in the sixteenth century, may be a corruption of the Abnaki name for the area around Bangor, Maine. Like the name Atlantis, it sparkled with legends of vanished gold, crystal, and pearls and mysterious people and animals, so a good choice for Horsford's Norse city in Massachusetts.)

It's easy to laugh at Eben. But even though he was not the first to speculate on the Viking discovery of America, he initiated the popularization and "shovel testing" of the Norse sagas. The archaeological discovery in 1960 of Newfoundland's L'Anse aux Meadows, settled around A.D. 985 by Vikings, has proved his underlying hypothesis correct. A pathfinder like the Senecas he had admired as a boy, Eben did not fear setting off on his own, seeking knowledge—proof—with robust Protestant self-assurance. In his own field, as a nutritional chemist, he became known as "the father of modern food technology." He contributed to increased food safety, and processes he developed, such as that for condensed milk, made dietary staples more affordable and accessible. Could he have imagined that the nation's industrialization he helped to develop would spawn today's GM corn, feedlots, manure lagoons, and McDonald's?

Evolution and Race

Classification was one of the main goals of nineteenth-century science, and the theory of evolution was in the forefront of that debate. Eben's Cambridge was convulsed by the topic. Asa Gray, the great American botanist at Harvard, played a major role in bringing the theory of evolution to America. Charles Darwin, who had utilized Gray's work on similarities between Japanese and American floras to support his thinking, wrote to Gray in 1857—before publishing *The Origin of Species* in 1859—laying out his reasoning on natural selection. Gray was convinced, albeit with reservations. He insisted that natural selection had to be directed by some supreme external force. A member, with Horsford, of the Shepard Church, he had thus found a way to reconcile Darwinism with Christianity. Gray himself arranged for American publication of *The Origin of Species*.

It's surprising that Horsford's papers give no evidence that he took part in the debate even though it so deeply engaged one of his closest colleagues, Louis Agassiz, as well as his friend Gray, Agassiz's chief opponent on the subject of creation and evolution. Agassiz, a charismatic Swiss who had arrived like a thunderclap on the American educational scene in 1846, became Horsford's trusted confrère. Sometimes they wrote to each other in German, Agassiz addressing Horsford as "Lieber Herr

Kollege" (colleague) and signing his letters "Your friend." In 1848, Agassiz was appointed founding professor of zoology and geology at the Lawrence Scientific School, where Horsford held the chemistry chair. Recognized as a brilliant zoologist and paleontologist, Agassiz held out for the standard religious view of creation. Following his teacher and mentor, the French paleontologist Georges Cuvier, he argued that God had fashioned each species in a single immutable form, without any heretical assistance from organic evolution. "Time," he wrote, "does not alter organized beings." In order to make sense of abundant fossil remains, Agassiz credited a series of Ice Ages with the repeated wipeout of the natural world, and God with its repeated creation.

The present-day scholar of American letters Louis Menand describes Agassiz as not only a thrilling scientific popularizer recognized nationwide, but also "personally thrilling . . . a large, handsome, self-assured man" whose "command of English was deliciously imperfect." That the Saturday Club, the leading literary society of Cambridge was often called "Agassiz's Club" measures the regard he enjoyed, given that members such as Emerson and Hawthorne were then at the height of their fame.

The establishment of the Lawrence Scientific School marked "the beginning of the professionalization of American science." Modern research practices that Agassiz and Horsford introduced to Harvard included hands-on observation followed by strict induction from the facts. It was to be, as Menand explains, a comparative approach—not a process "of enumerating facts, but of making sense of facts by putting them in relation to other facts." The scientist is "simply assembling reliable data and generating testable hypotheses. A personal preference for one outcome or another is not being permitted to override the evidence of the senses." The trouble lay in the variable meaning of "the evidence of the senses." The confidence inspired by a command of "the facts" as based on such evidence—skewed by what Menand describes as "unacknowledged preferences"—led Agassiz to promulgate racist theories based mostly on the work of a scary but well-respected Philadelphia anthropologist, Samuel Morton. Morton amassed a collection of more than six hundred human skulls (known as the "American Golgotha") from whose comparative dimensions he formulated a scale of racial capacities, ranking Caucasians first and "the Ethiopian" last. Agassiz, who had felt physically revolted by the first American blacks he encountered after his arrival in the United States—the staff of a Philadelphia hotel—was easily convinced.

And as a prominent scientist he could authoritatively spread the word about the innate inferiority of blacks. Agassiz wrote to Samuel Gridley. Howe (whose wife, Julia, the antislavery activist, wrote "The Battle Hymn of the Republic") that a biological catastrophe would ensue from racial interbreeding, which constituted a form of incest. During the fraught decade leading up to the Civil War, the Southern apologists for slavery fell on Agassiz's theories with relief.

In time, Agassiz was pushed to the sidelines of science, not for his bigotry, which would help support a century of nationwide segregation after the Civil War, but for his insistence on what we would call creationism, the doctrine of the immutability of species. Eben's silence on the closely linked topics of evolution and race leave us no clues as to his thinking, but the "scientific" arguments of Morton and Agassiz formed the backdrop for his unexpressed views as much as did the opinions of his friend Asa Gray, or out-and-out abolitionists such as William Lloyd Garrison (publisher of *The Liberator*, the abolitionist newspaper) and the freed slave Frederick Douglass, or middle-of-the-roaders, natural conservatives, of whom there were many, who believed that the westward expansion of the United States would eventually cause slavery to die out.

The Peculiar Institution

Agassiz was far from the only Northerner convinced of the natural superiority of whites; this widespread albeit tacit article of faith gained force from the daily disregard for the rights of free blacks. At first, abolitionists made little headway against the comforting sense that slavery was not the North's problem, or against Yankee economic interests. Owners and backers of mills that spun Southern cotton feared for their profits; thousands of millworkers feared losing their jobs. Animus against the South swelled after the passage of the Fugitive Slave Act in 1850, however. Even though the capture and return of runaways had been legal since 1730, only now did enforcement in the North become shockingly visible as federal marshals pursued fugitives onto the streets of Boston, then jailed them until they were shipped back to the South by court order. Northerners perceived such actions as infringements of their own states' rights.

A change of public opinion came about only over the course of several years. Cornelius Conway Felton, a professor of Greek at Harvard and later the university's president—the Horsfords gave his resounding name to their youngest daughter, Cornelia Conway Felton Horsford—was pro-slavery and opposed abolition in the 1850s. That is, until Senator Preston Brooks of South Carolina caned abolitionist Senator Charles Sumner of Massachusetts nearly to death on the U.S. Senate floor in 1856. That event, the Dred Scott case of 1857, the hanging of John Brown in Virginia in 1859, and finally the Southern assault on Fort Sumter in 1861 at last transformed lukewarm Northerners into warriors.

Eben threw himself into the Union cause with characteristic zest and expertise. He helped plan the defense of Boston Harbor, devised barnacle protection for ironclad submarines, and formulated and manufactured rations for the Union Army, which ordered many thousands of his rather fancifully named foot-square slabs of desiccated "bread" and "roasted whole beef." Alas, Amos B. Eaton, Commissary General of Subsistence for the United States Army, politely rejected them for military use, though without stating why they failed the field test.

Despite the effort Eben put into beating the South, he was uncertain what to think of slavery, or indeed of black people. Like so many other New Englanders, he joined the war effort primarily to save the Union, not to free the slaves. In 1852, he had visited his wife's cousin Julia Gardiner Tyler and her husband, the former president John Tyler, at Sherwood Forest, their fifteen-hundred-acre Virginia plantation on the James River not far from Jamestown, where Nathaniel had loaded his Dutch ship with tobacco in the 1640s.

In a letter to his mother, Eben described being rowed up the river in a barge by six liveried slaves in blue and white checked shirts with straw hats painted to match. He thrilled to the romance of "slave territory": a fecund jungle, dark with grapevines, ivy, and holly; "vast flotillas of ducks and geese . . . one flock not less than a thousand"; and "a magnificent primitive oak forest." He remarked on "quantities of slaves' houses" and found the fences and fields in much better shape "than I had pictured to myself." He eventually arrived at his hosts' imposing three-hundred-foot-long house, where a handsome row of outbuildings extended "on either side some distance including . . . corncribs, dove cotes, milk house &c" in an arrangement not so very different from that of Sylvester Manor, though on a grander scale. The Tylers owned sixty slaves, thirteen of them house servants.

Eben was familiar with the dire image of slavery painted by abolitionist literature in general, and in particular by Harriet Beecher Stowe, whose *Uncle Tom's Cabin* was just then finishing its debut as a popular newspaper serial. But struck by the order and prosperity that he saw at Sherwood Forest, he determined to find out "all I can about the system . . . that I may form an intelligent judgement." He visited "some negro cabins" and (to be thorough about his investigations) a black Baptist church. Taking the moral ambiguities of the "peculiar institution" in stride, he seemed unable to condemn outright what he saw, instead describing "the system in its best form as 'a minority that never terminates.'" He observed that "the slaves are treated like children—punished when they deserve it, rewarded when they should be . . . all of them permitted to earn extra pay—cared for when sick, and I should think uniformly cheerful and happy—& by no means hard worked."

A Woman of Property

His Virginia experience reinforced Eben's belief that black people "treated like children" would be "cheerful and happy" if properly handled. Eben and his family treated Julia Johnson respectfully and lovingly, perhaps almost as much to reassure themselves that they were not prejudiced against blacks as to express the affection they felt for her. For the Horsfords, Julia was the other living relic besides Isaac Pharoah on the "plantation," as the Horsfords occasionally took to calling the manor once again. The honor they accorded her as a relic, and the kindly public recognition they offered her, embodied for them a resolution to the great conflict that had nearly torn the nation apart, as well as a rare public admission that slavery had existed in the North. She was also a useful focus for increasingly romanticized tales of the manor's past. Mary and Phoebe Horsford had known Julia as a household servant since their Gardiner childhood; their daughters had known her since birth. "Our walks led us through woods and footpaths, sometimes to Julia's, a negress whose parents had been slaves on the estate and whose house was on Dering Harbor," wrote Lilian Horsford in a memoir of her early years.

Eben perceived what was "best" for Julia through the curiously occluded eye that results from a fixed view—or greed. By the 1860s, the land she had inherited from Comus and Dido stood in the way of Eben's plans for the manor. He was intent on developing several hundred acres of the property as a summer resort to be called Dering Park, a residential development complete with a hotel and restaurant owned and operated by "a consortium of gentlemen." In order to create an attractive seaside road from the public ferry landing to the new houses and cottages, Eben would need to acquire the strip of land along the east side of the harbor and build a bridge across the mouth of Dyd Creek. On a hot day, the porch of Julia's unpainted one-room frame house would have been a nice place to sit. (Lilian's careful pencil sketch of Julia's well and pump gives an idea of the pleasantly run-down condition of her property.) But Eben was selling ambience as well as real estate. The sight of a poor old black woman catching the breeze wouldn't have suited his pitch for a local "community of marked character and individuality" descended from Puritans and Pilgrims who had "always been the devoted friends of civil and religious freedom."

Julia doubtless had no one to advise her on the wisdom of selling her property except for the people who wanted to buy her out—her employers. She could pen a neat signature on a sale document, but was she up to comprehending the long-term benefits of hanging on to her land? Probably not. The waterfront land she sold is now worth millions: three big white houses shoulder each other on the site, fronting the fabled harbor view. If she acted independently, what was she thinking? Did she need cash more than she valued the security and status of property ownership, the gold standard of a rural society like Shelter Island's? As she aged, did she find the property too much to manage? Julia's son, Manford, appears once in the census records, in 1850, when he was a seventeen-year-old sailor. Was he lost at sea? Did he go to the city and leave Shelter Island behind, as other African Americans did? Perhaps, like Giles Sylvester, Julia thought of her acres as a bank account to draw on until it was spent. Evidence that she was reluctant to sell, however, may exist in the length of time—thirty years—it took her to dispose of piece after piece, some as small as half an acre. She first sold ten acres to the Gardiners in 1836, shortly after the death of her mother. By 1865, Julia had sold her house and every bit of property to the Horsfords. Whatever arguments Eben used to convince himself that he acted in Julia's best interests, this final sale left her as landless as the freedmen of Sherwood Forest became after the Civil War.

Like his Puritan forefathers, Eben believed that making money while benefiting others was unequivocally a good thing. His resort would offer visitors healthful relaxation and give islanders gainful employment, and yes, Eben stood to pocket a tidy profit. The multiple components of his plan, only partially implemented during his lifetime, included eighteen half-acre villa sites in the area immediately north of Julia's house, to be sold at $600 apiece for a total of almost $11,000. Even a cautious estimate suggests that the price of island real estate between 1836 and 1865 averaged $41 an acre. Over roughly the same period, the manor family paid Julia an average of $17.66 per acre. Her grand total of $757 amounted to only $57 more than Comus Fanning had paid Sylvester Dering for all twenty-one acres. It looks as if the Horsfords took advantage of Julia, to put it mildly.

The day I found the photograph of Julia, which now seems very long ago, I caught the ferry to Sag Harbor late in the afternoon. Although the sky was clear, a powerful west wind had whipped the narrow strait into whitecaps. A huge semitrailer painted with the name of a big moving and storage company, Cassone, boarded next, hogging the center of the deck and making the ferry sink perceptibly lower. The trailer's sleek metal sides were glossed with what looks like the same creamy enamel as the safe in the vault. Cassone. In Italy, a *cassone* is a rich and showy chest, which may be inlaid or carved and painted. A cassone holds a family's treasures and is supposed to keep them secure forever. The value of such treasures often depends on what they mean to the collector. For the manor archaeologists, the treasures are the thousands of pins, the Spanish coin inscribed with the Indian thunderbird sign. For Sylvester family descendants, the house itself, as well as the locks of hair and Ezra L'Hommedieu's gold watch, are precious. For someone living in the attic—an African replicating remembered religious rituals?—the picture frame that Bob Hefner found hidden under the floorboards at the northwest corner of the attic, near the chimney, with a worn gilt button carefully placed inside one corner, perhaps had special meaning. Irony and sadness shadow such repositories—who will value what someone once valued?

The ferry wheeled defiantly southwest, apparently heading straight for Long Beach, miles away from the landing on the other side of the crossing. This blunt-bowed boat was tacking! The stern suddenly heaved up at least two feet higher than the bow, which pushed nose-down. Then we were broadside, rocking wildly, horsing around in the swells. I didn't dare look up at the captain in the wheel cabin. Salt spray slashed my windshield. Foam-ridged water slopped onto the few feet of open loading zone that lay in front of my car, slipped under my wheels, then hissed back into the surf. I'd never felt seasick on this short trip before. I'd never wondered whether these docile vessels could capsize.

As we crashed heavily into the slip, the captain throttled the engine down to a low grind. The waves broke on the sandy spit nearby. Like the whisper of the glassy braid of tide running out under the stone bridge at the manor, this is the sound of time rushing. On the sliver of beach that is the manor's past, the thin lines of the years weave over each other, crisscrossing in the sand. Sea wrack—bits of seaweed, seashell, sea-bleached wreckage, and seaworn glass—lies on the high-tide rim. The manor safely holds the sea wrack of its history.

20

Ladies of the Manor

Cornelia

Up in the manor attic, a half dozen antique cameras speak of the Horsfords' love of photography. And scattered everywhere in the vault, bundled with string or housed in fat envelopes, are photographs: cartes de visite, cabinet photos, tintypes, stereotypes, glass lantern slides, postcards, even a few daguerreotypes. From the 1860s on, the family recorded one another taking part in rural activities such as haying, when all hands turned out to scythe and the air carried the sweet smell of cut timothy grass or tumbled alfalfa. Such lovely—and self-conscious—images are part of the Colonial Revival movement, when, after the Civil War, Americans looked back for the first time and saw they had a history. They felt more than nostalgia for a rural life already disappearing amid the advance of industrialization. What Americans needed was "a usable past . . . to give shape and substance to national identity" after the Civil War destroyed their sense of a shared mission. True or false, posed or candid, the photographs of the era shape our understanding of a vanished America.

Eben Horsford had served as a commissioner at the 1876 Philadelphia Centennial Exhibition, which celebrated the nation's first hundred years. The exposition looked forward, showing off American progress and industrial might, but it also glanced backward at American history. Celebrating colonial hearth and home gave women organizers at the fair, many of them the descendants of Pilgrim and Puritan families, the opportunity to play a public role. Their historical focus was the "Olde Tyme" kitchen and the log cabin that housed it. Besides offering "substantial New England cheer," the cabin display and restaurant aimed to "illustrate the domestic life and habits of the people, to whose determined courage, sustained by their faith in God, we owe that government, so dear to every loyal heart." The impact of the exhibit (which Cornelia and her sisters attended) was tremendous and spawned many other expositions, producing an outpouring of Colonial Revival style in architecture, gardens, and interior design that would last right through the 1950s.

During that summer and many the others that followed, guests at Sylvester Manor sat solemnly for plein air photographic portraits and had their visits meticulously noted in a guest book. The annual sojourners included Longfellow's and Lowell's children as well as eminent jurists and lawyers, classical scholars, architects and painters, and relatives with names familiar in American history, such as the descendants of New York's Dutch patroons the Van Rensselaers and President John Tyler. They strolled on the lawns, played croquet, lawn tennis, and golf. They sailed around Shelter Island (a full day's excursion) in the *Minnie Rogers*. In 1872, twenty-year-old Gertrude, the third Horsford daughter, "fell overboard, and was rescued with some difficulty," says the guestbook. The less adventurous rowed placidly around Gardiners Creek, disembarking onto steps built into the historic land bridge or tying up at the board dock that replaced Nathaniel's long-lost warehouse and wharf. Archery, touted as beneficial for women's lungs and the development (and display) of their corseted figures, was popular. Hammocks strung between the elms in front of the house invited dreaming. The house party atmosphere acted as a romantic hothouse: many young women in the Horsford circle brought admirers to court them decorously among the boxwoods, later returning to the island as young matrons with their children. The dearly beloved homebody Phoebe Horsford, the mistress of the manor, rocked on the porch, embroidery in hand, with some of the older contingent. In the afternoon, silver spoons clinked against porcelain cups, and the murmur of conversation and bursts of laughter sounded in the garden, where tea was taken among the old roses and flotillas of the latest and brightest annuals. The sporty set bicycled dusty island roads or trotted off with Cornelia, an able horsewoman. They strolled to the top of the North Peninsula, then a bald pasture, where a rustic gazebo and chairs overlooked the busy harbor and distant Greenport and Connecticut.

The manor's guest roster also reflects the handoff from theology to

From atop a wagonload of hay, a young woman in a straw boater, perhaps Cornelia Horsford, watches the farm crew pitch up the last forkfuls. The far horse wears muslin caps on its ears to keep the flies off.

science as the great preoccupation of nineteenth-century America, particularly in New England and above all at Harvard. Down through the manor generations, beginning with George Fox, the most notable visitors had been preachers. By contrast, the Horsfords collected an exceedingly clubbable fraternity of scientists. Asa Gray, "the father of American botany" and Darwin's champion, was the best known and most distinguished. During his thirty years at Harvard he became the de facto coordinator of American botany, receiving specimens from all over the nation and corresponding with colleagues worldwide. His *Manual of Botany* survives as a standard reference work, and his many textbooks gave two generations of American schoolchildren their first glimpse of natural history. Sylvester Manor tradition pictures him arriving with a sapling copper beech in 1877 and planting it himself. The huge tree—the tree that so amazed me on my first visit—stands at the water's edge today. Gray also took an interest in the younger Horsfords: in the vault, a tiny yet heavy metal spirit level, whose green bubble still doggedly floats to dead center in the glass, bears the label "To Cornelia Horsford from Asa Gray." It's as if the botanist recognized Cornelia not only for her interest in gardens and houses, which had become the American woman's domain, but also for an ability to appraise her physical surroundings with a precision any man might emulate. Cornelia, who stuck the red-edged schoolroom label to the level, clearly treasured this acknowledgment.

Meaning and Memory

Except for Cornelia, who entered the world in September 1861, the Horsford girls were born in the run-up to the Civil War. All of them spent their early childhood in the anguished atmosphere of wartime Cambridge. As children, their playmates and schoolfellows (both boys and girls) at local private elementary schools included many of the offspring of Cambridge and Harvard luminaries. Growing up together, the children became lifelong friends, forming a close-knit second generation of Cambridge society. In the fall of 1861, Cambridge's women and girls, including Longfellows, Danas, and Horsfords, formed a sewing circle like many others in the North, where they made clothes and bandages for soldiers.

As young adults visiting Shelter Island in the 1870s and '80s, some of the girls' closest friends would have gazed with special intensity at the somber burying ground near the big white oak (which still stands) silhouetted against the farm barns. (No white pine plantation had yet been planted to enclose the graveyard in its own private shield of darkness.) For Richard Henry Dana III and his sisters, Rosamund and Lily, and for Benjamin Robbins Curtis Jr., the cemetery and its memorial embodied what the historian Michael Kammen has called "the imperative of memory," as opposed to "the comfort of amnesia."

The Danas' father, Richard Henry Jr., a founder of the antislavery Free-Soil Party, had eloquently—and futilely—defended Anthony Burns, who fled slavery in Virginia only to be put on trial in Boston in 1854 under the Fugitive Slave Act. The elder Dana subsequently watched as the entire Boston militia was called out to prevent the outraged citizenry from freeing Burns as he was marched, surrounded by guards armed with swords and revolvers, to the ship taking him back to Virginia. All three Dana children went to elementary school in the Longfellow House on Brattle Street, which neighborhood children of both sexes attended. Rosamund and Lily Dana were among the Horsford girls' closest friends and schoolmates.

Benjamin Robbins Curtis Jr., who married Mary Gardiner, the Horsfords' eldest daughter, in 1877, was the son of a Supreme Court justice who had filed one of the two dissents in the infamous Dred Scott case twenty years before. Scott, a slave, sued for his freedom in 1847 on the grounds that he had lived both in Illinois, a free state, and in Wisconsin, then part of federal territories and not yet a state. Ten years later, the issues before the Supreme Court were whether it had jurisdiction to hear the case and whether Scott could qualify as a citizen of the United States. (The great unspoken issue was, of course, the spread and the legitimacy of slavery.) Chief Justice Roger B. Taney, in a manifestly pro-Southern majority decision, stated that the framers of the Constitution viewed blacks as "a subordinate and inferior class of beings who . . . had no rights or privileges but such as those who held the power and the Government might choose to grant them." The decision also overturned the Missouri Compromise of 1820, by whose terms Congress in 1850 had limited slavery's westward expansion in the territories that had not achieved statehood.

The senior Curtis, a legal conservative—and no abolitionist—first noted in his dissent that at the time the Constitution was ratified, some African Americans had been recognized as citizens in states both North and South and thereby had automatically enjoyed federal citizenship, and that therefore Taney's "jurisdictional" objection was ill-founded. Curtis went on to state that since Congress on a number of occasions had legislated with respect to slavery in the territories, the Missouri Compromise was a valid exercise of Congress's authority. He thereby held that Scott's residence in Wisconsin, not then a state, had made him a free man. (Curtis's views on slavery, property rights, and legal process were complex: he had once argued that a slave owner could restrain his human property when in a free state, and in 1862 he attacked Lincoln for issuing the Emancipation Proclamation on the grounds of abuse of executive power.)

Curtis released his opinion, which was published at once; Taney withheld his opinion "for revision" and refused to let Curtis see it for a month, claiming that Curtis's intention was to discredit him. The Court's decision, although hardly the cause of the Civil War, further inflamed passions on both sides of the political divide. The personal breach between the justices over the case became so rancorous that Curtis soon resigned and returned to the practice of law in Massachusetts. Scott was manumitted by his owners' sons shortly after the decision came down. He died nine months later. The Thirteenth Amendment, passed by Congress with difficulty in 1865, abolished slavery; the Fourteenth, passed in 1868, made all people born within the United States citizens of the nation.

Many Cambridge men of the elder generation, such as Oliver Wendell Holmes and Wilkie James, William and Henry James's brother, had gone to war to save the Union, not to free the slaves. Nonetheless, they had taken part in the terrible slaughter. At Sylvester Manor, the children of that generation stood in one of the few places where the fact of slavery in the North—obliterated almost everywhere else—was inescapable. By then in New England and New York, African Americans were a visible part of society, particularly in the cities. However, the manor memorial brought sharply into focus not only the slaves who had lived in the North for two centuries, but also generations of those who had kept them in bondage.

The North, as it retreated into an idealized New England past, seldom acknowledged the apparition of Northern slavery except as it was displayed in iron hitching post figures the size of small children, often disfigured as dwarves, often in livery or comic dress, with distorted faces like gargoyles. At most eighteenth-century New England properties where slaves had created the original basis of prosperity, once the system was abolished, the entire visible apparatus—the garrets and slave kitchens and other occasional housing, the ephemeral gardens—simply fell down, grew up into weeds, or became appropriated for different purposes, just as happened on Shelter Island.

The Horsfords—whatever their private ruminations and reservations—wished to do justice somehow to the complex conflicting memories clustered around their place. They inscribed the big glacial boulder near the burying ground with the words THE COLORED PEOPLE. Today, this phrase is so linked with segregation that it raises our hackles. For the Horsfords in 1884, however, the words managed to confer a dignity and humanity that "slaves" would not have done. Moreover, referring to "colored people" rather than "Negroes" described the reality of the site, a reality in which we now can read the long, mingled history of blacks and Native Americans.

The business of commemorating the Sylvester family swung into high gear in 1884. On a beautiful July afternoon, the Horsfords, along with their relations and friends (including many from Cambridge) and the general population of Shelter Island, trooped to the head of Gardiners

A big crowd, dressed in their best, came to the old cemetery at the head of Gardiners Creek to celebrate the 1884 dedication of the monument to the Sylvester family and the Quakers.

Creek. There, in the small eighteenth-century cemetery that has come to be called the Quaker Graveyard, stood a freshly carved table monument to Nathaniel Sylvester, surrounded by a motley collection of old grave markers recently fenced for the unveiling. The top of the brownstone tablet on its stout legs memorialized Nathaniel, by then dead for some two centuries, as the Quaker Protector. The steps that surround it are dedicated to the early Friends who visited Shelter Island. Inscriptions on the treads detail the executions, scourges, maiming, mutilations, and imprisonments that Quakers endured at the hands of Boston Puritans. The first part of the inscription on the tabletop displays the Brinley crest and an encomium of Nathaniel as a faithful, intrepid, and hospitable Englishman. Beneath the table, the supporting base lists the succession of Shelter Island's proprietors, beginning with the Manhansetts, and traces a descent through the female line from Anne Wase Brinley, Auditor Thomas's wife. This inscription recognizes the "Daughters of Mary & Phoebe Gardiner Horsford, Descendants of Patience, daughter of Nathaniel Sylvester" who have set up "with Reverence and Affection . . . a memorial to the good name of their ancestor."

Only one other living woman was publicly recognized at the creekside graveyard. After the minister blessed the monument and Eben spoke at length, and after descendants of Mary Dyer and the Southwicks read poems, including stanzas that James Greenleaf Whittier had composed especially for the occasion, Eben called on Julia Havens to rise in the audience. He then addressed her in what a local newspaper called "one of the pleasantest incidents" of the proceeding. "This venerable colored woman, now in the neighborhood of 80, has been a faithful servitor . . . For the last sixty-five years, there has not been an event of sorrow or joy in these three families in which she has not participated."

Julia had sold the last of her land to Eben almost twenty years before. The 1880 census finds her in Greenport, home to a growing black population. It is quite likely she lived in the manor house as custodian from time to time, because Eben Case, that revered twentieth-century repository of island memory, handed down a description of her presence there as "fierce and feared." In a supreme irony, she had effectively become mistress of the empty manor during the nine months of the year when the Horsfords were in Cambridge.

The Picture of the Past

Like her sisters, Cornelia studied drawing and painting. More than proficient, she produced landscapes, still lifes, and architectural compositions. The history of Sylvester Manor could be similarly "composed." Her canvas was the manor itself, where she amassed and sorted objects—Queen Anne chairs and Georgian silver with the marks of renowned colonial smiths—as well as legends, hearsay, and fragments of history. Noble Indians? Youghco and Wyandanch could be conjured up by the waterside shell mounds and the stone points spaded up by ethnologist Cushing on the North Peninsula. Loyal African slaves? They spiced Cornelia's sagas of sugar, rum, and tropical mahogany, of brave mariners, bold entrepreneurs, and dashing planters. No question about who suffered for their faith—somewhere on the property the Quakers Lawrence and Cassandra Southwick rest in peace. A handsome horseman in lace and velvet? Brinley Sylvester fit the bill. Ladies in panniers and mobcaps? The Horsford collection of heirloom satin-stitched samplers evoked delicate fingers plying their needles. Heroes of a young republic? Ezra L'Hommedieu, Thomas Dering, and General Sylvester Dering led the charge. Horticultural talismans of antiquity? Gnarled boxwoods hulked along the garden path. Venerable customs? To the amusement of island natives, Cornelia devised folk "traditions" such as the annual Baptism of the Calves, at which the young animals were garlanded with flowers on the manor house lawn by the local minister while their disconsolate mothers bawled in a nearby field.

"Being a custodian of the past is primarily its own reward," writes Michael Kammen, and Cornelia, unmarried at a time when spinsterhood could be as incapacitating as a broken leg, rewarded herself well. She married her house, a serviceable, if sometimes lonely, union. Emboldened by a father who played fast and loose with history, and by the ample supply of relics surrounding her, Cornelia freewheeled through the generations. Like many nineteenth-century women of her class with limited education, she seems to have had few outlets for her curiosity, intelligence, and energy. She chose historical fantasy. She concocted the unlikely romance of a barge rowed by slaves (quite probably a detail borrowed from her father's trip up the James River to the Tylers') carrying the Sylvester girls to the Congregational church in Southold, where, as Quakers, they would probably not have been welcomed. And she conjured, among other fantasies, a grateful Charles II bestowing an inlaid traveling knife and fork on Auditor Brinley; a tubercular Latimer Sampson nobly relinquishing his betrothed (Nathaniel's eldest daughter) and sailing away, never to return; and a modest Mary Burroughs Sylvester telling the local minister that she prized her sewing skills more than all her wealth and standing.

Most of Cornelia's yarns have some historical basis, however, and all have survived and thrived into the present day in print and online. To her credit, she put enough stock in the documented past to obtain a copy of Nathaniel's 1680 probate inventory and other records from surrogate court archives. In England she visited Datchet and the Sylvester tombs in Burford, and she hired a professional genealogist to research the Brinleys (his report rather savagely debunked some of her assertions). Cornelia also directed her architect, Henry Bacon, to draw up detailed plans of the existing manor house before starting renovations. And in 1915 she agitated for an official marker to commemorate the spot revered by Native Americans as the place where Youghco's funeral procession rested for the night on its way to Montauk in 1652.

Cornelia squeezed every drop of memory from the place as if it made her more real to herself, which, of course, it did. For her, the past was always as present as the here and now, and, as often happens with lonely people, her retelling of "memories"—even when she had only read about an event—grew ritualistic and ever more elaborate. A remarkably detailed letter she wrote when she was seventy-three lays out her obsessive preparations for East Hampton visitors. As part of their visit, she wrote, the guests would be asked to pass the family's seventeenth-century silver tankard from hand to hand to drink the health of "the loved and the absent."

She cherished even her smallest adventures. Early one spring, Cornelia made a foray to the island from Cambridge, bringing pine tree seedlings—probably the pines that shade the burying ground today, which Alice said were planted in 1900. In a letter to her mother she described how, aboard the sailboat ferry from Greenport, she saw the low wooded shore by Dyd's Creek where "the cherry & shad [blow] trees were white, looking like clouds caught among the trees." The island oaks were in flower, she wrote. "The box borders [were] covered with tiny light green leaves . . . the asparagus was delicious . . . Violets by the roadside . . . it is raining but warm." She closed with the news that "Julia is poorly I have not seen her yet."

Cornelia didn't date her letter, but it can be bracketed by the age of the pines and the death of her mother in 1903. Julia, in her mideighties or perhaps even ninety, was living somewhere on the island. Before 1907 she moved to Sag Harbor, where she had relatives, and there, apparently, she died. An anonymous letter printed in an issue of *The Friend*, a Quaker publication, mentions the Burying Ground of the Colored People as part of the manor's history. Dated August 28, 1908, and possibly the work of Cornelia's sister Katherine, the letter states that Julia "died at Sag Harbour eighteen months ago; by her request her remains were brought here to be laid with those of her forebears." Julia left no known descendants. Her grave is unmarked. Recognized in life as a "faithful servitor," in death she remains anonymous, like all the rest of those interred there.

Both Cornelia and her sister Lilian occasionally felt burdened by the weight of history, and by a disquieting suspicion that some things might not have been exactly as they imagined. They felt the sorrow of learning about the instability that lies at the heart of all things. Such emotions must have ghosted up in stray remarks and slight gestures, stirring the supernatural, magnetic strangeness that every visitor to Sylvester Manor feels. Lilian, who observed, recorded, and recalled more objectively than her sister (her lucid pencil sketches contrast markedly with Cornelia's impressionistic watercolors) wrote a memoir that she read aloud at a Shelter Island Historical Society meeting. She told of her fear as an eight- or nine-year-old—as real as childhood can make such fears—when she threw a pebble against a glacial boulder in a field, a spark flashed, and then she sniffed a "slight smell—of what? We thought it was brimstone." Her memoir went on, "We thought the flash was the fire of Hell and that we had discovered an entrance . . . We never played there again. We never spoke of it again."

Alice

Alice and I are looking at the portrait of Cornelia as a little girl that hangs at the bottom of the front stair. Cornelia's eyes do not waver. They appear to be fixed on the gauzy middle distance so beloved of Victorian portrait painters. But Cornelia's gaze is not gauzy—never mind that she is wearing a little pink frock with a frilled neckline, or that she is only about ten years old. If this girl turned her head, she would stare through Alice and me, backward through history. As an adult and with nineteenth-century certitude, Cornelia had firmly reshaped the house and gardens to suit herself and her ideas of what the place had been.

Henry Bacon, Cornelia's chosen architect and the architect of the Lincoln Memorial, arrived in 1908. From the start, both he and his client revered the hallowed fabric of the manor as more than walls and roof, and intended to make alterations they felt were historically appropriate. Bacon's most noticeable changes, all of which survive, include the removal of Samuel Gardiner's circa 1840s pillared front porch to add a small portico; the addition of twin piazzas crowned with Chippendale-style lattice on either side of Brinley's house; and the doubling of the north, or rear, section of the house to make a splendid long living room. The east piazza, garlanded with climbing roses, faces the garden, and the west piazza looks out across the creek. To a large extent the roofs of those outdoor living spaces now replace the shade of vanished American elms on the lawns, where the Horsfords once rested and read, knitted and talked in their rocking chairs. The living room (which obliterated the old kitchen where Isaac Pharoah once dozed by the fire) had an alcove for musicians. Both the piazzas and the new living room are much larger than any of the older rooms; they are where life goes on today. Bacon also added an amenity that most single ladies of his generation might not have asked for: Cornelia wanted a wine cellar, and she got it!

Alice Fiske, in her customary mobcap and standing a bit shorter than the black snakeroot at left, leans confidently on the gate to the garden where she spent so many hours. (Courtesy of Lissa Williamson and Roswitha Wisseman)

Alice loved the portrait of Cornelia as a young girl—she loves all the family portraits in the house—but she felt especially close to Cornelia. "We divided a hundred years between us in this garden," she said. It's true: Cornelia started ordering garden seeds in 1890 and died in 1944. Alice came to the manor in 1952 and died in 2006. Fifty-four years apiece.

Every day, beginning the Monday after Thanksgiving, Alice and Andy's house would fill with the warm smell of baking. Alice and Roswitha Wisseman, the manor housekeeper, began their task of making thousands of dainty Christmas cookies. Miss Rose, as Alice (and all of us) called her, sang Christmas carols in her beautiful church choir soprano. Silver and brass, floors and furniture, were polished. Every bedroom, every painting, was hung with greens. The aromas mingled, becoming the incense of a well-kept house. Glittering angels flew across paneled walls, danced on mantels. Then the tree was brought in. Decorating it took days—but no tinsel. "Very bad taste," said Alice.

Finally, the house was ready for "Tea and Tree." Alice and Andy held this party annually on the day after Christmas, and Alice continued it after his death. All day, platters piled high with tiny sandwiches in fancy shapes were meticulously prepared. "Cucumber, of course," Miss Rose told me recently, "and watercress, chicken, and Underwood ham paste. Thin bread and thick butter so the filling wouldn't bleed through." In the kitchen, as they worked, Alice always announced, "That's how the queen likes her sandwiches." Elizabeth II, that is.

Guests began to arrive as dusk fell, around four o'clock. "They didn't stay that long," Miss Rose remembers, "but there were waves of people—in all, about two hundred fifty. If you were special and you stayed later, you got a drink." Few were accorded the privilege, and they knew who they were. For most, it was tea and a look at familiar faces one hadn't encountered since perhaps the Christmas before. All the guests were pleased with themselves: they had donned tweed jackets and holiday dresses and escaped their own houses filled with small children (this was a grown-ups' party), half-assembled toys, and crumpled Christmas wrap. Shelter Islanders of almost every almost description—builders, bus drivers, farmers, members of the yacht club, plumbers, country gentry, and weekenders from New York City, the entire social order—were delighted to be invited to tea by the lord and lady of the manor.

As an off-island guest myself, writing a book about a place that had been a slave plantation for half of its long existence, I could not help comparing the present with the past. I noted the lack of even a single black face in the tea party crowd. Perhaps this was simply Shelter Island demographics, a reflection of the small size of the African American community on Shelter Island, which had dwindled so drastically at the end of the nineteenth century? Alice would have pooh-poohed me if I'd accused her of racial prejudice. In the few conversations we had about race, she and I generally stuck to the past, to slavery, so we were safely able to condemn it—but also to say that what was done was done. Nathaniel only did what others did, she said, and someone had to farm all that land . . . For Alice, and for many in her generation, the rights guaranteed by the Civil Rights Act of 1964 and the Voting Rights Act of 1965 had no bearing on the right to choose your own society.

Steve made efforts to attract African Americans to the dig, but few came; maybe the manor was not a romantic place to spend the summer for a black college undergraduate. Alice welcomed all the young diggers in her usual kindly and inventive fashion: she rented kayaks for outings on Gardiners Creek, for instance, and attended the annual field school whiffleball tournament. Ever tactful and polite about the opinions of others, she detested argument and kept her own counsel. It seems futile to question her enormous generosity because her broad-mindedness didn't extend to race. Her racial attitudes could not have been rooted in dislike; African Americans just didn't fit into her world of tea sandwiches and Queen Elizabeth.

Alice died in 2006. With her demise, Steve Mrozowski decided that the first active phase of the University of Massachusetts's six-week-long summer field schools (nine in all) should conclude. The team moved their efforts to Boston, to the Fiske Center for Archaeological Research at the university, which was endowed by Alice in memory of Andy; there they began the analysis (still ongoing as of 2013) of the thousands of artifacts from the digs. "Lab analysis takes ten times as long as fieldwork," says Kat, so who knows when it will all be completed. I began to write this book once all, or almost all, of my research and travels were concluded.

One of Andy's nephews, Eben Ostby, Eben Horsford's namesake, inherited the manor. Eben, who has been at Pixar Animation Studios since the company's start-up days in 1983 and is now the supervising technical director, lives in California and has no desire to recast himself as a Shelter Island squire. Fortunately, his sister's son, Bennett Konesni, now thirty-one years old, a farmer, musician, and the latest in the long line of Sylvester family members to steward the manor, was eager to take on the job. He moved into the manor house and set up an organic farm where more than a hundred families (at last count) pick up weekly shares of vegetables. Fields fallow since the nineteenth century are now alive with young farm staff members and summer volunteers who learn—and teach—the arduous methods of organic farming. They plant garlic, nurse seedlings, stake tomatoes, make pickles and compost, tend poultry and porkers, and host hundreds of visitors to demonstrate that agriculture doesn't have to be agribusiness. Near the 1810 windmill and the newly fenced four-acre windmill field, now a corduroy patchwork of crop rows, sits a new farm stand built with volunteer labor. A welcome addition to an island community where in previous years almost the only vegetables to be found were canned or frozen, the stand offers hardy salad greens beginning in April and stays open well into winter, selling the potatoes and turnips and onions that have been cold-weather mainstays over the centuries for rich and poor, black and white.

Exuberant, kindly, and earnest, Bennett promulgates a modern, youthful vision of the manor, a place where, as he has said on the Sylvester Manor website, sylvestermanor.org, "food continues to play a pivotal role in life [through] the arts of the field, kitchen, and table." He gives the evils of the past a cautious nod, acknowledging that "joy has not always been a part of our landscape." He counts on future UMass archaeologists to excavate the more than eighty footprints of early buildings along the manor shore in order to uncover evidence of the nameless people who worked here.

Once again, some of the labor is unpaid, but now the people farming the land choose to be there. Tea and Tree lives on, but with much thicker sandwiches and a multiethnic crowd. However, the manor still cannot support itself by farming alone. Maintained with land sales over the centuries, as well as sugar, rum, slaves, baking powder, patented chemicals, and natural gas residuals—and recently with gains from Disney stock—the place has now become Sylvester Manor Educational Farm, a nonprofit foundation incorporated in 2009 that is dedicated to preserving and sharing the manor's precious assets and its long history.

In 2009 Eben donated to the Peconic Land Trust (a Long Island land preservation nonprofit) a conservation easement extending over twenty-two acres on the North Peninsula overlooking Gardiners Creek and Dering Harbor. In 2012 he donated eighty-three additional acres to the Educational Farm, which will preserve his extraordinary gift forever as farmland through conservation programs of Shelter Island Town, Suffolk County, and the federal government. In 2013, three hundred and sixty years after Nathaniel and Grizzell moved to the island, the young foundation has grown sturdy enough for Eben to entrust it with the gift of the manor house, its outbuildings, and most of the manor's remaining acres.

In Alice and Andy's day, the only crop was flowers. (Occasionally a few fields were rented out to a local farmer.) Alice planted the landscape with specimen trees and tended the mighty boxwoods. Now the box are dying. Nematodes feast on their roots; borers nest in their leaves. The stress of climate change (drought, flood, excessive heat) has made them prey to many other diseases as well. The ancient garden next to the house is overgrown and overrun with deer. The house, now 276 years old, and its gardens are in hiatus, as though undergoing a kind of penance and review. Will the place regenerate? In what form? At the long dining table, Bennett and his farmers eat the food they have grown and kick back in Neo-Georgian chairs. Miss Rose fusses at the loosened-up housekeeping and hustles off to yard sales to find extra furnishings for the summer interns. A plaster ceiling crumbles and falls. The house needs a fresh coat of yellow paint. But the place rings with music (the farmers sing work songs; many of them are also musicians). Bennett plays the banjo, the African instrument that came to America with slavery. The long song of the manor is finding another tune.

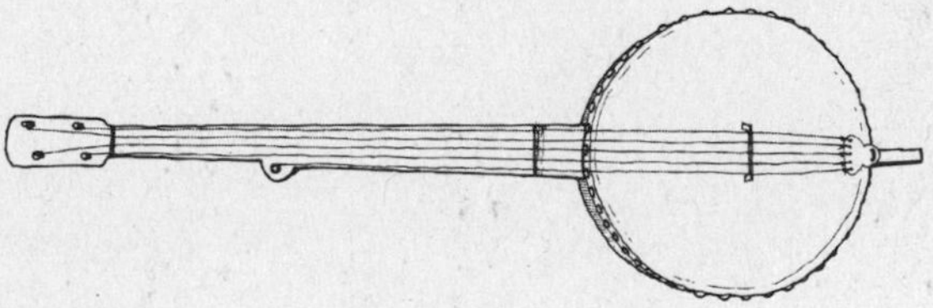

(Edith Gawler, 2012)

The Immigrants

The Sylvesters of Amsterdam, Barbados, and Shelter Island

Giles Sylvester of Charlton Adam, Somerset, and Amsterdam (c.1584–before 1652) and Mary Arnold Sylvester (1594/5–after 1662), who married in Amsterdam in 1613, produced seven children, birth order unknown, all born in Amsterdam

Constant (c.1615–1671) of Barbados and Brampton, England, married Grace Walrond
Grace (c.1618) married Robert Kett, moved to Barbados
Nathaniel (c.1620–1680) of Shelter Island married Grizzell Brinley (1636–c.1687)
Mercie (c.1628–after 1666) married Isaac Cartwright of Aspley Guise, Bedfordshire
Joshua (c.1626–1706) moved to Shelter Island, then to Southold, Long Island
Peter (c.1631–will proved in London 1658) married Mary Brinley, Grizzell Brinley's sister
Giles II (c.1632–before April 1671) of London married Anne Burrell

Tammero and Oyou of Africa and Shelter Island

Tammero and Oyou, whose origins in Africa are unknown, were by 1680 enslaved on Shelter Island and the parents of four children. One son, Obium (d. after 1757), was sold to a Boston owner, escaped, was caught in 1693, then was returned to Lloyd Neck, Long Island, to live there for the remainder of his life. He is the father of Jupiter Hammon (1711–before 1806), the first black writer to be published in America.

The Brinleys of London and Datchet, England, Rhode Island, and Shelter Island

Thomas Brinley (1591–1661) of Exeter, England, Auditor of the Revenue for Charles I and Charles II, and Anne Wase (c.1606–1670) of Petworth, his wife, lived in London and Datchet, Buckinghamshire, where they produced twelve children, of whom four went to America

Francis (1632–1719), born in London, moved to Rhode Island, married Hannah Carr, died in Roxbury, Massachusetts
Anne (1632–1708), born in London, married Governor William Coddington of Rhode Island, died in Newport
Grizzell (1636–1687), born in London, moved to Newport, married Nathaniel Sylvester of Shelter Island in 1653, died on Shelter Island
William (1647–death date unknown), born in Datchet, moved to Rhode Island

Sylvester Manor Time Line

1651 Nathaniel Sylvester (c.1620–1680) and three partners purchase on June 1, 1651, the 8,000-acre island from Stephen Goodyear, former deputy director of New Haven Colony to provision the West Indies with foodstuffs, livestock, and barrel staves for molasses and rum. Labor is provided by enslaved and impressed local Manhansetts and enslaved Africans who in 1680 number 24, the largest African slave population in New England.

1653 Following a formal protest by the Manhansetts stating that Goodyear's sale was invalid without their consent as owners, the four partners purchase the island from the tribe.

1666 Richard Nicolls, governor of New York Colony, awards Nathaniel and his brother Constant royal manor status for the island, which remains undivided at 8,000 acres.

1680 Grizzell Brinley Sylvester, Nathaniel's widow (1636–1687), is his executor and the manor's life tenant.

1680 Giles Sylvester (1657–1704), eldest son of Nathaniel and Grizzell, inherits the house and 40 acres. The remainder is entailed to him and his four brothers jointly. By 1700 the brothers have broken the entail and are beginning to sell off land.

1691 Manor status ceases to have any legal standing under New York Colony law. The Sylvesters still hold unofficial "lord of the manor" status for many generations.

1704 Giles dies without offspring and leaves the manor property to his executor, William Nicoll of Islip (1657–1722), to pay Giles's debts. Nicoll retains the residue of the estate (still approximately half the island).

1719 Brinley Sylvester (1694–1752), grandson of Nathaniel and Grizzell, moves to Shelter Island from Newport.

1730 The town of Shelter Island is formed. Twenty landowners (including William Nicoll's son, William) divide the island acreage.

c.1737 After a long lawsuit with the Nicoll family concludes, Brinley is awarded the old "mansion house late of Nathaniell Sylvester" and 1,000 acres.

1737–45 Brinley levels his grandfather's old house and builds the elegant existing dwelling.

1752 Brinley dies intestate. The daughters of Brinley and Mary Burroughs Sylvester (c.1702–1751), Mary Sylvester (1724–1794) and Margaret Sylvester Chesebrough of Newport, Rhode Island, divide the 1,000-acre property.

1757 Death of Obium of Shelter Island, father of Jupiter Hammon.

1762 Thomas Dering (1720–1785) and his wife, Mary Sylvester Dering, move to the manor. Margaret Chesebrough and her husband, David Chesebrough, of Newport rent their half of the property to Thomas.

1760s–70s The Derings extend the house by adding another kitchen.

1776–83 The Derings, along with other Long Islanders, flee to Connecticut after Long Island is occupied by the British during the Revolutionary War. Slaves, servants, or tenants care for the house and farm in the Derings' absence. The manor lies neglected.

1785 Sylvester Dering (1758–1820), eldest son of Thomas and Mary Dering, inherits the property. A model farmer who uses Enlightenment farming methods (but continues to use enslaved labor), he strives to restore the manor to productivity and wealth but never catches up with his debts.

1820 The seven children of Sylvester and Esther Sarah Havens Dering (1763–1839) inherit the property. A week before Sylvester Dering's death, Comus Fanning, a freed African American, purchases 21 acres of manor land from Dering. London, last of the manor slaves, is manumitted by Esther Dering.

1827 On July 4, slavery finally ends by law in New York State.

1827 Mary Catherine L'Hommedieu Gardiner (1806–1838) and her husband, Samuel Smith Gardiner (1789–1859), purchase the property, by this time 578 acres, and the house for $10,400 at public auction in Sag Harbor for estate and other debts. Mary is a great-great-granddaughter of Nathaniel and Grizzell through Patience Sylvester L'Hommedieu (1664–1719).

1840s Samuel Gardiner makes extensive alterations to the house shortly after his second marriage, to Susan Mott of Brooklyn.

1859 Mary, Phoebe, and Frances Gardiner, Samuel and Mary Catherine's three children, inherit jointly. Eben Norton Horsford (1818–1893), who first marries Mary (1824–1855) and then Phoebe (1826–1903), takes the lead in managing the estate.

1859 On Samuel Gardiner's death, the manor becomes a summer residence; the Horsford family lives in Cambridge, Massachusetts, where E. N. Horsford teaches at Harvard.

1865 E. N. Horsford purchases the last of Comus Fanning's 21 acres from Julia Dyd Havens Johnson (c.1809–1907), the manor housekeeper and the daughter of Fanning's wife, Dido.

1872–91 Cambridge's intellectual community visit every summer. Longfellow, Whittier, Asa Gray, and Sarah Orne Jewett are among the guests.

1884 The slave graveyard is fenced and marked with a commemorative stone. The family graveyard is fenced and marked with a table monument honoring the Quakers.

1893 Widow Phoebe Dayton Gardiner Horsford (1826–1903) inherits.

1903 Cornelia Conway Felton Horsford (1861–1944), Phoebe's daughter, inherits.

1907 Julia Johnson is buried in the slave graveyard at her request.

1908 Cornelia engages Henry Bacon, the architect of the Lincoln Memorial, to renovate and enlarge the house. Bacon makes "actual state" drawings before commencing the work.

1944 Augustus Henry Fiske (1880–1945) inherits from his great-aunt Cornelia, but he dies only six months after her.

1944 Mary Katharine Fiske Drury (1916–1988), daughter of Augustus, inherits the manor.

1949 By agreement, the property, now approximately 250 acres, passes to Mary Katharine's brother, Andrew Fiske (1909–1992). Andrew lives at the manor year-round.

1992 At Andrew's Fiske's death, life tenancy is bequeathed to his widow, Alice Hench Fiske (1917–2006).

2006 Eben Fiske Ostby (b. 1955), Andrew Fiske's nephew, becomes the owner of the 243-acre estate on Alice Fiske's death.

2007 Bennett Konesni, Eben Ostby's nephew (b. 1982), arrives to live at the manor. With the start of an organic farm and educational programs, a new phase of manor life begins, continuing the property's history with a new focus on organic food production and community.

2009–13 Eben Ostby forms a 501(c)(3), Sylvester Manor Educational Farm, Inc.; Ostby and the Sylvester Manor Board will preserve the manor's heritage by selling agricultural easements and transferring most of the acreage to the new foundation.

Time Line of World Events

1588 English defeat of the Spanish Armada. Reign of Elizabeth I. Birth of Giles Sylvester in England

1600–1650 Smallpox and other European diseases reduce New England's native population by 90%

1600–1700 The Netherlands' "Golden Age": Dutch transatlantic and Caribbean trade increases exponentially

1607 Jamestown founded

1619 The first Africans arrive in Virginia

1620 Plymouth founded

1621 Dutch West India Company (WIC) founded

1627 Barbados settled by the English

1630 John Winthrop leads the Puritans to Massachusetts

1637–38 Pequot War in New England

1656–57 Quakers begin to visit New England and are persecuted. The Sylvesters become Friends.

1640–59 English Civil Wars (Charles I executed 1649) and Commonwealth rule

1651–96 British "Navigation Acts" progressively limit colonial trade

1660 Charles II is crowned. Quaker Mary Dyer is hanged in Boston.

1673 Quaker founder George Fox visits Shelter Island

1673–74 Third Anglo-Dutch War: the Dutch cede New York permanently to the English

1674–76 King Philip's War ends the independent power of Indians in New England

1741 Slave "conspiracy" in New York City, where one in five inhabitants was African American

1775–88 American Revolutionary War and founding of the nation

1783 Massachusetts passes an antislavery law

1790 First census of the United States: 4 million Americans, of whom 19% are African American. Indians were not counted, although there were likely more than 80 tribes with 150,000 members.

1799 Act for the Gradual Abolition of Slavery passed in New York, with all slaves freed in 1827

1844 Railroad arrives in Greenport, New York, across the Peconic Bay from Shelter Island

1861–65 American Civil War. Emancipation Proclamation, 1863.

1964 The Civil Rights Act is signed into law by President Lyndon Johnson

Notes

List of Abbreviations

AFMCAR Andrew Fiske Memorial Center for Archaeological Research, University of Massachusetts Boston
BMHS Barbados Museum and Historical Society
COG Colonial Office Group
CSP *Calendar of State Papers, Colonial Series, America and West Indies*
EHTR *Records of the Town of East-Hampton*
GBS Grizzell Brinley Sylvester
GSDD General Sylvester Dering II Document Collection
JBMHS *Journal of the Barbados Museum and Historical Society*
JWJr John Winthrop Jr.
LIHJ *Long Island History Journal*
MHS Massachusetts Historical Society
MoLAS Museum of London Archaeology Service
NAA Gemeentearchief Amsterdam, Notarial Archives
NEHGR *New England Historical and Genealogical Register*
NEQ *The New England Quarterly*
NGSQ *National Genealogical Society Quarterly*
NHCR *Records of the Colony or Jurisdiction of New Haven from May 1653 to the Union*
NS Nathaniel Sylvester
NYGBR *New York Genealogical and Biographical Record*
ODNB *Oxford Dictionary of National Biography*
PRO Public Record Office
RPI Rennselaer Polytechnic Institute
SIHS Shelter Island Historical Society
SMA, NYU Sylvester Manor Archive, Fales Library and Special Collections, Bobst Library, New York University, http://dlib.nyu.edu/findingaids/html/fales/sylmanor_content.html
STR *Southold Town Records Copied and Explanatory Notes Added by J. Wickham Case*
TB Thomas Brinley

TNA	The National Archives (Great Britain)
WIC	Dutch West India Company
WMQ	*William and Mary Quarterly*, 3rd series
WNYHS	Abstracts of wills, New-York Historical Society, published in 17 volumes
WP	*Winthrop Papers*

1. The Discovery

7 *bought the island:* Stephen Goodyear to Captain Thomas Middleton, Thomas Rous, Constant Silvester, and Nathaniel Sylvester, June 9, 1651. *Records of the Town of East-Hampton, Long Island, Suffolk Co., NY, with other Ancient Documents of Historic Value*, 2 vols. (Sag Harbor: John H. Hunt, Printer, 1887), 1:96–99; Benjamin F. Thompson, *The History of Long Island: from its Discovery and Settlement, to the Present Time, etc.*, 2nd ed. (New York: Gould, Banks, 1843), 1:364.

9 *bed hangings:* The Society for the Preservation of Long Island Antiquities has the rest of this set.

10 *original parchment charter:* Enfranchisement for Shelter Island, Richard Nicolls to Constant and Nathaniell Sylvester, March 31, 1666. Sylvester Manor Archive, Fales Library and Special Collections, Bobst Library, New York University (SMA, NYU), Series A, Box 140, Folder 6; New York State Archives, series A1895, New York Colonial Manuscripts, 38:155.

11 *ten thousand people:* Sherrill D. Wilson, "African Burial Ground," in *Slavery in New York*, ed. Ira Berlin and Leslie M. Harris (New York: New Press, in conjunction with The New-York Historical Society, 2005), 7.

11 *419 human remains:* Wilson, 7.

13 *"Captain Nathaniell Sylvester":* The term may be a "gentry honorific," such as that of Captain, then Colonel, Lewis Morris of Barbados. In 1640s Dutch records, vessels in which Nathaniel Sylvester acted as a merchant factor were captained by professionals, a relationship spelled out as "the said captain and merchant." In 1651, as one of the purchasers of Shelter Island, he is "Captain Nathaniell Silvester." In 1652 he signs without a rank in a dispatch for payments to military forces on Barbados, but in 1655 he is called "Captain Nathiell Silvister" in a Connecticut court deposition. Thereafter, on Shelter Island, he frequently becomes "Captain." William Nicoll and Brinley Sylvester, contract, Suffolk County Deeds, Liber B, part 1:169; Kristen Block, *Ordinary Lives in the Early Caribbean: Religion, Colonial Competition, and the Politics of Profit* (Athens: University of Georgia Press, 2012), 149,167; NAA 1289, fo. 101v–102v; NAA 1293/30, March 22, 1646; September 20, 1652, GSDD 1:2; TNA, PRO, CO 1/11 no. 57.1 [ff.157-8]; *EHTR*, 1:91–93; Richard Smith to Governor John Winthrop, Jr., Sept. 5, 1673, in Daniel Berkeley Updike, *Richard Smith, First English Settler of the Narragansett Country, Rhode Island, with a Series of Letters Written by His Son Richard Smith, Jr., etc.* (Boston: Merrymount Press, 1937), 100–101.

16 *slavery in the North:* Richard Shannon Moss, "Slavery on Long Island: Its Rise and Decline During the Seventeenth Through the Nineteenth Centuries," Ph.D. dissertation, St. John's University, 1985; A. Leon Higginbotham Jr., *In the Matter of Color: Race and the American Legal Process; The Colonial Period* (New York: Oxford University Press, 1978), 61–100, 100–150; Grania Bolton Marcus, *Discovering the African-American Experience in Suffolk County, 1620–1860* (Mattituck, NY: Amereon House, for the Society for the Preservation of Long Island Antiquities, 1995).

16 *more human chattel:* Moss, *Slavery on Long Island*, iii.

16 *half the workforce:* Moss, *Slavery on Long Island*, 110–12.

16 *"Negro man Joseph":* General Sylvester II Document Collection, receipt, "Sylvester Dering to Joseph Hedges for negro man Peter, 1810," 2:52, Shelter Island Historical Society (SIHS).

16 *London, the last of the slaves:* Manumission certificate for London from Esther Sarah Dering, April 16, 1821, SIHS.

16 *for an article:* Mac Griswold, "Sylvester Manor: A Colonial Garden Becomes a Colonial Revival Garden," *Journal of the New England Garden History Society* 5 (Fall 1997), 25–34.

18 *"the spread of European cultures":* James Deetz, *In Small Things Forgotten: An Archaeology of Early American Life* (New York: Anchor Books, 1996), 5.

20 *fences, roads, and buildings:* Stephen A. Mrozowski, Katherine Howlett Hayes, and Anne P. Hancock, "The Archaeology of Sylvester Manor," 1–15; Hayes, "Field Excavations at Sylvester Manor," 34–50; and Kenneth L. Kvamme, "Geophysical Explorations at Sylvester Manor," 51–70; in *The Historical Archaeology of Sylvester Manor*, ed. Katherine Howlett Hayes and Stephen A. Mrozowski, special issue, *Northeast Historical Archaeology* 36 (2007).

21 *Nathaniel and his partners:* Articles of Agreement, Capt. Thomas Middleton, Constant Silvester, Capt. Nathaniell Silvester, Ens. John Booth, September 20, 1652, GSDD 1:2. Only Nathaniel Sylvester did not sign the contract. On July 30, 1652, he was on Barbados to witness "An Account of What Sugar Sir George Ayscue and Capt Michall Pack Have Ordered to Be Paid for the Use of the States Fleet," where he may have remained longer. TNA: PRO, America and West Indies Colonial Papers, CO 1/11 no. 57.1 [ff.157–58].

22 *Giles:* Henry B. Hoff, "The Sylvester Family of Shelter Island," *New York Genealogical & Biographical Record* 125, no. 1 (January 1994) 13–18; no. 2 (April 1994): 88–93.

23 obosom: The Besease shrine appears to have been created as a tourist attraction, but that is not entirely clear. For a seventeenth-century description of an *obosom*, see "Wilhelm Johannes Muller's Description of the Fetu Country, 1662–69," in *German Sources for West African History, 1599–1669*, ed. Adam Jones (Wiesbaden: Franz Steiner Verlag GMBH, 1983), 159, note 96; see also Michael A. Gomez, *Exchanging Our Country Marks: The Transformation of African Identities in the Colonial and Antebellum South* (Chapel Hill: University of North Carolina Press, 1998), 111.

2. Living with the Indians

25 *The Manhansetts:* Kathleen J. Bragdon, *Native People of Southern New England, 1500–1650* (Norman: University of Oklahoma Press, 1996), xi–xiii; Faren R. Siminoff, *Crossing the Sound: The Rise of Atlantic American Communities in Seventeenth-Century Eastern Long Island* (New York: New York University Press, 2004), 16–17.

25 *clasping hands:* It's debatable whether Indians shook hands with each other as a sign of agreement before the white man came. John A. Strong, pers. comm., Aug. 24, 2005.

25 *"The confrontation":* Karen Ordahl Kupperman, *Settling with the Indians: The Meeting of English and Indian Cultures in America, 1580–1640* (London: J. M. Dent, 1980), vii.

26 *bloodbath:* Jonathan I. Israel, *The Dutch Republic: Its Rise, Greatness, and Fall, 1477–1806* (Oxford: Clarendon Press, 1995), 159–60.

26 *"fingers and thumes"*: William Coddington to John Winthrop Jr. (JWJr), Newport, August 5, 1644, *WP*, vol. 4, 1638–44, ed. Allyn Bailey Forbes (Boston: MHS, 1944), 491.

27 *colonists feared:* Kupperman, *Settling*, viii.

27 *Algonquian accusations:* John A. Strong, *The Algonquian Peoples of Long Island from Earliest Times to 1700* (Hempstead, NY: Long Island Studies Institute, Hofstra University, 1997), 118.

27 *"make water burn"*: William Wood, *New England's Prospect: A True, Lively and Experimental Description of That Part of America, Commonly called New England* (London: Tho. Cotes, 1634), quoted in Strong, *Algonquian Peoples*, 117.

27 *"one of his visits"*: E. N. Horsford, Drafts, notes, and miscellaneous materials for a genealogical manuscript, SMA, NYU IV/A/11/111/20,21 and 112/1–6; Cushing/Horsford correspondence, SMA, NYU IV/A/1/a/58/54; National Anthropological Archives, Washington, DC.

29 *"aloof, impersonal"*: Strong, *Algonquian Peoples*, 111.

32 *"threatened to be forced off"*: William Wallace Tooker, *John Eliot's First Indian Teacher and Interpreter, Cockenoe-de-Long Island, and the Story of His Career from the Early Records* (New York: F. P. Harper, 1896), 26.

32 *a second time*: See Siminoff, *Crossing the Sound*, 41, for Dutch customs; also Patricia Seed, *Ceremonies of Possession in Europe's Conquest of the New World, 1492–1640* (Cambridge: Cambridge University Press, 1995).

32 *"For though hee hath no Kingly Robes"*: Wood, *New England's Prospect* (London, 1643), 79–80; quoted in Kupperman, *Settlement*, 143–44.

32 *"a great bunch of hayre"*: "muppacuck," "neyhommauog": Roger Williams, *A Key into the Language of America* (London: 1643; reprinted, ed. John J. Teunissen and Evelyn J. Hinz, Detroit: Wayne State University Press, 1973), 186.

33 *wampum:* Daniel K. Richter, *Before the Revolution: America's Ancient Pasts* (Cambridge, MA: Belknap Press of Harvard University Press, 2011), 141–42.

33 *"They are a very understanding generation"*: Kupperman, *Settling*, quoting from Alexander Whitaker, *Good News from Virginia* (London, 1613), 86.

33 *"Cloth, inclining to white"*: Williams, *Key*, 216; also see *Settling*, 33–44.

33 *"according to the usual custom"*: Confirmation of a deed of sale, March 23, 1653, signed by John Herbert, Robert Seeley, Daniell Lane, and Giles Sylvester, recorded Jan. 28, 1661. *Southold Town Records Copied and Explanatory Notes Added by J. Wickham Case*, 2 vols. (New York: S. W. Green's Sons, 1882, 1884), 158–59.

33 *permanent underclass:* John Strong, "Indian Labor During the Post-Contact Period on Long Island, 1626–1700," in *To Know the Place: Exploring Long Island History*, ed. Joann P. Krieg and Natalie A. Naylor (Interlaken, NY: Heart of the Lakes, 1995), 23.

34 *the island seemed preferable:* "Ambusco late Sachem of South-hold hath liberty to remove wth his family to Shelter Island to abide there with Mr. Sylvesters permission, but no others to be admitted to come on, or to follow him, wthout particular leave," Oct. 16, 1675. Edmund Bailey O'Callaghan and Berthold Fernow, eds., *Documents Relative to the Colonial History of the State of New York: Procured in Holland, England, and France* (Albany: Weed, Parsons, 1853–87, 1858), 14:703.

34 *Unlike Wyandanch:* Lion Gardiner, *Relation of the Pequot Warres* (Hartford, CT: Acorn, 1901), 27, 29, http://digitalcommons.unl.edu/etas/38.

34 *fire-hardened tips:* Strong, *Algonquian Peoples*, 86. Strong bases his description on an excavation in New Jersey.

34 *"deny entrance"*: For housing, see Strong, *Algonquian Peoples*, 86–88.

35 *Indian domestic fires burned:* For the details of daily life in this passage, see Bragdon, *Native People*, 106–7.

35 mâuo: Bragdon, *Native People*, 106.

35 *Huge bonfires:* Gardiner, *Relation of the Pequot Warres*, 26.

35 *"warm and thicke woodie bottomes":* Williams, *Key*, 128.

35 *"half a hundred":* Paul J. Lindholt, ed. *John Josselyn, Colonial Traveler: A Critical Edition of Two Voyages to New-England* (Lebanon, NH: University Press of New England, 1988), 91.

35 *civil society:* Kupperman, *Settling*, 4–5, 141–48.

36 *"Indian barnes":* For food preparation and storage, see Strong, *Algonquian Peoples*, 100–104.

36 *"All the neighbors":* Williams, *Key*, 170.

36 *three feet across:* Strong, *Algonquian Peoples*, 96.

36 *Indians didn't deserve their land:* See William Cronon, *Changes in the Land: Indians, Colonists and the Ecology of New England* (New York: Hill and Wang, 1983), 54–81.

36 *"choaking weede":* Wood, *New England's Prospect*, 94.

37 *Hobbemok:* See Bragdon, *Native People*, 236, for Indian graveyards located near or within sight of water.

37 *"a generall Custome":* Williams, *Key*, 191.

37 *step across the threshhold:* James Hammond Trumbull, "Natick Dictionary," *Bureau of American Ethnology Bulletin* 25 (Washington, DC, 1903), quoted in Bragdon, *Native People*, 193.

37 *"description solidifies":* John Updike, *Self-Consciousness*, quoted by Paul A. Robinson in "Lost Opportunities: Miantonomi and the English in Seventeenth-Century Narragansett Country," in *Northeastern Indian Lives 1632–1816*, ed. Robert S. Grumet (Amherst: University of Massachusetts Press, 1996), 15.

38 *ninety thousand Indians:* Bragdon, *Native People*, 25–28; Siminoff, *Crossing the Sound*, 76.

38 *God had deserted the Indians:* Kupperman, *Settling with the Indians*, 5–6, 115–18.

38 *"from the Birth":* Williams, *Key*, 97.

38 *"Shall I sleep here?":* Williams, *Key*, 106; "Cuppaimish," Williams, *Key*, 216. Williams compiled his "dictionary" on his way back to England on a visit; he wrote his observations when the book was about to be published, and his comparisons between the Indians and his own countrymen are often to the detriment of the English, who were then in the midst of civil war and social upheaval.

39 *a Spanish "cob":* Jack Gary, "Material Culture and Multi-Cultural Interactions at Sylvester Manor," in Hayes and Mrozowski, *Historical Archaeology of Sylvester Manor*, 100–12, 106.

39 *The spoken language:* Bragdon, *Native People*, 28–29; Siminoff, *Crossing the Sound*, 16.

39 *two English traders:* John Stone and John Oldham. See Strong, *Algonquian Peoples*, 154–56, and Richter, *Before the Revolution*, 161–68.

39 *as slaves:* See Margaret Ellen Newell, "The Changing Nature of Indian Slavery in New England, 1670–1720," in *Re-Interpreting New England Indians and the Colonial Experience*, ed. Colin G. Calloway and Neal Salisbury (Boston: Colonial Society of Massachusetts, distributed by the University of Virginia, 2003) 106–36. For the persistence of Indian bound labor, see the case of an "Indian Boye called Sharper" employed as a servant by Brinley Sylvester in 1726, New Connecticut State Library,

Record Group 3, New London County Court, Native Americans (vol. 23, folder 21), June 1726, John Pickett v. John Buroughs re: Sharper.

39 *ineffectively enforced legislation*: New York Council Minutes, Dec. 5, 1679, *Documents Relative to the Colonial History of the State of New York*, 13:537.

39 *marriage of Indian women*: Newell, "Changing Nature," 127–28; John Wood Sweet, *Bodies Politic: Negotiating Race in the Colonial North* (Baltimore: Johns Hopkins University Press, 2003), 172–79.

39 *their final victory*: Siminoff, *Crossing the Sound*, 72–74.

40 *growth of the European fur trade*: See Richter, *Before the Revolution*, 151–60.

40 *six beads for a penny*: Wampum first became legal tender in New England in 1637, http://www.dickshovel.com/meto.html.

40 *"ye English"*: Gardiner, *Relation*, 25.

41 *King Philip's War*: See Eric B. Schultz and Michael J. Touglas, *King Philip's War: The History and Legacy of America's Forgotten Conflict* (New York: W. W. Norton, 2000).

41 *hard cider and West Indian rum*: In 1675, Sylvester complained to Governor Edmund Andros of New York Colony about the behavior of drunken Indians threatening violence "to the disquiet of others, not least himself & whole ffamily." Katherine Lee Priddy, "On the Mend: Cultural Interaction of Native Americans, Africans, and Europeans on Shelter Island, New York" (master's thesis, University of Massachusetts Boston, 2002), 38, and *Documents Relative to the Colonial History of the State of New York*, 14:703.

41 *"Before entering [a harbor]"*: Giovanni da Verrazzano, *The Voyages of Giovanni da Verrazzano, 1524–28*, ed. Lawrence C. Wroth (New Haven: Yale University Press, 1970), 137–38, quoted in Bragdon, *Native People*, 4–5.

42 *invasive rhizomes and extinction*: John L. Strong argues that the cattail analogy doesn't hold for Long Island's Algonquians in "The Reaffirmation of Tradition Among the Native Americans of Eastern Long Island," *Long Island Historical Journal* 7, no. 1 (Fall 1994): 42–67; and in *We Are Still Here: The Algonquian Peoples of Long Island Today* (Interlaken, NY: Empire State Books, rev. ed. 1998). On June 15, 2010, through the Bureau of Indian Affairs, the Shinnecock Nation received official recognition from the United States federal government.

3. AMSTERDAM

43 *The archaeologist Paul Huey*: New York State archaeologist Paul R. Huey, Office of Parks, Recreation, and Historic Preservation, at Sylvester Manor, June 2000.

43 *in Gouda*: Herman Janse, *Building Amsterdam* (Amsterdam: De Brink, 2001), 42–43; and "'Gouda' Bricks Found at Whippingham Church," http://freespace.virgin.net/roger.hewitt/iwias/gouda.htm.

43 *foundations and chimneys*: Anne P. Hancock, "The Changing Landscape of a Former Northern Plantation: Sylvester Manor, Shelter Island, New York" (master's thesis, University of Massachusetts Boston, 2002), 77.

44 *Atlantic slave trade*: See Herbert S. Klein, *The Atlantic Slave Trade* (Cambridge: Cambridge University Press, 1999); Johannes Postma, *The Atlantic Slave Trade* (Westport, CT: Greenwood Press, 2003); Johannes Postma, "A Reassessment of the Atlantic Slave Trade"; Henk den Heijer, "The West African Trade of the Dutch West India Company, 1674–1740," in *Riches from Atlantic Commerce: Dutch Transatlantic Trade and Shipping, 1585–1817*, eds. Johannes Postma and Victor Enthoven

(Leiden, The Netherlands: Brill, 2003), 115–38, 139–69; and Stuart B. Schwartz, "A Commonwealth within Itself: The Early Brazilian Sugar Industry, 1550–1670," in *Tropical Babylons, Sugar and the Making of the Atlantic World, 1450–1680*, ed. Stuart B. Schwartz (Chapel Hill: University of North Carolina Press, 2004), 158–200.

44 *Europe's center:* Jonathan I. Israel, *Dutch Republic* and *Dutch Primacy in World Trade, 1585–1740* (Oxford: Clarendon Press, 2002); Simon Schama, *The Embarrassment of Riches: An Interpretation of Dutch Culture in the Golden Age* (New York: Vintage Books, 1997), introduction, ch. 5, and appendices.

44 *English traveler:* Brereton, *Travels in Holland*, 1:65.

45 *flush the canals:* Paul Spies, Koen Kleijn, Jos Smit, and Ernest Kurpershoek, eds., *The Canals of Amsterdam* (The Hague: SDU Uitgeverij Koninginnegracht, 1993).

45 *Mary, nineteen:* For the civil marriage, July 6, 1613, see Jakob Gijsbert De Hoop Scheffer, *History of the Free Churchmen Called the Brownists, Pilgrim Fathers, and Baptists in the Dutch Republic, 1581–1701* (Ithaca, NY: Andrus & Church, 1922), 194; Hoff, "Sylvester Family," Part Two: "The Arnold Family of Lowestoft, Suffolk, England; Amsterdam; and Southold, Long Island," *NYGBR* 125, no. 2 (April 1994): 89–93.

45 *English merchants:* Jessica Dijkman, "Giles Silvester, An English Merchant in Amsterdam," research paper commissioned for the Sylvester Manor Project, Griswold Papers, Fales Library, NYU, February 2003.

45 *English-sounding* names: Dijkman, "Giles Sylvester", 13, and Appendix 2.

47 *documents:* Dijkman, "Giles Sylvester," Appendix 1, 25–26.

47 *400 to 800 pounds:* Arthur P. Middleton, *Tobacco Coast: A Maritime History of the Chesapeake Bay in the Colonial Era* (Newport News, VA: Mariners Museum, 1953, Maryland Paperback Bookshelf Edition, 1984), 113.

48 *"A dispute":* NAA 942/1171.

48 *merchant with an account:* Amsterdam Exchange Bank services included a free transfer service for account holders, bills of exchange, and the issue of a stable currency. Janse, *Building Amsterdam*, 6–7; Violet Barbour, *Capitalism in Amsterdam in the Seventeenth Century* (Baltimore: Johns Hopkins University Press, 1950; Ann Arbor: University of Michigan Press, 1966).

49 *business contacts:* See NAA 141/fo 48v–49 v; Keith L. Sprunger, *Dutch Puritanism: A History of the English and Scottish Churches of the Netherlands in the Sixteenth and Seventeenth Centuries* (Leiden, The Netherlands: Brill, 1982), 379; NAA 849/123, August 22, 1647.

49 *business dealings:* Giles sold saffron in Amsterdam to a German merchant on behalf of an English merchant, Hendrick Congem. NAA 134, fo 173v, February 7, 1614.

49 *New Merchants:* Robert Brenner, *Merchants and Revolution: Commercial Change, Political Conflict, and London's Overseas Traders, 1550–1653* (Princeton: Princeton University Press, 1993; new edition, London: Verso, 2003), 111–12, 114–15, 159–69; and Dijkman, "Giles Silvester," 17.

50 *tightrope act:* Schama, *Embarrassment*, 609.

50 *boundary-crosser's realm:* a term used to describe New England's liminality in the period. Siminoff, *Crossing the Sound*, 2.

50 *the law:* George Dennis vs.William Maskelyne & Company and Philip Best (with NS as attorney), on Sept. 29, 1665, "Transcript of Trial Involving Nathaniel Sylvester (Original 1665)," SMA, NYU IV/H/4/106/25. See a later appeal (undated) from Governor Richard Nicolls, who signed himself "your affectionate friend and loving servant," to induce NS to conclude the matter and render a lesser amount to Dennis.

50 *Virginian tobacco*: NAA NA 720/46, Feb. 6, 1626, Dijkman, "Giles Silvester," Appendix 1, 25.

50 *his wife, Mary*: Giles died either in the Netherlands or in England sometime between May 11, 1651 (NAA 1695/1093, last entry in the Amsterdam Archive for Giles), and Nov. 19, 1652, when "the widow and Heirs of Gyles Sylvester," apparently on Barbados, successfully petitioned the Committee for Plantation Affairs that they were "not to bee looked upon as Dutch but as English" (Cal. State Papers Col. Series 1574–1660, 393, Nov. 19, 1652). She returned to London before Jan. 26, 1658, when she is mentioned in the will of her son, Peter (British NA Prob 11/273).

50 *June 1664*: Mary died in London before June 28, 1664, see Giles Sylvester, Barbados, to JWJr, New London, June 28, 1664, MHS *Proc.*, ser. 2, 4 (1887–89): 280, and Robert C. Black III, *The Younger John Winthrop* (New York: Columbia University Press, 1966), 240–45.

50 *crisscrossing*: Letters (May 29, 1658; June 28, 1664; September 16, 1664; and May 30, 1666) from Giles II (c.1632–d. betw. May 2, 1670, and Apr. 7, 1671) to JWJr, illustrate the family's transatlantic traffic. Constant (c.1614–1671) is found in Barbados, New England, or the Netherlands in the 1650s, and later in London or Brampton, Yorkshire. Peter (c.1631–will proved Feb. 11, 1658) was also an Atlantic traveler; NS (c.1620–will proved Oct. 2, 1680), once on Shelter Island, apparently traveled only locally with the exception of a single trip in 1661 to England with his wife; Joshua (c.1626–d. June 21, 1706) moved to Shelter Island before Sept. 7, 1660. MHS *Proc.*, ser. 2, 4 (1887–89): 275–77 and 278–82; Hoff, "Sylvester Family," 13–18.

50 *trip to England*: P. W. Coldham, *The Complete Book of Emigrants, 1661–99: A Comprehensive Listing Compiled from English Public Records of Those Who Took Ship to the Americas, etc.* (Baltimore: Genealogical, 1990), 20.

51 *Charlton Adam*: "'[1613] July 6, Giles Silvester from Adamchartle,' List of Marriages of English People Living at Amsterdam, etc.," Scheffer, *History of the Free Churchmen*, 194; "[Giles] Silvester of Adam Charlton . . . now resident in Amsterdam," NAA 849/123, Aug. 22, 1647. After Giles's death, c.1651, his sons Constant and Peter stated that their father was "borne in Salisbery in ye County of W____ [Wiltshire]." Hoff, "Sylvester Family," 14.

51 *"Brownists"*: Scheffer, *History of the Free Churchmen*, 1–9; Michael E. Moody, "Browne, Robert (1550?–1633)" (*ODNB*, 2004), http://www.oxforddnb.com/view/article/3695.

51 *Vlooienburg*: "Flea Town," perhaps a reference to the district's low status.

52 *"Of this sect"*: Keith L. Sprunger, *Dutch Puritanism*, 68.

52 *double standard*: Howard H. Brinton, *Friends for 350 Years* (Wallingford, PA: Pendle Hill, 2002), 170–72.

52 *wife swapping*: The "Family of Love" basing their beliefs on the works of the mystic Hendrick Niclaes (c.1502–1580), held that the true believer "possessed the spiritual power of God." Since "non-Familist readers . . . read H. N. [Niclaes] as dispensing with the ordinary moral code," contemporary critics repeatedly slung accusations of sexual license at them. John Evelyn (1620–1706), diarist and gardener, stumbling on a Familist community in East Anglia, wrote that they thought of themselves as "a sort of refined *Quakers*." Nathaniel and Grizzell became Quakers around 1657. Christopher W. Marsh, *The Family of Love in English Society, 1550–1630* (Cambridge: Cambridge University Press, 1994), 20; John Evelyn, *The Diary of John Evelyn*, ed. E. S. de Beer (Oxford: Oxford University Press, 1959), 868, quoted in Marsh, *The Family of Love*, 260.

52 *into exile:* Scheffer, *History of the Free Churchmen,* 13; Michael E. Moody, "Johnson, Francis (bap. 1562, d. 1617)" (*ODNB,* 2004), http://www.oxforddnb.com/view/article/14877.

52 *"schism and bad manners":* Sprunger, *Dutch Puritanism,* 59, 80.

53 *one Elder:* Christopher Lawne, *The Prophane Schism of the Brownists or Separatists, with the Impiety, Dissensions, Lewd and Abominable Vices of That Impure Sect, Discovered 1612,* quoted in Keith L. Sprunger, *Trumpets from the Tower: English Puritan Printing in The Netherlands, 1600–40* (Leiden, The Netherlands: Brill, 1994), 106. "Mansfield the Stripper," as Lawne calls the Elder, was excommunicated after Lawne's pamphlet appeared.

53 *biblical authority:* Markus P. M. Vink, "Freedom and Slavery: The Dutch Republic, the VOC World, and the Debate over the 'World's Oldest Trade,'" *South African Historical Journal* 59 (2007): 19–46.

53 *John Paget:* Keith L. Sprunger, "Paget, John (d. 1638)" (*ODNB,* 2004), http://www.oxforddnb.com/view/article/21114.

53 *"Separatist assembly":* Sprunger, *Dutch Puritanism,* 70.

53 *three thousand guilders:* NAA 848/97.

54 *"birchen rod":* William Bradford, *Divers Recollections of Puritan Strictness* (1648), quoted in Scheffer, *History of the Free Churchmen,* 98.

54 *Henry Ainsworth:* Michael E. Moody, "Ainsworth, Henry (1569–1622)" (*ODNB,* 2004), http://www.oxforddnb.com/view/article/240.

54 *Book of Psalms:* For Ainsworth's *The Book of Psalmes, Englished Both in Prose and Meeter,* Imprinted at Amsterdam by Giles Thorp (1612), see Sprunger, *Dutch Puritans,* 58. Thorpe, a deacon and an elder of the church, had set most of Ainsworth's works in type. Sprunger, *Dutch Puritans,* 76. Joseph Thorpe aged twenty-four "from London" who in 1626 married Lydia, Mary Arnold Sylvester's sister, is probably the same Joseph Thorpe who signed the church loan document in 1634, and a relation of Giles Thorpe. Sprunger, *Trumpets,* 86; Hoff, "Arnold Family," 90.

54 *"secretary hand":* Ambrose Heal, *The English Writing-Masters and Their Copy-Books 1570–1800, A Biographical Dictionary & A Bibliography, with an Introduction on the Development of Handwriting by Stanley Morison* (Hildesheim: Georg Olms Verlagsbuchhandlung, 1962).

54 *nine surviving letters:* NS, Shelter Island, to JWJr, Pequitt (New London), Oct. 10, 1654, SMA, NYU I/A/140/3, and MHS collections.

55 *cut a quill:* Heal, *English Writing-Masters,* xvii; Jean F. Preston and Laetitita Yeandle, *English Handwriting 1400–1650: An Introductory Manual* (Asheville, NC: Pegasus Press, 1999), xi.

55 *John Canne:* Roger Hayden, "Canne, John (d. 1667?)" (*ODNB,* 2004), http://www.oxforddnb.com/view/article/4552.

55 *"is not to be found":* Quoted in Sprunger, *Dutch Puritans,* 76; *Trumpets,* 124.

55 *"for conscience' sake":* Quakers would not take oaths in God's name, using the phrase "for conscience' sake" instead.

55 *reading as a birthright:* Nathaniel's enterprising maternal aunt, Mercy Arnold Pelham Bruyning (Browning), inherited her husband Browning's printing business and bookshop; her printed catalogue is titled *A Catalogue of Theological, Historical and Physical [Medical] Books with Other Miscellanies Being a Part of the Books of Mercy Browning, Joseph Browning's Widow, at Her Shop at the Corner of the Exchange, in*

Amsterdam; with her brother, Elias Arnold, she purchased and profitably sold an edition of the Bible called the "6,000-error Bible." NAA 795/36; Sprunger, *Trumpets*, 88, 98–102, 211–12.

56 *probate inventory*: GSDD 1:1.

56 *Francis Brinley*: "Gentleman's Library of 1713," *New England Historical and Genealogical Register* (*NEHGR*) 12 (January 1858): 75–78.

56 *a great variety of ideas:* David Harris Sacks, "Francis Brinley and His Books, 1650–1719," presented at "American Origins: The Seventeenth Century," a workshop of the *WMQ* and the Early Modern Studies Institute, Huntington Library and University of Southern California, May 2006, 19–20.

56 *Münster Rebellion:* Hermann von Kerrsenbrock, *Narrative of the Anabaptist Madness: The Overthrow of Munster, the Famous Metropolis of Westphalia* (Leiden, The Netherlands: Brill, 2007). For the Amsterdam Anabaptist incident, see the Global Anabaptist Mennonite Encyclopedia Online, http://www.gameo.org/encyclopedia/contents/A4755.html.

56 *baptismal entries:* Minister John Paget described the sect in 1635 as "without Sacraments, and had neither Lords Supper nor Baptism administred in their Church, their children for many yeares, remayning unbaptized, and sundry dying unbaptized," quoted in Sprunger, *Dutch Puritanism*, 70.

56 *birth order:* Henry Hoff gives a conjectural birth order based on other surviving records for the children of Giles and Mary (Arnold) Sylvester as follows: Constant; Grace (Kett) b. 1618; Nathaniel b. c.1620; Mary (also Mercie, Cartwright); Joshua b. c.1626, Peter, b. c.1631; Giles, b. c.1632, Hoff, "Sylvester Family," 15–16.

56 *"infinite number"*: Brereton, *Travels in Holland*, 65, quoted in Sprunger, *Dutch Puritanism*, 43.

57 *the* fluyt: Richter Roegholt, *A Short History of Amsterdam* (Amsterdam: Bekking & Blitz Uitgevers b.v., 2004), 37.

57 *"ships' camels"*: Janse, *Building Amsterdam*, 30.

57 *Dutch environment:* Schama, *Embarrassment*, 10; also see Donna Merwick, "The Shame and the Sorrow: Interpreting Dutch-Amerindian Encounters in New Netherland," presentation at the Atlantic History Workshop, NYU, May 2004.

58 *11.5 million guilders:* Wim Klooster, *The Dutch in the Americas 1600–1800: A Narrative History with the Catalogue of an Exhibition of Rare Prints, Maps, and Illustrated Books from the John Carter Brown Library* (Providence, RI: John Carter Brown Library, 1997), 17–25;

58 *the WIC:* See Henk den Heijer, "The Dutch West India Company, 1621–1791," in Postma and Enthoven, *Riches from Atlantic Commerce*, 77–112.

59 *pinks:* "Pink" in Dutch means "little finger," or "pinkie," as in English slang. A pink's narrow stern and high bulwarks protected sheltered deck space, while bulging sides meant attackers found them hard to board; later pinks were built up to 400 tons, but early to the consistent design they were still called "pinks." The Museum of America and the Sea, Mystic, CT; OED.

59 *three-ton craft:* NS to JWJr, August 8, 1653, MHS *Proc.*, ser. 2, 4: 270; "ye Bay" could be either Boston or Narragansett Bay.

59 *buying tobacco:* NS had loaded tobacco aboard the *Seerobbe*, and had then gone ashore in April 1644. NAA 1289, fo. 101v–2v.

59 *Dutch traders:* During the English Civil War (1642–49), English colonists depended on Dutch suppliers. As part of the new British mercantilist policy to direct trade,

the British Navigation Acts of Trade (1651, 1660, 1663, 1673, 1696) restricted shipping to English colonies only in English vessels manned by Englishmen. John J. McCusker and Russell R. Menard, *The Economy of British America, 1607–1789* (Chapel Hill: University of North Carolina Press, 1985), 35–50; Thomas C. Barrow, *Trade and Empire: The British Customs Service in Colonial America* (Cambridge, MA: Harvard University Press, 1967), 4–35.

59 Oranjeboom: For the Dutch in Tidewater Virginia in the 1650s, see "The Calendar to Amsterdam and Rotterdam Notarial Acts Relating to the Virginia Tobacco Trade," comp. Dr. Jan Kupp, Special Collection, Library of the University of Victoria, B.C., Canada, http://library.uvic.ca/spcoll/book/Kupp_calendar.pdf.

60 *"glass of sack"*: David Pietersz. de Vries: *Voyages from Holland to America A.D. 1632 to 1644* (Alckmeer, The Netherlands, 1655), trans. Henry C. Murphy (New York: Billin & Bros., Printers, 1853), 50, https://play.google.com/store/books/details?id=2MJPAAAAcAAJ.

60 *February 1644:* NAA 1289, fo. 101v–2v.

60 *plantation wharves:* NS purchased 16,000 pounds of tobacco from William Edwards. Surry County, Virginia, Court Records 1652–63, 1:[125]–27.

60 *black faces:* For an estimate of three to five hundred enslaved blacks in Virginia in 1649, see John C. Coombs, "The Phases of Conversion: A New Chronology for the Rise of Slavery in Early Virginia," *WMQ*, 3rd ser., 68, no. 3 (July 2011): 332–60, 353.

60 *"sweet-scented tobacco"*: John Rolfe is credited with bringing seeds of a milder Caribbean variety to Jamestown in 1613.

60 *the tobacco market:* Russell R. Menard, "A Note on Chesapeake Tobacco Prices, 1618–1660," *Virginia Magazine of History and Biography* 84 (1976): 402–408; Menard, "The Tobacco Industry in the Chesapeake Colonies, 1617–1730: An Interpretation," *Research in Economic History* 5 (1980), 109–77.

60 *"He who wishes to trade here"*: David Pietersz de Vries: *Narratives of New Netherland 1609–1664* (Alckmeer, Netherlands, 1655), trans. Henry C. Murphy, ed. J. Franklin Jameson, (New York: Charles Scribner's Sons, 1909), 196.

60 *forty-three:* the ownership of the tobacco and the freight costs were disputed on arrival in Amsterdam, see NAA 1678/2051 and NAA 848/903.

60 *the colony's capital, "Jemston"*: See Karen Ordahl Kupperman, *The Jamestown Project* (Cambridge, MA: Belknap Press of Harvard University Press, 2007), and Martha McCartney, *Documentary History of Jamestown Island*, vol. 1, *Narrative History* (Williamsburg: National Park Service, 2000), http://www.nps.gov/history/history/online_books/jame/documentary_history.pdf; *Virginia Immigrants and Adventurers, 1607–35* (Baltimore: Genealogical, 2007); "An Early Virginia Census Reprised," *Quarterly Bulletin of the Archeological Society of Virginia* 54, no. 4 (December 1999): 178–96; and *Jamestown People to 1800: Landowners, Public Officials, Minorities, & Native Leaders* (Baltimore: Genealogical, 2012).

60 *"Commodytyes"*: This list of goods was typical of those shipped by Dutch merchants in the heyday of Atlantic trade. Internal evidence supports the writer's identification as Giles Sylvester II. "A Letter from Barbados by ye Way of Holland Concerning ye Condiccion of Honest Men There, August 9, 1651," Giles Sylvester, Barbados, to Giles Sylvester, Amsterdam, Tanner Mss. 54, ff.153–544, 44, in V. T. Harlow, ed., *Colonizing Expeditions to the West Indies and Guiana, 1623–67* (London: Hakluyt Society, 1924), 48–53.

61 *two London ships:* de Vries, *Voyages* (1853 edition), 185–86.

61 *"all the people"*: de Vries, *Voyages*, (1853 edition), 186.

61 *"is more Unhelthie"*: NS to JWJr, April 7, 1655, MHS *Proc.*, ser. 2, 4: 273–74; Karen Ordahl Kupperman, "Fear of Hot Climates in the Anglo-Colonial Experience," *WMQ*, 3rd ser., 41, no. 2 (April 1984): 213–40. Identification of NS's symptoms as malarial was made by Professor Harold Cook, Director of the Wellcome Trust Centre for the History of Medicine, University College London, 2003.

61 *noxious swamp vapors*: The name "malaria" comes from the Italian *mal aria*, literally "bad air." Malarial mosquitoes thrived in European marshes as well as the New World, so Nathaniel may have contracted the disease in the Netherlands rather than in America. M. J. Dobson, "History of Malaria in England," *Journal of the Royal Society of Medicine* 82, Supplement No. 17 (1989): 3–7.

61 *"his Sicknesse"*: NS to [JWJr?], after February 4, 1673, Winthrop Family Papers, MHS.

62 *Arent Gerritss*: NAA 1293/30, March 22, 1646.

62 *Reijer Evertsen*: NAA 1294/68, June 3, 1697.

63 *WIC duties*: NAA 1293/30, March 22, 1646.

63 *a duplicate report*: NAA 1923/30, March 22, 1646, has the marginal notation "June 4, 1649, duplicate to Mr. Bosschieter." Burgomaster Claes Pieterss Bosschieter, a WIC director from the North Holland chamber, requested this evidence, but the complaint was filed in the WIC's Amsterdam chamber.

4. The Other Island: Barbados

64 *bale seal*: "Sylvester Manor Artifact Descriptions," Andrew Fiske Memorial Center for Archaeological Research, University of Massachusetts Boston (AFMCAR), April 27, 2005, #22. Two bale seals with discernable marks were found, but no merchants with those seals were identified. Katherine Hayes, pers. comm., Apr. 12, 2012. See Diana DiPaolo Loren, *Archaeology of Clothing and Bodily Adornment in Colonial America* (Gainesville: University Press of Florida, 2010), 45–49.

64 *Sylvester insignia*: Constant Sylvester, Barbados, to JWJr, Connecticut, April 6, 1659, MHS *Proc.*, ser. 2, 4: 277.

64 *"Such Sugars"*: The sugar was accompanied by some "palm oile . . . brought us hither from Ginny" (Gold Coast, West Africa) and "barbados tarr," a thick bitumen from a Barbadian petroleum spring, prized for its medical properties and therefore an astutely chosen gift for JWJr, New England's premier physician. Constant Sylvester, Barbados, to JWJr, Connecticut, April 6, 1659, MHS *Proc.*, ser. 2, 4: 277; Richard Ligon, *A True and Exact History of the Island of Barbados, etc.* (London: 1657, 1673); ed. Karen Ordahl Kupperman (Indianapolis: Hackett, 2011), 174.

64 *Sylvesters of Burford*: Merchant marks of Edmund Sylvester (d. 1568), William (d. 1577), Thomas (d. 1586), and Thomas (d. 1650) resemble that of Constant Sylvester; Robert (d. 1601) and Thomas (d. 1624) used similar marks as coats of arms, illustrating their upward social mobility. Janet Kennish, "Burford Sylvesters Charts, One and Two," Griswold Papers, Fales Library, NYU; Lilian Horsford, London, to Eben Norton Horsford, May 30, 1884, SMA, NYU IV/I/2/112/5; see also Charles Hoppin, "Sylvester," n.p., n.d., who identifies the Sylvester insignia as similar to the "woolman's mark," indicating that the family belonged to a wool guild, Griswold Papers, Fales Library.

64 *Agnes Sylvester*: The sister (d. 1576) of Edmund Sylvester (d. 1571), she married Edmund Harman ca. 1539/40; her granddaughter Agnes married an Edmund Bray;

family ties persisted among the Sylvester/Harman descendants in St. Mary Aldermary Parish, London, into the 1630s. See Janet Kennish, *Burford Sylvesters* and associated research documents, Griswold Papers, Fales Library, NYU. Connections to the English poet and translator Joshuah Silvester (1563–1618) remain to be made with the Sylvesters of Amsterdam and England.

65 *family memorial:* Harman (c.1509–1577), as royal barber to Henry VIII, was well placed to have heard of English ventures in South America; his monument, whose figures have been identified as Tupinambas from coastal Brazil, may celebrate a successful investment in a 1540s English trade or slaving venture in the 1540s. Michael Balfour, "Edmund Harman: Barber and Gentleman," Tolsey Paper No. 6 (Burford, England: the Tolsey Museum, 1988); Stuart Piggott, "Brazilian Indians on an Elizabethan Monument," in *Ruins in a Landscape: Essays in Antiquarianism* (Edinburgh: Edinburgh University Press, 1976), 25–32; David Beers Quinn, "Depictions of America," in *The Maps and Text of the Boke of Idrography Presented by Jean Rotz to Henry VIII, Now in the British Library,* ed. Helen Wallis (Oxford: Roxburghe Club, 1981), 53–56; R. G. Marsden, "The Voyage of the 'Barbara' of London to Brazil in 1540," *English Historical Review* 24 (1909), 96–100; James A. Williamson, *Sir John Hawkins: The Time and the Man* (Oxford: Clarendon Press, 1927), 7–19; James A. Williamson, *Hawkins of Plymouth* (New York: Barnes & Noble, 1969), 26–33.

65 *naked men and women:* A plate by Flemish artist Cornelis Bos is the source of the monument's motif. See Sune Schéle, *Cornelis Bos: A Study of the Origins of the Netherland Grotesque* (Stockholm: Almqvist & Wiksell, 1965), pl. 50, no. 184; Peter Sherlock, *Monuments and Memory in Early Modern England* (Aldershot, England, and Burlington, Vermont: Ashgate, 2008), 197–202.

65 *"the Indies":* Refers to the European expectation that the Americas were either Asia (hence the "East Indies") or would produce a western sea route there.

66 *plot for a warehouse:* Barbados National Archive, Deeds, RB3/2, p. 68; Frederick H. Smith, "Disturbing the Peace in Barbados: Constant Silvester of Constant Plantation in the Seventeenth Century," *JBMHS* 44 (1998): 38–54; NAA 1294/68.

65 *smoothly transitioning:* Barbados Department of Archives documents indicate the percentage of sugar used in commercial transactions rose from 8 percent in 1644 to 100 percent in 1652, the years that Constant began to transform himself from commodities merchant to sugar planter. John J. McCusker and Russell R. Menard, "The Sugar Industry in the Seventeenth Century: A New Perspective on the Barbadian 'Sugar Revolution,'" in Schwartz, *Tropical Babylons*, 289–330, Table 9.1, 292.

66 *Constant Plantation:* Constant and adjacent Carmichael plantations in St. George's Valley; another in Christ Church Parish. Richard Ligon's map of Barbados, first published in 1657, does not depict them because Ligon probably based his map on an earlier one of 1638, which does not include all the properties of those who arrived in the 1640s. The Richard Ford 1674 map depicts 844 plantations with the names of their owners and shows their various mills. Both the Ford map and that of Philip Lea (1685) show two windmills and a mansion on each estate. The Christ Church estate mentioned in the census of 1679 does not appear on the maps. Smith, "Disturbing the Peace," 4; Peter F. Campbell, "Ligon's Map," *JBMHS* 34 (1973): 108–12; William Blaythwayt, comp., *The Blaythwayt Atlas*, John Carter Brown Library, Brown University, Providence, RI, ca. 1683; repr. *The Blaythwayt Atlas*, John Carter Brown Library, Providence, 1970.

66 *an eighteenth-century house:* The third on the site, it replaces one built after a c.1647 cane fire, which in turn also burned "about the year 1770." Nathaniel Lucas, "Lucas Manuscript in the Barbados Public Library," *JBMHS* 25, no. 3 (May 1958): 149; Ligon, *True and Exact History*, 95.

66 *were exiled:* Sylvester, *A Letter from Barbados*, 48–51; Smith, "Disturbing the Peace," 5–7.

66 *bloodless siege:* For an account of the events of 1650–52, see Carla Giardina Pestana, *The English Atlantic in an Age of Revolution, 1640–61* (Cambridge, MA: Harvard University Press, 2004), 92–111.

66 *From the first:* NS, "Last Will and Testament, March 19, 1680," *General Sylvester Dering Documents*, 1:6. SIHS; New York County Wills, 2:191, 250.

66 *The concept of human chattel:* Edgar McManus, *Black Bondage in the North* (Syracuse: Syracuse University Press, 2001), 57.

67 *Richard Ligon:* Ligon knew all the Barbados-based players in the Shelter Island story: he mentions Thomas Middleton, Thomas Rous, James Drax, and Humphrey Walrond.

67 *"The nearer we came":* Ligon, *True and Exact History*, 20, 21.

68 *"humble Bee":* Ligon, *True and Exact History*, 61.

68 *Amerindian population:* See Jerome S. Handler, "The Amerindian Slave Population of Barbados in the Seventeenth and Early Eighteenth Centuries," *Caribbean Studies* 8, no. 4 (1969): 38–64.

68 *thirty-four Africans:* David Watts, *The West Indies: Patterns of Development, Culture and Environmental Change Since 1492* (Cambridge: Cambridge University Press, 1984), 183.

68 *two hundred Africans:* Father Antoine Biet, "Father Antoine Biet's Visit to Barbados in 1654," Jerome S. Handler, trans. and ed., *JBMHS* 32 (1967): 50–76, 69; http://jeromehandler.org/wp-content/uploads/2009/07/Biet-67.pdf.

68 *models:* Ligon refers to Sir James Drax and Col. Humphrey Walrond as the most successful planters on Barbados.

68 *innovative techniques:* Ligon, *True and Exact History*, 69; Justin Roberts, "Working Between the Lines: Labor and Agriculture on Two Barbadian Sugar Plantations, 1796–97," *WMQ*, 3rd ser., 63, no. 3 (July 2006): 551–86.

68 *price of slaves:* See Herbert S. Klein, "The Atlantic Slave Trade to 1650," in Schwartz, *Tropical Babylons*, 201–36, 226; Larry Gragg, "'To Procure Negroes': The English Slave Trade to Barbados, 1627–60," *Slavery and Abolition* 16 (1995): 1, 74.

68 *first Africans:* Jerome S. Handler and Frederick W. Lange, *Plantation Slavery in Barbados: An Archaeological and Historical Investigation* (Cambridge, MA: Harvard University Press, 1978), 15.

69 *A 1645 census:* Watts, *West Indies*, 151.

69 *2,030 people:* Philip D. Curtin, *The Atlantic Slave Trade: A Census* (Madison: University of Wisconsin Press, 1969), 55–56, Table 13, Fig. 2.

69 *tenfold:* Watts, *West Indies*, 187. According to Ligon the increase in cost per acre between 1647 and 1650 for a plantation set up to make sugar rose from £1 4s to £28. John J. McCusker and Russell R. Menard have charted the increase and the average prices of Barbadian land in the formative years of sugar, 1638–50. Ligon, *True and Exact History*, 86; McCusker and Menard, "Sugar Industry," Fig. 9.1, Table 9.5, 298, 299.

69 *67-acre Barbadian working plantation:* John Pierson to Constant Sylvester, Barbados National Archive, Deeds RB3/2, 782–83; Smith, "Disturbing the Peace," 4.

69 *quarter of a teaspoonful:* The partners may have paid in actual Barbadian sugar, or as a bill of exchange, a promise to pay by a certain date. Like other staple crops, or like beaver or wampum, sugar became a form of "commodity money." The price of sugar per hundredweight rose by a fifth of its value in just one year (1652–53), then fell by more than half by 1673, shortly after Constant's death. Russell R. Menard, *Sweet Negotiations: Sugar, Slavery, and Plantation Agriculture in Early Barbados* (Charlottesville: University of Virginia Press), 2006, Table 15, 69.

69 *Dutch capital:* Absent any commercial records, occasional references supply the only information. Giles (1584–1651/2) was a member of the Amsterdam Exchange by 1627; his brother-in-law had been a member since 1625: without an exchange account a career in international trade was impossible. Constant Sylvester and a Charles Jacobson solicited financial aid directly from the Dutch in Amsterdam and acted as factors for handling incoming cargoes of colonial produce. Dijkman, *Giles Sylvester,* 5, 6; Carl Bridenbaugh and Roberta Bridenbaugh, *No Peace Beyond the Line: The English in the Caribbean 1624–90* (New York: Oxford University Press, 1972), 83; and Watts, *West Indies,* 148–49.

69 *"Little Barbados":* Eric Williams, *Capitalism and Slavery* (Chapel Hill: University of North Carolina Press, 1994), 54.

69 *trading network:* The scale of the four partners' endeavors was small compared to major Atlantic consortiums such as that of the Lascelles (East as well as West Indies, Africa). Frances, the wife of a Lascelles partner, Samuel Vassall, was the sister of lawyer Isaac Cartwright, Nathaniel's brother-in-law. The much smaller Sanford kinship network (Newport, Rhode Island) bought goods in London, paid London merchants in sugar shipped from Barbados, and shipped horses and provisions from New England credited against the sugar. S. D. Smith, *Slavery, Family, and Gentry Capitalism in the British Atlantic, 1648–1834* (Cambridge: Cambridge University Press, 2006), chaps. 1 and 2; St. Andrew's Undershaft Parish, London, births 1558–1634, 1634–82, microfilm #4107/1–3; same parish, W. H. Challen, transcriber, marriages, *Transcript of Parish Records,* 1935: v. 37; Hoff, "Sylvester Family," 15. For other English-based mercantile partnerships, see Brenner, *Merchants and Revolution,* 159–166, 181–95; *The Letter Book of Peleg Sanford of Newport Merchant (later Governour of Rhode Island) 1666–68,* ed. Howard R. Preston (Providence: Rhode Island Historical Society, 1928), esp. 11, 45, 57, 69;

70 *sugar, molasses:* Giles Sylvester II (1632–71/2) notes 50,000 pounds of sugar and 25,000 pounds of ginger aboard a family ship outbound from Barbados in 1651; the shipment was canceled due to English Civil War events, but indicates the scale of family operations. Constant sent gifts of sugar and rum to New England in 1659; a later letter from Giles is datelined Madeira; Nathaniel Sylvester, acting as factor for Thomas Middleton, with his brother, Peter Sylvester, loaded peas and pipe staves aboard the *Two Sisters* in New England for Barbados, then loaded sugar, but the ship was discharged at Fayall after storms pierced her hull and she was broken up in December 1657. Giles Sylvester, "A Letter from Barbados," 50; Bernard Bailyn, *The New England Merchants in the Seventeenth Century* (Cambridge, MA: Harvard University Press, 1979), 83–84; NAA 1294/68; Constant Sylvester, Barbados, to Governor JWJr, Connecticut, April 6, 1659, MHS *Proc.,* ser. 2, 4 (1887–89): 277; Giles Sylvester to JWJr, May 30, 1666, MHS *Proc.,* ser. 2, 4 (1887–89): 281; Peter Wilson Coldham, *English Adventurers and Emigrants, 1609–60* (Baltimore: Genealogical, 1984), 165.

70 *Salt:* Nathaniel dealt in salt from Nevis and stored it in a salt house on Shelter Island. As early as 1643, at least nine New England merchants had entered the wine trade, exchanging pipe staves, fish, and whale oil for wine and fruit; by 1644, if not earlier, the Sylvesters carried wines and spirits purchased in La Rochelle, France, to the West Indies; Will of NS; Bailyn, *New England Merchants*, 82–86, NAA 1294/68 (June 3, 1647).

70 *access:* As the family network grew into a permanent contractual partnership, the Sylvesters became as well placed in London as in Amsterdam: Giles (1632–71/2) based himself there after the death of his brother Peter in 1657, and in 1662 he and two other London merchants loaned £500 to Governor JWJr. of Connecticut, also then in London seeking the Connecticut patent. Both Thomas Middleton (a member of the Council for Foreign Plantations) and Constant belonged to the London sugar lobby established by James Drax, the "Gentlemen Planters in London"; Governor William Coddington and merchant and magistrate Frances Brinley of Newport, important both politically and commercially in Rhode Island, were Nathaniel's brothers-in-law; by 1671 Nathaniel was listed as a merchant of "Shelter Island & Newport" in Rhode Island documents. Giles Sylvester, Barbados, to JWJr, May 29, 1658, MHS *Proc.*, ser. 2, 4 (1887–89): 275–77; Black, *The Younger John Winthrop*, 230; Journal of the Council for Foreign Plantations CO 1/15, 142–70; Vincent T. Harlow, *A History of Barbados, 1625–85* (London and Oxford: Clarendon Press, 1926), 202–3, 203 n2; Watts, *West Indies*, 190–91; Carl Bridenbaugh, *Fat Mutton and Liberty of Conscience* (Providence: Brown University Press, 1974), Appendix III, "Rhode Island Merchants 1636–1690," 138.

70 *Oil:* Daniel P. Mannix and Malcolm Cowley, *Black Cargoes: A History of the Atlantic Slave Trade, 1518–1865* (New York: Viking Press, 1962), 128–30.

72 *251 Africans:* McCusker and Menard, "Sugar Industry," 303–5, Table 9.6, "Sale of Slaves from the ship Marie Bonaventure of London, Capt. George Richardson, Master, and Richard Parr, Merchant, at Barbados, 27 July–17 August 1644."

72 *Samuel Farmer:* Will of Constant Sylvester, entered Barbados, Jan. 24, 1671, Barbados National Archives, RB6/8/316.

72 *"90 slaves":* Gragg, "To Procure Negroes," 73, and Barbados National Archive, Deeds, R/B3/2, 219–22.

72 *"the strongest, youthfullest":* Ligon, *True and Exact History*, 97.

72 *"very few":* Ligon, *True and Exact History*, 103.

72 *Twenty-five:* Kenneth F. Kiple, *The Caribbean Slave: A Biological History* (Cambridge: Cambridge University Press, 1984), 64.

72 *"fixed melancholy":* Dehydration from diarrhea may have been a principal cause. Kiple, *Caribbean Slave*, 63. For a nonphysiological understanding of "melancholy" (depression), see Jeremy Schmidt's *Melancholy and the Care of the Soul: Religion, Moral Philosophy and Madness in Early Modern England* (Aldershot, England: Ashgate, 2007), 2.

72 *"When slaves come":* "A Swiss Medical Doctor's Description of Barbados in 1661: The Account of Felix Christian Spoeri," trans. and ed. Alexander Gunkel and Jerome S. Handler, *JBMHS* 33 (1969): 7, http://jeromehandler.org/wp-content/uploads/Spoeri-69.pdf.

73 *Laws enacted:* See Jerome S. Handler, "Slave Revolts and Conspiracies in Seventeenth-Century Barbados," *New West Indian Guide* 56, nos. 1–2 (Leiden, 1982): 5–42, 17,

http://jeromehandler.org/1982/01/slave-revolts-and-conspiracies-in-seventeenth-century-barbados.

72 *drums:* Such "loud instruments . . . to give sign or notice to one another of their wicked designs and purposes" were specifically forbidden in the legislation of 1676. Handler, "Slave Revolts," 17, quoting from "A Supplemental Act . . . for the Better Ordering and Governing of Negroes," Apr. 21, 1676, TNA: PRO, CO 30/2 [ff 114–25].

72 *music:* "In May 1683, Barbados's governor urged the mounted militia to diligently patrol on Saturday evenings and on Sundays 'to prevent the disorderly meeting of Negroes.'" Handler, "Slave Revolts," 20.

73 *public existence:* Hilary McD. Beckles, *Natural Rebels: A Social History of Enslaved Black Women in Barbados* (New Brunswick, NJ: Rutgers University Press, 1989), 72–89.

73 *victory or death:* Handler, "Slave Revolts," 12.

73 *as long as slavery lasted:* Handler, "Slave Revolts," 11, 35.

73 *"their bodies black":* Ligon, *A True and Exact History*, 169.

73 *black plots:* One of the largest plots discovered took place in 1676. At least 107 people were implicated of whom forty-two were executed. Handler, "Slave Revolts," 14–15.

73 *One old black man:* Handler, "Slave Revolts," 20, from "Extract of a Letter from Barbados, December 18, [1683]," TNA: PRO, CO 1/53, [ff 264–66].

73 *The biggest scare:* Handler, "Slave Revolts," 24–29.

73 *"many [of whom] were hang'd":* Handler, "Slave Revolts," 24, from Anon, "A Brief, but Most True Relation of the Late Barbarous and Bloody Plot of the Negro's in the Island of Barbados on Friday the 21 of October, 1692" (London, 1693).

73 *Alice Mills:* Handler, "Slave Revolts," 24, from Minutes of the Barbados Council, Jan. 24, 1693, *Calendar of State Papers, Colonial Series 1693–96*: 5.

73 *In New York Colony:* Moss, "Slavery on Long Island," especially "Slave Laws, Slave Reactions: Island Slaves Under the Law," ch. 4, 154–55.

73 *Constant's widow:* The daughter of Grace Seaman and the planter Humphrey Walrond, who had banished Constant from Barbados in 1651, Grace Walrond probably married Constant around 1660 or 1661, when her father was president of the King's Council in Barbados. Grace Sylvester (d. 1702) was the mother of Constant, Humphrey, Grace, and Mary. Both sons died young. Both daughters married Barbadian planters, Sir Henry Pickering and Richard Worsham. Constant had previously married (possibly in 1655) the unnamed daughter of an English merchant of Delft, Abraham Kick, who sheltered the regicides John Okey, Miles Corbett, and John Barkstead. It can only remain a conjecture that for Constant, a Dutch-born planter accused of being an Anabaptist and suspect for his Commonwealth associations, close links with Kick were dangerous enough by 1660 for him to ally himself with the Walrond family in 1660. Like many others at the Restoration, Constant adroitly managed the transition to loyal subject, retaining his land and his position as a representative to the Barbadian Assembly for the parish of St. George. Michael A. LaCombe, "Walrond, Humphrey (b. 1602, d. in or after 1668)," (*ODNB*, 2004), http://www.oxforddnb.com/view/article/28605. P. F. Campbell, "Two Generations of Walronds: Power Corrupts," *JBMHS* 39 (1991): 1–23; Smith, "Disturbing the Peace," 9; Delft Archive, inv. nr. 101, f. 1v; Ralph C.H. Catterall, "Sir George Downing and the Regicides," *American Historical Review* 17 (1912): 268–89; Johnathan Scott, "Downing, Sir George, first baronet (1623–84)" (*ODNB*, 2004), http://www.oxforddnb.com

/view/article/7981?docPos=1; Robert Needham, "To the King's most excellent Majestie. The humble Petition of Robert Needham Esquire," TNA: PRO, CO 1/33, No. 84 [?1660], Item 357, Vol. 9 (Addendum 1574–1667, p. 139); Calendar of Marriage Licence Allegations, 1660–1700, Books 25, 30, London, Dec. 12, 1685; Minutes of the Barbados Assembly of Representatives, TNA: PRO, CO 1/20 Part I [ff. 4–100].

73 *18,000 whites:* McCusker and Menard, *The Economy of British America*, 153, Table 7, 153.

73 *"Fortifications":* Ligon, *True and Exact History*, 75.

73 *"Lime Tree":* Ligon, *True and Exact History*, 125.

73 *"Water they save":* Ligon, *True and Exact History*, 75.

74 *"whole lands of Canes and Houses":* Ligon, *True and Exact History*, 95.

74 *still greater wealth:* "Madam Grace Silvester" is listed in the 1679–80 Barbadian census as owning a total of 695 acres, 260 African slaves, and eleven white servants, more land, servants, and slaves than any other planter listed except Col. Henry Drax. Colonial Office Group, Class I, Piece 44, 149–379, I/44, cited by Richard S. Dunn, "The Barbados Census of 1680: Profile of the Richest Colony in English America," *WMQ*, 3rd ser., 26 (1969): 3–30; COG 1/44 for Silvester listings, and see transcriptions in John Camden Hotten, *The Original Lists of Persons of Quality; Emigrants; Religious Exiles; Political Rebels; Serving Men Sold for a Term of Years; Apprentices; Children Stolen; Maidens Pressed; and Others Who Went from Great Britain to the American Plantations 1600–1700* (London: Public Record Office, 1874), 461, 485, https://play.google.com/store/books/details?id=VN_A5wlsjQQC&rdid=book-VN_A5wlsjQQC&rdot=1.

74 *well developed by the 1650s:* See Schwartz, *Tropical Babylons*, esp. McCusker and Menard, "Sugar Industry."

74 *"Ingenio":* Ligon, *True and Exact History*, 67, 148–55; Menard, *Sweet Negotiations*, for a seventeenth-century description of an operating sugar mill by planter Thomas Tryon, 15.

75 *Two hundred acres:* Watts, *West Indies*, 188–89; McCusker and Menard, "Sugar Industry," 300.

75 *37 percent:* Watts, *West Indies*, 188.

75 *axes:* Menard, *Sweet Negotiations*, 15.

75 *harness traces:* Bridenbaugh, *No Peace*, 93.

75 *draft animals:* For New England's production of heavy horses for West Indian sugar mills, starting with William Coddington of Rhode Island in the 1640s, see Bridenbaugh, *Fat Mutton*, 42–43, 57–59, 122–24; Lion Gardiner to JWJr, Apr. 14, 1949, SMA, NYU I/A/140/1 and printed in John Lion Gardiner, *The Gardiners of Gardiner's Island* (East Hampton, NY: Star Press, 1927), 17–18; Daniel A. Romani Jr., "The Pettaquamscut Purchase of 1657/58 and the Establishment of a Commercial Livestock Industry in Rhode Island," in *New England's Creatures: 1400–1900*, Annual Proceedings of the Dublin Seminar for New England Folklife (1993), ed. Peter Benes (Boston: Boston University, 1995), 45–60; Sylvester, "A Letter from Barbados," 52; Spoeri, "A Swiss Medical Doctor's Description," 3; Peleg Sanford, Newport, to William Sanford, Barbados, Dec. 28, 1668, in Peleg Sanford, *Letter Book*, 68–70.

75 *forty horses:* NS probate inventory, GSDD 1:1.

75 *slave huts:* Because slaves were responsible for their own housing, they were able to replicate some aspects of African architectural techniques and styles, as well as traditional floor plans. Wattle-and-daub structures with low doorways, low-hanging thatched eaves, and multiple tiny rooms resembled what European visitors to the

Gold Coast described. Jerome S. Handler and Stephanie Bergman, "Vernacular Houses and Domestic Material Culture on Barbadian Sugar Plantations, 1640–1838," *Journal of Caribbean History* 43 (2009): 1–36, 4, 19–23, http://jeromehandler.org/wp-content/uploads/House-09.pdf; Pieter de Marees, *Description and Historical Account of the Gold Kingdom of Guinea (1602)*, trans. and ed. Albert van Dantzig and Adam Jones (Oxford: Oxford University Press, 1987), 75–76; "Michael Hemmersam's Description of the Gold Coast, 1639–45," in *German Sources for West African History 1599–1669*, ed. Adam Jones (Wiesbaden, Germany: Franz Steiner Verlag GMBH, 1983), 97–259, 201–2.

75 *five acres:* Jerome S. Handler, "Plantation Slave Settlements in Barbados, 1650s to 1834," in *In the Shadow of the Plantation: Caribbean History and Legacy*, ed. A. Thompson (Kingston, Jamaica: Ian Randle Publisher, 2002), 121–58, 128, http://jeromehandler.org/2002/07/plantation-slave-settlements-in-barbados-1650s-to-1834.

75 *commonwealth:* "As in African communities, Barbadian slaves may have viewed their settlements 'as groups of people rather than as groups of buildings,' and in arranging their houses in the 'Negro yards' slaves placed emphasis on their social relationships." Jerome S. Handler, "Plantation Slave Settlements," 130, quoting from B. W. Higman, *Jamaica Surveyed: Plantation Maps and Plans of the Eighteenth and Nineteenth Centuries* (Kingston: Institute of Jamaica Publications, 1988), 244.

75 *two stones:* The 1640s Southold water mill was in ruins in 1651; it is not clear how quickly it was rebuilt before 1659, when John Payne owned a new mill there. NS had contracted for the mill privileges by 1667 to produce grain for himself, for commerce, and for Southold town. Malcolm Freiberg, ed., *Winthrop Papers* (*WP*), 6 (1650–54) (MHS, 1992), 131, 190.

75 *food for slaves:* Handler and Lange, *Plantation Slavery in Barbados*, 297 n2; Handler, "Plantation Slave Settlements," 133–34.

76 *"Negro garden":* May 7, 1856, "Planted Six rows of corn in the Negro garden," "Samuel Smith Gardiner Account and Day Book, 1844–58," n.p. but chronologically arranged, SMA, NYU III/A/3/45/2.

76 *a third area:* That little cultivated land on Barbados was devoted to food crops, hence the need for outside suppliers, appears to be based largely on a few striking quotes, such as "men are so intent upon planting sugar that they had rather buy foode a very deare rates than produce it by labour, soe infinite is the profitt of sugar workes after once accomplished." Demand did exceed local supply, but the "very deare rates" they could charge for all kinds of goods (including food) are what spurred New England provisioning merchants to enter the trade in the late 1640s, and the Sylvesters in the 1650s. However, Ligon states that in 1647, "In this Plantation [Col. Thomas Modyford's, which Ligon managed] of 500 acres of land, there was imployed for sugar somewhat more than 200 acres; above 80 acres for pasture, 120 for wood, 30 for Tobacco, 5 for Ginger, as many for Cotton wool and 70 *acres for provisions* [my italics]; viz. Corn, Potatoes, Plantines, Cassavie, and Bonavist [beans]." Ligon, *True and Exact History*, 67; Richard Vines to JWJr, July 19, 1647, Allyn B. Forbes, ed., *WP* 5 (1645–49) (MHS, 1947), 171–72, http://archive.org/stream/winthroppapers05wint#page/n3/mode/2up; Giles Sylvester, "A Letter from Barbados."

76 *portraits:* Karen Ordahl Kupperman, "Introduction," in Ligon, *True and Exact History*, 23.

76 *"Very good servants":* Ligon, *True and Exact History*, 93–94.

76 *gravely malnourished:* Jerome S. Handler and Robert S. Corruccini, "Plantation Slave Life in Barbados: A Physical Anthropological Analysis," *Journal of Interdisciplinary History* 14, no. 1 (Summer 1983): 65–90, 79–81, http://jeromehandler.org/wp-content/uploads/2009/07/PlantSlaveLife-83.pdf.

76 *two hundred and sixty:* Hotten, *Original Lists*, 461, 485.

76 *salt fish:* Badly cured fish were frequently "a mass of foetid matter" when the barrel was opened; if it had been stored too long in the tropical heat, the contents were likely to contain "as little nutrition as the brine in which they lie." Kenneth F. Kiple, *The Caribbean Slave: A Biological History* (Cambridge: Cambridge University Press, 1984), 80, quoting from James Stephen, *The Slavery of the British West India Colonies Delineated,* etc. (London: J. Butterworth & Son, 1824–30), 2:282.

77 *"If any cattle dyed":* Ligon, *True and Exact History*, 86.

77 *imported and homegrown supplies:* For population statistics that reveal the shocking results of long-term malnutrition see Kiple, *Caribbean Slave*, 105–6, citing figures from Curtin's *The Atlantic Slave Trade*, 71 and Table 18, 92; and H. S. Klein and S. I. Engerman, "The Demographic Study of the American Slave Population; with Particular Attention Given the Comparison Between the United States and the West Indies," unpublished paper presented at the International Colloquium in Historical Demography, 1975.

77 *"if att any time":* Peter Thompson, "Henry Drax's Instructions on the Management of a Seventeenth-Century Barbadian Sugar Plantation," *WMQ*, 3rd ser., 66, no. 3 (July 2009): 588. Constant had died when Henry Drax drew up his instructions, but Constant's longstanding trust in Drax is evidenced in Constant's will, signed in England on April 7, 1671. Drax and two others were charged with overseeing delivery to Constant's sons, Constant (Constantine) and Humphrey, of funds during their minority (both sons under fourteen at their father's death), and their inheritance at their majority.

77 *"very badly fed":* "Father Antoine Biet's Visit to Barbados in 1654," trans. and ed. Jerome S. Handler, *JBMHS* 32 (1967): 50–76, 67, http://jeromehandler.org/wp-content/uploads/2009/07/Biet-67.pdf.

77 *any punishment:* In New York Colony, what were called "the Duke of York Laws" of 1665 were the first to include slave laws under British rule in New York Colony; what became known as the "black code" was codified in 1702 as "An Act for Regulateing of Slaves." See *The Colonial Laws of New York* (Albany, NY: James B. Lyon, 1894), 18. "The New York Colony legislature explicitly provided that except for taking a slave's life or dismembering him, it was 'lawful for any Master or Mistress of slaves to punish their slaves for their Crimes and offenses at [the master's] Discretion.'" Quoted by Aloysius Leon Higginbotham, Jr., *In the Matter of Color, Race & the American Legal Process: The Colonial Period* (Oxford: Oxford University Press, 1978), 119.

77 *"the sweet air of England":* Ligon, *True and Exact History*, 67.

77 *English country sports and rambles:* Ligon, *True and Exact History*, 178–79.

78 *living hell:* Richard Dunn portrays 1680 Barbados as an almost uninhabitable tropical paradise where the mark of a successful planter "was his ability to escape from the island and retire grandly to England," the pattern Constant and Thomas Middleton followed. Larry Gragg counters that view, pointing out those who stayed on Barbados and established many aspects of a traditional English society. Dunn, "Barbados Census," 30; Larry Gragg, *Englishmen Transplanted: The English Colonization of Barbados 1627–1660* (Oxford: Oxford University Press, 2003).

78 *landed gentlemen:* Constant's landholdings have not been located in Brampton, Huntingdonshire; no reference to the place exists in his will. However, his younger son Humphrey died there as a minor two years after his father (Apr. 16, 1673), so it appears that the family maintained a residence there. Constant's eldest son, also Constant, born in London in 1662/63, attended the prestigious St. Paul's School for Boys, then St. John's College, Cambridge, in 1681, and trained as a barrister at Middle Temple (1682), one of the four exclusive English Inns of Court. Not listed as an heir to his father's Barbados estates in 1694, Constant II was certainly dead by 1702, when his sister Grace Pickering administered their mother's estate. Dame Grace (d. 1732) and Sir Henry Pickering (d. 1705) lived in Whaddon, Cambridgeshire, forty miles south of Brampton, at Whaddon Manor, a house with nineteen chimneys—fitting habitation for a woman with a gold repeating Tompion watch who described herself on her husband's tombstone as the "heiress of Constant Sylvester of the Island of Barbadoes." Mary, sister of Grace Pickering and Constant Jr., married Henry Pickering's nephew, Richard Worsham, produced two daughters, and died in England in 1733. Grace Pickering relinquished her rights as Constant's heir to Shelter Island to Henry Lloyd, Nathaniel Sylvester's grandson. Brampton Parish Records; Robert Barlow Gardiner, *Admission Registers of St. Paul's School from 1748 to 1876. Edited with Biographical Notices and Notes on the Earlier Masters and Scholars of the School from the Time of Its Foundation* (London: George Bell and Sons, 1884), 57, https://play.google.com/store/books/details?id=AQoCAAAAYAAJ&rdid=book-AQoCAAAAYAAJ&rdot=1; Will of Grace Pickering 1732/1739, TNA: Prob. 11/699; Nesta Evans and Susan Rose, *Cambridgeshire Hearth Tax Returns Michaelmas 1664* (London: British Record Society, 2000), 79; Smith, "Disturbing the Peace," 52; "A Schedule of Papers," SMA, NYUI/A/140/30; and New York Supreme Court of Judicature Minute Book: March 13, 1732/33–October 23, 1739, Patrick Lithgow *ex dem* (*ex demessione*, "on the demise"] Wm Nicoll et al. against Brinley Sylvester, 176, 180, 182, 189, Aug. 2, 1735–Oct. 25, 1735.

78 *Constant would die:* Business and politics may have led Constant to choose Brampton as his English country residence, where he died on Sept. 3, 1671, and was buried at St. Mary the Virgin on Sept. 4 (will proved London, Oct. 7, 1671; Barbados, Jan. 18, 1672). Thomas Middleton (d. 1672), Constant's partner and colleague, in 1664 became Naval Commissioner for Portsmouth under Samuel Pepys, the diarist and Chief Admiralty Secretary for Charles II and James I. The two men spent time together; Pepys knew Brampton from boyhood and kept a house there; Constant may have gravitated to Brampton through these connections. Constant's sister, Quaker Mercie Cartwright, lived in Aspley Guise, Bedfordshire, only thirty-five miles west of Brampton. Huntingtonshire was "Cromwell country," home to many with former Presbyterian leanings like Constant's. Brampton Parish Registers; Henry F. Waters, *Genealogical Gleanings in England*, 2 (Boston: New England Historical & Genealogical Society, 1901, repr. 1969), 1:17; William Page, Granville Proby, and S. Inskip Ladds, eds., *History of the County of Huntingdon, The Victoria History of the Counties of England* (London: St. Catherine Press, 1936), 3:12–20; Smith, "Disturbing the Peace," 45; Hoff, "Sylvester Family," 15; C. S. Knighton, "Middleton, Thomas (d. 1672)," (*ODNB*, 2004), http://www.oxforddnb.com/view/article/66463; *The Diary of Samuel Pepys: A New and Complete Transcription*, ed. Robert Latham and William Matthews (London: G. Bell & Sons, 1976), vols. 5, 7, 8, 9 for Middleton references; Claire Tomalin, *Samuel Pepys: The Unequalled Self* (New York: Vintage Books, 2003), 21–26.

78 *enduring legacies:* Constant Plantation descended in the family through Constant's daughter, Mary Sylvester Worsham, during most of the nineteenth century. In 1900 the property, then 491 acres, was purchased by S. S. Robinson and is now owned by Ian and Jean Robinson. It is still operated as a sugar plantation. Smith, "Disturbing the Peace," 9.

5. Nathaniel's Middle Passage

79 *the* Seerobbe: Evidence that Nathaniel, not Constant, was aboard the *Seerobbe* on this trip is circumstantial. In September 1644, NS was named as one of the owners of the *Seerobbe* (NAA 848/903); in July 1646 the *Seerobbe* arrived in Barbados from La Rochelle; an inserted clarification in the testimony of the Dutch steersman, Reijer Evertsen, states that NS was aboard in July 1646 (NAA 1294/68). "From there this ship went with English orders and crew, and also some French men, to the coast of Guinea. The said captain [Sijmon Dircxsz] came with it himself. There he, the witness, disembarked, the other Dutch crewmembers having already left before, at La Rochelle."

79 *"the coast of Guinea"*: The Amsterdam notary Hendrick Schaeff wrote "na de cust van Guinea werde gesonden" in 1647. Did he mean Guyana, a regular port of call for Atlantic traders and merchants? Schaeff had also taken a 1646 deposition regarding the same voyage, where he wrote "na de Wilde Cust." "The Wild Coast" was the other name for Guyana, so it seems probable that Schaeff knew the difference between Africa and South America, Guinea and Guyana. On the basis of the Seerobbe's stop in L'Orient, Brittany, a port specializing in textiles for the African trade, Herbert L. Klein confirms that in his view the trip was to Africa. NAA 1294/68, NAA 1293/30; Herbert L. Klein, Dec. 13, 2006, Apr. 10, 2012, pers. comms.

79 *Most slavers:* The direct slave trade out of New England and the West Indies began in the 1640s: in 1644, a Boston vessel discharged a load of wine barrel staves in the Canary Islands, then returned to Boston with wine, sugar, salt, and "some tobaco which she had at Barbados, in exchange for Africoes, which she carried" from the Cape Verde Islands. In 1645 three Bostonians invested in the *Rainbow* to the Madeiras, then to Guinea for slaves to sell in Barbados. *The Journal of John Winthrop 1630–49*, eds. Richard S. Dunn, James Savage, and Laetitia Yeandle (Cambridge, MA: Belknap Press of Harvard University Press, 1996), 573; Gragg, *Englishmen Transplanted*, 124.

80 *North Equatorial Countercurrent:* http://oceancurrents.rsmas.miami.edu/atlantic/north-equatorial-cc.html.

80 *eastbound Guinea Current:* "Upwelling off the coasts of Ghana and Cote d'Ivoire occurs seasonally, with . . . intense upwelling from July to September." Chika N. Ukwe, Chidi A. Ibe, Peter C. Nwilo, and Pablo A. Huidobro, "Contributing to the WSSD Targets on Oceans and Coasts in West and Central Africa: The Guinea Current Large Marine Ecosystem Project," *International Journal of Oceans and Oceanography* 1, no. 1 (2006): 21–44, www.vliz.be/imisdocs/publications/100130.pdf. Also see Albert van Dantzig, *Forts and Castles of Ghana* (Accra: Sedco Publishing, 1980; reprinted 1999), 17.

80 *nineteen English ships:* Gragg, *Englishmen Transplanted*, 121.

80 *effective control:* In the 1640s, Barbadian planters welcomed shipments of slaves from all sources, Dutch or British; African rulers equally welcomed all European

slavers, despite efforts by European countries or their monopoly companies to restrict trade. For English slaving companies between 1618 and 1688, see Gragg, *Englishmen Transplanted*, 120–23; A. W. Lawrence, *Trade Castles and Forts of West Africa* (Palo Alto: Stanford University Press, 1964), 26–27; Brenner, *Merchants and Revolution*, 163–65; http://www.bristolandslavery.4t.com/royal.htm.

81 *"count the seas"*: John Atkins, "A Voyage to Guinea, Brazil, and the West Indies, etc." in *A New General Collection of Voyages and Travels*, ed. Thomas Astley (London, 1743–47, 1745), 3:450.

81 *goods:* Most slaving ventures took on a precise, expensive mix of goods in Europe. East Indian printed cottons, embroidered velvets, European and North African "white goods," and other textiles made up half of the imports. The Sylvesters' last European stop before Barbados was "Larrante," or L'Orient, in Brittany, an important depot for the printed cottons Africans favored. Constant's warehouse, "Fiftye fotte in Length & nineteen foote broad," offered ample room for trade goods, including Barbadian rum and tobacco. Klein, *The Atlantic Slave Trade*, 86–89; Patrick Manning, *Slavery and African Life: Occidental, Oriental, and African Slave Trades* (Cambridge: Cambridge University Press, 1990), 100; Deeds of Barbados, Barbados National Archives, contract signed by John Crispe and Constant Silvester, Nov. 14, 1645, recorded Jan. 1647.

81 *Orchards and kitchen plots:* See Thomas Astley's illustrations, "Views of Dixcove and English and Dutch Forts at Sakkundi," where the solid fort walls look down on cultivated slopes laid out in neat plots. Astley, *A New General Collection*, 2: plate 59; Lawrence, *Trade Castles and Forts*, 37–39; Alfred W. Crosby Jr., *The Columbian Exchange: Biological and Cultural Consequences of 1492* (Westport, CT: Greenwood Press, 1973), ch. 5, 170, for a list of New World foods.

81 *"Dinner being over"*: Thomas Phillips, "A Journal of a Voyage Made in the Hannibal of London, Ann. 1693, 1694, from England, to Cape Monseradoe in Africa and Thence Along the Coast of Guiney to Whidaw, the Island of St. Thomas, and So Forward to Barbadoes," in *A Collection of Voyages and Travels, Some Now First Printed from Original Manuscripts, Others Now First Published in English*, ed. John Churchill and Awnsham Churchill (London, 1732) 6:169–239, 201, https://play.google.com/store/books/details?id=0FVEAAAAcAAJ&rdid=book-0FVEAAAAcAAJ&rdot=1.

82 *Ham was cursed:* Genesis 9:25–27, Genesis 10:1–32. See also Benjamin Braude, "The Sons of Noah and the Construction of Ethnic and Geographical Identities in the Medieval and Early Modern Periods," *WMQ* 54 (January 1997): 103–42.

82 *"dark" or "black"*: David M. Goldenberg, "The Curse of Ham: A Case of Rabbinic Racism?" in *Struggles in the Promised Land: Towards a History of Black-Jewish Relations*, eds. Jack Salzman and Cornel West (Oxford: Oxford University Press, 1997), 21–52, 24–25.

82 *bulkheads:* Charles Garland and Herbert S. Klein, "The Allotment of Space for Slaves Aboard Eighteenth-Century British Slave Ships," *WMQ*, 3rd ser., 42, no. 2 (Apr. 1985): 238–48. The allotment of spaces on seventeenth-century ships did not radically differ from those described by Garland and Klein. Herbert Klein, pers. comm., 2008.

83 *The* Seerobbe: A ship *Seerobbe*, used or hired by the chamber of the Noorderkwartier, the northern chamber of the WIC, measured 150/140 *last* (about 280/300 tons) and carried 16/20 cannon, 21/22 sailors, and 13/18 soldiers. The port of origin

for the trips made by the Sylvesters that were investigated by the WIC is the same port of Hoorn, which constitutes some slight evidence for identifying this *Seerobbe* as the same vessel later owned by the Sylvesters. In 1635 and 1636 the chamber of the Noorderkwartier had freighted the *Seerobbe* for trips to Dutch Brazil. Johannes de Laet, *Iaerlyck Verhael van de Verrichtinghen der Geoctroyeerde West-Indische Compagnie in Verthien Boeken* (Annual Report of the Activities of the Chartered West-Indian Company in Thirteen Books), eds. S. P. l'Honoré Naber and J.C.M. Warnsinck (The Hague: Martinus Nijhoff, 1937), part 4; References to the *Seerobbe* in *Brazilië in de Nederlandse archieven—O Brasil em arquivos Neerlandeses (1652–54): de West-Indische Compagnie: Overgekomen brieven en papieren uit Brazilië en Curaçao* (Brazil in the Dutch archives, 1652–54: the West-Indian Company: transferred letters and documents from Brazil and Curaçao), Mauritinia no. 2N, ed. Marianne L. Wiesebron (Leiden: Research School CWNS, 2005), indices August 2, 1635; June 12, 1636; March 26, 1637; March 19, 1639; April 10–May 1639; February and June 1642.

83 *interior*: Garland and Klein. "Allotment of Space," 238–48; Philip Morgan, re numbers of crew and captives, pers. comm., 2007.

83 *eighteen inches*: Garland and Klein. "Allotment of Space," Table III, 244.

84 *Central and South America*: See Richter, *Before the Revolution*, 67–87.

84 encomienda: John Thornton, *Africa and Africans in the Making of the Atlantic World, 1400–1680* (Cambridge: Cambridge University Press, 1992), 130–41; Richter, *Before the Revolution*, 79–82.

84 *Indian slavery*: Legislation in New York Colony officially outlawed Indian slavery on Dec. 5, 1679, but the legal understanding of who could be enslaved continued to expand nonetheless: By 1708 the owners of any "Indian or Negro slave or slaves" punished by death for their crimes were to be reimbursed to a maximum of £25, minus the cost of prosecution not to exceed £5. Examples of wills and inventories of Long Island's East End demonstrate the continued treatment of Indians as property. *Documents Relative to the Colonial History of the State of New York*, 13: 537; Higginbotham, *In the Matter of Color*, 122; *The Colonial Laws of New York from the Year 1664 to the Revolution*, Charles Zabine Lincoln, William Henry Johnson, Ansel Judd Northrup, New York (State) Commissioners of Statutory Revision (Albany, NY: James B. Lyon Co., 1894), 631, https://play.google.com/books/reader?id=d3U4AAAAIAAJ&printsec=frontcover&output=reader&authuser=0&hl=en_US&pg=GBS.PR3; Patricia and Edward Shillingburg, "The Disposition of Slaves on the East End of Long Island from 1680 to 1796," 2003, http://www.shelter-island.org/disposition_slave.html.

84 *Indian power*: Confirmation of a deed of sale, March 23, 1653, recorded January 28, 1661, *STR* 158–59; Mathias Nicolls to JWJr, March 7, 1675, Winthrop Family Papers, MHS.

84 *"Indian" and "negro"*: Berthold Fernow, comp., and A.J.F. van Laer, ed., "Calendar of Council Minutes 1668–1783," New York State Library Bulletin 58, History 6 (Albany: University of the State of New York, March 1902), 111–12, https://play.google.com/store/books/details?id=jFAOAAAAIAAJ&rdid=book-jFAOAAAAIAAJ&rdot=1.

84 *Within Africa*: Thornton, *Africa and Africans*, 72–97; Manning, *Slavery and African Life*, 88–102; Klein, *Atlantic Slave Trade*, 103–29.

84 *African slavery*: Klein, *Atlantic Slave Trade*, 47–73; Thornton, *Africa and Africans*, 72–116; Manning, *Slavery and African Life*, 110–25.

85 *"Coromantees"*: Thompson, "Henry Drax's Instructions," 285.

85 *Fort Amsterdam:* Lawrence, *Trade Castles and Forts*, 245–49. Following the loss of Fort Cormantine in 1665, permanent British headquarters were relocated to Cape Coast Castle, only ten miles from the Dutch WIC headquarters at Elmina.

85 *"Gold Coast guardians":* As many as fifty people per vessel, including women who apparently helped with food preparation aboard, were loaded onto various Royal African Company vessels in the last quarter of the seventeenth century. Stephanie E. Smallwood, "African Guardians, European Slave Ships, and the Changing Dynamics of Power in the Early Modern Atlantic," *WMQ*, 3rd ser., 64, no. 4 (Oct. 2007): 679–716, 686–91.

85 *"Eyes met eyes":* Kiple, *The Caribbean Slave*, 58, quoting Elizabeth Donnan, ed., *Documents Illustrative of the History of the Slave Trade to America* (Washington, DC: Carnegie Institution of Washington, 1930–35), 1:206–9.

86 *"strip them of all":* Willem Bosman, *A New and Accurate Description of the Coast of Guinea, Divided into the Gold, the Slave, and the Ivory Coasts*, etc. (London, 1705), 370, http://play.google.com/books/reader?id=uNkTAAAAYAAJ&printsec=frontcover&output=reader&hl=en&pg=GBS.PT5.

86 *"so wilful":* Phillips, *A Voyage in the* Hannibal, 219.

86 *Father Denis de Carli:* Michael Angelo and Denis de Carli, "A Curious and Exact Account of a Voyage to Congo in the Years 1666, and 1667," in *A Collection of Voyages and Travels, Some Now First Printed from Original Manuscripts,* ed. Awnsham Churchill and John Churchill (London, 1732), 1:577, http://www.canadiana.org/view/33297/9.

86 *seven months:* Kiple, *Caribbean Slave*, 59.

87 *African drums:* Klein, *Atlantic Slave Trade*, 95.

87 *how much water:* Current research estimates a generous 3 liters (about 6.5 pints) of drinking water per day as the minimum for survival. In 1684 Portuguese law prescribed 1.5 pints daily. The French estimated that one water cask per person, weighing between 65 and 66 kilograms, was required for a two-month voyage, or slightly less than two pints a day. Peter H. Gleick, "Basic Water Requirements for Human Activities: Meeting Basic Needs," in *Water International* 21, no. 2 (1996): 84; Thomas, *Slave Trade*, 421; Klein, *Atlantic Slave Trade*, 94.

87 *100 degrees Fahrenheit:* Thomas, *Slave Trade*, 422.

87 *Slave rations:* Klein, *Atlantic Slave Trade,* 93–96; Klein, pers. comm., Dec. 13, 2006.

87 *scurvy:* a medical condition caused by the lack of vitamin C whose symptoms include swollen bleeding gums and extreme weakness; Klein, *Atlantic Slave Trade*, 93.

87 *ventilate the hold:* Thomas, *Slave Trade*, 416–17.

89 *Fort Amsterdam exists:* Lawrence, *Trade Castles and Forts*, 246, fig. 19.

89 *"two . . . square bastions":* van Dantzig, *Forts and Castles of Ghana*, 22.

89 *Seventeenth-century coastal traders:* For the following passage, see de Marees, *Gold Kingdom of Guinea*, 24, 31, 35, 36–39, 54, 75, and "Wilhelm Johannes Muller's Description of the Fetu Country, 1662–69," 183, 188, 194, 201, 202–4. For African cloth consumption and preferences, see Thornton, *Africa and Africans*, 48–52.

90 *their Africas:* The first generation of captives in America defined themselves by their specific ethnicities, even as they began to forge a new collective identity. Gomez, *Exchanging Our Country Marks*, 185.

91 *galley slave*: for "just wars," see Karen Ordahl Kupperman, *Providence Island, 1630–41: The Other Puritan Colony* (Cambridge: Cambridge University Press, 1995), 177–79; for John Smith see Gwenda Morgan, "Smith, John (*bap.* 1580, *d.* 1631)" (ODNB 2004), www.oxforddnb.com/view/article/25835; for Lewis Morgan, see Block, *Ordinary Lives*, 160.

92 *"people were forced"*: Manning, *Slavery and African Life*, 123.

92 *"lubricated and disguised the flow"*: Manning, *Slavery and African Life*, 102.

92 *"no Quaker could keep a slave"*: From the 1758 Philadelphia Yearly Meeting deliberations to censure slaveholders. In his journal for 1758, the Quaker abolitionist John Woolman, in describing Quakers who participated in the French and Indian War (1754–63), warned that "a carnal mind is gaining upon us," and at the 1758 meeting he exhorted Friends to "set aside all self-interest" regarding slaveholders, lest "God may by terrible things in righteousness answer us in this matter." Woolman's appeal had "had little to do with the evil results of slavery," but was focused on the slaveholder's soul: if he felt discomfort at holding people in bondage, the foremost reason for freeing them was to "give him inward peace." Quaker religious decisions are made by consensus; finally, in 1778 the Yearly Meeting declared Quaker slaveholders were to be disowned by their meetings. Thomas, *Slave Trade*, 460; *The Journal of John Woolman* (Boston: Houghton Mifflin, 1871), chaps. 5–7, https://play.google.com/store/books/details?id=T8MOAAAAYAAJ&rdid=book-T8MOAAAAYAAJ&rdot=1; Howard H. Brinton, *Friends for 350 Years*, 127, 151.

6. Before the Whirlwind

93 *dusty metal button*: "Sylvester Manor Artifact Descriptions," #3.

93 *"suite and cloak"*: Harleian Manuscripts, MS 1576, folio 642, quoted in Prudence Leith-Ross, *The John Tradescants: Gardeners to the Rose and Lily Queen* (London: Peter Owen), 77.

93 *twelve children*: Of the twelve, ten survived childhood; the four who came to America were Anne (c.1626–1708), Francis (1632–1711), Grizzell (1636–after 1687), and William (1647–after 1685). Mary (b. 1633) married Peter Sylvester, Nathaniel's brother, in 1656, then married Joseph Denham after Peter's death in 1657, and remained in England, as did Patience (b. c.1628), Rose (b. before 1630), Thomas (1634–1672), Elizabeth (b. 1637), and another son for whom there is only circumstantial evidence.

93 *eighteenth-century church*: The original 1144 Augustinian nunnery church, St. Mary *de fonte* (after the *fonte*, or springs, which gave the "Clerks' well" its name), was adjacent to the Knights Hospitallers' priory of St. John Clerkenwell. Barney Sloane and Gordon Malcolm, *Excavations at the priory of the Order of Hospital of St. John of Jerusalem, Clerkenwell, City of London* (London: Museum of London Archaeology Service, 2004), 24–25, 272.

93 *Henry VIII*: Following King Henry's break with the Roman Catholic church in 1534, he dissolved more than 800 monasteries and nunneries before 1540.

93 *fortresslike gate*: Sloane and Malcolm, *Excavations*, 169–72.

93 *Knights Hospitaller*: The Order of the Knights of the Hospital of St. John of Jerusalem, built the priory at Clerkenwell in 1144. Sloane and Malcolm, *Excavations*, 1–3, 24–25.

94 *aristocratic club*: Sloane and Malcolm, *Excavations*, 225.

94 *William Cavendish*: Lynn Hulse, "Cavendish, William, first duke of Newcastle upon Tyne (bap. 1593, d. 1676)" (*ODNB*, 2004), http://www.oxforddnb.com/view/article/4946?docPos=5.

94 *Gothic cloister*: Walter Thornbury, *Old and New London: A Narrative of Its History, Its People and Its Places* (London: Cassell, Petter, Galpin, 1881), 329, http://play.google.com/books/reader?id=KZQNAAAAIAAJ&printsec=frontcover&output=reader&authuser=0&hl=en&pg=GBS.PR1.

94 *"the Fleet"*: For "the Rules of the Fleet," see Sloane and Malcolm, *Excavations*, 275; Thornbury, *Old and New London*, 404–16.

95 *The noble Berkeley family:* George, 8th Baron Berkeley (1601–1658), who owned the house (1629–47) when the Brinleys lived next door, inherited it from his father, who had purchased it from Sir Maurice Berkeley of Bruton (1508–1581). The Berkeley connections extended to Datchet, Bucks., home of Anne Wase Brinley's family and of Royal Auditor Richard Budd, for whom Thomas Brinley clerked. Andrew Warmington, "Berkeley, George, eighth Baron Berkeley (1601–58)" (*ODNB*, 2004), http://www.oxforddnb.com/view/article/2208?docPos=1; Janet Kennish, *Datchet Past* (Chichester, England: Phillimore, 1999), 28–31.

95 *a map of 1676:* John Ogilby and William Morgan, "Large and Accurate Map of the City of London," etc., survey 1676, published 1677, http://www.british-history.ac.uk/lmap.aspx?compid=18979&pubid=61.

96 *"a Dwelling house"*: E-mail from Colin Thom, Senior Historian, Survey of London, English Heritage, to Gordon Brindley and Yvonne Brindley Long, July 8, 2003; Sloane and Malcolm, *Excavations*, 274.

96 *fallow deer:* Sloane and Malcolm, *Excavations*, 270–71.

97 *"The Best and Surest Herbe"*: John, Parkinson, *Paradisi in Sole, Paradisus Terrestris; or, A Garden of All Sorts of Pleasant Flowers Which Oure English Ayre Will Permitt to Be Noursed, etc.* (London: Humphrey Lownes and Robert Young, 1629, reprinted as *A Garden of Pleasant Flowers*, New York: Dover Publications, 1991), 6.

97 *Clipped specimens:* John Schofield, "City of London Gardens, 1500–c.1620," in *Garden History: The Journal of the Garden History Society* 27, no. 1 (Summer 1999): 79; John Harvey, *Medieval Gardens* (Beaverton, OR: Timber Press, 1981), 125.

97 Buxus sempervirens: Records suggest that until the 1500s, *Buxus sempervirens* was used for edging, clipped to about twelve inches.

97 *strains of box:* Jan Woudstra, "What Is Edging Box? Towards Greater Authenticity in Garden Conservation Projects," *Garden History* 35, no. 2 (Winter 2007): 229–42.

98 *"French or Dutch Boxe"*: Parkinson, *Paradisi in Sole*, 6.

98 *organic compound:* Takatoshi Tominaga and Denis Dubourdieu, "Identification of 4-Mercapto-4-methylpentan-2-one from the Box Tree (*Buxus sempervirens* L.) and Broom (*Sarothamnus scoparius* (L.) Koch," *Flavour and Fragrance Journal* 12, no. 6 (Nov./Dec. 1997): 373–76.

98 *rooted cutting:* If rooted boxwood cuttings arrived on Shelter Island safely, they were probably "containerized" without earth, packed in moss or grasses. Sir Thomas Hanmer, "How to Packe Up Rootes and Send Them to Remote Places," in Hanmer's *Garden Book* (1659, first pub. 1933), cited by Leith-Ross, *The John Tradescants*, 110

98 *"the Child's Corall"*: The will of Grizzell Brinley Sylvester, May 7, 1685, SMA, NYU I/A/140/19. Nathaniel Sylvester II gave his name to his eldest child, who died after 1714. Grizzell's probate inventory (October 12, 1687) lists a "silver coral with bells," but what happened to it is unknown. Acknowledgment/promissory note, Nathaniel Sylvester III to his mother, Margaret Hobert Sylvester, May 17, 1714, Hannah and Frederick Dinkel Collection of Family Papers, Shelter Island, NY; transcriptions, SMA, NYU, and SIHS; Kenneth Scott and James A. Owre, *Genealogical Data from Inventories of New York Estates 1666–1825* (New York: New York Genealogical and Biographical Society: 1970), 148.

98 *"walking up and downe"*: Dydymas Mountain (Thomas Hill), *The Gardeners Labyrinth* (London, 1577; reprint, New York: Garland, 1982), 24; pers. comm., David Jacques, Aug. 8, 2007.

99 *"strawberries"*: William Lawson, *The Countrie House-Wife's Garden for Herbs of Common use. Their Virtues, Seasons, Ornaments, Variety of Knots, Models for Trees, and Plots, for the Best Ordering of Grounds and Walks* (London, 1617; reprint with William Lawson, *A New Orchard and Garden: or, The Best Way for Planting, Graffing, and to Make Any Ground Good for a Rich Orchard, etc.* London: Cresset, 1927), 64.

99 *branches:* Early-fruiting trees were planted against a south-facing wall. Parkinson, *Paradisi in Sole*, 537; David Jacques, pers. comm., 2007; Sloane and Malcolm, *Excavations*, 258–59, 276.

99 *"answerable"*: Parkinson, *Paradisi* (*A Garden of Pleasant Flowers*), 3.

99 *"Bee-house"*: Lawson, *Countrie House-Wife*, 64.

99 *"Bird pots"*: Sloane and Malcolm, *Excavations*, 276–77.

100 *"Weeding"*: Lawson, *Countrie House-Wife*, 86.

100 *"comforting the spirits"*: Lawson, *Countrie House-Wife*, 81.

100 *compost pit:* Sloane and Malcolm, *Excavations*, 267.

100 *"servants and apprentices"*: Alan Macfarlane, *The Family Life of Ralph Josselin, a Seventeenth-Century Clergyman* (Cambridge: Cambridge University Press, 1970), 146, quoted in Ann Kussmall, *Servants in Husbandry in Early Modern England* (Cambridge: Cambridge University Press, 1981), 3.

100 *"family"*: Kussmall, *Servants in Husbandry*, 6–8; F. P. Leverett, *New and Copious Lexicon of the Latin Language* (Boston: J. H. Wilkins and R. B. Carter, 1839).

101 *"lytle Blackamore"*: Marika Sherwood, "Blacks in Tudor England," in *History Today* 53, no. 10 (October 2003), http://www.historytoday.com/marika-sherwood/blacks-tudor-england.

101 *ineffectively illegal:* The 1569 Cartwright case, about an Englishman's Russian slave, was "the first proceeding in which slavery was found to be inconsistent with English traditions," but the question of freedom would not be directly confronted until 1772. Higginbotham, *In the Matter of Color*, 321–55.

101 *"blackamoors"*: Sherwood, "Blacks in Tudor England"; Kathleen M. Brown, *Good Wives, Nasty Wenches & Anxious Patriarchs: Gender, Race, and Power in Colonial Virginia* (Chapel Hill: University of North Carolina Press for the Omohundro Institute of Early American History and Culture, 1996), 37–41.

101 *altar-tomb:* Thornbury, *Old and New London*, 339.

101 *Royal Exchequer:* G. E. Aylmer, *The King's Servants: The Civil Service of Charles I, 1625–42* (New York: Columbia University Press, 1961), 32–40; Madeleine Gray, "Land Revenue in the Late Sixteenth and Early Seventeenth Centuries," *Archives: The Journal of the British Records Association* 20, no. 87 (April 1992): 45–62.

102 *Richard Budd:* Budd's sister, Christina (b. 1556), married William Wase (b. 1554), whose granddaughter Anne married Auditor Brinley. See the genealogical chart "Wase, Budd, Brinley, Hanbury, Wheeler," comp. Janet Kennish, Griswold Papers, Fales Library, NYU.

102 *real estate agents:* Madeleine Gray, "Exchequer officials and the Market in Crown Properties 1558–1640," in *The Estates of the English Crown 1558–1640*, ed. R. W. Hoyle (Cambridge: Cambridge University Press, 1992), 112–36.

102 *Vermuyden:* Joan Thirsk, "Vermuyden, Sir Cornelius (1590–1677)" (*ODNB*, 2004), http://www.oxforddnb.com/view/article/28226.

102 *12,459 acres:* Charles I to Cornelius Vermuyden and his partners, William Courteine, knight, Robert Cambell, Charles Harbord, Thomas Brinley, John Lamote, and Timothy Vanvleteren, confirming a lease of December 27, 1628. Confirmation of

lease by royal letters patent, SY648/Z/1/1, March 24, 1634/5, http://www.nationalarchives.gov.uk/a2a/records.aspx?cat=197-sy648z&cid=1#1.

102 *acreage:* The grant is described as "massive." Madeleine Gray, "Exchequer officials," 113, 126.

102 Albion's Triumph: Graham Parry, *The Golden Age Restor'd: The Culture of the Stuart Court, 1603–42* (New York: St. Martin's Press, 1985), 185.

103 *Gardeners, scientists, scholars:* Henry Lowood, "The New World and the Catalog of Nature," in *America in European Consciousness, 1493–1750*, ed. Karen Ordahl Kupperman (Chapel Hill: University of North Carolina Press for the Institute of Early American History and Culture, 1995), 295–99.

103 *free inquiry:* Bacon's *The advancement of learning* was first published in 1605; and see Michael Hunter, "Boyle, Robert (1627–91)" (*ODNB*, 2004), http://www.oxforddnb.com/view/article/3137.

103 *John Winthrop Jr.:* Walter W. Woodward, *Prospero's America: John Winthrop, Jr., Alchemy and the Creation of New England Culture, 1606–76* (Chapel Hill: University of North Carolina Press for the Omohundro Institute of Early American History and Culture, 2010), 14–74.

103 "world of wonders": Woodward, *Prospero's America*, 306.

103 *"all parts of nature":* Susan Scott Parrish, *American Curiosity: Cultures of Natural History in the Colonial British Atlantic World* (Chapel Hill: University of North Carolina Press, 2006), 42.

104 *"comforting sameness":* Carol Berkin, *First Generations: Women in Colonial America* (New York: Hill and Wang, 1996), 6.

104 *"recognized the power":* Parrish, *American Curiosity*, 20–21.

104 *bestselling account:* Mary Rowlandson, "A True History of the Captivity and Restoration of Mrs. Mary Rowlandson" (London, 1682); reprinted in *Colonial American Travel Narratives*, ed. Wendy Martin (New York: Penguin Books, 1994); Laurel Thatcher Ulrich, *Good Wives: Image and Reality in the Lives of Women in Northern New England 1650–1750* (New York: Alfred A. Knopf, 1980; Vintage, 1991), chaps. 9–12.

104 *female characters: STR 1; Records of the Colony or Jurisdiction of New Haven from May, 1653, to the Union* (NHCR), ed. Charles J. Hoadly (Hartford: Case, Lockwood and Co., 1858), https://play.google.com/store/books/details?id=7PwPAAAAYAAJ&rdid=book-7PwPAAAAYAAJ&rdot=1; and for examples of the use of these voices, see Ulrich, *Good Wives,* and Martha Saxton, *Being Good: Women's Moral Values in Early America* (New York: Hill and Wang, 2003).

104 *Thomas:* Thomas Jr. (1634–1672), at King's College, Cambridge, by 1643, probably belonged to Benjamin Whichcote's group of clergymen and philosophers, the Cambridge Platonists, who read the works of the mystical Jakob Boehme and Henrik Niclae. Sarah Hutton, "Whichcote, Benjamin (1609–83)" *ODNB*, 2004), http://www.oxforddnb.com/view/article/29202; Sacks, "Francis Brinley and His Books," 22–23.

104 *Francis:* Francis Brinley (1632–1719) apparently left England in 1650 or 1651 for Barbados. Brinley briefly acted as secretary to his brother-in-law Governor William Coddington of Rhode Island before becoming a merchant and landowner. Bridenbaugh, *Fat Mutton and Liberty of Conscience*, 97.

105 *His 217 books:* Brinley, "A Gentleman's Library of 1713," 75–78; Sacks, "Francis Brinley and His Books," 3–4, 19–22.

105 *"human reason"*: Sacks, "Francis Brinley and His Books" (2006), 21.
105 *literate:* She had her own Bible, according to her will. Will of GBS, 1685.
105 *"fatal curiosity"*: Parrish, *American Curiosity*, 17, 174–214.
105 *"tedious prescriptions"*: Rebecca Bushnell, *Green Desire: Imagining Early Modern English Gardens* (Ithaca, NY: Cornell University Press, 2003), 9.
105 *"apparelled with plants"*: John Gerard's dedication to his patron William Cecil in *The Herball or Generall Historie of Plants* (London, 1597), cited by Bushnell, *Green Desire*, 100.
106 *regular city sight:* Leith-Ross, *The John Tradescants*, 14–15.
106 *"full improvement"*: Charles Hoole, *A New Discovery of the old Art of Teaching Schoole* (London, 1660), 284–85, quoted in Arthur MacGregor, "The Tradescants as Collectors of Rarities," in MacGregor, ed., *Tradescant's Rarities: Essays on the Foundation of the Ashmolean Museum, 1683, with a Catalogue of the Surviving Early Collections* (Oxford: Clarendon Press, 1983), 22–23.
106 *light craft:* Jennifer Potter, *Strange Blooms: The Curious Lives and Adventures of the John Tradescants* (London: Atlantic Books, 2007), 195.
106 *sixpence admission charge:* MacGregor, "The Tradescants as Collectors," 23, note 27.
106 *cultural world:* Ken Arnold, "Trade, Travel and Treasure: Seventeenth-Century Artificial Curiosities," in Chloe Chard and Helen Langdon, eds., *Transports: Travel, Pleasure, and Imaginative Geography, 1600–1830* (New Haven: Yale University Press, Studies in British Art 3, 1996), 263–85.
106 *whale ribs:* In 1638 the German visitor Georg Christopher Stirn saw them lying in the courtyard; the antiquarian John Aubrey described them as an arch later in the century. MacGregor, "The Tradescants as Collectors," 21; John Aubrey, *The Natural History and Antiquities of the County of Surrey* (London, 1719), 1:12–13, cited by Jennifer Potter, *Strange Blooms: The Curious Lives and Adventures of the John Tradescants* (London: Atlantic Books, 2006), 361.
106 *"little boat"*: MacGregor, "The Tradescants as Collectors," 17–23.
106 *1656 catalogue:* The catalogue is printed in full in Leith-Ross, *The John Tradescants*, 231–93; the coat is listed on p. 245.
107 *"the "robe"*: "'Powhatan's Mantle' . . . need not necessarily have been worn as a garment," http://www.ashmolean.org/ash/amulets/tradescant/tradescant07-13.html.
107 *They eagerly consumed:* For English interest in exotic experience, see Kupperman, *Jamestown Project*, 109–44.
107 *"a Bedstead"*: Kupperman, *Jamestown Project*, 132. Smith quotes are from John Smith, *The Generall Historie of Virginia, New-England, and the Summer Isles: with the Names of the Adventurers, Planters, and Governours from Their First Beginning An. 1584 to This Present 1624* (London, 1624), reprinted in *Captain John Smith: A Select Edition of his Writings*, ed. Karen Ordahl Kupperman (Chapel Hill: University of North Carolina Press for the Omohundro Institute of Early American History and Culture, 1988).
108 *"could not trust them"*: Karen Ordahl Kupperman, *The Jamestown Project* (Cambridge, MA: Belknap Press of Harvard University Press, 2007), 225.
108 *"Weroances"*: Gregory A. Waselkov, "Indian Maps of the Colonial Southeast," in *Powhatan's Mantle: Indians in the Colonial Southeast*, ed. Peter H. Wood, Gregory A. Waselkov, and M. Thomas Hatley (Lincoln: University of Nebraska Press, 1989), 292–343, 306–7.
109 *"girdles"*: The quotes in this paragraph are from MacGregor, *Tradescant's Rarities.*

109 *The two John Tradescants:* Arthur MacGregor, "Tradescant, John, the elder (d. 1638)" (*ODNB*, 2004); Arthur MacGregor, "Tradescant, John, the younger (bap. 1608, d. 1662)" (*ODNB*, 2004).

109 *American species:* MacGregor does not credit John the younger with the *introduction* of many American plants, assuming rather that most such plants arrived via other intermediaries. However, John the younger collected many plants in Virginia that may have been introduced previously. Arthur MacGregor, "The Tradescants: Gardeners and Botanists," in *Tradescants' Rarities*, 11–13; Potter, *Strange Blooms*, 265, citing J.A.F. Bekkers's introduction to *Correspondence of John Morris with Johannes de Laet, 1634–49* (Assen, The Netherlands: Van Gorcum & Comp., NV, 1970), 3; Potter, *Strange Blooms*, note 18, 420.

109 *American flowers:* Roger Torey Peterson and Margaret McKenny, *A Field Guide to Wildflowers of Northeastern and North-central North America* (Boston: Houghton Mifflin Co., 1968).

109 *bloodroot:* Bloodroot might possibly be the "Indian" plant that a collector in England put on his "wish list": "A small roote of a fingers bignes as red as blood wherewith they dye their mattes." The size is right, and bloodroot's root is a pale reddish color. Cited by Potter from Goodyer MS 11, fol. 21, and published in R. T. Gunther, *Early British Botanists and Their Gardens* (Oxford: Oxford University Press, 1922), 70–71.

7. The World Turns Upside Down

111 The title of Christopher Hill's book *"The World Turns Upside Down": The World Turned Upside Down: Radical Ideas During the English Revolution* (London: Temple Smith, 1972; reprinted London: Penguin, 1991)—the source for the chapter title—was taken from an old ballad.

111 *The will of Grizzell:* May 7, 1685, SMA, NYU, I/A/140/19.

111 *first Grizzell:* In 1630 a Grizzell and a Dorothy Wase received a £400 bequest from Auditor Richard Budd, Kennish, chart, Wase, Budd, Brinley, Hanbury, Wheeler, Chart, Griswold Papers, Fales Library, NYU.

111 *fairy tale:* William A. Wheeler, *An Explanatory and Pronouncing Dictionary of the Noted Names of Fiction, etc.* (Boston: James R. Osgood, 1872), 159; Clyde Furst, *A Group of Old Authors* (Philadelphia: George W. Jacobs, 1899), chapter 2, "A Medieval Love Story: Chaucer's Tale of Griselda."

114 *The Irish:* Ireland's bloody reduction was the first exercise of imperial British power. Nicholas Canny, *Making Ireland British* (Oxford: Oxford University Press, 2001).

114 *bouts of war:* The English Civil War was waged in Scotland and Ireland as well as England, and it had three phases: the first, 1642–46; the second, 1648–49; the third, 1649–65.

114 *two auditors:* William Gwyn Jr. and Richard Kinsman joined the king at Oxford in 1643. Gray, "Land Revenue," 59. Thomas Brinley II, Thomas Brinley's great-grandson, wrote that Auditor Brinley went to Oxford and followed Charles II into exile, but no confirmation exists. Thomas Brinley II (Boston?) to William Bollan, London, June 23, 1755, partial transcription input in 2000 at Sylvester Manor as Serial #197, Sylvester Manor FileMakerPro Database, Fales Library, NYU.

114 *Cavaliers and Roundheads:* In the 1950s and '60s, Laurence Stone and Christopher Hill, used the social sciences (and in Hill's case, Marxist theory) to enrich and deepen the standard political "what happened" rendering of the Civil War, set forth

by nineteenth-century "Whig" historians such as Thomas Macauley and G. M. Trevelyan. In the 1970s historian Conrad Russell and others took issue, viewing the unsuccessful settlement of Civil War issues as a complicated, unclear process resolved only in 1688. Conrad Russell, *The Causes of the English Civil War* (New York: Oxford University Press, 1990).

115 *out-and-out Parliamentarians:* Parliamentarians had to be very convinced of their cause in 1642, when it was unclear that the "revolution" would succeed. Aylmer, *The King's Servants,* Table 49, 405.

115 *"Lady Bullock's house":* Thornbury, *Old and New London,* 332.

115 *English lives:* Ann Hughes, "The Execution of Charles I," http://www.bbc.co.uk/history/british/civil_war_revolution/charlesi_execution_01.shtml.

115 *"man of blood": A Remonstrance of His Excellency Thomas Lord Fairfax, Lord General of the Parliaments Forces and of the General Councell of Officers Held at St. Albans the 16. of November, 1648* (London: Partridge, 1648), http://oll.libertyfund.org/?option=com_staticxt&staticfile=show.php%3Ftitle=2183&chapter=201180&layout=html&Itemid=27.

116 *Charles I:* Mark A. Kishlansky and John Morrill, "Charles I (1600–1649)" (*ODNB,* 2004), http://www.oxforddnb.com/view/article/5143?docPos=1.

116 *Henry Ireton:* Ian J. Gentles, "Ireton, Henry (bap. 1611, d. 1651)" (*ODNB,* 2004), http://www.oxforddnb.com/view/article/14452.

117 *four thousand troops:* Thomas signed a petition in nearby Eton to protest hardships caused by troops quartered in the area. Janet Kennish, *Datchet Past* (West Sussex: Phillimore, 1999), 41–43; "Petition from Parishes in Stoke Hundred to Parliament, Dec. 7, 1647," Centre for Buckinghamshire Studies, D/X 1205.

117 *surrounding landscape:* "The Royal Village: 16th and 17th Centuries," in Kennish, *Datchet Past,* 23–31 and figs. 20, 34; John Rocque, "County of Berkshire" (map), 1761, TNA: MPZ 1/1.

117 *manor house:* Thomas Brinley, who may have moved to Datchet by 1647 when his son William was baptized there, still gave his address as Clerkenwell in 1646. Earlier, he apparently lived in Eton, where he wrote his will, but at his death in 1661 he was probably living in Datchet Manor House. William Brinley, baptism 1647, no month or day given, Datchet Parish Register; Testimony of Richard Budd, 1621, Eton College, Miscellaneous Estates 49/155, Case of College v. Helen Foster relict of John Foster, Vicar of Datchet; "Inventory of Thomas Brimley [*sic*], 26 Nov 1661," *Buckinghamshire Probate Inventories, 1661–1714,* Michael A. Reed, ed. (Buckinghamshire Record Society, 1988), 11–12.

117 *royal business:* On March 1, 1640/1, "Mr. Auditor" TB certifies receipt of some £67 or so from fines levied on Henrietta Maria's properties in co. York. W. D. Hamilton, ed., *Calendar of State Papers, Domestic Series, of the Reign of Charles I, 1640–41* (London: Longmans, 1882), 528.

117 *lose everything:* Brinley salvaged lands and rents for his wife and sons, and portions for at least some of his daughters. Will of Thomas Brinley of Datchet, Buckinghamshire, filed December 11, 1661, Prerogative Court of Canterbury, PROB 11/306. Will of GBS.

117 *£600 annually:* Based on the income of Brinley's successor in the office, Richard Aldworth, in 1661, see *Westminster in the House of Commons, 1660–90,* ed. Basil Duke Henning (London: History of Parliament Trust, 1983) 1:525, in Sacks, "Francis Brinley and His Books 1650–1719" (2006).

118 *John Bland:* An Atlantic World merchant based in London, Bland had a brother in Spain in the 1640s. Other family members in Jamestown, Virginia, owned a warehouse there and received a large shipment of goods in 1644, when NS was also there.

118 *Anne was not the only wife:* Alice Clark, *Working Life of Women in the Seventeenth Century* (London: Routledge & Kegan Paul, 1919, reprinted 1982), 20–24.

119 *Boscobel:* http://www.british-civil-wars.co.uk/timelines/1651.htm.

119 *genealogical researcher:* Charles A. Hoppin was hired by the Horsfords in 1904. Thomas Brinley II, Thomas Brinley's great-grandson, wrote that Auditor Brinley went to Oxford and followed Charles II into exile, but no confirmation exists. Thomas Brinley II (Boston?) to William Bollan, London, June 23, 1755, partial transcription input in 2000 at Sylvester Manor as Serial #197, Sylvester Manor FileMakerPro Database, Fales Library, NYU; full paper copy, Griswold Papers, Fales Library, NYU.

119 *Thomas's grant holdings:* The papers on compounding Thomas Brinley's estate listed in 1880 at the PRO as First Series xxxi–651 were reclassified in 1895 as G91-959-1019-1 to 11. Circa 1904 these documents could not be found; a recent (2002) search confirms their absence. Legal efforts to reclaim property by generations of Brinley descendants were unsuccessful. Charles Hoppin, "Brinley," 40; Rachel Judith Weil, "Thinking about Allegiance in the English Civil War," *History Workshop Journal* 61 (Autumn 2006): 183–91.

120 *Presbyterian:* One whose church is governed by a synod of lay elders, not bishops. By the 1640s, "Presbyterian" was used as a political term, meaning a moderate Puritan opponent of the Crown. For distinctions between the Presbyterians of London and the "Independents" (more radical and more hostile to the king), see Valerie Pearl, "London's Counter-Revolution," in *The Interregnum: The Quest for Settlement, 1646–60*, ed. G. E. Aylmer (London: Archon Books, 1972), 29–56.

120 *right kind:* Laurence Brinley left a £30 bequest to the radical Presbyterian minister Edmund Calamy and another "for poor ministers put out of their places." Will of Laurence Brinley, Haberdasher of London, December 3, 1662. TNA: PRO PROB 11/309; Hoppin, "Brinley," 52–53.

120 *forefront:* During the war, Lawrence collected money, plate, and horses for the parliamentary financial machine. During the Interregnum, his ties to other intercolonial merchants may have helped shield Thomas. Brenner, *Merchants and Revolution*, 430, TNA: PRO, State Papers 16/491/47; Sacks, "Francis Brinley and His Books," 35–36.

120 *more lenient treatment:* As a London County Commissioner, Laurence had enough influence with the Commonwealth government in 1651 to assist a suspected Royalist, James Badham, with the return of his property; Laurence may have shielded his brother in the same way. Committee for Compounding Vol. G.1, Sept. 15 and Sept. 24, 1651; Hoppin, "Brinley," 40–41.

120 *assets:* Thomas also invested funds (a total of £200) toward the purchase of lands in Ireland. John P. Prendergast, *The Cromwellian Settlement of Ireland*, 2nd ed. (London: Longmans, Green, Reader, and Dyer, 1870), 431, 447, 448, https://play.google.com/books/reader?id=RmoBAAAAQAAJ&printsec=frontcover&output=reader&authuser=0&hl=en&pg=GBS.PR1.

120 *helped Anne and Grizzell:* See Sacks, "Francis Brinley and His Books," 35, for an interpretation of how Laurence may have assisted Patience (1653) and Elizabeth (1655) and Mary with shelter in London, based on a reading of their marriage licenses and banns in 1653, 1655, and 1656.

120 *Atlantic community:* Through Lawrence, Brinleys and Sylvesters could have met, via business, family and religious linkages, both Craddock and Vassall, leaders in the trades with New England, Virginia, the West Indies, and Africa. Troy O. Bickham, "Cradock, Mathew (c.1590–1641)" (*ODNB*, 2004), http://www.oxforddnb.com/view/article/6562; Brenner, *Merchants and Revolution*, 138; John C. Appleby, "Vassall, Samuel (bap. 1586, d. 1667)" (*ODNB*, 2004), http://www.oxforddnb.com/view/article/28120.

120 *William Coddington:* Virginia DeJohn Anderson, "Coddington, William (1601?–78)" (*ODNB*, 2004), http://www.oxforddnb.com/view/article/5794.

120 *fourth-richest citizen:* Bridenbaugh, *Fat Mutton*, 15.

120 *Stephen Winthrop:* Returning to Rhode Island, Coddington wrote to JWJr describing the jubilation he found in Commonwealth London. William Coddington, Rhode Island, to JWJr, Pequit, February 19, 1652, Freiberg, *WP* 6:173–76.

121 *January 1650:* "Coddington, William, esq. of the Isle of Rhodes, beyond seas, widower, about 40 and Anne Brindley, about 24, daughter of Thomas Brindley, of Eaton, co. Bucks., esq. alleged by John Mayer, of St. Bennet, Paul's Wharf, London, Gent—at Datchett, co Bucks 12 Jan 1649/50 F." Faculty Office of the Archbishop of Canterbury.

121 *"my loving Brother in Law":* Will of GBS.

121 *back to England:* Coldham, *Complete Book of Emigrants*, 20.

121 *Church of England:* Thomas leaves nothing to any church or minister, commends his soul to God in conventional language appropriate to a member of the Church of England, and is buried in St. Mary's, the Church of England parish church of Datchet. See Sacks, "Francis Brinley and His Books," presented in "Recovering the Record: Sylvester Manor in the Atlantic World, ca. 1650–1750," Session 20, American Historical Society Association Annual Meeting, January 7, 2005, Seattle, WA, note 45.

121 *brood of twelve:* Kennish, chart: "Wase, Budd, Brinley, Hanbury, Wheeler," Griswold Papers, Fales Library, NYU.

121 *"I have but them two":* Anne Brinley, London, to Francis Brinley, Newport, RI, April 20, 1665, holograph copy, original unknown, East Hampton Library. Anne Brinley's literacy does not mean her daughters were literate as well. Grizzell was "signature literate," meaning she could sign her name; her ability to read is evidenced by her ownership of a Bible. Anne Coddington wrote a remarkable letter in 1660 to Governor Endicott of Massachusetts shortly after the hanging of Mary Dyer, printed in Joseph Besse, *Collection of the Sufferings of the People Called Quakers: for the testimony of a good conscience, etc.* (London: Luke Hinde, 1753), 2:207–8, http://dqc.esr.earlham.edu:8080/xmlmm/docButton?XMLMMWhat=builtPage&XMLMMWhere=E6875814B.P00000204-207&XMLMMBeanName=toc1&XMLMMNextPage=/printBuiltPage.jsp.

8. "TIME OF LONGING"

123 *"the garden of New England":* "An Account Taken from Mr. Harris of New England," *Calendar of State Papers, Colonial Series America and West Indies* (*CSP*), eds. W. Noël Sainsbury et al. (London: Public Record Office, 1860–1994), 9:222, quoted in Antoinette F. Downing and Vincent Scully Jr., *The Architectural Heritage of Newport, Rhode Island, 1640–1915* (New York: Clarkson N. Potter, 1967), 472 n9.

123 *left Barbados:* After 1647, no records have been found of the Sylvesters' *De Seerobbe*.

123 *decommissioned by the Dutch:* The *Swallow*'s last Dutch-owned trip ended in New Amsterdam. The Company's directive instructed: "On arriving in New Netherland, the ship, *Swol*, being old, ought to be sold." O'Callaghan and Fernow, *Documents Relative to the Colonial History of the State of New York*, 1:165–67.

123 *such cabinets:* Huon Mallalieu, ed., *The Illustrated History of Antiques* (Philadelphia: Running Press, 1995), 40–41; Joseph Aronson, ed. *The Encyclopedia of Furniture*, 3rd ed. (London: B. T. Batsford, 1965), 65–67; Jonathan L. Fairbanks and Robert F. Trent, *New England Begins: The Seventeenth Century* (Boston: Boston Museum of Fine Arts, 1982), 293–94, 527–28.

123 *"perceiving his cabbinet":* "Deposition of Stephen Daniel," April 28, 1653, *WP* 6 (1650–54): 284–85.

124 *"the Swallow":* "Deposition of Bernerd Collins before Lion Gardiner and Thomas Baker, February 25, 1655/56," *EHTR*, 1:91–93.

124 *"Captain Nathiell Silvister":* Collins, *EHTR*, 1:91–93.

124 *in the morning:* It appears the *Swallow* first ran aground in late afternoon or at night: Collins said it was "the next Morning yt [that] the afor sd Greenfeild Larrabies ship was cast away." *EHTR*, 1:91–93.

124 *"the rest of Capt: Nathaniell Silvesters servants":* This may be a rare mention of Sylvester "servants," meaning indentured whites, as opposed to "servants" who were enslaved blacks. However, since the Swallow was en route from Barbados, Africans may also have been aboard.

124 *first law of salvage:* Dr. Kathy Abbass, Director, Rhode Island Marine Archaeology Project, 2003, pers. comm. Despite Larrabie's wrongful application of the law of salvage, the case was apparently decided as a personal property issue (NS's cabinet) in court.

124 *"Consented unto the opening":* Collins, *EHTR*, 1:91–93.

125 *"Now Mr. Giles Silvister":* Collins, *EHTR*, 1:91–93.

125 *found guilty:* For the judgment, May 11, 1653, see *Records of the Particular Court of Connecticut, 1639–63* (Hartford: Connecticut Historical Society and Society of Colonial Wars in the State of Connecticut, 1928), 116–17.

125 *thriving plantation:* William Coddington, Rhode Island, to JWJr, Pequit (New London), April 20, 1647, quoted by Bridenbaugh, *Fat Mutton*, 50–51.

126 *"Nanhygonsett [Narragansett] Bay":* "An Account taken from Mr. Harris," in Downing and Scully, Jr., *Architectural Heritage of Newport*, 16.

126 *the Coddington house:* Coddington, builder of the only brick house in Boston before he left for Rhode Island in 1637, designed his Newport house as a stone-ender, a construction that draws on stone building traditions from the West and North of England with which Coddington, born in Lincolnshire, would have been familiar. Myron O. Stachiw, *The Early Architecture and Landscapes of the Narragansett Basin* (Newport: Vernacular Architecture Forum, 2001), 1:23; Downing and Scully, *Architectural Heritage of Newport*, 27.

126 *After her arrival:* Coddington returned to Newport with Anne, infant Nathaniel, and Grizzell before early August, when Roger Williams wrote to JWJr of Coddington's arrival. Freiberg, *WP*, 6:131–32.

126 *multilingual slaves:* Like the Puritans of Providence Island, pan-Atlantic merchants in New England by the late 1630s saw little objection to buying Africans as cheap, lasting labor. Lindholdt, *John Josselyn*, 24; Karen Ordahl Kupperman, *Providence Island*, 172.

126 *"charter generation" of slaves:* Ira Berlin, *Many Thousands Gone: The First Two Centuries of Slavery in America* (Cambridge, MA: Belknap Press of Harvard University Press, 1998), 104.

127 fala de Guiné: "Guinea speech," "negro speech," in Berlin, *Many Thousands Gone,* 20. Also Thornton, *Africa and Africans,* 214–15.

127 *ways to influence it:* Berlin, *Many Thousands Gone,* 26–27, 34–36.

127 *"time of longing":* Thomas Weld, quoted in Edmund S. Morgan, *The Puritan Family: Religion and Domestic Relations in Seventeenth-Century New England* (New York: Harper & Row, 1966), 59.

127 *could never love:* Saxton, *Being Good,* 48–49.

128 *"in and for the Lord":* Hugh Peter, *A Dying Father's Last Legacy to an Onely Child* (London, 1660), 34, quoted in Saxton, *Being Good,* 49.

128 *"the official 'prudishness'":* Berkin, *First Generations,* 36.

128 *"Food, drink, sleep, sex, safety":* Morgan, *Puritan Family,* 16.

128 *"could not restrain":* Morgan, *Puritan Family,* 33.

128 *Young women:* Saxton, *Being Good,* 36–44.

129 *"impudent whores":* Brereton, *Travels in Holland,* 55, quoted by Schama, *Embarrassment of Riches,* 471–73. For minority women in New England and forced sex, see Saxton, *Being Good,* 40–44.

129 *sex with female slaves:* Richard S. Dunn, *Sugar and Slaves: The Rise of the Planter Class in the English West Indies, 1624–1713* (New York: W. W. Norton, 1973), 228, 252–55.

129 *"The man whose heart":* Thomas Hooker, *The Soules Humiliation* (London, 1638), quoted in Morgan, *Puritan Family,* 62.

129 *higher ratio:* In New England between 1621 and 1651 there were four single men for each single woman. David Hackett Fischer, *Albion's Seed: Four British Folkways in America* (New York: Oxford University Press, 1989), 26–27; Berkin, *First Generations,* 25.

129 *four or five years younger:* Fischer, *Albion's Seed,* 75–76; Ulrich, *Good Wives,* 6.

129 *a date of 1620:* Hoff, "Sylvester Family," 16.

129 *a handful of portrait artists:* See Jonathan L. Fairbanks, "Portrait Painting in Seventeenth-Century Boston: Its History, Methods and Materials," in Fairbanks and Trent, *New England Begins,* 3:413–55; Abbott Lowell Cummings, "Seventeenth-Century Boston Portraiture: Profile of the Establishment," in *Painting and Portrait Making in the American Northeast, Annual Proceedings of the Dublin Seminar for New England Folklife 1994* (Boston: Boston University for the Dublin Seminar for New England Folklife, 1995), 17–29; and Lillian B. Miller, "The Puritan Portrait: Its Function in Old and New England," in *Seventeenth-Century New England, A Conference Held by the Colonial Society of Massachusetts* (Boston: Proceedings of the Colonial Society of Massachusetts, #63, 1984), ed. David D. Hall and David Grayson Allen, 153–84.

130 *"The Body is the Shell":* Francis Quarles, *Epigrammes* (London, 1695), 127, quoted by Aileen Ribeiro, *Fashion and Fiction: Dress in Art and Literature in Stuart England* (New Haven: Yale University Press for the Paul Mellon Centre for Studies in British Art, 2005), 159.

130 *"weareing your cloathes":* James Cleland, *Hero-paideia, or, The Institution of a Young Nobleman* (Oxford: Joseph Barnes, 1607), 125, quoted in Ribeiro, *Fashion and Fiction,* 181.

130 *"Skin-close" breeches:* Samuel Purchas, *Purchas His Pilgrim: Microcosmus, of the Historie of Man, Relating the Wonders of his Generation, Vanities in His Degeneration, Necessity of His Regeneration* (London, 1619), 267, quoted in Ribeiro, *Fashion and Fiction,* 185.

130 *"old Violett Coullered cloak"*: Copy of Bradford's probate in Plimoth Plantation, "Dossier for Alice Bradford," n.p.

131 *"For to Make a Hand som Woman"*: Seaborn Cotton, "Commonplace Book of Reverend Seaborn Cotton," MS A1454, R. Stanton Avery Special Collections Dept., New England Historic Genealogical Society, paraphrased in Martha Saxton, *Being Good*, 47–48, and note 9, 314.

131 *"Women of the gentry"*: See Ribeiro, *Fashion and Fiction*, 203–7, and the reproductions of "Hester Tradescant and her Stepson," 1645, oil on canvas, attributed to Emmanuel de Critz (Ashmolean Museum, Oxford) and "Winter," 1644, by Wenceslaus Hollar, for this quote and the succeeding paragraph.

131 Autumn: *Autumn*. Wenceslaus Hollar, in Ribeiro, *Fashion and Fiction*, 207.

132 *Hollar's drawings*: Ribeiro, *Fashion and Fiction*, 204, for Hollar's "Young Woman," 1645.

132 *near-transparency*: the sheerness of the fabric helps explain why, in the seventeenth century, "naked" usually meant "wearing a shift," while "stark naked" was used for complete nudity.

132 *best defense against pestilence*: Kathryn Ashenburg, *The Dirt on Clean: An Unsanitized History* (New York: North Point Press, 2007), 93–111.

132 *Robert Herrick's Julia*: Of the fifty-four poems about Julia in his *Poetical Works*, ed. F. W. Moorman (London: Humphrey Milford/Oxford University Press, 1921), eight are about how her body smelled, including "Upon Julia's unlacing her self" (156); "Upon Julia's sweat" (240); "On Julia's lips" (271); and "His embalming to Julia" (129).

133 *preserving the Englishness*: "Considering, amongst many other inconveniences . . . how like we were to lose our language and our name of English . . . how unable there to give such education to our children, as we ourselves had received." Edward Winslow, "Hypocrisie Unmasked" (London, 1646), reprinted in *Chronicles of the Pilgrim Fathers of the Colony of Plymouth from 1608 to 1625* (Boston, 1841, reprinted Baltimore: Clearfield, 1995), 381.

133 *"the usuall speech of the Court"*: Anonymous (attributed to George Puttenham), *The Art of English Poesie* (London, 1589).

135 *secular contracts*: Puritans in England, Europe, and New England restricted religious recognition of marriage to banns read in advance of the marriage—part of the struggle to set themselves apart from the Church of England. Chilton L. Powell, "Marriage in Early New England," *The New England Quarterly* (*NEQ*) 1, no. 3 (July 1928): 323, 324–25, http://www.jstor.org/stable/359877.

135 *Francis*: In early 1652 in Newport, Francis Brinley, identifying himself as "Secretary," copied an official letter for his brother-in-law William Coddington, who in 1652 was still governor under his 1651 commission. Freiberg, *WP* 6:182.

135 *"Sexual experience"*: Ulrich: *Good Wives*, 95.

135 feme sole: Dayton, *Women Before the Bar*, 19–20; MaryLynn Salmon, *Women and the Law of Property in Early America* (Chapel Hill: University of North Carolina Press, 1986), 81–119; Susan Staves, *Married Women's Property Rights in England, 1660–1833* (Cambridge, MA: Harvard University Press, 1990), 95–130; Linda Sturtz, *Within Her Power: Propertied Women in Colonial Virginia* (New York: Routledge, 2002), 20–24.

135 *"better comfortable livelyhood"*: Will of GBS.

136 *Under Nathaniel's will*: Will of NS.

136 *"So long as the husband and wife"*: Staves, *Married Women's Property Rights*, 149–50.

136 *larger expenditures:* A long-held rule that "the right to present enjoyment of a thing did not allow the owner to change its nature" meant a wife's annual allowance—"pin money"—could not be converted into real property or chattel without becoming something else, and therefore the husband's property. The rule of no arrears beyond a year minimized "the possibilities that women could take property intended for maintenance and use it as capital." Staves, *Married Women's Property Rights*, 150, 155.

137 *Jacquero:* The variety of European monikers by which Abee Coffu Jantie Seniees, a leading late-seventeenth-century politico and merchant at Cape Coast, was known (Jan Snees, Jacque Senece, Johan Sinesen, Jantee Snees) indicate that he worked with Dutch, Danish, and English traders. Berlin, *Many Thousands*, 23.

137 *"my Negro Girl Isabell":* Will of NS.

137 *"negotiated relationship":* Berlin, *Many Thousands Gone*, 2.

137 *"I give unto my five daughters":* Will of GBS.

9. Where They Lived

139 *"it hath pleased god":* NS, Shelter Island, to JWJr, August 8, 1653, *WP*, 6:20–21. JWJr was close by in New London (Pequit) at the time, Walter W. Woodward, pers. comm., Sept. 5, 2006.

139 *female relatives:* Anne Coddington, Grizzell's sister, was her only female relative in America.

139 *sociable community life:* Ulrich, *Good Wives*, 50–67.

139 *became a Quaker:* In 1657 when the Friends arrived in New England from Barbados, or soon thereafter, GBS and NS, and the Coddingtons, were convinced.

140 *"deputy husband":* Ulrich, *Good Wives*, 8–10.

140 *"moved freely":* For this quote, and "A New England woman" in the next paragraph, see Berkin, *First Generations*, 33.

140 *"Yongest Child":* NS to JWJr, Shelter Island, 6th of 8br [October 6], 1655, MHS *Proc.*, ser. 2, 4: 274–75.

141 *Winthrop's advice:* For Winthrop's role as regional physician, see Woodward, *Prospero's America*, 182–99.

141 *The baby:* Nathaniel's will lists eleven children born between 1654 and 1675 (Grizzell, Giles, Nathaniel, Peter, Patience, Elizabeth, Mary, Anne, Constant, Mercie, and Benjamin).

141 *"strong, self-contained":* Saxton, *Being Good*, 24.

141 *female domestics:* Ann Collins, perhaps the wife of John Collins, witnessed Nathaniel's will in 1680. A John Collins had contracted to barter island produce from Nathaniel in 1658. Anna Guillat, perhaps the wife of Jacques Guillot, witnessed Constant Sylvester's will in 1670. A John Collins and a "Jacquis Guillot" also witnessed NS's will. Sylvester Manor Account Book 1658–1768, East Hampton Library; Will of Constant Sylvester, Records of Barbados 6/8: 316.

141 *"to doe any busenes about ye house":* NS to JWJr., October 6, 1655. MHS *Proc.*, ser. 2, 4: 274–75.

142 *"That until such time":* Articles of Agreement, September 20, 1652, GSDD, SIHS.

142 *visit for a year:* Francis Brinley lived with the Sylvesters in 1654. Dorothy C. Barck, ed., *Papers of the Lloyd Family of the Manor of Queens Village, Lloyd's Neck, Long Island, New York, 1654–1826* (New York: New-York Historical Society, 1927), 1:219.

142 *unrelated men and women:* Multiple examples, often leading to rape as well as consensual sex, are cited from New England court records by Ulrich, *Good Wives*, and Saxton, *Being Good*.

142 *"starter house":* Eighty-four pre-1725 Massachusetts houses out of Abbott Lowell Cummings's sampling of 144 were first built on a one-room or half-house plan (an entrance hall with a chimney behind, and a single "parlor"); almost all were enlarged. Abbott Lowell Cummings, *The Framed Houses of Massachusetts Bay, 1625–1725* (Cambridge, MA: Belknap Press of Harvard University Press, 1979), 23.

143 *"a dynamic, multi-cultural landscape":* Mrozowski et al., "Archaeology of Sylvester Manor," 3–8.

143 *EDM:* For this explanation of how an EDM operates, pers. comm., Katherine Hayes, 10/15/12.

144 *"Record everything":* On the first day of each field school, Steve gathered the students to talk about the summer plan. Griswold Papers, Fales Library, NYU.

144 *"paint chips for dirt":* Griswold Papers, Fales Library, NYU.

145 *available histories:* The manor's library includes standard American and Long Island histories, as well as works of local interest such as William Wallace Tooker's *The Indian Place-Names on Long Island and Islands Adjacent with Their Probable Significations* (New York: G. P. Putnam's Sons, 1889; Knickerbocker Press, 1911), and memoirs by family members, such as Catherine E. Havens's *Diary of a Little Girl in Old New York* (New York: Henry Collins, 1919, reprinted Bedford: Applewood Books, 2001), Sylvester Manor Book Inventory, Sylvester Manor Educational Farm, Shelter Island, NY.

145 *hard facts:* See Cummings, *Framed Houses of Massachusetts Bay*, and Cummings, ed., *Rural Household Inventories: Establishing the Names, Uses and Furnishings of Rooms in the Colonial New England Home, 1675–1775* (Boston: The Society for the Preservation of New England Antiquities, 1964).

145 *tiled roof:* See Horsford, unfinished genealogical manuscript, SMA, NYU IV/I /2/111/ 20–21, 112/ 1–6; Martha J. Lamb, "The Manor of Shelter Island, Historic Home of the Sylvesters," *Magazine of American History* 18 (November 1887): 365–66; Rev. Jacob E. Mallmann, *Historical Papers on Shelter Island and Its Presbyterian Church* (New York: A. M. Bustard, 1899, reprinted Shelter Island: Shelter Island Public Library, 1985), 21–22, 47; Cornelia Horsford, "The Garden at Sylvester Manor, Shelter Island," in *Gardens of Colony and State: Gardens and Gardeners of the American Colonies and of the Republic Before 1840*, ed. Alice G. B. Lockwood (New York: Charles Scribner's Sons, 1931), 1:278–79; Ralph G. Duvall, *The History of Shelter Island, from its Settlement in 1652 to the Present Time, 1932* (Shelter Island Heights: privately printed, 1932), 21, 53; Cornelia Horsford, "The Manor of Shelter Island," address read before the annual meeting of the Order of Colonial Lords of Manors in America on April 23, 1931 (New York: privately printed, 1934), 6–7.

146 *The first printed Long Island history:* Silas Wood, *A Sketch of the First Settlement of the Several Towns on Long-Island with their Political Condition to the End of the American Revolution* (Brooklyn: Aldeu Spooner, 1828). Harold D. Eberlein's *Manor Houses and Historic Homes of Long Island and Staten Island* (Philadelphia: J. B. Lippincott Company, 1928) includes a description of Sylvester Manor, 58–67.

146 *"The twilight zone":* C. Vann Woodward, *The Strange Career of Jim Crow* (Oxford: Oxford University Press, 1955), viii, quoted by Michael Kammen, *Mystic Chords of Memory: The Transformation of Tradition in American Culture* (New York: Vintage, 1993), 31.

146 *"as it ought to have been"*: "By a curious paradox through the very fact of their respect for the past, people came to reconstruct it as they considered it ought to have been." Cultural historian Marc Bloch, *Feudal Society* (Chicago: University of Chicago Press, 1964), 1:102, quoted in Kammen, *Mystic Chords*, 30–31. For traditional accounts and folk history of the manor, see Hancock, "Changing Landscape," 12–14, 41–44.

146 *smaller wire mesh:* Katherine Howlett Hayes, "Field Excavations at Sylvester Manor," in *Historical Archaeology*, 34.

146 *Center for Archaeological Research:* The Andrew Fiske Memorial Center for Archaeological Research (AFMCAR) was established with a $650,000 gift from Alice Fiske in 1999, which was matched by the Commonwealth of Massachusetts for a total of a million dollars; http://www.fiskecenter.umb.edu.

146 *the technologies of magnetometry:* Magnetic gradiometry responds to iron in an iron tool or a brick or any heavily fired clay surface containing iron. Ground-penetrating radar sends pulses of radar energy into the ground to locate discontinuities between the pulses such as changes in stratigraphy and the evidence of walls, house or pit floors, rubble or midden deposits. All geophysical testing technologies require extensive processing of the data they produce. Kenneth L. Kvamme, "Geophysical Explorations," *Historical Archaeology of Sylvester Manor*, 51–70.

147 *"square corners"*: Griswold Papers, Fales Library, NYU. "Linear features, squares, rectangles, right angles, circles or ovals are not generally products of nature, but are culturally produced." Kenneth L. Kvamme, *Final Report of Geophysical Investigations Conducted at Sylvester Manor, Shelter Island, New York*, 2000 (Boston: Archeo-Imaging Lab, University of Massachusetts Boston, 2001), 11.

147 *major change in plantation layout:* Kvamme, "Geophysical Explorations at Sylvester Manor," 59–60.

149 *as many as eighty buildings:* Griswold Papers, Fales Library, NYU.

149 *shadowy footprints:* See Kvamme, "Geophysical Explorations," 59–60, for examples of how different technologies are used to check and enlarge results.

149 *ad hoc "first house"*: Before the Sylvesters arrived, James Farrett, the Earl of Stirling's agent, may have built a house in 1638 after he claimed both Shelter and nearby Robins Island as payment for his services in settling English colonists on Long Island, a patent that had been granted to William Alexander, the Earl of Stirling, by the Crown in 1636. After the earl's death in 1640, Farrett sold the islands to Stephen Goodyear (deputy governor of New Haven Colony) to pay for passage to Scotland in 1642. Until Goodyear's 1651 sale of the island to the four partners, no Europeans apparently lived there. See Hancock, "Changing Landscape," 69–70 and figure 9.

149 *"earth fast" structures:* Emerson W. Baker, Robert L. Bradley, Leon Cranmer, and Neill DePaoli, "Earthfast Architecture in Early Maine," presented at the Vernacular Architecture Forum Annual Meeting, Portsmouth, NH, 1992, http://www.salemstate.edu/~ebaker/earthfast/earthfastpaper.html.

151 *unfinished manuscript:* Horsford, unfinished genealogical manuscript, SMA, NYU/IV/I/2/111.

151 *the storytellers:* Eben W. Case (1918–2004) knew Cornelia Horsford and was revered as Shelter Island's "memory." The UMass team consulted him.

151 *personal sensitivity:* See David Presti and John D. Pettigrew, "Ferromagnetic coupling to muscle receptors as a basis for geomagnetic field sensitivity in animals," *Nature* 285, no. 5760 (May 8, 1980): 59–91, http://www.nature.com/nature/journal/v285/n5760/abs/285099a0.html.

152 *a stretch of the southeast lawn:* Sylvester Manor Project researcher Barbara Schwartz interviewed Eben Case twice about the possible "first house" location, then plotted his description to scale on graph paper and placed the scaled dowsing result over the Case plan. Case confirmed the location as what Cornelia Horsford had told him. Barbara Schwartz interviews with Eben Case, SIHS; Griswold Papers, Fales Library, NYU; Hayes, "Field Excavations," 47, 48.

152 *"closet or porchamber":* The rear section of the "cross" was often lacking, leaving only a projecting two-story lobby entrance on the front of a rectangular box. Will of GBS; Virginia and Lee McAlester, *A Field Guide to American Houses* (New York: Alfred A. Knopf, 2003), 105–6, line drawing, 107. Architectural historians agree that porch towers indicated wealth and status. Cummings, *Rural Household Inventories*, 1964), xiv; Cummings, *Framed Houses of Massachusetts Bay*, 35–36 and Appendix I, Table 3, numbers 224, 228, and 231; Richard L. Bushman, *The Refinement of America: Persons, Houses, Cities* (New York: Vintage Books, 1993), 103–4; William N. Hosley Jr., "Architecture," in *The Great River: Art and Society of the Connecticut Valley, 1639–1820*, ed. William N. Hosley Jr., and Gerald W. R. Ward (Hartford: Wadsworth Athenaeum, 1985), 73–74; Updike, *Richard Smith*, 66; *The Diary of Joshua Hempstead: A Daily Record of Life in Colonial New London, Connecticut, 1711–58* (New London: New London County Historical Society, 1999), 626–27; James D. Kornwolf and Georgiana V. Kornwolf, *Architecture and Town Planning in Colonial North America* (Baltimore: Johns Hopkins University Press, 2002), 2:1058, Figure 7.176b.

153 *ell:* A lean-to, sometimes one and a half stories, was often added (at Sylvester Manor, perhaps the "Long Room" described in GBS's will).

153 *postholes:* Hayes, "Field Excavations," 48.

153 *a new hypothesis:* Griswold Papers, Fales Library, NYU; Hayes, "Field Excavations," 48.

10. How They Lived

155 *his inventory:* Dean Failey, Senior Director of American Furniture and Decorative Arts at Christie's, and author of the authoritative decorative arts work for Long Island, *Long Island Is My Nation* (Albany: Mount Ida Press for the Society for the Preservation of Long Island Antiquities, 1998), observed that, among the period Long Island inventories with which he is familiar, "only Wm Tangier Smith's probate inventory even approaches the scale of Nathaniel's inventory." (William "Tangier" Smith, 1655–1705, Manor of St. George, Long Island.) He also noted that while "the greate glasse" that Grizzell mentions was a sign of wealth, "textiles were what really counted. The 10 beds is an extraordinary number as all had to be 'dressed.'" Dean Failey, pers. comm., April 2006.

155 *a couch:* A seventeenth-century couch was like a chaise longue, but angular and stiff, with hard-surfaced embroidered upholstery.

155 *baroque stone carpet:* When the late art historian Robert Hughes observed the pavement emerging from the ground, he drew the analogy between the diagonals emphasized by baroque painters and sculptors and the diagonal patterning of the pavement, presumably of the same period.

156 *No comparable example:* For other period pavement surfaces in New England that may be as early as 1690, see Anne A. Grady, *Historic Structure Report: Spencer-Pierce-Little House, Newbury, Massachusetts* (Society for the Preservation of New England Antiquities, Conservation Center, Waltham, 1992), section 3, 61–65.

156 *a few cobbles:* Hayes, "Field Excavations," 46.

156 *royal manor:* Sung Bok Kim, *Landlord and Tenant in Colonial New York: Manorial Society, 1664–1775* (Chapel Hill: University of North Carolina Press, published for the Institute of Early American History and Culture, Williamsburg, VA, 1978), 9–13.

158 *Steve said:* MKG Field Notes, Summer 2000, SMA, NYU.

158 *one archaeological stratum:* Hayes, "Field Excavations," 46–47; Gary, "Material Culture and Multi-Cultural Interactions at Sylvester Manor," *Historical Archaeology of Sylvester Manor,* 107–8.

158 *Pins also secured:* Mary C. Beaudry, *Findings: The Material Culture of Needlework and Sewing* (New Haven: Yale University Press, 2006), 8, and chap. 2.

158 *"long shell'd":* "The Second Voyage," in Lindholdt, *John Josselyn, Colonial Traveler,* 79.

159 Weskhunck, tackhunck: Williams, *Key,* 37; Bragdon, *Native People,* 104.

159 *pestle:* Mortar and pestle were sometimes buried with a woman, as hunting implements were buried with men. Strong, *Algonquian Peoples,* 102.

159 *roar of a mill:* NS's inventory lists a "horse mill," a pair of millstones, and a grindstone. Robert Hefner, author of *Windmills of Long Island* (New York: W. W. Norton and The Society for the Preservation of Long Island Antiquities, 1983), surmised that the manor's Upper Inlet would have provided enough flow. "An Inventory of the Estate of Nathaniel Sylvester taken the 22: September 1680," GSDD #1, SIHS.

159 *Joshua:* Born c.1626 in Amsterdam, naturalized as English with brothers Nathaniel and Giles in 1657, Joshua died in Southold June 21, 1706. He may have suffered from some physical disability: CS and NS made provisions in their wills for his upkeep, but soon after his arrival in America he was well enough to travel across Long Island Sound. Hoff, "Sylvester Family," 5; William A. Shaw, ed., *Letters of Denization and Acts of Naturalization for Aliens in England and Ireland, 1603–1700* (Lymington: Huguenot Society of London, 1911), 71; Joshua Sylvester, Shelter Island, to JWJr, Hartford, Sept. 7, 1660, MHS *Proc.*, ser. 2, 4: 277–78; will of CS, 1671; will of NS, 1680.

159 *at the same table:* Sarah Kemble Knight, "The Journal of Madam Knight," in *Colonial American Travel Narratives,* 64.

160 *port and madeira:* The Sylvesters stopped in the Azores as early as 1657 and in Madeira on at least one voyage. Coldham, *English Adventurers,* 165; Giles Sylvester II, Madeira, to JWJr, Hartford, May 30, 1666, MHS *Proc.*, ser. 2, 4: 281–82.

160 *Rhenish pottery jugs:* Salt-glazed stoneware jugs became part of Dutch Atlantic traders' standard stock-in-trade. Hancock, "Changing Landscape," 90; Charlotte Wilcoxen, *Dutch Trade and Ceramics in America in the Seventeenth Century* (Albany: Albany Institute of History and Art, 1987), 73.

160 *"case bottles":* Nathaniel's probate lists "1 Case with Bottles"; four case bottle fragments were found in the midden in front of the existing house. NS inventory; Hancock, "Changing Landscape," 59.

160 *Barbadian rum:* Entries for the 1680s, Sylvester Manor Account Book, 1658–1768, East Hampton Library.

160 *pewter plates:* Nathaniel's 1680 inventory lists a large amount of pewter, 280 pounds, but no silver. Mention of "all my plate" in Grizzell's will leads to a conjecture that the silver was considered her personal property; NS inventory, GSSD 1; Will of GBS.

160 *stew in pottery bowls:* Sarah Sportman, Craig Cipolla, and David Landon, "Zooarchaeological Evidence for Animal Husbandry and Foodways at Sylvester Manor," in

Historical Archaeology of Sylvester Manor*, 127–40; Elizabeth Therese Newman, "What's For Dinner: Distinctive Diets in New England," paper presented at annual conference of the Society for Historical Archaeology, Providence, RI, January, 2003.

160 nausamp: Nathaniel Sylvester presumably knew both Dutch and the English transliterations of the Indian word (the Narragansetts called it "nausamp"). Dutch chroniclers Isaac de Rasieres (1628) and Adriaen van der Donck (1655) both commented on "sappaen" or "samp." Samp is dried or parched corn, *yokeg*, soaked in a hot lye preparation, then pounded to a consistency that makes porridge when mixed with water. Bragdon, *Native People*, 102–3.

160 *Samp was reheated for days:* Alice Ross, "Corn the Food of a Nation," Alice Ross Hearth Studios, http://www.aliceross.com/journal/articles.html; Ross, pers. comms. April 2001, June 20, 2012.

160 *"niggering corn":* Ralph Ireland, "Slavery on Long Island: A Study in Economic Motivation," in *Journal of Long Island History* 6 (Spring 1966): 4.

160 *constantly redefined:* Ira Berlin makes the point that "historians have frozen their subject [slavery] in time. While they have captured an essential aspect of chattel bondage, they have lost something of the dynamic that constantly made and remade the lives of slaves, changing them from time to time and place to place." Berlin, *Many Thousands Gone*, 5.

160 *"slave societies":* For this distinction, Berlin, in *Many Thousands Gone*, 8, credits earlier works that focus on slavery in antiquity, such as Keith Hopkins, *Conquerors and Slaves: Sociological Studies in Roman History* (Cambridge: Cambridge University Press, 1978), 99; Moses I. Finley, "Slavery," in *International Encyclopedia of the Social Sciences* (New York: Macmillan, 1968); and Finley, *Ancient Slavery and Modern Ideology* (New York: Viking, 1980), 79–80.

161 *"the planting field:"* Will of NS, 1680.

161 *Jacques Guillot:* Last Testament and Will of Constant Sylvester, Oct. 26, 1695. SMA, NYU I/A/140/26.

161 *midden:* For a description and analysis of the slaughter pit and the remains it held, see Sportman et al., "Zoological Evidence," 137–38.

162 *as late as the 1670s:* Hayes, "Field Excavations," 48.

162 *Lab analysis:* According to David Landon at UMass, the pit contained mostly pig bones (65 percent), most of which (almost 90 percent) are head and foot bones, with few body bones, suggesting the meatier parts were barreled for shipment (barrels containing as little waste as possible). The smaller numbers of cattle and sheep bones, and of heads and feet, suggest that these animals were butchered for domestic Shelter Island consumption. Dr. David Landon, pers. comm., Sept. 27, 2005, Dec.11, 2012.

162 *Specific butchering cuts:* Sportman et al., "Zooarchaeological Evidence," 137–38.

162 *a large, smooth-bodied clay pot:* Gary, "Material Culture," 105; Katherine Howlett Hayes, "Race Histories: Colonial Pluralism and the Production of History at the Sylvester Manor Site, Shelter Island New York," Ph.D. dissertation, University of California, Berkeley, 2008, 156–62.

162 *Fort Shantock: Hayes:* "Race Histories," 143–45, 157, Laurence M. Hauptman and James Wherry, *The Pequots in Southern New England: The Fall and Rise of an American Indian Nation* (Norman: University of Oklahoma Press, 1993), 99.

162 *pan-Indian identity:* Hayes, "Race Histories," 235–37; Robert G. Goodby, "Reconsidering the Shantok Tradition," in *A Lasting Impression: Coastal, Lithic, and Ceramic*

Research in New England Archaeology, ed. Jordan E. Kerber (Westport, CT: Praeger, 2002), 141–54.

163 *quickly:* Sportman et al., "Zooarchaeological Evidence," 138.

163 *ate them:* for dog bones with butchering cuts, see Sportman, "Zoological Evidence," 131.

163 *For meat and hides:* Strong, *Algonquian Peoples*, 112–14.

163 *"mask being":* Strong, *Algonquian Peoples*, 112. Strong admits there is scant evidence for this assertion, but some evidence. John A. Strong, pers. comm., 2005.

163 *forced migrations:* Strong, *Algonquian Peoples*, 112. The Lenape were forced progressively westward, ending in Oklahoma, where they live today; http://www.ancestral.com/cultures/north_america/lenni_lenape.html.

163 *East End tribes revered:* Mesingw images had special powers and were ceremoniously "fed" every year. If they were damaged, they were given a ritual burial.

164 *a large mask:* William Wood describes war paint among the "Abergenians" (not yet clear who he's writing about) as "all black as jet, some red, *some half red and half black* [italics mine], some black and white, others spotted with diverse kinds of colors." Wood, *New England's Prospect*, 1977:103, quoted in Bragdon, *Native People*, 223.

164 *He watched the hunters:* Strong, *Algonquian Peoples*, 113.

164 *four or five times as many people:* In Southold, the closest town, according to the 1686 census, Isaac Arnold, Nathaniel's first cousin, owned six, John Conkling, five, and John Budd, a wealthy timber merchant, three. Of the 111 families listed, only nine others were slaveholders, owning one or two at most. Rufus King, "Early Settlers of Southold, Suffolk County, Long Island," *NYGBR* 30 (April 1899): 121.

164 *"bundle of silences":* Hayes, "Race Histories," 232.

165 *plantation-period examples:* Hayes, "Race Histories," 141–43, 153–90.

165 *common African smelting and ironworking practices:* Hayes, "Race Histories," 188, 242.

165 *"a flow of knowledge":* Hayes, "Race Histories," 246–47.

165 *"small acts of sharing":* Hayes, "Race Histories," 229, also 189–90.

165 *a deliberate act:* Hayes, "Race Histories," 240–42; Hayes to MKG, e-mail Oct. 3, 2012.

165 *"very sullen":* Matthias Nicolls to JWJr, March 7, 1675, Winthrop Family Papers, MHS.

166 *"Hindsight being 20/20":* Kat Howlett to Mac Griswold, August 6, 1999, fax, "Some notes on the readings" regarding differences between Northern and Southern slavery. For housing slaves in their owners' houses in the North, see William Dillon Piersen, *Black Yankees: The Development of an Afro-American Subculture in Eighteenth-Century New England* (Amherst: University of Massachusetts Press, 1988), 25–36; Joanne Pope Melish, *Disowning Slavery: Gradual Emancipation and "Race" in New England, 1780–1860* (Ithaca: Cornell University Press, 1998), 27. Later, in the eighteenth century, "where the holding was large, some had to be quartered in outbuildings at some distance from the main house"; see sale advertisements for farms with "Negro houses," Edgar McManus, *Black Bondage in the North*, 92.

166 *At Rich Neck Plantation:* The difference between the artifacts scattered around the Rich Neck house and the kitchen and quarters illustrates the increasing gulf between masters and black slaves, which was mirrored in increasingly restrictive legislation for blacks. Rich Neck was abandoned around 1700, leaving the

seventeenth-century site intact. David Muraca, Philip Levy, and John C. Coombs, "Masters, Servants, Slaves and Space: Exploring the Social Structure of Early Colonial Virginia" (annual meeting, Society for Historical Archaeology, 2002); John C. Coombs, "Building 'The Machine': The Development of Slavery and Slave Society in Early Colonial Virginia" (Ph.D. dissertation, College of William and Mary, 2003); Coombs, "One for the Negro Slaves: Houses, Homelots, and the Development of Slavery in Early Colonial Virginia" (annual meeting, Society for Historical Archaeology, 2007); Leslie McFaden, Philip Levy, David Muraca, and Jennifer Jones, with contributions by Dr. Douglas Owsley, D. Hunt, and Emily Williams, "Interim Report: The Archaeology of Rich Neck Plantation," Marley R. Brown III, Principal Investigator, Williamsburg: The Colonial Williamsburg Foundation, Department of Archaeological Research, 1999, 3–7, 23–26; Graham et al., "Adaptation and Innovation," 508.

167 *masters and slaves:* Bedding is listed in the "meel house," where flour was also kept, and in small spaces on other floors in the inventory of Brinley Sylvester (1694–1752). Administration on the estate of Brinley Sylvester, Sept. 13, 1762, East Hampton Library. Some Northern families with more than two or three slaves built separate "quarters" in the late eighteenth century. At least two such structures existed on Shelter Island, but because the term "kitchen" is sometimes used to describe them, it is unclear whether they were completely separate buildings or not. Nicoll Havens's Grand Central Mansion, since destroyed, had a "slave kitchen"; the Cartwright house, formerly located on the Henry Dering property, now on Coecles Harbor, was the house of London, a slave in the Thomas Dering family. For separate quarters in New York State during the eighteenth century, see John Michael Vlach, "Slave Housing in New York's Countryside," in *Slavery in New York*, eds. Ira Berlin and Leslie M. Harris, 72–73.

168 *various structures:* Besides Nathaniel Sylvester's 1680 inventory, a lease of 1693—when his eldest son, Giles, hired Edward Downing, "husbandman late of Boston," to farm the place and live in the west half of the house—presents most of the documentary evidence for the seventeenth-century operation. NS inventory; Giles Sylvester to Edward Downing, December 1, 1693, Suffolk County Deeds, Liber A: 161–62, Suffolk County Clerk's Office, Riverhead, NY.

168 *warehouse:* The warehouse apparently stored and preserved 150 hogsheads of perishable salt for at least thirteen months. A hogshead stands five feet high and 42 to 44 inches wide. "Transcript of Trial Involving Nathaniel Sylvester (Original 1665)," SMA, NYU IV/H/4/106/25; Chapman, *Weights, Money and Other Measures Used by Our Ancestors* (Baltimore: Genealogical, 1996, reprinted 1997), 47–62.

168 *Shuttling livestock:* In a letter to JWJr regarding the purchase of cattle for Shelter Island, NS writes "the sooner it is done better by reason ye yeare is passinge away," meaning the weather would make it dangerous to transport them. A case tried in the New Haven court on March 15, 1656, reveals the dangers of shipping livestock by water even on short trips: a mare the Sylvesters bought in Southampton fell and was killed on the trip to Shelter Island. NS, Shelter Island, to JWJr, Pequit (New London), October 10, 1654, SMA, NYU I/A/140/3; Hoadly, *NHCR* 2:193–94.

168 *"a prsell [of staves]":* NS, Shelter Island, to JWJr (Pequit?), March 15, 1654, MHS *Proc.*, ser. 2, 4: 272; for the quotation: NS, Rhode Island, to JWJr, July 27, 1654. Freiberg, ed. *WP* 6: 412; NS, Shelter Island, to JWJr, Pequit, April 7, 1655, MHS *Proc.*, ser. 2, 4: 274.

168 *thousands of staves:* NS acted as receiver in 1665 for 1,000 pipe staves (a "pipe" is a small barrel) and 1,768 hogshead staves in 1666 for the account of Thomas Revell, merchant of New England and Barbados, and in 1665 as attorney for Revell regarding an outstanding order for 700 hogshead staves. In 1686, when James Lloyd, NS's son-in-law and one of the executors of his estate, tallied his final "Accounts with the Sylvesters of Shelter Island," he listed twenty hogsheads of molasses and four hogsheads and twelve tierce of rum, as well as 5,350 pipe staves ready for shipping, indicating that NS's Caribbean trade was thriving at the time of his death. *STR* 1:366 and 1:420. Barck, *Papers of the Lloyd Family*, 1:112, 113.

168 *African identity:* According to Long Island history researcher Reginald Metcalf, Tammero's origins may be Igbo, based on a reading of the name of his son Obium as a variant of the Igbo female name Obia. Charla E. Bolton and Reginald H. Metcalf, Jr., "The Migration of the Jupiter Hammon Family: A Notable African American Journey," *LIHJ*, May 2013.

168 *proudly acknowledged:* John Thornton states that "Records and inventories that give ethnonyms of slaves for the sixteenth and seventeenth centuries are rare," but several of the names in NS's will and other Sylvester documents appear to be of ethnic origin. Thornton, *Africa and Africans*, 195.

170 *Oyo Empire:* See Thornton, *Africa and Africans*, "West African States," map, vii, and xxiv–xxv for territory and brief history.

170 *collective identity:* See "Talking Half African, Middle Passage, Seasoning, and Language," in Gomez, *Exchanging Our Country Marks*, 184–85.

170 *"Whereas Tammero":* Will of NS.

170 *Tammero:* "My Negro Tammero and his wife Oyou to my son Peter," will of NS, is the first mention of the couple. On September 26, 1687, "Tomeo and O You," with their son "Opium" (Obium), with another Sylvester slave, Tony, noted by Isaac Arnold (NS's first cousin and an executor of Nathaniel's estate), are valued at £83 New York money in a bill of sale to James Lloyd (Boston merchant and husband of Grizzell Sylvester Jr.), which also mentions £9 as due to Constant Sylvester's estate (evidently as part of the original agreement in which Tammero was "yeelded to goe into partnership"), SMA, NYU I/A/140/21. On September 11, 1688, son Peter Sylvester, who was setting up his own farm on Shelter Island, bought the couple back from Lloyd for £38 New York money, SMA, NYU I/A/140/22. The will of Peter Sylvester (1663–1696) (Suffolk County Abstract of Wills, 2: 1665–1707) does not mention the two slaves, although he leaves the "improved part" to his brother, Constant. Constant mentions Peter as a beneficiary in his own will, dated October 26, 1695, SMA, NYU I/A/140/26, but Constant died in 1697. Tammero and Oyou may then have been returned to Lloyd, although this is unclear. In 1687 Tammero was valued at only £16 (so he was perhaps an old man), while the price for his wife was £22; see "James Lloyd's Accounts with the Sylvesters of Shelter Island," Barck, *Papers of the Lloyd Family*, 1:115.

170 *"socially stratified":* Gomez, *Exchanging Our Country Marks*, 154.

170 *"good fraight":* Richard Smith to Fitz John Winthrop, MHS *Colls.*, Letter 31, April 2, 1674, quoted in Emily Coddington Williams, *William Coddington of Rhode Island: A Sketch* (Newport: privately printed, 1941), 78.

171 *lady's maid:* Two "smothing irons" are listed in NS's 1680 inventory.

171 *winter isolation:* The seventeenth century marked the nadir of the Little Ice Age; ships avoided sailing in winter, as they could get trapped and damaged in the ice. For effects of the Little Ice Age, see Karen Ordahl Kupperman, "Climate and Mas-

tery of the Wilderness in Seventeenth-Century New England," in David D. Hall and David G. Allen, eds., *Seventeenth-Century New England* (Boston: Colonial Society of Massachussetts, 1984).

171 *naming a child:* Slaves' names, often taken from the Bible, or from classical antiquity—Hercules, Juno—were given to slaves by their captors.

171 *One scholar:* John Pulis, pers. comm., August 2001.

171 *baptismal and death records:* In his will, NS spells the name of the elder woman as Semmie, and the girl as Semenie. For the 1698 listing, see Edmund Bailey O'Callaghan, *Lists of Inhabitants of Colonial New York, Excerpted from the Documentary History of the State of New York* (Baltimore: Genealogical, 1979), 51, http://books.google.com/books?id=4XzO6xwgyYoC&printsec=frontcover&source=gbs_atb#v=onepage&q&f=false; "my Negro girl [Simone]" (brackets original) is mentioned in the will of John Conkling II of Southold, January 15, 1705/6, copy, SMA, NYU I/A/140/27; for a Simene, "negro servant of Widow Seth Parsons," bap. May 20, 1736, and a Simene, "servant of Widow of Deacon Mulford," Sept. 16, 1736, as well as her three children in 1739, 1742, and 1745, see "Baptisms of Black Residents of East Hampton Township," compiled by Dorothy Zaykowski, in a folder labeled "East Hampton Township . . . Deaths and Baptisms—Black Residents," Sag Harbor History Room, John Jermain Memorial Library, Sag Harbor, NY; for the admission of a Semonie in 1791 as one of the first fifteen members of the Presbyterian Church in Sag Harbor, see Presbyterian Church Records, copy, East Hampton Library; and for the death on September 12, 1805 (b. 1750) of Simmany, "Esq. Fordhams negro woman" in "Deaths of Black Residents of East Hampton Township," also East Hampton Library, but a different list from the above. Referring to slaves, T. H. Breen observes: "East Hampton's colonial blacks appear in the records like subatomic particles in a physics experiment . . . All that we have are their names: Bess, Jack, Peter, Rose, Bristo, Betty, Hannah, and Simene." T. H. Breen, *Imagining the Past: East Hampton Histories* (Reading, MA: Addison-Wesley, 1989), 181–82.

171 *no dictionary of proper names*: "An Alphabetical Table of the Proper Names in the Old and New Testaments" in a 1792 edition of the Bible, although a late source, offers a possibility on page 4 of the table for the choice of the name Semie or Semnie, from the Hebrew meaning "hearing" or "obedient." Rev. John Brown, *The Self-Interpreting Bible: Containing the Sacred Text of the Old and New Testaments* (New York: Hodge and Campbell, 1792).

171 *Guyanese Indian woman:* Peter. F. Campbell, *Some early Barbadian History: as well as the text of a book published anonymously in 1741 entitled 'Memoirs of the first settlement of the island of Barbados . . .': and a transcription of a manuscript entitled 'The description of Barbados' written about the year 1677 by Major John Scott* (St. Michael, Barbados: Caribbean Graphics, 1993), 146.

172 sêminí *or* osêminí: *"sêminí* (sometimes *osêminí*) = *Komantí* spirits (collectively)." The plural word sêminí invokes or means a gathering of the *Komantí*, "the ultimate Saramake warrior and curing gods." The word Komantí, meaning both spirits and a Saramakkan language, is derived from "Cormantine" (for the local Coromantees), the name the English gave to the Gold Coast (Ghanaian) slave fort. Richard Price, *Travels with Tooy: History, Memory, and the African American Imagination* (Chicago: University of Chicago Press, 2008), 345, 341; Richard Price, pers. comms., July 26, 2006, June 26, 2012. Dutch records on Guyanese slavery online begin with the late eighteenth century; nineteenth-century manumission records produced five slave women by the

name of Semiere, or Semmie. www.nationaalarchief.nl/vrij-in-suriname and www.surinamistiek.nl IBS (Instituut ter bevordering van de 'Surinamistiek').

172 *old "Poppy" Terry:* Information from Shinnecock Becky Genia and from Elizabeth Thunder Bird Haile, tribal elder of the Shinnecock Nation, 2005.

11. IN THE GROUND

173 *Her letter is dated:* Cornelia Horsford to unknown, August 26, 1915, copy, SMA, NYU IV/H/1/98/9.

175 *burial without markers:* Gaynell Stone, "Spatial and Material Aspects of Culture: Ethnicity and Ideology in Long Island Gravestones, 1670–1820" (Ph.D. dissertation, State University of New York at Stony Brook, 1987), 146, 148. Margaret Fell Fox, George Fox's wife, was buried without a headstone in 1702. Her last words were "I am in Peace."

175 *"social death":* Orlando Patterson, *Slavery and Social Death* (Cambridge, MA: Harvard University Press, 1982).

175 *Jerome Handler and Ira Berlin:* Handler and Lange, *Plantation Slavery in Barbados,* 171–215, esp. 173, "The Negroes . . . bury one another in the ground of the plantation where they die," wrote Barbados's governor (Jonathan Atkins) in 1676, "and not without ceremonies of their own"; 195, "Under normal circumstances, plantation management apparently did not interfere with interment and postinterment behavior"; and 215, "'However one may choose to define a generalized West African "heritage" shared by the slaves transported to any New World colony . . .' the West African homelands clearly influenced the mortuary patterns of Barbadian slaves to a considerable degree," Handler and Lange quoting Sidney W. Mintz and Richard Price, "An Anthropological approach to the Afro-American Past: a Caribbean Perspective," ISHI *Occasional Papers in Social Change* 2 (Philadelphia: Institute for the Study of Human Issues, 1976), 5–7; Berlin, *Many Thousands Gone,* 62–63.

175 *sole authority:* NS appealed for outside governance in 1672, to the New York court for power to arrest the island's Indians who "have presumed in their Drink to breed Disturbance . . . ye occasion of great ffrights and trouble in his family." O'Callaghan, *Documents Relative to the Colonial History of New York,* 14:713.

175 *"a preventive strategy":* Smallwood, "African Guardians," 700.

175 *in New York City:* The first large-scale rebellion in New York did not occur until 1712; the second, more conspiracy than revolt, was in 1741. As on Barbados, legislative response to the discovery of slave plots, rumors of rebellion, or the revolts themselves offer a way to gauge the strength of white fears and rumors against the presence of a rising number of blacks in the city. Edgar McManus writes, "Slave disturbances were so common that the streets of most towns were not safe." Jill Lepore, "The Tightening Vise: Slavery and Freedom in British New York," in Berlin and Harris, *Slavery in New York,* 58–69, 78–87; Jill Lepore, *New York Burning: Liberty, Slavery, and Conspiracy in Eighteenth-Century Manhattan* (New York: Alfred A. Knopf, 2005); Higginbotham, *In the Matter of Color,* 119, 131–35; McManus, *Black Bondage in the North,* 79.

176 *many ways to retaliate:* Berlin, *Many Thousands Gone,* 11.

176 *carved monuments:* Marcus, *Discovering the Black Experience in Suffolk County,* 117.

177 *the body of an infant:* Description of graves 335 and 336 at the African Burial Ground, http://legacy.www.nypl.org/research/sc/afb/shell.html.

177 *No stone confirms:* No stonecutter's receipts have been found. So it is not clear whether Cornelia commissioned the burying ground monument as indicated in her letter or whether it was carved at the same time as the Quaker monument, whose inaugural celebration took place in July 1884. Another stone with lettering similar to that of the slave burial ground monument is located near the spring on the east side of the top of Gardiners Creek. Visible only from a boat or by standing in the creek, the inscription reads "Yoko," surely a reference to the canoe-borne life of the sachem Youghco. Another stone on the north side of a maple just a few yards from the front drive circle offers a disagreeable start: inscribed "Sambo," the lettering commemorates a pet, who was at least honored with his name.

177 *The list, if it existed:* The burying ground is on private property, so there was no official requirement to list the interments in the town record. Griffing may have kept his own list, if such a list was indeed maintained.

178 *"Planted Six rows of corn":* Samuel Smith Gardiner Daybook No. 3 "commenced September 4, 1844" 1844–1858, SMA, NYU III/A/3/45/2.

178 *"Negro garden":* Fields often have long-lived names, derived from use or location. Obsolete language also often continues in use: a good late example being the word "pitle," a small lot, often irregularly shaped, a word E. N. Horsford used in writing to the manor superintendent Jesse Preston, "At present you might keep all the sheep in the pitle." Horsford to Preston, Cambridge, October 28, 1884, SMA, NYU IV/A, 1a, 67, 44.

178 *"For the enabling Negroes":* Jerome Handler makes clear the distinctions between "Negro Garden" (also sometimes known as the "Negro Ground") and the two other areas where slaves grew food for their own sustenance, the "provision ground" and the house plots that surrounded the slave village huts. Slaves sold their own produce and sometimes animals (pigs, chickens) on Barbados and Long Island, where legislation forbidding slave markets was enacted as early as 1684. Peter Thompson, "Henry Drax's Instructions on the Management of a Seventeenth-Century Barbadian Sugar Plantation," *WMQ*, 3rd ser., 66, no. 3 (July 2009): 585; Handler, "Plantation Slave Settlements," 133–34; Handler, pers. comm., Dec. 1, 2008; Higginbotham, *In the Matter of Color*, 117.

179 *Indian corn, or maize:* Crosby, *Columbian Exchange*, 185–86.

179 *as blanks:* The erroneous idea of incoming slaves as "blanks" persisted: see Jerome S. Handler, untitled review of Sidney M. Greenfield's 1966 *English Rustics in Black Skin: A Study of Modern Family Forms in a Pre-industrialized Society* (New Haven, CT: College and University Press, 1966), in *American Anthropologist*, New Ser., 71, no. 2 (April 1969), 335–37, http://jeromehandler.org/wp-content/uploads/GreenfieldReview69.pdf.

179 *Indian land management:* Cronon, *Changes in the Land*, 34–53.

179 habitus: Pierre Bourdieu, *Outline of a Theory of Practice*, trans. Richard Nice, *Cambridge Studies in Social Anthropology* 16 (Cambridge: Cambridge University Press, 1977), 85; Bourdieu, *The Logic of Practice* (Cambridge: Polity Press, 1990), 53; Fernand Braudel, *On History* (Chicago: University of Chicago Press, 1980), 25–84; Elizabeth Terese Newman, "San Miguel Acocotla: The History and Archaeology of a Central Mexican Hacienda" (Ph.D. dissertation, Yale University, 2008), 7–8.

179 *callaloo:* Callaloo is a general descriptive term for a number of edible leafy greens from the amaranthus, chenopodium, and phytolacca plant families. See B. W. Higman, *Jamaican Food: History, Biology, Culture* (Jamaica: University of the West Indies Press, 2008), 100–109, and Sidney W. Mintz, "Food Enigmas, Colonial and Postcolonial," *Gastronomica* 10, no. 1 (Winter 2010): 149–54.

180 *cassava:* Cassava, *Manihot esculenta*, of which one variety, the bitter cassava, yields triple the caloric value of maize, thrives in poor soils; produces a heavy crop and several harvests from one planting; is drought resistant and not eaten by herbivores, as it is poisonous until processed; and keeps well in the ground, like turnips. Grown by Amerindians and domesticated in Brazil and Central America four thousand years ago, it was imported into Africa by the Portuguese in the sixteenth century. Cassava cakes, by the 1680s, were a favored food in the West Indies; one writer called cassava "the common bread" of planters and servants in Jamaica. Higman, *Jamaican Food*, 61–64. Also see Jane G. Rubin and Ariana Donalds, eds., *Bread Made from Yuca: Selected Chronicles of Indo-Antillean Cultivation and Use of Cassava 1526–2002* (New York: InterAmericas, 2003).

180 *"a disposition to recollect"*: Oliver Sacks, "The Landscape of his Dreams," in *An Anthropologist on Mars: Seven Paradoxical Tales* (New York: Vintage Books, 1996), 169.

181 *"the spring and the end of the graveyard"*: Horsford, unfinished genealogical manuscript, SMA, NYU-IV-I-2-111.

181 *"clay colander"*: Griswold Papers, Fales Library, NYU.

181 *a piece of a European utensil*: AFMCAR.

181 *"Ground-truthing"*: For "ground-truthing," see Joanne Bowen, "Historical Ecology and the British Landscape," and R. Marley Brown III, "Pervasive Factionalism and Identity Politics in the Early English New World: Archaeological Examples from the Colonies of Virginia, Bermuda, and Barbados," both papers presented at the annual meeting of the Society for Historical Archaeology in Mobile, Alabama, 2002; for how ground-truthing works at its best and can be distilled in print to reveal how archaeology can be "sensitive to questions of general cultural significance," see Deetz, *In Small Things Forgotten*, 44–49.

183 *Peter Banks:* Interview with Peter Banks, professional plowman and heavy horse trainer, Herefordshire, England, Sept. 30, 2001.

184 *a GIS (Geographic Information System) program:* Pers. comm., David Landon, Oct. 18, 2012; http://blogs.umb.edu/fiskecenter/2012/07/23/geographic-information-systems.

184 *to "observe the landforms"*: A. Wayne Cahilly and Todd Forrest, "Observation of Landforms, Hawthorns, and other Genera at Sylvester Manor," New York Botanical Garden report, 2000, Griswold Papers, Fales Library, NYU.

185 *the scientists concluded:* Cahilly and Forrest, "Observation of Landforms," 8.

185 *Erosion patterns:* The North Peninsula drops a mere twenty feet from the hill crest over the length of a generous 200 to 300 feet to reach the broad curve of the Upper Inlet shore near a spring at the western end of the inlet. "Erosion seldom occurs in forested areas, and when it does the resulting depressions are deep and narrow, more on the nature of a defile . . . Some of the areas eroded from the plateau [the top of the North Peninsula] to the marsh are now little more then concave linear depressions recognizable only by their descending orientation" and thus don't display the patterns characteristic of erosion on forested land, indicating that this area has been cleared for a long time. Cahilly and Forrest, "Observation of Landforms," 6.

186 *The UMass team:* Hayes, "Field Excavations," 40.

188 *in New York City:* Lepore, "The Tightening Vise," 60.

188 *slaves to New Netherland:* Christopher Moore, "A World of Possibilities: Slavery and Freedom in Dutch New Amsterdam," in Berlin and Harris, *Slavery in New York*, 29–56.

188 *in Charleston:* Lepore, "The Tightening Vise," 60.

188 *Duke's Laws: The Colonial Laws of New York,* 1:18; see also Higginbotham, *In the Matter of Color,* 115–16; Edgar J. McManus, *A History of Negro Slavery in New York* (Syracuse: Syracuse University Press, 1970), 1–22; and Ira Berlin, *Generations of Captivity: A History of African-American Slaves* (Cambridge, MA: Belknap Press of Harvard University Press, 2003), 31–36.

188 *Over the decades:* The Duke's Laws defined the concept of inherited slave status: the children of slave mothers were slaves for life, so manumission became the only option for slaves to become free.

188 *By 1698:* See Berlin, *Many Thousands Gone,* 52–59, for seventeenth-century slavery in New York Colony; also see Shillingburg and Shillingburg, "The Disposition of Slaves": "The New York colony had more slaves than New England, New Jersey, and Pennsylvania combined. About 20% of the population of Suffolk County in 1698 was African and most of them were slaves." For an extended overview of slavery on Long Island, see Moss, "Slavery on Long Island."

188 *Shelter Islanders:* O'Callaghan, *List of Inhabitants,* 51.

188 *half the slaves:* Moss, *Slavery on Long Island,* 110–11.

188 *colossal by East End standards: Abstracts of Wills 1665–1787,* Suffolk County Surrogate's Court, Riverhead; Kenneth Scott, "Early New York Inventories of Estates," *National Genealogical Society Quarterly* (*NGSQ*) 53 (June 1965): 133–43, and Scott, "New York Inventories, 1665–1775," *NGSQ* 54 (Dec. 1966): 246–49.

188 *Solely to him:* By paying a fine of £500 against his partners' interests to the Dutch government in 1674, NS was thereby considered the owner of those interests under Dutch law. In both will and inventory—written under English law seven years later—listing what was owned in partnership must have been a protective legal stratagem.

189 *"the said Moyetie":* Will of NS.

189 *renounced her claim:* Barck, *Papers of the Lloyd Family,* 1:292–94; SMA, NYU I/140/30.

189 *William Brenton:* Brenton's livestock herds at Point Judith in the Narragansett region were double or triple the size of the Shelter Island herds (more than 1,600 sheep to NS's 427, and eighty horses versus forty), except for cattle, where NS's much larger herd of two hundred against Brenton's forty-nine may indicate an interesting difference in how they made their money, in wool or in salt meat for export. As compared to NS's twenty-four slaves, Brenton listed only five Africans and one Indian. William Brenton will and inventory, Brenton-Mumford Manuscripts, Box 5, Newport Historical Society, cited in Romani, "The Pettaquamscut Purchase," 60.

189 *larger estates:* See Dunn, "The Barbados Census of 1680."

190 *Nathaniel's annual income:* Sample trading activity records, 1654–72: NS, Shelter Island, to JWJr, March 15, 1654, mentions a ship of "300 tunnes" due to arrive soon with salt and English trade goods; NS wishes to load a "psell of staves." MHS *Proc.,* ser. 2, 4: 271–72; NS to JWJr from Rhode Island, July 27, 1654: "Its my hartie desire there may be a trade betwixt us." *WP,* 6:412. NS to JWJr from Shelter Island, October 10, 1654, mentions cattle to be shipped from Fishers Island to Shelter Island, SMA, NYU I/A/140/3. JWJr, Hartford, to Thomas Lake, April 15, 1661, "There is a ship of 300 tunnes at Shelter Iland, fr° Barbados, consigned to Capt Sylvster (its said fr° ye Quakers)." MHS *Colls.,* ser. 5, 8 (1882): 73; Darrett B. Rutman, "Governor

Winthrop's Garden Crop: The Significance of Agriculture in the Early Commerce of Massachusetts Bay," *WMQ*, 3rd ser., 20, no. 3 (July 1963): 409. In Southampton, NS sold goods to Reneck Garison and was to be paid in whale oil, through an agent, Thomas Backer of East Hampton, June 10, 1672, *EHTR* 1: 345–46. Caribbeanist John Pulis made the suggestion that breeding and selling slaves could have been part of the Shelter Island operation. The proposal is not out of the question, since slaves were at a premium in this early period and the practice was not unknown. See Josselyn, *John Josselyn*, 24, for colonist Samuel Maverick's intention to breed Africans for use as slaves. The dollar calculation was made on December 12, 2012, using TheMoneyConverter.com.

190 *the income stream:* On at least one occasion Grizzell assisted a child directly, her second son, Nathaniel II (1661–1705), Brinley Sylvester's father. Contrary to usual practice regarding a jointure or pin money (see Staves, *Married Women's Property Rights*, 155), she helped Nathaniel purchase a house (perhaps in East Hampton, where he lived until 1700 after his marriage to Margaret Hobert of East Hampton) "out of the Rents issues and profits of my jointure." She also gave him "some household stuffs w.ch is now in his possession." Will of GBS; Hoff, "Sylvester Family," 17.

190 *Nathaniel sold a firkin:* Shelter Island Account Book 1658–1768, East Hampton Library, n.p. Side B, page 8, the earliest entry.

190 *Hog Neck:* "Option on Horse Neck Given to Nathaniel Sylvester by John Richbell, 1664[–65]," *Lloyd Papers*, 1:15–16.

190 *the mill at Tom's Creek: STR* 1: 429–30.

190 *other lots:* North Fork and on Block Island. Will of NS.

190 *land in New Jersey:* Edwin Salter, *History of Monmouth and Ocean Counties, New Jersey* (Bayonne: F. Gardner & Son, 1890), 10–25.

190 *A merchant of Newport:* Bridenbaugh, *Fat Mutton*, "Appendix III Rhode Island Merchants 1636–90," 139.

191 *sixty-five acres:* "the planting feeld behinde the Orchard Containeing about fourtie akers and the planting feeld called Mannanduck Containing about twentie five akers." Will of NS, 1680.

191 *meadows and mowing land:* Entry dated April 6, 1678, in *The Second Book of Records of the Town of Southampton, Long Island, N.Y. . . . Including the Records from 1660 to 1717*, William S. Pelletreau, transcriber and ed. (Sag Harbor, NY: John H. Hunt, Printer, 1877), 69–70.

191 *moldboard plow:* Four plows, plowshares and collars, six yokes, and seven iron chains were inventoried for a total value of £4.14.0. Inventory of NS, 1680.

191 *the manor today:* With the exception of tidal marsh, and a few areas labeled "Muck" on the 1978 USDA soil map, the entire 243 acres of Sylvester Manor today—which would have been considered the home grounds—consist of prime soils for agriculture, part of the "Montauk series," mostly fine sandy or silty loams.

191 *"longer than a week":* Interview with Peter Banks.

191 *big, handsome Major:* Both riding and draft horses, almost all of mixed breeds in the colonies, rarely exceeded fifteen hands (the measurement of the breadth of a palm, four inches) or five feet at the withers in the seventeenth century. James E. Kences, "The Horses and Horse Trades of Colonial Boston," *The Dublin Seminar for New England Folk Life, Annual Proceedings* 18 (1993): 73.

12. "Oppression upon the Mind"

193 *The inscription:* For the 1884 monument, see Edward Doubleday Harris, "Ancient Burial Grounds of Long Island, NY," *NEHGR* 54 (1900): 59–61, and Katherine Howlett Hayes, *Slavery Before Race: Europeans, Africans, and Indians at Long Island's Sylvester Manor Plantation, 1651–1884* (New York: New York University Press, 2013), 145–47; Hayes, "Race Histories: Colonial Pluralism and the Production of History at the Sylvester Manor Site, Shelter Island New York," Ph.D. dissertation, University of California, Berkeley, 2008.

193 *slave traders:* Quaker merchant John Grove of Barbados was one of the largest importers of slaves to Barbados, bringing in 1,362 people between 1700 and 1704. Smith, *Slavery, Family, and Gentry Capitalism*, 29–30 and note 76.

193 *"There is that of God in every man":* George Fox, *A Collection of Many Select and Christian Epistles, Letters and Testimonies, Written on Sundry Occasions, by That Ancient, Eminent, Faithful Friend and Minister of Christ Jesus, George Fox* (London, 1698), 117.

193 *"To Friends Beyond Sea":* George Fox, "To Friends Beyond the Sea, That Have Blacks and Indian Slaves," Number 153 (1657), in *The Works of George Fox* (Philadelphia: Marcus T. Gould: 1831), http://www.qhpress.org/texts/oldqwhp/gf-e-toc.htm.

193 *"He that is called in the Lord":* Delivered by Fox in the Barbados Quaker meetinghouse in 1671, the epistle was printed as *Gospel Family-Order, Being a Short Discourse Concerning the Ordering of Families, Both of Whites, Blacks and Indians* (London, 1676), quoted in J. William Frost, *The Quaker Origins of Antislavery* (Norwood, PA: Norwood Editions, 1980), 49.

194 *"Consider with your selves":* Fox, *Gospel Family-Order*, quoted in Frost, *Quaker Origins*, 51.

194 *"the Negars to rebel":* Fox, *To the Ministers, Teachers and Priests (so called and so stileing yourselves) in Barbadoes* (London, 1672), quoted in Kristen Block, "Faith and Fortune: Religious Identity and the Politics of Profit in the Seventeenth-Century Caribbean," Ph.D. dissertation, Rutgers University, 2007, 239.

194 *a few doubts:* Alice Curwen, Letter to Martha Tavernor, delivered on Barbados in 1676, in Curwen, *A Relation of the Labours, Travails and Suffering of that Faithful Servant of the Lord Alice Curwen* (London, 1680), 18; Morgan Godwin, *The Negro's and Indians Advocate, Suing For Their Admission into the Church* (London, 1680); Francis Pastorius, *The German Mennonite Resolution Against Slavery* (Germantown, PA, 1688) (the first formal protest against the practice to be made in the British American colonies); and Aphra Behn, *Oroonoko, or, the Royal Slave* (London, 1688).

194 *"a flash of wit":* Williams and Edmundson held four debates about Quaker tenets in Rhode Island in 1671. Roger Williams, *George Fox Digg'd Out of his Burrowes* (Boston, 1676). For Williams's quote, see Richard L. Greaves, "Edmundson, William (1627–1712)" (*ODNB*, 2004), http://www.oxforddnb.com/view/article/8508.

194 *the first American attack:* Edmundson's attack was preceded by that of Samuel Rishworth on Providence Island, in the Caribbean, in 1633, where English Puritans had founded a colony in 1630 and imported slaves. Kupperman, *Providence Island*, 168–69.

194 *"And many of you":* "A Paragraph of an Epistle from William Edmundson, Dated at Newport the 19th of 7th mo. 1676," *The Friend, or, Advocate of Truth* 3, no. 1 (1834): 9.

197 *"Offensive Carriage Concerning the Saboth":* *NHCR* 2:93.

197 *"prepared ground"*: Rufus M. Jones, *The Quakers in the American Colonies* (London: Macmillan, 1923), 215.

197 *Nathaniel would have been open:* It seems likely that NS knew of the visit to Barbados in 1655 of Ann Austin and Mary Fisher, the first Quakers to visit the American colonies. Both NS and Constant knew Lieut. Col. Lewis Morris, a Barbadian planter, who in 1650 with Constant and Thomas Middleton was punished as a Parliamentarian. Morris escaped to England, and on his return to Barbados he invited the Quaker missionary Henry Fells to visit his plantation; Fells convinced him. Nathaniel's relationship with Morris lasted a lifetime: he interceded on Morris's behalf with the Dutch in New York during the Third Anglo-Dutch War (1673–74); Morris witnessed NS's 1680 will. Lieut. Col. Thomas Rous, a Shelter Island partner in 1651, was convinced as early as 1655 by Fisher and Austin. His son, John, already a Quaker, sailed from Barbados for Rhode Island in October 1657, then traveled in early 1658 from Newport to Southold and New Haven. Therefore it seems extremely likely that by February 1658, NS was already familiar with Quaker doctrine through Morris, or the Rouses, father and son, or was already a Quaker himself. Barbara Ritter Dailey named Constant Sylvester as a Quaker, but there is no evidence; Constant was buried in St. Mary's, the Anglican church in Brampton, Yorkshire, England. Barbara Ritter Dailey, "Morris, Lewis (1613?– 91)" (*ODNB*, 2004), http://www.oxforddnb.com/view/article/71108; I. Gadd and Steven C. Harper, "Rous, John (d. 1695)" (*ODNB*, 2004), http://www.oxforddnb.com/view/article/24175. Also Jones, *Quakers in the American Colonies*, 61–62; Barbara Ritter Dailey, "The Early Quaker Mission and the Settlement of Meetings in Barbados, 1655–1700," *JBMHS* 39 (1991): 27, 29; Larry Gragg, *The Quaker Community on Barbados: Challenging the Culture of the Planter Class* (Columbia: University of Missouri Press, 2009).

197 *opportunity to vote:* Most New England settlements were also governed by a church member "elect." The East End's distance from the center, New Haven, increased opportunities for open dissent. *NHCR* 2:47–51 (November 22, 1653) and *NHCR* 2:58–59 (March 22, 1653).

197 *"high miscariages"*: *NHCR* 2:17, 51.

197 *Ensign John Booth:* By 1652, when the articles of agreement for Shelter Island were signed, Thomas Rous's quarter rights from the 1651 purchase of Shelter and Robins Island had been turned over to John Booth. Booth's descendants still live in Southold today.

197 *"garrison at Southhold"*: *NHCR* 2:51.

197 *Similar threats of revolt*: This paragraph and the next draw on courtroom descriptions in *NHCR* 2:76 and *NHCR* 2:92–93.

198 *eight English Quakers:* William Brand, John Copeland, Christopher Holder, Thomas Thurston, Mary Prince, Sarah Gibbon, Mary Weatherhead, and Dorothy Waugh. Almost all became leaders in the Quaker movement in America. Michael Tepper, ed., *Passengers to America: A Consolidation of Ship Passenger Lists from the New England Historical and Genealogical Register* (Baltimore: Genealogical, 1977), 462; also Jones, *Quakers in the American Colonies*, 36–38; and James Savage, *Genealogical Dictionary of the First Settlers of New England, Showing Three Generations of Those Who Came Before May 1692* (Boston: Little, Brown, 1860), 1:255, https://play.google.com/store/books/details?id=HWEblLuls8kC&rdid=book-HWEblLuls8kC&rdot=1.

198 Speedwell*'s westward voyage:* "Francis Brinsley," Tepper, *Passengers to America*, 462.

198 *"night-journeys"*: See Carla Gerona, "'Like a Horse by the Bridle': Mapping a New World in the Second Half of the Seventeenth Century," Chap. 3 in *Night-Journeys: The Power of Dreams in Quaker Culture*, 70–95 and Introduction (Charlottesville: University of Virginia Press, 2004), for Quakers' interpretations of their dreams and the uses to which they put them.

199 *"a horse by the head"*: Jones, *The Quakers in the American Colonies*, 45–53, quoting Quaker testimony about the voyage of the tiny, unseaworthy *Woodhouse* from Portsmouth, England, to New York.

199 *"In his story"*: Barry Levy, *Quakers and the American Family: British Settlement in the Delaware Valley* (New York and Oxford: Oxford University Press, 1988), 56.

199 *"the flaming sword"*: Fox, *Journal of George Fox*, ed. Nickalls, 27, quoted by Hugh Barbour, *The Quakers in Puritan England* (Richmond, IN: Friends United Press, 1985), 35.

199 *"painful travel [travail]"*: Robert Barclay, *An Apology for the True Christian Divinity, etc.* (London, 1678), Proposition 11, #8, as quoted by Hugh Barbour, *The Quakers in Puritan England* (New Haven: Yale University Press, 1964; Richmond, IN: Friends United Press, 1985), 36.

199 *"an heir to His kingdom"*: Humphrey Norton, writing about his convincement. Humphrey Norton and John Rous, *New England's Ensigne* (London, 1659), one of the first published accounts of the sufferings of the Quakers in New England, quoted in Jones, *Quakers in the American Colonies*, 52.

199 *"It is under my hand"*: Quaker William Brend, in Norton and Rous, *New England's Ensigne*, quoted by Jones, *Quakers in the American Colonies*, 37.

200 *(about $16,000 today)*: Calculated as the buying power of £100 for commodities. But if the value of the sum is calculated against the earnings of the average person in Britain in 1660, then the amount escalates to approximately $222,038. Calculations from Measuringworth.com.

200 *Resident Quakers:* In July 1656, Massachusetts had punished Ann Austin and Mary Fisher under a general law against heretics: in September 1656, New Haven passed legislation forbidding entry to Quakers, Ranters (another radical nonconforming sect), and other heretics, but without specifying punishment. In May 1657, New Haven passed another law, retroactively justifying Norton's punishment. The penalties in New Haven for those who brought Quakers into the colony were half those of Massachusetts and "permitted Quakers to enter . . . to dispatch their lawful business . . . to lose no penny of profit which might accrue to the merchants of the colony through trade with the proprietors of Shelter Island." In October 1657, New Haven passed more repressive legislation. In September 1658, the New England Confederation (which included all the colonies except Rhode Island) was the first to recommend the death sentence for "that accursed and permisious sectt of heretiques." Isabel Macbeath Calder, *The New Haven Colony* (Hamden, CT: Archon, 1970), 95–98; *NHCR* 2:217, 238–41; *Plymouth Colony Records* 10, 155–58, http://plymouthcolony.net/resources/pcr.html.

200 *Puritan apologia:* John Norton, *The Heart of New England Rent* (Cambridge, MA, 1659; London, 1660).

200 *Quakers so toxic:* See Carla Gardina Pestana, "The City upon a Hill Under Siege: The Puritan Perception of the Quaker Threat to Massachusetts Bay, 1656–61," *NEQ* 56 (1983): 323–53, 327–42; Pestana, *Quakers and Baptists in Colonial Massachusetts* (Cambridge, MA: Harvard University Press, 2004), 120–44; Pestana, "City upon a Hill Under Siege," 326, note 6; and for meetinghouse disturbances, 330–31.

200 *Quakers also rejected:* See Mary Maples Dunn, "Saints and Sisters: Congregational and Quaker Women in the Early Colonial Period," in *Women in American Religion*, Janet Wilson James, ed. (Philadelphia: University of Pennsylvania Press, 1980), 27–46, 42, for female Quaker preachers traveling alone; for Fox's beliefs on original sin and the curse of Genesis, see Dunn, "Saints and Sisters," 41 and note 20. After the Restoration, when Quakers united under George Fox to become less radical, women again took second place in the hierarchy. For changes in Quaker attitudes toward women Friends and their domestic and public roles over the next century, see Levy, *Quakers and the American Family*, 5–18.

201 *Quakers were often suspected of witchcraft:* Pestana, "The City upon a Hill Under Siege," 336.

201 *civil disobedience*: See Jonathan Chu, *Neighbors, Friends, or Madmen: The Puritan Adjustment to Quakerism in Seventeenth-century Massachusetts Bay* (Westport, CT: Greenwood Press, 1985), for how the Quakers appeared to Boston authorities; also Jonathan Beecher Field, "The Grounds of Dissent: Heresies and Colonies in New England, 1636–63," vol. 1., Ph.D. dissertation, University of Chicago, 2004. In Barbour, *Quakers in Puritan England*, see chap. 2, "'The Lamb's War': The Quaker Awakening," 33–71, for a summary of the Quakers' formative years.

202 *"The word of ye lord"*: Henry Fell in Barbados to Margaret Fell, January 19, 1656/7. Ms.1.68 Tr. 2, 111, Typescript #366, Library of the Society of Friends, London; printed in Geoffrey F. Nuttall, *Early Quaker Letters from the Swarthmore Mss. to 1660*, Calendared, Indexed, and Annotated by Geoffrey F. Nuttall (privately printed, Library of the Society of Friends, London, 1952), http://www.hallvworthington.com/Persecutions/Part-2.html.

202 *"loose and wild spirit"*: Pestana, "City upon a Hill Under Siege," 333, quoting from Williams's *George Fox Digg'd Out of His Burrowes*.

202 *"they heard me soberly"*: John Taylor, *An Account of Some of the Labours, Exercises, Travels and Perils, by Sea and Land of John Taylor, of York* (London, 1710), 6–7.

203 *"They would . . . pray"*: John Winthrop, "A Short Story of the Rise, Reign, and Ruine of the Antinomians, Familists & Libertines," quoted in David D. Hall, ed., *The Antinomian Controversy, 1636–38: A Documentary History* (Durham, NC: Duke University Press, 1990), 204–5.

203 *"an ocean of darkness and death"*: George Fox, *Journal*, ed. Nickalls, 12, quoted by Barbour, *Quakers in Puritan England*, 35.

203 *whipped:* See Calder, *New Haven Colony*, 96–97; Arthur J. Worrall, *Quakers in the Colonial Northeast* (Hanover, NH: University Press of New England, 1980), 22–24; Humphrey Norton, John Rous, and John Copeland, *New England's Ensigne* (London, 1659); Steven C. Harper and I. Gadd, "Norton, Humphrey (fl. 1655–60)" (*ODNB*, 2004), http://www.oxforddnb.com/view/article/20344.

204 *"I see you say"*: Depositions of John Youngs, Thomas Moore, and John Budd, February 3, 1658; of Edward Preston, same date; and George Deakins, February 12, 1658, *STR* 1:466–68.

204 *"all the ministers"*: Deposition of Giles Sylvester, February 28, 1658, *STR* 1:467–68.

204 *"A Place Called Shelter Island"*: William Robinson to George Fox, July 12, 1659. Ms. vol. 366, Library of the Society of Friends, London.

204 *"Sinke"*: John Woodbridge Jr. to Richard Baxter, in "Woodbridge-Baxter Correspondence," ed. Raymond Phineas Stearns, *NEQ* 10 (1937): 573.

205 *independent status:* Griswold, "Nathaniel Sylvester of Amsterdam and Shelter Island," 1–3. Faren Siminoff, author of *Crossing the Sound*, concurs, saying, "I agree that neither New Haven nor Connecticut would have had any claim of jurisdiction to Shelter Island . . . There is no legal nexus that I can see between Shelter Island to New Haven despite the fact that New Haven may have later regretted passing on the island and then tried to take jurisdiction through 'the back door' so to speak. The precedent for Shelter Island and the other areas on Long Island as being able to voluntarily align (or not) themselves with a southern New England colony is seen both on Gardiners Island as well as Southampton." Siminoff, pers. comm., July 16, 2008.

205 *"As the Lord gives the opportunity"*: Thomas Brucksupp of Little Normanton, July 1, 1664, to John Bowne, Flushing, Long Island. Norman Penney, ed., *The Journal of the Friends' Historical Society* 9 (London: Swarthmore Press, 1912), 13–14.

205 *"in much Love and Tenderness"*: Taylor, *An Account of Some of the Labours*, 8.

205 *Lawrence and Cassandra Southwick:* Will of Lawrence Southwick, written July 10, 1659, "in presence of Nathaniell Silvester" and recorded November 29, 1660. Savage, *A Genealogical Dictionary*, 4:91. See Carla Giardina Pestana, *Quakers and Baptists*, 25–31, for Salem Quakers and the Southwicks. For other versions of their story, see Jones, *Quakers in American Colonies*, 67–70, and Quaker poet James Greenleaf Whittier's "Cassandra Southwick" and "Banished from Massachusetts. 1660. On a Painting by E. A. Abbey," *The Writings of John Greenleaf Whittier* (Boston: Riverside Press, 1888), 1:65–75, 419–21, http://books.google.com/books/reader?id=iCIqAAAAYAAJ&printsec=frontcover&output=reader&pg=GBS.PA366. Whittier was a close friend of the Horsfords and visited them on Shelter Island.

205 *she had traveled further*: Given the freedom that women found as Quakers, and the equality of status Quakers held out to women, one may consider the possibility that Grizzell was the first of the couple to be convinced.

206 *on the Quaker map*: "I suppose you have heard of the Quakers ship that arrived at Capt. Silvesters + came over wth him to New London and thence to Rhode Island . . . they were but 7 weeks as I heare from England." JWJr to John Richards, Hartford, December 12, 1659, MHS *Colls.*, ser. 5, 8 (1882): 55; "There is a ship of 300 tunnes at Shelter Iland, fro Barbados, consigned to Capt Sylvester (its said fro ye Quakers)," JWJr to Thomas Lake, Hartford, April 15, 1661, MHS *Colls.*, ser. 5, 8 (1882): 73.

13. Quaker Martyrs, Quaker Peace

207 *Antinomian Controversy:* Martin Luther coined the term to condemn teachings by his former follower, John Agricola, who (in Germany in 1535) countered the Vatican's emphasis on works as the means of salvation by stating, as the Reverend Walter Farquhar Hook wrote, "that good works do not promote salvation, nor evil works hinder it." Hook, *A Church Dictionary* (London: John Murray, 1858), 33. The doctrine surfaced again in seventeenth-century England, where it provided the background for the Massachusetts Puritans to condemn the Hutchinsonians as dangerously immoral. Flung about loosely, the term became an epithet used against those whose politics as well as religious beliefs were unorthodox. John Milton grouped Anabaptism, Familism, and Antinomianism together as "fanatick dreams." Milton, *The Doctrine and Discipline of Divorce* (London, 1644; London: Pickering, 1851).

207 *Anne Hutchinson:* Anne Hutchinson's challenge to the Boston hegemony was not the first; Roger Williams was banished in 1636 for, among other points, denying the

colony's right to compel obedience to the Puritan church, and for questioning the limits of ministerial authority, a point Hutchinson also made. Besides arguing for the effects of grace, she also spoke out for the rights of a congregation to appoint its own ministers, rather than having them appointed by the state. See Berkin, *First Generations*, 37–41. Bernard Bailyn and other historians take the view that the Massachusetts schism also reflected a major struggle between the merchant contingent in Boston and the public authorities over the definition of the limits of acceptable business conduct. Bailyn, *The New England Merchants in the Seventeenth Century* (Cambridge, MA: Harvard University Press, 1979), 39–41. See Hall, *Antinomian Controversy, 1636–38* for all documents relevant to the controversy and an understanding of the process.

207 *"a haughty and fierce carriage"*: John Winthrop, *A Short Story of the Rise, Reign, and Ruine of the Antinomians, Familists & Libertines* (London, 1644), in Hall, *Antinomian Controversy*, 263–64.

207 *found Hutchinson guilty*: "A Report of the Trial of Mrs. Anne Hutchinson Before the Church in Boston," in Hall, *Antinomian Controversy*, 372.

208 *Winthrop circulated*: Although the print version of the "monstrous births" was not published until 1644, the news was quickly circulated by JWJr (and doubtless by others) in private correspondence in 1638. For various contemporary views of the two births at a time when monstrous births were being attributed to natural explanations (thanks to "the new science") as well as to older beliefs crediting supernatural intervention or the appearance of "marvels," see Anne Jacobson Schutte, "'Such Monstrous Births': A Neglected Aspect of the Antinomian Controversy," *Renaissance Quarterly* 38, no. 1 (Spring 1985): 8, n9 and 85–106.

208 *"30. [sic] monstrous births"*: Thomas Weld, Preface, added to the second edition of Winthrop's *A Short Story*, Hall, *Antinomian Controversy*, 214.

209 *"comely young woman"*: Winthrop, *A Short Story*, 280. A quarter century later, the Quaker leader and polemicist George Bishop described her as "a comely and grave Woman, of goodly personage and of good report." George Bishop, *New-England Judged by the Spirit of the Lord in Two Parts* (London, 1661; Philadelphia: Thomas William Stuckey, Printer, ca. 1885), https://play.google.com/books/reader?id=67kTAAAAYAAJ&printsec=frontcover&output=reader&authuser=0&hl=en&pg=GBS.PA103, 119.

209 *"person of no mean extract"*: Gerard Croese, *The General History of the Quakers* (London: John Dunton, 1696), quoted in Ruth Talbot Plimpton, *Mary Dyer: Biography of a Rebel Quaker* (Boston: Branden, 1994), 11. Croese, writing some thirty years after Dyer's death, probably drew on Bishop's descriptions of Dyer in *New-England Judged*.

209 *Quakers from all over New England*: Pestana, *Quakers and Baptists*, 32–33.

209 *"hand in hand"*: Bishop, *New-England Judged*, 103.

210 *to Boston*: In a letter to the Boston authorities pleading for his wife's life, William Dyer stated, "I have not seen her above this half yeare . . . so itt is from Shelter Island about by Pequid [New London] Narragansett and the Towne of Providence she secrettly and speedyly journyed, and as secretly from thence to y^{or} jurisdiction." William Dyer to the Boston Magistrates, May 27, 1660, Portsmouth, Rhode Island, quoted in Plimpton, *Biography of a Rebel Quaker*, 184.

210 *"She did hang as a Flag"*: Edward Burrough, *A Declaration of the Sad and Great Persecution and Martyrdom of the People of God called Quakers in New-England, for the Worshipping of God* (London: Robert Wilson, 1661), 30, http://digitalcommons.unl.edu/cgi/viewcontent.cgi?article=1023&context=etas.

210 *English Friends:* Chu, *Neighbors, Friends, or Madmen*, 86. The earliest petition, dated December 19, 1660, was held by the Council for Foreign Plantations for five months. The injunction against further persecution of Quakers reached Massachusetts after Leddra's execution.

210 *to the king:* "Petition of the Quakers at the Court at Whitehall the Viiith day of April 1661," TNA: PRO, America and West Indies Colonial Papers, 1661, CO 1/15 31 (ff.60–61). Giles, the only Long Islander to sign, and much less prominent in Friends' affairs than the other three, quite possibly had been an eyewitness to the Boston executions.

211 *the petition ground its way:* For progress through the bureaucracy, see entries for meetings on March 25, April 1, April 25, May 20, June 17, and June 23, 1661, all attended by Thomas Middleton. TNA: PRO, America and West Indies Colonial Papers, 1661, *Journal of the Council for Foreign Plantations,* CO1/15 (ff.153–58).

211 *appended to which was a note:* Field, "The Grounds of Dissent," 267.

211 *mandamus:* The writ was signed by Charles II on September 8, 1661. Called after the Latin verb *mandamus*, meaning "we command," a writ of mandamus is a court order from one court or official to another court or official to perform a certain action. In this case, the command was to cease capital punishment and other corporal persecution and to send any accused to England for trial instead of standing trial in Massachusetts.

211 *"The King's Missive": Writings of John Greenleaf Whittier,* 1:381–86, http://books.google.com/books/reader?id=iCIqAAAAYAAJ&printsec=frontcover&output=reader&pg=GBS.PA366.

211 *"With a prosperous gale:" George Fox: An Autobiography,* ed. Rufus M. Jones (Philadelphia: Ferris & Leach, 1903), 161, https://play.google.com/books/reader?id=SsthpbX3ZyUC&printsec=frontcover&output=reader&authuser=0&hl=en&pg=GBS.PA160.w.0.3.0.

211 *"Governor John Endicott's door": George Fox: An Autobiography,* 161.

212 *"We shall obey":* The entire previous paragraph is taken virtually word for word from *George Fox: An Autobiography,* 161.

212 *exclusively Puritan rule had ended:* After Charles II's show of tolerance, persecution of Quakers increased over the next decade in England, concluding with the Conventicle Act of 1670 in England, which forbade gatherings of sects not in accordance with the Anglican Church.

212 *"slanderous & blasphemous letter":* The timing of NS's letter—which unfortunately has not been found—and the collecting of New Haven's accusations against him for this court sitting suggest that New Haven considered that the Quaker situation was moving rapidly out of control and that Shelter Island had become an important sanctuary. *NHCR* 2:364, 380, 416.

212 *"written with his owne hand": NHCR* 2:364, 380, 416.

213 *Nathaniel failed to turn up:* October 17, 1660, *NHCR* 2:380; May 27, 1661, *NHCR* 2:412.

213 *"divers persons under the Government":* Giles outlines the history of the sale as the basis for the island's separate jurisdictional status, concluding that when New Haven "endeavored to bring the Petitioner and other Inhabitants on the Island under their Jurisdiction . . . your Petitioner well knowing they had not right so to do did refuse to yield obedience thereunto." That the petition frames the sale of Shelter Island to "Colonel Thomas Middleton Esq. who by himself and partners did at their very great charges settle a Plantation upon the said Island" reinforces the idea that Giles and

Middleton worked together in London on Shelter Island's behalf. Middleton sat on the Council for Foreign Plantations when Giles's petition was submitted. "The Humble Petition of Gyles Silvester, Merchant for and on behalf of himself and divers other of the inhabitants of Shelter Island near the Colony of New Haven in New England," TNA: PRO, America and West Indies Colonial Papers 1660, CO 1/14 No. 65 (f.189).

213 *Captain Ralph Goldsmith:* In 1665 in Southold, Ralph Goldsmith, "Sea Captain of London," purchased more than three hundred acres of land, a meadow lot, and eight acres of "upland . . . and meadow" near the point "apposite to the ____[?] necke of Shelter Island." One of the deeds was witnessed by Joshua Sylvester and one "Sampson," perhaps Latimer Sampson, who styled himself "of Oysterbay upon Long Island" and who partnered with NS in the purchase of Horse Neck, now Lloyd's Neck, near Oyster Bay, New York, and had been engaged to marry Grizzell Sylvester before his death in 1668. It is possible that the Sylvesters were attempting (unsuccessfully) to shape their own East End Quaker community. Goldsmith was "received as an inhabitant so behaving himself as a naybor" in Southold, but he never built a house or lived there. See *STR* 1:233–35, 357; 2:150, for Goldsmith deeds.

214 *"After we had stayed"*: George Fox, *The Journal*, ed. Nigel Smith (London: Penguin, 1998), 458.

215 *"in a great barn full of people"*: For this quote, and quotes in the following paragraph, see Fox, *Journal* (Smith edition), 456–58 and 461–62.

215 *"and yet by the continued coming in"*: Ibid., 426.

215 *"tender Plants"*: Public Friend Alice Curwen addressed "An Epistle to Nathaniel Sylvester and his Wife, at Shelter-Island" in which she exhorted the Sylvesters, as "Friends" and as "those who are Parents," to "watch over your Children in the Fear of the Lord, and keep them to Plainness of Speech." Curwen, *A Relation of the Labours*, 13.

216 *"at Shelter Island"*: Fox, *Journal* (Smith edition), 459.

216 *"many of the world"*: Ibid.

216 *"a very great fog"*: Ibid.

217 *Fewer than a thousand:* Richter, *Before the Revolution*, 286.

217 *"So must we be one as they are"*: Gardiner, *Relation of the Pequot Warres*, 25.

217 *Winthrop's emissary:* Matthias Nicolls to JWJr, March 7, 1675, Winthrop Family Papers, MHS.

217 *"The Spirit of Christ"*: Barbour, *Quakers in Puritan England*, 206.

14. "A Duchman in His Hartt"

219 *"provisions of the country"*: For this paragraph, see O'Callaghan and Fernow, *Documents Relative to the Colonial History of the State of New York*, 2:587–88. The Dutch confiscated NS's partners' shares on the grounds of damages they had suffered when the English conquered New Netherland in 1664. The rest of the list of goods was compiled from Winthrop Family Papers, Calder's *New Haven Colony*, and Southold and New Haven town records as being typical of what would have been at the manor in February 1674.

219 *"Horses and Mares, Cattle, sheep, hogs"*: Will of NS.

220 *Long Islanders had chafed:* Donald Shomette, "Empire Strikes Back: On the East End in 1674," lecture delivered at East Hampton Library, East Hampton, NY, Sept. 12, 1998, http://www.easthamptonlibrary.org/pdfs/history/lectures/19980912.pdf.

221 *"houses, lands, movables"*: O'Callaghan and Fernow, *Documents Relative to the Colonial History of the State of New York*, 2:587.

221 *pragmatic realignment with the Dutch*: Morris and Gardiner had none of NS's obvious Dutch connections; there is no evidence they were viewed as traitors. O'Callaghan and Fernow, *Documents Relative to the Colonial History of the State of New York*, 2:645, 664 for Morris, and 2:587 for Gardiner. Morris was a witness to NS's will.

222 *"I understand Captt Sylvester"*: Richard Smith Jr., in Wickford, September 5, 1673, to JWJr, in Updike, *Richard Smith*, 100–1.

222 *"submit as dutiful subjects"*: O'Callaghan and Fernow, *Documents Relative to the Colonial History of the State of New York*, 2:645.

222 *"the Poore in their Cottages"*: Quoted by Shomette, "Empire Strikes Back."

222 *"reduce or destroy"*: Fitz John Winthrop, in Southold, report to Captain John Allyn, February 25, 1674. MHS *Colls.*, ser. 5, 8 (1882): 30:91.

223 *"himself in no condition"*: Ibid.

223 *"prevent the shedding of blood"*: Fitz John Winthrop report to Captain John Allyn, MHS *Colls.*, ser. 5, 8 (1882): 30:91.

224 *"Capt. Sylvester being returned"*: Winthrop, February 25, 1674, in Southold to Capt. John Allyn, MHS *Colls.*, ser. 5, 8 (1882): 30: 91.

224 *persuaded the Dutch*: Other details of the engagement from Shomette, "Empire Strikes Back," and from O'Callaghan and Fernow, *Documents Relative to the Colonial History of the State of New York*, 2:656. For a possible construction of Dutch commander Eewoutsen's motives, see Shomette: "But for troops in open boats, Eewoutsen considered, the defender's fire was all too hot. Thinking better of conducting a costly assault on a town that would only continue to refuse subjugation, he called off the attack. Soon afterwards he ordered anchors raised and all sail made for New Orange."

224 *"Favoirs that have so liberally"*: NS, Shelter Island, May 9, 1674, to JWJr, Hartford, MHS *Proc.* 2, 4 (1887–89): 274. This letter, delivered by Nathaniel's first cousin, Isaac Arnold, tells Winthrop (who was probably already aware of the news) that the English and Dutch have made peace.

225 *sensitivity:* To ward off any threat to their autonomy, the Sylvesters retained the slippery Captain John Scott as an overseas agent 1661–62, presumably to ward off attempts to include Shelter Island in the Connecticut Patent. Scott, generally regarded as a transatlantic con artist, lost favor with the Sylvesters, however; by 1664 Giles Sylvester wrote to JWJ about Scott's "Unhuman and Unheard of perfidiones" and his "lying and Wicked Corses." Black, *Younger John Winthrop*, 236; Giles Sylvester, June 28, 1664, Barbados, to JWJr, Hartford, MHS *Proc.* 2, 4 (1887–89): 280; Giles Sylvester, S Jr., Hartford, MHS *Proc.* 2, 4 (1887–89): 278.

225 *"uncomfortable oppositions"*: "But if any misunderstanding hath beene in any kinds, I beseech you to forbeare any further proceedings, about M[r] Sylvesters or parts towards the Dutch, or any other places, in respect whereof these may be uncomfortable opositions and litigious controversies raised." JWJr, London, March 4, 1662 (3?), to John Mason, Deputy Governor, Connecticut, Hartford. MHS *Colls.*, ser. 5, 8 (1882): 77, quoted in Black, *Younger John Winthrop*, 239.

225 *"fitt testimony"*: JWJr to Fitz John Winthrop, Hartford, October 23, 1673, MHS *Colls.*, ser. 5, 8 (1882): 158.

225 *By May 1674*: See Shomette, "The Empire Strikes Back," for a full account of the peace treaty contracted overseas, the arrival of a copy of the document, and the

arrival of Edmund Andros, the incoming English governor, who had been appointed in July 1677.

225 *end of the Dutch empire:* The treaty was ratified by the Dutch State-General on March 4, 1674. Because communications by sea were uncertain and slow, on February 23–24, when the Southold engagement took place, the participants were unaware that a peace treaty between Great Britain and the Netherlands had been signed in England. For background to the war, see Henry L. Schoolcraft, "The Capture of New Amsterdam," *English Historical Review* 22, no. 88 (1907): 674–93, http://ehr.oxfordjournals.org/content/XXII/LXXXVIII/674.citation.

226 *customs inspectors:* The seventeenth-century Navigation Acts were intended to restrict the nationality of vessels and the kinds of goods that could be shipped, and how. The first Act (1651) was intended to injure the Dutch trade; gradually emphasis shifted to control of the relationship between colonists and the mother country: trade was supposed to benefit Britain, not the colonists.

226 *Shippers and merchants:* The long colonial coastline made enforcement expensive and almost impossible, however, so that the Acts were an irritant but not a bar to what became a deep-rooted habit of illegal trade. See Calder, *New Haven Colony,* 166–68; Victor Enthoven and Wim Klooster, "The Rise and Fall of the Virginia-Dutch Connection in the Seventeenth Century," in *Early Modern Virginia: Reconsidering the Old Dominion,* eds. Douglas Bradburn and John C. Coombs (Charlottesville: University of Virginia Press, 2011), 105–14; and Barrow, *Trade and Empire,* 4–19.

226 *"an auxiliary to landowning":* Bernard Bailyn, *New England Merchants,* 55, 102.

227 *"as if the said Child so doeing":* Will of NS.

227 *left all his property to his fiancée:* Will of Latimer Sampson, Oct. 18, 1666. SMA, NYU I/A/140/7. For Sampson's connections to Bristol, see Roger Hayden, "The Records of a Church of Christ in Bristol, 1640–1687" (Bristol: Bristol Record Society 23 [1974]).

227 *Patience:* Patience (1664–1719) married Benjamin L'Hommedieu in 1684. Giles and Hannah Savage Gillam were married in 1686 by Laurent van der Bosch, the first Anglican minister in Boston. Nathaniel II (1661–1705) was baptized in January 1683 by New York Colony's English chaplain, Dr. John Gordon. Nathaniel's witness was William Nicoll, his brother Giles's executor. Hoff, "Sylvester Family," 17, 18; Washington Chauncy Ford, "Ezekiel Carré and the French Church of Boston," MHS *Proc.* 3, 52 (1918–19): 122–24; mimeograph copy of Nathaniel II's baptismal certificate, "Legal affirmation #402," SIHS. All three married or converted after NS's death but before that of GBS (1687).

227 *married a Matthew Carey:* D. Brenton Simons, "Bigamy in Boston: The Case of Matthew Cary and Mary Sylvester," *NEHGR* 159 (Jan. 2005): 5–11.

227 *brother Giles petitioned:* See Simons, "Bigamy in Boston," petition of Gyles Sylvester, stating that Matthew Carey, acquitted of the charge of bigamy for want of evidence, "continues to live with the sister of the petitioner, and asking that it be prevented till proof is received that the other wife is dead, etc.," dated Nov. 17, 1698. For desertion and divorce in Massachusetts, see Saxton, *Being Good,* 71–74.

15. "Children of the Founders"

229 *"the ultimate goal":* Dennis Piechota, "The Laboratory Excavation of a Soil Block from Sylvester Manor," *Historical Archaeology of Sylvester Manor,* 84.

232 *When organic matter:* Piechota, "Soil Block," 92; Griswold Papers, Fales Library, NYU, 2003.

232 *she did not swear:* A typed version dated Dec. 11, 1911, of NS's inventory states: "I, Grissell [*sic*] Sylvester, widdow and executrix . . . doe testifie that in March last past 1680 I did give into the Apprizers . . . a full and just inventory of the estate of my husband deceased for the truth of which (being a person that cannot take an oath for conscience sake) I have here-unto sett my hand this 3 day of Nov. 1681 on Shelter Island." SMA, NYU, V/A/118/28.

232 *We don't know:* Directions to prove her will were issued on Sept. 10, 1687, with a probate inventory for her taken by a William Brinley, either her youngest brother or her nephew, on Oct. 12, 1687, on Shelter Island. Barck, *Papers of the Lloyd Family* 1:113; Hoff, "Sylvester Family," 16–17; *Books of General Entries of the Colony of New York 1674–88*, ed. Peter R. and Florence A. Christoph (Baltimore: Genealogical Publishing Co. for the Holland Society of New York, 1982), 390; Scott, *Genealogical Data*, 148.

232 *His brothers Peter and Constant:* Peter died at thirty-three, Constant at twenty-five. Will of Peter Sylvester, Feb. 22, 1696, proved Suffolk County, Mar. 14, 1696, New York County Wills 5:152; will of Constant Sylvester, October 26, 1695, proved Mar. 2, 1697, SMA, NYU I/A/140/26.

233 *died of unknown causes:* His share of land was transferred to the common land of his four brothers.

233 *sporadic accounts of payments for farm work:* Giles's dealings with Black John, who was mentioned as a slave in NS's 1680 will, were set up as a separate "line" in a farm account book. But only two entries are noted, both in September (harvest time) 1688, each for two shillings and paid in cider. That he was paid underlines the variability of a slave's status: was he paid as a slave for extra labor, or as a freedman? Shelter Island Account Book, 1658–1768, East Hampton Library.

233 *"husbandman":* Giles Sylvester to Edward Downing, December 1, 1693, Suffolk County Deeds, Liber A:161, Riverhead County Clerk's Office, Riverhead, NY.

234 *The historian David Hackett Fischer:* Fischer, *Albion's Seed*, 98.

234 *sold off:* In the 1680s, Long Island land prices rose in light of new demand for grain. Instead of branching out to other West Indian markets besides Barbados (where demand was lessening) and increasing the island's own grain production, Giles and Nathaniel responded to the pressure to produce more grain by selling land to others who wished to take advantage of the new markets. See Sung Bok Kim, *Landlord and Tenant in Colonial New York*, 27–28.

234 *"sometime of Shelter Island":* Simons, "Bigamy in Boston," 7; Massachusetts State Archives, Suffolk Files, case 3766, second paper.

234 *"The children of the Founders":* Bailyn, *Merchants*, 109, note 89, 216.

234 *a judge of the Court of Common Pleas:* Wills of six Southampton or Southold residents were proved before Giles Sylvester, Esq., in 1706 and 1707. Abstracts of wills, New-York Historical Society (*WNYHS*), 1:425, 427–29, 434, 438.

235 *Giles fought back:* On July 16, 1692, the New York Council ordered Suffolk County to desist from levying taxes. The question should have been moot by 1692, as manors had been incorporated into a colonywide administrative system by means of the act of May 13, 1691. But perhaps because there were many gray areas concerning manor patents in general, the Sylvesters' 1692 petition was granted. Giles Sylvester III, Shelter Island, to Fitz John Winthrop, New London, October 27, 1683, MHS *Proc.* 2, 4 (1887–89): 29;

NY Council Minutes 5:87; N.Y. Col. Mss. 38:155; *Journal of General Assembly*, I:77–79; *NY Council Min.* 6:111/2; NY Col. Mss. 38:155. (*N.Y. Col. Laws*, I: 237–38.)

235 *letters he wrote*: Giles Sylvester III, Shelter Island, Oct. 1, 1674, to Fitz John Winthrop, in New London, *WP* 19:27; Giles Sylvester III, Shelter Island, Aug. 19, 1677, to Wait Winthrop, Boston, MHS *Proc.* 2, 4 (1887–89): 287.

235 *"English as only British colonials can be English"*: Bailyn, *New England Merchants*, 194.

235 *"As for Mr. Sylvester's living"*: Hannah Sylvester, in Boston, to William Nicoll, April 25, 1709, SIHS 1973.31–103.

235 *"the ideal of a cultivated"*: Bushman, *Refinement of America*, xii.

235 *"Brother G: S: [Giles] owed Camble"*: Barck, *Papers of the Lloyd Family*, 1:116.

236 *"all that messuage"*: Giles Sylvester to Ephraim Savage and James Lloyd, August 10, 1689, GSDD 10. Savage was Hannah's father and Lloyd was Giles's brother-in-law, married to Grizzell Sylvester.

237 *all his remaining property*: Will of Giles Sylvester, March 12, 1707, proved June 19, 1708, *NY Co. Wills* 7:375.

237 *"after my said Debts are paid"*: Will of Giles Sylvester.

237 *"the mansion house of Capt. Nathaniel Sylvester"*: February 5, 1719, Suffolk County Deeds, Liber B part 1:169.

237 *one of the four children*: The four were not identified by name in NS's will, but two, Obium and Tom, are later named in the trail of documents during the 1680s and '90s transferring the boys from one Sylvester family member to another. Will of NS.

237 *It was not uncommon*: Philip D. Morgan, writing about later colonial South Carolina runaways, states, "Those said to be visiting relatives, friends, or acquaintances outnumbered those attempting permanent escape by about four to one." The Connecticut slave and later freedman Venture Smith ran away twice, returning the first time (1754) to his former master, and the second, in the 1760s, when he was to be sold upstate, finding a new master in Stonington, where most of his family lived. Philip Morgan, "Colonial South Carolina Runaways: Their Significance for Slave Culture," in *Slavery & Abolition: A Journal of Slave and Post-Slave Studies* 6:3 (1985), 57–78, 67. Venture Smith, *A Narrative of the Life and Adventures of Venture Smith, etc.* (Whitefish, MT: Kessinger Publishing, 1996), chap. 2.

237 *the stretch of New England*: Legitimate travels on a master's business (in addition to sales from one owner to another), along with interactions with the large free black population in the North and with indentured whites, gave many slaves during the first century of Northern colonial slavery (1650–1750) a surprisingly wide knowledge of seventeenth-century geography: its roads, ports, county towns, and countryside. See Berlin, *Many Thousands Gone*, 56–60 and note 29 (chap. 2).

237 *"to find the horse"*: Barck, *Papers of the Lloyd Family*, 1:144; *Boston News-Letter*, no. 87, Dec. 17, 1705.

238 *"negro man named Obium"*: Ibid., 1:121, "Inventory of James Lloyd's Estate . . . September 22, 1693."

238 *"unwilling to part with us"*: Nelson to Lloyd, January 31, 1710, in Barck, *Papers of the Lloyd Family*, 1:187–88.

238 *"practical consciousness"*: Anthony Giddens, *The Constitution of Society* (Berkeley: University of California Press, 1984), xxiii, quoted by Fitts, "Northern Bondage," 59.

239 *more clothes*: See Hodges and Brown, *"Pretends to be Free:" Runaway Slave Advertisements from Colonial and Revolutionary New York and New Jersey* (New York: Taylor & Francis, 1994), xxxii. On the other hand, Edgar McManus writes that in various

periods "slaves were well clad for all sorts of weather," that "clothes were a considerable expense of slaveholding," and that some masters "provided their slaves with 'Sunday clothes' for special occasions besides ordinary working clothes for the job." McManus, *Black Bondage*, 93.

239 *"A Great Coate"*: Nelson to Lloyd, January 31, 1710, Barck, *Papers of the Lloyd Family*, 1:187–88.

239 *"curious old hymnbook"*: "Curious Old Hymnbook and Buried Golden Treasure at Huntington, the Volume that Once Belonged to a Slave," *The Brooklyn Eagle*, September 16, 1888.

240 *Recent research:* Sondra S. O'Neale, *Jupiter Hammon and the Biblical Beginnings of African American Literature* (Metuchen, NJ: American Theological Library Association and the Scarecrow Press, 1993), 20–22; also see Margaret A. Brucia, "The African-American Poet, Jupiter Hammon: A Home-born Slave and His Classical Name," *International Journal of the Classical Tradition* 7, no. 4 (Spring 2001): 517; Bolton and Metcalf, "The Migration of the Jupiter Hammon Family," *LIHJ*, May 2013.

240 *"if any be afflicted"*: James 5:13.

241 *a "single event"*: On June 4, 2002, Steve Mrozowski characterized as rapid deposition the fill in some of the postholes in front of the house as against the spread of the midden which took place over time: "Its consistency (of the fill) tells you it was a single event—and this one was fairly fast." Griswold Papers, Fales Library, NYU.

241 *The house and everything around it:* The description in this and the next sentence is based on Hayes, "Field Archaeology," 42, 45, 46, and Gary, "Material Culture," 101.

241 *Brinley is a thrifty man:* Gary, "Material Culture," 101.

242 *hauled out:* Timbers cut and shaped for new construction were used quickly because the joints would tighten together as the green wood dried, Robert Hefner, pers. comm., 2006. The dendrochronology data collected in 2004 on construction timbers for seven East End houses indicated that most were utilized within a year of felling. Sylvester Manor, one of the two inhabited houses in the sample, was unable to supply enough datable timbers because it was decided that the investigation would have caused too much household upheaval for Mrs. Fiske. D.W.H. Miles and M. J. Worthington, with Edward Cook and Paul Krusic, "Oxford Dendrochronology Laboratory Interim Report 2006/47: 'The Tree-Ring Dating of Historic Buildings from Eastern Long Island, New York'" (Oxford: Oxford Dendrochronology Lab, December 2006), http://www.hvva.org/Long%20Island%20dendro%20report.pdf.

16. Illusion and Reality

243 *coterie:* Berkeley's planned college in Bermuda was never granted funding. The English portraitist John Smibert, who painted Dean Berkeley and "the Bermuda group," also painted Brinley's cousin, Colonel Francis Brinley, and his wife; David Chesebrough, Brinley Sylvester's son-in-law; and Andrew Oliver, Brinley's cousin.

243 An Essay Towards a New Theory of Vision: *An Essay Towards a New Theory of Vision* was first published in 1709; M. A. Stewart, "Berkeley, George (1685–1753)" (*ODNB*, 2004), http://www.oxforddnb.com/view/article/2211.

244 *rational dominion:* Until the last quarter of the eighteenth century, the American elite generally admired landscape views from the safety of a drive, or from a formally planted enclosure.

244 *from the front door to the main road:* See "Shelter Island in 1870," ca. 1928, attributed to Ralph G. Duvall, for Brinley's original drive.

244 *moved to Newport:* Nathaniel II and Margaret Hobert Sylvester may have lived with relatives. See an indenture between Francis Brinley (Nathaniel's uncle) and Francis and James Carr, Aug. 19, 1701, for the division of a house "by ye harbour" owned in common, as well as two parcels of land into two parts, each with "two cellars, two lower rooms, two chanbers [*sic*] and two garrets." "Abstracts from Rhode Island Colonial Land Evidence," *Newport Historical Magazine* 2 (1881–82): 223–26.

244 *"landskips":* Essayist Joseph Addison (1672–1719) first wrote on the theory of "natural gardening" in 1712 in *The Spectator.* Americans followed the English lead some forty years later. Horace Walpole, *A History of the Modern Taste in Gardening* (1771 / pub. 1780), reprinted in John Dixon Hunt and Peter Willis, eds., *The Genius of the Place, etc.* (New York: Harper & Row, 1975), 313.

245 *The local library:* For books purchased in London by Abraham Redwood for the lending library named after him in Newport, see Alice Brayton, "Rhode Island," in *Gardens of Colony and State* I: 221.

245 *prenuptial agreement:* Giles Sylvester to Ephraim Savage and James Lloyd, August 10, 1689, GSDD 1:10; Col. Francis Brinley (II) to Brinley Sylvester, Mar. 14, 1720, GSDD 11. See also William Sanford (cousin), Newport, to Brinley Sylvester, Apr. 19, 1720, East Hampton Library.

245 *a new will:* Will of Wm. Nicoll, March 19, 1719—probate Aug. 27, 1723, NY Co., NY Will Book vol. 9, 565, and "The Nicoll Family of Islip Grange, etc.," Rosalie Fellows Bailey (Order of Colonial Lords of Manors in America, n.d.).

245 *The sell-off:* For land sales 1652–1733, see Barbara Schwartz and Mac Griswold, in cooperation with the University of Massachusetts Boston, and the Shelter Island Historical Society, "Shelter Island, New York, Land Acquisition and Dispersal, 1652–1733," 2000, typescript, SIHS.

245 *continued to live on the North Fork:* Rev. Jacob E. Mallmann, *Historical Papers on Shelter Island and Its Presbyterian Church* (Shelter Island: Shelter Island Public Library, 1985 reprint. First published New York: A. M. Bustard, 1899), 39–40.

246 *no town government was set up:* Until 1666, when the island was confirmed as a manor, Shelter Islanders had recorded deeds in Southold and attended that town's annual meetings, but they had no voting privileges.

246 *commanded the handful:* Mallmann, *Historical Papers on Shelter Island*, 39–40. In November 1683 the island was set off as a township, but no action was taken to form a government until 1730, when it was forced to do so by the act passed on July 12, 1729.

246 *"Mr. Silvester's island": The Diary of Joshua Hempstead*, 206. By the time Brinley regained his confirmed possession of property on Shelter Island in 1735, the island had been incorporated as a town in 1730. Without insisting on any manorial rights per se, Brinley nonetheless became de facto "lord of the manor," serving in local and regional positions all his life.

246 The Sea Lions: Cooper probably visited the Nicoll family at Sachem's Neck. Wayne Franklin, author of *James Fenimore Cooper: The Early Years* (New Haven: Yale University Press, 2007), pers. comm. 2005.

246 *in 1735, the verdict:* "Wednesday Oct 22nd, 1735, Brinley Sylvester ag. Patrick Lithgow *ex dem* [on the demise of] Wm Nicoll . . . On Motion of Mr. Murray the Court gives Judgement for the plaintiff for four fifths of the Tenements in the Declaration," New York Supreme Court of Judicature Minute Book: March 13,

1732/33–October 23, 1739, p. 189, Municipal Archives, New York City; Dwight, Ruth, vs. Sylvester Brinley, Feb. 1735, Supreme Court Judgments, P-216B-1 (Ruth Dwight was William Nicoll's mistress and mother of John Nicoll, William's illegitimate son, who would have inherited the manor had Nicoll won the case), New York Judgment Index Retrieval System; "Legal documents: Patrick Lithgow, Heir to William Nicoll, Son and Heir to Benjamin Nicoll vs Brinley Sylvester," SMA, NYU I/140/36, 37; legal opinion, B. Sylvester v. Wm. Nicoll 1735, GSDD 15.

246 *Nicoll:* William Smith Pelletreau, *A History of Long Island: From Its Earliest Settlement to the Present Time* (New York: Lewis Publishing Company, 1905), 2:234–36.

246 *the last nineteenth-century Indian:* "Church Records of the Presbyterian Church Shelter Island N.Y. 1806–65 inclusive," "Records of Deaths: BettyToby [*sic*] Ceaser AE 75 February 2 an Indian woman 1834." SIHS 2004.59.

246 *"a very handsome man":* Lodowick Havens's (1774–1854) undated memoir quotes Mrs. Nicoll Havens, Desire Brown Havens (1744–1828), who could have remembered Brinley Sylvester from childhood. More likely her description is a composite memory, compiled from other Shelter Islanders' recollections. Lodowick Havens, Journal, n.d., SIHS.

246 *"rhone [roan] stallion":* October 28, 1745, entry for £139.10.6 to Capt. Nath. Pollan. Shelter Island Account Book 1738–46 (Brinley Sylvester), East Hampton Library.

247 *multiple positions:* He served variously as supervisor, assessor, clerk, and overseer of the poor: as clerk and overseer in 1738, 1740, 1743; as clerk and supervisor in 1744, 1745, 1746, 1749; and as clerk and assessor in 1750, 1752, the year of his death. Mallmann, *Historical Papers*, 155.

247 *"investigate the complaints of Indians at Montauk": NY Col. Mss* 68:151.

247 *"pieces of Gould":* Record for October 9, 1745: cash paid to Brinley Sylvester by Matthew Steward of New London for "6 Ram Lambs" includes these currencies as well as bills of "New England money." Shelter Island Account Book 1738–146, East Hampton Library.

248 *convulsions:* Edmund S. Morgan, *The Gentle Puritan: A Life of Ezra Stiles, 1727–1795* (New Haven and London: Yale University Press, 1962), 22.

248 *"Newtonian stratosphere":* Christopher Hill, "God and the English Revolution," in *The Collected Essays of Christopher Hill*, vol. 2, *Religion and Politics in 17th-Century England* (Amherst: University of Massachusetts Press, 1986), 333.

248 *"this amiable shepherd":* Frances M. Caulkins, *Memoir of the Rev. William Adams, of Dedham, Mass., and of the Rev. Eliphalet Adams, of New London, Conn.* (Cambridge, MA: Metcalf and Company, 1849), 47.

248 *"Guinea trade":* Sarah Deutsch, "The Elusive Guineamen: Newport Slavers, 1735 74," *NEQ* 55, no. 2 (June 1982): 229–53.

249 *"Only a few of New England's merchants":* Bernard Bailyn, "Slavery and Population Growth, in Colonial New England," in *Engines of Enterprise: An Economic History of New* England, ed. Peter Temin (Cambridge, MA: Harvard University Press, 1979), 256.

249 *"I want to make Sum money":* Brinley Sylvester, Shelter Island, to "my Dear Kinsman," November 1, 1750, Dinkel Coll.

249 *The sloop* Hampton: James Truslow Adams, *History of the Town of Southampton (East of Canoe Place)* (Bridgehampton, NY: Hampton Press, 1918), 141.

250 *"Beachman's Drops":* Brinley Sylvester, Shelter Island, to Joel Bowditch, December 6, 1745. Shelter Island Account Book, 1738–46, East Hampton Library.

250 *"the Best of Tarr"*: Brinley Sylvester, Shelter Island, to "my Dear Kinsman," November 1, 1750, Dinkel Coll.; George Berkeley, *Siris: A Chain of Philosophical Reflexions and Enquiries Concerning the Uses of Tar-Water* (London, 1744, reprinted Whitefish, MT: Kessinger Publishing, 2008).

250 *"rum"*: Draft by Col. Geo. Bennett of Jamaica (British West Indies) on ? (Mr. Brinley Sylvester), directing money payable to him on account, to be paid to Richard Bill, Boston Merchant (Bennett's Boston agent). Discharged June 17, 1720. East Hampton Library.

250 *James Fanning*: June 2, 1739, Shelter Island Account Book 1738–46, East Hampton Library.

250 *"the genteel ideal"*: Bushman, *Refinement of America*, 25.

250 *largest entry:* The number may have been somewhat greater or less, since the breakdown of men, women, children, and the aged or infirm is unknown. Sales were computed in different currencies: when Joshua Hempstead of New London sold a young black woman in Southold for £90, in 1735 the amount was perhaps paid in printed currency of lesser value, such as the money of Connecticut or New York, not sterling. Inventory of the Estate of Brinley Sylvester, Esq., May 9, 1753, East Hampton Library; Hempstead, *Diary*, 287; see George Mumford of New London, September 1, 1756, lists fourteen slaves by name, sex, age, and valuation for a total of £426. Inventory of the Estate of George Mumford; New London 1756 Probate Files #3779.

250 *the average price for a slave:* Moss, "Slavery on Long Island," Table VI, 73.

251 *to inflict punishment:* Moss, *Slavery on Long Island*, 147, 155–57; Higginbotham, *In the Matter of Color*, 117–23.

251 *"the visitations of God"*: *New-York Weekly Journal*, January 5, 1735/6, quoted by McManus, *Black Bondage in the North*, 91.

251 *The code:* Sources for this paragraph include Moss, "Slave Laws, Slave Reactions: Island Slaves Under the Law," chap. 4 in "Slavery on Long Island," 147–202; McManus, "The Law and Order of Slavery" and "Life at the Bottom," chaps. 5 and 6 in *Black Bondage in the North*, 72–107; Higginbotham, "The Early New York Experience," chap. 4, section 2 in *In the Matter of Color*, 114–35; and Lepore, "The Tightening Vise," 59–89.

252 *these two wedding gifts:* The 1915 gift of General Sylvester Dering II to the Metropolitan Museum of Art included a 1690–1700 covered porringer (Acc. #15.98.3 a,b); two Vernon porringers, (Acc. #15.98.1) dated 1720–35 and (Acc. #15.98.2) dated 1700–30; and a tankard (Acc. #15.98.4) dated 1705–15.

252 *"of Newport"*: The ties with Newport strengthened again as the Sylvesters' daughters grew up; they were sent to Boston for their education, but "resided a part of the time at Newport, for the education of his [*sic*] two only daughters Margaret and Mary." "Narrative of the life of Thomas Dering," unknown (mailed from Utica, New York), Oct. 19, n.d., to Eliza P. Brumley and R. Brumley Esq., Seamans Savings Bank, Wall St., New York, Dinkel Coll.

253 *Brinley had his dog shipped:* William Sanford, Newport, to Brinley Sylvester, Southold, August 5, 1719. Dinkel Coll.

253 *agreement with Nicoll:* Suffolk County Deeds Liber B, part 1: 169. See also Schwartz and Griswold, "Shelter Island, New York, Land Acquisition and Dispersal," Map 4 and List of Residents in 1708.

253 *affidavits:* Colonel Francis Brinley, Roxbury, to Brinley Sylvester, Shelter Island, March 14, 1720, GSDD 1:11, SIHS.

253 *ejectment*: Receipt, Brinley Sylvester to William Smith, Oct. 1, 1727, Newport, for actions of ejectment, for £4, East Hampton Library; Receipt, Brinley Sylvester to David Corey for William Nicoll for £182.12.3, October 11, 1736, for two actions of ejectment brought by William Nicoll, SMA, NYU I/A/140/37.

253 *"Mrs. Sylvester came from the west end"*: Lodowick Havens, Journal, SIHS.

255 *The inventory*: Inventory of the Estate of Brinley Sylvester.

255 *murdered*: Moss, *Slavery on Long Island*, 147–49.

255 *"be Dilgent"*: Mary Sylvester, Shelter Island, to Margaret Sylvester, in Boston, December 8, 1737; Chlo: Brinley Sylvester to Margaret Sylvester Chesebrough, December 5, 1749, Dinkel Coll.; earthquake: Mary Sylvester to Margaret Sylvester, December 8, 1737, Dinkel Coll.

256 *"what God is a bout"*: Mary Sylvester to daughter, probably Margaret Sylvester, in Boston, December 8, 1737, Dinkel Coll.

256 *"the Melancholy tidings"*: Brinley Sylvester to Margaret Sylvester Chesebrough, December 5, 1749, Dinkel Coll.

256 *"a Jugg of Sweet Cream"*: Mary Burroughs Sylvester to daughter, probably Margaret Sylvester, in Boston, December 8, 1737, Dinkel Coll.

256 *"Butter Cups"*: Brinley Sylvester, Shelter Island, to Captain Wiggins, Shelter Island, November 2, 1750; Adams's wig: John Cotton to Brinley Sylvester, Shelter Island, June 13, 1748, Dinkel Coll.

256 *"I am very sorry"*: Brinley Sylvester, Shelter Island, to Margaret Chesebrough, Newport, June 22, 1750, Dinkel Coll.

256 *A "linnen wheel"*: Brinley's inventory lists four spinning wheels for linen and three for wool, a measure of the importance of textiles to the manor economy. William Conoll (perhaps "Connolly") applied to Brinley in 1741 for work as a weaver and for lodging. Given the number of wheels, it seems likely that Connoll, or another weaver, was employed to weave what the household spun. William Conoll to Brinley Sylvester, June 22, 1741, East Hampton Library.

256 *the "Dorey"*: Inventory of the Estate of Brinley Sylvester.

257 *"He was a most tender Husband"*: Rev. William Throop, "A Sermon on the Death of Brinley Sylvester" (Boston, 1753), 8. The biblical reference is to Proverbs 11:17: "The merciful Man doth Good to his own Soul."

257 *"dear departed friend"*: William Adams, New London, to Thomas Dering, Boston or Newport, January 23, 1761, Sylvester Dering Letter Collection #2012.302.1–8, SIHS.

257 *"We are sorry"*: Thomas Hutchinson, Boston, to Brinley Sylvester, Shelter Island, July 27, 1742, Dinkel Coll.

257 *"a Piece of Skill"*: Franklin Bowditch Dexter, *Biographical Sketches of the Graduates of Yale College with Annals of the College History, Oct. 1701–May 1745* (New York: Henry Holt, 1885), 360; Charles W. Baird, *Chronicle of a Border Town: History of Rye, Westchester County, New York, 1660–1870* (New York: Anson D. F. Randolph, 1871), 166. https://play.google.com/store/books/details?id=qXsVAAAAYAAJ&rdid=book-qXs-VAAAAYAAJ&rdot=1.

258 *"She is with us"*: Dr. John Smith, Rye, to Brinley Sylvester, Shelter Island, April 3, 1744, Dinkel Coll.

258 *"grows very fleshy"*: "Given such patchy information, it's almost impossible for us to diagnose Mary's ailment. Late-onset bipolar disorder? Schizophrenia? Perhaps an organic syndrome such as Cushing's disease ('she grows very fleshy')?" Dr. Anna Fels, pers. comm., May 25, 2009.

258 *"wait with patience"*: Smith, Dr. John, Rye, to Brinley Sylvester, Shelter Island, May 28, 1744, Dinkel Coll.

258 *"supernatural drama"*: Mary Ann Jimenez, "Madness in Early American History: Insanity in Massachusetts 1700–1830," *Journal of Social History* 20 (1986): 29.

258 *"seton"*: Laurel Thatcher Ulrich, "Derangement in the Family: The Story of Mary Sewall, 1824–25," *Dublin Seminar for New England Folklife Annual Proceedings* 1990, 168–84. Also, Virginia Bernhard, "'Cotton Mather's Most Unhappy Wife': Reflections on the Uses of Historical Evidence," *NEQ* 60, no. 3 (1987): 341–62; Elizabeth Prendergast Carlisle, *Earthbound and Heavenbent: Elizabeth Porter Phelps and Life at Forty Acres (1747–17)* (New York: Scribner, 2004), 98–101.

259 *"the dark room"*: For the mentally ill, "a strict regimen, a total confinement from all company . . . sometimes to a dark room, severe discipline and subjection to a degree of fear and some medicine [were recommended as] the most effective ways of treating such a person." "Letter from Robert Treat Paine to Joseph Palmer about Mr. Leonard's Mental Illness," September 1762, MHS, Boston, quoted in Jimenez, "Madness in Early American History," 32.

259 *tried hard:* "Madness seems not to have been viewed as a permanent state in eighteenth-century Massachusetts; rather it was seen as episodic. When a person who was once mad acted normally, he seems to have been treated as a sane person, not as a latent lunatic." Jimenez, "Madness in Early American History," 27.

259 *"Your poor mother"*: Brinley Sylvester, Shelter Island, to Margaret Chesebrough, Newport, June 22, 1750, and December 5, 1749, Dinkel Coll.

259 *"an agreeable woman"*: B. Sylvester, Shelter Island, to Andrew Oliver, Boston, August 18, 1752, East Hampton Library.

259 *left to tenants:* First to a Thomas Fanning of Southold, then to his brother, Phineas, of Laurel, near Riverhead.

17. THE DOORS

261 *"fantastic nightgowns"*: Horace Walpole, quoted by Anne Hollander, *Seeing Through Clothes* (New York: Viking, 1978), 58.

261 *loves both portraits:* Joseph Blackburn, "Mary Sylvester" (1754), MMA 16.68.2, and "Mrs. David Chesebrough" (1754), MMA 16.68.3, gifts of General Sylvester Dering II in 1916.

262 *black-and-white photo:* The photograph is included in the SMA, NYU.

262 *the Dering brothers' firm to fail:* Thomas Dering was forced to mortgage his wife's half of the Sylvester estate to London merchants Lane & Booth; he rented the other half from his brother-in-law, David Chesebrough, who was initially unwilling to have the Derings as tenants because he feared the rent would never be paid. Margaret Chesebrough tried to prevent such a sale and evidently was successful. The mortgage "was after his death discharged by his children." Mr. Jacobson (of Lane & Booth), London, to Thomas and Henry Dering, Boston, April 21, 1762, Sylvester Dering Letter Collection, SIHS 2012.302.1–8; contract: Thomas Dering and Mary Dering, Shelter Island, with Thomas Lane and Benjamin Booth, May 23, 1767, Gen Sylvester Dering Docs. 21, "for one equal undivided half part of all that certain Farm . . . on the said Shelter Island"; Margaret Chesebrough, Newport, to Thomas Dering (Boston?) April 6,

1762, Sylvester Dering Letter Coll. "Narrative of the life of Thomas Dering," Dinkel Coll.

263 *Thomas Paine's* Common Sense: Thomas Paine, *Common Sense: Addressed to the Inhabitants of America, etc.* (Philadelphia: R. Bell, Jan. 10, 1776), SMA, NYU, Spec. Coll. E211, p. 1235, 1776b.

263 *new American government:* L'Hommedieu served in many positions throughout his life; Dering was a delegate to the New York Provincial Convention, which adopted the Declaration of Independence passed by the Provincial Congress on July 4, 1776. After the battle of Long Island, like many other Long Islanders, he was granted a leave of absence to go home to look after his affairs. "Narrative of the Life of Thomas Dering," Dinkel Coll.

263 *"colonial dark ages":* Jon Butler, *Becoming America: The Revolution Before 1776* (Cambridge, MA: Harvard University Press, 2000; first paperback ed. 2001), 7.

263 *L'Hommedieu:* Elizabeth van Beek, "Ezra L'Hommedieu (Aug. 30, 1734–Sept. 27, 1811)," http://www.anb.org/articles/01/01-00487.html?a=1&n=Ezra%20L%27Hommedieu&d=10&ss=0&q=1.

263 *William Floyd:* Eugene R. Fingerhut, "William Floyd (Dec. 17, 1734–Aug. 4, 1821, http://www.anb.org/articles/01/01-00290.html?a=1&n=William%20Floyd&d=10&ss=0&q=1.

264 *spent his own money:* Van Beek, "Ezra L'Hommedieu."

264 *"developed novel arguments":* See Patricia U. Bonomi, *Under the Cope of Heaven: Religion, Society and Politics in Colonial America* (Oxford: Oxford University Press, 1986), 153.

264 *"The institutional disruptions":* Bonomi, *Under the Cope of Heaven*, 153.

264 *young missionary friend:* Thomas Dering, Shelter Island, to Charles Jeffrey Smith, June 18, 1767, Dinkel Coll. Smith was a protégé of the Reverend Eleazar Wheelock, who founded Dartmouth College.

264 *George Whitefield:* George Whitefield, Boston, to Thomas Dering, Shelter Island, May 2, 1764, Dinkel Coll.

264 *political and intellectual Boston circles:* "Mr. Dering who . . . was early informed of all that was there [Boston] going on took a decided stand for Liberty and a deep interest in the establishment of our independence." "Narrative life of Thomas Dering," Dinkel Coll.

264 *"O poor New England!":* Boyd Stanley Schlenther, "Whitefield, George (1714–70)" (*ODNB*, 2004), http://www.oxforddnb.com/view/article/29281.

265 *"the Most alarming News":* Thomas Fosdick, New London, to Nicoll Havens, Shelter Island, April 27, 1775, Dinkel Coll.

265 *"whatever Measures may be recommended":* "Shelter Island Declaration of Independence": Printed form for the New York State "General Association . . . subscribed by the Freeholders, etc.," May 1775, reproduced in Mallmann, *Historical Papers*, 64; original, SIHS, 1974.81.1.

265 *Connecticut was held:* New London, and some other towns such as Fairfield, were destroyed. *Suffolk County Historical Society Register* 4, no. 3 (Dec. 1978): 41–56, 47–48.

265 *twenty-one cartloads of goods:* Frederic Gregory Mather, *The Refugees of 1776 from Long Island to Connecticut* (Albany, NY: J. B. Lyon, 1913), 248, 369, 744–49, https://play.google.com/store/books/details?id=fId2AAAAMAAJ&rdid=book-fId2AAAAMAAJ&rdot=1.

266 *more than three thousand British troops:* Mather, *Refugees of 1776*, 176.

266 *they fired without warning: Diary of Ebenezer Miller of Miller Place, Long Island, New York*, 1762–68, ed. Margaret Davis Gass and Willis H. White (Miller Place, NY: W. H. White, 1996), 3.

266 *In the usual way of occupiers:* For the war and its aftermath on Long Island and Shelter Island, see Mather, *Refugees of 1776*; Gaetano L. Vincitorio, "The Revolutionary War and Its Aftermath in Suffolk County, Long Island," *LIHJ* 7, no. 1 (Fall 1994): 68–85; Helen Otis Lamont, *The Story of Shelter Island in the Revolution* (Shelter Island, NY: Shelter Island Historical Society, 1975); and Sylvester Dering's 1779 correspondence with his father, Sylvester Dering Letter Coll.

268 *"We . . . are returned":* Sylvester Dering, Shelter Island, to Mrs. Ann Monk, July 15, 1783, East Hampton Library.

268 *wood cut on the property:* "Account of Wood Taken, British Forces Rhode Island to Thomas Dering 3,500 cords of wood £1400, 1783," GSDD, 30, and "Memorial S. Dering to Sir Guy Carlton, for wood 1783," GSDD, 34.

268 *"three thousand cords of wood":* Timothy Dwight, *Travels in New England and New York*, ed. Barbara Miller Solomon, 4 vols. (Cambridge, MA: Belknap Press of Harvard University Press, 1969), 3:214.

269 *Up the Connecticut River Valley:* Amelia F. Miller, *Connecticut River Valley Doorways: An Eighteenth-Century Flowering, An Illustrated and Annotated Checklist of 220 Doorways* (Boston: Boston University for the Dublin Seminar of New England Folklife, 1983), introduction, 14, and "Checklist of Doorways." 48, 56, 57, 60, and 106. Many of the scroll-pedimented doorways noted were added to earlier houses between 1749 and 1795, with the 1750s and 1760s the decades favored for their construction.

270 *"Tea Table," and the "6 Teaspoons and Tongs":* Inventory of the Estate of Brinley Sylvester.

270 *the local historian Ralph G. Duvall: The History of Shelter Island*, 53.

271 *"so the paper":* Griswold Papers, Fales Library, NYU.

271 *"There are carpenter's marks":* Griswold Papers, Fales Library, NYU.

271 *Duvall had also written:* Duvall, *History of Shelter Island*, 53.

272 *"historic research":* "Historic Structure Report, Progress Report, June 15, 2001," and Robert Hefner, "Sylvester Manor: Brinley Sylvester's c.1737 House, 80 North Ferry Road, Shelter Island, N.Y," Historic Structure Report, Architecture Component, prepared for Sylvester Manor Educational Farm, Inc., March 2013.

272 *the tactical masterpiece:* Terry Golway, *Washington's General: Nathanael Greene and the Triumph of the American Revolution* (New York: Henry Holt, 2005), 241.

273 *"Are you going":* Griswold Papers, Fales Library, NYU.

18. Family and Slavery

275 *papers:* Records of the sale (1827) and the settlement (1828) between Samuel S. Gardiner and Esther Dering. SMA, NYU III/A/4/46/12; Liber K Ass't Clerk's Book, 144–47, Riverhead, NY.

275 *the 1,312-acre farm:* In 1796 Henry Packer Dering released half of the acreage of the manor to Sylvester, apparently in exchange for land of equal value in Montgomery County, New York. Contract, S. Dering with Henry P. Dering re estate settlement 1792, GSSD 42, Contract, Henry P. Dering to S. Dering, release of land 1796, GSSD 46.

275 *public auction:* For the sale in chancery 20 Oct. 1827, see Suffolk County Liber K Ass't Clerk's Book, 144–47.

275 *Mrs. L'Hommedieu:* She detailed the debts owed to her, to the estate of Ezra L'Hommedieu (her late husband), and to Samuel Smith Gardiner (her son-in-law) as well as some notes on the auction and on sales from her husband's estate such as Robins Island. SMA, NYU II/C/2/29/24.

275 *the Nicoll family:* Patricia Shillingberg, pers. comm., Sept. 21, 2012.

276 *the family rift:* The matter remains unresolved. See Charles T. Dering testimony, Supreme Court proceeding, "In the matter of the appeal of Samuel S. Gardiner from the admeasurment of the dower of Esther Sarah Dering widow," May 19, 1828, SMA, NYU III/A/4/46/12; Liber K Ass't Clerk's Book, 144–47, Riverhead, New York.

278 *Thomas Dering's 1786 probate inventory:* "An Inventory and Apprisement of the Personal Estate of Thomas Dering Late Deceased, This 2nd Day of June 1786 by Ezra L'Hommedieu Esq. Mr. James Howell & Mr. William Bowditch." Shelter Island NY Papers Acquired Dec. 12, 1993, Queens Borough Public Library.

278 *Comus was purchased:* Hepzibah Edwards, Boston/Marshfield?, to Thomas Dering, Shelter Island, n.d., between Dec. 1762, the date of the Derings' arrival on Shelter Island, and July 1765, when Comus is listed in an inventory. Sylvester Dering Letter Coll., SIHS.

279 *"as you say nothing of Comas":* Ibid.

279 *"Dear Brother I must tel you":* Margaret Chesebrough, Newport, to Thomas Dering, Boston, April 6, 1762, Sylvester Dering Letter Coll., SIHS.

279 *"Dear Coz":* Hepzibah Edwards, Boston, to Thomas Dering, Shelter Island, October 22, n.d., but after Dec. 1762 and before July 1765. Dinkel Coll., SIHS.

279 *"Inventory of Personal effects":* A Comus, Cato, Judith, Matilda, a man, London, and a "negro male child," London, were listed in 1765; absent from the list in 1786 is "a man, London," who apparently had died; London, the child, had by then become "a young negro Man"; "Negro woman Hagar" was retained by Thomas Dering's widow as her property in 1787. "Inventory of Goods of Thomas Dering," July 12, 1765, Long Island History Room, East Hampton Library; "Mary Sylvester Dering, List of Goods retained from the estate," GSSD 41.

279 *The season began with currants:* List of trees and flowers in bloom on Shelter Island, 1797, 1799, 1804, probably compiled by Mary Catherine Havens L'Hommedieu, wife of Ezra L'Hommedieu and sister of Esther Sarah Havens, wife of the then owner of the manor, Sylvester Dering. SMA, NYU, Record Group II, Series B, Subseries 9, Box 28, Folder 23.

279 *"English cherries":* See *The Diaries of Augustus Griffin, 1792–1852*, ed. Fredrika Wachsberger (Orient, NY: Oysterponds Historical Society, 2009), 93; Lilian Horsford Farlow, "Memories of Samuel Smith Gardiner" (June 1923), SIHS L.S.F. Names/Gardiner.

279 *"yielded under a skillful husbandry":* Dwight, *Travels in New England and New York*, 3: 215.

280 *first Federal Census:* Helen Otis Lamont, *The Story of Shelter Island in the Revolution* (Shelter Island, NY: SIHS, 1975), 61; *First Census of the United States, 1790, New York*, "Names of Heads of Families, Queens County to Westchester County, Shelter Island Town," 165.

280 *Presbyterian church:* A strict hierarchy based on wealth and status—as well as race—was observed in the assignment of pews. Comus was also baptized on his

admission. "Church Records of the Presbyterian Church Shelter Island N.Y. 1806–65," SIHS 2004.57, Book Box 49.

280 *"Among other possessions"*: Mallmann, *Shelter Island and Its Presbyterian Church*, 59–60.

281 *The subtext is resistance*: The historian William D. Pierson writes that for such jokes to work, "the slaves had to communicate the foolishness of the white position by using the master class's own logic against it," and also notes that since "West Africans traditionally used proverbs both in legal argument and as a rhetorical device in resolving family and village controversies, we should understand the use of proverbial wisdom by black bondsmen before the bar of New England public opinion to be a continuation of an African form of resistance to injustice." Piersen, *Black Yankees*, 156, 147.

281 *Comus's African American dialect*: For an early-eighteenth-century New England exchange between whites, blacks, and an Indian in which all "speak Negro," see Knight, "The Journal of Madam Knight," 63–64; for African immigrants' need to create their own lingua franca as a language distinguished from that of their captors, see "Talking Half African," in Gomez, *Exchanging Our Country Marks*, 154–85.

281 *"secure approval"*: Moss, *Slavery on Long Island*, 77–78.

281 *The legislative progress of emanicipation*: http://www.slaveryinnewyork.org/PDFs/Laws_Affecting_Blacks_in_Manhattan.pdf and Higginbotham, *In the Matter of Color*, 128–50.

282 *"Few enslaved people got free"*: Sweet, *Bodies Politic*, 227.

282 *"Sparks of Compassion"*: Sweet, *Bodies Politic*, 141, quoting an unnamed Rhode Islander, in the *United States Chronicle*, Jan. 29, 1784.

282 *the central problem of race relations*: Sweet, *Bodies Politic*, 228.

282 *three generations*: Samuel and Mary Gardiner, E. N. and Mary Horsford (and Phoebe Horsford, second wife of Eben), Cornelia Horsford. On January 22, 1811, Sylvester Dering sent Dido, mother of Julia, to Ezra L'Hommedieu for medical treatment for her child, possibly Julia, who is "very much afflicted with sores about her neck." SMA, NYU II/B/1/3/4.

283 *an 1887 magazine article*: Lamb, "The Manor of Shelter Island," 361–89.

283 *Captain Phineas Fanning*: Will of Phineas Fanning (1724–96), Suffolk County Wills, Liber A 460–61;Walter Frederic Brooks, *History of the Fanning Family: A Genealogical Record of the Descendants of Edmund Fanning*, 2 vols. (Worcester, MA, 1905), 1:147, 148. Phineas Fanning rented Sylvester Manor, 1760–62, immediately before the Derings moved to the island.

284 *the census*: See "Shelter Island notes re slaves and freed blacks," comp. Mac Griswold, 2004, SIHS. By 1818 Fanning owned a small piece of land; his name appears in the assessments list of that year, Helen Zunzer Wortis, *A Woman Named Matilda* (Shelter Island: SIHS, 1978), 31.

284 *Sylvester Dering sold Comus*: For a full property description see an indenture dated September 30, 1828. The record dated Oct. 20, 1827, of the property sale by New York Chancery to Samuel Gardiner had described Comus's property as "exclusive of the part sold to Comus Fanning which . . . contains twenty acres and three quarters of land or thereabouts." The 1828 document was recorded in Suffolk County Deeds, Liber G: 340.1–4, July 29, 1837; the 1827 document in Liber K Ass't Clerk's Book, pp. 144–47, Riverhead, NY. SMA, NYU III/A/4/144/16.

284 *signed another document:* This confirming deed between "Esther Sarah Dering widow . . . and executrix . . . of the first part [and] the only heirs at law of the said Sylvester Dering deceased, of the second part, and of Comus Fanning of Shelter Island farmer of the third part" includes Widow Dering's indenture to Fanning, Aug. 21, 1821 (the document that omitted mention of the dollar amount Fanning paid). Confirmation, September 30, 1828, and recorded Suffolk County Deeds, Liber G: 340.1,2.3.4, 29 July 1837.

284 *badly torn hand-colored map:* 1867 Map and Survey of "The Farm Late of Samuel S. Gardiner, Esq." SIHS: 1867 Map, 2002.1.

285 *Comus's will:* Will of Comus Fanning, Suffolk County Records, Liber F, 299–301.

285 *"my wife the woman I now live with":* Will of Comus Fanning. The phrase "the woman I now live with" may have been used to indicate that Dido was Comus's second wife. Included in Comus's probate file are names of heirs-at-law and next of kin: an ex-wife, Jennie, remarried before his death; a daughter Ruth, of Boston (no surname given, presumably Fanning); a daughter Hepsibah, wife of Elimas Derby, of Sag Harbor.

285 *the largest freehold:* In 1831 Comus's property, listed as twenty-five acres, was assessed at $350.00. In Brookhaven, Long Island (a much larger township of 340,165 acres compared to Shelter Island's 7,676.5 acres), by April 1, 1815 tax receipts list seven black landowners with properties ranging from a quarter acre to two hundred and seventy acres, with property values from $100.00 to $515.00. "Assessment of the town of Sheltr [*sic*] Island made by Lodowick Havens includes acreage, real and personal property, 73 taxables." (1831) Dinkel Coll; Fire Island National Seashore, William Floyd Estate, Mastic Beach, NY, FIIS 9669, Box 3.

286 *only two black families:* Crank (no last name given), with a family of five, and Cade Moore, with a family of nine. Lamont, *The Story of Shelter Island in the Revolution*, 61, and see Griffin, *Diaries*, 218.

286 *restricted voting rights:* To vote, 1811 state legislation required black men (no women yet had suffrage) to present an endorsed certificate of freedom. In 1822, when property requirements were abolished for white men who had served in the militia or paid taxes, the requirement for blacks was increased from $100 to $250. See Patrick Rael, "The Long Death of Slavery," in Berlin and Harris, *Slavery in New York*, 113–46, 131–33; Higginbotham, *In the Matter of Color*, 146–47.

286 *"the said Matilda":* "Henry Dering's Accounts of Dealings with 'Matilda, A Free Black Woman,'" East Hampton Library; Wortis, *A Woman Named Matilda*, 48–58.

287 *"In them days":* Havens, Journal.

287 *a Dido, aged sixty-two:* Church Records 1806–65.

287 *Julia was known as Julia Dyd:* The matronymic persisted in the name of the creek: "Dyd's Creek" and in the church records for 1838 where "Julia Dido" is named as the mother of a child who died in infancy, no father listed. One later document uses two different surnames: Julia is first "Julia A. Johnson" (she married a Morris Johnson at an unknown date and gave birth to a son named Manford), then "Julia Johnson," then elsewhere "Julia Havens." Church Records 1806–65; "Statement as to the Comus Fanning (or Julia Havens's) property on Shelter Island," land sales recitation, Davis & Worth for Charles Eustis Hubbard, from "Prof. Horsford," July 5, 1836–Nov. 8, 1865. SMA NYU IV/A/3/76/23, 29, 38; Suffolk County Deeds, Liber 134, 66.

287 *her grave in 1834:* A copy of Dido's will, in which she is named as "Dido Fanning," using Comus's last name, was apparently drawn up by Samuel S. Gardiner. It may be the original, as it appears never to have been filed officially but was retained by Gardiner in his papers. SMA, NYU III/A/4/46/5.

19. SUMMER COLONY

288 *a woman's hair:* As late as 1937, a Dr. M. Kershaw declared that "When the hair grows long the general capacity to endure is weakened . . . It has been definitely shown that long hair saps strength. Hair drains vital material from the body in the form of oil." "U.S.C. Psychologist Poohs Idea of Strength in Lengthy Locks," *The News and Courier*, June 6, 1937, p. 10, http://news.google.com/newspapers?nid=2506&dat=19370606&id=zztJAAAAIBAJ&sjid=oggNAAAAIBAJ&pg=3749,4563533.

288 *postmortem list of her clothes:* SMA, NYU II/C/2/30/3.

289 *his attire:* Horsford, "Memories of Samuel Smith Gardiner."

289 *his academic career:* Samuel Rezneck, "The European Education of an American Chemist and Its Influence in 19th-Century America: Eben Norton Horsford," *Technology and Culture* 11, no. 3 (June 1970): 366–88; Pat Munday, "Horsford, Eben Norton," *ANB*, http://www.anb.org/articles/13/13-00791.html; Robert V. Bruce, *The Launching of Modern American Science, 1846–76* (Ithaca, NY: Cornell University Press, 1988).

289 *three years before:* Mallman, *Historical Papers*, 251, 265.

290 *the nineteenth-century mind:* To date (2012), 3,150 books have been inventoried, along with some 500 journals, diaries, portfolios, and scrapbooks previously shelved with the books. Email, Cara Loriz, Executive Director of Sylvester Manor Educational Farm, Sept. 26, 2012.

290 *Eben's thin notebooks:* The current count (2012) for these notebooks is "around twenty-five." Cara Loriz, Sept. 26, 2012.

290 *launching business ventures:* George F. Wilson and Eben Horsford incorporated the Rumford Chemical Works on May 31, 1859, with an authorized capital of $10,000. *History of Rumford Chemical Works*, Weaver Memorial Library, East Providence, RI, n.d., but after 1977.

291 *private railroad car:* The railroad car party in 1880–81 included H. F. Durant, Julian Taylor, Annie Longfellow, and Lilian and Cornelia Horsford. Rensselaer Polytechnic Institute, Institute Archives and Special Collections, Troy, NY, Horsford Family Papers.

291 *Helen Hunt Jackson:* Jackson (1835–85), née Fiske (a relation of Andrew Fiske, m. Gertrude Horsford 1878), lived in Colorado. In 1881, after publishing *A Century of Dishonor*, an exposé of Indian mistreatment, she was appointed special commissioner for the Mission Indians of California, http://www.anb.org/articles/16/16-00836.html?a=1&n=Helen%20Hunt%20Jackson&d=10&ss=0&q=1; SMA NYU IV/A/1/63/34, IV/B/1/94/13, IV/E/1/100/6 and 7; for travels to the West, IV/H/5/107.

291 *new entrance gates:* In 1915, the estate landscape designer and civil engineer James Greenleaf designed for Cornelia Horsford the manor gates and the water gate at the land bridge, which also exists today. Landscape plans and detailed construction plans, SMA, NYU, IV/H/7.

291 *the Cambridge intelligentsia:* A manor guestbook recorded summer visitors' names between 1872 and 1891. SMA, NYU IV/A/3/97/13.

292 *Horsford, the president of the Board of Visitors:* Horsford persuaded former Harvard colleagues to teach at Wellesley and gave funds, advice, and rare books, including more than two hundred dictionaries, grammars, and translations of the Bible into North American Indian languages. *President's Report*, Wellesley College 1888, 4; www.Wellesley.edu/Library.

293 *a mantelpiece to Shelter Island:* Both armchair and mantel remain at the manor today.

293 *Eadweard Muybridge's photographic series:* His first successful serial photographs of fast motion were taken in 1877 in California.

293 *"El Dorado":* Zuber Cie, the French wallpaper manufacturer, first blocked "El Dorado," a view of the snowy peaks of the Andes above a wide band of tropical flowers, in 1848. Eben Horsford invested in Mexican gold mines and Peruvian guano mines, so the choice of "El Dorado" seemed appropriate. See Catherine Lynn, *Wallpaper in America: From the Seventeenth Century to World War I* (New York: W. W. Norton, 1980), 196.

293 *Isaac Pharaoh, a Montauket:* Indenture, Isaac Pharaoh to Sam'l S. Gardiner, Shelter Island, November 10, 1829. A Shelter Island binding certificate for both Isaac and eight-year-old William, his older brother (who, according to local tradition, ran away and whose later whereabouts remain unknown), was issued to Gardiner by local official Caleb Loper on November 18, 1829. Neither indenture states provisions for education or skills, which were standard clauses in white servants' indentures. Indenture, SMA, NYU III/A/4/46/14; Binding Certificate, SIHS Acc.#3/Location Ledger Box #3; Strong, "Indian Labor," 19.

293 *In winter he lived:* Lilian Horsford Farlow, "Memories of Samuel Smith Gardiner."

294 *"figures in literary aspic": "Interview with a Friend . . .* Meet Marilyn Richardson," *Longfellow House Bulletin* 5, no. 1 (June 2001): 3, http://www.longfellowfriends.org/bulletins/Vol5No1.pdf.

294 *"savage fellows":* H. W. Longfellow, Cambridge, to Margaret Potter, October 29, 1837, in "Longfellow's Early Interest in Indians," *Longfellow House Bulletin* 5, no. 1 (June 2001): 4.

295 *"last of his royal race":* Eben Horsford, "Song of Shelter Island," August 28, 1872, *Bulletin of the Shelter Island Historical Society* 1, no. 1 (June 1924): 5–6.

295 *Frank Hamilton Cushing:* Jesse D. Green, "The Man Who Became an Indian," a review of Cushing's seminal work, *Zuni Breadstuff*, republished by the Museum of the American Indian and the Heye Foundation, 1974. *New York Review of Books*, May 1975, 31–32, http://www.nybooks.com/articles/archives/1975/may/29/the-man-who-became-an-indian.

295 *"participant observer":* Participant observation is "a method of qualitative research in which the researcher understands the contextual meanings of an event or events through participating and observing as a subject in the research." Wayne B. Jonas, *Dictionary of Complementary and Alternative Medicine* (St. Louis: Elsevier Mosby, 2005).

295 *Cushing whetted Horsford's interest:* Cushing correspondence in the Bureau of American Ethnology in Washington, DC, is datelined from Shelter Island and from 27 Craigie Street in Cambridge. He stayed four months in one of the resort cottages on Shelter Island in the summer of 1885, courtesy of Eben Horsford, and then traveled to Boston to stay with the family. Horsford's manuscript history of the family and of Shelter Island describes Cushing's visit to the North Peninsula. SMA, NYU IV/A/11/111/20, 21 and 112/1–6, and Cushing letters, IV/A/1/a/58/54.

295 *issued publications:* Eben Norton Horsford, *The Problem of the Northmen: A Letter to Judge Daly, the President of the American Geographical Society, on the Opinion of Justice Winsor, that "Though Scandinavians may have reached the Shores of Labrador, the Soil of the United States has not one Vestige of their Presence"* (Cambridge: John Wilson and Son, 1889); Julius E. Olson, *Review of the Problem of the Northmen and the Site of Norumbega by Professor Olson of Madison University, Wisconsin [sic] and a Reply by Eben Norton Horsford* [privately pub., 1891?]. *The Boston Transcript*, Jan. 2, 1893, 4, published a separate article on Horsford and the Norse hypothesis the same day that his obituary was printed, stating, "With that fervent 'scientific imagination' which marks all leaders in research he may have taken some eager strides beyond solid ground."

296 *the Senecas:* Rev. Epher Whitaker, "Sketch of the late Prof. Eben N. Horsford," *The Traveler*, Southold, NY, March 10, 1893; Richard R. John, "Brief Life of an Enterprising Antiquarian, 1818–93: Eben Norton Horsford," *Harvard Magazine* (Sept.–Oct. 1988), 44.

296 *"the father of modern food technology":* Carl Westerdahl, "Honoring Achievement: Rensselaer Alumni Hall of Fame Announces New Honorees," *Rensselaer Alumni Magazine*, 2001, 3, unattributed quotation as "the father of American food technology."

296 *Asa Gray:* For Gray's life and his struggle with Agassiz, see A. Hunter Dupree, *Asa Gray: American Botanist, Friend of Darwin* (Baltimore: Johns Hopkins University Press, 1988).

296 *Agassiz:* My description of Agassiz and the debate over evolution owes much to Louis Menand's *The Metaphysical Club: The Story of an American Idea* (New York: Farrar, Straus and Giroux, 2001); also see Stephen Jay Gould, *The Mismeasure of Man* (New York: W. W. Norton, 2006), 63–70, and Christoph Irmscher, *The Poetics of Natural History: From John Bartram to William James* (New Brunswick, NJ: Rutgers University Press, 1999), 236–82.

296 *"Lieber Herr Kollege":* Louis Agassiz, Cambridge, to Eben Norton Horsford, n.d., Horsford Family Papers, Agassiz, 1:12. RPI.

297 *"Time," he wrote:* Louis Agassiz, *Contribution to the Natural History of the United States of America* (Boston: Little, Brown, 1857–62), 1:25, quoted in Menand, *Metaphysical Club*, 106.

297 *"personally thrilling":* For this quote and quotes in the following paragraph, see Menand, *Metaphysical Club*, 98–101.

297 *Samuel Morton:* Stephen Jay Gould, "Morton's Ranking of Races by Cranial Capacity," *Science* 200 (1978): 503–9.

298 *Agassiz wrote to Samuel Gridley Howe:* Louis Agassiz to Samuel Howe, August 9, 1863. Agassiz letter quoted in Menand, *Metaphysical Club*, 114–15; writer Henry Wiencek stated that by 1863, mulattoes already made up the majority of people of color. Henry Wiencek, *An Imperfect God: George Washington, His Slaves, and the Creation of America* (New York: Farrar, Straus and Giroux, 2003), 404.

298 *Owners and backers of mills:* New England was the American cotton milling center; New York's merchants dominated the export trade. Southern publisher James DeBow wrote in 1860 that New York was "almost as dependent upon Southern slavery as Charleston itself." David Quigley, "Southern Slavery in a Free City: Economy, Politics and Culture," in *Slavery in New York*, 283.

298 *Fugitive Slave Act:* Passed by Congress on September 18, 1850, the act made federal

marshals liable for a $1,000 fine for not arresting an alleged runaway slave; a claimant's sworn testimony was all that was needed to make an arrest; the suspect could not ask for a jury trial or testify on his or her own behalf; those who helped a runaway were subject to six months' imprisonment and a $1,000 fine; and officers who captured fugitives were entitled to a promotion or a bonus. Many free blacks were enslaved since they had no rights in court. For the impact of the act in New York, see Graham Russell Hodges, *Root & Branch: African Americans in New York & East Jersey, 1613–1863* (Chapel Hill: University of North Carolina Press, 1999), 256–57; for Massachusetts, see Menand, *Metaphysical Club*, 9–11, and Albert J. von Frank, *The Trials of Anthony Burns: Freedom and Slavery in Emerson's Boston* (Cambridge, MA: Harvard University Press, 1998).

299 *Cornelia Conway Felton Horsford:* The Horsford, Agassiz, and Felton families were close. Felton's second wife, Mary Louisa Cary, was the sister of Elizabeth Cabot Cary Agassiz (Agassiz's second wife), the founder of Radcliffe College and a close friend of Lilian Horsford, who gave money to and worked tirelessly for Radcliffe from its founding until her death in 1927.

299 *Northerners into warriors:* See Menand, *Metaphysical Club*, 27–29.

299 *formulated and manufactured rations:* See Horsford Family Papers, Series 2A, and E. N. Horsford to Brigadier General Amos B. Eaton, Commissary General of Subsistence, United States Army, New York, March 15, 1865, SMA, NYU IV/A/1d/74/3.

299 *a letter to his mother:* Horsford, "President Tyler's Sherwood Forest," to Maria Chary Horsford, Feb. 14, 1852, Rensselaer, Horsford Family Papers 1:6.

300 *the moral ambiguities:* William Still, a freeborn black who in the 1840s–50s spent fourteen years in the Underground Railroad Service, viewed Tyler's plantation differently. Edward P. Crapol, *John Tyler: The Accidental President* (Chapel Hill: University of North Carolina Press, 2006), 249–53; E. N. Horsford to Maria Chary Horsford; source unknown of the quote "a minority that never terminates."

300 *"Our walks":* Lilian (b. 1848) remembered her grandfather (d. 1859) during his last years. Farlow, "Memories of Samuel Smith Gardiner."

300 *the land she had inherited:* The first sale was to Samuel Gardiner in 1836: "Julia A Johnson cash paid you on a/c of land to be conveyed to me having contracted with her for 2 acres more at $20 per acre, $20 per acre, $5.00" (October 15, 1836). SMA, NYU, III/A/44/5.

301 *a summer resort:* In his prospectus, Horsford paints the locals as a historical tourist attraction. The wooded "shore of Havens Creek [Julia Dyd's Creek] . . . would provide grand views of land and water scenery" for the planned 170-lot development. The open area north of Havens Creek woods comprised some sixty acres. Part of the hotel development parcel, Horsford valued it at $40,000, or $666.66 per acre, with $20,000 for development cost. "Shelter Island Parks: A New Watering Place, On Shelter Island in Gardiners Bay, Opposite Greenport the Terminus of the Long Island Railroad, 94 Miles from New York and 130 from Boston," n.d. but probably 1867, the date of a map that includes development plats and roads. SMA, NYU IV/A/3/76/47.

301 *careful pencil sketch:* SMA, NYU IV/D/3/99/22.

301 *Julia's son, Manford:* Manford Johnson, no age given, is first noted in 1842 in Samuel Gardiner's Daybook 1836–44, in which Gardiner charges Julia Johnson board "for your boy" while Julia is nursing Gardiner's mother-in-law. In the 1850 census, mother

and son are listed in the household of Purple Jennings: "Julia Johnson, black, aged 35, & Manford Johnson, black, age 17, seaman." Gardiner Daybook, SMA, NYU III/A/3/44/5; Shelter Island Census 1850.

302 *eighteen half-acre village sites:* SMA, NYU IV/A/3/76/47.

302 *a cautious estimate:* Estimates of land prices according to location but without taking into account market fluctuations, including those of the Civil War, averaged $41 per acre between 1840 and 1872. Eben Horsford bought another vital link in his resort scheme in 1872: 18.75 acres "with dwelling house and other outbuildings" for $6,000, which included the area where Winthrop Road (one of the development roads) would cross the mouth of Dering Harbor. Winthrop Road eliminated a long detour to the south around Gardiners Creek for those arriving on the North Ferry from Greenport (the Long Island Railroad terminus). Edward Shillingberg, e-mail communication, October 26, 2009.

20. LADIES OF THE MANOR

304 *daguerreotypes:* While teaching at the Female Academy in Albany in 1841, Horsford established the first daguerreotype gallery there in partnership with Thomas Cushman. H. S. Van Klooster, "Liebig and His American Pupils," *Journal of Chemical Education* 33, no. 10 (October 1956): 493–95.

304 *"a usable past":* Kammen, *Mystic Chords of Memory*, 6.

304 *"substantial New England cheer":* Rodris Roth, "The New England, or 'Olde Tyme,' Kitchen Exhibit at Nineteenth-Century Fairs," in *The Colonial Revival in America*, ed. Alan Axelrod (New York: W. W. Norton, 1985), 159–83, 162. Also see Celia Betsky, "Inside the Past: The Interior and the Colonial Revival in American Art and Literature, 1860–1914," in the same volume, 241–77.

305 *The annual sojourners:* The paragraph below draws on annual guest book entries, family scrapbooks, garden plans, and photographs of the manor. SMA, NYU IV/A/3/97/13; IV/I/5, 7; VI/B.

307 *Cambridge's women and girls:* Henrietta Channing Dana Skinner, *An Echo from Parnassus: Being Girlhood Memories of Longfellow and His Friends* (New York: J. H. Sears, 1928); Mary Towle Palmer, *The Story of the Bee* (Cambridge, MA: Riverside, 1924); Anita Israel, Archives Specialist, Longfellow National Historic Site, pers. comm., Dec. 2009.

307 *"the imperative of memory":* Kammen, *Mystic Chords of Memory*, 101.

307 *The Danas' father, Richard Henry Jr.:* The elder Dana is better known as the author of *Two Years Before the Mast*. Charles Francis Adams, *Richard Henry Dana: A Biography* (Boston: Houghton, Mifflin, 1890), 263–96; von Frank, *The Trials of Anthony Burns*; Lawrence Lader, *The Bold Brahmins: New England's War Against Slavery, 1831–63* (New York: E. P. Dutton, 1961), 204–16.

308 *Benjamin Robbins Curtis Jr:* Proud of his father's life and works, Curtis Jr. wrote the preface to an 1879 memoir of his father, written by his uncle, George Ticknor Curtis, the federal commissioner charged with enforcing the Fugitive Slave Act in Massachusetts. In the 1850s, like Daniel Webster, their ally in Congress, both Curtis brothers acted to strengthen Southern concerns (including the return of fugitive slaves) in order to keep Northern industrial and banking interests profitable. George Ticknor Curtis, *A Memoir of Benjamin Robbins Curtis, LL.D., with Some*

of his Professional and Miscellaneous Writings Edited by His Son, Benjamin R. Curtis, vol. 1 (Boston: Little, Brown, 1879), https://play.google.com/books/reader?id=XP08AAAAIAAJ&printsec=frontcover&output=reader&authuser=0&hl=en&pg=GBS.PP4; Menand, *Metaphysical Club,* 10–12.

308 *the infamous Dred Scott case:* Don E. Fehrenbacher, *Slavery, Law, and Politics: The Dred Scott Case in Historical Perspective* (Oxford: Oxford University Press, 1981), 145–237; Michael Boudin, Chief Judge of the Court of Appeals for the First Circuit Massachusetts Court of Appeals (2001–2008), pers. comm., Nov. 2009; Daniel Hulsebosch, New York University School of Law, pers. comm., Dec. 2009.

308 *Curtis's views on slavery:* In 1836, Curtis argued that Med, a six-year-old black girl from New Orleans, was the property of her Louisiana owner who was visiting Massachusetts. He lost the case in Massachusetts Supreme Court, which ruled that a slave brought into a free state was freed on the moment of arrival. (Massachusetts had abolished slavery in 1783.)

310 *Quaker Graveyard:* The family burying ground became known as "the Quaker graveyard" when the monument was erected and the remains and slabs of Brinley and Mary Sylvester were removed to the island's Presbyterian cemetery. The earliest burial of the remaining ten was that of Jonathan Hudson of Shelter Island, d. April 5, 1729, whose son, Samuel, married Grizzell L'Hommedieu, daughter of Patience Sylvester and Benjamin L'Hommedieu of Southold. According to descendant Shirley Hudson, Jonathan Hudson came first to Connecticut from Barbados in 1680, and may have been a Quaker. See "Shelter Island," extracts transcribed by Jane Devlin from Harris, "Ancient Burial Grounds of Long Island," 54–58; also Mallman, *Historical Papers of Shelter Island,* 203, 310, 307; pers. corresp., Shirley Hudson to MKG, Jan. 4, 2007.

311 *"This venerable colored woman": The Long-Islander,* Huntington, Long Island, July 25, 1884.

312 *Baptism of the Calves: Shelter Island Historical Society Bulletin,* April 1984 and Spring 2001.

312 *"a custodian":* Kammen, *Mystic Chords,* 10.

312 *unlikely romance:* Eben and Cornelia both circulated "traditional accounts" that appeared in magazine articles about the manor and in local histories: Lamb, "The Manor of Shelter Island," 1887; Mallmann, *Historical Papers,* 1899; and Ralph Duvall, *The History of Shelter Island* (Shelter Island Heights, NY: no publisher indicated, 1932). They became part of the "history" of the island. Also see Alice Morse Earle, *Old-Time Gardens* (New York: Macmillan, 1901); Louise Shelton, *Beautiful Gardens in America* (New York: Charles Scribner's Sons, 1915); Cornelia Horsford, "The Garden at Sylvester Manor, Shelter Island"; and Cornelia Horsford, "The Manor of Shelter Island."

312 *detailed plans:* Sylvester Manor plans for C. Horsford, twenty-seven sheets of Henry Bacon, actual state, alterations, and additions for four floors, all 1908. SMA, NYU IV/H/7.

312 *the spot:* Cornelia Horsford to "Mrs. Strong," June 16, 1928, "Three Photocopies of Letters from Cornelia Horsford," SMA, NYU IV/H/1/104/68A.

312 *A remarkably detailed letter:* Cornelia Horsford, to "Mr Jefferys," August 17, 1934, "Three Photocopies of Letters from Cornelia Horsford," SMA, NYU: IV/H/1/104/68A.

313 *a letter to her mother:* SMA NYU IV/C/1/93/13.

313 *"died at Sag Harbour"*: Mary K. Horsford (attrib.), "A Pilgrimage to Shelter Island," *The Friend* (Aug. 28, 1908): 576.

314 *"slight smell"*: Farlow, "Memories of Samuel S. Gardiner."

319 *Nematodes:* Mary Ann Hansen, "Major Diseases of Boxwood," 450–614, Virginia Cooperative Extension, http://pubs.ext.vt.edu/450/450-614/450-614.html.

Bibliography

Abstracts of Wills 1665–1787. Suffolk County Surrogate's Court, Riverhead, NY.

Adams, James Truslow. *History of the Town of Southampton (East of Canoe Place)*. Bridgehampton, NY: Hampton Press, 1918.

Anonymous. "Extracts from the Annual Letters of the English Province of the Society of Jesus." In *Narratives of Early Maryland, 1633–84*, edited by Clayton C. Hall. New York: Charles Scribner's Sons, 1910.

Anonymous (attributed to George Puttenham). *The Arte of English Poesie*. Edited by Edward Arber. London, 1869, https://play.google.com/store/books/details?id=ThEJAAAAQAAJ&rdid=book-ThEJAAAAQAAJ&rdot=1. First published in London, 1589.

Arnold, Ken. "Trade, Travel, and Treasure: Seventeenth-Century Artificial Curiosities." In *Transports: Travel, Pleasure, and Imaginative Geography, 1600–1830*, edited by Chloe Chard and Helen Langdon. New Haven: Yale University Press, 1996, 263–85.

Astley, Thomas, ed. *A New General Collection of Voyages and Travels*. 4 vols. London, 1745.

Atkins, John. "A Voyage to Guinea, Brazil, and the West Indies." In *A New General Collection of Voyages and Travels*, edited by Thomas Astley, 3:450. London, 1745.

Austin, John O. *Genealogical Dictionary of Rhode Island: Comprising Three Generations of Settlers Who Came Before 1690*. Albany: Genealogical, 1995.

Aylmer, G. E. *The King's Servants: The Civil Service of Charles I, 1625–42*. New York: Columbia University Press, 1961.

Bacon, Francis. *Chymical, Medicinal, and Chyrurgical addresses made to Samuel Hartlib, Esquire*. London, 1655.

Bailey, Rosalie Fellows. "The Nicoll Family and Islip Grange." Address before the Order of Colonial Lords of Manors in America, April 21, 1938.

Bailyn, Bernard. *Atlantic History, Concept and Contours*. Cambridge, MA: Harvard University Press, 2005.

———. "Slavery and Population Growth in Colonial New England." In *Engines of Enterprise: An Economic History of New England*, edited by Peter Temin, 253–59. Cambridge, MA: Harvard University Press, 2000.

———. *The New England Merchants in the Seventeenth Century*. Cambridge, MA: Harvard University Press, 1979.

Baird, Charles W. *Chronicle of a Border Town: History of Rye, Westchester County, New York, 1660–1870.* New York: Anson D. F. Randolph, 1871, https://play.google.com/store/books/details?id=qXsVAAAAYAAJ&rdid=book-qXsVAAAAYAAJ&rdot=1.

Balfour, Michael. "Edmund Harman, Barber and Gentleman." Tolsey Paper no. 6. Burford: The Tolsey Museum, 1988.

Barbour, Hugh. *The Quakers in Puritan England.* Richmond, IN: Friends United Press, 1985. First published New Haven: Yale University Press, 1964.

Barbour, Violet. *Capitalism in Amsterdam in the Seventeenth Century.* Ann Arbor: University of Michigan Press, 1966. First published Johns Hopkins University Press, 1950.

Barck, Dorothy C., ed. *Papers of the Lloyd Family of the Manor of Queens Village, Lloyd's Neck, Long Island, New York, 1654–1826.* 2 vols. New York: New-York Historical Society, 1927.

Barrow, Thomas C. *Trade and Empire, The British Customs Service in Colonial America.* Cambridge, MA: Harvard University Press, 1967.

Batdorf, Lynn R. *The Boxwood Handbook: A Practical Guide to Knowing and Growing Boxwood.* Boyce, VA: The American Boxwood Society, 1997.

Beckles, Hilary McD. *A History of Barbados: From Amerindian Settlement to Nation-State.* Cambridge: Cambridge University Press, 1990.

———. *Natural Rebels: A Social History of Enslaved Black Women in Barbados.* New Brunswick, NJ: Rutgers University Press, 1989.

Behn, Aphra. *Oroonoko, or, The Royal Slave.* London, 1688.

Benes, Peter, ed. *New England's Creatures, 1400–1900.* Dublin Seminar for New England Folklife. Boston: Boston University Press, 1995.

Berkin, Carol. *First Generations: Women in Colonial America.* New York: Hill and Wang, 1997.

Berlin, Ira. *Generations of Captivity: A History of African-American Slaves.* Cambridge, MA: Belknap Press of Harvard University Press, 2003.

——— and Philip D. Morgan. "Labor and the Shaping of Slave Life in the Americas." In *Cultivation and Culture: Labor and the Shaping of Slave Life in the Americas.* Charlottesville: University of Virginia Press, 1993.

———. *Many Thousands Gone: The First Two Centuries of Slavery in America.* Cambridge, MA: Belknap Press of Harvard University Press, 1998.

——— and Leslie M. Harris, eds. *Slavery in New York.* New York: New Press and the New-York Historical Society, 2005.

Bezemer Sellers, Vanessa. *Courtly Gardens in Holland, 1600–50.* Amsterdam: Architectura & Natura Press, 2001.

Bishop, George. *New-England Judged by the Spirit of the Lord. In Two Parts.* London, 1661, 1703; Philadelphia: Thomas William Stuckey, Printer, ca. 1885, https://play.google.com/books/reader?id=67kTAAAAYAAJ&printsec=frontcover&output=reader&authuser=0&hl=en&pg=GBS.PA103.

Black Robert C. III, *The Younger John Winthrop.* New York: Columbia University Press, 1966.

Blakely, Allison. *Blacks in the Dutch World, The Evolution of Racial Imagery in a Modern Society.* Indianapolis: Indiana University Press, 1993.

Blaythwayt, William, comp. *The Blaythwayt Atlas.* John Carter Brown Library, Brown University, Providence, RI, ca. 1683. Reprint, *The Blaythwayt Atlas,* John Carter Brown Library, Providence, RI, 1970.

Block, Kristen. "'Merchantmen of the Precious Truth': Barbados Quakers and Evangelization of Slaves in the Late 17th Century." Chapter 4. "Faith and Fortune: Religious Identity and the Politics of Profit in the Seventeenth-Century Caribbean." Ph.D. dissertation, Rutgers University, 2007.

———. *Ordinary Lives in the Early Caribbean: Religion, Colonial Competition, and the Politics of Profit*. Athens: University of Georgia Press, 2012.

Bolton, Charla E., and Reginald H. Metcalf, Jr. "The Migration of the Jupiter Hammon Family: A Notable African American Journey. *Long Island History Journal*, May 2013.

Bonomi, Patricia U. "The African Diaspora, Christianity, and the Law in Colonial British America." Presented to the Atlantic History Seminar, New York University, December 4, 2007.

———. *Under the Cope of Heaven: Religion, Society and Politics in Colonial America*. New York and Oxford: Oxford University Press, 1986.

Bosman, Willem. *A New and Accurate Description of the Coast of Guinea, Divided into the Gold, the Slave, and the Ivory Coasts*, etc. London, 1705, http://play.google.com/books/reader?id=uNkTAAAAYAAJ&printsec=frontcover&output=reader&hl=en&pg=GBS.PT5.

Bragdon, Kathleen J. *Native People of Southern New England, 1500–1650*. Norman: University of Oklahoma Press, 1996.

Brandow, James C., ed. *Genealogies of Barbados Families*. Baltimore: Genealogical Publishing, 1983.

Braude, Benjamin. "The Sons of Noah and the Construction of Ethnic and Geographical Identities in the Medieval and Early Modern Periods." *WMQ* 54 (January 1997): 103–42.

Braudel, Fernand. *Civilization & Capitalism, 15th–18th Century*. Vol. 1. *The Structures of Everyday Life, New York: The Limits of the Possible*. New York: Harper & Row, 1981.

Brayton, Alice. "Rhode Island." In *Gardens of Colony and State: Gardens and Gardeners of the American Colonies and of the Republic Before 1840*. Edited by Alice G. B. Lockwood. New York: Charles Scribner's Sons, 1931, 1: 174–221.

Breen, T. H. *Imagining the Past: East Hampton Histories*. Reading, MA: Addison-Wesley, 1989.

Brenner, Robert. *Merchants and Revolution: Commercial Change, Political Conflict, and London's Overseas Traders, 1550–1653*. London: Verso, 2003. First published by Princeton University Press, 1993.

Brereton, Sir William. *Travels in Holland and the United Provinces, England, Scotland, and Ireland*. Edited by Edward Hawkins. Vol. 1. Printed for the Chetham Society, 1844.

Bridenbaugh, Carl. *Fat Mutton and Liberty of Conscience*. Providence, RI: Brown University Press, 1974.

———, and Roberta Bridenbaugh. *No Peace Beyond the Line: The English in the Caribbean 1624–90*. New York: Oxford University Press, 1972.

Brinley, Francis. "A Gentleman's Library of 1713." *NEHGR* 12 (January 1858): 75–78.

Brinton, Howard H. *Friends for 350 Years*. Wallingford, PA: Pendle Hill, 2002.

Brown, Kathleen M. *Foul Bodies: Cleanliness in Early America*. New Haven: Yale University Press, 2009.

———. *Good Wives, Nasty Wenches, and Anxious Patriarchs: Gender, Race, and Power in Colonial Virginia*. Chapel Hill: University of North Carolina Press for the Omohundro Institute of Early American History and Culture, 1996.

Brucia, Margaret A. "The African-American Poet, Jupiter Hammon: A Home-Born Slave and His Classical Name." *International Journal of the Classical Tradition* 7, no. 4 (Spring 2001): 516–22.

Buckinghamshire Probate Inventories, 1661–1714. Edited by Michael A. Reed. Buckinghamshire Record Society, 1988.

Burrough, Edward. *A Declaration of the Sad and Great Persecution and Martyrdom of the People of God Called Quakers in New-England, for the Worshipping of God.* London: Robert Wilson, 1661, http://digitalcommons.unl.edu/cgi/viewcontent.cgi?article=1023&context=etas.

Bushman, Richard L, ed. *The Great Awakening: Documents on the Revival of Religion, 1740–45.* Chapel Hill: University of North Carolina Press, 1969.

———. *The Refinement of America: Persons, Houses, Cities.* New York: Vintage Books, 1993.

Bushnell, Rebecca. *Green Desire: Imagining Early Modern English Gardens.* Ithaca: Cornell University Press, 2003.

Butler, Jon. *Becoming America: The Revolution Before 1776.* Cambridge, MA: Harvard University Press, 2000. First paperback edition, 2001.

Cadbury, Henry J. "The Captain of Shelter Island." *The Friend* (London) 3 (March 20, 1953): 257–58.

Cahilly, A. Wayne, and Todd Forrest. "Observation of Landforms, Hawthorns, and Other Genera at Sylvester Manor." New York Botanical Garden report, 2000, Griswold Papers, Fales Library, NYU.

Calder, Isabel MacBeath. *The New Haven Colony.* Hamden, CT: Archon, 1970.

Calloway, Colin G., and Neal Salisbury, eds. *Reinterpreting New England Indians and the Colonial Experience.* Boston: The Colonial Society of Massachusetts, 2003.

Campbell, Gwyn, Suzanne Miers, and Joseph C. Miller, eds. *Women and Slavery: Africa, the Indian Ocean World and the Medieval North Atlantic.* Athens: Ohio University Press, 2007.

Campbell, Peter F. "Ligon's Map," *JBMHS* 34 (1973): 108–12.

———. *Some early Barbadian History: as well as the text of a book published anonymously in 1741 entitled 'Memoirs of the first settlement of the island of Barbados . . .' : and a transcription of a manuscript entitled 'The description of Barbados' written about the year 1677 by Major John Scott.* St. Michael, Barbados: Caribbean Graphics, 1993.

———. "Two Generations of Walronds: Power Corrupts." *JBMHS* 39 (1991): 1–23.

Canny, Nicholas. *Making Ireland British.* Oxford: Oxford University Press, 2001.

Case, J. Wickham. *Southold Town Records Copied and Explanatory Notes Added by J. Wickham Case.* 2 vols. New York: S. W. Green's Sons, 1882–84.

Catterall, Ralph C. H. "Sir George Downing and the Regicides." In *American Historical Review* 17 (1912): 268–89.

Caulkins, Francis Manwaring. *History of New London, Connecticut, from the first Survey of the Coast in 1612, to 1852.* New London, CT: published by the author, 1852.

Chapman, Colin R. *Weights, Money and Other Measures Used by Our Ancestors.* Baltimore: Genealogical Publishing, 1996.

Christoph, Peter R., and Florence A. Christoph, eds. *Books of General Entries of the Colony of New York 1674–88.* Baltimore: Genealogical Publishing, for the Holland Society of New York, 1982.

Chu, Jonathan M. *Neighbors, Friends or Madmen: The Puritan Adjustment to Quakerism in Seventeenth-Century Massachusetts Bay.* Westport, CT: Greenwood Press, 1985.

Church Records of the Presbyterian Church 1806–65, Shelter Island, New York.

Clark, Alice. *Working Life of Women in the Seventeenth Century.* London: Routledge & Kegan Paul, 1982. First published in 1919.

Cogswell, Thomas, Richard Cust, and Peter Lake. "Revisionism and Its Legacies: The Work of Conrad Russell." In *Politics, Religion and Popularity in Early Stuart Britain: Essays in Honour of Conrad Russell*. Cambridge: Cambridge University Press, 2002.

Coldham, Peter Wilson. *English Adventurers and Emigrants, 1609–60: Abstracts of Examinations in the High Court of Admiralty with Reference to Colonial America 1609–60*. Baltimore: Genealogical Publishing, 1984.

———. *The Complete Book of Emigrants, 1661–99: A Comprehensive Listing Compiled from English Public Records of Those Who Took Ship to the Americas for Political, Religious, and Economic Reasons; of Those Who Were Deported for Vagrancy, Roguery, or Non-Conformity; and of Those Who Were Sold to Labour in the New Colonies*. Baltimore: Genealogical Publishing, 1990.

The Colonial Laws of New York from the Year 1664 to the Revolution. Vol. 1. *1664–1719*. Introductory note by Charles Zabine Lincoln, William Henry Johnson, Ansel Judd Northrup, New York (State) Commissioners of Statutory Revision. Albany: James B. Lyon Co., 1894, https://play.google.com/books/reader?id=d3U4AAAAIAAJ&printsec=frontcover&output=reader&authuser=0&hl=en_US&pg=GBS.PR3.

Coombs, John C. "One for the Negro Slaves: Houses, Homelots, and the Development of Slavery in Early Colonial Virginia." Annual meeting, Society for Historical Archaeology, 2007.

———. "The Phases of Conversion: A New Chronology for the Rise of Slavery in Early Virginia." *WMQ* 3rd series, 68, no. 3 (July 2011).

Coughtry, Jay. *The Notorious Triangle: Rhode Island and the African Slave Trade, 1700–1807*. Philadelphia: Temple University Press, 1981.

Croese, Gerard. *A History of the Quakers*. London: John Dunton, 1696.

Cronon, William. *Changes in the Land: Indians, Colonists, and the Ecology of New England*. New York: Hill and Wang, 1983.

Crosby, Alfred W., Jr., *The Columbian Exchange: Biological and Cultural Consequences of 1492*. Westport, CT: Greenwood Press, 1973.

Cummings, Abbott Lowell, ed. *Rural Household Inventories: Establishing the Names, Uses and Furnishings of Rooms in the Colonial New England Home, 1675–1775*. Boston: The Society for the Preservation of New England Antiquities, 1964.

———. *The Framed Houses of Massachusetts Bay, 1625–1725*. Cambridge, MA: Belknap Press of Harvard University Press, 1979.

Curtin, Philip D. *The Atlantic Slave Trade: A Census*. Madison: University of Wisconsin Press, 1969.

Curwen, Alice. *A Relation of the Labours, Travails and Suffering of that Faithful Servant of the Lord Alice Curwen*. London, 1680.

Dailey, Barbara Ritter. "The Early Quaker Mission and the Settlement of Meetings in Barbados, 1655–1700." *JBMHS* 39 (1991): 24–47.

Davis, David Brion. *The Problem of Slavery in Western Culture*. New York: Oxford University Press, 1966.

Davis, Paul. "Abraham Redwood and the West Indies Trade." *Providence Journal*, March 12, 2006.

Day, Lynda R. "Friends in the Spirit: African Americans and the Challenge to Quaker Liberalism, 1776–1915." *LIHS* 10, no. 1 (Fall 1997): 1–16.

Dayton, Cornelia Hughes. *Women Before the Bar: Gender, Law, and Society in Connecticut, 1639–1789*. Chapel Hill: University of North Carolina Press, 1995.

de Carli, Denis, and Michael Angelo. "A Curious and Exact Account of a Voyage to Congo in the Years 1666, and 1667." In *A Collection of Voyages and Travels, Some Now First Printed from Original Manuscripts*. Edited by Awnsham Churchill and John Churchill. Vol. 1. London, 1732.

Deetz, James. *In Small Things Forgotten: An Archaeology of Early American Life*. New York: Anchor Books, 1996.

de Jong, Erik. *Nature and Art: Dutch Garden and Landscape Architecture, 1650–1740*. Philadelphia: University of Pennsylvania Press, 2001.

De Laet, Johannes. *Iaerlyck Verhael van de Verrichtinghen der Geoctroyeerde West-Indische Compagnie in Derthien Boeken* (Annual Report of the Activities of the Chartered West-Indian Company in Thirteen Books). Edited by S. P. l'Honoré Naber and J.C.M. Warnsinck. The Hague: Martinus Nijhoff, 1937.

de Marees, Pieter. *Description and Historical Account of the Gold Kingdom of Guinea (1602)*. Translated and edited by Albert van Danzig and Adam Jones. New York: Oxford University Press, 1987.

den Heijer, Henk. "The West African Trade of the Dutch West India Company, 1674–1740." In *Riches from Atlantic Commerce: Dutch Transatlantic Trade and Shipping, 1585–1817*, edited by Johannes Postma and Victor Enthoven. Leiden, The Netherlands: Brill, 2003, 139–69.

DeRiggi, Mildred Murphy. "Quakerism on Long Island: The First Fifty Years, 1657–1707." Ph.D. dissertation, SUNY, Stonybrook, 1994.

Dering, Sylvester. Sylvester Dering Letter Collection. SIHS #2012.302.1–8.

Deutsch, Sarah. "The Elusive Guineamen: Newport Slavers, 1735–74." *NEQ* 55, no. 2 (June 1982): 229–53.

de Vries, David Pietersz. *Narratives of New Netherland 1609–64*. Alckmeer, The Netherlands, 1655. Edited by J. Franklin Jameson. New York: Charles Scribner's Sons, 1909. https://play.google.com/store/books/details?id=VAYTAAAAYAAJ.

———. *Voyages from Holland to America A.D. 1632 to 1644*. Alckmeer, The Netherlands: 1655. Translated by Henry C. Murphy. New York, Billin & Bros., 1853, https://play.google.com/store/books/details?id=2MJPAAAAcAAJ.

Dijkman, Jessica. "Giles Silvester: An English Merchant in Amsterdam." Research paper commissioned for the Sylvester Manor Project, February 2003. In Griswold Papers, Fales Library, New York University.

Dinkel, Hannah, and Frederick Dinkel. Collection of Family Papers. Shelter Island, New York; transcriptions,SMA, NYU, and SIHS.

Dixon Hunt, John, and Peter Willis, eds. *The Genius of the Place: The English Landscape Garden, 1620–1820*. New York: Harper & Row, 1975.

Dobson, M. J. "History of Malaria in England." *Journal of the Royal Society of Medicine* 82, supplement no. 17 (1989): 3–7.

Donnan, Elizabeth, ed. *Documents Illustrative of the History of the Slave Trade to America*. Vol. 1. Washington, DC: Carnegie Institution of Washington, 1930.

Downing, Antoinette F., and Vincent Scully Jr. *The Architectural Heritage of Newport, Rhode Island, 1640–1915*. New York: Clarkson N. Potter, 1967.

Drake, Francis S. *The Town of Roxbury, Its Memorable Persons and Places, Its History and Antiquities, with Numerous Illustrations of Its Old Landmarks and Noted Personages*. Boston: Municipal Printing Offices, 1908.

Drax, Henry. "Instructions which I would have observed by Mr. Richard Harwood in the Mannagment of My plantation according to the Articles of Agreement betwene us which are heare unto Annexed." Rawlinson Mss A348, fol. 10v, Bodleian Library, University of Oxford.

Dunn, Mary Maples. "Saints and Sisters: Congregational and Quaker Women in the Early Colonial Period." In *Women in American Religion*, edited by Janet Wilson James, 27–46. Philadelphia: University of Pennsylvania Press, 1980.

Dunn, Richard S. *Sugar and Slaves: The Rise of the Planter Class in the English West Indies, 1624–1713*. New York: W. W. Norton, 1973.

———. "The Barbados Census of 1680: Profile of the Richest Colony in English America." *WMQ* 3rd ser., 26 (1969): 3–30.

Dupree, A. Hunter. *Asa Gray: American Botanist, Friend of Darwin*. Baltimore: Johns Hopkins University Press, 1988.

Duvall, Ralph G. (Attrib.) Shelter Island in 1870. Written about 1928. http://www.shelter-island.org/duvall_tour.html.

———. *The History of Shelter Island, from Its Settlement in 1652 to the Present Time, 1932*. Shelter Island Heights, NY: Privately printed, 1932.

Dwight, Timothy. *Travels in New England and New York*. Edited by Barbara Miller Solomon. Vol. 3. Cambridge, MA: Belknap Press of Harvard University Press, 1969.

Dyer, William Allen. "William Dyer, a Rhode Island Dissenter." *Rhode Island Historical Society Collections* 30 (1937).

Earle, Alice Morse. *Old-Time Gardens*. New York: MacMillan, 1901, https://play.google.com/store/books/details?id=XukYAAAAYAAJ&rdid=book-XukYAAAAYAAJ&rdot=1.

Edmundson, William. *A Journal of the Life, Travels, Sufferings and Labour of Love in the Work of the Ministry of That Faithful, Worthy Elder and Faithful Servant of Jesus Christ, William Edmundson*. London: Harvey & Darton, 1829, https://play.google.com/store/books/details?id=NQ9NAAAAcAAJ&rdid=book-NQ9NAAAAcAAJ&rdot=1.

Edney, Matthew H., and Susan Cimburek. "Telling the Traumatic Truth: William Hubbard's *Narrative* of King Philip's War and His Map of New-England." *WMQ* 61 (2004): 317–48.

Eltis, David, and David Richardson. *Atlas of the Transatlantic Slave Trader*. New Haven: Yale University Press, 2010.

Enthoven, Victor, and Wim Klooster. "The Rise and Fall of the Virginia-Dutch Connection in the Seventeenth Century." In *Early Modern Virginia: Reconsidering the Old Dominion*, edited by Douglas Bradburn and John C. Coombs, 90–127. Charlottesville: University of Virginia Press, 2011.

Failey, Dean F. *Long Island Is My Nation*. 2nd ed. Albany: Mount Ida Press for the Society for the Preservation of Long Island Antiquities, 1998.

Fairbanks, Jonathan L., and Robert F. Trent. *New England Begins: The Seventeenth Century*. Vol. 3. Boston: Museum of Fine Arts, 1982.

Farlow, Lilian Horsford. "Memories of Samuel Smith Gardiner." Literary Essay no. 21, SIHS.

Farnell, J. E. "The Navigation Act of 1651, the First Dutch War, and the London Merchant Community." *Economic History Review*, 2nd ser., 16, no. 3 (1963–64): 439–54.

Fehrenbacher, Don E. *Slavery, Law, and Politics: The Dred Scott Case in Historical Perspective*. Abridged. Oxford: Oxford University Press, 1981.

Ferguson, Leland. *Uncommon Ground: Archaeology and Early African America, 1650–1800*. Washington, DC: Smithsonian Institution, 1992.

Fernow, Berthold, comp., A.J.F. van Laer, ed. "Calendar of Council Minutes, 1668–1783," *New York State Library Bulletin* 58, History 6. Albany: University of the State of New

York, March 1902, https://play.google.com/store/books/details?id=jFAOAAAIAAJ&rdid=book-jFAOAAAIAAJ&rdot=1.

Field, Jonathan Beecher. "The Grounds of Dissent: Heresies and Colonies in New England, 1636–63." Ph.D. dissertation, University of Chicago, 2004.

Fischer, David Hackett. *Albion's Seed: Four British Folkways in America*. New York: Oxford University Press, 1989.

Fitts, Robert K. "The Landscapes of Northern Bondage." *Historical Archaeology* 30, no. 2 (1996): 54–73.

Foster, Nicholas. *A Briefe Relation of the Late Horrid Rebellion Acted in the Island Barbadas, in the West-Indie. Wherein Is Contained, Their Inhumane Acts and Actions, in Fining and Banishing the Well-affected to the Parliament of England (Both Men and Women) Without the Least Cause Given Them So to Doe: Dispossessing All Such as Any Way Opposed These Their Mischievous Actions. Acted by the Waldronds and Their Abettors, Anno 1650*. London: Printed for I.G. for Richard Lowndes on Ludgate Hill, and Robert Boydell in the Bulwarke neere the Tower, 1650.

Fox, George. *A Collection of Many Select and Christian Epistles, Letters and Testimonies, Written on Sundry Occasions, by That Ancient, Eminent, Faithful Friend and Minister of Christ Jesus, George Fox*. London, 1698.

———. *An Autobiography*. Edited by Rufus M. Jones. Philadelphia: Ferris & Leach, 1903, https://play.google.com/books/reader?id=SsthpbX3ZyUC&printsec=frontcover&output=reader&authuser=0&hl=en&pg=GBS.PA160.w.0.3.0.

———. *The Journal*. Edited with notes by Nigel Smith. London: Penguin Books, 1998.

———. *The Works of George Fox*. Philadelphia: Marcus T. Gould: 1831.

Frost, J. William. *The Quaker Origins of Antislavery*. Norwood, PA: Norwood Editions, 1980.

Games, Alison. *Migration and the Origins of the English Atlantic World*. Cambridge, MA: Harvard University Press, 1999.

Gardiner, John Lion. *The Gardiners of Gardiner's Island*. East Hampton: Star Press, 1927.

Gardiner, Lion. *Relation of the Pequot Warres*. Hartford, CT: Acorn, 1901, http://digitalcommons.unl.edu/etas/38.

Gardiner, Robert Barlow. *Admissions Registers of St. Paul's School from 1748 to 1876. Edited with Biographical Notices and Notes on the Earlier Masters and Scholars of the School from the Time of Its Foundation*. London: George Bell and Sons, 1884, https://play.google.com/store/books/details?id=AQ0CAAAAYAAJ&rdid=book-AQ0CAAAAYAAJ&rdot=1.

Garland, Charles, and Herbert S. Klein. "The Allotment of Space for Slaves Aboard Eighteenth-Century British Slave Ships." *WMQ* 3rd Series, 42, no. 2 (1985): 238–48.

Gary, Jack. "Material Culture and Multi-Cultural Interactions at Sylvester Manor." In *The Historical Archaeology of Sylvester Manor*, edited by Katherine Howlett Hayes and Stephen A. Mrozowski. Special issue, *Northeast Historical Archaeology* 36 (2007): 100–112.

Gapar, Barry David. "Slave resistance in Antigua, West Indies, 1700–1730." Presented to the 94th Annual Meeting of the American Historical Association, New York, 1979.

Gellman, D., and D. Quigley, eds. *Jim Crow New York: A Documentary History of Race and Citizenship, 1777–1877*. New York: New York University Press, 2003.

General Sylvester Dering II Document Book, SIHS.

Gerona, Carla. *Night-Journeys: The Power of Dreams in Quaker Culture*. Charlottesville: University of Virginia Press, 2004.

Gleick, Peter H. "Basic Water Requirements for Human Activities: Meeting Basic Needs." *Water International* 21, no. 2 (1996): 83–92.

Godwin, Morgan. *The Negro's and Indians Advocate, Suing for Their Admission in the Church*. London, 1680.

Goldenberg, David M. "The Curse of Ham: A Case of Rabbinic Racism?" In *Struggles in the Promised Land: Towards a History of Black-Jewish Relations*, edited by Jack Salzman and Cornel West. Oxford: Oxford University Press, 1997.

Golway, Terry. *Washington's General: Nathanael Greene and the Triumph of the American Revolution*. New York: Henry Holt, 2005.

Gomez, Michael A. *Exchanging Our Country Marks: The Transformation of African Identities in the Colonial and Antebellum South*. Chapel Hill: University of North Carolina Press, 1998.

Gordon-Reed, Annette. "Reading *White on Black*." *William and Mary Quarterly*, 3rd series, 69, no. 4 (October 2012): 853–57.

Grady, Anne H. *Historic Structure Report: Spencer-Pierce-Little House, Newbury, Massachusetts*. Waltham: Society for the Preservation of New England Antiquities, Conservation Center, 1922.

Gragg, Larry. *Englishmen Transplanted: The English Colonization of Barbados 1627–60*. Oxford: Oxford University Press, 2003.

———. *The Quaker Community on Barbados: Challenging the Culture of the Planter Class*. Columbia: University of Missouri Press, 2009.

———. "'To Procure Negroes': The English Slave Trade to Barbados, 1627–60." *Slavery and Abolition* 16 (1995).

Graham, Willie, Carter L. Hudgins, Carl R. Lounsbury, Fraser D. Neiman, and James P. Whittenburg. "Adaptation and Innovation: Archaeological and Architectural Perspectives on the Seventeenth-Century Chesapeake." *WMQ* 3rd series, 64, no. 3 (July 2007): 451–522.

Gray, Madeleine. "Exchequer Officials and the Market in Crown Property." In *The Estates of the English Crown, 1558–1640*, edited by R. W. Hoyle. Cambridge: Cambridge University Press, 1992.

———. "Land Revenue in the Late Sixteenth and Early Seventeenth Centuries." *Archives, the Journal of the British Records Association* 20, no. 87 (April 1992): 45–62.

Griffin, Augustus. *The Diaries of Augustus Griffin*. Edited by Fredrika Wachsberger. Orient, NY: Oysterponds Historical Society, 2009.

Griswold, Mac. Griswold Papers, 1997–2012. Fales Library, New York University.

———. "Nathanial Sylvester of Amsterdam and Shelter Island." Paper presented March 20, 2009, at "The Worlds of Lion Gardiner, ca. 1599–1663: Crossings and Boundaries." Stony Brook University, Stony Brook, NY, March 20–21, 2009.

———. "Sylvester Manor: A Colonial Garden Becomes a Colonial Revival Garden." *Journal of the New England Garden History Society* 5 (Fall 1997): 25–34.

Grumet, Robert S., ed. *Northeastern Indian Lives, 1632–1816*. Amherst: University of Massachusetts Press, 1996.

Gunther, R. T. *Early British Botanists and Their Gardens*. Oxford: Oxford University Press, 1922.

Hall, David D., ed. *The Antinomian Controversy, 1636–38: A Documentary History*. Durham, NC: Duke University Press, 1990.

Hamilton, Alexander. *Gentleman's Progress: The Itinerarium of Dr. Alexander Hamilton, 1744*. Edited by Carl Bridenbaugh. Chapel Hill: University of North Carolina Press, 1948.

Hancock, Anne P. "The Changing Landscape of a Former Northern Plantation: Sylvester Manor, Shelter Island, New York." Master's thesis, University of Massachusetts Boston, 2002.

Handler, Jerome S. "Father Antoine Biet's Visit to Barbados in 1654." *JBMHS* 32 (1967): 50–76, http://jeromehandler.org/wp-content/uploads/2009/07/Biet-67.pdf.

———. "Plantation Slave Settlements in Barbados, 1650s to 1834." In *In the Shadow of the Plantation: Caribbean History and Legacy*, edited by Alvin O. Thompson. Kingston, Jamaica: Ian Randle, 2002, 121–58, http://jeromehandler.org/2002/07/plantation-slave-settlements-in-barbados-1650s-to-1834.

———. "Slave Revolts and Conspiracies in Seventeenth-Century Barbados." *New West Indian Guide* 56, nos. 1–2 (Leiden, The Netherlands, 1982): 5–42.

———. *Supplement to A Guide to Source Materials for the Study of Barbados History, 1627–1834*, Providence, RI: John Carter Brown Library and the Barbados Museum and Historical Society, 1991.

———. "The Amerindian Slave Population of Barbados in the Seventeenth and Early Eighteenth Centuries." *Caribbean Studies* 8, no. 4 (1969): 38–64, http://jeromehandler.org/wp-content/uploads/2009/07/AmerindSlaves-69.pdf.

———. Untitled review of Sidney M. Greenfield's 1966 *English Rustics in Black Skin: A Study of Modern Family Forms in a Pre-industrialized Society*. New Haven, CT: College and University Press, 1966. In *American Anthropologist*, New Ser., 71, no. 2 (Apr. 1969), 335–37, http://jeromehandler.org/wp-content/uploads/GreenfieldReview69.pdf.

——— and Stephanie Bergman. "Vernacular Houses and Domestic Material Culture on Barbados Sugar Plantations, 1650–1838." *Journal of Caribbean History* 43 (2009): 1–36, http://jeromehandler.org/wp-content/uploads/House-09.pdf.

——— and Robert S. Corruccini. "Plantation Slave Life in Barbados: A Physical Anthropological Analysis." *Journal of Interdisciplinary History* 14, no. 1 (Summer 1983): 65–90, 79–81, http://jeromehandler.org/wp-content/uploads/2009/07/PlantSlaveLife-83.pdf.

——— and Frederick W. Lange, *Plantation Slavery in Barbados: An Archaeological and Historical Investigation*. Cambridge, MA: Harvard University Press, 1978.

Harlow, Vincent T., ed. *Colonizing Expeditions to the West Indies and Guiana, 1623–67*. London: The Hakluyt Society, 1924. Reprinted, Nendeln/Liechtenstein: Kraus Reprint Limited, 1967.

———. *A History of Barbados, 1625–85*. London and Oxford: Clarendon, 1926.

Harris, Edward Doubleday. "Ancient Burial Grounds of Long Island, N.Y." *NEHGR* 54 (1900).

Harvey, John. *Medieval Gardens*. Beaverton, OR: Timber Press, 1981.

Havens, Lodowick (1774–1854). Journal, n.d. SIHS.

Hayden, Roger. "The Records of a Church of Christ in Bristol, 1640–87." *Bristol Record Society* 23 (1974).

Hayes, Katherine Howlett. "Field Excavations at Sylvester Manor." *The Historical Archaeology of Sylvester Manor*, edited by Katherine Howlett Hayes and Stephen A. Mrozowski. Special issue, *Northeast Historical Archaeology* 36 (2007): 34–50.

———. "Race Histories: Colonial Pluralism and the Production of History at the Sylvester Manor Site, Shelter Island, New York." Ph.D. dissertation, University of California, Berkeley, 2008.

———. *Slavery Before Race: Europeans, Africans, and Indians at Long Island's Sylvester Manor Plantation, 1651–1884*. New York: New York University Press, 2013.

Heal, Ambrose. *The English Writing-Masters and Their Copy-Books, 1570–1800: A Biographical Dictionary & a Bibliography with an Introduction on the Development of Handwriting by Stanley Morison*. Hildesheim: Georg Olms Verlagsbuchhandlung, 1962.

Hefner, Robert. "Sylvester Manor: Brinley Sylvester's c. 1737 House, 80 North Ferry Road, Shelter Island, N.Y." Historic Structure Report, Architecture Component, prepared for Sylvester Manor Educational Farm, Inc., March 2013.

Hemmersam, Michael. "Michael Hemmersam's Description of the Gold Coast, 1639–45." In *German Sources for West African History 1599–1669*, edited by Adam Jones. Wiesbaden, Germany: Franz Steiner Verlag GMBH, 1983.

Hempstead, Joshua. *The Diary of Joshua Hempstead: A Daily Record of Life in Colonial New London, Connecticut, 1711–58*. New London, CT: The New London County Historical Society, 1999.

Higginbotham, A. Leon, Jr. *In the Matter of Color, Race and the American Legal Process: The Colonial Period*. Oxford: Oxford University Press, 1978.

Higman, B. W. *Jamaican Food: History, Biology, Culture*. Jamaica: University of the West Indies Press, 2008.

Hill, Christopher. *The Collected Essays of Christopher Hill*. Vol. 2, *Religion and Politics in 17th Century England*. Amherst: University of Massachusetts Press, 1986.

———. *The World Turned Upside Down: Radical Ideas During the English Revolution*. London: Penguin Books, 1991. First published London: Temple Smith, 1972.

Hill, Thomas. *The Gardeners Labyrinth*. London, 1577. Reprinted New York: Garland, 1982.

Hinsley, Curtis M. *The Smithsonian and the American Indian: Making a Moral Anthropology in Victorian America*. Washington, DC: Smithsonian Institution, 1981.

Hoadly, Charles J., ed. *Records of the Colony or Jurisdiction of New Haven from May 1653, to the Union*. Hartford, CT: Case, Lockwood, 1858, https://play.google.com/store/books/details?id=7PwPAAAAYAAJ&rdid=book-7PwPAAAAYAAJ&rdot=1.

Hodges, Graham Russell. *Root & Branch: African Americans in New York and East Jersey, 1613–1863*. Chapel Hill: University of North Carolina Press, 1999.

———, and Alan Edward Brown, eds. *"Pretends to Be Free:" Runaway Slave Advertisements from Colonial and Revolutionary New York and New Jersey*. New York: Garland, 1994.

Hoff, Henry B. "The Sylvester Family of Shelter Island," *NYGBR* 125, no. 1 (January 1994): 13–18.

———. "The Sylvester Family of Shelter Island," Part 2, "The Arnold Family of Lowestoft, Suffolk, England; Amsterdam; and Southold, Long Island," *NYGBR* 125, no. 2 (April 1994): pp. 89–93.

Hollander, Anne. *Seeing Through Clothes*. New York: Viking, 1978.

Hook, Rev. Walter Farquhar. *A Church Dictionary*. London: John Murray, 1858.

Hoppin, Charles A. "Brinley." Unpublished research paper commissioned by the Horsford family, ca. 1904. Copy, Griswold Papers, Fales Library, NYU.

Horsford, Cornelia. "The Garden at Sylvester Manor, Shelter Island." In *Gardens of Colony and State: Gardens and Gardeners of the American Colonies and of the*

Republic Before 1840, edited by Alice G. B. Lockwood, 1:276–79. New York: Charles Scribner's Sons, 1931.

———. "The Manor of Shelter Island." Address read before the annual meeting of the Order of Colonial Lords of Manors in America on April 23, 1931. New York, privately printed, 1934.

Horsford, Eben Norton. "Drafts, notes, and miscellaneous materials for a genealogical manuscript." SMA, NYU IV/A/11/111/20, 21 and 112/1-6

———. "Exercises at the Unveiling of the Monument to Nathaniel Sylvester, on Shelter Island, Thursday, 2:30 PM, July 17, 1884." University Press, John Wilson and Son, Cambridge, 1884. Also published in the *Brooklyn Eagle*, Jul. 17, 1884. Reprinted in *Friends' Intelligencer* 41, no. 28 (Aug. 1884): 436–37, https://play.google.com/store/books/details?id=cLlNAAAAMAAJ&rdid=book-cLlNAAAAMAAJ&rdot=1.

———. "President Tyler's Sherwood Forest," letter to Maria Chary Horsford, February 14, 1852. Rennselaer Polytechnic Institute, Troy, NY: Horsford Family Papers 1:6.

———. *The Problem of the Northmen: A Letter to Judge Daly, the President of the American Geographical Society, on the Opinion of Justice Winsor, that "Though Scandinavians may have reached the Shores of Labrador, the Soil of the United States Has Not One Vestige of Their Presence."* Cambridge: John Wilson and Son, 1889.

Horsford Family Papers. Archives and Special Collections, Rensselaer Polytechnic Institute, Troy, NY.

Horsford, Mary Katherine (attributed). "A Pilgrimage to Shelter Island," *The Friend* (Aug. 28, 1908): 574–76.

Hotten, John Camden. *The Original Lists of Persons of Quality; Emigrants; Religious Exiles; Political Rebels; Serving Men Sold for a Term of Years; Apprentices; Children Stolen; Maidens Pressed; and Others Who Went from Great Britain to the American Plantations 1600–1700*. London: Public Record Office, 1874, https://play.google.com/store/books/details?id=VN_A5wlsjQQC&rdid=book-VN_A5wlsjQQC&rdot=1.

Houghton, Raymond W., David Berman, and Maureen T. Lapan. *Images of Berkeley*. Dublin: Wolfhound Press, 1986.

Hughes, Ann. "The Execution of Charles I." http://www.bbc.co.uk/history/british/civil_war_revolution/charlesi_execution_01.shtml.

Inventory of the Estate of Brinley Sylvester, Esq., May 9, 1753, East Hampton Library.

Ireland, Ralph. "Slavery on Long Island: A Study in Economic Motivation. " *Journal of Long Island History* 6 (Spring 1966): 1–12.

Israel, Jonathan I. *Dutch Primacy in World Trade, 1585–1740*. Oxford: Clarendon, 2002.

———. *The Dutch Republic: Its Rise, Greatness and Fall, 1477–1806*. Oxford: Clarendon, 1995.

Jacques, David. "Who Knows What a Dutch Garden Is?" *Journal of the Garden History Society* (Winter, 2002): 114–30.

Janse, Herman. *Building Amsterdam*. Amsterdam: De Brink, 2001.

Jaray, Cornell, ed. *Historic Chronicles of New Amsterdam, Colonial New York and Early Long Island*. New York: Ira J. Friedman, 1968.

Jimenez, Mary Ann. "Madness in Early American History: Insanity in Massachusetts 1700–1830." *Journal of Social History* 20 (1986): 25–44.

Jones, Adam, ed. *German Sources for West African History, 1599–1669*. Germany: Franz Steiner Verlag GMBH, 1983.

Jones, David S. "Virgin Soils Revisited." *WMQ* 3rd ser., 60 (2003): 703–42.
Jones, Rufus M. *The Quakers in the American Colonies*. London: Macmillan, 1923.
Jordan, Winthrop D. "The Influence of the West Indies on the Origins of New England Slavery." *WMQ* 18 (1961).
———. *White over Black: American Attitudes Toward the Negro, 1550–1812*. Chapel Hill: University of North Carolina Press, 2012.
Kamensky, Jane. *Governing the Tongue: The Politics of Speech in Early New England*. New York: Oxford University Press, 1997.
Kammen, Michael. *Mystic Chords of Memory: The Transformation of Tradition in American Culture*. New York: Vintage, 1993.
Kences, James E. "The Horses and Horse Trades of Colonial Boston." In *The Dublin Seminar for New England Folklife, Annual Proceedings* 18 (1993): 73–82.
Kennish, Janet. "Brinley Family Charts" (2001); "Sylvester Family Charts " (2001); "Burford Sylvesters Chart" (2007); and "Wase, Budd, Brinley, Hanbury, Wheeler Chart" (2005). SMA, NYU.
———. *Datchet Past*. West Sussex: Phillimore, 1999.
Kerssenbrock, Hermann von. *Narrative of the Anabaptist Madness: The Overthrow of Münster, the Famous Metropolis of Westphalia*. Translated with introduction and notes by Christopher S. Mackay. *Studies in the History of Christian Traditions* 132. Leiden, The Netherlands: Brill, 2007.
King, Rufus. "Early Settlers of Southold, Suffolk County, Long Island." *NYGBR* 30 (Apr. 1889).
Kiple, Kenneth F. *The Caribbean Slave, A Biological History*. Cambridge: Cambridge University Press, 1984.
Klein, Herbert S. *The Atlantic Slave Trade*. Cambridge: Cambridge University Press, 1999.
———. "The Atlantic Slave Trade to 1650." In Schwartz, *Tropical Babylons*, 201–36.
——— and S. I. Engerman. "The Demographic Study of the American Slave Population; with Particular Attention Given the Comparison Between the United States and the West Indies." Unpublished paper presented at the International Colloquium in Historical Demography, 1975.
Klooster, H. S. Van. "Liebig and His American Pupils." *Journal of Chemical Education* 33, no. 10 (October 1956): 493–95.
Klooster, Wim. *The Dutch in the Americas 1600–1800, A Narrative History with the Catalogue of an Exhibition of Rare Prints, Maps, and Illustrated Books from the John Carter Brown Library*. Providence, RI: The John Carter Brown Library, 1997.
Knight, Sarah Kemble. "The Journal of Madam Knight." In *Colonial American Travel Narratives*, edited by Wendy Martin, 50–75. New York: Penguin, 1994.
Kohler, Lyle. *A Search for Power: The "Weaker Sex" in Seventeenth-Century New England*. Chicago: University of Illinois Press, 1980.
Kolodny, Annette. *The Land Before Her: Fantasy and Experience of the American Frontiers, 1630–1860*. Chapel Hill: University of North Carolina Press, 1984.
Krech, Shepard, III. *The Ecological Indian: Myth and History*. New York: W. W. Norton, 1999.
Kupperman, Karen Ordahl, ed. *America in European Consciousness, 1493–1750*. Chapel Hill: University of North Carolina Press for the Institute of Early American History and Culture, 1995.
———. "Climate and Mastery of the Wilderness in Seventeenth-Century New

England." In David D. Hall and David G. Allen, eds., *Seventeenth-Century New England*. Boston: Colonial Society of Massachusetts, 1984.

———. "Fear of Hot Climates in the Anglo-Colonial Experience." *WMQ* 3rd Ser., 41, no. 2 (April 1984): 213–40.

———. *Providence Island, 1630–41: The Other Puritan Colony*. Cambridge: Cambridge University Press, 1995. First published in 1993.

———. *Settling with the Indians: The Meeting of English and Indian Cultures in America, 1580–1640*. London: J. M. Dent & Sons, 1980.

———. "The Changing Definition of America." In *America in European Consciousness, 1493–1750*. Chapel Hill: University of North Carolina Press for the Institute of Early American History and Culture, 1995.

———. *The Jamestown Project*. Cambridge, MA: Belknap Press of Harvard University Press, 2007.

———. "The Puzzle of the American Climate in the Early Colonial Period." *The American Historical Review* 87, no. 5 (1982): 1262–89.

Kussmall, Ann. *Servants in Husbandry in Early Modern England*. Cambridge: Cambridge University Press, 1981.

Kvamme, Kenneth L. *Final Report of Geophysical Investigations Conducted at Sylvester Manor, Shelter Island, New York, 2000*. Boston: ArcheoImaging Lab, University of Massachusetts Boston, 2001.

———. "Geophysical Explorations at Sylvester Manor." In *The Historical Archaeology of Sylvester Manor*, edited by Katherine Howlett Hayes and Stephen A. Mrozoswki. Special issue, *Northeast Historical Archaeology* 36 (2007): 51–70.

Lamb, Martha J. "The Manor of Shelter Island, Historic Home of the Sylvesters." *Magazine of American History* 18 (November 1887): 361–89.

Lamont, Helen Otis. *The Story of Shelter Island in the Revolution*. Shelter Island: SIHS, 1975.

Latham, Roy, "Phragmites," *The Long Island Naturalist*, 1957, reprinted in *Long Island Botanical Society Newsletter* 7, no. 2 (1997).

Lawrence, A. W. *Trade Castles and Forts of West Africa*. Palo Alto: Stanford University Press, 1964.

Lawson, John. *A New Voyage to Carolina; Containing the Exact Description and Natural History of That Country, etc.*, London, 1709. This work is the property of the University of North Carolina at Chapel Hill, http://docsouth.unc.edu/nc/lawson/lawson.html.

Lawson, William. *The Countrie House-Wife's Garden for Herbs of Common Use. Their Virtues, Seasons, Ornaments, Variety of Knots, Models for Trees, and Plots, for the Best Ordering of Grounds and Walks*. London, 1617; reprint with *A New Orchard and Garden: or, The Best Way for Planting, Graffing, and to Make any Ground Good for a Rich Orchard, etc*. Preface by Eleanor Sinclair Rohde. London: Cresset, 1927.

Leith-Ross, Prudence. *The John Tradescants, Gardeners to the Rose and Lily Queen*. London: Peter Owen, 1984.

Lepore, Jill. *New York Burning: Liberty, Slavery and Conspiracy in Eighteenth-Century Manhattan*. New York: Alfred A. Knopf, 2005.

———. "The Tightening Vise: Slavery and Freedom in British New York." In *Slavery in New York*, edited by Ira Berlin and Leslie M. Harris. New York New Press, 2005, 58–89.

Leverett, F. P. *New and Copious Lexicon of the Latin Language*. Boston: J. H. Wilkins and R. B. Carter, 1839.

Levine, Gaynell Stone, ed. "Languages and Lore of the Long Island Indians." *Readings in Long Island Archaeology and Ethnohistory* 4 (1980). Suffolk County Archaeological Association. Massachusetts: Ginn, 1980.

Levy, Barry. *Quakers and the American Family: British Settlement in the Delaware Valley.* New York and Oxford: Oxford University Press, 1988.

Ligon, Richard. *A True and Exact History of the Island of Barbados, Illustrated with a Map of the Island, as Also the Principal Trees and Plants There, Set Forth in Their Due Proportions and Shapes, Drawn Out by Their Several and Respective Scales, etc.* London: 1657, 1673. Edited by Karen Ordahl Kupperman. Indianapolis: Hackett, 2011.

Lindholdt, Paul J., ed. *John Josselyn, Colonial Traveler: A Critical Edition of Two Voyages to New-England.* Hanover and London: University Press of New England, 1988.

Lipman, Andrew. "'A Meanes to Knitt Them Togeather': The Exchange of Body Parts in the Pequot War," *WMQ* 65, no. 1 (January 2008): 3–28.

Loren, Diana DiPaolo. *Archaeology of Clothing and Bodily Adornment in Colonial America.* Gainesville: University Press of Florida, 2010.

Lowood, Henry. "The New World and the European Catalog of Nature." In *America in European Consciousness, 1493–1750*, edited by Karen Ordahl Kupperman. Chapel Hill: University of North Carolina Press for the Institute of Early American History and Culture, 1995.

Lucas, Nathaniel. "Lucas Manuscript in the Barbados Public Library," *JBMHS* 25, no. 3 (May 1958): 139–49.

Luccketti, Nicholas. "Archaeological Excavations at Bacon's Castle, Surry County, Virginia." In *Earth Patterns, Essays in Landscape Archaeology*, edited by William M. Kelso and Rachel Most. Charlottesville: University of Virginia Press, 1990.

Lydon, James G. "New York and the Slave Trade, 1700 to 1774." *WMQ* 35, no. 2 (April 1978): 375–94.

MacGregor, Arthur, ed. *Tradescant's Rarities: Essays on the Foundation of the Ashmolean Museum 1683 with a Catalogue of the Surviving Early Collections.* Oxford: Clarendon, 1983.

Mak, Geert. *Amsterdam.* Translated by Phillip Blom. Cambridge, MA: Harvard University Press, 2000.

Mallalieu, Huon, ed. *The Illustrated History of Antiques.* Philadelphia: Running Press, 1995.

Mallmann, Rev. Jacob E. *Historical Papers on Shelter Island and Its Presbyterian Church.* New York: A. M. Bustard, 1899. Reprinted, Shelter Island: Shelter Island Public Library, 1985.

Manning, Patrick. *Slavery and African Life: Occidental, Oriental, and African Slave Trades.* Cambridge: Cambridge University Press, 1990.

Mannix, Daniel P., and Malcolm Cowley. *Black Cargoes: A History of the Atlantic Slave Trade, 1518–1865.* New York: Viking, 1962.

Marcus, Grania Bolton. *Discovering the Black Experience in Suffolk County 1620–1860.* Mattituck, NY: Society for the Preservation of Long Island Antiquities, Amereon House, 1995.

Markham, Gervase. *The English Housewife, Containing the Inward and Outward Virtues Which Ought to Be in a Complete Woman, etc.* Edited by Michael R. Best. Montreal: McGill–Queen's University Press, 1986.

Marsden, R. G. "The Voyage of the 'Barbara' of London to Brazil in 1540." *The English Historical Review* 24 (1999): 96–100.

Marsh, Christopher W. *The Family of Love in English Society, 1550–1630*. Cambridge: Cambridge University Press, 1994.

Martin, John Frederick. *Profits in the Wilderness, Entrepreneurship and the Founding of New England Towns in the Seventeenth Century.* Chapel Hill: University of North Carolina Press, 1991.

Mather, Frederic Gregory. *The Refugees of 1776 from Long Island to Connecticut*. Albany: J. B. Lyon, 1913, https://play.google.com/store/books/details?id=fId2AAAAMAAJ&rdid=book-fId2AAAAMAAJ&rdot=1.

McCartney, Martha W. "An Early Virginia Census Reprised." *Quarterly Bulletin of the Archeological Society of Virginia* 54, no. 4 (December 1999): 178–96.

———. *Documentary History of Jamestown Island.* Vol. 1, *Narrative History.* Williamsburg: National Park Service, 2000, http://www.nps.gov/history/history/online_books/jame/documentary_history.pdf.

———. *Jamestown People to 1800: Public Officials, Minorities, and Native Leaders*. Baltimore: Genealogical Publishing, 2012.

———. *Virginia Immigrants and Adventurers, 1607–35*. Baltimore: Genealogical Publishing, 2007.

McCusker, John J. *Money and Exchange in Europe and America, 1600–1775: A Handbook*. Chapel Hill: University of North Carolina Press for the Institute of Early American History and Culture, 1978.

———, and Russell R. Menard. *The Economy of British America, 1607–1789*. Chapel Hill: University of North Carolina Press, 1985.

———. "The Sugar Industry in the Seventeenth Century: A New Perspective on the Barbadian 'Sugar Revolution.'" In Schwartz, *Tropical Babylons*, 289–330.

McManus, Edgar J. *Black Bondage in the North*. Syracuse: Syracuse University Press, 2001. First published in 1973.

———. *A History of Negro Slavery in New York*. Syracuse: Syracuse University Press, 1970.

Melish, Joanne Pope. *Disowning Slavery: Gradual Emancipation and Race in New England*. Ithaca: Cornell University Press, 2000.

Menand, Louis. *The Metaphysical Club: A Story of Ideas in America.* New York: Farrar, Straus and Giroux, 2001.

Menard, Russell R. *Sweet Negotiations: Sugar, Slavery, and Plantation Agriculture in Early Barbados*. Charlottesville: University of Virginia Press, 2006.

Merwick, Donna. "The Shame and the Sorrow: Interpreting Dutch-Amerindian Encounters in New Netherland." Presentation to the Atlantic History Workshop, NYU, May 2004.

Meyers, Amy R. W., and Margaret Beck Pritchard, eds. *Empire's Nature: Mark Catesby's New World Vision.* Chapel Hill: University of North Carolina Press, 1998.

Middleton, Arthur P. *Tobacco Coast: A Maritime History of the Chesapeake Bay in the Colonial Era*. Newport News, VA: Mariners Museum (1953), Maryland Paperback Bookshelf Edition, 1984.

Miller, Amelia F. *Connecticut River Valley Doorways: An Eighteenth-Century Flowering.* Boston: Boston University for the Dublin Seminar for New England Folklife, 1983.

Miller, Ebenezer. *Diary of Ebenezer Miller of Miller Place, Long Island, New York, 1762–68*, edited by Margaret Davis Gass and Willis H. White. Miller Place, NY: W. H. White, 1996.

Miller, Naomi F., and Kathryn L. Gleason. *The Archaeology of Garden and Field*. Philadelphia: University of Pennsylvania Press, 1994.

Milton, John. *The Doctrine and Discipline of Divorce*. London: Pickering, 1851. First published London, 1644.

Mintz, Sidney W. "Food Enigmas, Colonial and Postcolonial." *Gastronomica* 10, no. 1 (Winter 2010): 149–54.

———. *Sweetness and Power: The Place of Sugar in Modern History*. New York: Penguin, 1985.

Moore, Christopher. "A World of Possibilities: Slavery and Freedom in Dutch New Amsterdam." In *Slavery in New York*, edited by Ira Berlin and Leslie M. Harris. New York: New Press and the New-York Historical Society, 29–56.

Morgan, Edmund S. "Slavery and Freedom: The American Paradox." *JAH* 59, no. 1 (1972): 5–29.

———. *The Puritan Family: Religion and Domestic Relations in Seventeenth-Century New England*. New York: Harper & Row, 1966.

Morgan, Philip D. *Slave Counterpoint: Black Culture in the Eighteenth-Century Chesapeake & Lowcountry*. Chapel Hill and London: University of North Carolina Press, 1998.

———. "The Caribbean and the Atlantic World, c. 1500–1800." Columbia Seminar in Early American History, 2003.

Moss, Richard Shannon. "Slavery on Long Island: Its Rise and Decline During the Seventeenth Through Nineteenth Centuries." Ph.D. dissertation, St. John's University, 1985.

Mowrer, Lilian T. *The Indomitable John Scott: Citizen of Long Island 1632–1704*. New York: Farrar, Straus and Cudahy, 1960.

Mrozowski, Stephen A., and Mary C. Beaudry. "Archaeology and the Landscape of Corporate Ideology." In *Earth Patterns: Essays in Landscape Archaeology*, edited by William M. Kelso and Rachel Most. Charlottesville: University of Virginia Press, 1990, 189–208.

Mrozowski, Stephen A., Katherine Howlett Hayes, and Anne P. Hancock. "The Archaeology of Sylvester Manor." In *The Historical Archaeology of Sylvester Manor*, edited by Katherine Howlett Hayes and Stephen A. Mrozowski. Special issue, *Northeast Historical Archaeology* 36 (2007): 1–15.

Muller, Wilhelm Johannes. "Wilhelm Johannes Muller's Description of the Fetu Country, 1662–69." In *German Sources for West African History, 1599–1669*, edited by Adam Jones, 132–59. Wiesbaden: Franz Steiner, 1983.

Needham, Robert. "To the King's Most Excellent Majestie. The Humble Petition of Robert Needham Esquire." CO 1/33, No. 84 [? 1660], item 357, vol. 9. (Addendum 1574–1667) 139.

Newell, Margaret Ellen. "The Changing Nature of Indian Slavery in New England, 1670–1720." In *Re-Interpreting New England Indians and the Colonial Experience*, edited by Colin G. Calloway and Neal Salisbury. Boston: The Colonial Society of Massachusetts, distributed by the University of Virginia, 2003, 106–36.

Newman, Elizabeth Terese. "San Miguel Acocotla: The History and Archaeology of a Central Mexican Hacienda." Ph.D. diss., Yale University, 2008.

———. "What's for Dinner: Distinctive Diets in New England." Paper presented at annual conference of the Society for Historical Archaeology, Providence, RI, January 2003.

Norden, John. *A Description of the Honour of Windesor . . . in Anno 1607*. Reprinted in

Raymond South, *Royal Castle, Rebel Town: Puritan Windsor in Civil War and Commonwealth*. Buckingham, England: Barracuda Books, 1981.

Norton, Humphrey, John Rous, and John Copeland. *New England's Ensigne*. London, 1659.

Norton, John. *The Heart of New England Rent*. Cambridge, MA: 1659; London, 1660.

Nuttall, Geoffrey F. *Early Quaker Letters from the Swarthmore Mss. to 1660*. Calendared, Indexed, and Annotated by Geoffrey F. Nuttall. Privately printed, Library of the Society of Friends, London, 1952.

O'Callaghan, Edmund Bailey, and Berthold Fernow, eds. *Documents Relative to the Colonial History of the State of New York; Procured in Holland, England, and France*. 15 vols. Albany: Weed, Parsons, 1853–87.

———. *Lists of Inhabitants of Colonial New York, Excerpted from The Documentary History of the State of New York*. Indexed by Rosanne Conway. Baltimore: Genealogical Publishing, 1979, http://books.google.com/books?id=4XzO6xwgyYoC&printsec=frontcover&source=gbs_atb#v=onepage&q&f=false.

Ogilby, John, and William Morgan, "Large and Accurate Map of the City of London," etc., survey 1676, published 1677, http://www.british-history.ac.uk/lmap.aspx?compid=18979&pubid=61.

Olson. Julius E. *Review of the Problem of the Northmen and the Site of Norumbega by Professor Olson of Madison University, Wisconsin* [sic] *and a Reply by Eben Norton Horsford*. Privately published, 1891(?).

O'Neale, Sondra A. *Jupiter Hammon and the Biblical Beginnings of African-American Literature*. Metuchen, NJ: American Theological Library Association and the Scarecrow Press, 1993.

Page, William, S. Inskip Ladds, Herbert E. Norris, and Granville Proby, eds. *History of the County of Huntingdon, The Victoria History of the Counties of England*. Vol. 3. London: St. Catherine Press: 1936.

Paine, Thomas. *Common Sense: Addressed to the Inhabitants of America, etc.* Philadelphia: R. Bell, January 10, 1776. Copy inscribed by Ezra L'Hommedieu: http://bobcat.library.nyu.edu/primo_library/libweb/action/dlDisplay.do?vid=NYU&afterPDS=true&institution=NYU&docId=nyu_aleph003403479.

Palfrey, John Gorham. *A History of New England from the Discovery by Europeans to the Revolution of the Seventeenth Century, Being an Abridgement of His "History of New England During the Stuart Dynasty,"* 5 vols. Boston: Little, Brown & Co., 1858–1890.

Palmer, Frédéric. "Hempsted House in New London." In *The Connecticut Antiquarian* 10, no. 1 (July 1958): 6–33.

Parkinson, John. *Paradisi in Sole, Paradisus Terrestris; or, A Garden of all Sorts of Pleasant Flowers which Oure English Ayre Will Permitt to be Noursed, etc.* London: Humphrey Lownes and Robert Young, 1629. Reprinted as *A Garden of Pleasant Flowers*. New York: Dover Publications, 1991.

Parrish, Susan Scott. *American Curiosity: Cultures of Natural History in the Colonial British Atlantic World*. Chapel Hill: University of North Carolina Press for the Omohundro Institute of Early American History and Culture, 2006.

———. "Richard Ligon and the Atlantic Science of Commonwealths," in *WMQ* 67, no. 2 (April 2010): 209–48.

Parry, Graham. *The Golden Age Restor'd: The Culture of the Stuart Court, 1603–42*. New York: St. Martin's, 1981.

Parry, M. H. *Aak to Zumbra: A Dictionary of the World's Watercraft*. Newport News, VA: Mariners' Museum, 2000.

Pastorius, Francis. *The German Mennonite Resolution Against Slavery*. Germantown, PA, 1688.

Patterson, Orlando. *Slavery and Social Death*. Cambridge, MA: Harvard University Press, 1982.

Pearl, Valerie. "London's Counter-Revolution." In *The Interregnum: The Quest for Settlement, 1646–1660*, edited by G. E. Aylmer, 29–56. London: Archon Books, 1972.

Pelletreau, William Smith. *A History of Long Island: From Its Earliest Settlement to the Present Time*. Vol. 2. New York: Lewis Publishing Company, 1905.

———, transcriber and ed. *The Second Book of Records of the Town of Southampton, Long Island, N.Y. . . . Including the Records from 1660 to 1717*. Sag Harbor, NY: John H. Hunt, Printer, 1877.

Penn, William. *No Cross, No Crown: A Discourse Shewing the Nature and Discipline of the Holy Cross of Christ, and That the Denial of Self, and Daily Bearing of Christ's Cross, Is the Alone Way to the Rest and Kingdom of God*. London, 1668.

Penney, Norman, ed. *The Journal of the Friends' Historical Society* 9. London: Swarthmore, 1912.

Pepys, Samuel. *The Diary of Samuel Pepys: A New and Complete Transcription*. Edited by Robert Latham and William Matthews. Vols. 5, 7–9. London: G. Bell & Sons, 1976.

Pestana, Carla Gardina. "A West Indian Colonial Governor's Advice: Henry Ashton's 1646 Letter to the Earl of Carlisle." *WMQ* 60 (2003): 382–421.

———. *Quakers and Baptists in Colonial Massachusetts*. Cambridge: Cambridge University Press, 2004.

———. "The City upon a Hill Under Siege: The Puritan Perception of the Quaker Threat to Massachusetts Bay, 1656–61." *NEQ* 56, no. 3 (1983): 323–53.

———. *The English Atlantic in an Age of Revolution, 1640–61*. Cambridge, MA: Harvard University Press, 2004.

Peterson, Roger Tory, and Margaret McKenny. *A Field Guide to Wildflowers of Northeastern and North-central North America*. Boston: Houghton Mifflin, 1968.

Phillips, Thomas. "A Journal of a Voyage Made in the *Hannibal* of London, Ann. 1693, 1694, from England, to Cape Monseradoe in Africa and Thence Along the Coast of Guiney to Whidaw, the Island of St. Thomas, and So Forward to Barbadoes." In *A Collection of Voyages and Travels, some Now First Printed from Original Manuscripts, Others Now First Published in English*, edited by Awnsham Churchill and John Churchill. London, 1732, 169–239, https://play.google.com/store/books/details?id=oFVEAAAAcAAJ&rdid=book-oFVEAAAAcAAJ&rdot=1.

Piechota, Dennis. "The Laboratory Excavation of a Soil Block from Sylvester Manor." In *The Historical Archaeology of Sylvester Manor*, edited by Katherine Howlett Hayes and Stephen A. Mrozowski. Special issue, *Northeast Historical Archaeology* 36 (2007), 83–99.

Piersen, William Dillon. *Black Yankees: The Development of an Afro-American Subculture in Eighteenth-Century New England*. Amherst: University of Massachusetts Press, 1988.

Piggott, Stuart. "Brazilian Indians on an Elizabethan Monument." In *Ruins in a Landscape: Essays in Antiquarianism*. Edinburgh: Edinburgh University Press, 1976.

Plimpton, Ruth Talbot. *Mary Dyer: Biography of a Rebel Quaker*. Boston: Branden, 1994.

Porter, Robert. "The Crispe Family and the African Trade in the Seventeenth Century." *The Journal of African History* 9, no. 1 (1968): 57–77.

Porter, Val. *British Cattle*. England: Shire Publications, 2001.

Postma, Johannes. "A Reassessment of the Atlantic Slave Trade." In *Riches from Atlantic Commerce: Dutch Transatlantic Trade and Shipping, 1585–1817*, edited by Johannes Postma and Victor Enthoven. Leiden, The Netherlands: Brill, 2003, 115–38.

———. *The Atlantic Slave Trade*. Westport, CT: Greenwood Press, 2003.

Potter, Jennifer. *Strange Blooms: The Curious Lives and Adventures of the John Tradescants*. London: Atlantic Books, 2007.

Preston, Jean F., and Laetitia Yeandle. *English Handwriting 1400–1650*. North Carolina: Pegasus, 1999.

Price, Richard. *The Convict and the Colonel: A Story of Colonialism and Resistance in the Caribbean*. Boston: Beacon, 1998.

———. *Travels with Tooy: History, Memory, and the African American Imagination*. Chicago: University of Chicago Press, 2008.

Price, Sally, and Richard Price. *Maroon Arts: Cultural Vitality in the African Diaspora*. Boston: Beacon, 1999.

Priddy, Katherine Lee. "On the Mend: Cultural Interaction of Native Americans, Africans, and Europeans on Shelter Island, New York." Master's thesis, University of Massachusetts Boston, 2002.

Quinn, David Beers. "Depictions of America." In *The Maps and Texts of the Boke of Idrography Presented by Jean Rotz to Henry VIII Now in the British Library*, edited by Helen Wallis. Oxford: Roxburghe Club, 1981, 53–56.

Rael, Patrick. "The Long Death of Slavery." In *Slavery in New York*, edited by Ira Berlin and Leslie M. Harris. New York: New Press and the New-York Historical Society, 2005, 111–147.

Rawls, Walton H, ed. *The Century Book of the Long Island Historical Society*. The Long Island Historical Society, 1964.

Records of the Particular Court of Connecticut, 1639–63. Hartford: Connecticut Historical Society and Society of Colonial Wars in the State of Connecticut, 1928.

Records of the Town of East-Hampton, Long Island, Suffolk Co.,Y., with other Ancient Documents of Historic Value. 2 vols. Sag Harbor: John H. Hunt, Printer, 1887.

Rezneck, Samuel. "The European Education of an American Chemist and Its Influence in 19th-Century America: Eben Norton Horsford." *Technology and Culture* 11, no. 3 (June 1970): 366–88.

Ribeiro, Aileen. *Fashion and Fiction: Dress and Art in Stuart England*. New Haven: Yale University Press for the Paul Mellon Centre for Studies in British Art, 2005.

Richter, Daniel K. *Before the Revolution: America's Ancient Pasts*. Cambridge, MA: Belknap Press of Harvard University Press, 2011.

Roberts, Judith. "The Gardens of the Gentry in the Late Tudor Period." *Garden History: The Journal of the Garden History Society* 27, no. 1 (Summer 1999): 89–108.

Roberts, Justin. "Working Behind the Lines: Labor and Agriculture on Two Barbadian Sugar Plantations, 1796–97." *WMQ*, 3rd Ser., 63, no. 3 (July 2006): 551–86.

Robinson, Paul A. "Lost Opportunities: Miantonomi and the English in Seventeenth-Century Narragansett Country." In *Northeastern Indian Lives 1632–1816*, edited by Robert S. Grumet. Amherst: University of Massachusetts Press, 1996, 13–28.

Rocque, John. "A Topographical Map of the County of Berks. By John Rocque, Topographer to His Sacred Majesty George the Third." London, 1761.

Rodriguez, Junius P. *The Historical Encyclopedia of World Slavery*. 2 vols. Oxford: ABC-CLIO, 1997.

Roegholt, Dr. Richter. *A Short History of Amsterdam*. Amsterdam: Bekking & Blitz Uitgevers b.v., 2004.

Romani, Daniel A., Jr. "The Pettaquamscut Purchase of 1657/58 and the Establishment of a Commercial Livestock Industry in Rhode Island." In *New England's Creatures: 1400–1900*, Annual Proceedings of the Dublin Seminar for New England Folklife (1993), edited by Peter Benes. Boston: Boston University, 1995, 45-60.

Ross, Alice. "Corn, the Food of a Nation." Alice Ross Hearth Studios, http://www.aliceross.com/journal/articles.html.

Rowlandson, Mary. "A True History of the Captivity and Restoration of Mrs. Mary Rowlandson." In *Colonial American Travel Narratives*, edited by Wendy Martin. New York: Penguin Books, 1994, 1–48. First published in London, 1682.

Rubin, Jane, and Ariana Donalds, eds. *Bread Made from Yuca: Selected Chronicles of Indo-Antillean Cultivation and Use of Cassava 1526–2002*. New York: InterAmericas, 2003.

Rutman, Darrett B. "Governor Winthrop's Garden Crop: The Significance of Agriculture in the Early Commerce of Massachusetts Bay." *WMQ* 3rd ser., 20, no. 3 (July 1963): 396–415.

———. *Husbandmen of Plymouth: Farms and Villages in the Old Colony, 1620–92*. Boston: Published for Plimoth Plantation by Beacon, 1967.

Sacks, David Harris. "Francis Brinley and His Books, 1650–1719." Presented in "Recovering the Record: Sylvester Manor in the Atlantic World, ca. 1650–1750," Session 20, American Historical Society Association Annual Meeting, January 7, 2005, Seattle, Washington.

———. "Francis Brinley and His Books, 1650–1719." Presented at "American Origins: The Seventeenth Century," a workshop of the *WMQ* and the Early Modern Studies Institute, Huntington Library and University of Southern California, May 2006.

———. *The Widening Gate: Bristol and the Atlantic Economy, 1450–1700*. Berkeley: University of California Press, 1991.

Sacks, Oliver. "The Landscape of His Dreams." In *An Anthropologist on Mars: Seven Paradoxical Tales*, 153–87. New York: Vintage Books, 1996.

Sainsbury, W. Noël, et al., eds. *Calendar of State Papers, Colonial Series, America and West Indies*. 45 vols. (1574–1738). London: Public Record Office, 1850–1994.

Salter, Edwin. *History of Monmouth and Ocean Counties, New Jersey*. Bayonne: F. Gardner & Son, 1890.

Samford, Patricia. "The Archaeology of African-American Slavery and Material Culture." *WMQ* 53, no. 1 (January 1996): 87–114.

Sanford, Peleg. *The Letter Book of Peleg Sanford of Newport Merchant (Later Governour of Rhode Island) 1666–68*. Edited by Howard R. Preston. Providence: Rhode Island Historical Society, 1928.

Savage, James. *A Genealogical Dictionary of the First Settlers of New England, Showing Three Generations of Those Who Came Before May 1692*. 4 vols. Boston: Little, Brown, 1860–62, https://play.google.com/store/books/details?id=HWEblLuls8kC&rdid=book-HWEblLuls8kC&rdot=1.

Saxton, Martha. *Being Good: Women's Moral Values in Early America*. New York: Hill and Wang, 2003.

Schaefer, Patricia M. *A Useful Friend: A Companion to the Joshua Hempstead Diary 1711–58*. New London, CT: New London County Historical Society, 2008.

Schama, Simon. *The Embarrassment of Riches: An Interpretation of Dutch Culture in the Golden Age*. New York: Vintage Books, 1997.

Scheffer, Jakob Gijsbert de Hoop. *History of the Free Churchmen Called the Brownists, Pilgrim Fathers and Baptists in the Dutch Republic, 1581–1701*. Ithaca, NY: Andrus & Church, 1922.

Schéle, Sune. *Cornelis Bos: A Study of the Origins of the Netherland Grotesque*. Sweden: Almqvist & Wiksell, 1965.

Schmidt, Jeremy. *Melancholy and the Care of the Soul: Moral Philosophy and Madness in Early Modern England*. Aldershot, England: Ashgate, 2007.

Schofield, John. "City of London Gardens, 1500–c. 1620." *Garden History: The Journal of the Garden History Society* 27, no. 1 (Summer 1999): 73–88.

Schultz, Eric B., and Michael J. Tougias. *King Philip's War: The History and Legacy of America's Forgotten Conflict*. New York: W. W. Norton, 2000.

Schwartz, Barbara, and Mac Griswold, in cooperation with The University of Massachusetts Boston and The Shelter Island Historical Society. "Shelter Island, New York, Land Acquisition and Dispersal, 1652–1733," 2000. SIHS.

Schwartz, Stuart B. "A Commonwealth Within Itself: The Early Brazilian Sugar Industry, 1550–1670." In *Tropical Babylons, Sugar and the Making of the Atlantic World, 1450–1680*, edited by Stuart B. Schwartz. Chapel Hill: University of North Carolina Press, 2004, 158–200.

Scott, Kenneth. "Early New York Inventories of Estates." *NGSQ* 53 (June 1965): 133–43.

———. "New York Inventories, 1665–1775." *NGSQ* 54 (December 1966): 246–49.

———, and James A. Owre. *Genealogical Data from Inventories of New York Estates 1666–1825*. New York: New York Genealogical and Biographical Society, 1970.

Seed, Patricia. *Ceremonies of Possession in Europe's Conquest of the New World, 1492–1640*. Cambridge: Cambridge University Press, 1995.

Seeman, Eric R. "Reassessing the 'Sankofa Symbol' in New York's African Burial Ground." *WMQ* 67, no. 1 (January 2010): 101–22.

Sellars, John R., and Patricia Molen Van Ee. *Maps and Charts of North America and the West Indies 1750–89: A Guide to the Collections in the Library of Congress*. Washington, DC: Library of Congress, 1981.

Sellers, Vanessa Bezemer. *Courtly Gardens in Holland, 1600–50*. Amsterdam: Architectura and Natura, 2001.

Shaw, William A., ed. *Letters of Denization and Acts of Naturalization for Aliens in England and Ireland, 1603–1700*. Lymington: Huguenot Society of London, 1911.

Shelter Island Account Book, 1658–1768. East Hampton Library.

Shelter Island Account Book, 1738–46 (Brinley Sylvester). East Hampton Library.

Shelton, Louise. *Beautiful Gardens in America*. New York: Charles Scribner's Sons, 1915.

Sherlock, Peter. *Monuments and Memory in Early Modern England*. Aldershot, England, and Burlington, VT: Ashgate, 2008.

Sherwood, Marika. "Blacks in Tudor England." *History Today* 53, no. 10 (October 2003), http://www.historytoday.com/marika-sherwood/blacks-tudor-england.

Shillingburg, Patricia, and Edward Shillingburg. "The Disposition of Slaves on the East End of Long Island from 1680 to 1796." 2003, http://www.shelter-island.org/disposition_slave.html.

Shomette, Donald. "Empire Strikes Back: On the East End in 1674." Lecture delivered Sept. 12, 1998, East Hampton Library, East Hampton, NY, http://www.easthamptonlibrary.org/lic/lectures/donaldshomettelecture.htm.

Shorto, Russell. *The Island at the Center of the World*. New York: Doubleday, 2004.

Silverman, David J. "'We Chuse to Be Bounded': Native American Animal Husbandry in Colonial New England." *WMQ* 60 (2003): 511–82.

Siminoff, Faren R. *Crossing the Sound: The Rise of Atlantic American Communities in Seventeenth-Century Eastern Long Island.* New York: New York University Press, 2004.

———. "How Dominant Were European Settlers?" *LIHJ* 17, nos. 1–2 (2005): 222–26, http://dspace.sunyconnect.suny.edu/bitstream/handle/1951/6616/LIHJSpring2005.pdf;jsessionid=0F08C19EEC96AEA8FB5B3E6638B088E6?sequence=1.

Sirkin, Les. *Eastern Long Island Geology.* Rhode Island: Book and Tackle Shop, 1995.

Sloane, Barney, and Gordon Malcolm. *Excavations at the Priory of the Order of the Hospital of St. John of Jerusalem, Clerkenwell, London.* London: Museum of London Archaeology Service, 2004.

Smallwood, Stephanie E. "African Guardians, European Slave Ships, and the Changing Dynamics of Power in the Early Modern Atlantic." *WMQ* 3rd ser., 64, no. 4 (Oct. 2007): 679–716.

Smith, Frederick H. "Disturbing the Peace in Barbados: Constant Silvester of Constant Plantation in the Seventeenth Century." *JBMHS* 44 (1988): 38–54.

———. "Holetown: Archaeological Investigations at the Site of the First British Settlement in Barbados." *JBMHS* 50 (Dec. 2004): 49–65.

Smith, John. *The Generall Historie of Virginia, New-England, and the Summer Isles: with the Names of the Adventurers, Planters, and Governours from Their First Beginning An. 1584 to This Present 1624.* London, 1624. Reprinted in *Captain John Smith: A Select Edition of His Writings.* Edited by Karen Ordahl Kupperman. Chapel Hill: University of North Carolina Press for the Omohundro Institute of Early American History and Culture, 1988.

Smith, Simon David. *Slavery, Family, and Gentry Capitalism in the British Atlantic: The World of the Lascelles, 1648–1834.* Cambridge: Cambridge University Press, 2006.

Smith, Venture. *A Narrative of the Life and Adventures of Venture, A Native of Africa, but Resident Above Sixty Years in the United States of America.* Whitefish, MT: Kessinger, 1996. First published in New London, CT: Printed by C. Holt, 1797.

Smuts, R. M. "The Puritan Followers of Henrietta Maria in the 1630s." In *The English Historical Review* 93 (1978): 26–45.

Soderlund, Jean R. *Quakers and Slavery: A Divided Spirit.* Princeton: Princeton University Press, 1985.

Southold Town Records, Copied and Explanatory Notes Added by J. Wickham Case. 2 vols. New York: S. W. Green's Sons, 1882, 1884.

Spicer, Joaneath. "The Renaissance Elbow." In *A Cultural History of Gesture,* edited by Jan Bremmer and Herman Roodenburg. Ithaca, NY: Cornell University Press, 1991.

Spies, Paul, Koen Kleijn, Jos Smit, and Ernest Kurpershoek, eds. *The Canals of Amsterdam.* Amsterdam: SDU Uitgeverij Koninginnegracht, 1993.

Spoeri, Felix Christian. "A Swiss Medical Doctor's Description of Barbados in 1661: The Account of Felix Christian Spoeri." Translated and edited by Alexander Gunkel and Jerome S. Handler. *JBMHS* 33 (1969): 3–13, http://jeromehandler.org/wp-content/uploads/Spoeri-69.pdf.

Sportman, Sarah, Craig Cipolla, and David Landon. "Zooarchaeological Evidence for Animal Husbandry and Foodways at Sylvester Manor." In *The Historical Archaeology of Sylvester Manor,* edited by Katherine Howlett Hayes and Stephen A. Mrozowski. Special issue, *Historical Archaeology* 36 (2007): 127–40.

Sprunger, Keith L. *Dutch Puritanism: A History of the English and Scottish Churches of the Netherlands in the Sixteenth and Seventeenth Centuries*. Leiden, The Netherlands: Brill, 1982.

———. *Trumpets from the Tower: English Puritan Printing in The Netherlands, 1600–1640*. Leiden, The Netherlands: Brill, 1994.

Staves, Susan. *Married Women's Property Rights in England, 1660–1833*. Cambridge, MA: Harvard University Press, 1990.

Stearns, Raymond Phineas, ed. "Woodbridge-Baxter Correspondence." *NEQ* 10 (1937): 573.

Stone, Gaynell. "Spatial and Material Aspects of Culture: Ethnicity and Ideology in Long Island Gravestones, 1670–1820." Ph.D. dissertation, State University of New York at Stony Brook, 1987.

Stout, Harry S., and Peter Onuf. "James Davenport and the Great Awakening in New London." *JAH* 71, no. 3 (Dec. 1983): 556–78.

Strong, John A. "How Dominant Were European Settlers?" *LIHJ* 17, nos. 1–2 (2005): 214–21.

———. "Indian Labor During the Post-Contact Period on Long Island, 1626–1700." In *To Know the Place: Exploring Long Island History*, edited by Joann P. Krieg and Natalie A. Naylor, 13–39. Interlaken, NY: Heart of the Lakes, 1995.

———. *The Algonquian Peoples of Long Island from Earliest Times to 1700*. Hempstead, NY: Long Island Studies Institute, Hofstra University, 1997.

———. "The Reaffirmation of Tradition Among the Native Americans of Eastern Long Island." *LIHJ* 7, no. 1 (Fall 1994): 42–67.

———. *We Are Still Here: The Algonquian Peoples of Long Island Today*. Published for the Long Island Studies Institute, Hofstra University, Hempstead, NY; Interlaken, NY: Empire State Books, revised edition 1998.

———. "Wyandanch: Sachem of the Montauks." In *Northeastern Indian Lives 1632–1816*, edited by Robert S. Grumet. Amherst: University of Massachusetts Press, 1996, 48–73.

Strong, Roy. *The Renaissance Garden In England*. London: Thames and Hudson, 1979.

Sung Bok Kim. *Landlord and Tenant in Colonial New York: Manorial Society, 1664–1775*. Chapel Hill: University of North Carolina Press, published for the Institute of Early American History and Culture, Williamsburg, VA, 1978.

Sweeney, John A. H. *Grandeur on the Appoquinimink: The House of William Corbit at Odessa, Delaware*. Newark: University of Delaware Press, 1989.

Sweet, John Wood. *Bodies Politic: Negotiating Race in the American North, 1730–1830*. Baltimore: Johns Hopkins University Press, 2003.

———. "Venture Smith and the Law of Slavery." In *Venture Smith and the Business of Slavery and Freedom*, edited by James B. Stewart, 83–128. Amherst: University of Massachusetts Press, 2010.

Sylvester, Constant. Last Testament and Will of Constant Sylvester, proved London, Oct. 7, 1671, Barbados, Jan. 18, 1672. Barbados National Archive, RB/6/8, p. 316.

Sylvester, Constant (son of Nathaniel Sylvester). Last Testament and Will of Constant Sylvester, Oct. 26, 1695. SMA, NYU I/A/140/26.

Sylvester, Giles, Barbados, to Giles Sylvester, Amsterdam. "A Letter from Barbados by ye Way of Holland Concerning ye Condiccion of Honest Men There. 9 Aug. 1651." Tanner Mss 54ff. 153–54. In Harlow, *Colonizing Expeditions to the West Indies and Guiana 1623–67*, 49–53.

Sylvester, Grizzell Brinley. Will of Grizzell Brinley Sylvester, May 7, 1685, SMA, NYU I/A/140/19.

Sylvester, Nathaniel. "Last Will and Testament, March 19, 1680." General Sylvester Dering Documents 1:6. SIHS, proved Oct. 2, 1680, New York County Wills 2:191, 250.

Sylvester documents from the Amsterdam Archives, translations and transcriptions. In Griswold Papers, Fales Library, New York University.

Sylvester Manor, Shelter Island, New York. Field Manual. AFMCAR, 2000.

Sylvester Manor Archive. Fales Library and Special Collections, Bobst Library, New York University. http://dlib.nyu.edu/findingaids/html/fales/sylmanor_content.html.

Taylor, John. *A Short Recital or Journal of Some of the Travels, Labours and Sufferings of John Taylor, Late of York.* London, 1710.

Temin, Peter, ed. *Engines of Enterprise: An Economic History of New England.* Cambridge, MA: Harvard University Press, 1979.

Tepper, Michael, ed. *Passengers to America: A Consolidation of Ship Passenger Lists from the New England Historical and Genealogical Register.* Baltimore: Genealogical Publishing, 1977.

Thomas, Hugh. *The Slave Trade: The Story of the Atlantic Slave Trade, 1440–1870.* New York: Simon & Schuster, 1997.

Thompson, Benjamin F. *The History of Long Island; from Its Discovery and Settlement, to the Present Time. With many important and interesting matters; including notices of numerous individuals and families; and a particular account of the different churches and ministers.* 2 vols. New York: Gould, Banks, 1843.

Thompson, Peter. "Henry Drax's Instructions on the Management of a Seventeenth-Century Barbadian Sugar Plantation." *WMQ* 66, no. 3 (2009): 565–604.

Thornbury, Walter. *Old and New London: A Narrative of Its History, Its People, and Its Places.* London: Cassell, Petter, Galpin, 1881, http://play.google.com/books/reader?id=KZQNAAAAIAAJ&printsec=frontcover&output=reader&authuser=0&hl=en&pg=GBS.PR1.

Thornton, John. *Africa and Africans in the Making of the Atlantic World, 1400–1680.* Cambridge: Cambridge University Press, 1992.

Tomalin, Claire. *Samuel Pepys: The Unequalled Self.* New York: Vintage Books, 2003.

Tominaga, Takatoshi, and Denis Dubourdieu. "Identification of 4-Mercapto-4-methylpentan-2-one from the Box Tree (*Buxus sempervirens* L.) and Broom (*Sarothamnus scoparius* (L.) Koch." *Flavour and Fragrance Journal* 12, no. 6 (Nov.–Dec. 1997): 373–76.

Tooker, William Wallace. *John Eliot's First Indian Teacher and Interpreter, Cockenoe-de-Long Island, and The Story of His Career from the Early Records.* New York: F. P. Harper, 1896, https://play.google.com/store/books/details?id=0TizR-rLnGoC&rdid=book-0TizR-rLnGoC&rdot=1.

Ukwe, Chika N., Chidi A. Ibe, Peter C. Nwilo, and Pablo A. Huidobro. "Contributing to the WSSD Targets on Oceans and Coasts in West and Central Africa: The Guinea Current Large Marine Ecosystem Project." *International Journal of Oceans and Oceanography* 1, no. 1 (2006): 21–44, www.vliz.be/imisdocs/publications/100130.pdf.

Ulrich, Laurel Thatcher. *A Midwife's Tale: The Life of Martha Ballard, Based on Her Diary, 1785–1812.* New York: Vintage Books, 1991.

———. *Good Wives: Image and Reality in the Lives of Women in Northern New England, 1650–1750.* New York: Vintage Books, 1991. First published New York: Alfred A. Knopf, 1980.

Updike, Daniel Berkeley. *Richard Smith, First English Settler of the Narragansett Country, Rhode Island, with a Series of Letters written by His Son Richard Smith, Jr., etc.* Boston: Merrymount, 1937.

Upton, Dell. *Holy Things and Profane*. New Haven: Yale University Press, 1997.

———. "Imagining the Early Virginia Landscape." In *Earth Patterns: Essays in Landscape Archaeology*, edited by William M. Kelso and Rachel Most, 71–86. Charlottesville: University of Virginia Press, 1990, 71–86.

van Dantzig, Albert. *Forts and Castles of Ghana*. Accra: Sedco, 1980; reprinted 1999.

Vincitorio, Gaetano L. "The Revolutionary War and Its Aftermath in Suffolk County, Long Island." *LIHJ* 7, no. 1 (Fall 1994): 68–85.

Vink, Markus P. M. "Freedom and Slavery: The Dutch Republic, the VOC World, and the Debate over the 'World's Oldest Trade.'" *South African Historical Journal* 59 (2007), 19–46.

Von Frank, Albert J. *The Trials of Anthony Burns: Freedom and Slavery in Emerson's Boston*. Cambridge, MA: Harvard University Press, 1998.

von Kerrsenbroch, Hermann. *Narrative of the Anabaptist Madness: The Overthrow of Munster, the Famous Metropolis of Westphalia*. Leiden, The Netherlands: Brill Academic, 2007.

Walpole, Horace. *A History of the Modern Taste in Gardening*. London, 1771, published 1780. Reproduced in *The Genius of the Place, etc.*, edited by John Dixon Hunt and Peter Willis. New York: Harper & Row, 1975.

Waselkov, Gregory. "Indian Maps of the Colonial Southeast." In *Powhatan's Mantle: Indians in the Colonial Southeast*, edited by Peter H. Wood, Gregory A. Waselkov, and M. Thomas Hatley, 292–343. Lincoln: University of Nebraska Press, 1989, 292–343.

Waters, Henry F. *Genealogical Gleanings in England*. Vol. 1. Boston: New England Historical & Genealogical Society, 1901, reprinted 1969.

Watts, David. *The West Indies: Patterns of Development, Culture and Environmental Change since 1492*. Cambridge: Cambridge University Press, 1984.

Weaver, Joyce Rosnel. "Far Distant from Friends: The 17th and 18th Century Quakers of Setauket, NY." *Suffolk County Historical Society Register* 23, no. 3 (1997): 70–90.

Weigand, Philip C. "How Advanced Were Long Island's Native Americans? A Challenge to the Traditional View." *LIHJ* 17, nos. 1–2 (2005): 101–18.

Weigold, Marilyn E. *The Long Island Sound*. New York: New York University Press, 2004.

Wharton, Katharine Johnstone. "An Old Newport Loyalist." *Bulletin of the Newport Historical Society* 32 (April 1920): 1–14.

Whittier, James Greenleaf. *The Writings of John Greenleaf Whittier* (Boston: Riverside, 1888), http://books.google.com/books/reader?id=iCIqAAAAYAAJ&printsec=frontcover&output=reader&pg=GBS.PA366.

Wiesebron, Marianne L., ed. *Brazilië in de Nederlandse archieven / O Brasil em arquivos Neerlandeses (1652–54): De West-Indische Compagnie: Overgekomen brieven en papieren uit Brazilië en Curaçao (Brazil in the Dutch archives, 1652–54: the West-Indian Company: transferred letters and documents from Brazil and Curaçao)*, Mauritinia no. 2N, ed. Leiden, The Netherlands: Research School CWNS, 2005.

Wilcoxen, Charlotte. *Dutch Trade and Ceramics in America in the Seventeenth Century*. Albany: Albany Institute of History and Art, 1987.

Williams, Emily Coddington. *William Coddington of Rhode Island: A Sketch*. Newport: privately printed, 1941.

Williams, Eric. *Capitalism and Slavery*. Chapel Hill: University of North Carolina Press, 1994.

Williams, Roger. *A Key into the Language of America*. London: 1643. Reprint edited by John Teunissen and Evelyn J. Hinz. Detroit: Wayne State University Press, 1973.

———. *George Fox Digg'd Out of His Burrowes*. Boston, 1676.

Williamson, James A. *Hawkins of Plymouth: A New History of Sir John Hawkins and of the Other Members of His Family Prominent in Tudor England*. London: Black, 1949; New York: Barnes & Noble, 1969.

———. *Sir John Hawkins: The Time and the Man*. Westport, CT: Greenwood Press, 1970. First published Oxford: Clarendon, 1927.

Wilson, Sherrill D. "African Burial Ground." In *Slavery in New York*, edited by Ira Berlin and Leslie M. Harris. New York: New Press and the New-York Historical Society, 8.

Winiarski, Douglas L. "Souls Filled with Ravishing Transport: Heavenly Visions and the Radical Awakening in New England." *WMQ* 61 (2004): 3–46.

Winthrop, John. *The Journal of John Winthrop 1630–49*. Edited by Richard S. Dunn, James Savage, and Laetitia Yeandle. Cambridge, MA: Belknap Press of Harvard University Press, 1996.

Winthrop Family Papers. 6 vols. Boston: Massachusetts Historical Society.

Witek, John Charles. "The Lives and Identities of the Indians of Shelter Island, 1652–1835." *LIHJ* 4 (Spring 1992): 173–84.

Woodward, C. Vann. *American Counterpoint: Slavery and Racism in the North-South Dialogue*. Boston: Little, Brown, 1971.

Woodward, Walter W. *Prospero's America: John Winthrop, Jr., Alchemy, and the Creation of New England Culture, 1606–76*. Chapel Hill: University of North Carolina Press for the Omohundro Institute of Early American History and Culture, 2010.

Woolman, John. *The Journal of John Woolman*. Boston: Houghton, Mifflin, 1871, https://play.google.com/store/books/details?id=T8MOAAAAYAAJ&rdid=book-T8MOAAAAYAAJ&rdot=1.

Worrall, Arthur J. *Quakers in the Colonial Northeast*. Hanover, NH: University Press of New England, 1980.

Wortis, Helen Zunzer. *A Woman Named Matilda*. Shelter Island: SIHS, 1978.

———. "An Early Visitor to Shelter Island." In *America: History and Life*. Haverford, PA: Haverford College Press, 2004.

———. "Black Inhabitants of Shelter Island from First Settlement to Manumission." *Long Island Forum* 37, no. 8 (Aug. 1973): 146–53.

———. "Blacks on Long Island: Population Growth in the Colonial Period." *LIHJ* 11, no. 1 (Autumn 1974). 35–46.

———. "Shelter Island and Barbados." *America: History and Life*. Haverford College: 2004.

Woudstra, Jan. "What Is Edging Box? Towards Greater Authenticity in Garden Conservation Projects." *Garden History* 35, no. 2 (Winter 2007): 229–42.

Wrightson, Keith. *Earthly Necessities: Economic Lives in Early Modern Britain, 1470–1750*. London: Penguin Books, 2002.

Wulf, Karin A. "'My Dear Liberty': Quaker Spinsterhood and Female Autonomy in Eighteenth-Century Pennsylvania." In *Women and Freedom in Early America*, edited by Larry D. Eldridge, New York: New York University Press, 1997, 83–108..

Yamin, Rebecca, and Karen Bescherer Metheny, eds. *Landscape Archaeology*. Knoxville: University of Tennessee Press, 1997.

Acknowledgments

"The hardest thing about writing is writing," as the late Nora Ephron so truthfully said. My friends, colleagues, mentors, allies, and family have been partners throughout years of researching, writing, and rewriting this book, and I am so grateful to them all.

First, thanks go to the University of Massachusetts archaeology team, Stephen A. Mrozowski, Katherine Howlett Hayes, David Landon, Heather Trigg, and Dennis Piechota, who grounded my work in the manor's soil. For intellectual guidance and friendship, I owe much to Herbert S. Klein, David Harris Sacks, Karen Ordahl Kupperman, John Wood Sweet, Robert Hefner, Jennifer Anderson, and Philip Morgan, who all contributed important pieces of the puzzle or a path to follow. For details of Sylvester Manor's history, I thank Michael Austin, Therese O'Malley, David Jacques, Elizabeth Terese Newman, Dean F. Failey, Frederick H. Smith, Marley R. Brown III, Martha McCartney, Martha Saxton, Walter Woodward, Antonia Booth, Carrie Rebora Barratt, Gaynell Stone, Margaret Brucia, Jason Green, the late Eben Case, Jennifer Snodgrass, John Thornton, Peter Benes, the Lamont family, Jonathan Foster, Henry B. Hoff, Andrew H. Lee, Kwame Anthony Appiah, John G. Waite, Robert Forbes, David Lichtenstein, Reginald H. Metcalf Jr., Charla E. Bolton, Gordon Brindley and Yvonne Brindley, Richard Westmacott, and Elisabeth Sifton. For help in Barbados I thank Jerome S. Handler, Karl S. Watson, Harold Hart, and the staff of the Shilstone Memorial Library at the Barbados Museum and Historical Society. For legal questions I turned to Judges Michael Boudin and Pierre N. Leval, and to Daniel Hulsebosch and Faren Siminoff. In the Netherlands, Victor Enthoven and Jessica Dijkman were my guides.

Organizations of many kinds supported this project, including the Sylvester Manor Project Committee, especially Ashton Hawkins, Jane Gregory Rubin, and Joan Kaplan Davidson. Guidance from Bonnie Burnham and Frank Sanchis at the World Monuments Fund was invaluable. Charles Birnbaum and Nord Wennerstrom of the Cultural Landscape Foundation have freely shared their intellectual capital with me. Generous grants to study the manor house, to organize and preserve the family papers, to speed the slow progress of my writing, and to improve the book were provided by the J. M. Kaplan Fund and the Furthermore Program of the J. M. Kaplan Fund, the Interamericas Program at the Reed Foundation, the Jessica E. Smith and Kevin R. Brine Charitable Trust, the Moore Charitable Foundation, the Gilder Lehrman Institute of American History, and the Arthur Ross Foundation. I thank Elizabeth Barlow Rogers and the Foundation for Landscape Studies for recognizing my work on Sylvester Manor with a Place Keeper Award. A Guggenheim Fellowship permitted me to travel to Amsterdam and Ghana.

At libraries and institutions of learning, my heartiest thanks go to Carol Mandel, dean of the Division of Libraries at New York University; to Marvin Taylor, director of the Fales Library and Special Collections at NYU; to Colin Wells and Noah Gelfand; and to Lisa Darms and Liza Harrell-Edge. Thanks also go to the Atlantic World Workshop at NYU, where I met Kristin Block, Lauren Benton, Jenny Shaw, Christian Crouch, Martha Hodes, Michael Gomez, and Nina Dayton, among others; and to NYU's Sylvester Manor Working Group, especially Karen Kupperman and Patricia Crain. I'm grateful to Plimoth Plantation's John Kemp; to Amy Rupert at the Rennselaer Institute Archives and Special Collections; to Anita Israel at Longfellow House; and to the staffs of the Library of the Religious Society of Friends, London; the Friends Historical Library at Swarthmore College; and the Barbados National Archives.

For opportunities to present ongoing research, I thank among others the American Historical Association, the American Antiquarian Society, the Society of Architectural Historians, the Decorative Arts Trust, Longfellow House/Washington's Headquarters, the Brooklyn Historical Society, Wyck Historic House/Garden/Farm, and the Atlantic History Program at Johns Hopkins University.

For research, support, and long-standing friendship I thank Louise

Green, Beverlea Walz, Phyllis Wallace, Nanette Breiner-Lawrenson, and Belle Lareau at the Shelter Island Historical Society. At Sag Harbor's John Jermain Memorial Library I single out Catherine Creedon, Patricia Brandt, Susan Mullen, and Susan Smyth. I thank Hannah and the late Frederick Dinkel for access to their collection of Sylvester family papers. At the East Hampton Library, thanks go to Diana Dayton Deichert, Gina Piastuck, and Steve Boerner; at the Newport Historical Society, to Bert Lippincott III; at the Massachusetts Historical Society, to Anna Cook. Major thanks also go to the New York Botanical Garden, especially Gregory Long, Todd Forrest, and Wayne Cahilly; to the John Carter Brown Library, especially Norman Fiering, director and librarian emeritus; to Paul Gunther at the Institute for Classical Architecture & Classical America; and to Wendy Schnur at the G. W. Blunt Library, Mystic Seaport. Conversations with Lynda Kaplan and Richard Rabinowitz at the American History Workshop and with Dr. Rex M. Ellis, Associate Director for Curatorial Affairs for the National Museum of African American History and Culture at the Smithsonian Institution, were critical.

First among friends and companions I thank Frederick Seidel, who rowed me up Gardiners Creek, made electrifying suggestions for each chapter, and found the patience and love to read the manuscript at least three times. Vast gratitude also goes to my readers Douglas Brenner, Carol Williams, Steven Kossak, Christopher Mason, Richard Rabinowitz, Lorin Stein, Anne Isaak, Catherine Cochran, and Wendy Gimbel. For insights, wisdom, criticism, comfort, useful introductions, good food and drink—and encouragement—I am also indebted to the late Richard Poirier, Jamaica Kincaid, Sarah Plimpton and Robert Paxton, Susan Weitz, Joe Lelyveld, Richard Brookhiser, Tim Lovejoy, Christian Brechneff, Susan Rowland and the late Charles P. Sifton, the late Robert Hughes, Alan Kriegel, Victoria Hughes, Johnnie Moore, Isabel Fonseca, Liz Addison, Miguette Chapin, Douglas Reed and Will Makris, Sam Sifton, Eleanor Weller Reade, William Buice, Grace Tankersley and Nicholas Quennell, Barbara Goldsmith, Suzanne McNear, Leslie Close, Jeanie Blake, Barbara Dixon, Esther and Chris Pullman, Susana Leval, Peter Andersen, Barbara Paca, Vivienne Simpson, and Barbara Schwartz. I cherish my New York City book group, especially Susan Galassi, Anna Fels, and Anka Begley, for help and encouragement. In England I happily owe debts to Janet Kennish, Elizabeth and Lawrence Banks, Peter Banks, Jane Brown, and Patrick Driscoll.

At my swift and elegant publisher, Farrar, Straus and Giroux, profound thanks go to Jonathan Galassi, who rescued the book and always believed in it; and to my remarkable editor, Courtney Hodell, who found the book in the book; and to those who helped it become a reality, including Mark Krotov, Taylor Sperry, Susan Goldfarb, Debra Helfand, Emily DeHuff, Charlotte Strick, Jonathan Lippincott, and Sarita Varma, among others. Andrew Bush's photographs powerfully present the manor's lights and shadows. For technical support I thank Charles Grubb, Sheryl Heller, and Michael Avery. Frances Tenenbaum at Houghton Mifflin was the first to recognize Sylvester Manor as a stirring subject. For encouragement and standing by me in every crisis, I salute Jeff Posternak and Andrew Wylie at the Wylie Agency.

On Shelter Island, my profound gratitude goes first to the late Alice and Andrew Fiske, and to their daughters Lissa and Sue, and then to Bennett Konesni for breathing new life into this old place, Edith Gawler for her grace and draftsmanship, Susan Brady for encouraging children's programs, Leila Ostby for sharing family memories, and most of all to Eben Fiske Ostby, who has preserved his family's history by generously giving it away. I hail Rose Wisseman and Gunnar Wisseman for their stories and stewardship. I also thank the board of Sylvester Manor Educational Farm, especially David Kamp, Sara Gordon, and Edith Landeck, and the staff, Cara Loriz, Maura Doyle, and Melissa Mundy.

Last, for their love and support, I thank my daughters, Anna Brown Griswold and Belinda Griswold and her husband, Robert Lee; my brothers, Christopher and Dennis Barlow Keith and their spouses and children; and my Shelter Island family, Felicity Seidel and Daniel, Daisy, and Enzo Siegel. I dedicate this book to my granddaughter, Emma Tara Johnston Lee, now two years old, counting on her to be a lover of history someday.

Index

Page numbers in *italics* refer to illustrations.

Illustration Credits

ii Photographer unknown. Julia Dyd Havens Johnson. Originally photographed for Martha J. Lamb, "The Manor of Shelter Island, Historic Home of the Sylvesters." *Magazine of American History* 18 (November 1887): 361–89. Photographic print, courtesy of the Sylvester Manor Archive, Fales Library and Special Collections, New York University.

4 Photographer unknown. Sylvester Manor boxwood garden before 1908. Courtesy of the Sylvester Manor Archive, Fales Library and Special Collections, New York University.

19 Jack Gary. Map of shovel test pit exploration, 1999–2006. Courtesy of the Andrew Fiske Memorial Center for Archaeological Research, University of Massachusetts Boston.

26 Wyandanch signature, detail from a Deed of Sale: Horseneck, with American Indian Signatures (Wyandanch), 1658. Courtesy of the Sylvester Manor Archive, Fales Library and Special Collections, New York University.

48 Balthazar Floritzoon von Berckenrode, detail from *Bird's-eye View of Amsterdam* (1625). © Amsterdam City Archives.

49 Pieter van der Keere, *Profile of Amsterdam Seen from the IJ* (1618). Copyright © Amsterdam City Archives.

54 Nathaniel Sylvester to John Winthrop, August 8, 1653, detail. Winthrop Family Papers. Courtesy of the Massachusetts Historical Society.

65 Constant Sylvester to John Winthrop Jr., April 6, 1659, detail. Winthrop Family Papers. Courtesy of the Massachusetts Historical Society.

67 Richard Ford, *A New Map of the Island of Barbadoes* (1674). Courtesy of the John Carter Brown Library at Brown University.

70 Richard Ford, *A New Map of the Island of Barbadoes* (1674), detail. Courtesy of the John Carter Brown Library at Brown University.

88 *Fort Amsterdam, Kormantine.* From Albert van Dantzig, *Forts and Castles of Ghana.* Courtesy of Sedco Publishing Ltd.

91 *Prospect of the Coast from El Mina to Mowri,* detail. Engraving by Jean Barbot, in *Description of the Coasts of North and South Guinea* (London, 1732), II:589. Copyright © The British Library Board/V9733, vol 2, pg 589.

94 Gilded metal button with tulip motif. Courtesy of the Andrew Fiske Memorial Center for Archaeological Research, University of Massachusetts Boston.

95 *Gatehouse of the Hospital of St. John of Jerusalem, Clerkenwell,* etching by Wenceslaus Hollar (1661). Courtesy of the British Museum. 1880, 1113.4811-AN789524.

96 Survey of the City of London, by John Ogilby and William Morgan, on a scale of 100 feet to the inch. London, 1676.

107 "Scythian Lamb." From Henry Lee's *The Vegetable Lamb of Tartary* (London, 1887), after Claude Duret (1605). Copyright © The Natural History Museum/The Image Works.

112 Detail, Grizzell Sylvester, Last Will and Testament (May 7, 1685). Courtesy of the Sylvester Manor Archive, Fales Library and Special Collections, New York University Library.

134 From John Gorham Palfrey, *A History of New England*, etc. (Boston: Little, Brown & Co., 1858–1890), 5 vols., 2:62. Courtesy Library of Congress.

141 "The Children of my Brother Nathaniel Sylvester" (n.d.). Courtesy of the Sylvester Manor Archive, Fales Library and Special Collections, New York University.

152 From *A Field Guide to American Houses* by Virginia and Lee McAlester. Copyright © 1984 by Virginia Savage and Lee McAlester.

157 Photograph of a cobblestone pavement. Courtesy of the Andrew Fiske Memorial Center for Archaeological Research, University of Massachusetts Boston.

174 "Burying Ground of the Colored People of the Manor Since 1651." Photograph by Andrew Bush. Courtesy of Mac Griswold.

180 Map of the excavation of a possible African Garden site. Redrawn with the permission of the University of Massachusetts. Courtesy of the Andrew Fiske Memorial Center for Archaeological Research, University of Massachusetts Boston.

185 Photographer unknown. North peninsula and land bridge, c.1900. Courtesy of the Sylvester Manor Archive, Fales Library and Special Collections, New York University.

187 Inventory of the estate of Nathaniel Sylvester, detail (1680). Courtesy of the Shelter Island Historical Society, New York University.

195 George Fox, *Gospel Family-Order* (1676). Courtesy of Friends Historical Library of Swarthmore College.

220 Coat of Arms, Willem III of Orange. Copyright © Barry Vincent/Alamy.

230 Photographs of soil block, South Lawn, Sylvester Manor. Courtesy of Dennis Piechota.

240 Robert Hefner. Sylvester Manor south front restored, elevation drawing. Courtesy of Sylvester Manor Educational Farm.

252 Silver porringer. Copyright © Metropolitan Museum of Art/Art Resource.

254 Robert Hefner, Sylvester Manor first floor plan, conjectural restoration. Courtesy of Sylvester Manor Educational Farm.

260 Nathaniel Hurd, bookplate of Thomas Dering (1749). Engraving. Gift of William E. Baillie, 1920 [20.90.11(72)]. Copyright © Metropolitan Museum of Art/Art Resource.

267 Robert Hefner, Sylvester Manor two-leaf door to north attic room. Courtesy of Sylvester Manor Educational Farm.

269 Detail of former front door. Photograph by Andrew Bush. Courtesy of Mac Griswold.

277 *A Plan of the Dwelling House, Dooryard and Outhouses Late the Property of Sylvester Dering Deceased,* detail. Courtesy of the Sylvester Manor Archive, Fales Library and Special Collections, New York University.

289 Photographer unknown. Woman walking in Sylvester Manor garden (n.d.). Courtesy of the Sylvester Manor Archive, Fales Library and Special Collections, New York University.

292 Photographer unknown. E. N. Horsford with family and visitors at Sylvester Manor (n.d.). Courtesy of the Sylvester Manor Archive, Fales Library and Special Collections, New York University.

294 Isaac Pharoah. Penknife carving on wooden dormer board. Photograph by Andrew Bush. Courtesy of Mac Griswold.

294 Line drawing. Richard C. Youngken, *African Americans in Newport* (Newport, RI: Newport Historical Society, 2nd printing, 1998).

306 Photographer unknown. Haywagon and farm crew at Sylvester Manor (n.d.). Courtesy of the Sylvester Manor Archive, Fales Library and Special Collections, New York University.

310 Photographer unknown. Dedication of the monument of Nathaniel Sylvester in the family graveyard, since known as the Quaker graveyard (1884). Courtesy of the Sylvester Manor Archive, Fales Library and Special Collections, New York University.

315 Alice Fiske at the Sylvester Manor garden gate, about 1985. Photograph by Roswitha Wisseman. Courtesy of Lissa Williamson and Roswitha Wisseman.
319 Edith Gawler. Ink sketch of a modern tackhead banjo (2012). Courtesy of Edith Gawler.

Insert

1 Sylvester Manor on Gardiners Creek. Photograph by Andrew Bush. Courtesy of Mac K. Griswold.
2 The manor house from the water tower. Courtesy of the Sylvester Manor Archive, Fales Library and Special Collections, New York University.
3 View of a garden pergola. Photograph by Andrew Bush. Courtesy of Mac K. Griswold.
4 Rose trellises and arches. Photograph by Andrew Bush. Courtesy of Mac K. Griswold.
5 The garden privy. Photograph by Andrew Bush. Courtesy of Mac K. Griswold.
6 The graveyard table monument dedicated to the Sylvesters and to the Quakers persecuted in Boston. Photograph by Andrew Bush. Courtesy of Mac K. Griswold.
7 *Mary Sylvester,* by Joseph Blackburn. Copyright © Metropolitan Museum of Art/Art Resource. Gift of Sylvester Dering, 1916 (16.68.2).
8 "Paneled parlor," mantel detail. Photograph by Andrew Bush. Courtesy of Mac K. Griswold.
9 *The Horsford Girls.* Courtesy of the Sylvester Manor Archive, Fales Library and Special Collections, New York University.
10 Bennett Konesni on the farm road. Photograph by Andrew Bush. Courtesy of Mac K. Griswold.
11 Upstairs "hall chamber," mantel detail. Photograph by Andrew Bush. Courtesy of Mac K. Griswold.
12 "Landscape Parlor" and the door to the slave staircase. Photograph by Andrew Bush. Courtesy of Mac K. Griswold.
13 The second-floor staircase to the attic. Photograph by Andrew Bush. Courtesy of Mac K. Griswold.
14 "Isaac's Room," attic. Photograph by Andrew Bush. Courtesy of Mac K. Griswold.
15 Gardiners Creek at sunset. Courtesy Cara Loriz.